Freelance film-maker Kim Traill got her start in documentary making with *Race Around the World*, where she was runner-up for the main prize. She has worked for SBS's *Dateline* and ABC's *Foreign Correspondent*, where she specialised in stories about the former Soviet Union. Kim has spent much of the past nineteen years living, working and travelling in Eastern Europe, Asia, and the US. She lives in Sydney with her son, Nik.

RED SQUARE BLUES

KIM TRAILL

A beginner's guide to
the decline and fall
of the Soviet Union

FOURTH ESTATE • *London, New York, Sydney* and *Auckland*

Fourth Estate
An imprint of HarperCollins*Publishers*

First published in Australia in 2009
by HarperCollins*Publishers* Australia Pty Limited
ABN 36 009 913 517
www.harpercollins.com.au

HarperCollins*Publishers*
25 Ryde Road, Pymble, Sydney, NSW 2073, Australia
31 View Road, Glenfield, Auckland 0627, New Zealand
A 53, Sector 57, Noida, UP, India
77–85 Fulham Palace Road, London, W6 8JB, United Kingdom
2 Bloor Street East, 20th floor, Toronto, Ontario M4W 1A8, Canada
10 East 53rd Street, New York NY 10022, USA

National Library of Australia Cataloguing-in-Publication data:

Traill, Kim.
    Red Square blues : a beginner's guide to the
    decline and fall of the Soviet Union / Kim Traill.
    ISBN: 978 0 7322 8566 1 (pbk.)
    Glasnost.
    Soviet Union–History–1985–1991.
    Soviet Union–Social conditions–1970–1991.
    Soviet Union–Description and travel.
    Russia–History.
    Russia–Social conditions.
    Russia–Description and travel.
947.0854

Cover design and illustration by Marcelle Lunam
Typeset in 11.5/16pt Bembo by Kirby Jones
Printed and bound in Australia by Griffin Press
70gsm Classic White used by HarperCollins*Publishers* is a natural, recyclable product made from wood
grown in sustainable forests. The manufacturing processes conform to the environmental regulations
in the country of origin, Finland.

5 4 3 2 1   09 10 11 12

To Nik

To run away is not glorious, but very healthy.

Russian proverb

PROLOGUE

Moscow, February 2004

It's twenty below zero and I'm standing on the arched, cobblestone bridge behind Moscow's White House, surrounded by skinheads waving swastikas. Next to me, a motley group of youths brandish red flags, emblazoned with the moustachioed mug of Joseph Stalin. Nearby, others carry Orthodox crosses and icons; the saintly painted faces gazing serenely over the mayhem.

'Russia for Russians,' the skinheads chant menacingly.

Then the leaders start up a new refrain: 'Glory to Russia', 'Glory to Russia'.

Hundreds of black boots stamp furiously in the snow. I beckon aside a pair of pimply teens in worn black leather jackets. One carries a cheap printed icon of the Virgin Mary pasted to a board. I fit a lapel microphone to his jacket collar, point my camera at him and press record.

'What's going on?' I bellow over the racket.

'The government has to get all the black-arses from the Caucasus out of Russia. They are destroying our country,' he yells. 'It's because of them that there are no jobs for our young people. They have taken over the markets and businesses, and if the government doesn't get rid of them, then we will kill them ourselves.'

Damn. He's shouting so loudly the sound levels are distorting. I rewind a fraction and listen to the replay. His voice is an incomprehensible crackle. I'll have to ask him to say it again and I'm running out of time. An icy breeze is blowing up from across the Moscow River. I can't operate the camera with gloves on and I've already lost all sensation in my fingers. My camera batteries are about to run out. More worryingly, it's almost time for Nik to wake up. I put my foot on the back of his pram and push it back and forth, hoping the motion will keep him asleep a little longer. Okay, time for take two.

I'm shooting a film about the rise of xenophobia in post-Soviet Russia and its become a terrifying insight into the darkest recesses of the human psyche. So far I've filmed a nineteen-year-old devotee of Hitler who'd proudly shown me a collection of gold teeth he'd wrenched from the gums of Georgians and Chechens he'd beaten up in Moscow's metro. I've been to a bizarre initiation ceremony in a forest outside Moscow with some teenage members of the extreme right-wing People's National Party, led by self-professed 'Russist/racist', Alexander Sukharevsky. I've also met an Armenian woman whose husband had died in hospital after being mugged by a gang of skinheads.

It isn't really a project compatible with child rearing. But as I have no one else to look after fourteen-month-old Nik, I've dragged him along with me in a pram clearly unsuited for use in heavy snow. With his blue eyes and bald head, the Aryan supremacists love little Nik — as much as a band of xenophobes could love anyone. But I am beginning to wonder if I'm going too far.

I reassure myself that one day Nik will get a chuckle from the fact that while still in nappies he'd been to London to interview the alleged Chechen terrorist Akhmed Zakayev, one of Russia's most wanted men. Or that just after his first birthday, he'd been let loose around the set of a controversial Russian reality TV show called *Golod* (*Hunger*), whose starry-eyed contestants were deprived of food and sent out into the streets of Berlin to fend for themselves for the entertainment of their countrymen.

I look down at Nik's sleeping baby face, pink cheeks flushed with cold. I kiss him on the nose and turn back to the spotty skinhead.

'OK, can I just get you to say that again ...'

I'd first come to Russia in 1990, as the Soviet empire was in its final death throes. I was hooked immediately. Not on the terrible weather, dire food, infuriating bureaucracy and sadistically rude service — but on the kindness and hospitality of the ordinary people and the intrigue of their histories. I returned again and again, first as a traveller, later as a film-maker; bearing witness to the extreme political and social upheaval which has rocked that vast region since the collapse of the USSR. I would find myself at collective farms, overcrowded communal apartments, soirees for the obscenely wealthy, military academies, nuclear bases, international marriage agencies, Arctic and desert outposts. I would observe the horrific effects of war, nuclear accidents, drug and alcohol addiction and ethnic rivalries. I would see some of my Russian friends find lucrative jobs, buy flash cars, fancy houses and travel the world, while others would struggle to feed their families. And I would watch on as corruption, repression and injustice were established as integral elements of the new Russian society.

The craziness of Russia was in my blood and not even motherhood had managed to cure me.

PART ONE

Back in the USSR

1

Into the Red

What's the difference between Aeroflot and a Scud missile?
Aeroflot kills more people.

August 1990

At its height, the Soviet empire stretched from its satellite state of East Germany, south to the puppet government of Afghanistan and east to the vassal state of Mongolia. Its influence extended as far as Cuba, Angola, Yemen and Vietnam. But for me, it started at Singapore airport, in the Aeroflot check-in queue. I was the only Westerner in a crowd of grim-faced Soviet citizens dressed in 1960s-style fashion and clutching plastic bags bulging with duty-free bottles, food, clothing, cassette players and even VCRs. Everyone, including the check-in staff, ignored the large signs indicating weight and volume restrictions on hand luggage, including the check-in staff.

I too wrestled with an 8 kilogram bag of shampoos, skin creams and toilet paper I had offered to deliver to one Ludmilla in Moscow — the mother of the girlfriend of a friend of my dad. So far I had schlepped the rapidly disintegrating plastic carrier from Melbourne to Singapore, around Singapore for a day, and now back to the airport.

Lizzi, an Australian friend of mine who'd been to Leningrad, had reported that Russians were obsessed with all things Western. She'd advised me to bring Levi's, chewing gum and Marlboro cigarettes —

apparently a sure-fire way to win friends and influence people in the economically torpid Soviet state.

I was a rabid anti-smoker but I wedged a carton of duty-free Marlboros under the seat in front of me and lowered my backside to await takeoff. The Soviet national airline had an impressive reputation for lax safety standards and obnoxious service and I wasn't disappointed. As soon as my rear hit the seat, the whole thing collapsed, leaving me squatting on the metal frame. I showed the detached seat base to a scowling stewardess who snapped ferociously and ordered me to do up my seat belt. It was my first lesson in the Soviet way: 'Don't complain because we're not going to do anything about it.'

The prospect of fourteen hours balancing on a wobbly seat only momentarily abated my excitement. I was twenty-one, and going to the USSR was almost an act of rebellion for me. I'd been relishing the shocked reactions — 'You're going where?!?' — when I told people I'd bought a ticket to Moscow. Many of my musician friends from college were heading overseas to study in the cradles of Western classical music — Vienna, Amsterdam, Cologne, Paris, Budapest and London. But the cafés and civility of Europe held little appeal to me. I wanted to do something radical, something different. I hadn't realised that I was on my way to one of the most conformist societies on the planet. That revelation came at dinnertime.

'I ordered a vegan meal,' I complained, in pathetic pidgin Russian to the same sneering stewardess. 'No meat, no dairy.' I pointed to the words in my phrase book.

'Nyet,' she snapped, slapping down a standard issue in-flight meal — a slice of tinned meat resembling dog food, a mushy tomato, half a pickle and a dried hunk of black bread I couldn't even get my teeth into. Fortunately I had plenty of fat reserves, but for the first time I worried about how bad the notorious food shortages might be. How many weeks could I survive on stale black bread and mushy tomatoes? How was it that all my fellow passengers were so generously proportioned?

Until now, most of what I knew about the USSR had come from the evening news and James Bond movies. I was a closeted, unworldly classical music student who read little but musical scores. My knowledge of world politics and history was a sorry vacuum, and I'd never left Australia. To me, the world's largest empire was a caricature — a secretive superpower with endemic queues, shortages of consumer goods, bitter winters, exploding nuclear reactors and scary KGB men. But I was obsessed with Russian music. With the certainty of the totally ignorant, I was confident that anywhere that spawned such virtuosic musicians and inspired composers couldn't be all bad. I might even find myself a Russian clarinet teacher.

It had all begun with my childhood 'ballerina phase'. I'd lock myself in the living room with Mum's Tchaikovsky records blaring, practising pirouettes until my toes blistered, ankles caved in and knees knocked. But sadly the size of my bum ruled out a future in ballet. So I took up the clarinet. As a gawky teenager I listened to Stravinsky and Prokofiev, Shostakovich and Rimsky-Korsakov — savouring the dramatic, angst-ridden and really loud bits. My parents' hopes of their daughter having a useful career in scientific research were dashed. I practised, got a place at the Victorian College of the Arts and then in the Australian Youth Orchestra (AYO). A trombonist taught me Cyrillic on tour bus rides. I found my grandfather's 'Learn to speak Russian' cassettes, purchased for a trip there in the 70s and memorised useful phrases like, 'Excuse me, where can I find a mule?' But if I hadn't got to know Olga, I never would have found the courage to travel on my own to the USSR.

Olga was the first Russian I met who still lived there. Her father, Vladimir Verbitsky, was engaged to conduct the AYO for a month-long season in January 1990 and Olga came with him. That year, orchestra members were spending a scorching summer living and rehearsing at Geelong Grammar, a boarding school outside Melbourne that was vacant for the school holidays. Fresh off the plane from frost-bitten Leningrad, Olga was shell-shocked by the heat, jet lag and rowdy Aussie teenagers. She cut a striking figure; nineteen-years-old, nearly six feet tall, long-limbed and lanky with pale blue Slavic eyes, high cheekbones and blonde streaked hair.

I approached her as she sat timidly by the school's pool, wondering whether to warn her that her translucent northern winter skin would fry in seconds in the blazing Australian sun. She was bewildered by the Aussie accent and dumbfounded by our slang. 'Wanna cuppa?' apparently wasn't on the syllabus of Leningrad State University's English course. She was shy and hesitant with her English but we could communicate. Over the next few weeks I sought her out between rehearsals, nosily probing her for details of life in her enigmatic land and raving enthusiastically about the genius of Soviet musicians. I couldn't tell what she thought of my endeavours at conversation, but when I invited her to my family home in Melbourne after the camp, she agreed to come. After she returned to Leningrad we wrote to each other, despite our letters taking months to cross the globe.

I'm still not sure if she actually meant to invite me, or if she was merely politely returning my attempts at hospitality, never imagining that I would really take her up. Either way, when Olga suggested I visit her in Leningrad, I leapt at the offer. She told me that she lived with her grandmother on an island in the Neva River and her parents were often away travelling. She would enjoy the company. In a spur of the moment decision, I booked a plane ticket to Moscow. My mum was bemused. She couldn't understand why anyone would choose to go to a place that didn't have shampoo or toilet paper.

Olga began the complicated process of wrangling with Soviet bureaucrats to issue a visa invitation. I had no idea that this entailed her spending hours in queues at the spooky sounding 'Ministry of the Interior', waiting for rude officials on constant tea breaks to put stamps on stacks of documents. Or that she would then idle away many more hours in bank queues waiting to pay processing fees. Back in Melbourne I obsessively checked the letterbox for word of her progress, wondering why it was all so difficult. What sort of a place was this that could string a simple request out for months? Had I known how time-consuming it would be for her I would never have put her through it all — and both our lives would have turned out very differently.

A Soviet tourist visits a Western home and sees there is a kitchen, bedrooms, living rooms, children's area and more. 'We have all this too,' he says. 'Only without partitions.'

Through a convoluted web of friends and relatives I had an invitation to visit Moscow before heading to Leningrad to stay with Olga. The exact arrangements were murky, but I had been assured someone would meet me at the airport.

My welcome to Soviet soil was as warm as an Aeroflot stewardess's snarl. I cheerfully tried out my Russian greetings on Moscow's Sheremetyevo Airport staff, shamelessly butchering 'Hello', the tongue-mangling *Zdravstvuitye*. The surly passport control officers and customs officials appeared to have studied customer relations techniques with the hosties, grunting and snorting as they flicked suspiciously through my documents.

Deflated by the onslaught of unfriendliness, I hauled my luggage outside and stood blinking in the hazy afternoon sun. Seconds later, I was smothered in an avalanche of affection by two middle-aged women. To someone who'd grown up in the stiff Anglo-Aussie tradition of handshakes and personal space it was quite a shock.

'I Yulia, I have car. Come!' one stammered, pulling my arm between frantic puffs on a half-crushed cigarette. She gestured over the cracked and cratered car park to a tall, dark man standing by a miniature car.

'Svetlana, mother,' said the other eagerly, tugging at my other arm. 'I Ludmilla. You stay me.'

I recognised Yulia's face from a photo I had seen in Melbourne. She was gaunt and wiry, with a shock of wavy hennaed red hair, piercing brown eyes and exuded nervous energy like a miniature tornado. Her best friend, Elena, had emigrated from Moscow to Melbourne several years earlier. Elena's son, Michael, played the violin, her daughter Alissa sang, and I had often seen them busking on one side of Bourke Street Mall, while I tootled on my clarinet on the other. Later Michael and I played in an orchestra together. Learning of my plans to visit his homeland, Michael introduced me to his mother, who called Yulia in Moscow and told her I was coming.

Ludmilla was petite — in a cuddly way — with a beaming smile and hair raked back neatly into a bun. Our connection was similarly convoluted. Her daughter, Svetlana, had worked as an interpreter for Fred Schepisi's adaption of John Le Carre's spy novel *The Russia House*, which had been filmed recently in Moscow. Svetlana had met an Australian cinematographer friend of my father's during the shoot and since moved to Melbourne. It was she who had passed on the sack of shampoos I'd just lugged halfway around the world. Ludmilla was desperate for news of her only child, but I'd never met Svetlana in person. All I could offer in compensation was the now dripping and slimy bag of lotions.

An animated discussion ensued over who could take this slightly malodorous foreigner home. Finally, Ludmilla yielded, kissed me on the cheeks and left. Yulia beckoned to the man by the car. He strode over, an unsmiling beanpole with a thinning black comb-over, whom she introduced as 'her son's father', her ex-husband, Sasha. Sasha hoisted my 20-kilogram backpack onto his shoulder and carried it to a rusty Matchbox-toy-like Lada, where it filled the entire boot and caused the back of the car to sink alarmingly. Yulia prised the carton of Marlboros from under my arm and gazed at it longingly.

'For you,' I nodded, grinning uncomfortably at presenting her with such a cancerous gift. She was elated.

'Russia cigarette very bad,' she spluttered, following her pronouncement with a coughing fit as if to emphasise her point. 'This good cigarette!'

The potholed road from the airport was almost deserted, bar a few lumbering khaki trucks and the occasional ancient bus. I gazed out at the dense pine forests flanking the road while Yulia fumbled with the plastic wrapping on her new healthy fags. Soon the road led us into Soviet 'suburbia'; a homage to the central planning bureau's love affair with concrete. Rows of grey high-rise apartment blocks poked from unkempt fields towards the washed-out sky, like a 1970s Stonehenge. These gigantic oblongs of ugliness rolled on for kilometre after kilometre, before giving way to edifices of an earlier era as we neared the city centre.

The blandness of it all was striking. There wasn't an advertisement to be seen: no posters, billboards or neon lights. The only colour came from large red cloth banners with bold white slogans strung across façades of intimidatingly huge official buildings, and multistorey-high murals painted up the narrow windowless ends of apartment blocks — some depicting muscular workers with chiselled cheekbones brandishing shovels, others towering images of Lenin, fist raised to the sky.

Yulia's flat was a couple of kilometres south of Moscow's heart — the Kremlin and Red Square — in a shabby older-style building with blistering turmeric yellow paint. Neighbours milled around in the warm summer night, staring and blinking at the alien wrenching a bulky blue backpack from the boot of Sasha's Lada. Across the road a queue snaked along the footpath, past a bus shelter and down steps to a subterranean door. At regular intervals, men emerged from the door, clutching small boxes, which, Yulia informed me, were nasty Soviet cigarettes.

Sasha removed the windscreen wipers and cassette player from the car — so no one would steal them. I followed Yulia up several flights of worn stone stairs. The walls of the stairwell were a flaking and scungy green, the windows thick with dust. Six floors up we stopped before a heavy door, covered in padded leather with metal studs. Yulia rang a bell and I heard a second door being unlocked behind this one. The doors opened and an enormous slobbering black and brown dog leapt up at us, almost pulling over the teenage boy and old woman in a floral smock trying to hold onto its collar. Yulia's diminutive mother locked me in an another embarrassingly ardent embrace. Dima, a super-cerebral looking lad with round glasses greeted me shyly in polite accented English and pointed to a rack.

'Put your shoes here,' he said. 'And take *tapochki* … what is *tapochki* in English?'

'Slippers,' I replied, glancing at the objects in question. I undid my shoelaces and noticed Dima and Yulia staring aghast at my Doc Marten boots. After a pause Dima spoke.

'We buy new comfortable shoes for you, lady shoes. They better in Soviet Union.'

I protested that my boots *were* comfortable, but they were unconvinced. It would be some time before I understood their concern was nothing to do with comfort. It was my non-conformity that bothered them. Women simply did not wear such awfully unfeminine footwear. My unsightly clodhoppers were intended for men in uniform and it would only be a rare and subversive punk-type female who would dare to wear army-style boots in public. Convention dictated that Soviet women should dress meticulously, femininely, with particular attention to enhancing their womanly attributes.

Sasha left and Dima took me to his room, generously offering me his space 'for as long as I wanted to stay'. I hadn't realised I would be taking over his room and felt decidedly uncomfortable, but he seemed not to mind. He showed me the couch, which folded out into a bed he would share with his grandmother (babushka) in the living/dining room next door. Privacy seemed a foreign concept here. There was one other room, which Yulia used as a bedroom/study. The kitchen and bathroom were tiny, with none of the normal appliances of modern life in the West that I took for granted: washing machines, microwaves, toasters and other labour-saving devices. Washing dripped from lines strung across the bath, more soaked in plastic buckets in the tub. Jars of home-pickled vegetables lined the corridor. The whole flat would have fitted into my parents' very average suburban living and dining room. It was a snug space for three Russians, a pony-sized canine and a guest.

The kitchen table was laid out with a mystifyingly large quantity of food for a country with a much publicised dearth of comestibles. While I pondered its origins, Grandma piled my plate with fat slices of salami, a big hunk of butter, a pickled tomato and more slabs of black bread. Through Dima I explained I didn't eat meat or dairy food. There was a shocked silence. 'But why?' Dima asked.

'Ummm, I am sad for the animals,' I replied.

My empathy for edible beasts was apparently as outlandish as my boots. I didn't want to appear unappreciative or critical of their carnivorous ways, so to change the subject I bit into the tomato. It exploded, sending mushy tomato innards all over the table and hitting poor Grandma in the face. The pickling process had turned the tomato into a bomb, a tough skin filled with liquid waiting to burst. My first Russian meal was not going well. Grandma bustled around and brought out some *kapusta* (shredded pickled cabbage), soup and potatoes. Each time I thought I'd finished, she refilled my plate. I tried to object and they looked offended.

'Eat now, Leningrad no food,' implored Yulia.

I took a deep breath. I could sense I needed to make some radical changes to my attitude if I was going to survive here. I would have to learn to graciously accept being hugged by strangers, having my dietary preferences, possessions and op-shop/grungy hippy/punk dress sense constantly scrutinised — and develop a taste for pickled cabbage.

It was already 9 pm, but Moscow being so far north, the sky was still bright. I peered out the window and bleared into the fug of rancid tobacco smoke floating up from the bustling street below. I was dizzy and disoriented from jet lag and fatigue, but could see I would disappoint my eager hosts by doing something as antisocial as falling asleep. Besides, I desperately needed to shake down some of Grandma's *kapusta*.

Yulia phoned the obliging Sasha and asked him to return with his Lada to take us to Red Square. It was just as I imagined. I felt a strange thrill as I gawped at the red stars glowing like Christmas decorations from atop the towers on the Kremlin walls. From somewhere inside the fortress, the General Secretary of the Communist Party, Mikhail Gorbachev, ruled 250 million people: hundreds of different nationalities, living in fifteen republics defended by a four-million-strong army and an arsenal of weapons that could destroy the planet. It was a daunting thought.

Tonight, the cobblestoned Red Square on the Kremlin's eastern side was teeming with evening sightseers: swarthy Georgians and Armenians from the Caucasus; Central Asians with their more Oriental features; blonde, blue-eyed, high-cheekboned Slavs and blends of the above. At the southern end of the square, photographers stood in front of the eccentric spotted and striped onion domes of St Basil's Cathedral, displaying faded samples of their work on easels. Groups of giggling Central Asian women in colourful dresses, baggy pants and headscarves lined up for snaps, writing their addresses on envelopes for the photographers to forward once the pictures were developed. No one had their own cameras. I felt ashamed of my indecent wealth and kept mine in my bag.

Dima related a gory tale of Tsar Ivan the Terrible, a 'great ruler' who had ordered that the architect behind St Basil's have his eyes gouged out, so he could never design anything like it again. A pity, I thought, that the central planners responsible for Moscow's unsightly suburbia hadn't been treated to a similarly grisly fate. Across the square, stony-faced soldiers with bayonets goose-stepped, changing guard outside the red and black polished granite mausoleum where Lenin lay, pickled and wax-like.

Next Sasha took us to Old Arbat Street, a popular hangout in central Moscow. Artists sketched charcoal portraits of prim young women, guitarists strummed, a jazz band with accordion, trumpet, saxophone and tuba bopped and stalls sold *matryoshki* — the ubiquitous Russian nesting dolls — and Red Army paraphenalia. Pedestrians promenaded: men in polyester suits worn shiny at the knees, the ladies in knee length skirts and puffy blouses with neck ruffles and bows. With hair sprayed into bouffants and faces slathered in thick foundation, bright blue eye shadow and painted lips, they looked just like the *matryoshki*.

Yulia had already exhausted her English vocabulary and I realised that the stock phrases of Grandpa Traill's Russian tapes weren't going to go far. Dima took my dictionary and waved at a queue so long we couldn't even see what people were lining up for. 'Turn,' he said pointing to the dictionary entry. 'We say *ochered*. There are many turns in Soviet Union. You must to learn this word.' I followed his fingertip. *Ochered* did mean 'turn', as in 'to take one's turn'. Down the list of alternatives was 'queue'. I wrote it in my notebook in English and Cyrillic. It was my very first new word.

'Money,' Yulia added, her pick of essential vocabulary. '*Dengi*? How I get money?'

I would soon find money was a topic of great fascination. Like most Soviet citizens, Yulia earned the standard wage of 200 roubles a month as a pharmacist, approximately AUD\$20. It was enough for the basics. Her flat, electricity, water and phone were all paid for by the state, while food, clothing and other goods were heavily subsidised. But there was no opportunity to do more than make ends meet, and she was exhausted by the daily grind of work and queuing. She wanted her son to lead her to a better life. Elena had told me that Yulia was desperate to emigrate — even more so after a visit to her friend in Australia. She just needed to find a country willing to take her. Yulia's hopes were pinned on the mathematically gifted Dima winning a scholarship to study elsewhere. As he was so young, she and her mother would move with him. She was trying for South Africa, or maybe Germany.

For me, matters financial were remarkably simple. In the morning a man arrived with a bag of banknotes, for what would be my very first black market transaction. He counted out 4,000 roubles in ten rouble notes onto Yulia's kitchen table, flicking them deftly with his thumbs and forefingers. Dima watched, bug-eyed. This was twenty months wages for a Soviet citizen, yet it had cost me the embarrassing equivalent of a couple of days teaching clarinet back home. Officially, the rouble to US dollar rate was one to one. But everyone knew their national currency was worth little more than the paper it was printed on and many were ready to pay a premium to change theirs into dollars, Deutschmarks, pounds, or any other kind of 'hard currency'. These currencies that were actually worth something were called *valyuta*.

Valyuta was vital for those citizens able or required to travel, for savings, or to spend in special 'hard currency' only shops. Poetically named Beriozka — meaning 'birch tree' — these stores were shrines to the luxuries of capitalism, purveying otherwise unavailable and exorbitantly priced imported alcohol, chocolates, watches, souvenirs and perfume to foreign tourists and locals with *valyuta*. But few Soviet citizens had legal access to foreign currency. The black market rate for Australian dollars, Elena had informed me, was ten roubles to a dollar. She knew plenty of people who would happily pay that for mine. So back in Melbourne I'd given her AUD$400 and now here was my sack of Monopoly money. I felt vaguely uneasy, but no one else involved in the transaction seemed bothered. I stuffed a few notes into my money pouch and announced I wanted to explore the city.

Yulia was horrified when I said I'd like to go alone. She and Dima accompanied me to the palatial entrance of the nearby Serpukhovskaya underground metro station and reluctantly showed me how to purchase tokens. She clung to Dima, and shook her head as I pushed my way through the turnstile. 'You mother how let you go away?' she shuddered. 'You Westerners very strange. My Dima stay me.' Her protectiveness was almost overbearing. I'd always craved independence, and my mother had encouraged it. But familial relations here seemed somehow closer. I couldn't imagine my brother agreeing to share a bed with our grandma in a million years. Perhaps it was the cramped living spaces, or perhaps it was the culture? Whatever the reason, I supposed it was just something I'd have to get used to.

A near-vertical escalator funnelled stony-faced commuters deep into the bowels of the capital. Another brought them up, a conveyor belt of expressionless automatons spewing back out into the daylight. There wasn't a single smiling face. My token for the trip cost five kopecks: half an Australian cent. Feeling fantastically wealthy, I watched the train I'd just missed disappear into the blackness. An LED display at the end of the platform counted the seconds until the next arrived — an awesomely efficient ninety seconds later.

Using the miniature metro map Yulia had lent me, I navigated my way around the system. It was remarkably easy to follow: a 20-kilometre long 'Ring' line circumnavigates the city centre, with Red Square and the Kremlin as its central point. From this hub, spokes criss-cross through the old centre and radiate out into the suburbs. Magnificent underground stations punctuated the web of tunnels: intricate mosaics portraying communist uprisings in one, twice life-sized bronze statues of glorified workers in another, backlit stained glass flowers like an underground cathedral in another — each as architecturally marvelous as the suburban jungle was hideous.

Following Yulia's directions, I made my way to Red Square and took out my camera. Instantly I was surrounded by ragged and filthy gypsy children, who grabbed at me, gesturing that they were hungry. I opened my money pouch revealing my stash of ten-rouble notes. I handed one to a grubby girl, calculating it was more than an adult's daily wage and that they could split it. But she darted off, and the others went wild, grasping at the waistband of my money pouch. A glowering policeman stalked over, thumping his truncheon on his palm. The kids scattered.

The policeman eyed me curiously. I slunk off, feeling uneasy, and thought about Yulia's concern for me wandering around alone. Despite several years of Gorbachev's glasnost (openness), I knew lone foreigners visiting the USSR were still rare. Tourists arrived in easily controllable tour groups: met by Intourist (the state-run tourist agency) guides at the airport, neatly corralled into buses and chaperoned to Intourist hotels. They were taken on two excursions daily, and to the theatre or circus at night, seeing only what the guides were instructed to show them. Foreigners would rarely wander off alone. Every night of their stay was recorded and stamped by a department of the Ministry of the Interior.

My unkempt clothing, clompy boots and bulky camera made me instantly identifiable as an *inostranka,* an 'other country person'. So did my facial expressions. Soviet citizens had a blank, almost haunted look — indeed a smile in public was as out of place as a kangaroo in Bourke Street Mall. I noticed they rarely made eye contact with strangers and would consciously recoil from an accidental flicker of a connection. If I were to go unnoticed I would have to do the same. Over the next week as I wandered around, exploring Moscow's overgrown monasteries, bare department stores, phenomenal art collections and grandiose monuments to the glorious achievements of the Soviet state, I practised staring straight through people as if they didn't exist, and kept my camera in my bag. But I just couldn't bring myself to wear a frilly shirt and shoes with heels.

A few days after my arrival in the Soviet capital, an acrobat from the Moscow Circus named Kharis tracked me down at Yulia's. He'd toured Australia recently where he'd met Svetlana, now working as an interpreter for visiting Soviets Down Under. Svetlana had told him that I was in Moscow and now he was calling with an invitation to see the circus with him. He arrived at Yulia's to collect me, took one look at my feet, and offered to buy me new shoes.

The compact and muscly Kharis was proud of his circus, but not of his country. As we strolled along, he pointed at the rusting Ladas and Zhigulis, belching smoke as they puttered along the boulevards.

'In Australia, you good cars,' he sighed with envy. 'This country no good.'

He stroked his stubbly chin. 'You know, we have man in space, but no razor blades.'

The USSR may have had inferior automobiles and a paucity of shaving gear, but the acrobats were incredible. My cabbage-bloated stomach lurched as Kharis and I watched lycra-clad trapeze artists make death-defying leaps from wobbling ladders with no safety nets, effortlessly form human pyramids, cartwheel along tightropes and spin themselves into blurs holding a rope by their teeth 15 metres up.

The precision and excruciating difficulty of the acrobatic displays was almost superhuman. Even the child performers were like miniature adults, focused and intense. I recalled a performance I'd heard years earlier by some young visiting Soviet Bloc musicians. At twelve they flawlessly performed works I could only just manage at eighteen. Their teacher gave a ruthless masterclass to some of my classmates and I understood that such achievement did not only come from a nurturing of natural ability, but something more Darwinian. Teachers demanded perfection, and those who couldn't keep up were eliminated.

'Our acrobats very good. They best!' declared Kharis as we applauded, his chest puffed out with pride. 'That one People's Artist USSR. He medal.'

'People's Artists', Kharis explained, came in many varieties: dancers, singers, musicians and conductors. There were also state medals, titles and prizes for high-achieving sportsmen, scientists, architects, authors and military men. The State couldn't provide its heroes with a decent salary, but they could dangle tacky badges and the glory of a title as incentive. And if they were really lucky, the real tangible reward for excellence was a bigger flat, or a move up the waiting list for a car or a telephone. At the time I thought it simply wonderful that the USSR placed such a high value on encouraging its people to excel in the arts and sciences. If only we did the same.

Kharis might have impressed Australian audiences with his awesome aerial stunts, but he was equally blown away by the material abundance of the West. Like all Soviet stars travelling abroad, the circus performers were accompanied by KGB minders, but they couldn't fail to notice the striking disparity in living standards between their nation and that of their Cold War foes. He told me how many picked up extra money by bringing back desirable items purchased on tour: a VCR, some Western videos and a couple of pairs of Levi's that would each sell for a month's wages. With the proceeds of their trading, many could save for cars.

Compared to the mundane lives of the average *homo sovieticus*, it was worth practising very hard.

But Kharis was discontent with his occasional opportunities to see the world from the confines of a tour group. I sensed he envied Svetlana's chance to escape the USSR through her Australian romance and had hopes that this odd Aussie with the appalling taste in footwear might fall for him as the Melbourne cameraman had fallen for her. Not wanting to lead him on, I thanked him for taking me to the performance and decided to be careful not to appear too enthusiastic about further meetings.

What is the nationality of Adam and Eve?
　Russian of course. Why else would they think they're in Paradise when they were homeless, naked, and just had one apple for both of them?

I continued my meanderings, baffled by the contradictions I found at every turn. The grand façades of the GUM (Glavny Universalny Magazin) and TSUM (Tsentralny Universalny Magazin), the main and central universal department stores respectively, *the* mega-shopping malls of the USSR, disguised rundown warrens of almost empty shops painted in an insipid mint. The few items available — tractor parts, buttons, cheap plastic combs — were displayed in locked glass cases. Queues for the basics were hundreds long. The whole city was like a giant machine shuddering to a halt. But I looked on the bright side.

To the locals, Moscow might have been a place of deprivation and frustration. But to this idealistic middle-class Australian, consumed with indignation at the rampant materialism of home, and its resulting landfill, Moscow's economically stagnant misery was pleasing to my greenie sensibilities. Well yes, the shops were empty, but there was no litter on the streets. There was no excess packaging because there was no packaging at all. If you wanted to buy vegetable oil, you took your own bottle. If you needed vegetables, you took a cloth bag. Surely we wasteful Westerners could learn from this? Shops were in basements and every amenity was within walking distance. Public transport was a dream; fast, frequent, cheap and widespread. Buses weren't held up by traffic, because there were almost no cars. And wasn't it great that everyone was equal? Poor by Australian standards, yes, but at least they were equally poor — or so it seemed to my naïve and uninformed brain. This communist caper didn't seem a bad thing at all.

Despite my rose-coloured glasses, I could see some drawbacks. Roads were crumbling, buildings half-derelict and salespeople bad-tempered. If no one owned anything, there was little incentive to keep places spruce or be nice. And it was hardly a constructive use of time for people to spend their entire working days standing in queues.

'We pretend to work, and they pretend to pay us,' was the oft-quoted description of the Soviet economy.

Some things were changing, thanks to a new law sponsored by Mikhail Gorbachev in May 1988, which permitted limited private enterprise. Old women hawked their garden produce outside metro stations — flowers, potatoes, apples and bunches of parsley. Enterprising 'shuttle' traders journeyed to Poland, Turkey and China to buy up consumer goods and flog them on Moscow streets. They were expensive compared to the ridiculously low state-subsidised prices in the department stores, but at least the queues weren't so long. A little over two and a half years earlier such activities would have been illegal.

But change wasn't coming fast enough for Yulia. She was adamant she and Dima had no future here; she was bored and frustrated by her work at the pharmacy and perturbed that her ageing mother was forced to spend her days lining up for basic goods. The prospects for Dima, even with his remarkable intellect, were not much better than for everyone else.

I became infuriatingly and fervently encouraging about life in Moscow, giving Yulia glowing daily reports on my adventures and revelations. I praised the public transport and the respect for artists, scientists and teachers. I admired the closeness of families. It felt so safe here, unlike St Kilda, the last place I'd lived in Melbourne. There were no homeless people, no drug addicts and no prostitutes. Communism was great, and the USSR was the best country in the world! And I should know. I'd been here a whole week. Yulia squinted at me as if I were half mad. I assumed it was the language barrier.

Yulia asked me to help her fill in an immigration application for South Africa. I did so, concerned that if granted an interview, her minimal spoken English would betray a native English speaker as the author. She said she didn't care. She was desperate and deception was acceptable. But she didn't even get an interview.

Dima had spent his long summer break huddled over textbooks and Yulia wanted him to get some sun. She called Sasha and asked him to take us on a trip to the country. We all crammed into the Lada, Grandma and mammoth dog too. Our first stop was the petrol station, or more precisely half a kilometre before the petrol station. Two hours of queuing later we were able to fill up.

Our destination was a 'sanatorium', which I imagined to be a kind of convalescent home. In fact it was a Soviet-style holiday camp, a rundown four-storey concrete building standing incongruously in a clearing in a pine forest. A group of boys were playing ball on a cracked concrete sports court. Middle-aged couples strolled through the forest to the river, a nondescript brown waterway where some corpulent men rested fishing rods on their paunches. Everyone seemed content and relaxed — except Yulia.

'Not beach Australia,' she sniffed, waving her arm dismissively over the scene.

I tried to be upbeat. It *was* little more than a concrete box in an insect ridden wood, hardly the golden sands of an Australian beach, but to me it seemed nice that people went away together and enjoyed the simple pleasures. Dima chased the dog through the trees and we watched the fishermen haul flaccid sardine-sized fish from the sludgy river. Enthusiastically I thanked Yulia for bringing me here. 'It's lovely,' I gushed. And I really meant it.

But Yulia was no fool. She knew there could be more to life than this. And I suppose deep down, so did I, only I didn't want to let it spoil my delusions just yet. As it turned out, Yulia and Dima would find a way to leave the country of their birth in which they could see no future. And I would keep finding ways to come back.

2

Tourism in the Tundra

What's the difference between socialism and capitalism?
Under capitalism one person exploits another person, and under
socialism, the opposite.

I was on a high. I hadn't opened my clarinet case in a week, and after years of practising every day, I realised I wasn't missing it at all. There *was* a world out there, beyond the soundproofed practice cells, fluoro-lit rehearsal halls, and dim, dark orchestra pits of my past few years. I was like a prison escapee on speed — I wanted to see and do anything and everything.

Moscow was mind-boggling, but Olga, Leningrad and the Arctic beckoned. In Olga's last letter, she wrote that not long after I was due to arrive, she and some friends were going on a trek in the tundra, north of the Arctic Circle. I was welcome to join them. I called her from Moscow and over a crackly line she shouted that they already had a train ticket for me, departing from Leningrad on the following night. Yulia, Grandma and Dima watched on as I packed, clearly perplexed as to why anyone would choose to go somewhere so remote and desolate for fun.

The next morning, Yulia took me to Leningradsky Station in Moscow to help me buy a ticket for the eight-hour journey to Moscovsky Station in Leningrad. Like everything in the USSR, train travel was heavily subsidised. A comfortable bunk bed in a plush four-person compartment cost less than one Australian dollar. Sheets were optional and could be 'hired' for a few extra kopecks. Officially I should have paid more, as there was a two-tiered price system — one for locals, another, many times more expensive for foreigners. But I couldn't buy a foreigner's ticket as I hadn't yet registered my visa — which had to be done with Olga as the 'inviting party' in Leningrad. Yulia was worried about my lack of an official stamp and nervously chaperoned me past the wagon attendants who manned each carriage to check tickets, hand out bed sheets and keep the water boiler full.

Soviet long-distance train travel was remarkably luxurious — a fortunate fact for the millions of citizens who relied on rail to get from A to B, which was often a very, very long way away. It could take six days for descendants of Siberian exiles to travel several thousand kilometres to visit relatives in the Ukraine. Or perhaps eight days for engineers who'd opted for the higher pay of work in the freezing far north to get to their sanatoriums on the Black Sea, also many thousands of kilometres away. Fortunately, central planners had decided that travellers should be comfortably accommodated on their marathon trips, and this was reflected in the uncharacteristically jovial moods of people forced to spend days on end in confined and bumping spaces. Or perhaps they were pleased at the break from pretending to work.

Whatever the reason, those icy expressions melted away and once on the train the dour automatons of the streets and metro magically morphed into affable and laid-back human beings. Even before the train left the station, passengers removed their street outfits to slip into something more comfortable: slippers, rayon tracksuits in various hues of blue for men, floral cotton wraparound dresses for women. The fold-out laminate tables between the bunks were piled with bread, cheese and pickles, tea glasses, sugar cubes and vodka bottles, a feast-on-wheels to savour while watching the countryside rattle by. My joy at the prospect of an eight-hour period without being force-fed was short-lived. Cramming food into strangers was apparently a Russian obligation — and the more the better. The amiable young couple and their little daughter who shared my *coupe* were no exception, plying me with ginger biscuits and sickly sweet tea.

The Moscow–St Petersburg train line passed quaint villages, shimmering blue lakes and tidy birch forests with gleaming white trunks, all in a dead straight line — almost. Legend has it that back in 1842 when the track was in the planning stages, engineers and officials couldn't agree on which towns the new railway should pass through. Tsar Nikolai I took a ruler and drew a straight line on the map between Moscow and St Petersburg, with a bump around his own finger. Too afraid to question the all-powerful Tsar, the planners ordered the line to be built as per his instructions, with a 17-kilometre bend near the city of Novgorod for no apparent reason.

Olga was waiting for me on the crowded platform of Moscovsky Station. After a brief and flustered 'hi' amidst swarms of reuniting relatives, baggage trolleys, and officious railway staff, she grabbed my bag and darted off into the melee. I struggled not to lose her, my eyes glued to her bobbing blonde head as she dodged through the hordes into the central hall of the station.

Here we were greeted by an incongruous sight: under a huge marble bust of Lenin on a pillar was a shrine to a man with a mullet. Hundreds of teary-eyed youths clasping flowers and candles squatted around a framed poster of a twenty-something Eurasian man. Olga identified him as a rock singer, Viktor Tsoi, who had been killed that day in a car crash in Latvia.

Tsoi had been one gutsy guy, a Soviet artist brave enough to discuss politics and social problems in his lyrics. His band, Kino (Cinema) had become famous with a song called '*Elektrichka*' ('Suburban train'), about a man stuck in a train taking him where he didn't want to go. I didn't really understand why at the time, but it was a blatant metaphor for life in the Soviet Union and the authorities banned it. Instantly, Tsoi became a hero of the youth anti-establishment movement. Kino's fame spread 'underground', as fans secretly copied and passed on his forbidden cassettes. And although the government supported 'approved' artists, providing housing, studios and distributing their recordings, rock was stereotyped as the music of drug addicts and delinquents. So despite his soaring popularity 'underground', Tsoi continued his job in the boiler room of a Leningrad apartment building. In the days after his death, sixty-five distraught fans would commit suicide.

Olga had liked Tsoi's music, but with a wink, told me she preferred the Beatles. Until recently their 'capitalist music' had also been prohibited, but her dad had brought her back records from his overseas tours. The only approved Western artists, she told me, were ABBA and Boney M, and the most popular song by the latter was the one that went: 'Ra, ra, Rasputin, lover of the Russian Queen'. Apparently this fitted nicely with the Soviet state's portrayal of the Tsars as morally compromised, ruthless exploiters of the Russian people. The last Tsaritsa, the German Empress Alexandra, had been particularly reviled, so it was unsurprising that Soviet authorities would wholeheartedly approve of a song accusing her of infidelity with a deranged monk. Olga had seen queues three hundred long waiting to snap up Boney M and ABBA records. There was also a thriving black market in the music and paraphernalia of Kiss and the Scorpions. Soldiers, sailors, and travelling performers would smuggle it in, to be onsold by shifty-eyed youths known as *fartsovchiki*. I would see them soon enough, pacing up and down outside Gostiny Dvor department store on Leningrad's main street, hissing, '*Pssst, Kiss khochesh?*' ('Do you want Kiss?') at passers-by.

We took the metro out to Primorskaya, the end station on the Vasilievsky Island line, and emerged into another jungle of ugly grey apartment blocks, identical to those on the outskirts of Moscow, standing sentinel-like against a dull northern sky. I'm not exactly sure what I expected when Olga had told me she lived on an island, but this concrete forest on the Gulf of Finland wasn't it. Still, I prattled away, eagerly relating tales of my Moscow adventures and extolling the virtues of her motherland. Unlike Yulia, who obviously thought I was a beetroot short of a borsch, Olga seemed genuinely pleased by my praise. But she was very quiet and I worried that perhaps she was uncomfortable with this Australian invasion.

We lugged my bags onto a crowded trolleybus, a strange bus–tram hybrid, and I pressed my face to the dust-streaked window. I remembered her telling me back in Melbourne how much more beautiful Leningrad was than Moscow. Right now I couldn't see it. She read my mind and whispered, conscious that half the passengers on the trolleybus were staring at us: 'Wait until you see the centre, the Winter Palace and Nevsky Prospekt. Then you will understand how special our city is. People say it is like Venice.'

Vasilievsky Island, where Olga lived with her grandmother, was a large land mass between the Neva River — the main waterway that sliced through the city — and the Baltic Sea. Their flat was in a district developed in the 1930s: Stalin's heyday, when buildings were built to impress, with sculpted façades, high ceilings and stone balconies. Sixty years on, the lemon, tangerine and rose paint jobs were blistering badly, pipes were corroding and pavements cratered; a 'renovator's delight', like the rest of the country. Olga led me down an alleyway lined with car-sized rusting metal boxes which she explained were used as garages, and into the yard in front of her building. Children played on a warped slide, painted long ago in happy primary colours, now peeling and neglected.

The lift to her flat was a rickety wire cage with inward opening doors that had to be completely closed before it would start. We only just managed to squash my bag and us in far enough to close the doors. At last it lurched upwards with a spine-tingling rattle. Olga apologised, as though she were personally responsible. Despite her evident pride in her city and country, she appeared acutely aware of how run-down and inefficient the place must seem to me.

Olga's grandmother, Vera Nikolayevna, and their ginger and white cat, Rizhok, came to the door. Vera regarded me suspiciously with a pair of intense deep-set pale blue eyes, tugging nervously at her wig as Olga introduced us. She ignored me and spoke sharply to Olga, whose reply seemed to appease her.

Like Yulia's place, Olga's flat had 'three rooms'. The usual way to describe the size of a Soviet dwelling was by the number of rooms, without including the utilitarian kitchen and bathroom. Living and sleeping were done in the same place, so there was no delineation between bedrooms and living rooms. A three-room flat was regarded as a luxury, even if it was accommodating three generations. The rooms in Olga's flat were bigger than Yulia's, but considering her father was an internationally renowned conductor, it was a humble place.

She showed me around. Her room, which she said would be mine for as long as I wished, boasted an impressive collection of plush marsupials and Australian postcards. She would move across the corridor into her parents' room, as they would be away on tour for many months to come. I peeked in and noticed the soft toy platypus presented to her father by the AYO, in one of a row of floor-to-ceiling glass-fronted wooden cabinets, stacked with yellowing collections of musical scores, concert programs and other mementos of her father's travels. Vera Nikolayevna had retreated into her space and shut the door, and Olga indicated that it was a no-go zone, even for her.

But there was no time to settle in. We were off to the Arctic. Olga's three-month summer holidays were almost over, and in a fortnight she would be back to the daily grind: studying Russian language and literature at night, and working as a lecturer's assistant by day, both at Leningrad University's Philology Faculty. A week's trekking in the tundra seemed the perfect way to chill out.

Our train would be leaving in a few hours. Olga heaved my pack off the floor and politely suggested I leave some of my possessions behind. I contemplated my enormous bag, feeling shamefully bourgeois for having so much, yet unable to imagine going without a daily change of clothes, let alone my clarinet and score of Nielsen's Clarinet Concerto. I removed some books and a couple of items of clothing as a token gesture. Fortunately Olga had sensibly packed useful things, like food and camping gear. We scoffed a rushed supper of black bread, tea and ginger biscuits with her grandma who glared at me disapprovingly and bombarded Olga with questions. I could pick up enough to recognise that she was bothered by the presence of this incoherent stranger.

Now sated (yet again) and repacked, we were ready to return to the station. I was about to open the front door when Olga did a curious thing. She sat down on her pack, told me to do the same and put her finger to her lips. After a minute's silence, she stood up. I raised an eyebrow.

'It's our tradition,' she explained. 'We have a lot of superstitions in Russia. When we go on a journey we always must do this before we can leave so we have good luck.'

Vera Nikolayevna watched us leave, staring at me in surprise, as if she'd never seen me before. '*Kto eta?*' she demanded of Olga. 'Who's that?'

Olga spoke to her and I recognised snippets of phrases from her supper conversation. Vera Nikolayevna nodded.

'Is it a problem for me to be here?' I asked Olga as we battled with the lift doors.

'No, not at all, just babushka forgets things all the time.'

We gave up on the lift and raced down the six and a half flights of stone stairs and retraced our route to Moscovsky Station. Her four friends were waiting on the platform, loaded up with bulging rucksacks, baskets of food and even a guitar. They handed Olga a couple of tickets and hustled us onto the train, which was just about to leave.

'Don't say anything,' Olga whispered. 'We only have ordinary ticket for you, Russian price. You must pretend.' I shuffled aboard with the others. The wagon attendant glanced at my ticket, looked me up and down and nodded. Olga looked relieved. We found our bunks and flopped onto them. 'It's OK,' she whispered. 'I didn't think she would guess we had an Australian with us! It is not a usual thing here.'

Olga introduced me to our *sputniks* (which I discovered weren't just satellites, but 'travelling companions' too). Masha and Natasha were old friends from high school. They had graduated together three years ago, and now Masha (the serious one), and Natasha (the smiley one) were studying at the Pedagogical Institute. Masha was specialising in geography, Natasha in mathematics. Andrei was Masha's boyfriend and he'd brought along his friend, Anton, a cheery student of puppetry at the Theatrical Institute and a guitar. Anton had a mischievous twinkle in his eye and always seemed to be making everyone laugh. Only Masha and Olga spoke English, but I got the feeling it wasn't going to matter.

It was blue rayon tracksuit and slipper time again. While everyone was changing, Masha examined my new backpack, squeezing the padded harness and tugging the straps.

'I've seen pictures of backpacks like this, but never a real one. I think it is very strong and comfortable.' She spoke with a heavy accent, rolling her r's and l's. Later I learned that not even her teachers had ever heard English spoken by native speakers.

'There is nothing like this here. Even if there was something, it is badly made.'

She showed me her rucksack, which she'd sewn herself from material brought by friends from Poland. She'd made everything else too: the other's rucksacks, tents, coats, pants and even sleeping bags. Barely able to sew on a button myself, I was impressed.

For the first time since our reunion that afternoon, Olga began to relax. She confessed she'd been worrying for weeks that her English wouldn't be good enough for us to communicate — and what would she do then? She was amazed we could understand each other so well. And although we'd met a few times in Australia, having me arrive on her doorstep was a daunting prospect. We came from such different worlds. How would we get on? We both laughed — and I was sure it would all be fine.

Our carriage for this trip was less fancy than the one I'd taken from Moscow to Leningrad. Then, I'd been in a *coupe* wagon, the Soviet equivalent of second class, with a carpeted corridor down one side and ten individual compartments each with four bunks, two up, two down. First class, or *lux*, had only two bunks per compartment. But for this trip we were travelling *platscart,* the cheapest 'third class' option favoured by students, workers and pensioners. *Platscart* wagons were open plan, arranged in a similar configuration to the *coupe* wagons, only without walls and doors to each four bunk compartment. This enabled an extra two bunks to be squeezed into the corridor. Luggage was stowed on a third level and under the bottom bunks.

The biggest drawback in *platscart* class was that sixty people shared the toilet. The first challenge in using the bumping convenience was that the seat was not designed to sit on, but rather to squat on, with moulded shoe holes and a hand rail. Our journey was a short one by Soviet standards, only forty hours north through Karelia and up the Kola Peninsula to the mining town of Apatity. But with sixty passengers whose chief entertainment for the duration was eating and drinking, the toilet was up for a flogging. The first time I needed to go I picked my way in my socks past the travellers picnicking in the aisles. Masha looked at me quizzically, and offered me her *tapochki*. 'No problem,' I replied. 'It's not cold.'

I waited patiently, but just as my turn came, the wagon attendant locked the door, and looked oddly at my feet. A few minutes later the train ground to a halt at a station. I went back to Olga who looked embarrassed. 'The … ummm, kaka falls through on the track, so you can't use toilet at station,' she whispered. 'You can go back when it's five minutes out from the platform. And here, take my *tapochki*.'

Russians were paranoid about cold — about getting cold feet, a cold head, about draughts, and about walking on cold surfaces. Even though it was still summer, with temperatures in the twenties, Yulia had been worried about me going out in a T-shirt in Moscow. I thought Olga was being motherly, concerned I might get sick from having cold feet. But when I got to the toilet, all became clear. Balancing in a squat position on the toilet seat of a lurching wagon, with a cold wind blowing up from beneath is no mean feat. Judging by the state of the floor, many of my predecessors had not been entirely successful. Socks were a bad idea.

Back in our carriage, Andrei passed his guitar around. Most of the group knew the chords to at least a few songs and all knew the lyrics: ballads about travelling, trekking, weather and even soldiers' songs from the decade-long war in Afghanistan in the 1980s. Everyone sang and munched away happily, laughing and proposing toasts. Masha hacked into bricks of black bread, topping them with slabs of butter as thick as the bread. She offered me a slice of *salo*, a chunky rectangle of solid pork fat, and again I had to explain I was a vegetarian. 'But why?' she asked.

Masha listened incredulously to my explanation, while continuing to saw into a fat length of *kolbasa,* a salami type cold sausage. The USSR had a reputation for having some of the world's best heart clinics and surgeons. Now I could see why. With a diet like this there'd be plenty of candidates to practise on. 'There will never be vegetarians here,' she declared. 'It's too cold. We need the fat.'

I asked Masha about her studies, and what she hoped to do when she finished her geography teaching degree. She looked glum. 'It's only because I have to get some kind of higher education. I looked at the faculty of foreign languages, but it's a *blatnoi fakultet*. That means all the students are only there because they have connections,' she muttered ruefully. 'My family doesn't have high connections so I couldn't get in anyway, even though my marks were enough. So I picked geography because it's easy.'

Masha's mother was an engineer, but her father had no higher education. He operated printing machines for a publisher. 'We don't have so many opportunities here in the Soviet Union,' she explained. 'There are only a small number of paths you can choose. But if we want to travel and work in some other country then the government will refuse to let us come back here. Probably I will have to be a teacher. Olga is very lucky that she had a chance to visit other countries.'

I had no idea what Masha meant by 'connections'. Surely in a communist country everyone had equal opportunities? Even in 1980s capitalist Australia, gaining admission to university depended on what you knew, not who you knew or how much money you had. But, as I was learning, in the USSR, the reality was poles apart from the rhetoric. Obtaining anything, from food, to a job, to a place in a university, relied on being part of a complicated network of people who could do you favours. You needed friends in high places — *apparatchiks*, communist party members, the *nomenklatura*, who could pull strings for you. And you needed to have something to offer them in exchange. These back-scratching networks offered innumerable opportunities for corruption and bribery. In fact, existence here was impossible without it. Honesty did not pay. Creaming a bit off the top for oneself was perfectly legitimate and absolutely the norm.

At a small regional station rotund babushki (which I now knew meant any older woman, whether she was a grandma or not) waited on the platform selling steaming *pirozhki*, deep fried buns stuffed with potato, meat or cabbage, from enamel buckets covered in tea towels. We bought a pile and passed them around the wagon. It was still light at 11 pm when I drifted off, watching the ever-shrinking forests rolling past my dusty window. The further north, the shorter the trees. Even the forests were conformist: orderly and organised, dead straight trunks standing to attention. Australian bush seemed anarchic in comparison.

Our journey was very much a social affair. By morning the neighbouring passengers knew they had a foreigner in their midst and through Olga, assailed me with questions about Australia. 'Do kangaroos really hop around in the streets?' enquired a weather-beaten old man, stirring four sugar cubes into a teacup of black leafy water. 'Do you really have no winter?' asked a woman with a gravity defying ginger hairdo.

Olga translated, I responded. Soon I would hear the same questions so many times I could understand and answer them myself.

'How much money do people get paid in Australia?'

'Ummmm,' I hesitated, wondering how I could avoid the subject. 'Well, it depends what your job is. If you're a doctor you get more than a garbage collector.'

Olga translated and our audience moved closer. 'But what about you?' they asked. 'What do you do?'

Uncomfortably aware of my relative wealth, I found myself deliberately trying to make life in Australia sound as difficult as possible. I explained that as a music teacher I didn't get a monthly wage, rather I was paid hourly and how much I got depended on how much I worked. From this I had to pay tax, rent, phone, water and electricity, and everything else was much more expensive than it was here.

Glancing around I sensed a mixed reaction to my answer. Under a socialist system, the masses could live their lives secure in the knowledge that the state would look after all its children from cradle to grave, no matter what their contribution. Housing was free, as was water, electricity and gas. Those who had phones paid a nominal sum. Medical services and education were covered by the state, there were almost no taxes and everything else was heavily subsidised.

But while these basics were guaranteed, it was at the most minimal level. Central planners had deemed that each citizen should be allocated 9 square metres of living space. Frequently, however, this was unavailable and a hundred million citizens were still waiting for their own 9 square metres. Waiting periods for new or bigger flats ranged from twenty years to never. Divorced couples would be forced to continue to share rooms for years on end, newlyweds would have no alternative but to live with parents and in-laws, even after the kids came and grandma was still there.

Over fifty million Soviet citizens lived in *kommunalki*, communal flats where up to three generations of each family would be allocated one room and up to twelve families would share a single toilet, sink and kitchen. There were ten-year waiting lists for cars and even telephones, unless of course you happened to have the right connections.

And you certainly couldn't complain. You were either with the communists or against them. And if you were against them, it was best not to say it too loudly. Expression of discontent was tantamount to betrayal, and traitors were dealt with by the state's most powerful organisation, the Komitet Gosudarstvennoy Bezopasnosti, or KGB. The Committee for State Security was the 'sword and shield' of the nation, entrusted with weeding out dissenters and monitoring 'harmful acts'. Until recently these could have been as innocuous as listening to pop music, watching foreign videos, or talking openly about the system. No matter how badly I tried to portray my situation back home, there was no comparison.

'But how much money do you earn as a music teacher?' 'How many rooms do your parents have in their house?' 'Do you have a car and do you we have a VCR?'

Reluctantly I confessed that I'd been earning the equivalent of twice a Soviet monthly wage *an hour* teaching clarinet from the age of eighteen, I didn't know how many rooms my parents had, both my mother and father had their own cars and yes we had a VCR. Gasps of envy followed and a discussion broke out. Olga translated what she could. One man was angry at this confirmation that they had been cheated out of a decent living. 'We should be a rich country. We have oil, coal, natural gas, diamonds, gold, timber, black soil for agriculture.

So why is it that we are living so badly and in a far-off land of convicts — excuse me — a music teacher can afford to travel?'

'Because no one is working,' answered someone else. 'We are all waiting for the leaders to fix things and nothing is getting better.'

The socialist empire was on the brink of collapse, but no one yet knew if and when it would happen. Five years earlier, in March 1985, the relatively young and sober Mikhail Gorbachev was elected to the position of General Secretary of the Communist Party after his elderly and ailing predecessors — Leonid Brezhnev, Yuri Andropov and Konstantin Chernenko — had dropped off the perch in quick succession. By the time Gorbachev took the helm, it was obvious that the Soviet-style centrally planned economy was a dismal failure.

According to Marxist-Leninist ideology, communism was destined to reshape human society, to establish a classless, stateless social organisation based on common ownership of the means of production. Once communism was achieved, there would be no need for leaders or even money in this paradise on earth. But something had gone drastically wrong with Marx and Lenin's recipe for utopia. With no other way to vent their frustrations, the economic and political system had become a source of humour for despairing Soviet citizens.

A speaker explains the advantages of communism to the residents of a lunatic asylum. Everybody applauds except for one guy standing at a distance.

'Why aren't you clapping?' asks the speaker.

'I'm a nurse,' he answers, 'not a madman.'

By 1986, Gorby had bravely acknowledged that the USSR's economy was a corrupt and stagnant mess. Still a staunch Lenin-loving communist at heart, Gorbachev introduced radical new concepts of perestroika (restructuring) and glasnost (political openness). This prompted a new *anekdot*, lampooning the contributions of Soviet leaders to the advancement of their motherland:

Stalin, Khrushchev, Brezhnev and Gorbachev were travelling together in a railway carriage, when unexpectedly the train stopped. Stalin put his head out of the window and shouted, 'Shoot the driver!' But the train didn't start moving. Khrushchev then shouted, 'Rehabilitate the driver!' But still it didn't move. Brezhnev then said, 'Comrades, comrades, let's draw the curtains, turn on the gramophone and pretend we're moving!' Gorbachev finally suggests, 'Let's get out and push!'

The state was bankrupting itself to keep its superpower status — pouring nonexistent funds into the military, the KGB and subsidies to the nations of the communist world. Farms, factories, transport services and stores had practically ceased to perform their designated functions, leading to severe shortages of consumer goods. This in turn had led to a thriving and well-developed black market run by entrepreneurial Mafia groups, which often included corrupt party officials. Most of the food on Soviet tables didn't come from the state shops, but found its way there via workplaces, friends or family connections. While on paper everyone received a roughly equivalent salary, it hardly mattered, as there was almost nothing to buy. Differences in living standards were determined by the perks and privileges that came with a job or connections, and how these could be traded. The insanity of the situation was common knowledge, discussed at kitchen tables across eleven time zones, from Brest (in the far west) to Vladivostok (in the Far East).

But in the parallel universe of state-controlled media, the rosy portrayal of Soviet life continued, with endless good news stories of bountiful harvests and important decisions taken by sage leaders. According to the propagandists, nothing bad ever happened in the USSR, there were never any accidents, there was no crime, no drugs, no prostitution, no poverty and no one ever went hungry. By contrast, the United States was an abominable place where a fantastically rich minority exploited the poverty-stricken masses. Olga and Masha saw no point in following the news, finding reruns of *Skippy*, *Lassie* and *Flipper* infinitely more believable.

By the time Gorbachev introduced his glasnost, the press had long been the butt of jokes by an aggrieved populace with no other way to express their frustrations.

'Rabinovich,' a friend asked, 'do you read communist newspapers?'
'Sure I do,' he replied. 'How else could I know what a happy life I lead?'

What is the difference between the two newspapers The Truth (Pravda) *and* The News (Izvestia)*?*
In The Truth *there is no news, and in the* The News *there is no truth.*

The advent of glasnost was particularly pleasing to the thousands of prisoners and occasional dissident Gorbachev ordered to be released from Soviet jails. The media began to report on the hitherto officially nonexistent seedy matters of drug addiction, prostitution and abuse of power by police. Then came the shocking images of the Chernobyl disaster and the controversial and unpopular invasion of Afghanistan. Without the propaganda machine in action to cover up the chaos, many in the Communist Party presciently feared they would lose their grip on power.

Olga, Masha and co had little interest in politics. At school they'd learned to recite minute details of the agendas of every Party Congress for the past seventy-three years, biographies of their great leaders and memorised slabs of socialist, communist, Marxist and Leninist theory. Soviet politics had for so long been a theatre show with no audience participation. To them it was boring, irrelevant and the likelihood of real change seemed as remote as the chance of finding a pineapple in a state shop. No one seemed aware of how much these policies — anti-communist to the core — were eroding the very foundations of the Communist Party's control of the country.

Thankfully they weren't interested in discussing money either, finding the subject distasteful and uncultured. I was pleased to avoid the issue, aware that although we were all about the same age, I'd earned enough for an overseas trip. Even if they'd been free to leave, foreign travel was prohibitively expensive. Not that they seemed bothered. Their own country was vast, travel was cheap and easy and there was plenty of excitement to be had right here on the Kola Peninsula.

After our second night on the train we disembarked in the morning at Apatity, a grey and dismal mining town picturesquely situated by a behomothic decrepit and clanking factory. It was surrounded by grey quarries, grey scree slopes of tumbling grey boulders, grey tundra, with grey apartment buildings to one side, all under a grey sky. Clouds of black smoke belching from the chimney stacks provided a welcome change of colour.

Gawping at the steel giant before me, I replayed a Shostakovich symphony in my head. The composer had been writing about battles, oppression and suffering, but his sometimes brutal and hammering musical language could have been a soundtrack to this scene of industrial hell. I could see the grinding machinery in his relentless, pounding rhythms, and discordantly screaming piccolos and trumpets. His sinister harmonies were the perfect sonic reflection of the hideousness of Soviet industrialisation. And this was where we were coming for a holiday adventure?

'Tourism', Olga called it. And we were 'tourists'. Later I found the following 'Advice for Tourists' in a textbook called *Russian for Beginners*:

Tourists are people who walk when they could go by
transport, and work when they could be relaxing. On a tourist
expedition we advise you to walk in a row with the strongest
at the end. He can carry things as his comrades drop them.
On the expedition one needs to eat more. The more one eats,
the lighter your rucksack. Overall, a tourist expedition has the
advantage that after it, any work seems like a holiday.

Olga and Masha did a quick recce of the food baskets and announced that we needed to stock up on rations and have a good meal. After what felt like forty hours of constant consumption on the train, I would have been happy to fast for the next week. Yet again I heard the refrain, 'You must eat up now because you will need it.'

Everyone was afraid that supplies might run out at any moment. Food was a national obsession and all opportunities to consume had to be taken. *Gostepriimstvo* — showing hospitality to guests — was a time-honoured Russian tradition, best done by constant force-feeding, rather like a French goose destined for a fine pâté. I was living in a country with empty shops, yet in my first four months in the USSR I would put on ten kilos. People would offer everything they had — the more your guests' waistlines bulged, the better you had undertaken your hosting duties.

The only place to eat was the factory canteen, a barn of a building with warped chequered linoleum tiles, wonky plastic tables and a bank of bain-maries. Portly matrons in white coats and chef's hats stirred steaming garbage-bin-sized saucepans, gruffly dolloping shredded pickled cabbage, grey boiled meat and potato slop onto our grimy plates.

Masha's plan was for us to trek over the Khibiny Massif, a horseshoe shaped range lying between Lake Imandra in the west and Lake Umbozero in the east. The Kola Nuclear Power Plant was about 60 kilometres away, but I didn't know that. Nor did I or anyone else know that there had been some 'serious operational disturbances' at that nuclear plant right before our visit. Glasnost had apparently not yet come to Apatity and it would be years before a Norwegian-based environmental research organisation called Bellona would begin to delve into the malfunctioning of Russia's decrepit nuclear facilities on the Kola Peninsula.

Bellies bulging with grey slop, we began our ascent of the barren rocky slopes behind the town. It was immediately obvious that the Westerner with the fancy backpack and hiking boots was embarrassingly less fit than the Russians. Once we passed easy picking distance from the town, smiley Natasha found clusters of fat dark purple berries growing close to the ground — blueberry-ish in taste and appearance — which we gorged by the handful. Patches of snow still lingered from the previous winter, even though it was now the end of summer. Anton found some bear footprints, but the others didn't share my enthusiasm for an encounter with a hungry beast.

After several hours, Masha and Andrei downed packs in a gully by an icy stream and we set up camp by a clump of straggly birch saplings, which gave us some protection from the wind. Natasha picked mushrooms the size of dinner plates and Andrei sautéed them like steaks. We collected basketfuls of whoppingly huge fungi, which we sliced, threaded onto strings and dried over the fire to take back to Leningrad for winter. We gathered jarfuls of juicy berries to be made into jam 'because they have lots of vitamin C'. As with their camping gear, if they couldn't buy it in the shops, my resourceful new friends found some way to obtain what they wanted regardless. (Ten years later, back on the Kola Peninsula to make a film about the state of Russia's nuclear facilities, I would find myself wondering whether the proximity of the nuclear power plant had anything to do with the extraordinary dimensions of the Arctic flora I'd gorged myself with on this trip.)

Masha had been here last in winter, skiing over slopes metres deep in snow. For years there had been a deficit of skis, but some young students had recently returned to Leningrad from a trip to the Crimea reporting they'd seen some skis in a shop there. They were promptly dispatched to return to the Ukraine, a two-day train trip, to buy up all they could.

After dinner Anton and Andrei played songs around the fire from a band called Mashina Vremeni (Time Machines) while the others sang along. Using goofy charades, Anton taught me useful words: *gusinitsa* (caterpillar), *griby* (mushrooms), *dim v glaza* (smoke in eyes), *krutoi* ('cool' in a Rambo kind of a way). I wrote them in my notebook as the others laughed at Anton's antics and my mispronunciations. None could believe I hadn't seen *Rambo*. It had been one of the first Western movies to hit Soviet cinemas and young people had flocked to watch it in droves. Here it had been an event, an insight into the world beyond Soviet borders. For me it had just been another daft American movie I couldn't be bothered with.

I squeezed my calves, aching from the day's trek. For Masha, this 'tourism' was kid's stuff. Her great dream was to be an *alpinist*, a serious mountain climber who used ice picks and ropes to scale the USSR's great peaks: Peak Communism and Peak Lenin in Kirghizia, Mount Elbrus in the Caucasus. I looked at her in amazement. 'Are you serious?'

'This was nothing,' she said, gesturing the way we'd come. 'I take my children on *this* walk.'

She and Natasha worked as 'Pioneer leaders' at their local 'Pioneer Palace' back on Vasilievsky Island, organising outdoor activities, training and competitions for children. The Young Pioneers was a movement for children aged from ten to fifteen, set up shortly after the Bolshevik revolution. 'Give me four years to teach the children and the seed I have sown will never be uprooted', Vladimir Ilyich had famously proclaimed, followed by 'Give us the child for eight years and it will be a Bolshevik forever'. In theory, membership was voluntary, but in reality, every Soviet child became a pioneer, wearing a red neck-scarf, a pin-on badge with the cherubic face of the child Lenin inside a silver star, and swearing allegiance to Lenin and the Communist Party. Their motto was 'Always prepared'. At sixteen they would move on to join the Komsomols (Communist Youth League).

Masha assured me that these days the organisation was no longer focused on propaganda and brainwashing. Rather her role was to teach the children useful skills in co-operation, initiative and survival. But ten years earlier, Lenin had still been a hero and becoming a Young Pioneer was a rite of passage, a pre-teen affirmation of the faith like that of a Catholic confirmation.

Olga's recollections of her initiation were tinged with nostalgia for a childhood where everything seemed so much clearer. She described how proud she'd felt, how the teachers had prepared them for months beforehand, telling them of their responsibilities to Lenin and the Communist Party. Then on Lenin's birthday she and all the other ten year olds had donned white shirts for the big ceremony. Her mother had even taken her out to a restaurant for the first time in her life that night. 'Back then in 1980, going to a restaurant was a very special thing to do,' she said wistfully.

I found it all a bit eerie. 'But wasn't it strange as a ten year old to be told you had responsibilities to Lenin and the Communist Party?'

She sighed. 'I know it's hard for you to understand, but from the time I was five years old, all the children's stories I read were about Lenin. Little Volodya behaved so well and studied so hard with only the best marks. They were written in a very positive way, and I really liked them. To me he was like a very positive hero and we all felt love and admiration for him.'

At almost midnight the sun was only just below the horizon, moving horizontally around our little world. Masha and Andrei shared a tent with Anton. Olga and Natasha produced a communal sleeping bag for our girl's tent, yet again challenging my concept of personal space. I said nothing, feeling guilty for my individualistic ways.

We spent a week exploring the tundra, never seeing another soul. The ever-entertaining Anton and Andrei made a mini black-and-white silent film on a wind-up camera, taking turns to shoot and act out monsters and bears chasing each other through the woods and icy stream. Anton carved a puppet's head from a birch branch and had us all in hysterics with a puppet show using nothing more than a tea towel.

There was a very good reason why trekking and alpinism had become popular Soviet pastimes in the 1960s, 70s, and 80s, particularly amongst intellectuals. Not everyone in the USSR felt the same love and admiration for Grandfather Lenin and his communist ideology as the young Olga. Not loving Lenin was a risky business and talking about it was even riskier. While walls, ashtrays and light fittings had 'ears', the mountains did not, and sitting around a campfire at 6,000 metres above sea level was the perfect location to discuss taboo subjects. The extreme challenge of scaling the towering peaks of the Pamirs, Altai, Caucasus and Tien Shan appealed to those who were trapped in oppressive jobs, controlled by lumpen-headed bureaucrats. On such an expedition they could take command of their own lives. Better still, if they were members of the Federation of Alpinists they could get state permission to take time off work and still get paid.

Our week over, we hiked back to Apatity, laden with mushrooms and berries, to wait for our train to come through in the wee small hours from Murmansk in the north. In the station, a group of teenage boys sat on post-trek dusty packs around a Jesus-lookalike with a wispy beard. He introduced himself as Alexander Karasyov, the Soviet Union's first Scout Leader. The tired and muddy boys were its first Scout Troop. Olga, Masha and co were mystified, but I was excited to find something familiar. I asked Olga to tell Alexander that I'd been a girl guide. His eyes lit up. He explained that there had been scouts in Russia before the revolution, but they'd been banned in the 1920s so all children could devote themselves to the Pioneers. Alexander had been reading about the scouting movement and had just established the Federation of Russian Scouts in Leningrad.

'But you must be a communist,' he exclaimed on hearing my name. 'Or at least your parents were. K.I.M is the acronym for Kommunisticheskaya Internatsionalnaya Molodyozh (the International Communist Youth).'

I laughed, and decided against telling him the real reason — that my father thought the American actress Kim Novak had nice legs.

Olga was suspicious of these scouts and seemed uncomfortable. 'Why do we need to bring some foreign experience into our country when we have our own such groups? I am against this.'

Her protective patriotism fascinated me as much as Alexander's enthusiasm for the new and foreign. The Soviet Union was at last opening up to outside influence, but not everyone was ready to have the old order completely shaken.

The City of Revolution

The seven miracles of the Soviet Authority:
1. There is no unemployment, yet nobody works.
2. Nobody works, yet the Grand Scheme is carried out.
3. The Grand Scheme is carried out, yet there is nothing to buy.
4. There is nothing to buy, yet there are queues everywhere.
5. There are queues everywhere, yet everyone has everything.
6. Everyone has everything, yet everyone is dissatisfied.
7. Everyone is dissatisfied, yet everyone votes 'Yes'.

Back in Leningrad, Olga and I had to visit one of the nightmares of the Soviet Authority: the OVIR (Department of Visas and Registration). This was the branch of the Ministry of the Interior charged with the task of making sure its citizens and visiting 'other country people' were all exactly where they were supposed to be. Everyone who went anywhere other than their 'registered' address, had to inform the kind comrades at OVIR. As with all Soviet ministries, employment by this department required advanced skills in rudeness and inefficiency, and the comrades at the Vasilievsky Island branch had graduated with first-class honours.

We stood for hours in slug-paced queues of locals trying to arrange invitations for friends and relatives. I twitched and paced with frustration while Olga and the others waited patiently, missing days of work with resigned expressions and fatalistic shrugs. Twice we made it to the counter after three-hour waits, only to have the window shut in our face. When we finally submitted my documents, poor Olga was interrogated about why I hadn't come within three days of arriving in the country. I paid a minuscule fine and several more forms later, a surly woman with bright blue eyeshadow stamped my visa. But it wasn't over yet. She sent us to the bank to buy a *gosposhlina*, a five-kopeck square of sticky paper, which meant another morning of queuing. Then we had to queue for another day at OVIR to show it to her.

By then I had refined my own deadpan stare. The sheer tedium of trying to carry out simple tasks either drove people mad, or turned them into zombies. While anger achieved nothing but high blood pressure, at least humour soothed the soul. As I too began to be dragged down by the oppressively inefficient bureaucracy, my collection of *anekdots* grew.

A man is queuing for food. Finally he's had enough. He turns round to his friend and says, 'That's it. I'm going to kill that Gorbachev,' and marches off. Two hours later he comes back.

'Well,' says the friend, 'did you do it?'

'No,' replies the other, 'there was an even longer queue over there.'

A Muscovite ordered a car and was told it would be delivered in five years, on the second Monday in September. 'Will that be in the morning or afternoon?' he asked.

'What does it matter after five years?' asked the salesman.

'It's just that the plumber is coming in the morning,' he replied.

A customer asks at a shop, 'What's this, you don't have any meat again?'

'That's not true! There's no meat in the shop opposite. We don't have fish.'

Hoping to make life easier for Olga, I asked her to teach me a few basic phrases so I could at least do the shopping. But just ducking down to the corner store to pick up a loaf of bread was impossible. Central planning committees had seen to that, devising ludicrously time-consuming ways of carrying out what should have been the simplest of procedures. The daftest idea was the *kassa*, or cashier system. Instead of queuing once in each shop, you had to queue twice, and sometimes even a third. The first queue was to tell the bad-tempered saleswoman behind the glass counter what you wanted. If you were lucky, she'd write down the prices, and hand you a piece of paper, which you would then take to the next queue, the cashier. If not, you'd have to remember it. The cashier would add the figures with an abacus and bark the total. Once you'd paid and got a receipt, you returned to the first queue, to hand over the receipt and pick up your lump of stale bread, plastic bag of milk, or half-mouldy cabbage. This could take up to two hours in any one shop, and there were individual shops for bread, dairy, vegetables, cooking oil and everything else.

It was perfectly possible to spend a full day queuing to get just a few ingredients for one meal. Most of the people also standing in the queues were supposed to be at work. While everyone was queuing, nothing else was getting done. Olga had missed days of her work assisting a university lecturer with classes because she had no other time to buy food for herself and her grandmother. It was no wonder office opening hours were so short, and lunch breaks so long. It was the only chance most people had to get food and other essential items, and even then it wasn't enough.

There was only ever one kind of toothpaste, shampoo, soap, etc, available, if you could find it at all. At first, I found the lack of choice preferable to the confusing excess of my local Safeways in Melbourne, with its thirty brands of toothpaste. Then Olga explained that most Soviet goods had no production standards. The typical off-the-shelf shampoo was likely to be some random chemical concoction that would cause the user's hair to fall out and skin to come up in a blistering rash. Olga's parents had brought her an impressive collection of soaps, cleansers, moisturisers, perfumes and cosmetics from their travels and I noticed she would often save empty bottles for the curiousity value of their shape or exotic labels.

Near the Primorskaya Metro station there was a 'supermarket', a novel place where foodstuffs were left unguarded and customers could push a flimsy wire trolley through aisles of metal rack shelves and help themselves. But the only item available in the entire 'Super' market was super-sized glass jars of shredded pickled beetroot. At least it was a vegetable. We bought three — 12 litres of pickled purple.

When we needed cooking oil, Olga rummaged for half an hour through the kitchen cupboards in search of a bottle to take to the shop, muttering about the 'poor organisation' in her country. I chirpily remarked how great I thought it was that so much was recycled. She looked at me as though I were a madwoman. But my optimism had limits. For a vegetarian, the vegetable and fruit shops were the most depressing. The potatoes were shrivelled and black, carrots tiny, muddy and withered, and apples mushy and brown. Sometimes there were a few puny cabbages and cauliflowers, in such an advanced state of decay I couldn't bring myself to buy them. We mostly lived on black bread and soup made from the unhappy vegetables. Even the sausages Olga bought for Rizhok the cat had to be boiled for hours to kill the salmonella.

Ostensibly I had come to the USSR to study music, but already I was finding the daily rituals of practice tedious. My enthusiasm for hours of scales and arpeggios was evaporating, and I was beginning to wonder if blowing down a wooden tube was indeed my calling. Each time I played, my fingers were stiffer, bottom lip sorer and face muscles floppier. And I still had a thesis to finish for a post-graduate degree — 20,000 riveting words about reeds, the little half-shaved slices of bamboo that are the bane of every clarinet player's life. Perhaps life was too short?

I threw myself into studying Russian and exploring Leningrad. I bought a guide booklet in English — published by the Central Advertising and Information Bureau — from which I learned that Leningrad was 'the city of revolution which has by right been given the name of the great Lenin'. I read that there were over '270 memorial places in Leningrad relating to Lenin's name' and how 'dear everything related to Lenin is to Leningraders, same as to all Soviet people'. Tsar Peter I, the man responsible for founding the city in 1703 barely rated a mention. Being a Tsar, he was naturally dismissed by Soviet historians as nothing but an evil autocrat.

Peter had indeed been an evil autocrat, and at six foot eight, a scary one at that. And like Ivan the Terrible, he was rumoured to have been an inspiration to communist leaders. Stalin in particular was said to have been impressed by Peter's use of forced labour — known as *katorga* — of convicts and serfs to construct factories, roads and fortresses, and ultimately one of the world's most spectacularly beautiful cities on a fetid swampland at the mouth of the Neva River. The site was appalling, weather even worse, and workers died like flies. Peasants were conscripted in their tens of thousands from all parts of the country, expected to provide their own tools and walk hundreds of kilometres shackled and escorted by military guards just to get there. Half died on the way. Peter hired German engineers, Italian architects, and ordered every stonemason in Russia to help build his new Amsterdam, or 'Venice of the North'.

Almost three hundred years on, despite decades of neglect, Leningrad was still magnificent. Grand Italianate palaces adorned with columns, statues and vases, façades painted in fading pastels, lined the boulevards and waterways of the centre like crumbling wedding cakes. In a stroke of genius, one of Peter's successors, Catherine the Great, had decreed that with the exception of church domes and bell towers, no buildings could be constructed higher than the roof of the Winter Palace. Fortunately, no one since had dared defy his orders and the heart of the USSR's second largest city retained its original elegance and harmonious proportions, with not a skyscraper or office block in sight.

Peter's transformation of the mosquito-infested swamp into a sophisticated metropolis revolved around the vast Neva River. Flowing majestically through the northern capital — from Lake Ladoga in the east to the Gulf of Finland in the west — the Neva and its sixty-five tributaries and canals dissect Leningrad into 101 islands. These are connected by 365 bridges; some of which are raised at night to allow ships to pass, others ornate footbridges decorated with sculptures and wrought iron. Just before entering the Gulf, the river splits into three, slicing Vasilievsky Island and the Petrograd district off from the mainland. The main streets of the old centre radiate out from the Admiralty building and Winter Palace on the banks of the Neva across from Vasilievsky Island.

Olga showed me how to use the metro, tram and trolleybus to get to the palaces, museums, galleries and theatres on the Neva's southern bank. I wandered the streets where Dostoyevsky had lived and imagined Raskolnikov, anti-hero of *Crime and Punishment*, roaming along the canals, his soul tortured with guilt from his macabre and grisly crime. And I explored the Peter and Paul Fortress, the city's first building and at one time the most dreaded prison of Tsarist Russia.

With dictionary and notebook in hand, I spent days meandering through the grandiose baroque Winter Palace, marvelling at the majestic reception halls and gilded chambers of the Tsars, decorated with malachite, agate and other semi-precious stones, with intricate mosaic and parquet floors, silk-upholstered furniture and glittering chandeliers. The adjoining Hermitage buildings had been commissioned by Catherine the Great in 1764 to house her art works and provide 'a place of seclusion' for her to entertain on a smaller scale to the vast Winter Palace. Now the Palace Hermitage displayed collections spanning the entire history of world culture: ancient Egyptian artifacts, Graeco-Scythian antiquities, Western European jewellery, silver, porcelain, carpets, arms and armour, galleries overflowing with the works of the great European masters. Entire rooms were dedicated to Picasso, Cézanne, Matisse, Rubens, Rembrandt or Raphael. It wasn't hard to imagine how such ostentatious wealth and luxury had infuriated hungry peasants and workers.

Groups of primary school children, the girls in pinafores with pigtailed hair and puffy white bows, filed neatly around the Palace listening attentively to stooped babushki rattling off dates and details. I loitered nearby and eavesdropped, jotting down unfamiliar words to look up in my pocket dictionary. Soon I could decipher the gist of their narratives, tales of the Bolshevik's storming of the palace, and how, thanks to grandfather Lenin, these treasures now belonged to the people. 'Good on the revolutionaries,' I thought approvingly. 'Far better that it was now owned by the state for everyone to enjoy.'

Black-and-white photos showed young women preparing the

priceless collections for evacuation to Siberia as the Nazis rained bombs down on the city during the 'Great Patriotic War', as the Soviets called World War II. Other grainy images showed Hermitage workers cultivating cabbages and potatoes in the palace gardens during the 900-day blockade of the city. More than forty-five years on, many of the survivors still worked here, most noticeably as 'security grannies'. They sat, perched on chairs at the entrances to each of the more than one thousand rooms of the seven-building complex, hunched and irritable in dark cardigans, ready to snap at recalcitrant visitors. And everyone knew better than to mess with an eagle-eyed, acid-tongued granny.

Pavlina, a doe-eyed university friend of Olga's, wanted to practise her English on the resident antipodean guinea pig. She took me around the Russian Museum, resplendent with enormous canvases portraying proud moments in the expansion of the Russian empire. I found Surikov's *Conquest of Siberia* especially confronting: a heroic depiction of the sixteenth century Cossack leader Yermak Timofeyevich and his army of gun-toting Slavs slaughtering terrified indigenous Siberians clad in animal skins, armed only with bows and arrows. In 1990 in Australia we had not yet apologised to our Aborigines, but I couldn't imagine any museum curator hanging a wall-sized oil painting graphically illustrating their massacre.

She led me to masterpiece after masterpiece: 'our' Vereshchagin's exotic Central Asian marketplaces, 'our' Vasnetsov's grand historical scenes, 'our' Mikhail Vrubel's fairytale characters and 'our' Kuindzhi's magically atmospheric landscapes. Back on the street Pavlina talked about 'our' poets, 'our' architects and 'our' composers. I was intrigued by her constant use of the word 'our'. It never would have occurred to me to speak of 'our Henry Lawson', or 'our Tom Roberts'. To me this seemed yet another indicator of the radically different East vs West mindset. In the West we were brought up to be individuals first and foremost. Here, people were Soviet citizens. Whatever gifts and talents they may have belonged to the nation.

Determined to soak up the abundant brilliance around me, I frequented the concert halls and theatres. For just a few roubles I could watch extraordinary performances of ballets and operas at the Kirov Theatre, or listen to world-class soloists and conductors at the Philharmonia. Audiences were packed with people of all ages. There may have been little to sate the appetite, but there was plenty of nourishment for the soul. At least an inspirational performance by the Leningrad Philharmonic could help people forget the daily torture of accomplishing life's basics.

Olga was back at university now, working during the day and studying at night. We barely saw each other, beyond preparing a late night supper together. After trying to make a meal from whatever scraps we'd managed to acquire, we'd sit at her wobbly kitchen table, swap stories and gossip, laugh at the latest jokes and worry about Vera Nikolayevna's increasingly eccentric ways. Olga particularly enjoyed hearing my exuberant reviews of whatever cultural activity I had engaged in that day. Much about her motherland was mind-numbingly maddening, and I think she was relieved I was having a glass half-full experience.

One night she invited me to sit in on some of her lectures at the Philology Faculty where she was studying Old Church Slavonic and ancient Russian. The subjects hadn't been her first choice. She wanted to study Czech after spending two years in Prague and Bratislava as a teenager while her father was chief conductor of the Bratislava Symphony Orchestra. But her marks weren't high enough, so her dream of finding a way back to Czechoslovakia was put on hold. English was an option, but interest and patriotism led her to Slavic languages. Old Church Slavonic was the original idiom of the Russian Orthodox Church, the Slavic equivalent of Latin to the romance languages. In class, students read parables from the Bible and the ancient writings of Orthodox monks. I was surprised to learn that this subject, so integrally connected with religion, had never been banned by the communists.

Most of the students at the Philology Faculty had similar motivations to Olga, to use their second and third languages as a way to travel or work in another country. One friend was studying Albanian, with a master plan of finding a husband and new life in Tirana. Proficiency in the lingo, she hoped, would increase her chances.

Between lectures we visited the bathroom. It was freezing and putrid, with squat toilets and broken doors. None of the toilets flushed properly, but that was standard. There were plenty of capable people who could have sorted out the nation's woeful plumbing, but they'd been put to work on more pressing projects, like nuclear submarines or weapons manufacture. The girls checked their make-up and adjusted their clothing before a cracked spattered mirror. A glass jar on the sink top contained a fresh cigarette. There was a note taped on the mirror above the jar which read: 'If you have cigarettes, please leave one here for those who don't. If you don't have any, then please take one.'

I was astounded by such extraordinary anonymous charity. Cigarettes were among the most precious and difficult to obtain commodities and to me, that sign summed up the generous spirit of the ordinary Mr Ivan Soviet.

'You'd never find anyone doing something like that in Australia,' I remarked to Olga. 'People are so much nicer here. The system makes people look after each other.'

She seemed surprised I'd even noticed. It was just how things were. There wasn't much around, but people were happy to share, even with total strangers.

Even scarcer than cigarettes was toilet paper. There wasn't any. Empty wire baskets hung optimistically on the walls dividing the squat holes: totally pointless toilet paper holders. The Soviets had sent Gagarin into orbit back in 1961, but couldn't provide their citizens with anything to wipe their bottoms. I often pondered this while scouring my bag for something to get me out of a tricky situation. No matter where you were — a theatre, train station, museum, restaurant or university — you had to bring your own. The paper mills had other more important priorities. A joke at the time went:

Can you wrap a bus in a newspaper?

Yes, if the newspaper has just published a speech by the General Secretary.

The dearth of derriere-dabbing material had given print journalism a special role in the Soviet Union. After reminding the people how well everything was going, it came into its own and became truly useful; shredded and stashed in receptacles on the backs of toilet doors in private flats or workplaces. But your average *Pravda* didn't go far. Soviet papers had no advertising and there were usually only one or two broadsheet pages — unless the General Secretary had been on the job — printed in a lethal black ink which left one's hands looking like a coal miner's. I preferred not to think what they did to other points of contact. The used paper would block the sewerage pipes, so you couldn't flush it down, instead leaving it in a filthy basket by the loo.

The rest of Russia's paper pulp was diverted to the printers of books, postcards and posters. These all served the same purpose as the papers — to tell everyone how great their motherland/communism/ Lenin was and how lucky they were to live here. Leningrad's biggest bookshop, Dom Knigi (House of Books), was on Nevsky Prospekt, the city's main street which runs perpendicular to the Neva River from the Winter Palace, and west to Moscovsky Station. I regularly spent hours browsing through the multistorey rabbit warren of a store with its treasure trove of Soviet propaganda. For a country that prided itself on its technological prowess, little effort had gone into developing printing presses. Picture postcards were blurry and pixellated, in bright unnatural colours, giving an alien quality to the featured Soviet architecture and monuments. And why anyone would want to send a snap of a 500-room concrete box hotel in Murmansk or a statue of bayonet-waving soldiers was a complete mystery to me.

I bought a collection of textbooks designed for foreigners to learn Russian. Practice dialogues involved kind Soviet students showing the aliens around their cities, pointing out the beautiful boulevards, modern amenities and locations of heroic deeds. The foreign student would learn to enthusiastically exclaim how they had nothing like that in their country. Other sample translation exercises described the USSR's superior medical and education systems, the genius of its sportspeople, and its scientific and literary achievements. The triumph of the Red Army in the Great Patriotic War was also a common theme.

That war still obsessed the nation. While reminders of the 45-year-old victory were omnipresent, there was no mention at all of the humiliating withdrawal of Soviet troops from Afghanistan a year earlier, in 1989. Propagandists worked hard to keep the memory of the defeat of the Nazis fresh, as if trying to distract the people's attention from the rotting food on the almost empty shelves. I bought a set of posters reprinted only months earlier designed to be put together as a wall mural in schools. Entitled 'How they Fought for the Motherland', the posters were social realist images of soldiers with chiselled cheekbones waving flags with pronouncements such as: 'Under the banner of Lenin — Forward for the Motherland for our Victory' and 'Our Work is Truth. Victory will be Ours'.

I filled postcards (depicting vast hotels and bronze war memorials) with excitable rants about every extraordinary detail of my new life, and braced myself for the ordeal of sending them home to friends and family. There was only one place in Leningrad — a city of five million people — to post letters out of the country: the Central Post and Telecommunications Office. The 'international' counter operated for three hours a day, three days a week. Several times I waited a full three hours in line to be turned away with a snarl on the stroke of 1 pm.

After a month and a half I received my first letter from home, sent two days after my departure. It had been torn open and roughly taped back together. Olga told me that all the letters I'd sent to her had been opened as well. I hoped Mum had received some of my letters before now but phoning to check was next to impossible. International, even intercity, calls had to be booked five days in advance and the telephone exchange would choose the time to make the connection, probably at a time convenient to whoever wanted to listen in on our chat. It was all too hard.

Olga's friends, Masha and Andrei from the tundra trek, decided to tie the knot. Both were twenty, the optimal age for marriage in the Soviet Union. But the imminent wedding of a friend posed a pressing problem for Olga. What could she get for a present? She knew her adventurous friend was desperate for a pair of ski boots. After weeks of searching every bare-shelved sporting goods shop in Leningrad, she finally located a pair for only fifty-five roubles, a week's wages. 'They are even Masha's size,' she told me ecstatically.

Some days later, the wedding party assembled at the local 'Wedding Palace'. Like Pioneer Palaces, Wedding Palaces were another monolithic Soviet institution, a production line facility designed to ensure that each amorous union was cemented in as equally bland and unromantic manner as possible. Anxious couples congregated with their guests in the drab marble foyer of what had once been a sumptuous nobleman's mansion on the Neva embankment, waiting for their turn on the nuptial conveyor belt. Andrei joked around and Masha looked nervous as the buxom celebrant officiously ushered the groups in and out of the former ballroom. Their turn came. I stood at the back with Olga while a stocky babushka with a heaving chest rushed them through the oaths.

'This is a big decision, for the rest of your life. Are you ready to spend all your lives together?' Olga translated in a whisper.

The ceremony was over in minutes. Masha and Andrei agreed, signed the papers and exchanged rings. We all filed meekly out of the hall, to the accompaniment of some scratchy taped Tchaikovsky. Bride, groom and guests squeezed into a couple of rented cars and headed off for the mandatory photo session in front of a towering row of bronze soldiers brandishing bayonets, out on the road to the airport. Several other couples and their entourages stood around, waiting for their turns. A brisk wind whipped snow around the high-heeled and sheer-stockinged ankles of the shivering brides and their maids of honour. It was a Soviet tradition, explained Olga, to have wedding photos taken in front of significant monuments, usually those dedicated to soldiers killed in the Great Patriotic War. 'It is to express gratitude for the fact that we are alive and free. If not for them, then we would not be here now.'

The most important part of the occasion was the celebration afterwards and the parents of the newlyweds must have been saving and queuing for months to put on such a banquet in Masha's family's cramped flat. A long table was spread with traditional foods: *selyotka pod shubi* ('herring in a fur coat', pickled fish with shaved vegetables on top), cold meats, salads of grated beetroot, peas and ham drowning in mayonnaise, cheeses, breads and dishes of bonbons. There was sweet berry liqueur, *Sovietskoye Shampanskoye* — sickly sugary bubbly wine, passed off as Soviet Champagne — and vodka toasts chased with fat pickles. The guests shouted '*Gorko, gorko!*', meaning bitter. Andrei and Masha had to kiss, 'to make it sweet'.

Masha's father eagerly showed me his slide collection, bought on his travels throughout the USSR. I examined each one with genuine interest, ooohing and aaahing at the miniature images of gold fountains, palaces and theatres, along with, of course, the obligatory concrete hotels and war memorials. How silly I was. He bundled a boxful together and pressed it into my hands, his treasured images of his beloved country collected over decades, for me to take home to Australia. I protested. I couldn't possibly take them. He looked mortified and I didn't know what to do. I didn't want to deprive him of his collection, yet feared he would be offended if I refused. I gulped and gratefully accepted his gift, making a mental note to self: 'Be careful what you admire, because you may just end up with it.'

Predictably, the conversation turned to marriage in Australia. How old were people when they got married? How old was I? 'Twenty-one!' When was I planning on getting married and having children? It was time. If I didn't find a man soon then I would be too old and no one would want to marry me. Perhaps they could find me a Russian man? They were shocked to hear that women often didn't marry until thirty or older. 'But they are old women by then!' 'What man would want to marry an old woman?'

The panic was on. Youth and beauty had to be capitalised on before a woman's use-by date was up and she would miss out altogether. Personally, I couldn't see why a woman would be in such a rush to marry. Sure the local men were delightfully gentlemanly, they opened car doors, carried women's bags and helped them on and off with their coats. But most Russian men never cooked, cleaned, washed clothes, looked after the kids or shopped. After one day as a fluffy centre of attention, a bride faced an interminable future of waiting on her hubby, cooking *kasha* (porridge) and cutlets, emptying out the toilet paper basket and washing smelly shirts by hand in a bucket in the bath. To top it off she would have either her or her husband's parents sleeping only metres away, with only a thin plaster wall between them. Masha and Andrei were to move into Masha's room in her family's cosy flat, along with her parents and granny. They were divorced within a year.

Masha and Andrei weren't the only ones whose relationship was facing insurmountable obstacles. Svetlana, the *Russia House* interpreter who'd moved to Melbourne, called me at Olga's. With a broad Australian accent, she told me she'd left her cameraman boyfriend and was back in Russia again. She was staying with her mother and grandmother in their flat near the Tushinskaya Metro station on Moscow's northern outskirts, and wondered if I'd be able to visit.

Technically I wasn't allowed to stay anywhere but Olga's flat on Vasilievsky Island, without first seeking permission from the Ministry of the Interior. So to avoid another torturous series of visits to OVIR, I bought a train ticket from one of the scalpers lurking outside the Moscovsky Station in Leningrad. These budding entrepreneurs never asked to see passports, and you never had to queue. Shady characters in black leather jackets, the scalpers had running deals with the official sellers, buying up train-fulls worth of state-subsidised tickets and onselling to the public at inflated prices, direct from their jacket pockets. It was illegal of course, but a percentage of profits slipped to the station cops made sure the system ran like a finely tuned machine. The cumbersome bureaucracy was so painful that people happily paid extra to circumvent the system. The black market worked.

Back in Moscow I took the metro out to Tushinskaya, a bleak *spalny raion* (sleeping district), so-called because there are no amenities, only residential flats. Built in the 1980s, the twenty-storey blocks were like anthills, shelter for hordes of identical scurrying workers. Bringing a new standard to 'cheap and nasty', their rushed construction was already evident. The poor quality concrete slabs were cracking and crumbling, the balconies — piled high with junk — hung precariously, and dribbles of rust stained the walls. I wedged myself into a packed minibus at the metro station and counted the stops as per Svetlana's instructions. This wasn't a place I wanted to get lost.

I had never met Svetlana in person, but I recognised her at once, waiting in the cold at the bus stop near her building. She was a younger version of her mother, petite, with *matryoshka* doll features: wide, high cheekbones, delicate nose and round eyes with thick lashes. Ludmilla was ecstatic to have her back. Australia was far away and Sveta was her only child. But it wasn't to be for long. Before leaving, Sveta had met a wealthy Sri Lankan–Dutch businessman on holiday in Australia. He'd showered her with expensive clothes, jewellery and perfumes and was calling her daily in Moscow trying to convince her to move to Sri Lanka. She thought she was in love and chattered away enthusiastically about her new beau's manly attributes. At least until her 'old friend', Alexei called and invited her out.

Sveta went into a spin. She spent the afternoon washing, blow-drying, curling and uncurling her hair, testing different eyeshadows and trying on outfits. Finally she settled on the most bust-enhancing option. Through her job at a Moscow Beriozka (hard currency) store, Ludmilla had a mink coat, which Sveta donned with a flourish. She insisted I come along, the pudgy companion in an op-shop skirt, holey tights and dowdy black hand-knitted jumper. Alexei arrived in a chauffeur-driven black ZIL limousine, 'The favourite car of every one of our leaders since Stalin,' Sveta explained. 'There aren't so many of them, and they are only for important people in the Government.' It looked like something out of a 1950s American gangster movie. I was bemused. It was the first time I had seen evidence of real wealth here, and it didn't fit my nice picture of everyone living equally, and modestly.

For someone who had just been telling me about the new love of her life, Sveta flirted up a storm with her 'old friend'. Alexei spoke no English and they had a lot to catch up on. I stared out the tinted windows in silence, feeling like a spare leg and wondering who this Alexei was and why he had such a fancy car and chauffeur? Why was Sveta so keen to impress him? I couldn't bring myself to ask. After all, I was their guest.

We pulled into a circular driveway, under a colonnaded portico of a grand building in central Moscow. Sveta waited for Alexei to help her out. An obsequious doorman ushered us into a foyer carpeted in rich red and another set of obliging hands took our coats. Oozing deferential charm to Alexei, the mâitre d' guided us into a massive banquet hall. A band played rousing songs, and couples swung each other around on a parquet dance floor. The tables groaned with dishes of caviar, baked fish, even suckling pigs with apples wedged in their mouths. Each place was set with a row of ornately engraved pink crystal glasses in different sizes. Eagle-eyed waiters circulated keeping the pretty goblets filled with liqueurs, wines and spirits. The room buzzed with loud laughter and general gaiety. Unlike the sullen masses on the streets, the well-fed and well-dressed men and women in this hall were having a great time. A singer with greased back hair crooned into a microphone, accompanied by an accordion, while the couples held each other close and swayed around the dance floor. Alexei took Sveta by the hand and gazed smitten into her eyes.

Everyone was so drunk and preoccupied I may as well have been invisible, which was fine by me. Marvelling at the luxury and extravagance, I almost wished I were brave enough to sample the dish of red and black caviar in front of me. But determined to remain true to my vegetarian principles I contented myself with the dish of tinned peas and cheese cubes drowned in mayonnaise that passed for salad. When Sveta at last came over, I asked what the occasion was.

'These are just some work colleagues of Alexei's, you know, just getting together for a party with some friends,' she said cryptically.

Just as I began to enquire into Alexei's line of work, Sveta flounced off for another dance. I was afraid to ask again. A year later I found a copy of George Orwell's *Animal Farm*, only just translated into Russian, and this mysterious night of excess came into my mind. Some animals really were more equal than others.

4

Soviet Disunion

To Glory, our free Fatherland
The stronghold of the friendship of peoples
Party of Lenin is the power of the people
It leads us to the triumph of Communism
Chorus of the national anthem of the Soviet Union

Forty-six years after Sergei Mikhalkov penned the lyrics to the Soviet national anthem, its message still rang true with Olga: the 'union of free republics' was indeed 'the stronghold of the friendship of the peoples'. 'Some people speak different languages, but really the USSR is all one big friendly country,' she enthused. 'It doesn't feel like there are borders at all between our republics.'

I was back from Moscow and we were planning a trip to Ukraine, in the far southwest of the USSR and the second largest republic after Russia. But while Olga was anticipating a warm reception from the Ukrainians, we had some local unfriendliness to deal with first. At the State Railways Ticket Office on Griboyedov Canal, we purchased *coupe* class tickets to the western Ukranian city of Lvov at the bargain price of the rouble equivalent of AUD$2 each for a two-night journey. We returned home to discover the tickets were missing, along with Olga's internal passport and chequebook. Devastated, she reported the theft at the local police station. A sneering cop looked her up and down, obviously neither believing her nor caring. Eventually he agreed to make a note which read: 'she says she lost her passport'. He then told her she was too ambitious and waved us away. Olga was fuming; insulted, offended and frustrated. It was her first encounter with the *militsiya,* and had shattered her childhood illusions of good, brave and helpful policemen.

The bank was only marginally more helpful. Olga was informed that because she had lost her chequebook, her account would be closed for the next three years. She would be unable to withdraw money for this period, but they could give no guarantee that whoever had stolen her chequebook wouldn't be able to use it. Once the three years were up she would be given a new number and could access her money, assuming no one had taken it in the meantime. Fortunately she had some traveller's cheques at home to tide her over. We had to buy new train tickets too.

The passport was less problematic. Soviet citizens had to carry passports at all times. There were two kinds: internal — for use within the USSR — and *za-gran* or 'beyond border' passports. Not everyone could get a *za-gran* passport, but Olga had one because her father's work involved travel. Luckily it was her internal passport that was stolen, as it was easier to get a new one. When she went to get photos taken, I got one done too. After a couple of takes the photographer emerged from his black shroud and glared at me. 'Do not smile. It is forbidden to smile for a passport photo.'

We were going to the Ukraine with one of Olga's closest friends, Natasha, another Russian language student at Leningrad State University. For the past three years Olga and Natasha had worked together on summer holiday research projects. The first was in the Novgorod region, 180 kilometres south of Leningrad, where they visited ancient churches in and around the thousand-year-old city, recording and deciphering recently discovered graffiti written by monks in Old Church Slavonic. Their second project was collecting healing spells used in lieu of modern medicine by babushki in the villages around Leningrad. The experience had been an eye-opening one. It was their first encounter with poverty, and they were horrified to learn that most of the village men were either in prison or drunkards. On their third trip they collected dialects in the villages around the town of Staraya Russa, a further 60 kilometres on from Novgorod. Now, a fellow student in her mid-thirties named Valya had invited Olga and Natasha to visit her at her home in Lvov. When she'd heard about Olga's 'Australian', she'd extended the invitation to me too.

Five precepts of the Soviet intelligentsia: Do not think. If you think — do not speak. If you think and speak — do not write. If you think, speak and write — do not sign. If you think, speak, write and sign — don't be surprised.

Natasha was the grand-daughter of an army general, petite, dark and serious, with a scholarly demeanour. She wore no make-up, dressed ultra-conservatively and lived with her mother and grandparents in a three-room flat in Leningrad's Petrograd district, another large island adjacent to Vasilievsky. Her mother, who I'll call Irina as she was afraid to be identified, was an academic and lecturer in English at a Leningrad Military Academy. Her parents had divorced when she was six and she rarely saw her father, a professor of French. Mother and daughter spoke in exceedingly gracious Queen's textbook lingo, and I couldn't help but smile when Natasha asked ever so politely, 'Wouldn't you like a cup of tea?'

Thanks to her grandfather's former post in the army, followed by a position as a Professor of Radio Technology, Natasha was the only student in her school class who didn't live in a *kommunalka*. The family had a car, a dacha (country house), a bigger flat than most, and money problems were unheard of. She knew she was lucky, she knew the 'everyone is equal' propaganda was a load of baloney, and she knew that everyone else knew it too. Natasha showed me a pair of coveted genuine Levi's, neatly folded and apparently unworn. A classmate of her mother's who worked on a ship had brought them for her, but Natasha was afraid to wear them. 'I'm uncomfortable that I have such things and others don't,' she confessed quietly. 'So I just get them out sometimes and touch them.'

When General Secretary Leonid Brezhnev died in 1982, Natasha was an impressionable ten-year-old. 'Everyone cried, because we thought there would be an atomic war the next day. We really believed that the US wanted war with us. But now almost no one believes in the anti-Western propaganda. We were always told that in the West there were a few very, very rich people and everyone else was exploited by them and lived in poverty. I used to believe it. But now, people visit relatives in Israel and America and they see it isn't true. They come back, tell others and the word gets around.'

Natasha still remembered the day Olga brought her a tub of yoghurt from her return flight from Australia. 'It was the first time I'd ever tasted yoghurt. It was like a cultural event. I didn't think there could be anything so tasty in the world.' Natasha had longingly perused Olga's photos from my 'exotic' homeland. But for her, a trip to Australia seemed as likely as visiting Mars.

Her mother and grandfather were keen followers of political developments in the country. Remarkably her grandfather — an ex-military man and Communist Party member — was not only supportive of perestroika and Gorbachev's political and economic reforms, but now called himself a democrat. Natasha didn't find this at all strange. 'It was only for his career,' she explained matter-of-factly. 'He had to obey orders and say all the right things to keep his job. But in his heart he has always been a democrat.'

Irina's grandmother, Natasha's great-grandmother, had been a democrat too. Born in 1892, she was twenty-five years old at the time of the Bolshevik revolution. Irina remembered her grandmother's tales of Tsar Nikolai, of how weak he was as a leader, and how he allowed the country to fall apart while he worried about his wife and son. But grandma had hated the communists, and called Stalin a 'bandit'. She became a Russian teacher in Baku, in the Caucasian republic of Azerbaijan, and one day was given a bust of Stalin as a prize. Although the population was quivering in fear of Stalin's henchmen, gutsy grandma told everyone that 'she wasn't taking this rubbish home', and left it on a windowsill.

Great-grandma lived long enough to see the beginning of perestroika and had great hopes for a democratic future. But Natasha was completely apolitical, rebelling against her mother and grandparents by having no interest in contemporary events whatsoever. As an aspiring academic, she approved of freedom of speech and removal of censorship, which would give her legal access to foreign literature, but all the rest seemed irrelevant. Gorbachev might have been trying to change the system, but she'd still had to memorise and recite the works of Lenin to get her place at university.

Loaded up with food and carefully clutching our new tickets, Olga, Natasha and I boarded our train at Leningrad's Vitebsky Station and rattled off through the forests. Ten hours later we crossed an invisible border into the Soviet Socialist Republic of Byelorussia. Natasha had been to the Byelorussian and Ukrainian republics many times before and like Olga she considered their territories an integral part of her Soviet motherland. But a horrendous accident four years earlier had got some locals thinking differently.

We were halfway across Byelorussia when a pale and gaunt teenage boy took the fourth bunk in our *coupe*. Olga and Natasha offered him food and tea. Pavel came from a village near the town of Gomel, a region in the southeast of Byelorussia severely affected by fallout from the explosion at the Chernobyl nuclear power plant in 1986. Many of his neighbours and relatives had moved away from the blighted area, 'but a lot have nowhere else to go.'

Olga recounted how she'd heard of the accident on the TV and radio. 'It was such an unusual situation, because before this time any incident had been hidden from us. Gorbachev was very brave to tell the truth about this very dangerous and terrible thing that happened. So we knew that the scale of the tragedy was huge and that many people got sick and there was a terrible effect on the environment.'

I was surprised by Olga's praise for Gorbachev's bravery and openness. I dimly remembered that the rest of the world had condemned him for withholding information. In fact, the Soviet leadership had gone to extraordinary lengths to keep it quiet. The first the West knew of the accident at the Chernobyl nuclear plant on 26 April was on Monday, 28 April 1986, when at 9 am, technicians at a Swedish nuclear power plant noticed disturbingly high levels of radiation. Scientists in Finland, Norway and Denmark picked up the same signals, and their suspicions quickly turned to the USSR. But Moscow persistently denied anything was wrong. Then, at 9 pm that day, three days after the reactor meltdown had occurred, the following announcement was made on state TV: 'An accident has taken place at the Chernobyl power station, and one of the reactors was damaged. Measures are being taken to eliminate the consequences of the accident. Those affected are being given assistance. A government commission has been set up.' That was it.

After the accident it took over a day before residents were evacuated from the town of Pripyat, which housed plant workers and their families only two kilometres from the reactor. Not even the town of Chernobyl itself, 20 kilometres from the plant, was evacuated until 2 May. And in Kiev, 150 kilometres away, the May Day holiday parade was held as usual, despite dangerous levels of radiation in the streets. Tens of thousands of people marched in intense heat, celebrating communism and the glory of the USSR, playing music and listening to speeches by party officials. There were vague rumours of a terrible accident, but in order to avoid mass panic, officials and the state press continued their spin: 'Our nuclear plants do not represent any risk. We could have built them at Red Square. They are safer than our samovars.' (Literally 'self-boiler', a samovar is a traditional water heater used in and around Russia.)

It would be eighteen days before the then General Secretary Gorbachev publicly acknowledged the gravity of the disaster that had destroyed the power station in the Ukraine and spread radioactive fallout across the globe. 'For the first time,' Gorbachev announced, 'we have confronted in reality the sinister power of uncontrolled nuclear energy.' For Olga, a little bit of honesty was a tremendous act of bravery on behalf of a Soviet leader. But to the rest of the world, Gorbachev's silence showed that despite his rhetoric of transparency, he was still very much a product of his Soviet indoctrination.

The colourless, odourless radioactivity was an insidious enemy. Militiamen and soldiers were called in to combat the invisible foe, with promises of wages doubled, tripled, or even multiplied by six if they would work close to the plant. Helicopter pilots flew over the burning plant in masks left over from the Second World War, dropping bags of sand onto the exploded reactor core, vomiting from the extreme levels of radioactivity. Army reservists wore makeshift lead aprons to protect themselves as they used shovels and wheelbarrows to remove radioactive graphite dust from the roof of the reactor next to the explosion site. While they were dreaming of their future dachas and cars, their bodies were silently irradiated beyond hope.

Our new *sputnik*, Pavel, told us how his father had been one of thousands conscripted to help with the clean-up operation, spraying roads, fields and villages with decontaminant liquid, and bulldozing houses into the ground. Their so-called 'protective' clothing was completely inadequate and the workers and soldiers inhaled huge quantities of radioactive dust. The Soviet government refused offers of international assistance, preferring to sacrifice its own people rather than endure the humiliation of accepting outside help. Now, four-and-a-half years on, many of the 'liquidators' and firefighters were already dead. Pavel's father had undergone a bone marrow transplant but the prognosis was grim. Yet incredibly, the Soviet government had only just declared Byelorussia an ecological disaster zone.

Across Russia, superstitions and rumours about the radiation spread like wildfire. Olga described how a friend of her brother Igor had been on tour in the Ukraine with a children's choir when it happened. 'When he came back, his mum took all his clothes and hung them on the balcony so the radiation wouldn't get inside their flat.' Natasha nodded. 'Some people were saying that you had to mix iodine with sugar — depending on your age you had to take a certain amount — and that if you drank that, it would get the radiation out. Others believed that drinking vodka would prevent irradiation.'

It was also vital to avoid getting rainwater on one's hair and skin. 'After Chernobyl,' Olga recalled, 'everyone became paranoid. Before, people used to think that rain was good clean water, that it was good for your hair, but after the disaster, people said it was dangerous. Grandma always wears a plastic bag on her head now and everyone tries very hard not to get wet with rain. You know, we heard all kinds of stories about how the plants and animals are changing, that the mushrooms are growing like crazy, and that someone saw a butterfly with two-metre wings!'

Olga and Natasha knew men in Leningrad and other cities who were deployed to the site of the disaster. 'They were sent there by the military commanders as it was an emergency situation,' Olga explained. 'Their radiation levels would be measured every day and once they got to a certain amount they would be sent back home again. It was like military service, they had no choice but to go. Now all these people receive a special pension because of this work. Have you seen in the shops how there is a list for people who don't have to stand in queues and get very cheap prices for things? That is for invalids from the Great Patriotic War and also those who worked at Chernobyl.'

Slowly the truth about Chernobyl would come out: the lies, cover-ups, incompetence and arrogance of the administration. But the families of most of those who died while trying to secure the reactor never received an explanation as to how their loved ones had perished. Their poisoned corpses were immediately sealed in zinc coffins to prevent radiation from spreading. Relatives were unable to see the bodies, let alone give them a proper burial. Families of the dead and desperately ill survivors received little compensation. Hundreds of thousands of people were unable to return to their homes. With no savings, their homes were all they had. A few hundred elderly people refused to leave their abandoned villages. They had nowhere to go.

The Chernobyl disaster, and the state's botched response to it, was not only a disaster for the millions of people in the fallout zone. It was a litmus test for glasnost, and it failed, exposing the true nature of the party officials and their propaganda to the people. For many, whatever faith in their leaders and media remained was profoundly shaken. Emboldened, closet democrats like Natasha's grandparents were coming out. But curiously to me, Olga and Natasha had little interest in these momentous political changes. And because I was seeing the country through their eyes, with no access to news beyond what they passed on to me, I barely knew about them until much later.

A woman selling apples by the roadside calls out, 'Chernobyl apples for sale. Come and buy my Chernobyl apples!'

A man stops and says, 'Don't say that. No one will buy them.'

'On the contrary,' the woman replied. 'Some buy them for their mother-in-law, some buy them for their wife …'

A spray of graffiti defaced a wall of Lvov Station. 'Welcome to Hell,' Natasha translated. It was a loud anonymous declaration of discontent, a sign that not everyone was prepared to remain silent about the Communist Party's oppressive control over their lives.

Olga and Natasha's friend Valya and her mother, Anya, met us on the platform. A handsome woman in her early thirties, Valya had thick wavy dark hair and a warm smile. Anya was only nineteen years older and looked young enough to be her sister. We took a trolleybus through the cobblestone streets of the twelfth-century town centre and Valya pointed out Lvov's majestic Opera and Ballet Theatre, with its Corinthian columns, stucco garlands and winged bronze figures, symbolising Glory, Poetry and Music, crowning the roof. Constructed over the Poltava River between 1897 and 1900, the building's foundations had apparently begun to sink shortly after its completion. The architect fell into a depression, and legend has it that he hung himself in humiliation. The foundations soon stabilised, and ninety-one years on, the theatre still stood proud.

Squabbled over for centuries, Lvov had been a principally Polish settlement before the Soviets deported most of the Poles to Siberia during the Second World War. After the war, Lvov had become part of the Ukrainian Soviet Socialist Republic, its remaining population now predominantly ethnic Russians and Ukrainians. A pall of gloom hung over what must have once been a vibrant city. Ragged old women queued impassively outside a bakery. A *Technika* shop, the Soviet equivalent of Dick Smith Electronics, displayed old-fashioned wooden radios with brass mesh over the speakers, just like the one my grandfather had. It wasn't an antique shop, but the place to come for the latest technology on offer.

Valya and Anya shared a one-room flat in a shabby 70s block in the burbs. For most of the day there was no water at all, and hot water for only a couple of hours each evening. They kept plastic buckets full in the bath to use for flushing the toilet and washing their hands. Sugar and animal fats were rationed. In the kitchen, Anya served tea, Russian style, from the samovar: first pouring a splash of *zavarka* (very strong tea) from a small teapot sitting atop the samovar, then filling it up with boiling water from the tap at the bottom. She piled the kitchen table with dishes of brightly wrapped sweets, ginger biscuits and slices of watermelon, and began to bombard me with all the usual questions about life in my land at the bottom of the world. 'How many rooms do you have?' 'Do you have a car?' 'How much do you earn?' 'Is there really no winter?'

Already embarrassed at her mother's inquisitiveness, Valya turned crimson when Anya began to ask about marriage Down Under. I knew from Natasha and Olga that Valya was getting a hard time from her mum about her single status. To be still unmarried in her early thirties most likely meant a life sentence of spinsterdom. Anya was aghast to hear that in Australia, many women didn't marry until their late twenties, thirties and sometimes not at all.

'So old?' She glared at Valya. 'You must try harder. Otherwise, what will happen to you? And how will I get grandchildren?' It seemed a bit hypocritical for Anya, a long-time single mum, to be criticising Valya for her lack of a partner. But apparently it was more socially acceptable to be a divorced single mother than never to have married. Valya sighed. Teachers, especially of the humanities subjects as she was, were almost exclusively women. Apart from her students and superiors, there were simply no men around to meet.

Valya taught Russian stylistics at the Lvov 'Military-Political' Academy, which trained 'military journalists' from twenty-two socialist countries — including Cuba, Angola, Libya, Vietnam and Mongolia — as part of a Soviet program run by the ominously titled Department of Ideological Works of the Head Political Administration of the Soviet Army and Navy.

Olga, Natasha and I went along to have a stickybeak. It was like a mini United Nations summit — Asians, Africans, Latinos and Europeans — only all were immaculately attired in the khaki-grey uniform of the

Soviet Army. The academy director, General Major Pushnov, was a jocular fellow with a fleshy face and neatly clipped moustache. He gave us a personal tour of the institute, even ordering the troops to be brought out for inspection by the visitor from afar. Row after impossibly straight row of young men stood to attention, shaven to within an inch of their lives, staring at the shoddily dressed newcomer. The General Major made a long-winded speech and I heard the word 'Avstralii' barked repeatedly. He finished and gestured to me to give a response. Even with Olga as a translator I was tongue-tied with nerves. I thanked them for their kindness at our warm reception and before I knew it, we were exchanging vows of eternal friendship between various People's Republics worldwide and the great land of Avstralia.

General Major presented me with a souvenir copy of the academy magazine, *Politrabotnik* (*Party Man*), with my very own personal dedication. It was a special issue celebrating 120 years since the birth of Lenin and forty-five years since the 'Victory', automatically understood by all as referring to the defeat of Nazi Germany. One article was entitled 'Be a Real Communist', another 'The 45th Spring', accompanied by black-and-white photos of the authors, stern-jawed colonels and lieutenants with receding hairlines, coats dripping with medals.

'We have a powerful weapon in our hands', I read. 'The pen of a journalist must be used to defend the ideals of socialism and internationalism, as well as to strengthen our State — the Union of Soviet Socialist Republics.' Obviously the role of 'journalist' in the USSR didn't come with the sort of job description it had back home. Rather than reporting objectively on events and issues, these scrubbed new soldiers had been groomed to be *politruks,* literally 'political hands' or propagandists. Their task was to encourage 'correct thought' amongst the members of the armed forces: loyalty to the Party, the state and to the ideals of communism.

A set of pages was devoted to final-year students returning to their home countries, and I picked out some of the faces in Valya's class. 'We're leaving, but not saying farewell', by an East German, and 'We will never forget', co-authored by a Libyan and Namibian. Olga saw nothing sinister in the USSR sponsoring students from afar to come to the

USSR for a propaganda-filled education — in how to write propaganda. 'They come from poor countries, so it is good that we can help them with schooling,' she thought. At the time, I supposed she was right.

But the academy had a pressing problem. Its primary function was to train the future preachers in the necessity and virtues of communism and internationalism. But even as they studied, that very system was crumbling into irrelevancy around them. It had once been illegal to wave the blue and yellow national flag of the Ukraine, but since the Chernobyl disaster, Ukrainian nationalists were brazenly brandishing their banner in defiance of the outraged communists. From 1987, there had been demonstrations demanding the abolition of the Communist Party, the public release of documents related to Chernobyl and even the resignation of the government. Rebellion was fomenting and by 1990, the pen of the party man was about as powerful as a water pistol.

Naturally the colonels were deeply worried. If the Party was to lose control, then what would happen to them? They had devoted their lives to serving an ideal. In return it had provided them with a livelihood, with jobs, perks and privileges. In desperation, they filled their academy magazine with encouragement to the young graduates. In one article I read:

> This author was entrusted with his Party Card in a different era. But the orders are still the same now as then: 'You must take political culture to the mass of soldiers, and be a conduit for the communist idea, and for this you need to be a real communist.'

The generals could no longer ignore the challenges ahead. Gorbachev's glasnost had unleashed the critics and the republics were seething with decades of repressed resentment, which the magazine despairingly acknowledged.

> In many regions of our country the situation is very difficult, contradictory, unique. Our graduates will be sent to all corners of the Soviet Union … and it will be most challenging for

those going to serve in the Pri-Baltics (Latvia, Lithuania and Estonia), the Caucasus and the Central Asian regions. There you will be required to pay close attention to the formation of the correct inter-nationality relationship between the military servicemen, keeping in yourself the high principles of Soviet Internationalism and patriotism.

The newly graduating *politruks* would be in for a tough time, but no one, not even the nationalists, could have predicted just how quickly their four years of training would be rendered redundant.

Valya had heard from Olga that I enjoyed 'tourism'. She'd arranged for a friend, Igor, to take us on a trek in the Carpathian Mountains, near the Romanian border. A serious young man with a black moustache, Igor arrived with a tattered backpack, and train tickets to the town of Ivano–Frankovsk. From there we took a bus to a pretty village at the foothills of the mountains. Shriveled babushki in cardigans and flowery scarves wandered down stony roads prodding bumbling cows in the backside with big sticks. Low bells rang out from the swaying bovine necks. Flower-filled gardens surrounded brightly painted wooden houses with ornately carved window frames, and dark needled pine forests covered the slopes behind the village.

We ascended the rocky summit of Mount Khomyak and had just a moment to enjoy the spectacular views before a bank of black thunderclouds rolled in. A violent storm lashed into us as we stumbled along rocky ridges in search of the hut we were supposed to be staying in overnight. But for some reason Igor hadn't brought a map or compass. We were soon completely lost, freezing, sodden and bruised. In the wee small hours we came across a cowshed and crammed in to wait out the storm. By morning the sky was clear and we dried off in the sunshine on the way to the nearby village. I remembered the last part of the 'Advice for Tourists' in my Russian book: 'Overall, a tourist expedition has the advantage that after it, any work seems like a holiday.'

At least there was some truth in that.

5

Red Terror

*In 1937, as Stalin's terror was raging through Moscow, a man packed
his bags every night before he went to sleep, in case he should have to
escape. Finally, one night, sure enough. Knock! Knock! He gets up
out of bed, kisses his wife, takes his bag and leaves.
A few minutes later, he's back. His wife looks at him, 'What happened?'
'It's nothing,' he replies. 'Just the house on fire.'*

Each time I returned to the Verbitskys' flat on Vasilievsky Island, Vera
Nikolayevna quizzed Olga about this alien in their midst. 'Who is
she?' 'Why is she here?' She often came running into my (Olga's)
room in the small hours, shouting that there was someone at the
door. When she saw me she would gasp with panic, as if I were an
intruder.

'Babushka lived through terrible times,' Olga explained. 'I think
now sometimes that in her mind she is back in the 1930s and 40s,
when everyone was living with the terror of Stalin's purges. So she still
believes it is dangerous to communicate with a foreigner. She is afraid
you are a spy and she will be in trouble.'

On her good days when she remembered who I was, Vera
Nikolayevna invited me to drink tea with her. She told the same
stories over and over, each time as if she'd only just thought of it,
giving me a chance to look up words and gradually nut out what she
was saying. '*Povtoreniye, mat ucheniya* (Repetition is the mother of

learning),' Vera would tell me. Sometimes she understood that I wasn't Russian and tried to say a few words to me in German.

Between Vera and Olga (along with the works of dissident writer Alexander Solzhenitsyn), I began to piece together Vera's life story, and with it, the often bloody history of their nation. She was born in the western Siberian town of Tobolsk in July 1914, just days before the deeply unpopular Tsar Nikolai II ordered the mobilisation of Russian forces to support Serbia in what would become the First World War. As the woefully unprepared troops were slaughtered in their millions, outrage against the Tsarist regime escalated. Many thousands of disgruntled workers and peasants began to join revolutionary groups called *soviets* (councils).

While Tsar Nikolai was away at the front, furious peasants and workers rioted against severe food shortages, inflation and unemployment and demanded the cessation of the war. By March 1917, even the army had turned against the Tsar. It was the first Russian Revolution of 1917. Nikolai II, Emperor and Autocrat of All the Russias, was forced to abdicate, marking the end of the Romanov family's 300-year imperial rule of Russia. After four months under house arrest in a palace near Petrograd (the future Leningrad), the Romanovs were moved by train to the Governor's mansion in Vera's hometown of Tobolsk. Vera was just three years old.

The provisional government put in place after the Tsar's abdication faced strong opposition from the workers' *soviets*. When Vladimir Ilyich Lenin, leader of the Bolshevik faction of the Russian Social Democratic Labour Party, returned to Russia from exile, he fired up the workers with slogans: 'Bread, Peace and Land' and 'Down with the Provisional Government — All Power to the Soviets!' Supported by the Bolsheviks, the workers held strikes, the peasants revolted and armed workers' militias, calling themselves Red Guards, held anti-government demonstrations. In October 1917, pro-Bolshevik soldiers and their Red Guards stormed the Winter Palace in Petrograd, arresting members of the provisional government, in what would later become known as the Great October Socialist Revolution.

Under Lenin's leadership, the Bolsheviks proceeded to appoint themselves heads of government ministries. The Red Guards were coordinated into a Red Army, and promptly set about seizing control of the country. A secret police organisation called the Cheka was established to eliminate those who questioned the infallibility of the great Lenin and his grand plan to spread harmony, equality and worker's rights throughout the empire. Under the command of 'Iron' Felix Dzerzhinsky, the Cheka had its own special status to act without consultation with police, the government, or regard to any law — all for the good of the people. The Tsar and his family were in trouble. In April 1918 the Bolsheviks relocated the Romanovs from Tobolsk to Ekaterinburg. In July, the entire family was executed.

By now the country was gripped in civil war: the Bolsheviks' Red Army against everyone else — the White Army (a loose amalgamation of monarchists and liberals), peasant landowners (*kulaks*), bourgeois capitalists, priests and even other socialist factions, including the Mensheviks, Anarchists and Social Revolutionaries. In September 1918, Lenin announced a campaign of mass repressions, which he called the 'Red Terror'. He declared that 'anyone who dares to spread the slightest rumour against the Soviet regime will be arrested immediately and sent to a concentration camp'.

With so many 'enemies of the revolution', the already overcrowded jails were soon overflowing and an imaginative solution was needed. That stroke of genius came in 1918. When Russia released its two million prisoners of war at the end of World War I, the empty POW camps were turned over to the secret police, to be used as concentration camps. Soon the Cheka were rounding up anyone and everyone who wasn't a die-hard Bolshevik, and sending them off to camps to be 'humiliated and taught a lesson about hard work', while being 'put to work in service of the new state'.

This was the beginning of what would eventually become known as the GULAG, or Glavnoye Upravleniye Ispravitelno-trudovykh Lagerei i Kolonii (The Chief Administration of Corrective Labour Camps and Colonies). The Gulag system grew rapidly. At the end of 1919 there were twenty-one camps, a year later there were over one hundred. Eventually the Gulag would spread across the furthest reaches of the Soviet empire: Siberia, the Arctic and the Far East.

Ultimately the Bolsheviks were victorious. In 1922, the civil war ended, and the USSR was created. After the revolution, Vera's father, Nikolai Verbitsky, moved the family to Gorelovo, a town near Petrograd, which would be renamed Leningrad after Lenin's death in 1924. Nikolai's brother, Ivan, eventually relocated his family to Leningrad too, where he took up a post with the Grain Board. Vera's musically talented Uncle Ivan did relatively well. He even managed to purchase a piano for the family's two-room flat on Fifth Soviet Street, which his son Igor loved to play. Vera met her cousin Igor, two years her junior, for the first time in Leningrad. Years later, in 1942, they would marry.

Nikolai and Ivan watched on as their children were indoctrinated with Bolshevik propaganda. In 1924, when Vera was ten, and Igor eight, Joseph Stalin succeeded Lenin as the General Secretary of the Communist Party. Both Igor and Vera were fervent believers in the revolution and Marxist-Leninist ideology. Vera's first job was as a schoolteacher in Gorelovo, grounding pupils in the minutiae of Russian and communist history. Igor began to work for the successor to the Cheka, the NKVD (Narodny Komissariat Vnutrennikh Del or People's Commissariat for Internal Affairs).

In 1935, when Vera was twenty-one, Stalin — a self-given pseudonym meaning 'Man of Steel' — began to suffer paranoid delusions that traitors within party ranks were plotting to overthrow or assassinate him. Ordering the elimination of anyone he suspected of disloyalty, Stalin's first targets were those who worked in key Soviet institutions: the Communist Party, the army and, ironically, the NKVD, who themselves were charged with responsibility for political repressions. Igor Verbitsky had every reason to feel fearful.

As Stalin's paranoia worsened, the purges spread into wider society. By the late 1930s, ordinary citizens were urged to assist in 'cleansing' the country of traitors, capitalists and 'enemies of the revolution'. Desperate to prove their own patriotism, people denounced neighbours and work colleagues. Thousands were executed. Millions of these 'political prisoners' were sent to the Gulag, which by now had grown to become a significant part of the Soviet economy — its labour force used for mining, forestry, farming, road and railroad construction. There was no shortage of workers either, thanks to a vague and ever-changing definition of 'enemy of the people'. As Lenin, and later Stalin, tried to put communist economic principles into practice with disastrous results, they were in constant need of 'enemies' to blame for the chaos. Lenin called them 'saboteurs' and 'wreckers'. Stalin spoke of 'vermin', 'poisonous weeds' and 'filth to be purified'.

Initially the professional criminals — thieves, murderers and pickpockets — were kept apart from the politicals, in separate prisons run by the Commissariat of the Interior. But by 1925 they all ended up together. Although many of the politicals may have done little more than tell an inappropriate joke, they were considered far more 'socially dangerous' than ordinary felons. Lenin had even viewed the common convicts as allies, believing that they would cease their nefarious ways once society had become more just.

The politicals were treated with brutal contempt by guards and criminal prisoners. Guards even encouraged the criminals, who called themselves *vory* (thieves), to terrorise and intimidate the politicals. The camps were hell on earth. Inmates were tortured, interrogated, humiliated and forced to toil for long hours in freezing temperatures with inadequate food and clothing. Many were denied contact with friends and relatives. Tuberculosis, typhus and other diseases were rife. For many, internment in the Gulag was a death sentence. The mass arrests, exiles and executions continued until Stalin's death in 1953.

This was the backdrop to Vera and Igor Verbitsky's married life. Despite their impeccable communist credentials, they never discussed politics or any other subject that might incur the suspicion of the authorities. No one trusted anyone. Every night Vera locked the heavy metal door of her flat, wondering if the secret police would come at 4 am to eliminate one of their own, her husband Igor.

Now, decades later, Vera was gripped by the same fear and paranoia. She worried about having me, a foreigner, in her house. She also worried Rizhok the cat wasn't getting enough to eat, forgetting that Olga had already fed him. Often we came home to find our entire cauldron of soup painstakingly prepared from rotting vegetables and weevil-ridden rice, after hours of queuing to acquire the ingredients, had been ladled out in saucers all over the flat. Vera herself lived on little more than sugary tea and black bread, which she dipped in the tea to soften so her false teeth wouldn't get stuck. She spent her days at the tiny kitchen table, listening to news on the radio, shaking her head in despair.

As Vera Nikolayevna's dementia worsened, she began to wander the streets. Sometimes she left all the gas burners on the stove turned up on full flame, worried we might run out of matches and be unable to light the stove to cook and boil water. Tap water was unsafe, so no gas flame meant imminent thirst. It was impossible to reassure Vera Nikolayevna that our match supply was in no danger. Olga thought this was another of her flashbacks, to the time of the Leningrad Blockade during the Great Patriotic War.

To Soviet citizens, World War II is their 'Great Patriotic War' or 'Great War of the Fatherland', and the USSR's victory over Nazi Germany remains one of the nation's defining glories. When the Germans invaded in June 1941, Vera was twenty-seven and still working as a schoolteacher. She was in charge of twenty students on a holiday excursion in the city of Novgorod, 180 kilometres from Leningrad, when they learned of the invasion. Vera was petrified. All trains had stopped running and the only way she could return the students to their families was by hiding them in a goods truck.

By September, the Nazis had completely surrounded Leningrad, beginning an almost three-year total siege of the city. Food supplies were quickly exhausted and ravenous Leningraders were reduced to eating whatever they could find: horse chaff, bread made from sawdust, soup made from glue. There was no power and no fuel for heating. During the long, bitter winters people burned their furniture to stay warm. As hundreds of thousands of citizens starved and froze to death, many of the living had no choice but to tear pieces from emaciated corpses piled in the streets.

Despite the horror around them, Vera fell pregnant. One day she heard a radio announcement calling urgently for new students to enroll at the Leningrad Medical Institute. The besieged city was overflowing with the sick, wounded and starving, and there was a severe deficit of doctors. Despite her pregnancy, Vera applied to study medicine, seeking a distraction from the daily struggle to find bread she feared was driving her crazy. Vera was accepted into the course, and not long into her studies was called up to meet the Dean. Trembling with nerves, she did as she was bade. But instead of the anticipated reprimand, the Dean asked if she could memorise the Physiology and Anatomy subjects and teach them to new students. She did so, and soon became a respected teacher at the Institute.

Vladimir Igorovich, Olga's father, was born in October 1943. It was just over two years into the siege, yet Vera was fortunate to have enough breast milk to feed her baby son, and even be able to donate some to other new mothers. Not long after Vladimir's birth, Igor was badly injured in an explosion and lost his sight. The family lived in one room — 10 square metres — of a *kommunalka* not far from the Winter Palace, sharing a kitchen and bathroom with three other families. Often Vera walked nearly 15 kilometres to help build defences against the German tanks. When the blockade was finally lifted on 27 January 1944, almost nine hundred days after it had begun, it was estimated that more than one million people had perished. Leningrad was hailed as a 'Hero-City'.

The siege survivors, known as *blokadniki*, had been honoured ever since. On each anniversary of the lifting of the blockade they visited schools to remind students of the horrors they endured at the hands of the 'evil fascists'. With defiant lines of pain and struggle etched into their faces, they displayed their medals proudly. The *blokadniki* told of their heroism in defending the motherland and its revolution. Olga and her friends were gripped by these accounts, appalled by the barbarity of the invaders, full of respect and gratitude to their elders.

'We can't even imagine how awful it was,' she sighed. 'Sometimes babushka doesn't even recognise me, but she never forgets the names of all the anatomy that she had to remember back during the war, and the history of the revolution that she was teaching when the war started.'

★　★　★

By the time young Vladimir was five years old, it was clear that he had inherited his grandfather Ivan's prodigious talent for music. Ivan presented him with the family piano and Vladimir soon became a competent pianist. At the age of seven he was accepted into the Leningrad Kapella, Russia's oldest choral school, just across the square from the Winter Palace. Originally established as a private choir back in 1479 by Tsar Ivan III, the Kapella was moved to St Petersburg when the city was founded in 1703. It was still the premier training ground for gifted young choristers and musicians in 1950, and Vladimir spent the next twelve years there honing his musical skills. He excelled in his studies and entered the prestigious Leningrad Conservatoire, where Tchaikovsky, Shostakovich and Prokofiev had studied. In addition to piano, he began to study symphonic, operatic and choral conducting.

As part of his practical studies, he worked as chorus master and accompanist for the Leningrad University choir, where he met twenty-year-old Ninel, a student of mathematics and mechanics from the Nizhni Novgorod region, who loved to sing. (Ninel, 'Lenin' backwards, was a popular name for girls.) They married in 1965 and settled in Leningrad. In 1967, they had a son, named Igor after his grandfather. Olga arrived in 1969.

Vladimir studied with Yevgeny Mravinsky, Chief Conductor of the Leningrad Philharmonic, and became guest conductor for Evgeny Svetlanov's USSR State Symphony. He travelled all over Europe, the Americas and Asia with the orchestra, and was awarded the title of 'People's Artist of Russia'. There were always KGB spooks amongst the touring musicians — perhaps the French horn player was eavesdropping on the double bassist? No one knew for sure who they were, but everyone knew they were under constant surveillance.

Young Igor, Olga's brother, also soon began to show musical talent. He played the piano and listened to his father's classical records, waving his arms around to Bizet's *Carmen*, imagining he was conducting. At seven he too entered the Leningrad Kapella where he sang in the choir. When Vladimir was offered a job as principal conductor of the Voronezh Philharmonic, the family moved south of Moscow. Igor decided to stay on at the Kapella and moved in with his grandparents in their new and bigger flat on Vasilievsky Island. Studies at the Kapella were as rigorous as ever — both music and academic subjects — with classes from 8 am to 6 pm. Expectations were high, competition intense, but Igor was determined. By the end of the course only seven students of the original twenty-eight remained. Igor was one of them.

The two Igors, grandfather and grandson, were very close. But Igor the elder remained guarded while talking about his past, barely mentioning the war or his job in the Central Military Headquarters. Blind and unable to work, grandfather Igor spent his days glued to the radio. As it became possible to listen to Voice of America, Radio Liberty, BBC World and Deutsche Welle, both Igors were transfixed by these new perspectives on events in their country and the rest of the world. An uncle, Oleg, brought them prohibited books, obtained from acquaintances who had stealthily copied them on their workplace rotaprint machines. They in turn had received the banned manuscripts from others who had travelled abroad and sneaked them illegally into the country — sailors, traders and even diplomats. In this way, the Igors and much of the USSR's intelligentsia read the writings of the dissident Alexander Zinoviev, and Bulgakov's *The Master and Margarita*. Gradually they ceased to believe in the great utopian dream of the Soviet Union. But grandfather Igor was afraid, fearful that young Igor might gossip at school and get the family into trouble. Vladimir was a party member — essential for anyone in a high position such as his — and his teenage son's idle conversation could easily lose him his job.

Things were easier with Olga. In provincial Voronezh, she had little exposure to foreign influences beyond those deemed acceptable by the Soviet censors, which for the most part were TV serials revolving around cute talking animals. In 1982 her father took a two-year post as chief conductor of the Slovak Philharmonic in Bratislava. She moved to Czechoslovakia with her parents and was sent to a Russian boarding school in Prague, only seeing her parents every three weeks. Now in Leningrad with her grandmother, she asked few questions about the political system she had grown up under. If awful things had indeed happened, then they must have been necessary. It was just the way things were.

6

The Opium of the People

'Religion is opium for the people. Religion is a sort of spiritual booze, in which the slaves of capital drown their human image, their demand for a life more or less worthy of man.'
Vladimir Ilyich Lenin

On the Petrograd side of Vasilievsky Island, not far from the State University, was a passenger cruise ship port. One chilly day, Olga and I stopped at the ticket office, curious to see where the ships went. On a whim, we bought tickets for a five-day *putyovka*, an all-inclusive voyage through the lakes north of Leningrad. The highlight was to be a visit to an ancient Orthodox monastery on the island of Valaam in Lake Ladoga. Olga arranged a couple of days off work and quietly hoped her lecturers wouldn't notice her absence from night classes.

Our vessel was the *Sergei Kirov*, a holiday cruise boat named after a popular communist party leader who'd been assassinated in 1934, quite possibly on the orders of a jealous Stalin. But Stalin publicly mourned his 'friend' and it was Kirov's death that sparked the great purges as Stalin vowed to punish his assassin. Kirov had since been posthumously recompensed for his sorry end by having not only Leningrad's most famous opera and ballet theatre named in his honour, but five towns across the USSR, a Moscow metro station, a huge industrial plant, a speedskating prize, a class of battlecruiser and at least one ship.

To reach the lakes we had to sail east up the Neva River, which for all but two hours in the dead of the night is barricaded by a series of bridges. We boarded our 'snow-white beauty of a liner', as our ship was proudly described in the booklet provided to passengers, in the evening. At 2 am the bridges rose, like massive drawbridges over a giant moat, to allow the waiting vessels through. We peered out the porthole window of our shiny cabin at the darkened palatial façades lining the riverbank, dimly illuminated in the moonlight. In the ship's restaurant, coiffed couples, the women in lurid rayon blouses and men in patterned knits, swirled each other to the 'Lambada' under the blinking lights of the ship's disco mirrorball.

By morning we were 75 kilometres upriver in a 250-year-old man-made canal near the town of Shlisselburg, on the east bank of the Neva as it emerges from Lake Ladoga. Peter the Great had ordered the Ladoga Canal be built to protect ships from the frequent treacherous storms and high waves on the lake, and while we'd slept, the water level under us had been raised 2 metres. We now waited in a lock while water gushed out into specially constructed reservoirs, lowering our boat once again to the level of the lake. The sluice gates ground open and we sailed out into the biggest lake in Europe, Lake Ladoga, with barely a wave to be seen.

I knew all this because a woman with a megaphone herded all the passengers out on deck for a running commentary on every wondrous sight. A Soviet *putyovka* wasn't just a pleasure cruise, it was an educational tour, laden with statistics designed to inspire pride in the motherland. Olga did her best to translate the rapid-fire of facts and figures. 'Lake Ladoga was a very important place during the Great Patriotic War and blockade of Leningrad. At this place, the heroic Leningraders were resisting the fascist barbarians who caused immense damage to our city. There was a military barrier across the lake, heroically defending Leningrad from capture.'

Like obedient school children, our *sputniks* paid close attention. Even the guys with the slicked-back hair, who anywhere else would have been far too cool to look interested, kept their eyes riveted to the guide. We heard how the Russian soldiers made roads across the frozen lake in winter, and used boats in summer, to take food into the besieged city and evacuate hundreds of thousands of starving Leningraders. It was the only road from Leningrad to the rest of the country: the *Doroga Zhizni*, or Road of Life.

Gazing across the now peaceful cobalt expanse, it was hard to imagine it had been witness to such scenes of desperation. The sun shone in the unusually low cloudless sky as shores of hazy jade retreated behind us. A land of endless horizons, lakes and forest stretching from the White Sea to the Gulf of Finland, the now Autonomous Soviet Socialist Republic of Karelia had been immortalised in vivid orchestral imagery by the Finnish composer Jean Sibelius. In the 1890s, when most of Karelia was under the control of the Russian Tsar, the fervently nationalistic Sibelius hoped to foster Finnish culture in the border area near Russia. His *Karelia Suite* captured both the serene beauty of the landscape and the fighting spirit of the Finnish Karelians, defiant in the face of repressive Russian rule.

Realising they had a foreigner aboard, crew and passengers went out of their way to be friendly. Olga was naturally shy and uncomfortable with strangers, but like the owner of an unusual pet, she found that I was a conversation piece. Warming to her new role, she become more confident. 'You know, people are interested in talking to you because you are a Westerner,' she explained. 'We Russians feel that we are somehow less than foreigners, and that's why everyone wants to help you and give their best for you. This is our custom.'

Then we got to the ship's restaurant.

'The menu is mostly of Russian cuisine, its dishes being of high culinary virtues', boasted the tour guide booklet. Unless you were a vegetarian. The bewildered galley staff prepared a special menu for me: breakfast: black bread; lunch: beetroot and cabbage for entrée, followed by an entire plate of sliced beetroot for main course; dinner: mashed potato, half a tomato, black bread and beetroot caviar. I felt very special indeed.

It seemed odd to me that the people of a nation so obsessed with its heroes, glories and achievements could have an inferiority complex. But perhaps that partly explained the national fixation on their accomplishments? Did the omnipresent statues of Yuri Gagarin,

Bolshevik leaders and military heroes somehow aid in boosting Soviet egos?

We sailed northeast, out of Ladoga and up the Svir River to Lake Onega, past immense forests and swamps, home to elk, bear, lynx and partridge. Once on Europe's second largest lake, we headed for the island of Kizhi, the local Karelian word for 'playground'. Once upon a time, wild heathen celebrations had taken place on this barren isle. Now it was a tourist mecca. We joined the sightseers eagerly queuing to take snaps, posing in front of the island's pair of fairytale wooden churches. Built in 1714, the remarkable churches have twenty-two different sized cupolas arranged in five tiers, topped with layers of metal onion domes, each with an Orthodox cross on a spire. The entire buildings were constructed of pine, without a single nail. It is said that when the builder finished, he threw his axe into the water and declared: 'There has never been anything like this before, and there never will again.' Just like St Basil's in Moscow, a one-off never to be repeated masterpiece to be admired by generations to come.

Back on Lake Ladoga, we cruised north towards Valaam, a pine, asp and rowan-tree-forested archipelago. Gold Orthodox crosses glowed like bright flames against the sky. Until 1940, the border between Finland and Russia had been drawn through the lake and the Valaam archipelago had belonged to Finland. After the war the Finns lost Karelia to the USSR. Valaam was the site of thirteen ancient Orthodox monasteries, which just one year earlier had been permitted to resume their monastic activities. Young monks with wispy midriff length beards and heavy black robes strode between the whitewashed stone buildings of the monastery, tending livestock and cleaning their chapel.

Our guide herded us through the grounds, and cruise passengers regarded the religious men with curiosity. Olga was quieter and more thoughtful than usual. I asked her what she was thinking. 'I am very interested in this,' she mused, waving her hand at the scene of religious piety. 'I think there is some connection far back in my family. My brother has been baptised, and I think my father believes something, but my parents weren't brave enough to have me baptised.'

'Has Vera Nikolayevna ever talked to you about religion?'

'It's strange but she has never mentioned it to me. But I've noticed some strange things. We have a saying, "*Slava tebe gospodi*", that means "Thank the Lord". But babushka only says "*slava tebe*", as if she is afraid to say the word for Lord. I think she was taught not to say it. She was afraid because she was living in that time when she might be arrested.'

As we sailed back to Leningrad, autumn began to spread its amber and deep rust hues through the forests, reflected in perfect symmetry in the still black water. Back in the city, children collected elm leaves in courtyards and parks, threading them on strings to make crowns. Breezes from the Baltic became wilder and chillier, the days shorter and greyer. Olga bought an icon and placed it by her bed. She began to read about Orthodox rituals.

It was only after Vera Nikolayevna's death in 1993 that Olga learned the full story of her family's religious connections. Stashed amongst dusty piles of papers in Vera's room was a document signed by Vera's uncle and father-in-law, Ivan Verbitsky, in which he renounced his faith in the Russian Orthodox Church. Olga discovered that before the Bolshevik Revolution, Ivan had been the conductor of a church choir in a village near Nizhni-Novgorod. His brother, Nikolai Verbitsky, Vera's father, had been a village priest. So were Vera's grandfather and two more of her uncles.

The Bolshevik Revolution was dire news for the Russian Orthodox Church. In 1914 Russia, the Church had been a massive institution, with over 85,000 churches and chapels, around 115,000 clergy and more than 90,000 monks and nuns living in over a thousand monasteries and convents. Lenin well understood the power the Church held over the people and promptly declared it a counter-revolutionary organisation. 'Religion,' he stated, 'is opium for the people,' and the clergy were 'class enemies'.

Bizarrely, the atheist communist regime's official line was one of religious tolerance. But the reality was less savoury. The Bolsheviks set to work to eliminate the 'opium': confiscating church property, destroying churches and monasteries or converting them to secular use, ridiculing religion as superstition, harassing believers and propagating atheism and anti-religious propaganda in schools. The openly religious could not join the Komsomol or the Communist Party. Careers of believers were limited. Theological schools were closed down and Church publications were banned.

On fear of death, Vera's father and uncles were forced to deny their faith, leave their parishes and pledge support to the revolution and communist party. Clergy who refused to reject the Church were brutally persecuted: tortured, subjected to mind control experiments, arrested, sent to prison camps, mental hospitals. There were even reports of priests, monks and nuns being crucified, scalped, strangled, drowned in holes in the ice and thrown into cauldrons of boiling tar. Between 1917 and 1935, 95,000 priests were executed by firing squad.

Had Ivan and Nikolai Vasilyich not declared their loyalty to the communists, they would have no doubt joined them, ending Olga's family line in a pile of bones somewhere in a mass grave of enemies of the people. Incredibly, Vera had never spoken of her family's religious connections. Perhaps it was from fear, or perhaps from shame. But now it was too late to ask.

The abundant religious faith of the masses was masterfully re-routed by the Politburo towards reverence and worship of Vladimir Ilyich Lenin. When Lenin died in January 1924, his embalmed body was placed in a gleaming red granite mausoleum on the western side of Red Square, near the Kremlin wall. The Party immortalised him as a Christ-like figure. 'Lenin lived, Lenin lives, Lenin will live', became the catch-cry of the Cult of Lenin. His bald, goateed profile adorned metro stations, theatres and buildings of all kinds. Statues in bronze, marble, and iron — from life-size to colossal — took pride of place in city, town and village squares across the USSR. Marble plaques throughout the country proclaimed that he had once been here: given a speech, held a meeting, scratched his bum. His name was honoured by boulevards, collective farms, libraries and factories. The birth city of the October Revolution, Petrograd, became Leningrad.

An entire nation was indoctrinated with this fusion of political idolatry and religious ritual. Devotees of the new communist faith would soon become every bit as devout as the most fundamentalist of any religion. To many of the masses, the Cult of Lenin filled the void created by the destruction of the Church. Vladimir Ilyich Lenin was their prophet and supreme deity, the Communist Manifesto their Holy Book, the General Secretary of the Communist Party their Patriarch, and the Politburo their bishops and high priests. Through the Young Pioneer movement, children were taught to love the wise and kind Grandfather Lenin. Vera Nikolayevna did, and so did Olga. The 'opiate of the masses' had been replaced by a new drug.

But not even the Communist Party could eradicate religion entirely. Faith was so deeply ingrained in the Russian psyche that like the Mad Monk mystic Rasputin, it was next to impossible to kill. Two years into the war against Germany, Stalin had a radical change of heart, deciding that the best way to encourage patriotism and support for the war effort amongst his long-suffering people was to permit religious activity. Thousands of churches were reopened and a new patriarch was appointed, the first in twenty years. Patriarch Alexei, however, was little more than a puppet of the state. His every word was strictly supervised by the state and he could do nothing without permission from the chairman of the 'Council for the Affairs of the Orthodox Church', an NKVD operative. Patriarch Alexei promptly proclaimed Stalin to be a divinely appointed ruler, offering prayers for victory over the fascists and the good health of Comrade Stalin.

The NKVD-infiltrated Church grew rapidly and by 1957 there were over 20,000 active churches. But Stalin's successor, Nikita Khrushchev, was not impressed, reviving the persecutions and forcing around 12,000 churches to close. By the time Gorbachev came to power in 1985, there were fewer than 7,000 functioning churches, and most of the clergy had KGB connections. As part of his glasnost, Gorbachev began to return buildings to the Church for restoration. The year 1988 marked the millennial anniversary of the Christianisation of Russia, and throughout that year the government supported celebrations, reopened churches and monasteries, and lifted the ban on religious propaganda on state television.

On my first Sunday in Russia, I had wandered into the high white walled Danilov monastery complex near Yulia's flat in Moscow. Drawn by the sublime sound of chanting I tiptoed into a small chapel with a green onion-shaped dome. The walls were adorned with painted wooden icons in pressed gold frames. Babushkas with scarves tied tightly under their chins lit thin yellow candles and placed them on round brass holders, crossing themselves as they stepped back. An open coffin was brought in and laid on the floor, surrounded by quietly weeping relatives. A mass christening was taking place by a well in the monastery grounds. Several lofty, long-bearded priests in heavy black cassocks spoke to a group of about twenty people of all ages. They held out icons to be kissed, cut off locks of hair and commanded the initiates to walk down into a large marble pool until fully immersed.

In a separate chapel, another hirsute priest waved incense with one hand and made crosses in the air before three young couples standing at the front of the church. A further three couples filed past the priest, each holding up a large gold ring, first for him to kiss, then for the couples to be wedded. They stood behind the brides and grooms, holding the rings like haloes above their heads. Absorbed in the ethereal chanting, I watched as five, ten, then fifteen minutes passed. Still the ring holders kept their arms up, occasionally twitching and attempting a sneaking stretch. Nearly twenty-five minutes had passed and the ring holders looked as if they were about to collapse. I wondered whether they might not be happy for a bunch of bayonet-toting revolutionaries to burst through the door and relieve them.

Like Olga, her brother, Igor, never knew of his great-grandfather's religious beliefs or musical talents. But somehow he had chosen that same path. Now twenty-three, six-and-a-half-foot Igor was coming to the end of his studies at the Leningrad conservatorium. Not only was he studying choral conducting, he'd developed a deep interest in the Russian Orthodox Church. 'Anyone who performs music is in some way doing something spiritual,' he told me.

After the revolution, the Bolsheviks had banned the performance of religious music and replaced the Synodal Choir with the People's

Choir Academy. In the 1960s and 70s, lyricists were hired to change the words of liturgical music to 'rubbish about weather and nature', according to Igor. Even so, the music was awe-inspiringly beautiful. Igor studied the requiems of Western composers, travelled overseas and bought records in Bulgaria. But the real turning point for him came in 1982 when Sergei Rachmaninov's long prohibited settings of texts from the Orthodox All-Night Vigil ceremony were performed at the Leningrad Kapella. Composed and premiered in 1915, the work had been praised as Rachmaninov's finest achievement, as well as the 'greatest musical achievement of the Russian Orthodox Church'. Igor was hooked. He went to churches to listen to music, then he became interested in religion itself. In 1988 he was baptised in a small church in Estonia, along with twenty others. It was the beginning of a religious renaissance in the USSR.

Unlike Igor, Olga believed in Lenin. The masses believed in him. As recently as December 1989, an astonishing 72 per cent of Soviet citizens surveyed by the All-Union Centre for the Study of Public Opinion regarded Lenin as the greatest person who ever lived and the most outstanding scholar/scientist of all time. Yet now, less than a year later, the state which had preached his genius for almost three-quarters of a century was beginning to waver. Glasnost had freed the tongues of the doubters, and gradually their dissenting voices were seeping into the public consciousness, tainting the once sacred official history of the glorious Great October Revolution.

Lenin believed that people turned to religion because 'impotence of the exploited classes in their struggle against the exploiters inevitably gives rise to the belief in a better life after death'. What a bitter irony that seventy-three years after his revolution, the workers were still the impotent exploited classes, and little by little were turning back to religion.

7

The Republic of the Uzbeks — Soviet Style

To-morrow's fate, though thou be wise,
Thou canst not tell nor yet surmise;
Pass, therefore, not to-day in vain,
For it will never come again.
Omar Khayyam (Persian poet, mathematician
and astronomer c.1048–1131)

The Leningrad Tourism Club was probably not the sort of thing Omar Khayyam had in mind when he urged restless dreamers to fling themselves into the unknown. It was a drab tourist agency off Nevsky Prospekt displaying dusty and faded photos of popular holiday destinations — a cruise ship on the Volga, murky waves lapping at a stony beach on which voluptuous bikini-clad women stood in crucifixion poses. 'Sunbaking,' explained Olga helpfully. But for me Crimea's Black Sea coast couldn't compete with the alluring image of a mosaic-tiled mosque in the ancient town of Samarkand, in the Uzbek Republic.

I'd never imagined when I came to the USSR that a trip to Central Asia would be remotely possible. After all, the fabled desert oases of the Silk Road with deliciously exotic names like Samarkand, Bukhara, Khiva and Shakhrisabz were 3,500 kilometres southeast of Leningrad.

But here in front of us was a chance to take a tour to this far-flung corner of the Soviet empire — if only no one picked me as a foreigner. The idea of visiting Central Asia had never entered Olga's head, but she didn't take much convincing. My 'what the heck, let's just do it' mantra was starting to infect her too and like naughty schoolkids we rationalised that a few more missed classes wouldn't hurt.

The brusque tour agent regarded me suspiciously, even more so when I couldn't produce a passport. 'She's my guest from Estonia,' explained Olga. The woman nodded knowingly — Russians considered Estonians to be slow-witted — and handed us tickets for our Uzbek *putyovka*. The cost for a seven-night trip with flights, accommodation, excursions and meals for two: the rouble equivalent of $AUD61. Neither Olga nor I could bear the thought of more grovelling to rude officials at the OVIR office to get permission for me to leave Leningrad. So far, I'd managed to sneak onto trains and a ship unchallenged, so we decided to risk it and continue our dopey Estonian routine.

For some reason, our flight south was scheduled to depart from Leningrad Pulkovo Airport at the ultra-convenient hour of 2 am. So apparently were flights to everywhere else. Our group assembled in the crowded terminal and the guide began to panic. First, two Hungarian students turned up with tickets and then a yawning Estonian/ Australian. Olga smoothed the way and the foreigners were allowed aboard with the others: a young couple from Byelorussia, and some middle-aged engineers, drivers and teachers, off to sight-see in the distant colonies of the vast Soviet territory.

After takeoff, a snippy steward wheeled a dented metal trolley down the aisle, offering 'in-flight entertainment' in the form of grimy hand-held Donkey Kong video games, just one rouble for the flight's duration. The cabin soon filled with incessant electronic beeping. We refuelled in Ufa, capital of the Autonomous Republic of Bashkirian. A withered old man with a wispy snow-white beard, turban, stripey padded coat and knee-high leather boots boarded and sat in the spare seat beside Olga and I. He took a chicken from inside his coat and stroked it tenderly. No one gave him a second glance.

The distant peaks of the Pamir Mountains glowed in the pink dawn light as we descended into central Uzbekistan's Zerafshan Valley. Our guide herded us into a rickety bus for the short drive to Samarkand's vibrant central bazaar, a scene almost identical to Vereshchagin's paintings from a century earlier. Women wore the same multicoloured dresses with baggy pants, headscarves and heavy velvet overcoats in deep blues, purples and reds. They bustled and fussed over baskets of flatbreads, dried fruits and spices. The faces were a handsome blend of Asian and Middle Eastern, the combination softening the dominant features of each. Older men wore padded dressing-gown style coats with turbans, navigating donkey carts stacked with fresh fruits and vegetables. Younger men in *tubiteikas*, black skullcaps embroidered with white swirls, roared at bystanders as they backed exhaust-belching khaki Kamaz trucks loaded with melons into place. Others hacked into animal carcasses with axes, sorting the bloody pieces into fly-blown piles of ribs, legs, offal, heads, feet, tongues and tails. Olga and I bought *non*, steaming round flatbreads deftly hooked out of an anthill-like clay tandoori oven with a wire. We wandered through the bedlam, gawping and munching as vendors pounced on us tourists, pressing handfuls of dried raisins and apricots into our hands. There was no shortage of food here, or so it seemed on this sunny autumn morning.

Beyond the exotic hustle of the bazaar, much of the ancient town was crumbling to dust. Soulless homogenised Soviet concrete blocks sprung up amidst the ruins. Our hotel was one of the ugliest. I was assigned a room with the Hungarian girls, a tall fair Andrea and a petite dark Andrea, both studying Russian in Leningrad after learning it compulsorily since kindergarten in Budapest. Olga was put in with two single older women. She suspected that we foreigners had been put together so it was easier to keep an eye on us. The Andreas spoke excellent English and were appalled by the state of the room. There were three sagging midget-sized beds with broken springs, stained floral mattresses, and sheets apparently just vacated by sweaty, hairy miners. The bathroom was a mouldy tiled cupboard with a corroded pipe dripping reddish brown water, the toilet blocked and caked with faeces in various stages of dehydration. The flush button was jammed so we took the top off the cistern and pulled the wire by hand.

Our tour ran with military precision, following an exacting schedule to ensure we met our daily quota of historical landmarks. The Soviet tourists loved it, listening attentively to our schoolma'am guide bellowing into her grey megaphone. I struggled to follow so Olga and the Andreas took turns to translate for me. At each location the tourists donned spangly gold embroidered Uzbek costumes of lurid silks and velvets and posed with each other while photographers snapped away. When developed, the pictures would be sent on to Byelorussia and Leningrad to be shown to friends and family.

Once a prosperous city on the major trade route between Persia and China, Samarkand had borne witness to much of Central Asia's blood-splattered history. But according to the English language guidebook I'd purchased in the hotel shop, published in 1986 by the Amalgamated Publishers of the Communist Party of Uzbekistan, it had only found 'genuine happiness under the banners of the Great October Socialist Revolution in the freedom, friendship and fraternity of the peoples'. Samarkand had been founded in the seventh century BC, making approximately 2,600 years of misery before the socialists came along to cheer up the place.

Samarkand's main problem was its beauty and sophistication, along with an excellent location in a fertile oasis on the Zerafshan River. By the time Alexander the Great invaded in 329 BC, it was a highly developed city, with a substantial population, developed crafts, commerce and culture. Naturally Alexander tried to conquer the city for himself, as did every passing army for centuries to come. But the 'freedom loving people of the territory offered stubborn resistance to the invaders'.

And no wonder. In 1220, Genghis Khan and his hordes overran the Zerafshan Valley, described in the following thirteenth-century historian's eyewitness testimony: 'They pitied no one, slaughtering men, women, and children. They slit open the wombs of pregnant women and killed the foetuses. The flames of the massacre spread far and wide, and evil covered everything like a cloud driven by the wind.'

Samarkand was razed to the ground and the memory of the invaders was expressed in the following saying: 'They came, destroyed, killed, plundered and left.'

By the end of the fourteenth century, Samarkand had produced its very own nomadic warrior tyrant, Timur (also known as Tamerlane), who, my guidebook informed me, 'waged endless and bloody conquests creating an empire from the Volga to the Ganges and from the Tien-Shan to the Bosphorous'. Flourishing cities were razed to the ground and hundreds of thousands of people were annihilated. Timur dreamed of world supremacy and was quoted as saying: 'As there is one god in heaven, there must be one king on earth'.

During medieval times, Samarkand had been the cultural, intellectual and economic centre of Central Asia. The official city centre was a magnificent complex of mosques called the Registan, used by Timur to show off spiked heads of defeated enemies, to make pronouncements about his wars, for public executions and to show off loot from his various conquests. I recognised one of the mosques as the one in the Leningrad Tourism Club photo that had lured me here. The Registan was a breathtaking sight, a vast square, fronted on three sides by soaring mosaic-tiled mosques flanked by pairs of minarets with diamond-patterned mosaics in cobalt, turquoise and white. The central archways were decorated with intricate designs in glazed ceramic chips, one featuring a pair of striped lions chasing baby deer, curiously breaking Islamic tradition forbidding the representation of living beings. But the remarkable structures had been long neglected, tiles were missing and tufts of vegetation grew from disintegrating clay bricks.

Olga and I wondered at the incongruity of showing off severed heads before a place of religious study and worship. Behind the façades were *madrassahs*, Islamic boarding schools, where chanting pupils of Islam had lived and studied in a honeycomb of small cells on several levels around large paved central courtyards. Now a museum, they were abandoned: bare and silent apart from a few tourists whose whispers echoed off the stony walls. The once rich blend of Persian, Indian, and Mongolian culture that had made Samarkand unique had been sterilised out of existence by the Soviets in the name of progress, and judging by the approving nods of the tourists to the lady with the megaphone, I seemed to be the only person in the group who wasn't sure that was a good thing.

My guidebook, diligently keeping to the officially approved version of Soviet history, told how after building the Trans-Caspian rail line, the Tsarist empire had brought civilisation to this area. 'But Central Asia became a colony of Russian landlords and capitalists. Against the will of tsarism, the peoples of Central Asia established contacts with the mighty revolutionary force that was the Russian working class, and resolutely embarked on the path of national-liberation struggle.'

The Bolsheviks arrived in 1917 to aid the locals in their revolt against the evil capitalists, proclaiming the formation of the Autonomous Soviet Socialist Republic of Turkestan. But not all Central Asians were as pleased as the Soviet historians described. My guidebook conveniently omitted to mention the *basmachi,* guerrilla bands of fiery locals led by mullahs and tribal chiefs who fiercely resisted the Red Army. After being slaughtered in their tens of thousands, the *basmachi* were eventually suppressed.

The five Central Asian republics were created in 1924, their borders drawn by Lenin's Commissar for Nationalities, Joseph Stalin. The elongated Uzbek Soviet Socialist Republic (SSR) was in the middle, with the large Kazakh SSR to the north, Turkmen SSR to the southwest, Kirghiz and Tajik SSRs to the east and southeast, respectively. Samarkand was the first Uzbek capital. Later it was shifted to the more modern city of Tashkent. Until 1924, the sweeping territory of Central Asia had no distinct boundaries and had been populated by a hotchpotch of different ethnic groups, many of them nomadic. But now Moscow held strict political and economic control of the whole region, and my guidebook assured me that the people had never been so happy.

There is an Uzbek legend about a golden book in a golden casket which was buried in the ground at the time of the bloody invasions by evil tribes. Centuries passed and the people believed that a warrior would be born to find the book and return it to the people. There eventually came into this world a warrior whose mind was brighter than the sun, whose eyes were kind, whose smile instilled cheer and hope and refreshed the tired as a water spring in the desert, whose words were filled with wisdom. This warrior was the great Lenin. He found the golden casket with the wonderful book and opened it to the Uzbeks and the other enslaved peoples of the world.

The great Lenin's minions promptly set about modernising the 'backward outlying national areas' of the Muslim Central Asians. In the name of internationalism, almost all their mosques were destroyed. The Arabic script of their native tongues was first forcibly latinised, then transcribed into Cyrillic, isolating Muslims from their literature and religious texts. Ethnic Russians settled the territory in droves, and Russian became the official state language. The Uzbek SSR was designated as the Soviet Union's prime cotton-producing region and all other crops, including food, were discouraged. Vast tracts of land were destroyed through over-cultivation, soil erosion and overuse of pesticides, and despite what we'd seen in Samarkand's markets, the Uzbek SSR was struggling to feed itself. And for all the cotton being grown, by the time the manufactured products returned from the factories in the western republics, Uzbeks couldn't afford to buy them. The region that was once the heart of the Silk Road soon became the Polyester Route, as national costumes were mass-produced in cheap and nasty rayons. The native culture was reduced to quaint folk-dancing shows. Meanwhile Gorbachev proudly claimed that in the USSR, the nationalities question had been resolved. His country was the 'Great Union of Friendly Peoples'.

We were ferried around more ancient monuments; gravestones, an astronomical observatory and the majestic Guri-Emir mausoleum, built by Timur in 1404, for himself and his descendants. His desiccated cadaver was still in the underground crypt. Our guide informed us that the inscription on his tombstone warned against opening the grave. 'But on the 21st of June 1941, a team of Russian and Uzbek archaeologists opened it and found the remains of Timur.' She paused for dramatic effect. 'On the 22nd of June at 4 am, Hitler attacked the territory of Russia.' There was silence. To me, it seemed a mere unfortunate coincidence, but the superstitious Russians were less cynical. Suddenly music began to blare from a set of loudspeakers in the mausoleum. It was my comrade, our Kylie Minogue, singing, 'I Should Be So Lucky'.

From Samarkand, our rattly bus trundled along a deserted crumbling road, heading westwards through the steppe to the city of Bukhara. It was flat, parched, dusty and desolate, everything a shade of greyish beige: the sand, the low thorny bushes, even the sky. The only diversion was a group of two-humped Bactrian camels lurching lazily in the distance and a line of far-off snow-capped mountains making a pale blue ripple across the horizon. I thought of Alexander Borodin's *In the Steppes of Central Asia*. Composed in 1882 as Tsar Alexander was expanding his empire southwards, Borodin took a peaceful Russian song played on the clarinet and a mournful oriental melody on the English horn, blending the two in masterful counterpoint. At the time of composition, it was suggested that Borodin's vision of the empire was perhaps more idealistic than the reality, wishfully entwining the melodies of the disparate peoples in common harmony.

I was engrossed in mentally playing Borodin, and the tourists were sleeping off the previous night's toasts, when suddenly there was a terrible crash. Our driver had dozed off, drifted into the wrong lane and hit an oncoming truck. Fortunately the damage was relatively minor, a smashed windscreen and mangled frame, but the driver was badly cut and bleeding heavily. What happened next left me stunned. Instead of helping him, our tourists were furious, abusing him for being so careless and ruining their schedule. Olga and I tore up some clothes and bandaged his wounds while he sat in silence, more shamed than pained. A few hours later a new bus arrived to take us on to Bukhara.

The Intourist Hotel in Bukhara laid on a sumptuous banquet with soups, kebabs, *plov* (pilaf) — the Uzbek national dish of spicy rice cooked with pumpkin and lamb, naan breads, *samsa* (small pasties), stuffed vine leaves and peppers and a deliciously sweet yellowy-green fleshed melon called *dynya*. A trio of musicians played a *tanbur* (small fretted lute), *nai* (side-blown flute) and *daira* (tambourine like hand drum), accompanying a young woman who sang droning Middle Eastern modal melodies in a throaty nasal voice. Uzbek girls in voluminous Scheherezade pants with thick ebony plaits to their waists danced in a graceful fusion of belly and Balinese; all swirling hips and twirling fingers. A delicate, effeminate man called Rustam gave a recitation of works of the eleventh-century Persian poet Omar Khayyam in Persian, followed by translations in Russian. As far as I could tell, boozing seemed to be the bard's favourite theme. The tourists guffawed loudly and banged their glasses on the tables for the waiters to fill as Rustam continued:

And lately, by the Tavern Door agape,
Came shining through the Dusk an Angel Shape
Bearing a Vessel on his Shoulder, and
He bid me taste of it, and twas — the Grape!

Our hectic program offered little opportunity to talk to locals, although few of our group seemed interested in doing so. Despite the rhetoric of 'we're just one big happy family', I sensed the Slavic tourists saw the Central Asians as poor quaint colonials. Olga was more open-minded and we decided to introduce ourselves to Rustam. He invited us into a dimly lit den lined in crimson velvet, with carpet-covered cushions against the walls. Gesturing us to sit, he ordered a platter of fruit.

Rustam was a Tajik Jew, whose ancestors had come to Bukhara from Persia two thousand years earlier and claimed to be the city's oldest inhabitants. They even had their own special Tajik–Jewish language, one of seven tongues the erudite Rustam spoke fluently, along with Tajik, Persian, Russian, Uzbek, Yiddish, Polish and a good smattering of English. His main job was as a tour guide for visiting Poles. A plate piled with *dynya*, apricots, grapes and cherries arrived, along with another jug of wine. Rustam stood up, struck a pose and broke into verse. I couldn't understand a word and glanced at Olga. She shook her head. He finished and poured the wine. 'Omar Khayyam,' he explained. 'In the Persian original, naturally.'

Rustam looked at Olga and repeated the verse in Russian, which she then translated for me: 'Drink! For you know not whence you came nor why. Drink! For you know not why you go, nor where.'

So we did.

'Persian culture is high culture: of poetry, of love, of art, of civilisation,' he declared.

'This city, Bukhara and Samarkand, they are *Tajik* cities, cities of superior culture. They are *not* Uzbek cities. These Uzbeks ...' and he lowered his voice, 'they are warriors.' Rustam raked his thinning black hair across his skull with his fingers.

'Comrade Stalin was very clever you know,' he said, arching an eyebrow. 'Like a fox, how do you say?'

'Cunning?' I offered.

'Yes, cunning. The Romans said, "Divide and rule", and Comrade Stalin understood well. His borders put our Tajik cities — Samarkand and Bukhara — in Uzbek Republic, and many Uzbeks in Tajik Republic. Osh is Uzbek city in Kirghizia. This way people will not unite to fight Moscow.'

I was intoxicated by the sweet fruits, seductive music, exotic scenery and fascinating history — and frustrated by the restrictions of the tour group. I asked Rustam if it would be possible for me to come here alone. 'You are first Australian, first foreigner, I see here alone,' he replied, waggling a skinny finger. 'You no stay in hotel without group. But we find somewhere for you stay, no problem. You come and we look after you.'

Returning to our rooms I asked Olga what she thought of my plan. She looked at me as if I were crazy. 'How will you get here? You can't fly again as they will check your passport. The only way is by train and that is four or five days.'

'I'll have to go by train then. I won't talk and no one will guess. I'm sure it will be safe, they are such nice people. By the way, do you think Rustam is gay?'

'What?'

'You know, he likes men instead of women.'

'I don't know. I don't think we have any people like that in our country. It doesn't happen here I'm sure.'

★ ★ ★

Bukhara's centre retained much of its medieval character, with narrow alleyways and ancient clay buildings, dominated by the massive mud walls of the Ark fortress, the former palace of the Emir. Like Samarkand it was an oasis of green in the barren and prickly steppe, with elegant mosques and madrassahs covered in mosaics of different-hued, bright blue glazed tiles. At the heart of the old town, a pond reflected the façade of the most beautiful of the madrassahs. Wizened men played backgammon and dominoes, sitting cross-legged on low tables called *tapchans*, sipping green tea from the *chaikhanas*, in the shade of five 500-year-old trees.

Olga and I sat on a *tapchan* with the Hungarian Andreas, comparing our souvenirs over miniature cups of green tea. I'd bought some of the local skullcaps, which cleverly folded flat, and a ridiculous wedding hat: gold-embroidered with sequins that a gold-toothed babushka had urged me to buy. It was bakingly hot and I felt sticky in my T-shirt, yet the local men were wearing heavy coats stuffed with cotton padding, and the women had ankle-length velvet gowns. The theory was that they would sweat so much it would keep them cool.

Bukhara had an intriguingly gruesome history. We climbed the Kalyan minaret, built in 1127, and once the tallest structure in Central Asia. Dubbed the 'Tower of Death', legend had it that executions were performed by throwing the condemned from the top. Then there was the *Zindan*, a skin-crawling pit of a jail where two British officers had been infamously imprisoned. One had failed to provide appropriate gifts to the Emir of Bukhara on his visit in 1842, and the second was sent to see what had happened to him. They were kept in the creepily named Bug Pit then forced to dig their own graves before being ceremonially beheaded in front of the Emir's palace.

Before we left Bukhara, Rustam introduced me to a friend's nephew, Anwar. 'Tell me when you want to come back,' Rustam instructed. 'You must take train to Tashkent. I will send Anwar to meet you there and he will bring you here. He is a good boy and you can stay with him and his mother here for as long as you like.'

Back on Vasilievsky Island, I plotted my return to Central Asia. Olga still thought I was mad, but accepted that I was going to do it anyway.

She helped me buy tickets to Moscow, and then on to Tashkent, called Rustam and told him the time of my arrival.

Just before leaving I went to a concert at the Leningrad Kapella, the music academy near the Winter Palace where Olga's father and brother had studied. After the concert, I strolled out across Palace Square, heading for the trolleybus stop. Suddenly a distorted male voice bellowed from the blackness. I looked up and saw rows of missile launchers, tanks and APCs (armoured personnel carriers) whir into action, circling the Alexander Column in the centre of the square.

I had no idea what was happening, but I was sure I wasn't meant to be in the middle of it. There wasn't a civilian in sight. A man in military uniform with a megaphone waved furiously at me to move. I sprinted out of the way of the oncoming weaponry with its blaring sirens and hid behind a tree in the palace garden, wondering if perhaps World War Three had broken out. A note at the trolleybus stop said all transport was cancelled and I began the long walk home through empty streets to Olga's. She laughed to hear I thought there was a war. 'No, no. They are having rehearsals for the big parade next week. It is our famous holiday to celebrate the October Revolution. They always make a display of our weapons for this, so all the people can see how strong and powerful our country is.'

I was strangely disappointed. I think I was hoping to find myself in the middle of some history-making battle. But while there was to be no all-out war, people were already beginning to see through the illusory power of a street full of tanks and red flags.

8

Uzbek Republic Solo

'We are told that the communism is already seen at the horizon.'
'Then, what is a horizon?'
'The horizon is an imaginary line which moves away each time you
approach it.'

October 1990

The day after World War III had failed to begin, I set out on my solo trip back to the Uzbek SSR. It was the first time I'd been somewhere without Olga, Yulia or Sveta to hold my hand and cover for me and although this second unsanctioned trip to Central Asia was a potentially deportable offence, I was enjoying the adrenaline rush of defying what I considered to be completely pointless regulations. Bizarrely, I still believed communism was a noble ideology, for some reason making an illogical connection between the warmth of the ordinary people and their political system. But I doubt I would have lasted a week in the Soviet Union if I'd been a citizen, with Big Brother control-freak authorities monitoring every aspect of life.

I'd already adopted Russian superstitions, and sat on my bag for an extra minute before leaving Olga's for Moscow. The train to Tashkent departed the following evening from Moscow's Kazansky Station — the main hub for trains heading east to Siberia and southeast to Central Asia — across the road from the Leningradsky and Yaroslavsky Stations. The 'three stations' is a Moscow landmark, each building designed in the architectural style of its namesake destination city and connecting via underground tunnels with Komsomolskaya Station on the circle line of the metro. Named in honour of the Communist Youth Organisation, I was amused to note that every ornate pillar on the Komsomolskaya platform had 'KIM' at the top in glazed ceramic Cyrillic letters, the acronym for the Kommunisticheskaya Internatsionalnaya Molodyozh (Communist International Youth).

The labyrinth of tiled subterranean passageways between the stations pulsated with crowds of anxious travellers. Uzbeks and Tajiks dragged overloaded sacks of clothing, fruits and other goods. One man pushed a trolley laden with boxes of fragrant *dynya*, which he'd brought up on the train with him. It seemed a ridiculously inefficient way to get melons to the Moscow market. Pimply uniformed soldiers, barely out of their teens, stomped in unison. Stocky old women clutched plastic bags, incongruously printed with exotic tropical beach scenes or overflowing bowls of fruit. I waited, stomach churning, until the last possible minute, tied a scarf on my head and boarded.

The wagon attendant waved me through into the crowded carriage. Most passengers had already changed and settled in for the three-day trip. The fold-out tables were piled with the standard supplies: pickles, cheeses, sausage and black bread. There were Russians, Uzbeks, Tajiks, and many more I couldn't identify. I climbed onto my top bunk, hoping to be ignored, and peeked down at my *sputniks*: a jovial babushka under me, and a canoodling, giggling couple in their early twenties on the bunks opposite. I eavesdropped as they introduced themselves: Valentina Ivanovna from Tashkent, Lena and Timur from a town near Tashkent. Lena was a peroxide blonde with dark roots and a mouth half full of gold teeth. She was Russian, her jolly boyfriend, Timur, an Uzbek.

The portly Valentina wobbled off to fill her teapot from the urn and Lena called me to come down and join them. Instantly they realised there was something wrong. I could understand a lot more than I could say, and I understood that Lena and Timur thought I was some kind of semi-mute. They'd never met anyone who couldn't speak Russian well and quickly concluded I was retarded in some way. Valentina returned and spoke slowly at me. I decided it was pointless to pretend I was anything other than what I was. '*Ya iz Avstralii*,' I whispered. ('I'm from Australia.')

I might well have said I was a Martian. I was nervous, worried that this sensational gossip would spread and I would be found out. But Lena, Timur and Valentina loved the intrigue, and even seemed to enjoy their complicity in my unauthorised adventure. They showered me with hospitality, stuffed me with food and spoke slowly, waiting for me to look up unfamiliar words in my dictionary. I showed them photos of my family and friends, explaining who was who in grammatically mangled Russian.

The days passed and the forests and villages of the Russian Republic gave way to arid windswept steppe. When the police boarded the train at the Kazakh SSR border, Valentina conspiratorially ordered me onto my bunk to feign sleep. She told the *militsiya* 'her grand-daughter' was unwell and not to be disturbed. No one argued with Valentina Ivanovna. She prodded me when they'd gone and winked. 'Get down here and you might see some camels.'

We'd almost reached Tashkent when Timur returned excitedly from the restaurant car. He'd found another foreigner, and urged me to come. Lena and I followed him through the lurching train and I was surprised to see a young midnight-black man staring sadly out the window. I tapped him on the shoulder and he turned around. He was strikingly handsome, with a perfectly symmetrical face, high cheekbones, straight nose and wide eyes.

On hearing English, his face broke into a smile. Then he looked as though he might burst into tears. Solomon was from Ghana, on his way to begin a seven-year medical degree in Tashkent. For Africans, a degree from a European university was highly sought after. The richest went to London, Paris and other Western European capitals. The next step down was Poland or Moscow, and those unable to afford anything better went to the Uzbek capital. It was hardly Europe, but back in Ghana, a degree from Tashkent would get twenty-year-old Solomon further than anything he could earn in Africa. So far he'd been in Russia three days, didn't know a word of the language and was fed up with being stared and pointed at. He'd even been called a 'black monkey'. Poor Solomon wouldn't be able to afford a trip home until his degree was finished and he missed his family already. He showed me a photo of his parents and siblings, posing happily beside a banana palm in colourful cotton robes and sandals. Then he looked out at the bleak expanse beyond the mud-caked window and sighed with a mock shiver. It was the first time in his life he'd been cold.

At the station in Tashkent, Solomon took down my address at Olga's, and wrote out his own, care of the international students' house of Tashkent University's medical campus. He promised to write and let me know how he was going. Lena, Timur and Valentina squeezed me tearfully and gave me their phone numbers, with invitations to visit and stay with them. I echoed their offers, trying to visualise taking gold-toothed Lena for a walk down Bourke Street Mall. How would my land of abundance seem to her?

The deadpan Anwar was waiting at Tashkent Station, his status symbol denim jeans hitched high and belted around his belly button. He held tickets on to Bukhara, another day away. It would be my fifth consecutive night on wheels and this time I shared it with a cage of squawking chickens and several crates of watermelons. I tried to engage the taciturn Anwar in conversation, but soon found the chooks made far more entertaining travel companions.

At last we reached Bukhara. Anwar lived with his mother, who was fortunately considerably more animated than her son, in a dilapidated 1970s two-room flat on the ground floor of a low-rise concrete apartment block, close to the old centre of town. He was twenty but his mother could have been his grandmother, tiny and frail, with beady yet smiling almond eyes and skin heavily wrinkled from a life under the desert sun. She had a gentle sweetness about her, and wore a floral long-sleeved tunic over a pair of matching loose-fitting trousers. Her headscarf was tied tightly, but a few wisps of grey hair had escaped across her forehead.

'You can call me Bibigul,' she said shyly, in slow accented Russian. 'It means Grandma Flower.' Although Russian had been the official language of the Uzbek SSR for decades, for most non-ethnic Russians, it was still their second language. They spoke it slowly and used simpler words and grammar, making it much easier for me to understand than the rapid fire of the native speakers.

Bibigul poured boiling green tea into small dishes, swishing them and tipping out the first round to sterilise the cups. Anwar and I sipped tea while she ladled *plov* onto plates. A simple and trusting soul, Bibigul worked on night duty in the local *internat*, a boarding school and home for orphans and children whose parents live far away. 'Her' children were the five to ten year olds, and she spoke about them with moist-eyed affection.

'They miss their parents so much, but at least they are better off than your Western children.'

Bibigul knew of the West what the Soviet propagandists had decided she should hear, that is, that capitalist societies were run by a wealthy exploiter class, and the majority lived in slavish poverty. At school she'd studied Charles Dickens's *Oliver Twist*, interpreted by her teachers as documentary evidence of the evils of capitalism. Such exploitation of innocent children had upset her terribly. She wondered too why the Americans wanted to destroy the Soviet Union.

'They don't.'

'But our Government tells us they do.'

Fervour for communist ideals seemed more pronounced in this provincial region. Apparently Gorbachev's message of openness hadn't arrived in distant Bukhara, at least not in Bibigul's world. For her, the Cold War was still raging. She'd even been afraid of having a Westerner to stay, but had made a promise to Rustam, and her instinct for hospitality overrode her fears. Soon after my arrival she had a change of heart. 'You know, maybe what our government tells us about you Western people is not right. You are just like we are.'

During the day Bibigul curled up on her mattress on the floor to watch Soviet movies on her black and white television. I watched some with her, trying to follow the plots. They seemed to go like this: Boy meets girl while working on a collective farm. She's impressed with his strength and devotion to the Communist Party, and he is likewise impressed by her. Some wicked counter-revolutionary would get in the way, but ultimately the heroes would end up together, united by their common love for the communist cause.

Bibigul's nineteen-year-old niece, Marina, was half-Russian, half-Tajik, an attractive girl with black hair and blue eyes. Unlike most Tajik women, who wore their hair in fat waist-length plaits, hers was shoulder length and layered. She worked as a seamstress in a small, prefabricated concrete workshop on the outskirts of town, churning out knee-length dresses and baggy pants. Once these had all been made of traditionally patterned handwoven *atlas* silk, dyed with black-and-white diamond and arrow shaped geometric motifs, with stretched spots of bright yellows, reds, blues and greens. But these days, silk on the Silk Road was hard to come by, and they were mostly polyester and rayon.

Marina's real passion was 'modern' fashion. Her prized possessions were a bundle of dog-eared, ten-year-old magazines with pictures of Muscovite women in the latest straight woollen skirts, frilly blouses, and fluffy baby pink cardigans. Marina had carefully studied the grainy photos, made sketches, cut patterns and sewn herself a wardrobe of garments unlike that of any other woman in Bukhara.

The day of the long-anticipated parade of the year finally arrived. Marina invited me to watch it with her, her sister-in-law Galina, and Galina's family. It was now 7 November but confusingly, the anniversary of the Great *October* Socialist Revolution of 1917. This was because up until 1918, the Russian empire had followed the Julian calendar, while the majority of the world had adhered to the Gregorian for centuries. So in Russia it was 25 October, but everywhere else it was 7 November. After 1918 there were some radical experiments in calendar change, including a five-day week/six-week month arrangement designed to increase productivity. The government finally joined the rest of the world in using the Gregorian calendar in 1940, losing thirteen days.

Bukhara didn't have as fine a collection of military hardware to display as had been rehearsing in Leningrad, but the crowds made up for it in enthusiasm. The whole town turned out, dressed in their finest, to applaud the procession of marching bands and military vehicles decked with red billboards, some with hammers and sickles, others bearing slogans such as '1917', 'Proletarians of the World Unite', 'Long Live the Great October Socialist Revolution' and 'Long Live Marxism-Leninism'. Children and elderly waved red flags; war veterans strutted proudly, chests plastered with medals and ribbons. Marina and Galina jumped up and down like school children and even I waved a red flag. After the parade, Marina's family hosted a banquet. Her Russian father broke out the vodka in a blurry night of toasts to internationalism and eternal friendship between Bukhara and Australia.

Back on Bibigul's floor that night, I hazily read from the guidebook I'd bought on my first trip to Bukhara:

> The Great October Socialist Revolution of 1917 brought happiness into the home of every Uzbek. It meant freedom for the Uzbek people from social, economic and national oppression. The revolution overcame the bitter resistance of the exploiter classes, brushed aside the vestiges of medieval times and drew the masses into the struggle for the consolidation of the Soviet system and the construction of a new and happy life.

If today was anything to go by, people really were happy. Or perhaps it was the vodka? Or were they not only indoctrinated about what to think and do, but indoctrinated into being happy about it too?

I finally caught up with Rustam, who was busily guiding Polish tour groups staying at the Intourist Hotel. He invited me to tag along with one group on an excursion to the ruins of the ancient city of Varakhsha, now little more than wind- and time-ravaged mud walls rising from the steppe. I sat next to an English teacher from western Poland called Barbara, who told me how she felt a common bond with the Uzbeks, both being 'a proud people, suppressed by the Soviets'.

Poland had been the first Eastern bloc country to successfully stand up to the Soviet Union. It was now over a year since the burly Lech Walesa led his workers waving their flags of *Solidarnosc* (solidarity) painted in dripping blood red, to oust the communist leaders of the People's Republic of Poland. Walesa's victory had inspired the fall of the Berlin Wall in 1989, leading to the overthrow of Warsaw Pact Soviet satellite regimes in East Germany, Czechoslovakia, Hungary, Bulgaria and Romania.

But could the same thing happen here in Central Asia? Soviets had dominated this territory for three-quarters of a century, while Poland had only been reluctantly under Soviet control for a relatively short forty-four years, since the end of World War II. Many Poles still remembered life before communism, but the Central Asians had been comprehensively brainwashed for their entire lifetimes.

Despotic rulers had been the norm here for centuries: from Genghis Khan and Timur to a whole host of slightly less notorious but equally unsavoury emirs and khans. Society was fiercely tribal, with allegiances first and foremost to one's clan. As the reality of Soviet authority dawned in Central Asia in the aftermath of the Bolshevik revolution, clan leaders understood that what couldn't be beaten should be joined. Representatives of the dominant clans signed up to the Communist Party, paid lip service to whatever was required of them by Moscow and promptly directed money and employment to their own families. Except in name, the social structure barely changed. The First Secretaries of Central Asia's communist parties were still emirs and khans, albeit adorned with Soviet medals instead of traditional embroidered robes.

Rather than being despised by their people as corrupt dictators, they were admired for their cunning in defrauding the Soviets. When Moscow demanded the Uzbeks increase cotton production, First Secretary of the Uzbek Communist Party (from 1959 to 1983), Sharof Rashidov, responded by falsifying figures, managing to scam himself and his cronies around USD$2 billion in payments for nonexistent crops. When he was eventually caught out, Rashidov was dismissed, his minister for cotton production was executed, and almost three thousand officials were jailed. But his defiance of Moscow only increased his popularity at home. Eventually, in 1989, Moscow found a leader more to their liking in Islam Karimov, a gruff yes-man of Tajik–Uzbek parentage who had grown up in a state orphanage. Karimov had climbed the Party ranks through his hard-line support of Moscow, spoke poor Uzbek and had few ideas of his own. In short, he was the perfect candidate for the position of First Secretary of the Uzbek Communist Party.

Glasnost had permitted a limited revival of both Islam and nationalism in Central Asia, although the die-hard communist Karimov was too much the dictator to allow genuine freedom of speech. In late 1988, writers and intellectuals in the Uzbek SSR established a nationalist popular front called Birlik (meaning Unity). This was soon followed by similar groups in the Tajik, Kazakh, Kyrghyz and Turkmen republics. Birlik's first task was to demand the restoration of the fast-disappearing Uzbek language and in 1989 they organised a huge demonstration in Tashkent. Irate authorities arrested one hundred demonstrators, including Birlik's leader, but eventually did agree to restore Uzbek as the national tongue. Birlik's next demand was more threatening: a democratic and secular society. Unimpressed, Karimov realised he needed to bring Birlik under control. He engineered a split in the Party and began to cultivate an image of himself as an Uzbek nationalist. When the first elections were held in March 1990, Birlik was banned from running. The sour-faced Karimov was elected, unopposed, to the post of President of the Uzbek SSR. Central Asia looked set to continue its history of autocratic despotic rulers.

But for now, life in Bukhara still went on much as it had for decades. Oblivious to the political shenanigans going on in Tashkent, groups of old men gathered to chat, play chess or backgammon in the narrow alleyways of the ancient town. I set out each morning to explore, invariably finding myself taken hostage by curious and hospitable locals who dragged me into their lives and force-fed me with *plov*. One day I was wandering down a high mud-walled lane, when an old man grabbed my arm. He pulled me through a doorway into a courtyard, buzzing with women in action. One pounded something with a mortar and pestle, another rolled out sheets of dough. A third stirred a *plov*-filled super-sized wok. All wore traditional dress, albeit of the rayon variety. The man led me to two girls and grinned a gold-toothed grin. The girls beamed and one asked in stilted Russian. 'You come to our *svadba*?'

Noting my clueless expression they began to dance, stepping from side to side, twirling their arms and snapping their fingers. 'Man, woman, together,' said one, linking her forefingers and pushing them at my face. I got it — a wedding, today, now. The girls introduced themselves as Gulyam and Firuza, and gestured to a *tapchan* under a vine-covered trellis in the centre of the courtyard. 'Seet dowen pliz,' urged Gulyam. She burst into peals of hysterical laughter and spoke in Russian. 'That's the only English we learnt at school. Our teachers didn't even know any more than that!'

She brought me a cushion and dish of green tea. Children scampered around, the bigger ones dragging the smaller, like sacks of flour. They all wore what looked like black eyeliner painted thickly around their eyes. 'Kohl,' she explained, showing me a small conical black stone. She wet it and rubbed it on a cube of the same stone, then drew a thick line on her hand. 'It's so the bad spirits don't get in.' She drew thick lines around my eyes and put the stone in my pocket. '*Na pamyat*,' she said. 'To remember me by.'

I tried to help make *samsa* and they laughed at my clumsy attempts to fold triangles of dough around spoonfuls of meat and onion. The banquet was almost ready, and the women changed from their everyday outfits into velvet dresses adorned with mass-produced bangles, necklaces and earrings. The men arrived, awkward in ill-fitting suits, and we all piled into a couple of sputtering Ladas. Gulyam, Firuza and I shared the front seat. The frilly white bride was crammed in the middle of the back, black hair tumbling in ringlets down her lace and tulle bodice. She looked petrified. I offered her my congratulations, trying to elicit a smile. 'Today, good day!' Her bottom lip quivered and she looked about to cry. Gulyam waggled her finger at me and shook her head with a 'tsk, tsk' sound.

We squeezed out of the vehicles at another dusty old town alleyway where more revellers were waiting. The wedding party had now swelled to about thirty, including musicians. One played a drum, another an oboe-type reed instrument. They began to dance through the narrow street, arms outstretched, hands upwards, fingers clicking and wrists twirling. The bride, in the centre of the partying throng, kept her veil over her face and eyes down. Traditionally, a Tajik wedding took three days and even involved the slaughter of a goat. But Soviet influence had led the goat slaying to be replaced by the obligatory photo shoot at the town war memorial. This was the favoured time of year for weddings, post-harvest, when the fieldwork was complete. Several wedding parties vied for a spot near the red granite monument. Everyone seemed to be having a great time, except our bride, who looked desperately sad as she posed with her lanky groom in his polyester suit.

Snaps taken, the bridal entourage moved on to another house. The rooms were laid out with long plastic sheets along the length of the floor with mattresses and cushions against the walls. The bride and groom sat at the far end of the room. I, the guest of honour, was waved to a place next to the bride. Gulyam, Firuza and the other women brought out huge plates of steaming *plov*, freshly baked *samsa,* and bowls of grapes, melons and dried fruits. The men reclined, relaxed, snapping their fingers for food and vodka refills between picking meat from their teeth. The bride neither ate nor spoke and continued to appear thoroughly miserable. I tried to make eye contact and engage her in conversation, hoping to cheer her up. Eventually I asked Gulyam if everything was OK. She giggled.

'Don't worry. It's our custom. She must not smile or talk to anyone. Today she is leaving the house of her mother and father forever. She must be sad about it.'

Symbolically sad, or genuinely sad, I wondered. Probably both. As I watched her gawky new husband knocking back the vodka, I didn't envy her at all. Central Asian men made the Russians look positively SNAGgy. In the house of her new in-laws she would have to work harder than anyone else, waiting on not only her new husband, but the rest of his family too. There would be no sitting on the streets playing backgammon.

Winter was on its way and my thin Australian raincoat wasn't doing much to keep out the chill. I bought some thermal underwear from a remarkably queue-free army supplies shop near Bibigul's flat, and at a market a pair of second-hand Uzbek woman's baggy pants, made from garish purpley-pink silk with swirly gold embroidery around the ankles. From mid-thigh height upwards the material was what looked like offcuts from an old floral flannel sheet. This part was supposed to be covered by a dress, and without one, I was effectively exposing my underwear. I'm embarrassed to admit that my fashion sense was so dire that's just what I did. To top off my stylish new look, I purchased what

I considered to be a perfectly respectable quilted coat for the bargain price of ten roubles (AUD$1). Called a *telogreika,* it was made of durable grey cotton with vertically stitched channels stuffed with wadded cotton fibre. Bibigul was horrified. 'You can't wear a *telogreika!* That is for prisoners, soldiers and workers.'

Three weeks after my arrival in Bukhara I realised that my visa was about to expire. It was one thing to be 3,500 kilometres away from where I was registered, but an expired visa on top of it could get me into even more trouble. Rustam helped me buy tickets back to Leningrad and Marina, Galina, Bibigul and Anwar all came to the station to wave goodbye. Marina shook her head in despair at my new outfit. 'Come back soon and I'll sew you some nice clothes,' she implored. Bibigul cried, and Galina gave me some kohl as a present. Anwar merely hitched his high-pants even higher and looked as glum as ever.

I stopped in Tashkent to change trains and spent a few hours meandering around the city. A massive earthquake in 1966 had devastated almost everything of historical interest and Soviet planners had been hard at work ever since, replicating the architectural travesties of the *spalny raions* of Moscow, Leningrad and every other Soviet city. The only difference was that Tashkent's apartment blocks had mosaic-tiled geometric patterns down their sides. Washing fluttered from sagging balconies and the buildings were even more decrepit than in the northern cities. There were noticeably more ethnic Russians than in Samarkand and Bukhara, their pale skin and European dress oddly out of place in the desert. Everything about the city felt forced, incongruous: from the vertical slums to the 30-metre-high statue of Lenin in the main square.

'When I want to understand what is happening today or try to decide what will happen tomorrow, I look back', Omar Khayyam had written.

Bibigul, Rustam, Anwar and Marina could not have known that they had celebrated their last Great October Socialist Revolution Day Parade. Within less than a year, the Uzbek SSR would be an independent state, cut off from the umbilical cord of Mother Russia. Central Asia's past had been filled with blood and tyrants. Could it hold onto its 'genuine happiness, freedom, friendship and fraternity'? Did it even exist?

9

Restive 'Small Peoples': The Balts and the Tatars

*An American, a Russian, and an Estonian are riding in the same
compartment in a train. The American takes out a pack of
cigarettes, offers one to the others, and then throws the rest of the
pack out the window.*
'What did you do that for?' exclaim both the Russian and the Estonian.
'Ah, in America we have so many cigarettes,' replies the American.
*After a while the Russian takes out a bottle of vodka, offers it all around,
and then throws the rest of the vodka out the window.*
'What did you do that for?' ask the American and the Estonian.
'Oh, in Russia, we have so much vodka,' replies the Russian.
*Time goes by, and the Estonian sits in deep thought. Finally he throws
the Russian out the window.*

Olga burst out laughing when she saw me. I'd been so pleased at
solving my winter coat dilemma for only ten roubles, that I never
imagined people would find my peasant/workers' coat, floral headscarf
and baggy pink silk Uzbek pants so ridiculous. I opened my mouth,
hoping to impress her with my new improved Russian. She stifled a
chuckle. 'You sound like an Uzbek!' She was right. In the cultured
north, my Bukharan worker accent sounded as out of place as that of a
Queensland grazier in Oxford.

'But why did it matter?' I wondered. What about this equality and harmony amongst all nationalities and ethnicities? I noticed that when I wore my Uzbek/peasant garb on public transport, a space would appear around me. People whispered, '*Ostorozhno, Tsyganka*' ('Be careful of the gypsy'), and recoiled as I passed. Olga supposed people feared I would pick their pockets, as anyone with olive skin (as I have) and such outlandish clothes would be likely to do. In my jeans and an orange down coat of Olga's I was evidently so trustworthy I would be half crushed.

In Leningrad, temperatures plummeted and snow began to fall, only to be quickly squelched into brown sludge by the relentless pedestrian traffic. Olga and I once again queued for three days at OVIR and the bank, and I was granted an extra month in the country. The days became shorter, and by late November it was dark by half past four. I met two Canadian students, Tina and Katya, on a tram. Both were studying Russian at Leningrad University and lived in a student hostel one street away from Olga's. Tina was my age, a diminutive brunette of Slovenian descent, with a razor-sharp mind and penetrating gaze. She was a walking encyclopaedia of Soviet history and a polyglot to boot. Russian was her fourth language, after French, English and Slovene. I visited her in her seedy dormitory room, with its saggy bed and dirty green walls, glad that I hadn't come here as a student. On hearing of my Uzbek wanderings, Tina was initially incredulous, envious, then impatient to try a trip of our own. Over stale gingerbread and murky tea we hatched a plan to visit Riga, the capital of the Baltic republic of Latvia.

Just over six months earlier — in May 1990 — the Latvians had become the third union republic to demand independence from Moscow, following neighbouring Lithuania and Estonia in declaring that their territories had been illegally annexed by the USSR. But the Soviet Army had cracked down hard on the Lithuanians, and Gorbachev immediately and flatly put an end to their call for self-rule.

Unless you were reading Soviet history books, the Latvians, Lithuanians and Estonians had never been willing subjects of the Soviet empire. According to that version of events, the Red Army entered the Baltic lands in June 1940, in accordance with Stalin and

Hitler's Molotov–Ribbentrop Pact to divide Europe into 'spheres of influence'. There was no occupation because the Baltic governments (although newly installed by the Soviets) agreed to have Russian troops stationed on their territory. They then voluntarily decided to lose their statehood to their 'liberators' and formally applied to join the USSR. The fact that in the first year of the 'liberation', tens of thousands of opponents to Soviet rule were slaughtered or exiled to Siberia didn't rate a mention. Hundreds of thousands more, including 70,000 Latvian Jews, lost their lives when the Nazis occupied the territories during the Great Patriotic War.

The Soviets returned after the war, in 1944–1945, to forcibly collectivise and sovietise the Baltic nations. Many ethnic Balts fled to Europe and Sweden. Hundreds of thousands more were deported en masse to the Far East, while a huge influx of labourers, military personnel and administrators from the Russian and other Soviet republics flooded the small nations. Soon the Balts were almost minority groups in their own homelands. Their native languages were suppressed and supplanted by Russian, and ethnic Russians took over most key government positions.

Prompted by glasnost, in the late 1980s massive demonstrations began against the Soviet regime, which would become known as the 'Singing Revolution'. As in Central Asia, opposition popular fronts were created which received widespread support. The most spectacular protest took place on the fiftieth anniversary of the signing of the Molotov–Ribbentrop Pact. On 23 August 1989, an estimated two million people joined hands, creating a 600 kilometre human chain called the 'Baltic Way', stretching through Lithuania, Latvia and Estonia. It was only then that the Supreme Soviet, the highest legislative body of the USSR, backtracked and declared that perhaps the goings-on in the Baltics had in fact been an occupation, which was not technically 'in accordance with law', nor with the 'will of the Soviet people'. But that still didn't mean Gorbachev would concede to their demands for full independence.

Olga could see the logic in the rebellious Baltics' bid for independence, but as a patriotic Soviet citizen, she had mixed feelings about the best way to resolve what was now a very messy situation. 'The Baltic States say we occupied them by force. But now there are so many Russians there, it is a strange situation. On one hand it's logical for them to be independent. But in Lithuania there are almost 50 per cent Russians. What would happen to them? Where will they go?'

Tina was certain that sovereignty of the Baltic states was inevitable and imminent, and wanted to visit immediately, while there were still no border checks or separate visas required. An overnight train trip there, a day in Riga, and overnight back. Katya would tell their teachers that Tina had come down with a stomach bug. Again I bought tickets from scalpers hovering around the station in Leningrad. They eyed us with curiousity — me in my grey prison coat, Tina in her high-tech Canadian snow wear.

Only a fourteen-hour train journey from Leningrad, the Latvian SSR felt like a different world. Riga was a gingerbread town, picture-postcard cute with higgledy-piggledy cobblestone streets, wrought-iron street lamps and pastel terraced houses with window shutters and snow-covered flower boxes pressed together in narrow alleyways. People-sized and cosy, it was the antithesis of the austere and intimidating concrete horrors with which Soviet architects had surrounded the city. We could even buy tasty food without having to queue for it.

Between overindulging in scrumptious pastries, Tina and I chatted with locals: cake-shop patrons, the director of the Natural History Museum and the saleswoman in the musical instrument shop where Tina persuaded a music student to buy a state-subsidised cello for her to take back to Leningrad. Many of the ethnic Russians had spent most of their lives in Latvia. Their children had been born there and all connections to the Russian Republic were long severed. Yet few had seen the need to learn the native language, and judging from those we spoke to, they still felt confident that the mighty USSR would maintain the status quo. But the Latvians were not so happy. Nationalist sentiment was rising, and the patriotic students we spoke to were bursting to cut all ties with the Soviet Union. It was time for retribution, time to reinstate Latvian as the national language and time to expel the Russians and their military. The flood of protest unleashed by glasnost was drowning out all pretense of inter-ethnic harmony. No longer did the Latvians have to feign gratitude to their oppressive liberators.

> *An old Latvian is walking down the street and sees a person that has just been killed by a falling brick. 'What a pity that a Latvian dies when there are so few of us,' he complains. A bystander tells him that it is a Russian, not a Latvian. Again the old man complains, 'Damn! There are so many Russians here that there is not even room for a brick to hit the ground.'*

The Estonians shared the Latvians' affections for their Soviet masters:

> *Why did the Estonian put on a gas mask when a nuclear bomb landed on Moscow? To hide his smile.*

> *Did you know that our Estonia is the biggest country in the world?*
>   *Really? How's that?*
>   *The coastline's on the Baltic; the capital is Moscow; and the population's in Siberia.*

Back in Leningrad I had a call from an English student Rustam had introduced me to in Bukhara. Peter was studying Russian at the University of London's School of Slavonic and East European Studies (SSEES) and part of his course required spending a year in Russia. He and several others were living with Russian families in the city of Kazan; the capital of the autonomous republic of Tatarstan, 800 kilometres east of Moscow on the Volga River, where they took classes in Russian language and literature at the Kazan Chemical Technology Institute.

Peter was planning a day trip to Tallinn, capital of the Republic of Estonia. Like Latvia, this Netherlands-sized state on the Gulf of Finland was in the throes of a nationalist renaissance, which since March 1990 had progressed to a 'transitional phase to independence'. Gorbachev was displeased, but despite his protests and warnings, the Estonians had voted for local law to take precedence over Soviet legislature. The end of Soviet rule in Estonia seemed nigh.

I told Peter I'd love to join him and he arrived the next morning with a Welshman, Ian, along with the son of Ian's host family in Kazan, Sergei Stepanov. Sergei was a wide-eyed seventeen-year-old law student in his first year at Kazan State University. He spoke great English and had an infectiously enthusiastic manner, keenly following our conversations as we rattled through the snowy night from Leningrad to Tallinn. Well over six foot, with broad shoulders and angular jaw, he would have made an excellent model for a propaganda poster. But Sergei had other plans. He wanted to know about the world and had begged his parents to host a foreign student, even giving up his own room for the duration of Ian's stay. The reclusive Welshman, however, was proving a disappointment, cloistering himself away to study and barely speaking to the family.

From the age of seven Sergei had dreamed of representing the USSR in track and field. He began training as a long jumper in Kazan and soon began to win competitions in Tatarstan. In his teens, he answered an advertisement in *Sovietsky Sport*, calling for talented athletes to try out for the USSR's most prestigious sports boarding school. School No. 9 in Moscow trained four hundred students in twenty different disciplines, churning out world champions in everything from diving to chess, as well as requiring them to complete a full academic course. Sergei was summoned to the capital, passed their tests and was accepted.

From 1987 to 1989 he trained 'insane' hours, intensely motivated to achieve greatness alongside many of the nation's most celebrated athletes. It had been a non-stop high, until he came down with hepatitis. He was sent back to Kazan for six months to recuperate. When he recovered he realised that he didn't want the life of a 'superhero sportsman' after all. 'I needed to have some serious profession and not finish sport at twenty-eight or thirty,' he explained. 'And one of my greatest motivations for doing sport was to have the ability to travel, including abroad.' He hoped that now the country was beginning to open up, he might find some other opportunities to experience the world.

We arrived in Tallinn to find the town caught in a wild blizzard, its medieval charm almost invisible under the swirling whiteness. The availability of queue-free beverages was an enticing option for the alcohol-starved Brits, and the pubs were warm and cosy. We staggered from one to the next, appraising Baltic brews and conversing with the clientele. Peter told a young Estonian that he was studying in Russia. The Estonian curled his lip. 'I don't like Russians,' he said defensively.

Sergei looked at him. 'I'm Russian,' he said. There was silence and Peter changed the subject. But Sergei wasn't offended. He knew these territories on the Gulf of Finland were unhappy, but had little sympathy for the cause of Baltic nationalism. His Uncle Grigory from Kazan had fought in Estonia during the Great Patriotic War, later marrying an Estonian woman who rescued and cared for him after he was seriously wounded. They had a son and settled in Estonia. Grigory had even received an Order of Lenin for his services to Estonian road and bridge building. But when Sergei's mum, Tatiana, had visited recently, Grigory was on edge. Nationalistic Estonian youths now openly called him an occupant. His son had taken his mother's Estonian surname to disguise his half-Russian parentage and refused to speak in the language of the occupiers.

Estonian is a Finno–Ugric tongue from the Ural Mountains region, related to Finnish, Hungarian and other minority tongues from the area. It is an astoundingly complicated language with fiendishly tricky grammar, and only around a million speakers. I could see why ethnic Russians never bothered to learn it. Russians in the Russian Republic made fun of Estonians, telling jokes v-e-r-y s-l-o-w-l-y with a kind of Swedish Muppet Chef accent.

Two Estonians are sitting by the camp fire.

'Christmas is nice!' says one of them.

Half an hour later, the other one replies: 'Yes, Christmas is nice, but a woman is even nicer!'

Another half-hour later the first man replies: 'Yes, a woman is better, but Christmas comes more often!'

It was no wonder the Estonians wanted the Russians out. But the future looked grim for Sergei's uncle Grigory if the Russian-hating Estonian youth were to have their way. It was a complex situation with no straightforward solution and emotions were running high. 'Baltic people say that Russians invaded them and that they suffered,' said Sergei. 'But my parents and grandparents also suffered under the Soviet regime. So they are also angry at the "Russians", only they are Russians themselves. And even though I probably agree with the Baltic nationalists and their assessments of "Russian" actions, why should I be responsible for things that those "Russians" did?'

It wasn't only the Balts, Central Asians and Ukrainians who were growing increasingly resentful of Soviet control. Ethnic minorities all over the empire were twitching and restless as glasnost revealed and acknowledged the brutality and hypocrisy of the regime. Memories of centuries of bloody rivalry were being dredged up, wearing down the veneer of the happy *homo sovieticus*. Sergei's hometown of Kazan was the ancestral capital of one of the largest minorities in the USSR — the Tatars — an intriguing blend of Turkish and Mongol. But unlike the nations on the periphery of the empire, the Tatar homeland was slap in the middle of the European part of the Russian Republic, surrounded by Russia on all sides.

On the way back to Leningrad, Sergei invited me to visit his family in Kazan, just as soon as he checked with his mother. She agreed, and a few days later I once again handed over some roubles to a shifty entrepreneur outside Leningrad's Moscovsky Station, and slipped onto an overnight train to Moscow with my anonymous ticket. I repeated the same procedure the next day at Kazansky Station in Moscow, unwittingly booking myself a hellish night in a confined space with three blokes determined to empty three bottles of vodka between them. As the spirit level sank, the arguments and noise level rose until my reeking companions finally passed out, sprawled on their bunks, snoring like asthmatic lions.

At nearly midnight we pulled into the town of Gus Khrustalny. Snowflakes fluttered to the ground, sparkling in the bright station lights, and I was confronted by an extraordinary sight: people running up and down the platform, waving crystal chandeliers, crystal vases and boxes of goblets in etched pink glass. Noticing I was awake they pressed their cold-reddened fur-fringed faces against the window, gesturing to their unusual wares. The town's rouble-strapped crystal factory, it turned out, was paying workers in the wares they produced, which they were selling to travellers passing through on their way from Moscow to Siberia.

By morning the train crossed the frozen Volga River, pulling into Kazan soon after. My *sputniks* were stinking and subdued, and I made a mental note never to travel in a lockable compartment again with strangers. Sergei met me at the station and we took a rickety tram to his parents' flat on Sibirsky Trakt, the main road to Siberia, which begins another 800 kilometres further east beyond the Urals. He'd already warned his mother, Tatiana, about the strange girl he'd met in Leningrad, who wore army boots, a prison jacket and Uzbek underwear on the outside. But she hadn't warned the neighbours. While they looked on, asking her. 'Who is this homeless person?', Tatiana seized me in a tight embrace. She was forty-two and a classic Russian beauty. Sergei had inherited her high cheekbones and wide blue eyes. She fussed over me like a mother hen, her *gostepriimstvo* so overpowering I felt I'd been taken hostage.

It was 1 December 1990, and on that day in Kazan, ration cards were introduced for the first time since the Great Patriotic War. Each adult was allocated a monthly limit of 1.5 kg of meat, 1 kg of sausages, 0.5 kg of butter, 0.25 kg of vegetable oil, 10 eggs, 0.5 kg of flour and 1 kg of cereals or macaroni. Tatiana was unconcerned and plied me with slices of a deliciously calorific Tatar apple pie. 'The meat at the state shops is terrible anyway,' explained Sergei. 'It always looks as though the cow was killed last year and has only just now been brought to the shop. Mum buys our meat from the farmers in the villages.'

Tatiana was a proud and patriotic Soviet citizen, with connections that helped make life just that little bit easier. Her uncle had been the second secretary of the Communist Party in the Azerbaijani capital,

Baku. Her father had played football for the USSR, and her grandfather had been the director of a polyclinic — a medical centre — in Kazan. Her husband, Sergei's father, Anatoly, had been an engineer with a high-up position in a scientific institute: 'Something to do with producing optics for space ships and submarines,' Sergei mused. When perestroika began and entrepreneurial activities were permitted, Anatoly set up a 'co-operative', a two-pronged commercial business involved in developing and producing technologies for improving oil extraction, along with trading anything and everything from furs to oil. The Stepanov family were quite comfortably off, able to host Ian from Wales as their non-paying guest in their larger than average four-room flat. They could even afford to put up new wallpaper in honour of his stay.

Sergei moved back into his bedroom with Ian and Tatiana made the dining room fold-out couch into a bed for me. After working mornings as a preschool teacher, she devoted the rest of her time to my education, chattering incessantly about anything and everything. Whenever I reached for my dictionary she grabbed it. '*Nyet, ne nado* (You don't need that),' she would say, explaining what she meant in terms a four-year-old could understand. Like Yulia, her smothering, mothering instincts were overwhelming, and I now realised resisting a Russian woman on a mission was futile. It was my first experience of intact family dynamics in the USSR. Yulia, Olga, Valya, Natasha and Bibigul were all either single or separated. On one hand Tatiana ruled the roost, on the other she was the house servant. As a young woman, she had travelled all over the Soviet Union, and saw in me a kindred wandering spirit, at least to a degree. But the holes in my jeans and my lack of desire to acquire cooking skills disturbed her deeply. If I didn't learn to make *pelmeni* (ravioli) and *pirozhki* (pasties), then what kind of wife was I going to make the unfortunate fellow who got lumbered with me? Certainly no Russian male would tolerate such a useless spouse.

When the Bolsheviks came to power, propaganda posters had shown how communism would free women from domestic duties. Cooking and child rearing would be taken care of by communal kitchens and childcare centres. No longer would women be slaves to their families. Now they would be free to be slaves to their country. Women were mobilised to drive tractors, build railways, fight wars, staff factories and till fields. Posters showed muscular girls wielding a scythe, hammer or *kalashnikov* in one hand, clutching a rosy-cheeked toddler in the other. Women were to contribute to the greater good by both labouring as a man, and breeding a new generation of *homo sovieticus* to replace the twenty million lost in the Great Patriotic War. Medals of honour were presented to 'Heroine Mothers', those who had ten or more children.

But Lenin's grand scheme to release women from their domestic drudgery had been a miserable failure. The state had not been able to provide affordable and quality dining halls, laundries and childcare. Instead of producing washing machines, fridges and vacuum cleaners, factories had been devoted to making tanks, guns and submarines. Olga took her linen to a dingy local laundry, which took weeks to return her sheets and towels. Tatiana washed hers in a bucket in the bath. Both swept their flats with brooms made from a bunch of twigs and stored perishables on kitchen windowsills in the space between the double-glazing. Saddled with the double burden of housework, child-raising and outside employment, many women were exhausted and fed up. One thing was certain, Russian men weren't going to help. While Tatiana ran in circles, from school to the shops and around the flat, Anatoly slumped in front of the TV, waiting for her to bring him tea.

Gorbachev knew he had a problem. Overworked women were having fewer children, yet at the same time unemployment was rising. His solution was to encourage women back to their kitchens to free up jobs for men. A propaganda team set to work, introducing a course in 'The Ethics and Psychology of Family Life' into schools, with an accompanying TV broadcast. Teachers were urged to 'train girls to be girls and boys to be boys'. In his 1987 book, *Perestroika: New Thinking for our Country and the World*, Gorbachev argued that 'women no longer have enough time to perform their everyday duties at home — housework, the upbringing of children and the creation of a good family atmosphere. We should … make it possible for women to return to their purely womanly mission'.

Tatiana appeared to have no objections to this concept of a womanly mission.

'Don't Anatoly or Sergei ever help with anything?' I asked her one day as she set me to work peeling and grating boiled beetroot, while she wrung out dripping shirts over the bathtub. 'Hasn't anyone here ever heard of feminism?'

She looked shocked. '*Feministka*,' she explained, 'is a dirty word. It's an insult.' In the USSR, a feminist wasn't a woman who wanted equal rights, it was a woman who both wanted to be like a man, and who hated men. My aversion to fashion and the culinary arts was a bad look indeed. Women should cook, clean and wait on men, and in exchange men should open doors, help them out of cars and buy them flowers. It was all so very patriarchal and carried a hint of prudishness too. Sex had been a taboo subject in this ultra-conservative society, something married couples did to procreate but didn't otherwise mention. Homosexuality and prostitution officially did not exist, and pornography was banned.

Sergei took me to catch up with Tim, another of the SSESS students I'd met in Bukhara, and his photographer friend, Andrei Bogdanov, who had also been on the Central Asian tour to document the foreign students' activities. Intense and quiet, Andrei had rarely spoken, but snapped prolifically, roll after roll, to develop back in Kazan. We found Tim and Andrei in the Kazan State University darkroom, where Andrei was pegging out fresh dripping black-and-white prints of a leggy brunette in skimpy lingerie, reclining across a railway track running through a forest.

Sergei was transfixed and I had to stifle a smile. This was the second oldest university in Russia and considered one of the most prestigious. Leo Tolstoy had studied here, and the Grandfather of the Soviet people, Vladimir Ulyanov (later to change his name to Vladimir Lenin), had spent three months here before being expelled. Sergei was a student at the Faculty or Law, and Andrei was on his way to becoming a chemist. Yet they were using university facilities to produce what were for the USSR, highly radical images. Andrei fished around in a box and handed a dog-eared copy of *Vogue* to Sergei. A friend had smuggled the illicit magazine from Italy for him and it was obviously one of his prized possessions. Andrei had been studying the photos carefully and judging by the display folders Tim was flicking through, he had no shortage of volunteer models to practise his technique on.

Assuming I wouldn't be so enthusiastic about half-naked women, Andrei opened a manila folder of pictures for me to peruse: his record of the foreign students' trip to Uzbekistan. Tim and I featured heavily: purchasing watermelons, climbing weatherworn mud steps in a crumbling mosque in Shakrisabz. Andrei then handed me a book filled with pictures of fur-clad Eskimo-type peoples, taken by his father, a professional photographer, who'd spent fifteen years documenting the lives of indigenous peoples of far north Siberia, between his work snapping visiting communist dignitaries for *Zapolyarnaya Pravda* (*The 'Beyond the Pole' Truth*). Andrei's dad was still there, living in Norilsk, a former Gulag camp and now the coldest town on the planet — 200 kilometres north of the Arctic Circle.

Just as I was drawn to these snapshots of a remote and exotic unknown society, Andrei had a fascination with the hitherto forbidden fruits of Western culture. He told me how people brought VCRs from overseas and ran mini cinemas in bars, cafés, student houses or even private flats. For three roubles a head, up to twenty people would cram around the TV to watch smuggled movies featuring Bruce Lee, Sly Stallone and Jean-Claude Van Damme. When Andrei returned from army service in 1988, he'd seen *9½ Weeks* in a student hostel. Apparently it had been a smash hit in these illegal *videosalons*, which explained why so often when I said my name was Kim, people would nod knowingly and reply, 'Ah, da, Kim Basinger …'

VCRs were in such demand that Andrei recalled seeing an ad in a local paper in the mid-80s offering to exchange a one-bedroom flat for a second-hand player. The police of course knew who owned these evil machines. They also knew that at 8 pm the *videosalon* showed *Fantastika* — sci-fi and action — and at 10 pm the porno came out. So instead of just barging in to raid the place, the cunning cops would turn off the electricity to the premises, thus jamming the offending tape in the machine. If pornography was discovered, the owner of the VCR would be sent to prison.

Suspecting that a night of grainy thirtieth-generation dubbed American porn might not be my thing, Andrei and Tim took me to meet one of their friends. Zulfia Kadeyeva was a striking, voluptuous and bubbly Tatar — more Turk than Mongol — with large brown eyes, thick wavy dark hair and infectious smile. Her English was impeccable, thanks to a privileged education at a specialised school where from the very first year all subjects were taken in English. Remarkably, none of her teachers had ever left Russia, and very few had ever met native English speakers.

Zulfia's parents, Nai'ilya and Kayum, and her brother, Zofar, lived a few blocks from the university, on Karl Marx Street, which ran downhill from the Opera House. It was a fantastic central location, made possible due to Kayum's former post as head of the Department of Safety in Industry. The flat was filled with books and paintings, and patterned carpets in deep red hues hung on the walls behind the couches, giving the place a cosy, homely feel. Zulfia batted her eyelashes to the lads and her mother brought a giant steaming apple pie and a jug of thick, creamy and very cowish-smelling milk from a local village to the table. She was specialising in the study of vacuums at the Space Mechanics Faculty of the State Technical University, with plans for a future in cosmic research. With a wink she added to me, 'And don't you think that cosmonauts look very smart in their suits?'

What Zulfia didn't mention until I had known her for several years was that she was married at the time. When we met she was exactly one year younger than me — twenty. Her husband was eight years older, the son of one of her university lecturers. The lecturer had approached Zulfia one day and suggested she might like to marry her son. Zulfia had never even seen him, let alone met him, but agreed to an introduction. Despite her mother's advice to the contrary, she consented to the marriage. 'I'd already got my dress and ring and invited guests,' she told me sheepishly many years later. 'How could I back out?' When I asked what he'd looked like, she answered obscurely, 'I had a fever. I can't remember.'

I was dumbfounded. 'You mean for your entire marriage?'

'My memory is very strange,' she replied. 'I've completely blocked out everything about those two years, except that we were completely unsuited to each other. All I remember is that he expected me to do everything for him, and I didn't want to be doing that at the age of twenty.'

'So your mother was right?'

'Yes, of course she was. Mothers are always right.'

Zulfia and I arranged to meet again. She was a proud fountain of knowledge of the complex history of her Turkic–Mongol hybrid nation — the world's northernmost Muslims — and never tired of talking of her Tatar heritage.

The region — between the Volga River and the Ural Mountains — had been settled around 550CE by a Turkic tribe originating north of the Black Sea. Known as Volga-Bulgars, they were a trading and industrial people, who minted silver coins with Arabic inscriptions, smelted iron, worked gold, silver and leather. In 922, Volga-Bulgaria adopted Islam and began to erect mosques, schools, palaces, caravanserais and civic buildings. Kazan was transformed from a small frontier Bulgar town into a powerful citadel of the Khans. In 1236, Genghis Khan's grandson Batu swept across from the East, subjugating the Bulgars, along with other Turkic speaking tribes on the way. After attacking Moscow and Kiev, he continued on to Poland and Hungary. There he heard that his uncle, the Great Khan Ogodei, had died. He retreated with his warriors to the home of the Volga–Bulgars and set up an empire known as the Golden Horde. The Chinese had given the name 'Tatar' to the Mongol warriors. As the Mongols were absorbed into Kazan's population, the Volga–Bulgars became known as Tatars, and the entire region as Tataria. From the mid fourteenth century, the Golden Horde began to collapse. By the mid fifteenth century, several new states were formed, including the Khanate of Kazan, which inherited a mix of linguistic, religious and cultural traditions from both the Bulgars and the Golden Horde.

In 1552, Ivan the Terrible seized Kazan and annexed it to the Russian state. Russians flooded in and began a violent program of

Christianisation, ousting the Muslim Tatars to the suburbs. Zulfia and I wandered around the white stone walled Kremlin fortress on the Kazanka riverbank, built on the orders of Ivan the Terrible over the ruins of the castle of the Khans. There was a Russian Orthodox Church and bell tower, but no sign of the nation's Muslim heritage. In 1593, Tsar Theodore had ordered all mosques on the territory of Kazan to be destroyed. It would be nearly two hundred years before the Empress Yekaterina II (Catherine the Great) abolished the prohibition on mosque building, and more than another three hundred before a decree would be given to rebuild the mosque in the Kazan Kremlin.

The Bolshevik revolution led to the creation of the Tatar Autonomous Soviet Socialist Republic. As with everywhere in the USSR, ethnic Russians held the majority of important posts, and although Russians made up just under half the population, Russian was the official language. By the late 1980s, the Tatars began to take advantage of the loosening Soviet grip on their territory and culture. On 30 August 1990, the Supreme Council had declared Tatarstan a sovereign state. Tatar law took priority over that of the USSR, and property of the USSR was declared property of the republic. But this recent pronouncement of independence meant little to Zulfia.

'Practically nothing has changed. How can we be really independent if we are in the middle of Russia, surrounded by Russia on all sides? The only difference is that before Russia took one hundred per cent of the taxes, and now Tatarstan gets some.' But she was quickly being caught up in the excitement of change and opportunity and had ideas of becoming a government deputy.

Kazan — a Tatar word meaning 'cauldron' — was fifteen years off the one thousandth anniversary of its founding. The old centre of the city exuded a rustic charm: narrow winding streets lined with two- and three-hundred-year-old wooden houses, standing crooked in the deep snow with elaborately carved and painted window and door frames.

'In most of our cities these wooden houses have been destroyed to make way for new flats,' Zulfia explained as she led me up and down the steep hills around the university. 'Kazan is very special because it has preserved some of its history.'

In addition to her studies and political ambitions, Zulfia taught English to first-year students at a recently established Tatar–American college. She persuaded me to come and talk about Australia, assuring me that her class would be attentive and well behaved. It was like talking to a wall. They sat stonily still and I worried that they didn't understand me at all. But when Zulfia took over they were the same. They asked no questions, and answered hers as if by rote. I asked Zulfia after the class if they were always so quiet and unopinionated. 'This is our style of teaching,' she explained. 'This is how it's always been.'

As we packed up, a young girl approached us shyly. Ziyoda had been a student at the same special English school Zulfia had once attended, and had recently returned from a trip to London with her parents. Nodding in my direction, she told us she'd seen punks, hippies and people even 'weirder looking' than me. I asked her why they were all so fearful of talking.

'We are afraid that maybe we will have the wrong answer, or our grammar will be mistake. It is shame for us,' Ziyoda replied.

Zulfia went on. 'You have to understand that in Soviet Union, people have been brought up not to have their own opinion. So students listen to teachers and learn the correct answers and correct opinions.'

It was bitterly cold in Kazan, a daily average of minus twenty degrees or 'twenty degrees of frost' as the Russians called it. Each time I left the flat, Tatiana nagged me to dress more warmly, reprimanding me for walking several kilometres into town to see Zulfia. The nostril-burning, lip-splitting icy winds made the webs of skin at the base of my fingers crack and bleed when I stretched my hands. Tatiana — who seemed a little tetchy at the amount of time I was spending with Zulfia — wanted to buy herself a new jumper. The state shops were empty so she took me to the local bazaar, an icy yard near the main train station packed with trestle tables piled with poor quality Chinese and Turkish clothing and footwear. Women in fluffy woollen scarves, wrapped cabbage-like in layers of thick clothing, stomped their feet on the compacted snow to keep warm.

These *spekulyanti* (speculators) took advantage of connections and subsidised prices to buy up quantities of dirt-cheap goods from the state shops and factories, schlepping them by train to markets in other Eastern bloc countries. With the proceeds they bought either hard currency, or goods unavailable in the Soviet Union and brought them back to sell. Tatiana examined their wares and considered a ruffled purple knitted sweater. She heard the price and we left empty-handed.

It was a tough way to make a living, but many were doing well for themselves, sporting material possessions unheard of by their less enterprising comrades. On one hand Tatiana felt sorry for the *spekulyanti* at having to stand out in the cold all day. But she was also rather scathing, seeming to consider trading and bargaining for profit like these 'new capitalists' to be an undignified way to earn one's living. I got the impression she thought there was something 'uncultured' about wheeling and dealing, doing something purely for money with no greater good for society.

Tatiana, like other intelligentsia, often described people and behaviour she disapproved of as 'uncultured' or 'uneducated'. It was the worst kind of insult. Fortunately for Sergei, his academic achievements surpassed even his mother's expectations. On graduation from high school he'd been able to choose from the two most prestigious university degrees: medicine or law. The decision was a no-brainer. He 'didn't want to have to deal with dead people; doctors get miserly salaries and law is only five years while medicine is seven'.

Sergei's higher education came with a bonus — exemption from military service. In the USSR, all eighteen-year-old males who were not enrolled at university or deemed medically unfit, were obliged to serve in the Soviet Army for a minimum of two years, and the world's biggest army had a reputation as a tough place for a young recruit. It was never acknowledged publicly, but many divisions practised 'hazing' — beatings, humiliation, even torture. Sergei had no intention of being part of the action, and believed that in a post–Cold War world, a four-million-strong army was unnecessary. His older brother, Igor, hadn't been so fortunate.

Their father, Anatoly, had secured a place for Igor at the university's Faculty of Biology, with the primary purpose of keeping him out of the army. Igor only lasted a few months before dropping out. Immediately he was called up and sent to a town just south of Moscow to serve in the division responsible for Moscow's air defence. Luckily for Igor, his superiors did not look kindly upon the abuse of their low-ranking soldiers. Tatiana visited him every month, taking bags of food and money. But he was embarrassed at having things others didn't and asked her not to come. After two years, Igor returned from service, kilos lighter and desperate for ice cream, but otherwise unscarred. Tatiana and Anatoly enrolled him in the Veterinarian Institute, and again he gave up. Now twenty-one, Igor was married with a baby daughter. They lived with his wife's parents and he'd found work installing security systems in private flats and offices around Kazan. He had plenty of business, but whenever he came to visit his parents he seemed tense and unhappy, as though the strain of family responsibility was more than he could bear.

After a fortnight in Kazan, my second Soviet visa extension was coming to an end, and without an officially acceptable reason to stay on, I had to leave the USSR. Zulfia, Zofar, Andrei, Tatiana and Sergei all came to see me off from Kazan Station. Sergei presented me with his Red Youth Membership card, teary-eyed Tatiana packed a bag of potato-filled pasties, and Andrei brought a folder of copies of his Uzbek photos. Zulfia hugged me warmly, gave me a card, and begged me to return. They all waved and ran alongside the train as it pulled away from the platform. I was touched.

On my way through Moscow I dropped in to see Yulia, still unhappy and seeking a way out. I also called Ludmilla who passed on her sad news that Sveta had left for Sri Lanka with her new beau.

Back in Leningrad, Olga was scouring the shops for mayonnaise, the principal ingredient of most Russian salads. New Year was fast approaching and it was vital to have 'as rich a table as possible' on that night, as it was a certain indicator of the year to come. The presence of a bowl of tinned peas, cubed ham and cheese swimming in mayonnaise would doubtless improve one's chances of future prosperity. Her parents were away on tour and she was lucky to have some extra ration cards to help out her friends, but food shortages were worse than ever. Her empty fridge did not augur well.

I arranged to meet up with two Polish viola players — Anna and Piotr — who had played in the Australian Youth Orchestra in Melbourne that same season that Olga's father had been our conductor. Planning to return soon, I left most of my things at Olga's. She accompanied me in my prison coat to the Varshavsky (Warsaw) Station and waved me off to Poland, along with hundreds of shuttle traders and their boxes of tacky goods. The train clattered through the night, and I peered out the window, watching the powdery snow shimmering in the beams from the station lamps. Russian words jumbled through my head. I thought of the kindness so many people had shown me, a complete stranger from the other side of the world, and realised that I'd been infected with a terrible case of Russophilia.

Then we arrived at the Soviet–Polish border. Like everything else in the USSR, even leaving it was an ordeal. Customs officials and border police searched every wagon from roof to wheel, emptying bags and poring over and documents. Mechanics dismantled the entire train, carriage by carriage, lifting each in turn so the wheels could be adjusted from Soviet gauge to Polish. When the train arrived in Warsaw, it was like stepping out of a black-and-white movie into a world of colour. Blinking like a newborn I gazed dopily at bright poster-sized advertisements, kiosks stocked with magazines and sweets, and a fruit stand with boxes of gleaming ripe Ecuadorian bananas. The closest I'd come to a banana in the last five months was a squished and blackened skin lying on a path under the soaring monument to celebrate the USSR's conquest of space at the Moscow Exhibition Centre. The Soviet Union had won the space race and built an improbably impossible memorial to that achievement. But it could barely manage to get food from its own fields into its shops, let alone food from anywhere else. It had been a year and a half since Poland had ousted its communist leaders and the country seemed much healthier for it.

Anna and her parents, Henryk and Jadwiga, welcomed me enthusiastically and wondered what on earth had possessed me to spend almost five whole months with their awful Eastern ex-rulers.

But Jadwiga didn't want to talk politics. Tonight was a big night on Polish TV. *Dynasty* was on, and the entire nation stopped to watch. Jadwiga was an addict. She commanded us all to be silent for the duration, sighing and gasping with the changing fortunes of the characters, riveted by the extreme glamour and obscene wealth. 'This is real life in America, yes?' she asked me when it was over.

It wasn't hard to see why someone who'd spent their life in a miniature flat with leaky plumbing and dodgy electrics on the twelfth floor of a concrete tower overlooking a ten-lane road would be transfixed by these images of excess. Mundanity had been forced upon them and they were desperate to dream of more. Across the Eastern bloc a giant pendulum was swinging away from the strict order of communist central planning and political control. The desire for fantastic wealth and luxury was surging through the frustrated populations, who watched *Dynasty* as if it were a documentary on the benefits of capitalism. The Poles were already mesmerised, and the Soviets were about to be.

August 1990 – Picking giant fungi on our 'tourist expedition' in the Khibeni tundra. Back, left to right: Anton, Andrei, Olga (with mushroom). Front: Natasha.

November 1990 – Bukhara, Uzbek Soviet Socialist Republic. Marina the seamstress (second from right) and her family at the last annual October Revolution Day parade (celebrated in November!).

December 1991 – Olga shopping for shoes in a typically empty Soviet department store in newly renamed St Petersburg, just days before the USSR collapsed.

December 1991 – Nadia (left) and Tina (right) in Nadia's flat in Chertanovo, a 'sleeping district' in southern Moscow.

December 1991 – Outside Vildan the beekeeper's house in the village of Saya, Tatarstan. Left to right: Rustam (Vildan's Uzbek brother-in-law), Vildan with son Ruslan, a neighbour, Vildan's wife, Nai'ilya, Rustam's friend Rashid, and Tatiana.

December 1991 – Tatiana in front of a memorial to locals lost in the Great Patriotic War, in a village near the Tartarstan capital, Kazan.

New Year's Eve, 1991,
in Kazan, Tatarstan.
Back: two of Zulfia's
girlfriends and Marat.
Front: Zulfia, me, Zofar.

31 December 1991 –
Sergei and his friend
Katya in her flat in
central Kazan. Katya
is about to dress me
up for a big night out
at the Lenin Library
New Year disco.

January 1992 – Gulshat and her daughter, Gurnaz, in the kitchen of their house near Urgench, in the northwest of newly independent Uzbekistan.

January 1992 – Solomon, the Ghanaian student who was studying medicine in Tashkent. We were on a trip to the Kumushkan mountains, just outside the Uzbek capital.

September 1995 – Photographer Andrei Bogdanov on the island of Sviyazhsk in the Volga River near Kazan. During the Soviet era, some of the fifteen churches and monasteries on the island were used as psychiatric hospitals for political dissidents.

September 1995 –Yuri (left) and Oleg at Irkutsk train station, Siberia. Muscovites still in their teens, they had been sent by a Moscow bank to sell credit cards to Siberians.

October 1995 – With Zulfia (right) at Kazan Opera House.

November 1995 – Olga and me in the foyer of a newly opened Indian restaurant near the Admiralty in St Petersburg. Olga's father spent his early days in a nearby *kommunalka* (communal flat). (Photo: Mikhail Kulikov)

November 1998 – Trying to get warm in an icy hotel room in Ivangorod (on the Russian side of the Russian-Estonian border). The hotel had no water or heating and the receptionist suggested we stay elsewhere. (Photo: Eric Campbell)

November 1998 – The train platform at the town of Gus Krustalni on the Moscow-Kazan-Siberia/Central Asia line. The town's main industry is a crystal factory and unpaid workers ply their wares to passengers passing through.

February 2000 – Human rights activists Magomad Magomadov (left) and Viktor Popkov (right) at Magomad's family home in Sleptsovsk, Ingushetia. Viktor was fatally shot in April 2001 while delivering medical supplies to Chechen civilians. (Photo: Bentley Dean)

PART TWO

The Collapse and Chaotic Reign of Tsar Boris

10

The Wind of Change

I follow the Moskva
Down to Gorky Park
Listening to the wind of change
An August summer night
Soldiers passing by
Listening to the wind of change
From *Crazy World*, the 1990 album by German rock band, Scorpions

Since the fall of the Berlin Wall in November 1989, the Scorpions rock ballad 'Winds of Change' had become a smash hit all over Europe: the anthem to glasnost and perestroika, the soundtrack to the parting of the Iron Curtain. After the band recorded a Russian version of the song, 'Veter Peremen', even Gorby professed his admiration, summoning the hirsute, leather-clad Germans to tea at the Kremlin. By the time I made it back to the USSR in November 1991, lead singer Klaus Meine's rousing crooning was blaring from ghetto blasters everywhere.

The 'Wind of Change' had been blowing a gale in the ten months since I'd left Olga's place. The Soviet Union hadn't just changed — it was only weeks from disappearing altogether. Gorbachev had been overthrown as Communist Party leader, the Communist Party itself had been banned, the three Baltic republics had declared full independence and the other republics had made significant moves towards sovereignty. And I'd missed all the fun.

Back in January 1991, while I'd been practising Bartok at the Liszt Music Academy in Budapest and watching the Gulf War on BBC World, Gorbachev had ordered Soviet troops into Lithuania. Russian soldiers, led by the KGB's crack Spetsnaz group, Alfa, had stormed the TV tower in Vilnius, killing fourteen civilians and injuring hundreds. By February, the mind-bogglingly titled Chairman of the Presidium of the Supreme Soviet of the Russian Soviet Federative Socialist Republic, Boris Yeltsin, was accusing Gorbachev of dictatorship. In April, while I'd hitchhiked through Italy, the Caucasian republic of Georgia voted for independence. And in June, as I'd backpacked around Scandinavia, sleeping on park benches and in train stations, the Russian Republic held its first-ever democratic presidential elections. Boris Yeltsin won.

By August, many of the union republics had become festering hotbeds of anti-Soviet sentiment. In a desperate attempt to appease the restive regions, Gorbachev proposed a compromise deal — the New Union Treaty — in which the USSR would be converted into a federation of independent republics, with a common foreign and military policy, and a common president ... himself. This treaty was due to be signed on 20 August 1991. But communist hardliners — including the head of the KGB — feared this arrangement would encourage the republics to press for complete independence. On 19 August the hardliners staged a coup, taking over state TV and radio to denounce Gorbachev and his regime, and putting Gorbachev himself under house arrest in Crimea. As I hitched around Spain I saw dramatic images of Boris Yeltsin waving his fist on a tank in front of the White House. Two days later the coup collapsed. Gorbachev returned from Crimea to condemn its instigators. Seven were arrested, one committed suicide.

But things were still looking bleak for Gorbachev. Three days later, on 24 August, while I was talking my way barefoot through British Immigration at Dover, Yeltsin banned the Communist Party and forced Gorbachev to resign as its General Secretary. And as I busked in the London Underground to save money for a ticket back to see Olga, Boris took control of all the key Soviet ministries to become the most powerful man in Russia. And when a tour bus of a rock band I'd never heard of called Dire Straits offered me a lift from the M25 to Paris, the USSR finally recognised the independence of Estonia, Latvia and Lithuania. By the time I made it back to a snow-bound Vasilievsky Island in November, Gorbachev was a marked man. Without the Communist Party, and with three republics already gone, Lenin's empire and Great October Socialist Revolution looked about to be consigned to the dustbin of history.

And if this wasn't change enough, Olga even had a new address. She still lived on Opochinina Street, but in a referendum in June, the people of Leningrad voted to change the name of their city back to St Petersburg. I assumed this was in order to honour the city's giant-sized founder — who in Soviet Russia had been Peter I, but was now Peter the Great again — over the short and bald Vladimir Ilyich Lenin. Olga preferred a different theory. She'd heard that Peter the Great hadn't named the city after himself, but rather after St Peter. 'The first building he began in the city was the St Peter and Paul Cathedral and Fortress. So I think that because of this, the saints are looking after our city and the city is blessed.'

St Petersburg didn't seem particularly blessed at this moment. Thanks to continuing economic liberalisation, inflation was spiralling. This phenomenon, unheard of in the Soviet Union, had sent the price of most products up by around 160 per cent in the last year, resulting in longer queues and barer shelves than ever. It was still only possible to purchase many products with government issued *talony*, or ration cards. Olga's parents were touring again so she was able to pass their rations on to needy acquaintances. Possession of these precious scraps of cardboard did not, however, exempt one from the joy of five hours in a queue for a bag of milk.

Soviet communism had disintegrated faster and more completely than anyone could have imagined. But I still continued to delude myself that in principle it was a fine ideology. A chronic shortage of consumer goods wasn't a hardship, it was evidence of what a wonderfully anti-capitalist, anti-materialistic society the USSR really was. After ten months of study and wandering in Europe, I wrote to my mother of my disgust at its rampant materialism. 'All those shopping malls filled with useless stuff that no one needs. All that waste and rubbish. All that sickening commercialism.' As Olga and I peeled and chopped rotting vegetables in her St Petersburg kitchen, trying vainly to find an edible cubic centimetre for a soup, I still didn't blame the Soviet central planners for the fact that produce was decayed before it reached our shopping bags, or that I couldn't even buy a stamp to send my letter home.

Olga had never been able to comprehend my distaste for Western excesses. Her imported tea and shampoo collection had grown through regular contributions from her travelling parents. While still as patriotic a Soviet citizen as ever, she savoured the luxury of English infusions and French cosmetics. But change had come to the motherland and Olga already had a small part in it. The shops might have been empty, but the economy was freeing up.

In December 1990, the Swedish furniture giant IKEA had opened a small office in Leningrad/St Petersburg, one of the first Western companies to venture into business in the city. IKEA had been buying Russian timber since 1975. Now it not only had Siberia's forests in its sights, but several of the USSR's woodworking factories as well. Olga had heard through friends that the company was looking for an English-speaking secretary. Months of one-on-one English practice with me had given her the confidence to apply. She'd got the job and was very happy.

'Our office is so beautiful,' she gushed proudly. 'The Swedes are so nice to us, like a family. It's not like a Soviet office where the managers are dictatorial and always trying to show the workers their places. The Swedes like to discuss things and it's even possible to talk to a manager at IKEA. When they come from Sweden they bring chocolates, perfumes and other presents, things that are difficult to buy here.'

Olga invited me to visit her at work. Compared to the dank and dingy ambience of a typical Russian workplace, with dark patterned wallpapers, broken wooden chairs and shelves stacked with dusty tomes, IKEA's new St Petersburg headquarters were indeed a small square of bright and blonde Scandinavian order, hidden in the basement of a Stalin-era edifice. The Swedes had even hired a lady to shop and cook lunch for the staff.

'They really take care of us,' Olga enthused, still in disbelief at her good fortune. 'They don't want us to waste time standing in queues for bread, so they have even bought a bread-making machine. And look at this,' she pointed to some containers, 'teas, wines, special biscuits!'

There was a certain irony in Olga's happiness at her treatment by the kindly Swedes. The Bolshevik revolution had been supposed to bring about a worker's paradise, a communist utopia in which class divisions were broken down and everyone was equal. The 'evil capitalist exploiter classes', according to Lenin, were only fit to be shot or sent to the Gulag. But even patriotic Olga was happy to admit that her 'capitalist, exploiter' Swedish employers were far more egalitarian and respectful of their workers than her communist compatriots. The revolution might have done away with one set of dictatorial bosses, but it had soon replaced them with another.

I settled into life at Opochinina Street with Olga and Vera and absorbed myself in the complexities of Russian grammar and catching up with friends. Vera Nikolayevna's dementia was worsening. Night and day she wandered around the flat mumbling to herself. Whenever Olga returned from shopping Vera would demand to know the cost of each item, sinking into her chair and shaking her head in horror. She forgot everything moments after being told, and caring for her was taking its toll on Olga. But Vera became a great teacher for me. We sat together at the kitchen table and I read texts aloud from my tutor book. She was a mercilessly blunt critic of my pronunciation, declaring haughtily, 'I don't know what you're talking about!' whenever I got stresses in the wrong place or muddled my cases. She often became involved in the stories, frequently thinking I was talking about myself and stopping to ask about the village where she thought I worked as a doctor.

Masha from the tundra trip had separated from her husband, Andrei. She invited me to a slide show evening with the university alpinist's club: a series of spectacular images of scruffy triumphant youth, Masha amongst them, posing against a backdrop of soaring peaks in the Caucasus, Central Asia's Tien Shan, Siberia and the Urals.

Masha had already started saving her food ration cards to purchase provisions for her next escape from the humdrum of grey and queues, this time a winter skiing expedition to Khibeni.

Natasha from the Ukraine trip was now in her fourth year at the Philology faculty and wanted to practise teaching Russian to someone. I volunteered to be her guinea pig. The economic turmoil had wreaked havoc on her family's comfortable existence. Her ex-General democrat grandfather, who had initially been supportive of Gorbachev's reforms, had recently passed away at the age of seventy-two. His bank savings, once enough to purchase two cars and a flat (had they been available), had been completely wiped out by the triple digit inflation of the last year.

'There was just enough left for his funeral,' Natasha sighed wryly. 'He was happy that history was changing, but he didn't understand that all the money he'd earned and saved during his life was eaten by inflation. He died with nothing but disappointment.'

For the first time in Natasha's life, her family had money troubles. Irina's prestigious position as a military academy lecturer earned her what only a year ago had been the exceptionally large sum of 300 roubles per month. Since then, the cost of goods had increased 160 per cent while her pay hadn't gone up a kopeck. Right across the intelligentsia class — those who worked in the once respected and valued spheres of science, arts and education — people were doing it tough on desperately inadequate state salaries. For most there was no alternative. Natasha and Irina not only had no idea how to do *biznes,* they considered it a shameful and lowly way to make a buck. They watched on disapprovingly as bullish entrepreneurs, black marketeers and shuttle traders began to make fortunes, buying and selling everything from hard currency to videos, clothing, sausage and cars.

Despite its meagre financial rewards, Natasha was determined to pursue her calling to academia. She picked up a few roubles here and there teaching Russian and translating, but refused flatly to let me pay her. One day she arrived late to our meeting, flustered and annoyed.

'I've just been waiting in a queue for four hours to buy sausage. Four hours and it is twenty degrees of frost outside! The man I stood next to was eighty years old. Can you imagine that? In the end we had to write our names on a list and they told us to come back tomorrow to collect it. I am so ashamed of this country.'

The next time I saw her she was fuming again.

'You remember that sausage I told you about? When I finally picked it up, it was inedible.'

At the History of the Revolution museum, curators had been furiously updating their displays to keep pace with the latest twists in the saga of Soviet politics. Former Bolshevik and Communist Party idols had already been stripped of their hero status. An exhibition from the August coup attempt in Moscow honoured Boris Yeltsin, in an obvious snub to the commies. There was a sense that the final nail was being tapped into the Soviet coffin.

In a Ukrainian referendum on 1 December 1991, 90 per cent of voters opted for independence. A week later, Boris Yeltsin, President of the Russian Republic, met secretly with the leaders of the Ukrainian and Byelorussian republics in the Byelorussian village of Belovezha. Together they decided to dissolve the Soviet Union and replace it with a new union, to be called the Sodruzhestvo Nezavisimykh Gosudarstv. I couldn't even pronounce it, let alone translate it, and it would be some days before I learned I was now living in the Commonwealth of Independent States. The CIS was intended to be a free association of sovereign states with coordinated trade, finance, lawmaking and security. A furious Gorbachev declared the move unconstitutional but he was powerless to stop it.

On 12 December, the Russian Republic officially seceded from the Soviet Union, and denounced the 1922 Treaty of the USSR's creation. On 21 December, representatives of all the Soviet Republics but Georgia signed a protocol confirming the Soviet Union's extinction. On that same date, the five Central Asian states joined Armenia, Azerbaijan and Russia to sign up as members of the Commonwealth of Independent States. The Baltics wanted nothing to do with it.

His empire gone, Gorbachev had no choice but to resign as President. On 25 December, his powers were transferred to Yeltsin. That night, the red hammer and sickle flag was lowered over the

Kremlin for the last time. From now on the tricolour white, blue and red banner of the Russian state would fly in its place. The former Russian Republic was renamed the Russian Federation, and the Cold War was officially over.

The collapse of the empire they'd grown up with left Olga and Vera Nikolayevna in shock, almost bereaved. It was as though someone old and familiar had died. The death was not entirely unexpected, but the events of that December came as a surprise and left a gaping hole in the lives of many of those remaining. Olga seemed quietly stunned. Being a citizen of such a vast empire, of a superpower, had been somehow reassuring.

'It felt stronger,' she would tell me later. 'People don't feel so secure now that it's gone. This perestroika of Gorbachev's, it seemed natural and necessary, but we didn't think it would lead to the end of the Soviet Union.'

She could understand the loss of the hostile Baltic States, after all 'they'd never wanted to be a part of the Soviet Union anyway', but was astounded that Ukraine, Byelorussia and the other republics wanted independence.

'I think it is a mistake. We are such close nations, our language and people are so similar and now we need a visa to go there. And Central Asia too, although they are very different from us, they felt like a natural part of the Soviet Union. We were bringing them civilization and development. Before people were starving there, and it was only men who were important and they made the women stay at home.'

Olga was also concerned for the future of millions of ethnic Russians living in these newly 'foreign' countries. What would happen to them if local ethnic groups became resentful of their presence? Where could they go? Many had been there for generations and had no connections left in the Russian Federation.

The shock waves of the collapse hit the older generation the hardest. 'For their whole lives,' said Olga, 'they were taught that communism is the perfect ideal that we should be striving for. Now we are told that it was all wrong, and old people in particular feel cheated. Many devoted their whole lives to this cause, and now they find out it was for nothing. Of course they are lost and don't know what to believe in.' For the true believers in communism, the damnation of their demi-God Lenin was as distressing as Christians being told that Jesus was a mass murderer.

Olga had already found a way to fill the void left by the collapse of the communist regime. I noticed she had placed a number of small, glittering Orthodox icons by her bed: miniature, mass-printed copies of ancient originals, gold embossed bearded saints glued to rectangles of wood. Before going to sleep she would kneel before them, pray and cross herself repeatedly. Earlier that year, her brother, Igor, had taken her to a church near his house to be baptised. Now she was learning the 'very strict' rules of the Russian Orthodox Church. She flicked through a thick, well-thumbed paperback, running her finger down pages of instructions. 'There are so many times of the year when you have to fast, for example, which for us means that you can't eat meat and many other things. It's very hard to remember it all.'

Faith came easily to Olga. Deep down she suspected it had always been there, perhaps even in her DNA. But it wasn't only the Russian Orthodox Church that was attracting followers en masse. Representatives of numerous other faiths — Hare Krishnas, Mormons, Jehovah's Witnesses and Baptists among them — were flocking in like vultures to establish centres of worship and collect converts from amongst the hordes of spiritually bereft orphans of the Soviet motherland. Irina, a wild-eyed high-school friend of Olga's, told us excitedly about a newly established American-led evangelical church she'd been to on Vasilievsky Island. They sang boppy songs, clapped their hands a lot and Irina thought she'd like to become a born-again Christian. She had been to an Orthodox service with Olga, but found the experience less than satisfying.

'They wouldn't let her take communion as she'd eaten berries before the service, so I think she was offended,' said Olga. 'The priests are very critical and if you don't follow the rules exactly then they will tell you so in a not polite manner. So she went to the Americans. They aren't so particular and will just take anyone.'

Olga had been along to the American church with Irina to see what it was all about. She hadn't been impressed. 'It was so easy, in a big hall with lots of singing and jumping around and no special rules.' Olga believed that Russians should revive their own traditions rather than adopting some frothy Western fad. She was also suspicious of the Americans' motives in bringing their church halfway around the world. 'Probably,' she mused, 'there is some financial interest involved.' Even so, she was renting out a small flat that her parents owned near Primorskaya Metro station to an American couple, Roger and Margaret, who had come to St Petersburg to 'do the good work of the Lord'.

Roger and Margaret may or may not have tucked aside a few extra dollars from their Iowan collection bowls for themselves, but it was chicken feed in comparison to the loot President Yeltsin's cronies would rip off from their former comrades. Within days of the dissolution of the Soviet Union, President Boris Yeltsin set about dismantling the old administrative command system to create his new 'capitalist' Russia. It was a daunting task. The USSR's moribund and bureaucrat-heavy economy was a massive interconnected structure, which had taken decades to put in place. The system obviously wasn't working, but unravelling it wasn't going to be easy.

Firstly, the nation's obsession with the Cold War meant that a quarter of the economy was devoted to the defence sector. One in five of the working population, and in some areas up to half the workforce, were preoccupied with keeping the US out of the USSR. Now the Cold War was over it was clear serious spending cuts to Russia's bloated military-industrial complex were needed. Secondly, central planners had decided long ago that the establishment of 'single industry towns' made good sense. Around half the cities and towns in the former USSR worked on this model, whereby almost the entire working population of a city would be employed at the same factory. Factories were responsible for providing complete livelihoods to their workers, including housing, healthcare, education and childcare. Yet another looming problem was that while the population was exceptionally well educated in certain areas, business skills were not among them. Factory directors had become experts in fudging figures to comply with state-issued production quotas, but few had any idea how to run a business profitably and efficiently.

Following the advice of his 35-year-old deputy prime minister — a pudgy economist called Yegor Gaidar — Yeltsin had embarked on a radical program of 'shock therapy' two months before the USSR's collapse. Shock therapy had dispensed with the old system in one fell swoop. Government subsidies to farms and factories were cut and price controls were lifted. Foreign imports were permitted and restrictions on private trade and manufacture were removed. For workers locked into the state system, it was shocking indeed. Millions of livelihoods were at stake as entire industries ground to a halt, unable to pay their workers when state subsidies stopped.

For those 'outside' the official economy however, the new freedoms were a green light to make mega-bucks. Lenin's vision of a society in which the privileged classes would be abolished and the workers, peasants and soldiers would 'claim ownership of the means of production' had never materialised. Instead, those with power had found ways to abuse it, and corruption within the party had become endemic, continuing under Stalin, increasing under Khrushchev and escalating still further during Leonid Brezhnev's 28-year reign.

'When the final phase of socialism, namely communism, is built, will there still be thefts and pilfering?'
'No, because everything will be already pilfered during socialism.'

By the 1960s the party had grown into a massive self-serving bureaucracy, a vast hierarchy of ministries employing hundreds of thousands of officials with vague job descriptions, plenty of perks and numerous opportunities for graft. Caring and sharing as it purported to be, Marxist-Leninist economic theory just didn't work. Instead of creating a worker's paradise, the Communist Party had become a giant Mafia, little more than a vehicle for the personal gain of its members. The revolution was a sham, an outright hypocrisy. While the party continued to preach the virtues of Lenin's grand utopian dream of equality for all, in practice they lived the high life, with their own special stores, chauffeur-driven cars, flash country houses and lavish overseas trips. Just as it had been before the revolution, society was split into those with privileges and those without. And of course those with privileges — the Communist Party officials, *nomenklatura* and *apparatchiks* — had no intention of losing them.

> *A man parks his car in Red Square. A policeman rushes up to him,*
> *shouting, 'Are you crazy? This is where the government is!'*
> *'No problem,' answers the man, 'I've got good locks on my car.'*

Many ordinary people, the intelligentsia in particular, saw through the double standards, yet were powerless to do anything about it. The state's institutions were too potent, the elite too keen to hang onto power. Dissidents were dealt with harshly, and everyone knew it. Even so, many of the population did continue to believe in the fairytale of the socialist propaganda, soaking up slogans about happy workers and dear wise Grandfather Lenin who cared so much about the ordinary people.

While the elites lived it up, the official economy was as stagnant as a Siberian swamp. Central planners still dictated what, where and how much of anything was produced, with complete disregard to demand. The state had poured funds into heavy industry, defence in particular, while neglecting the production of consumer goods. There may have been plenty of nuclear submarines and tanks, but it was next to impossible to acquire razor blades, fridges or washing machines.

> *'What is the most permanent feature of our socialist economy?'*
> *'Temporary shortages.'*

The growth of the 'black market' was a response to unfulfilled demands for consumer goods. By the 1970s there was an entire 'shadow economy' in which those with connections — from factory directors to government officials — provided frustrated citizens with everything from bread to jeans, cassette players and car parts to apartments and healthcare — for a hefty price of course. Bribes and party connections had always been necessary for anything and everything in the USSR: from getting your children into a university and seeing a doctor, to having a telephone connected or buying a car. Unlike corruption in the West, survival in the Soviet Union was next to impossible without constantly infringing upon the laws. When I'd arrived in 1990, few thought twice about 'illegal' deals. It was just the way it was. But with the demise of the Soviet empire, corruption levels were about to soar to unimaginable heights. With the resources of an entire state up for grabs, it was a good time to be a thief. For decades the party elite had been showering itself with perks and privileges. Now those smart enough to join Yeltsin's democratic camp were in a position to steal the entire country.

Along with the officially employed crooks, the USSR had also been home to a flourishing underworld — *vorovskoi mir* (thief's world). Organised crime had a long and colourful history in Russia. *Urki* (professional criminals) and *vory* (thieves) had thrived under the Tsars and during the Bolshevik revolution. In the Gulags the thieves not only prospered, they often took over, encouraged by Gulag guards to intimidate and terrorise the politicals. After all, uttering a bad word about Lenin, Stalin or the great Soviet state was an infinitely worse crime than theft, extortion or murder. The thieves lived by their own laws, a 'code of honour' which, among other things, forbade them to work, to have a family or a house, or to take up arms on behalf of the state. The only acceptable means of survival was thievery. A *vor* would take punishment rather than work, even in prison, and kill to avenge an insult. Breaking the code was punishable by mutilation or death.

The toughest, smartest and most charismatic of the *vory* were given the title *vor-v-zakone*, literally 'thief-in-law', or one who follows the thief's code. They shunned 'normal' life, proudly spending most of their lives in Gulags and prisons — indeed, respect in the criminal community was directly proportional to prison sentence time. Like Mafia godfathers the *vory* practically ran the prisons from their cells: controlling the guards, organising for alcohol, drugs and women to be smuggled into the camps, taking their pick of parcels sent to the camps by relatives of the inmates and spreading their code amongst the inmates. Extortion was a favourite pastime, and the *vory* regularly took what little money the politicals received for their work in exchange for the privilege of not being killed. They spoke in their own jargon, called *fenya*, referred to themselves and others by nicknames, had their own gestures and even their own courts. Tattoos marked a *vor*'s acceptance into the brotherhood, his achievements and position in the underworld hierarchy. Those released would propagate the code in wider society, recruiting young men to take up a life of crime.

Far from operating in a vacuum, these criminal networks often came to develop a symbiotic relationship with the Soviet elite. When Gorbachev's perestroika permitted private enterprise, it was the corrupt officials, underground entrepreneurs and career criminals who had all the necessary connections in place to take advantage of the new freedoms. High-level officials were already siphoning off state funds into their own companies and bank accounts. The *vory* were actively recruiting and Mafia groups were flourishing. A new breed of Russian was in the making, the fabulously wealthy Novy Russky, literally 'New Russian'.

While Gaidar's shock therapy gave free rein to the canny and crooked, living standards of ordinary people would plummet. Deprived of subsidies, most industries would head towards bankruptcy. Wages would go unpaid and prices would continue to skyrocket. Hyperinflation would rage worse than ever as the Central Bank printed extra money. Life savings would be swallowed in days. Pensioners and those on fixed incomes would suffer the most. But for now, few could imagine what was to come, and surely the winds of change couldn't blow in anything worse than the communists?

'It will be even worse!' cries the pessimist.
'It can't get any worse,' the optimist answers.

Olga (the optimist) and I took a train together to Moscow where her father was conducting a concert at the Conservatorium. The next day I visited Yulia (the pessimist), still despairing and so far unsuccessful in her attempts to find a country to take her and Dima. She had heard of a German scholarship program for students gifted in science and mathematics and was endeavouring to get Dima a place, unfazed that all studies would be in German.

'He is very smart. He will learn fast,' she assured me.

'What about you and your mother? Won't it be hard for you to learn a new language and find work? Won't you miss your friends?'

She rolled her eyes and fidgeted with her cigarette lighter. 'I am ready for anything. Anything to leave here. Things are going to get much worse, I am sure of that.'

While Yulia couldn't get out quickly enough, Canadian Tina, like me, couldn't keep away. Tina had finished her studies in St Petersburg and moved to Oxford during the year. This winter she was spending her holidays working as an intern at the Canadian Embassy in Moscow. And it was here in the capital that she would introduce me to a remarkable woman by the name of Nadezhda, Russian for 'Hope'.

11

Nadia

A delegation from Georgia comes to visit Stalin. As they head out down the Kremlin corridor after the meeting, Stalin begins looking for his pipe. Unable to find it, he calls in Lavrenty Beria, the dreaded head of his secret police. 'Go after the delegation, and find out which one took my pipe,' he tells him. Beria scuttles off down the corridor.
Five minutes later Stalin finds his pipe under a pile of papers.
He calls Beria. 'Look, I've found my pipe.'
'It's too late,' Beria says. 'Half the delegation admitted they took your pipe, and the other half died during questioning.'

This was apparently one of the Man of Steel's favourite *anekdots*. But what was acceptable for the boss was no laughing matter for his subjects. According to historian Roy Medvedev, who examined the files of many of Stalin's political prisoners, more than 200,000 citizens were imprisoned in Gulags for nothing more than telling anti-Soviet jokes. Nadezhda Khaimovna Shenker has no idea which one her father told. All she knows is that he got an extra ten years of hard labour in Siberia for whispering a few lines such as this:

Three prisoners in the Gulag get to talking about why they are there. 'I am here because I always got to work five minutes late, and they charged me with sabotage,' says the first. 'I am here because I kept getting to work five minutes early, and they charged me with spying,' says the second. 'I am here because I got to work on time every day,' says the third, 'and they charged me with owning a Western watch.'

Nadia (diminutive of the name Nadezhda) Shenker was one of millions whose life had been turned upside down by the paranoia of the 'Great Architect of Communism'. Now fifty-nine, she lived alone in a one-room apartment in Chertanovo, a dreary *spalny raion* in the south of Moscow. From her twelfth-floor window, Nadia could gaze across a sea of identical bland high-rises — *novostroiki* — built over what had been a village until the 1970s. Unlike the typical plump babushka, she was petite and delicate, almost girlish in manner. Nadia was the aunt of Tina's Russian lecturer back in Canada, and practically bounced with excitement at seeing Tina again and having another foreigner to visit. She bustled us into her tiny, immaculately clean flat, poured tea and filled the table with biscuits.

Tina always made a point of visiting Nadia whenever she travelled to Moscow, and Nadia relished every minute of her company. On Tina's first visit in 1990, they queued together for three hours at the USSR's first McDonald's, so Tina could introduce the enthusiastic Nadia to the delights of a Bolshoi Mak and fries. Then they'd queued again at the first Baskin-Robbins store to taste ice cream shipped by truck from London. Nadia had never married. Her only relatives were a younger sister, Tanya, who had moved to Cuba, and Tanya's son (Tina's lecturer), who lived in Canada. Nadia and Tina thought highly of Gorbachev and his reforms, and despite the total dysfunction of the country, both were devastated by his ousting.

Unlike Olga, Nadia's faith in the Soviet regime had been crushed long ago. Her father, Khaim Shenker, was a Polish Jew and fervent communist. He'd migrated to Moscow in the 1920s, following the success of the Bolshevik revolution and its vow to end Tsarist persecution of Jews. Khaim joined the Communist Party and took out Soviet citizenship. Nadia's mother, Rosa, was born in the Siberian town of Tomsk and moved to Moscow in the 1920s to live with her aunt after her father remarried. Rosa and Khaim fell in love, married, and in 1924 Rosa gave birth to a son, Grigory, affectionately called

Grisha. Baby Nadia arrived in November 1932. Khaim was a boot maker and designer at Moscow's renowned Parisianskaya Commune factory, which produced boots so fine that they were exported to Western Europe. His salary afforded the young family a comfortable lifestyle: Nadia's mother could stay home with the babies and they were able to rent a dacha near Moscow for summer holidays.

But in December 1934 that happy family life was shattered, with the assassination of Leningrad Party Leader, Sergei Kirov. Although officially a loyal Stalinist, Kirov had made the mistake of becoming too popular, too independent and too powerful for Stalin's liking. Stalin himself was the obvious suspect as instigator of Kirov's murder, but in his typically mistrustful manner, he declared he had uncovered a conspiracy to assassinate the entire Soviet leadership. He ordered his secret police to begin arresting enemies, real and imaginary, en masse. Hundreds were executed, thousands more were sent to the Gulag.

On New Year's Day, 1935, the NKVD came for Khaim Isaakevich Shenker. Nadia related how he had protested his innocence, 'I wasn't in Leningrad, I've never held a pistol in my hand. How can I have any relation to this?' The investigator showed Khaim the tip of his little finger and said, 'Even if you were this much guilty then we would shoot you here and now …'

The secret police knew Khaim had nothing to do with Kirov's murder but arrested him anyway, under the dreaded Article 58 of the Russian Penal Code: engagement in counter-revolutionary activities. These were defined as 'any action aimed at overthrowing, undermining or weakening of the power of the governments of the USSR and Soviet and autonomous republics', a vague and broad definition which included a Gulag sentence for failing to report counter-revolutionary activities by others, and a decade of hard labour for telling a joke. Arrest under Article 58 instantly branded the arrestee as an 'enemy of the people'.

As Khaim awaited interrogation in Moscow's Butyrka prison, the dean of Leningrad University was brought in, shaking with terror and cold. He died there and then, in front of Nadia's father. Khaim was sentenced to five years of menial labour at a metallurgical factory in the town of Cherepovets, midway between Leningrad and Nizhny Novgorod. Wives and children of 'politicals' were frequently arrested too, and Rosa was strongly advised to divorce her husband. She had little choice but to do so, however she continued to visit him in Cherepovets for the five years he was imprisoned there. Little Nadezhda, then five years old, went to school and still had vivid memories of being singled out by her classroom teacher as 'the daughter of an enemy of the people'.

By 1939 Khaim had served his time and was a free man, almost. Because he'd been a 'political' prisoner, he was not permitted within 100 kilometres of major cities. The authorities gave him a list of places he could go to, and he chose Ryazan, 180 kilometres southeast of Moscow. A shoe factory offered him employment and Rosa travelled regularly to visit him, taking Grisha and Nadia with her. Tanya was born in 1940, and Rosa lived with the three children in a 12 metre square room of a *kommunalka*. But it was a good building, recalled Nadia, with one toilet between fourteen people, and a kitchen with a gas stove. Everyone was friendly and they all got on.

Nadia already understood that life was different for party members: they had separate flats, their own shops, tailors, sanatoriums for holidays and special discount prices. 'But still, we believed it all,' she said, shaking her head. 'They beat into our heads that we had to be grateful to Stalin for our happy childhood, for our free education, free pioneer camps, and free medical care.'

Rosa and Khaim were still divorced, but they decided to move the family to Ryazan and live together. On Friday 20 June 1941, Khaim made an illegal trip to Moscow. He planned to collect Rosa and the children and take them to Ryazan to show Rosa a flat he had found to swap for their room in Moscow. Khaim stayed in Moscow for the weekend and on Sunday morning took the family to Zatsepski Rinok, the huge covered central market. He bought nine-year-old Nadia a wind-up mechanical toy — a pig that played the violin. Suddenly they heard the voice of Molotov, the Soviet Foreign Minister, booming through the market, announcing the German invasion. The Shenkers raced to the station, bought a train ticket for Khaim and he returned immediately to Ryazan. But it was too late. He was arrested on arrival — again under Article 58 — and sent to Tavda in southern Siberia for ten more years. Nadia and her father exchanged letters, but as every word was scrutinised by the authorities, she learned little more than that her father was alive and clearing forests.

The war years were terrible for Rosa and the children. Rosa had no education and had only ever worked one job, making theatrical hats back in Tomsk. Since marrying she had looked after the children. With Khaim gone again, they had no source of income. To feed the family, Rosa found work as a cleaner, scrubbing cloakroom floors. But it wasn't enough and the family relied on handouts from others to survive. They even had to exchange their bed for a bag of potatoes. As the Germans approached to within a few kilometres of the capital, almost the entire population evacuated eastwards. Rosa stayed on. Nadia had no idea how they survived. She recalled how her mother would carry hot water up to their fifth-floor room while she and two-year-old Tanya huddled under threadbare blankets.

In 1943, nineteen-year-old Grisha volunteered for service and left for the front. His mother and sisters never saw or heard from him again. It would be years before they learned he had been killed within two months of joining the army. They were never told how or where it had happened. He simply disappeared. There were no letters, and no body.

Unfortunately for Khaim and his fellow Jews, the USSR hadn't turned out to be the haven it had promised to become in the early days of the Bolshevik revolution. Communism had vowed to eradicate all forms of national discrimination, including anti-Semitism, and indeed many men of Jewish origin held prominent posts in the Bolshevik government, the secret police in particular. This however did not endear them to the non-Jewish population, many of whom came to associate Jews with the most despised and feared organ of the Bolshevik government, the Cheka. As Cheka terror increased, so did anti-Jewish sentiment. Stalin's ascension to the leadership further inflamed the situation. Historians are still debating the degree of the 'Brilliant Genius of Humanity's' personal anti-Semitism, but what is certain is that anti-Jewish feeling in the population dramatically increased during Stalin's time in power.

During the Great Patriotic War, two million Soviet Jews were slaughtered by the Nazis, often with the assistance of local collaborators. But not wanting to arouse sympathy for the Jews, Soviet press reported these atrocities as mass killings of 'civilians', never as genocide. With the end of the war, surviving Soviet Jews hoped for an improvement in their lot. Instead, Stalin embarked on a campaign against what he called 'rootless cosmopolitans', closing down Yiddish cultural institutions and implying that Soviet Jews could not be trusted.

Nadia finished seventh class in 1946 and dreamed of continuing her education. But Rosa needed her to work so they could feed themselves and little Tanya. Nadia, now fourteen, enrolled in a typing course, and to pay for it Rosa exchanged their room in the *kommunalka* for a dingy 12 metre square basement flat, with just a sliver of window at the top of one wall. They would spend seventeen years in that tiny hole, their only view of passing feet. Nadia completed her course with fine results and heard that the Central Committee required typists for a certain government department. But her teacher, also a Jew, warned her that she had no chance of being offered work. For any job application she would be required to declare her ethnicity and show her passport, in which 'Jew' was clearly written on the fifth line. As if that wasn't handicap enough, her father was an Article 58, an enemy of the people.

She searched for work for six months. At her mother's bidding she told everyone her father was dead. Finally she met a girl from her school who had completed the same typing course and now worked at the Central Statistics Department. Nadia explained her predicament and the girl offered to speak with her boss who she knew was Jewish. Nadia was invited to an interview and somehow the sympathetic *nachalnik* managed to persuade his superiors to give her a job. It was 1948 and the now sixteen-year-old Nadia was thrilled to be able to help her mother at last.

In May of that year the state of Israel was established, a development which would bring further torment to the USSR's Jewish population. Initially Stalin had supported the creation of a Jewish homeland, viewing it as a way to help bring about the collapse of the British Empire by pushing the British out of the Middle East. He had not however reckoned on the strength of the links between the Zionists and the

United States. As it became clear that the US was Israel's greatest ally, Stalin switched sides to back the Arabs. Stalin regarded Zionism as an ideological foe — an American and Jewish tool for racist imperialism — and Israel became a sworn enemy of the USSR. In the USSR itself, he ordered Jewish organisations to be closed down. Only a few token synagogues remained, and these were kept under strict police surveillance.

'The Jews couldn't go up the ladder,' Nadia recalled. 'They were capable people and could have been anything: factory directors, professors ... but they were kept down.' They were often not allowed to enrol at universities and were only permitted to work in certain jobs. Jews were banned from the government and openly humiliated, often referred to by the derogatory moniker: *Zhid*. Many changed their names in an attempt to hide their identities. Numerous Jews were rounded up and executed or sent to labour camps. The period between 1948 and 1953 would become known as the 'Black Years'.

Meanwhile in Siberia, Khaim's sentence had been extended for telling a joke about Stalin. But soon, for once, luck would favour him. In 1949, the Polish government demanded the Soviets return all Polish prisoners of war. Polish officials scoured the camps of the Gulag for compatriots, and although Khaim was a Soviet citizen, he told them he was Polish. The Polish prisoners were loaded into cattle wagons and returned to their homeland. Somehow Khaim managed to get a message to Rosa that he would be passing through Moscow, and begged the family to come and see him at Byelorussky Station where they would be changing trains. Rosa and the girls waited for hours. Finally they caught a brief glimpse of Khaim, almost unrecognisably emaciated in his filthy rags, straining through the bars of the cattle cage. He didn't see them; his exhausted wife and his daughters, now seventeen and nine years old.

Khaim escaped just as anti-Semitism flared further. Demented with suspicion, Stalin pronounced all Jewish nationalists to be agents of the American Intelligence Service. 'Jewish nationalists think that their nation was saved by the USA (there you can become rich, bourgeois, etc.). They think they're indebted to the Americans. Among doctors, there are many Jewish nationalists,' he declared in late 1952. He promptly ordered the arrest of fifteen Jewish doctors who he claimed were 'filthy Zionist spies', plotting to poison him. Fortunately for the doctors, Stalin died shortly after, in March 1953, and they were released.

Safe in Poland, Khaim was grateful to be out of the camps where other politicals languished until Nikita Khrushchev took power after the death of Stalin. He began to write to Rosa and the girls, but they were too afraid to reply. Eventually Nadia approached her local raikom — the Regional Party Committee — and explained their situation. She was told that as Poland was now a socialist country, she could communicate with her father. Khaim wrote to Nadia of the terrible state he'd been in on his arrival in Poland. He'd lost all his teeth and his skin was 'practically falling off' as a result of vitamin deprivation after his years in the Gulag. A Polish woman had looked after him and when he was fit to work again he had begun to help her with her two children. He was also finally able to send money to his family back in Moscow.

Khaim sent repeated invitations to Nadia to visit him in Poland, but the Department of Visas and Registration (OVIR) at the Ministry of the Interior refused to grant her an exit visa. In despair, she wrote to the Presidium of the Supreme Soviet. A 'kind woman' there helped her rewrite her letter and within a month she was given permission to go. It was now November 1955, more than fourteen years since that fateful day in Zatsepski market when her father had bought her the wind-up toy pig. Nadia was beside herself with excitement as she waited for an acquaintance of her father's to bring money from Poland for her plane ticket. In February 1956 she was on her way, aboard a rickety YAK twenty-five seater aircraft, which heaved and shook as it was buffeted about in a blizzard all the way to Warsaw. By the time she landed, she was a quivering wreck. But her father was waiting, with his new wife — the Polish woman who had cared for him. The daughter Khaim had last seen as a little girl was now a 23-year-old woman. Nadia spent six weeks with Khaim and his new family, shocked to witness the post-war ruins of Warsaw, and horrified by the dire situation for the Jews of post-Holocaust Poland. She refused to board a plane again and took a train back to Moscow.

At the end of that year Khaim was allowed to visit her in Russia. As a bonus, he, along with hundreds of thousands of other politicals, was 'rehabilitated', meaning he was officially cleared of all charges against him. He was given a special certificate, which read: 'Khaim Isaakevich Shenker has been rehabilitated due to lack of evidence.' It was small consolation for all he and his family had been forced to endure. Not long after his trip to Russia, Khaim left Poland for Israel with his new family where he found work as a caretaker in Haifa. After his wife died, he sold their house and divided it between himself and her children before moving to Tel Aviv. Amazingly, Khaim still considered himself a Bolshevik. He joined the Communist Party in Tel Aviv and began a relationship with a local communist called Ester. He continued to send invitations to Nadia to visit him in Israel but most were confiscated by the Soviet authorities before she received them. When eventually she did apply for an exit visa to see him, the Ministry of the Interior refused her request with a vague excuse: 'because of the war'.

Nadia, Tanya and Rosa continued to live in their 12 metre square basement flat, which became even more crowded when twenty-year-old Tanya married and had a baby son. They couldn't afford a cot, so the baby slept on the table, while Tanya's husband, a film-directing student three years her senior, lived in a nearby dormitory. The baby was only a few months old when his father announced he'd married too young and wasn't ready to be either a husband or father. Tanya became very ill and Nadia took over the care of her nephew, 'as if he were my own son'. She had convinced herself that she would die in childbirth, and now at nearly thirty, had given up on the idea of marriage and of having her own family.

Stalin's death brought little relief to the USSR's Jews. His successor, Nikita Khrushchev, carried out yet another extensive campaign to eliminate what remained of Jewish religion and culture. In the early 1960s, a number of Jews were imprisoned or executed for committing 'economic crimes'. Soviet Jews began to apply to emigrate to Israel in ever increasing numbers. Most were rejected, and after Israel's triumph in the Arab Israeli Six Day War of June 1967, the Soviet government put an almost complete end to emigration. The most common excuse given by the Ministry of the Interior was that these persons had at some time in their careers been given access to information vital to

Soviet national security. This meant that anyone who had ever served in the army — which in the USSR was compulsory for all males — would automatically and immediately be turned down. Even to apply for an exit visa, applicants often had to quit their jobs in advance. Many Jews were arrested for merely expressing a desire to leave for the West, this being seen as confirmation of their disloyalty to the Soviet motherland. So when Nadia received yet another invitation from her father to visit, she too was denied permission to go, just in case she should decide not to return.

In October 1964 Leonid Brezhnev succeeded Nikita Khrushchev as General Secretary of the Communist Party. The country sank still deeper into stagnation, but Nadia, Rosa, Tanya and Tanya's son were finally able to move from their basement room to a slightly larger flat. Little else changed. Practising Jews were still unable to enter universities and were barred from becoming Komsomol or party members, a necessity if one was to have a respectable career. Spies kept watch on the synagogues, and those brave enough to continue practising did so in secret. Throughout the 1970s, hundreds of thousands of Soviet Jews applied to flee to Israel. Thanks to the granting of political and economic concessions to Soviet leaders by US and European governments, 250,000 Jews were given the right to leave, resulting in a mass exodus to Israel. Incredibly, despite the limitations placed on the Jews' tertiary education, they were still the most highly educated ethnic group in the Soviet Union. In an attempt to stem the 'brain drain', the Soviet government slapped a 'diploma tax' worth up to twenty annual salaries on émigrés who had obtained tertiary qualifications in the USSR.

While a quarter of a million Soviet Jews did leave, many more, particularly the young, were denied permission. They became known as *otkazniks,* from the Russian verb *otkazat,* 'to refuse', or *refuseniks* in English. The *refuseniks* were treated with disdain, asked scornfully by their OVIR interrogators: 'What? Is it really so bad for you here?' Many *refuseniks* had quit their jobs when they applied to leave and were now unemployed. This left them open to charges of social parasitism, a criminal offence in itself. Of those who made it to Israel, many found the searing desert heat and constant conflict with the

Arabs unbearable. While the majority moved on to the United States, some asked to return to the USSR. The Soviet authorities declined their requests. A friend of Nadia's tried to return and was told, 'You went there, you can stay there.'

In 1974, Nadia took out a government loan to buy her own flat: a bed-sit with a minuscule bathroom and kitchen in one of thousands of co-operative apartment blocks sprouting up on Moscow's outskirts. Muscovites flooded out from the crowded, fetid *kommunalki* and dormitories in the city centre to these new sleeping districts, while others moved in from other cities in search of work. A neighbouring building exclusively housed workers from the nearby ZIL (Zavod Imeni Lenina — Factory in the Name of Lenin) car factory, the illustrious manufacturer of limousines for the elite. Now forty-two, Nadia found her new neighbours less than ideal, but at least she had a little space of her own, for the first time in her life.

'They were used to having *militsiya* [police] around, day and night,' she said. 'And out here there was nothing and they went wild. They are simple, common people and there are so many drunks everywhere here.'

Tanya had proven to be a talented linguist and found work as a Spanish–Russian interpreter for visiting delegations from Cuba. Just as Nadia moved out, Tanya fell for a theatre director/composer/conductor from Havana she had worked for at a composers' conference in Moscow. The feelings were mutual and they corresponded for two years before marrying in Moscow in August 1976. But not even then, as the wife of a foreign national, could Tanya get permission to leave. Her new husband returned to Cuba without her while she made frantic calls to check on the progress of her application. 'What's the hurry?' she was always asked. 'Once you leave, you're never going to see the USSR any more …' Six months later, Tanya took off for Havana, leaving her sixteen-year-old son with Grandma Rosa.

By late 1979 the Cold War was hotting up afresh. The USSR's invasion of Afghanistan on 24 December sent relations with the West to a new low, and Jewish emigration was almost completely halted. Following in his mother's footsteps, Tanya's son entered the Moscow State Pedagogical University where he majored in Spanish. Soon after,

Rosa heard that *matzoh,* the traditional Jewish unleavened bread, was secretly available in Moscow and she began to send her grandson to buy it for them. For two years he did as she bade. By the third he refused, fearful that he would be caught and expelled from university. Nadia stopped work in 1981 and they all scraped by on Rosa's 44 rouble pension and the 100 roubles a month that Tanya was able to send from Cuba. Shortly after Tanya's son finished his diploma in 1982 he fled to Israel to live with his grandfather. It would be almost a decade before Nadia would see him again. A month after his defection, Rosa passed away and her now empty flat was taken back by the state. Nadia was now all alone in her tiny bedsit.

Khaim died in Israel in 1985 and his grandson moved to Canada where he found work teaching Russian language and literature at a university in Ottowa. With the advent of glasnost and perestroika, students flocked to learn Russian. Several of his protégés, including Tina, had been to visit Aunt Nadia when they finally made it to Russia. Nadia was always delighted to meet them, and kept treasured mementos of their visits: an ice-cream wrapper, an empty moisturiser bottle with 'exotic' English writing, a postcard from Canada.

She was now receiving a state pension of 89.45 roubles a month, which barely covered her flat payments, bread and milk. Perestroika had brought longer queues, emptier shelves and ration cards. As an officially acknowledged victim of political repression, Nadia was eligible for a food parcel from a nearby shop. Even so, she still had to queue for half a day to collect it. Nadia filled her days standing in lines, discussing politics with her neighbours, and sharing news of friends and relatives in the growing diaspora of Soviet Jews in Canada and Israel.

Nadia had every reason to have become bitter and twisted. But if she was, it didn't show. She was delicate, fragile and emotional perhaps, but in an optimistic and excitable way. Or maybe it was her recent news that made her seem so positive. President Yeltsin had just decreed that Stalin's secret archives would be opened to scholars, allowing them to probe for the first time into the long-locked labyrinth of files and documents that told the true story of the Soviet century. And her nephew was returning to Moscow to be with the first ones in.

12

A Toast to the New Year

Veselo veselye — tyazhelo pokhmelye.
Revelry might be jolly, but a hangover is heavy.
Russian proverb

December 1991

Sergei's mother, Tatiana, was a ditherer. For two hours now she had been fussing about, trying to conjure up presents for every person we might possibly run into on our country outing, along with laboriously preparing a bag of *pirozhki, pelmeni* and various other pallid, dough-based foodstuffs. I was beginning to worry that at this rate we would find ourselves still out in the dark, which fell at around 4 pm — not an enticing prospect considering we had no vehicle, it was close to thirty below zero and blowing a blizzard.

It was the day before New Year's Eve and I'd arrived back in Kazan a few days earlier to visit Sergei, Zulfia and Andrei. But within minutes, I'd been taken captive again by the force of nature that was Tatiana. Today she had decided we would make a mid-winter visit to her Tatar friends who lived in a village 50 kilometres from Kazan. She wanted me to 'experience the hardship of life for country people', although I suspected perhaps she also wished to show off the curious phenomenon that was her Australian 'daughter', or '*dochinka moya*', as she liked to refer to me. Fortunately, I discovered I still had a stash of clip-on koalas and postcards from Australia, so armed with stuffed marsupials and a bag of freshly made potato pasties, we trudged down Sibirsky Trakt through the biting winds and deepening snow to the bus station.

A friendship with Tatar countrysiders made Tatiana a rarity amongst ethnic Russians in Kazan who generally seemed to consider villagers and collective farm workers to be uncultivated and provincial, mere peasants.

'They are uneducated people who only know about cows and only eat potatoes and noodles. They don't know how to cook and certainly don't read literature,' was Tatiana's damning assessment of her rural neighbours. 'They have no intellect! But Vildan and Nai'ilya are different,' she assured me. 'They are intelligent.'

Tatiana had met the beekeeper Vildan and his wife, Nai'ilya, several years earlier. Frustrated by the dearth of goods in state shops, she had begun to travel to nearby villages to hunt out edible food and other treasures unavailable elsewhere. She'd been given a tip-off that the Tatar village of Saya was a good place to pick up a goat's fur scarf. The purveyor of scarves, Nai'ilya, offered her some honey ('the best you will ever taste', swore Tatiana) and they became friends.

As our decrepit bus headed out of Kazan into the white nothingness that was the main road northeast, Tatiana chattered with child-like excitement, teaching me different words to describe the way snow glistened, and telling me how she'd travelled all over the former Soviet Union when she was eighteen with her friends and sister. I looked around the lurching bus, packed solid with fur-clad folk in felt boots. Every single passenger was attired from top to toe in the sombre and discrete blacks and browns of bear and mink. All but me.

In line with my vegetarian principles I couldn't bring myself to wrap a dead sable pelt around me, and so Olga had lent me a *pukhovka*, a goose down filled coat, several sizes too large, in a fetching shade of bright orange. I stood out like a flaming beacon. Everyone — Natasha, Masha, Tina, Nadia, Sergei and Tatiana — had the same reaction to my distinctive outerwear: 'Gosh, [suppressed giggle] you look like an orange on legs.' So '*apelsin s nozhkami*', I was.

The blizzard was becoming wilder by the minute. Tatiana babbled on as I watched snowflakes smack horizontally into the bus windows.

After some time she stood up and began to elbow her way forward through the jam-packed aisle.

Suddenly she bellowed, 'Stop here, we're getting off!'

I thought she must be joking. There was nothing out there, nothing but a vast expanse of whirling, blinding snow. Seconds later we were standing right in it, just the two of us, watching the bus trundle off and disappear into the whiteout. I could just make out the top of a sign on the other side of the road poking up from the snow: 'Kazan — 40 kms'. An arrow pointed in the direction we had come from.

Tatiana pointed across the road and shouted. My ears were buried under layers of scarves she had insisted on bandaging my head with, and I could hear nothing but the wind.

'What?' I yelled.

'Saya is up that road,' she roared.

'What road?' I yelled back grumpily. Snow was flying into my face and my nose was so cold I feared it might snap off.

'Saya is about eight kilometres up there. We'll hitchhike.'

I did a slow 360-degree turn. My eyelashes had frozen and it seemed the rest of me wouldn't be long behind. There was not a vehicle in sight.

'We'll start walking and someone will come along,' Tatiana shouted cheerily. I nodded dubiously, my jaw locked with cold.

I plodded after her, thankful my aversion to animal slaughter hadn't extended to the local winter footwear. *Valenki* were thick solid felt 'socks' which I had tucked my thermals and jeans into. They were perfectly snug, unless temperatures rose to zero and the snow began to thaw — then they would become soggy and disintegrate. To prevent their *valenki* from literally dissolving, the locals wore rubber galoshes over the felt. I'd been out of luck though. With all the shortages, I'd been unable to find a pair of galoshes my size. Tatiana had been nudging me for the whole bus trip to keep my felt-clad feet out of the swamp of melted snow on the bus floor.

Now she was almost skipping, as much as was possible to do so in snow half a metre deep.

'Isn't this great? It's so beautiful. I love the winter, everything so clean and white.'

I tried to agree; but my frozen lips wouldn't move to answer. The icy air burned my throat and it even hurt to breathe. How anyone survived life in the Gulag, without decent clothing or footwear, little to eat and excruciatingly long hours of forced labour in these painful temperatures, was almost incomprehensible. And this was *only* around minus thirty. Further north and east where most of the camps were located, temperatures would frequently hover around fifty degrees of frost.

My mind wandered to a morbid snippet of information my freind Zulfia had thought I might find interesting. Every spring when the snow begins to thaw, cars appear by the side of country roads, their occupants still inside, stiff and dead. The vehicles had either broken down or been caught in blizzards — or both — and must have been completely buried by snow before anyone passed by to help. No one would know what had happened until the warmer weather arrived to reveal their snap-frozen fate.

Tatiana began jumping up and down and flapping her arms, interrupting my gloomy thoughts. A battered khaki truck was rattling up behind us. The driver had no choice but to stop or run Tatiana down. She opened the door and begged the reluctant man to take us. Finally she resorted to the 'and look, here's an Australian, you've never seen one of those out here' card. By now I was happy to be paraded as a freak show exhibit — anything to have a chance to sit in his warm cabin. We bumped across the icy fields, skidding and lurching alarmingly until we saw smoke rising from a cluster of wooden cottages on a nearby hillside. The truck could go no further and our relieved driver, who now knew all about kangaroos and Australia having no winter, let us out to walk.

The Zainullin family's log cabin (*izba*) was half-buried in snow, right up to its elaborately carved duck-egg blue window frames. There were no phones out here so there'd been no way to tell them we were coming. Nai'ilya was obviously surprised, and delighted, to find Tatiana and a giant orange person standing on her doorstep. She bustled us inside. Vildan looked equally bewildered and their three small boys peeked timidly at me from around a doorframe. Tatiana began handing out presents and they came to life, rushing around the room snapping at each other with koala arm clips. She asked the eldest boy, seven-year-old Ruslan, to bring his school geography book. Rushan, six, and Rustam, four, crowded around as she pointed to Australia. Vildan and Nai'ilya nodded blankly. Born in Saya, the furthest Vildan had been in his entire life was Kazan — and it was only 50 kilometres away. Australia was incomprehensibly far.

Noticing that I was still shivering, Vildan took me to an adobe wall in the centre of the cabin and put my hand on it. It was warm, very warm. On the other side was a wide adobe bench with a hotplate, and a wood burning stove underneath.

'This is the *pechka*, a kind of big oven,' Tatiana explained. 'You put wood in here [she opened a cast iron door] and when it burns it heats the hotplate and warms the wall and the house too.' Simple but effective.

It was only noon, but a bottle of vodka appeared on the table.

'Just 100 grams,' insisted Tatiana. 'For the meeting.'

Russians often referred to their national spirit this way, just giving the amount. Everyone knew exactly what '100 grams' meant. Vildan glanced at me expectantly, an almost cheeky glint in his eye. He looked to be in his mid-thirties, with ruddy cheeks, brown hair and the slightly almond shaped eyes of many Tatars. Nai'ilya was four years older, slightly built and energetic with a mouthful of gold teeth. She came from a town 700 kilometres away, in the Ural Mountains, and had married Vildan at the almost ancient age of twenty-eight. She was now busily setting out tumblers on the floral plastic tablecloth. It would have been insulting to refuse. Vildan filled the glasses, raised his and proposed a toast … 'to my visit'.

We clinked tumblers and gulped them down. It did feel good after the cold. Nai'ilya slapped a dish of home-grown, home-pickled cucumbers on the table. It was essential to crunch into some snack, called *zakuski*, after a toast. Not eating after drinking was a certain indicator of alcoholism, but as long as you scoffed a gherkin per shot you were fine.

Tatiana was in an excellent mood. She showed me the cellar where the Zainullins kept their winter store of potatoes, cabbages and apples.

It was her fantasy to live in the country like this one day: growing all her own food, preserving tomatoes and cucumbers from the garden, milking her own cow, collecting eggs and chopping wood for the fire. Looking at her now with her blue eyeshadow and fastidiously ironed clothing, I just couldn't see it. But I toyed with the idea and for months after this visit, Tatiana tried to convince me to buy an *izba* in a neighbouring village. For the first time in three-quarters of a century I could have done so. New privatisation laws were being introduced giving people legal ownership of their land and houses. This meant they could sell them too. Many people were keen to make a quick buck and five hundred Australian dollars seemed like an impossible fortune to a Tatar peasant in exchange for a hundred year-plus log cottage with an outdoor pit toilet.

'Now is the time to buy,' Tatiana urged. 'You can invite all your friends to come and stay.'

The sheer madness of becoming a landowner in the middle of nowhere in Russia was appealing, but finding five hundred dollars proved to be too complicated and I eventually shelved the idea. Meanwhile, the lid was off the vodka bottle and there was no way it was going back on.

'A toast to friendship between Australia and Saya,' proposed Tatiana.

Nai'ilya refilled my shotglass and Tatiana looked at me sternly. Oh, the pressure. Another round of clinks, and down it went.

'A toast to the New Year.'

My thoughts began to blur. Nai'ilya peeled potatoes and opened a huge jar of home-pickled cabbage. The boys bought me a photo album: grainy black-and-white photos of grandparents and great-grandparents, staring solemnly into the camera lens, with their Asiatic eyes and cheekbones, women in headscarves and men in skullcaps. There was a gritty defiance in their poses and expressions. The Soviets may have forced them off their ancestral lands but they seemed to sense a time would come when their nation would flourish again.

Vildan showed us his snow-covered beehives, and handed me a lump of honeycomb to suck. Tatiana recited my life story yet again and happily answered their questions on all matters Australian, namely the frequency of kangaroo sightings and the non-existence of winter. She loved to be an expert. By now I was almost incapable of remembering where I came from, let alone anything meaningful about it.

After lunch, Vildan's swaggering brother-in-law, Rustam, arrived with a friend, Rashid. Rustam was a sleazy Uzbek with devious eyes and permed curly hair in his early twenties who had married Vildan's younger sister, Gulshat. They lived with his family on a *kolkhoz* (collective farm) in the town of Urgench, in the mid-west of the Uzbek SSR near the border with the Turkmen SSR. Rustam was now staying with Vildan while negotiating the purchase of a Kamaz truck. Kazan boasted the biggest truck plant in the entire Soviet Union and their formidable dark khaki wares could be found lumbering everywhere from Cuba to Vietnam. Rustam fantasised about owning one of these monstrous vehicles and had brought his friend Rashid along to keep him company as they drove back across the steppes of Kazakhstan.

Rustam regaled his in-laws with tales of a winter-long supply of whopping watermelons and sweet green *dynya*. I listened, remembering my last train journey to Uzbekistan. I'd been itching to get out amongst the dust and camels, and I still wanted to see the ancient town of Khiva, which I knew wasn't far from Urgench. As if reading my mind, Rustam gestured to me. 'You can come with us if you like,' he offered.

I looked over at Tatiana whose jaw had dropped at the suggestion. For the briefest of moments there was silence. I knew that if I'd been her daughter there would be no way she would let me go off through Kazakhstan in a truck with a couple of hot-tempered southerners. She glared at me disapprovingly. I smiled at Rustam, and buzzing with alcohol-clouded judgement, I agreed.

The vodka continued to flow and a stack of empty bottles grew amongst the pickle and *pelmeni* dishes. By 3 pm when we staggered out into the near twilight, I was pleasantly oblivious to the cold and excitedly contemplating my upcoming Uzbek expedition. Tatiana was as high as a cosmonaut.

'They just love you,' she gushed. 'Do you realise they will still be talking about your visit in ten years from now?'

This to me was more of a reflection of the pace of life in provincial Tatarstan than the thrill factor of having your house crashed by a giant orange Australian bearing miniature fluffy toys. But it was nice to see Tatiana so cheerful.

I have no idea how we got back to the main road. All I know is that somehow we ended up at another village on the outskirts of Kazan. It was called Vysokaya Gora, meaning 'High Mountain' ... and it was completely flat. Not one to waste an opportunity, Tatiana wanted to visit a friend who worked in the state-run general store, just off the main road near the local train station. By now she had lost her disdain for trading for profit. As much as she hated to admit it, Tatiana understood that in the new market economy this was her only option to earn the extra money necessary to afford the steeply rising prices of basic goods.

'You can still find some mass-produced items from our Soviet factories in some of the village stores,' she had explained to me the day before. 'They are very cheap, at the pre-inflation prices. I want to buy them before the prices go up.'

Tatiana had quite a collection of these bargains now: a pile of kitchen towels from one village, some plastic hairbrushes from another. The rationale was that she should purchase everything she could afford, horde it until it could no longer be obtained, then sell it for a profit. Her master plan was to amass a load of tackily made treasures then join the other shuttle traders on the train to Poland, where they would sell them in the markets.

Flushed with cold and vodka, Tatiana launched herself into the almost bare store, greeting her shell-shocked friend Irina with a vice-like hug. Twenty minutes later her bag was stuffed with almost the entire contents of the shop: pins, bits of elastic, random buttons, combs. The bench-height glass cabinets that had displayed these humble items as though they were diamond rings at a jeweller's were now empty, bar a few handwritten price tags propped up on their dusty shelves. 'Comb: Ten kopecks'. A comb had cost ten kopecks for decades. The era of prices everyone could afford was over.

Irina was every bit as excitable as Tatiana. 'You must come and have a drink with us to celebrate the New Year,' she implored, hooking my arm in hers and dragging me out into the street. I was sobering slightly at last and wanted to keep it that way. My greatest wish was to flop down somewhere and pass out. Tatiana took me aside.

'We must go and have a quick visit. They are all so excited about meeting you.'

Irina lived in a two-roomed wooden cottage that had seen better days, with her boyfriend, a female friend, her eleven-year-old daughter, Zhenya, and a tribe of mongrel cats. They didn't have much, but emptied their cupboards onto the kitchen table. Another bottle of vodka appeared.

'How is our Russian hospitality?' Irina's boyfriend asked, ripping off the metal cap. I grinned dopily. It was every bit as extraordinary as their capacity to consume vast quantities of alcohol and remain reasonably coherent.

'Welcome to High Mountain,' said Irina, handing me a tumblerful.

Hours and bottles later we all stumbled into the now clear lamplit darkness. A few snowflakes drifted down from above, glittering in the light beams. Coloured fairy lights twinkled on New Year's *yolki* (decorated firs), the atheist's substitute for Christmas trees. We crunched through the fresh snow to the train station, Tatiana's and Irina's arms linked through mine in an attempt to keep me upright. Zhenya skipped along beside us. Irina and Tatiana were singing loudly. The whole village seemed to be out and about. Babushki towed toddler grandkids on wooden sleds, teenagers built snowmen and lobbed snowballs at each other. Empty vodka bottles bred in clusters by benches and under trees.

The train platform was packed. Irina and Zhenya clung onto us tearfully, pleading with Tatiana to stay for another bottle, more food … to sleep the night. The *elektrichka* to Kazan pulled in and we tried to ram ourselves into an already overflowing carriage. It was no use; another two bodies were not going to fit. Tatiana tottered up to the engine, pulling my drunken form behind her. She bellowed in at the driver.

'Let us ride in the engine. There's no room on the train and there isn't another train for an hour. Look, it's thirty-five below,' she shouted, pointing at the station's LED thermometer at the end of the platform.

The driver scowled. 'Look, I've got an Australian here,' Tatiana went on, pushing my face through the door. 'You can talk to her all about Australia. You don't get a chance to do that every day.'

That clinched the deal and we were hauled into the engine. By now I had consumed more alcohol than ever before in my entire life, quite possibly put together. The driver looked at me with interest, blew his whistle and the train began to move.

'So you don't have winter in Australia?' he asked.

'Ummm, the DOOR!' I yelped, lurching towards it and pushing with all my strength.

It opened just in time for me to hurl all over the platform before falling out, face first into the snow. The train screeched to a halt. Tatiana and the guard hauled me back in and propped my floppy body against the back of the engine.

'No, there's no snow in Australia,' replied Tatiana, as we headed off towards Kazan.

It was a bad start to New Year's Eve. I woke feeling like a Kamaz truck was backing and filling across my head. Sergei and Anatoly were horrified to find the women of the house so appallingly hungover, particularly when there were preparations for a New Year's feast to be carried out, which were, of course, women's work. I was completely incapable of rendering any meaningful assistance in the dough making, *pirozhki* stuffing, potato peeling and lard-slicing department. In fact, I could do little but mumble to myself that I should never, ever, ever touch the evil 'little water' again.

But it was New Year's Eve, and this was Russia. Sergei was going to a disco at the Lenin Library with a glamorous sixteen-year-old called Katya and some of her friends, and I was invited. Later we would go on to Zulfia's place, from where we would walk to the romantic sounding Chornoye Ozero (although slightly less romantic in English — 'Black Lake') to see in the New Year.

By evening I had recovered enough to contemplate going out, so long as no one offered me a drink. But I had nothing at all to wear to a disco. My only footwear were my *valenki* and by now extremely scruffy Doc Marten boots. My jeans were full of holes and my Uzbek pants got the thumbs down from Sergei. He called Katya and she promised to sort me out with something suitable.

An hour later I stood before her full-length mirror, profoundly dejected, a short and chubby sidekick to tall, slim glamourpuss Katya, with her huge blue eyes and real blonde hair. The only item in Katya's wardrobe that would squeeze over my bulging bits was a stretchy black dress. I looked like a badly misshapen sausage. Katya and her mother were most gracious, obviously noting yet saying nothing about my hairy legs.

'No, no, you look lovely,' they said as I tried to suck my *pirozhki* belly in. I couldn't possibly go out like this.

'Here, take these,' insisted Katya, pushing a pair of stockings and heels at me.

The horror. I lurched and teetered as if I'd just downed another bottle of the evil spirit. Further protest was futile. Katya sprayed my hair, painted on some *de rigueur* blue eyeshadow and red blush, then stepped back to admire her creation. I looked just like a salesgirl in a state food shop. All I needed was a white paper hat and apron. Sergei politely said I 'looked nice'.

Determined to avoid mirrors for the evening, I donned my giant orange coat and boots, putting the heels in a plastic bag to change into, as was the practice here. Together we trudged to the Lenin Library, an imposing palace of red granite, perched on the bank of the frozen Volga, presently resounding with a repetitive dull, 'doof doof' thumping. We entered the foyer. Coloured disco lights flashed in the dimness, casting eerie auras over the marble bust of the Grandfather of the Soviet People towering over us. Vladimir Ilyich's stone eyes glared disapprovingly at this desecration of a sacred site. I jiggled away to the Lambada, still Russia's favourite song, trying desperately not to move my feet too much lest I slip on the marble floor. There was something still sweet and almost innocent about it all, what I imagined a blue-light community disco for thirteen-year-olds would be like in Australia. The boys were gentlemanly, the girls demure in their ruffles and bows.

Still, I was quietly relieved when Sergei said it was time to go to Zulfia's and I could extract my blistered toes from Katya's high heels. Zulfia and her mother had laid on a banquet of epic proportions: with Tatar pies and cakes, salads swimming in the ubiquitous mayonnaise and trays piled with sliced meats. After stuffing ourselves, we skidded down icy paths from their flat on Karl Marx Street to the central park. It was nearly midnight, and a balmy twenty below. A giant fir tree, decorated with strings of tiny lights, stood in the centre of the park, and the lake swarmed with twirling and squealing skaters. Thousands of Kazanets wandered around, congratulating each other. Everyone seemed to know everyone, or at least Zulfia seemed to know everyone. At the midnight countdown there were fireworks, sparklers and the unison popping of hundreds of bottles of syrupy sweet *Sovietskoye Shampanskoye*.

Sergei's friend Marat, a lanky Tatar with a mischievous grin and wicked sense of humour, joined us. He was in Sergei's class at law school, and besides me seemed to be the only other person in Kazan with a brightly coloured down-filled coat. Until recently Marat's mother had worked as a barrister in the prosecutor's office, but had since ventured into activities of a more entrepreneurial nature. Business was booming and she had procured Marat his *pukhovka* on a trip abroad. She'd also bought him a car, which way too many of us squashed into on this freezing New Year's Eve. Marat's mum's former connections with the prosecutor's office would come in handy later that evening as he drove his packed vehicle at terrifying speeds on Kazan's iced roads. When a policeman waved us over, Marat confidently pulled a card out of his pocket and showed it to the cop, who sheepishly apologised for bothering us, and wished us all a Happy New Year.

And a Happy New Year it would be for Tatiana. Her beloved younger sister, Natasha, was due to arrive in Kazan for a rare visit, along with her handsome military doctor husband, Vitaly, and daughters, Lena and Vika. After their wedding in Kazan back in 1972, Doctor Vitaly had whisked Natasha off to Hungary where he was charged with keeping

Soviet troops healthy. Baby Lena was born in Budapest. The family was then relocated to Leningrad so Vitaly could undertake further study at the prestigious Kirov Military Medical Academy, and in 1977 Doctor Vitaly was posted to the Baikonur Cosmodrome in the Kazakh Republic. Natasha and Lena went with him.

Founded in 1955 as a testing centre for long-range ballistic missiles, Baikonur had eventually expanded to include launch facilities for space flight. The first Soviet satellite left earth from Baikonur in October 1957, and a month later the first Soviet dog was launched into orbit, sadly never to return. Yuri Gagarin, the first man in space, was more fortunate, blasting into space in April 1961 to land back on earth as one of the USSR's greatest heroes of all time. By the time Doctor Vitaly arrived in Baikonur, *Soyuz* spacecraft were making regular missions to a series of *Salyut* space stations. Tatiana almost burst with pride when telling me that her brother-in-law knew the crew of the *Soyuz T6* personally.

Vitaly and Natasha's second daughter, Vika, was born in Baikonur. After thirteen years in the Kazakh steppe, the family was moved again, this time to the Crimea. They now lived in the USSR's Ministry of Defence sanatorium in the spa town of Gurzuf on the Black Sea coast. Weary Soviet generals and military officials flocked to the stony beaches to rest and consult Dr Vitaly for treatment of their various ailments, most caused by an excess of vodka and caviar.

Tatiana went into a frenzy of preparation, scouring the flat and mixing troughs of dough to make into the mountains of *pirozhki* and *pelmeni* essential for the visit of such an important personage as Dr Vitaly. She spent hours on her eyeshadow, tried several different outfits, and when they finally arrived she went completely ga-ga. 'Doesn't he look smart in his uniform?' she whispered to me. When they left I had an invitation to Crimea. But first I had to take up my Uzbek offer.

13

Independent Uzbeks

'We have always been supporters of firm order and discipline.
A leadership that abandons order and discipline can never
return to power.'
Uzbek President Islam Karimov, August 1991

Islam Karimov's open backing of the communist hardliners' August 1991 coup against Gorbachev had proved an unwise move. Islamists and nationalists in the Uzbek SSR decried him as the same old anti-democratic communist puppet of Moscow he'd always been, who'd even refused to allow glasnost to penetrate his propaganda-saturated domain. Desperate to improve his flagging image at home, on 31 August, 1991, Karimov reluctantly ordered his parliament to declare Uzbekistan's independence. Soon after, he banned the Communist Party, and renamed it the People's Democratic Party of Uzbekistan. Of course everyone knew that being Karimov's party, there was nothing democratic about it.

On 29 December 1991, he held presidential elections, allowing a poet from Erk, the breakaway faction of the intellectual's party Birlik, to run against him, knowing full well he would cooperate with the regime. The real opposition — Birlik and the Islamists — were still banned. With a compliant propaganda machine slaving away to brainwash the voters, the election result surprised no one: a landslide victory for Islam Karimov.

Although Uzbekistan was already 'independent', the collapse of the USSR had come as a rude shock to Karimov and the other Central Asian leaders. They simply had no idea how to run their own countries. Since 1917, the once great trading route had been reduced to a production zone; supplying cotton, metals and other raw materials to the Soviet industrial machine. Electrical cables, telephone wires, oil pipelines, roads and railways all led to Moscow. The mighty Soviet army defended their borders. Central Asian Party leaders had only ever known subservience to, and reliance on, the centre. All of a sudden, the old certainties were gone. After decades of Soviet indoctrination about internationalism and friendship between peoples, the entire region had been abruptly cast away. The Slavs now viewed their southern neighbours as a drain on resources, a money sink for peoples who were culturally, racially and religiously apart from the Russian motherland.

The irony was that these peoples who had fought so bitterly against Soviet authority back in the 1920s were now daunted by having real independence thrust upon them. The place was seething with nationalism, and worryingly for Karimov and the other Central Asian leaders, anti-Russian sentiment amongst local populations. Ethnic Russian settlers provided most of the technical know-how to keep industries running, and the leaders understood that mass Russian emigration would be disastrous for their ailing economies. By January 1992, trouble was already brewing in the brand new country of Uzbekistan.

Back in Kazan I remained pleasantly oblivious to the dramas down south, amusing myself with matters less political. Sergei and I went on a trek across the four-kilometre wide frozen Volga, slipping and sliding in our felt boots, intrigued to find unlucky fish trapped mid-swim in the thick ice. Fishermen camped patiently by holes they'd hacked in the ice sheet. One had sat in the biting winds for three hours already and hadn't caught a thing. But at least his wife couldn't nag him out here, he told us with a grin. We hiked on to the Pioneer camp Sergei had been packed off to as a child, the rows of coloured wooden huts boarded up for winter. Communist slogans still adorned the main buildings.

I visited Andrei the photographer, who was trying to organise an exhibition of his semi-nude women portraits in the Lenin Cultural Centre. It wasn't looking likely. The director, while apparently keen to examine the photographs in detail, had declared that Andrei's images were 'too aggressively sexual' for the general public. And Zulfia had taken me to the new hot spot in town, a bar/café called Grotto. Even more revelatory than the faux concrete stalactites was that you could actually get coffee. In such a tea-based culture, this was sophistication indeed, and I did my best impression of enjoyment as we sipped at our grimy disposable plastic cups of lukewarm Nescafe 3-in-1.

A few days into the New Year, I received the call I'd been waiting for. Rustam and Rashid were ready to leave for newly independent Uzbekistan, but sadly not in their new Kamaz truck. With each passing day, hyperinflation was shrinking the population's rouble savings, and Rustam was no longer able to afford one. We were going to go by train instead. Inflation hadn't yet hit the railways, and our tickets for a 4,000 kilometre trip were still cheap: the equivalent of about AUD$1 for a *platzkart* bunk. More problematic was purchasing provisions for the journey. To get to Rustam and Rashid's hometown of Urgench, we first had to travel to Tashkent, almost three full days from Kazan. No matter how much cash one had, without ration cards you couldn't buy a thing, and only officially registered residents of Kazan were issued with *talony*. We discussed our dilemma while standing in the queue at the Kazan Station ticket office.

Rustam was annoyed. 'Things are much better in Uzbekistan,' he snorted, puffing up his chest. 'We have food, we have everything. You'll see.'

But we were in luck. The babushka in front of us overheard our conversation and offered us half her ration coupons. I was overwhelmed by her generosity. Rustam snatched them with barely a thanks and scuttled off with Rashid, returning with bread, pickles and vodka. I tried to give the old woman some money but she wouldn't hear of it.

The lid was off the vodka bottle before the train had begun to move. 'Of course we're Muslims, we're Uzbeks,' retorted Rustam when I queried their rush to get into the hard stuff.

'But aren't Muslims forbidden to drink?' I mumbled, knowing full well the answer. After all, it was only a week since Rustam's Muslim Tatar family had got me plastered. They shouldn't, but they did. The Soviets had confiscated their Korans and introduced them to 'little water'. Seventy years after the Union, few saw any problem with that, least of all Rustam who managed to down several shots by the time we hit the periphery of Kazan. To be fair, so had most of the other passengers to whom eating and drinking themselves into oblivion was the standard way of passing the time on a long train journey. But the addition of alcohol to Rustam-the-cool-dude's ego made him downright obnoxious. He tried to climb on my bunk and I pushed him off. He fell with a drunken thud onto the floor. The next morning I gave him a lecture, telling him how disgusted I was that we were on the way back to his family, and here he was being a lecherous creep. He behaved himself for the rest of the trip, but I could tell he didn't get it. Or perhaps it was me who didn't. I mentioned the incident to Zulfia when I got back to Kazan. She wasn't in the least surprised.

'Men in Central Asia and the Caucasus, they have a different attitude to women,' she explained. 'You know, hotter countries, hotter tempers. They treat women more like objects, without respect. They don't understand a woman who is travelling alone. They think it is not moral, so she is not moral.'

As we headed south the snow became patchier, but it was still bitterly cold. Winds whipped sand across the desolate Kazakh steppe and there wasn't a camel to be seen. We arrived in Tashkent in the morning and had a day to wait before our train to Urgench. I called Solomon, the African student I'd met over a year earlier. We'd exchanged several letters since our meeting and he was still finding his new life tough. Rustam wanted to catch up with his younger brother, Azad, a student at the Automobile and Roads Institute so I told Solomon to meet us there. He came quickly and I hurried to meet him at the entrance. When Rustam saw me approaching a black man, he was horrified. He and Rashid grabbed me by the arms.

'What are you doing? Who is this?' they demanded.

'This is my friend. His name is Solomon.'

'He can't be your friend. He's a black, a Negro. How can you talk to one of them?' shouted Rustam.

Solomon's face fell. After a year's intensive Russian study he understood everything. I apologised to him in English and the Uzbeks became even angrier.

'Don't worry, it's always like this for me here,' he said gloomily.

I gave Rustam a piece of my mind and he and Rashid stalked off. Furious and upset, I thought about abandoning the trip to Urgench, but Tatiana had asked me to go to see Vildan's sister, Gulshat. She had been in Uzbekistan for five years now and Vildan was worried about her. I decided to grit my teeth and stick it out.

Solomon and I found a streetside *plov* stand. After three days of pickles and black bread, a steaming plateful of spicy rice and pumpkin was just what I needed, even if the utensils were filthy. A bit of dirt would toughen me up. But poor Solomon was almost beyond cheering. He hated Uzbekistan, mainly because the Uzbeks hated him. Everywhere he went people stared and pointed. Sometimes they whispered amongst themselves about 'that monkey from Africa'. Sometimes they said it to him openly. The more Russian he learned, the harder it was to ignore.

The Uzbek economy was feeling the pain of losing its subsidies from Mother Russia. Hyperinflation was raging, and tempers were fraying. Livid locals were looking for anyone to blame, and a strikingly black Ghanaian was a handy scapegoat. It wasn't just him; all the African students were being harassed. Solomon missed home dreadfully yet still had six years before he could return. To leave any earlier would bring shame upon him and his family. I promised to visit again after Urgench, and he offered to try to get permission for me to stay in the university dormitories.

By the time I met up with Rustam and Rashid at the train station, a wave of nausea was washing over me. Our train to Urgench was a local, stopping-all-stations, and the 1,000-kilometre trip was to take over twenty-four hours. This was no longer the scrubbed comfort of the Moscow to Leningrad line. Swarthy men in *tubiteikas* lugged aboard crates of vegetables and boxes of clothing, piling them high in the aisles. A babushka on the opposite bunk stowed a litter of frisky puppies under her bed, giving me a gold-toothed grin as she shut the lid on her yapping brood. The stench of sweat-soaked clothing, stale cigarette smoke and rancid breath pervaded the tightly sealed and overheated wagon.

Not long into the journey my stomach began rumbling like a volcano. I staggered to the toilet and lost a kilo from each end. Soon I sank into a blurry daze, comatose on my bunk. Then my stomach gurgled again. I lurched back to lose more of my body weight on the tracks across the steppe. I was rapidly dehydrating, but there was nothing to drink. When we reached Urgench a day later, I was delirious. I dimly remember being dragged through the darkness and laid on a thin red mattress, a crowd peering at me.

A young woman in a headscarf with mournful eyes and several gold teeth brought me a small dish of lukewarm brown water with leafy things at the bottom. Faint and parched, I gulped it down greedily. I lay in a haze as women spread out a large square of plastic on the floor, bordered by red mattresses along the walls. There was no other furniture and the walls were painted with murals; a peaceful oasis scene on one, a mosque on another. The women piled the 'tablecloth' with dishes of *plov*, bowls of fruit and a bottle of vodka, then disappeared. Only when all was prepared did the men came in; an assortment including Rustam, Rashid and an older man wearing a *tubiteika*. Suddenly I felt another wave of rumbling within and pulled myself upright. Rustam, his mouth stuffed with food, bellowed from his reclining pose, 'Gulshat, come here.'

The woman with the sad eyes rushed in, pulled me up by the arm and led me out … out into the dirt-floored 'kitchen' where the women sat eating the leftovers, out the back door into a muddy courtyard and through the mud to some wooden steps which led to a rickety wooden door next to the cow's pen. She handed me some torn newspaper and opened the door. There was no light inside, but moonlight shone on the damp floor. A foul stench rose from a black hole of inestimable depth, which threatened to swallow me if I put a foot wrong.

I slept fitfully, tossing and turning, desperately thirsty. I dreamed of gleaming white porcelain toilet bowls floating in the air. I grabbed out at bottles of Perrier water and fresh oranges, which melted as I tried to catch them. I cried out as a fat frog hopped onto my face in the night. And I couldn't find my way out of the pitch-dark house when the next stomach rumble came in the small hours of the morning. Gulshat found me slumped against the kitchen door in the darkness. When I woke the next day I was dressed in her clothes. I stared at the ceiling, unable to move. What had I done? I hadn't told anyone but Tatiana where I was going. I didn't even really know where I was myself. There was no phone, and the closest place with a halfway decent hospital was Tashkent, twenty-four torturous hours away by train. And then what would I do? How could I explain my presence here, with my Australian passport and visa which explicitly stated that I was to reside with Olga in St Petersburg. I had again left without permission from OVIR and was now several thousand kilometres away from where I should have been. If I died, who would tell my parents?

Gulshat came to see me and I saw one of her eyes bore a fresh bruise. I also noticed for the first time that her chest was wrapped in a bandage, crushing one breast against her rib cage. Her bandaged breast was much larger than the other. 'It's very painful,' she whispered, wincing. 'I need my daughter to drink from it, but she won't. I need some medicine but I don't have any.' I felt terrible. She was in severe pain from mastitis, yet she was looking after me. I gestured to her eye. She grimaced. 'Him,' she said even more quietly. 'What? Who? Rustam?' She nodded slowly. I was shocked and sickened. 'But don't say anything, okay?' she begged, holding my arm.

For the next week Gulshat sat with me whenever she could take time off her household duties and I became her confidante. She was miserable. Rustam beat her, cheated on her, drank all the time, did nothing but play cards with his friends. It was expected that she would be his slave. As the 'imported' wife, she was also responsible for cooking for the entire extended family, milking and looking after the cows, feeding the chickens, cleaning, washing clothes by hand, and looking after their son and daughter: four-year-old Rashid, and two-year-old Gurnaz. Once I saw Rustam hit her because she hadn't cleaned the mud off his shoes. But her greatest sorrow was that she had no friends. As a Tatar, she was a social pariah. One day little Rashid ran in, shouting in Uzbek. Gulshat looked about to cry. 'He's repeating something the village children sing at him. They taunt him: "Your mother's a Tatar, your mother's a Tatar." I've heard it ever since I came here, but it's the first time he's said it to me.'

My stomach woes continued and Gulshat was concerned. I hadn't eaten in days and was losing weight fast. She insisted on calling a doctor, a shrunken old man with his *tubiteika* on a rakish angle. The doctor, who looked more Oriental than the Uzbeks, felt my pulse and nodded gravely, then handed Gulshat a greasy dark glass bottle. In heavily accented Russian he said to me, 'You take this three times a day.'

'What is it?' I asked, suspiciously.

'Distilled dog fat,' answered Gulshat. 'It will cure you.'

'But I'm a vegetarian. I can't eat dog,' I protested weakly.

They both looked at me as if I were mad and ungrateful, which I suppose I was.

'This good Korean medicine. You drink it, you get better,' he said sternly.

I couldn't bring myself to drink the thick yellow grease, but after another few days I began to be able to hold down food again. When I finally put my jeans on, they slid straight off. Gulshat punched four extra holes in my belt. The next time I stood on scales I was 8 kilos lighter.

It had been well over a week since I had washed. I was literally itching to do so, but the family had no facilities for such an undertaking. They wore the same clothes day and night, and no one else had washed or changed either, or seemed in the least bothered. Gulshat took me to the village bath house, the *banya*. A group of snotty-nosed kids followed us down the street, laughing and pointing at the strange white person with the Tatar. The washing cubicles were dank and slimy, but the water was warm and I blissfully poured jugfuls of tea-brown water over my stinking body. Suddenly a chorus of giggles broke out. I looked around to see a small ogling eyeball pressed against a hole in the wall.

Gulshat and Rustam lived in a 'state agricultural village' on Urgench's outskirts. Around six hundred families cultivated cotton and rice in the fields radiating out from the settlement, and most had their own cows, sheep and chickens. Urgench itself was a drab Soviet concrete town with the usual ugly monuments praising the glory of communism and the local 'white gold' (cotton). Bored youths kicked rocks around the dusty streets, grimy and forlorn in their winter greyness. The main industry was cotton production, but this was turning out to be both the life and death of the town.

Back in the 1930s, Comrade Stalin decided that the two great rivers of Central Asia, the Amu Darya and the Syr Darya — which flow from high in the Tajik Mountains and across the Uzbek steppe before finally draining into the Aral Sea — could be better utilised. He commanded Soviet planners to design irrigation canals to divert their waters out into the steppe, with the aim of making the Uzbek Soviet Socialist Republic one of the world's major cotton producers. The canals were built and cotton targets achieved, but at a disastrous cost to the environment. By 1960 the Aral Sea, once the world's fourth largest lake, began to shrink. Thirty years later it had split into two and lost well over half its volume. It was an ecological catastrophe.

Gulshat and I wandered along the canals running through the cotton fields around their home. Most of the canals were dry. Some contained a few inches of fetid green slime. 'Look at this,' she said pointing at the sludge. 'There is no water now. This is a bad place.' Toxic fertilisers, poured onto the soil for over half a century, were now blowing about in whirlwinds of dust, choking the lungs of the locals and their children. The harvest was long over, but much cotton remained unpicked.

The 'village' still ran on communist principles whereby workers received salaries regardless of output. At best there was little incentive to work hard, but now people were barely being paid at all. Morale was flagging. We teased tufts of cotton fluff from spiky seedpods and collected it in bags. It was an awful job, and our fingers were soon scratched and bleeding. Gulshat grimaced. 'Can you imagine,' she said, 'that every picking season, school children are sent into the fields to pick cotton too, instead of going to school.' Apart from her children, I couldn't see a single crumb of joy in Gulshat's life.

'Why don't you leave Rustam and go back to Tatarstan?' I asked.

'You know, in our Muslim religion, in our culture, it is bad for a woman to leave her husband. This is my life now,' she said dolefully.

'But your husband is not a real Muslim. He drinks, he has affairs, he beats you. He doesn't pray. Why can he be bad and you have to be good? That's worse than you leaving.' Her sorrowful eyes clearly doubted my radical Western feminist ideas.

A couple of weeks into my stay, Rustam's brother Azad arrived home unexpectedly from Tashkent. The Uzbek capital was in chaos, rocked by violent riots involving thousands of incensed students. Police had cracked down on them, seriously wounding many, and there were rumours that several had been killed. Authorities had suspended classes at Tashkent University — the biggest in Central Asia — and ordered students from the provinces to return to their homes. I feared for Solomon and was curious to see what was going on.

Gulshat and Rustam took me to the train station in Urgench, Rustam swaggering as ever, Gulshat tearful and begging me to stay. 'Be strong,' I whispered as I hugged her goodbye. She nodded, and I noticed a hint of defiance in the set of her mouth.

I arrived in Tashkent to find Solomon agitated and uptight, too afraid even to leave the campus. Yet somehow, despite the turmoil, he had managed to convince the university authorities that I was a visiting medical student from Australia, and I was given permission to stay with some of his female friends in the international student dormitories.

The International Student House was exclusively for foreigners, all of whom came from Africa or the Indian subcontinent. No Uzbeks or

Russians could enter without official permission. Each time I went in, guards would stop me and demand to check my papers. Solomon was offended. 'They are treating you as they treat a Russian prostitute,' he sniffed angrily. 'The only white-skinned women who try to come in here are prostitutes. The Uzbek guards hate them because there is nothing worse than a Russian girl who sleeps with black men for money.'

I was lucky that document checks were the extent of my troubles. A few months earlier a Kazakh girl, rumoured to be a prostitute, had been attacked, stripped and beaten by an angry mob. I bunked in with three Ghanaian girls, several mice and a colony of cockroaches in a room less than three metres square. We cooked on a two-burner gas stove on top of a wobbly mini fridge, and shared a communal sink and squat toilet at the end of the corridor with hundreds of others. They were too scared to go out and spent their days watching television and twisting tiny fake plaits onto each other's hair.

The tension in Tashkent's university campus was palpable. The riots had been triggered by bread, or rather the lack of it. After promising not to increase the price of his nation's staple food, President Karimov had not only upped its cost, but introduced a 'coupon' system, whereby it could only be purchased in conjunction with a state-issued ration card. Students had not been provided with coupons, and the bakeries refused to sell them anything. A queue of fifty or so hungry students outside the university's local bakery had been pleading to be allowed to buy bread. When it was discovered that some was being sold quietly behind the counter for a higher price, things turned nasty. The ravenous students returned to their hostels to muster others, the police arrived, stones were thrown and shots were fired. At least two students were killed. Hundreds were wounded and arrested.

Karimov's government wasn't the only target of the Uzbek students' fury. There was a general perception amongst the local students that the foreign students came from wealthy families. Many were reviled as profiteers too, bringing goods from their own countries to sell in Tashkent with a heavy mark-up. In contrast, Uzbek students from the regions existed on nothing but a miserly state stipend, and rather than receiving extra money from their families, the families relied on the students themselves to send money back from their mandatory cotton harvesting work. So when the foreign students were given certain privileges denied to the locals, such as being allowed to purchase meat cheaply once a month, it only inflamed the locals' anger. Solomon and his friends were petrified. He would spend another hellish year in Uzbekistan, before managing to transfer to St Petersburg, where he found that instead of being called a monkey, he had girls falling all over him.

With my romantic ideals of blue-tiled desert oases dashed, I decided it was time to leave. But first I had to wish my father a happy birthday. At the Central Telecommunications Office I was told phone calls had to be booked five days in advance. My only option was a telegram — in Cyrillic. I selected letters that looked most like 'Happy Birthday! (НАРРУ ВІЯТНДАУ). By the time the telegram reached him in Melbourne, it said: 'NARRU VNYATNAU'.

For the first part of my journey back to Kazan, I befriended a twenty-year-old medical student called Ludmilla. A gentle ethnic Russian, who had grown up in the Uzbek capital, Ludmilla, like millions of other Soviet students, undertook her tertiary studies in a city far from that of her birth. Apparently this had been another part of the grand Soviet master plan to homogenise the nation's disparate ethnic groups. She was now travelling back from her winter holidays in Tashkent to the Volga town of Kuibyshev where she was training to become a military doctor.

In Kuibyshev, a corpulent babushka took over Ludmilla's bunk. She immediately fell fast asleep, snoring and snorting like a walrus, her vast stomach slopping over the side of the narrow bed. It was now 10 pm and I noticed a pair of rough and ragged blokes pacing up and down in the aisle. The *muzhiks* didn't appear to have tickets and I watched as they slipped a few notes to the wagon attendant. One sat on the end of my bunk and I saw he had only two fingers on his right hand, which was more of a melted stump than a hand. The other sat at the babushka's feet. Both were unshaven, with tattooed knuckles and reeked of urine and body odour. I feigned sleep.

The man with the stump pulled a dog-eared packet of playing cards from his shabby coat pocket and waggled it at two men across the aisle. Soon a raucous game of cards was underway, punctuated by vodka toasts in plastic cups. After some time, the two bona fide passengers handed over what looked like a large sum to the stump man, before slumping onto the table amidst the empty vodka bottles. The smelly men packed their cards away. I sat up and made eye contact with stump man. He smiled a slightly scary rotten-toothed smile.

'I wish we didn't have to do this,' he whispered in a raspy voice. 'But we have no choice. We have nowhere to live, nowhere to go.'

'Do what?' I asked innocently.

'This ... play cards with passengers on trains.'

Yura and Boris had been prisoners in a Siberian camp since their early twenties. Now in their fifties, they had been freed recently: 'rehabilitated', they said.

'Look at us,' said Yura, flicking his hand and stump down his filthy clothing. 'No one will give a job to an ex-con, even if he has been rehabilitated. We can't get housing, we have no way to make a living. So we go from train to train. We pay the wagon attendants, play with the passengers and win money to buy food and vodka. Then we move on.'

Just before the next station, Yura and Boris stood up to get off. I reached into my bag, found a handful of roubles and pressed them into Yura's intact hand. He pushed them away.

'I'm not taking your money,' he said curtly and began walking to the door.

It was 4 am and the platform's LED thermometer showed minus twenty-eight degrees. I fished around again, raced down the aisle and caught them just as they stepped off the train.

'Okay, take this then. *Na pamyat* (For the memory).'

Giving gifts as mementoes of a meeting or occasion was a Russian obsession. The train began to move as Yura held the object I'd just given him up to the light. He looked mystified ... then gave a bemused smile.

'What the ...?' he shouted over the roar of the moving train. It was a clip-on koala.

Back in Kazan, I caught up with Zulfia. Somehow she had come into some money and we decided to go on a trip together with her brother Zofar, to the sanatorium town of Kislovodsk, in the northern Caucasus. Zulfia and Zofar booked into Russia's oldest health resort and organised flights for themselves. I went by train, first overnight to Moscow, then two and a half days on to the town of Mineralniye Vody (Mineral Water). From there it was a relatively short train trip, past Zheleznovodsk (Iron Water) and Goryachevodski (Hot Water) to Kislovodsk (Sour Water), which sprawled picturesquely over the foothills of the Caucasus Mountains. Zulfia and Zofar flew in from Kazan and checked into Kislovodsk's best hotel. By Western standards it might have just scraped up two stars. Checking in to a hotel required showing one's documents, which I couldn't do as I wasn't supposed to be there. Zulfia would have to smuggle me in and out, a tricky exercise in such a security conscious establishment as a sanatorium. Instead of being given room keys, guests were given *propuski* — cards with their personal and room details — which they would show to a hawk-eyed *dezhurnaya* (duty) babushka who sat on each floor monitoring the comings and goings of guests. Once the *dezhurnaya* was satisfied everything was in order, she would open the door for them.

The signboard outside the hotel boasted of the magical properties of Kislovodsk's bubbling mineral waters: 'They will return youth to the old, health to the sick and beauty to the ugly'.

The waters were reputed to cure all kinds of ailments: from 'illnesses of blood circulation and organs of breathing' to 'illnesses of osseous and muscular system and nervous systems'. Zulfia and I queued with throngs of overweight believers wearing ill-fitting dressing gowns to drink cups of foul tasting gassy liquid from frothing fountains in a faux-Greek temple. I found the Russian attitude to physical wellbeing rather bemusing. It was apparently fine to live on lumps of solid pig fat, sugar cubes and vodka for eleven months of the year, providing you spent a month soaking in concrete ponds of sulphurous bubbles afterwards.

Having supped our fill of stinky water, we decided to explore the region. We took a bus to a vantage point from where we could see the twin peaks of Mt Elbrus, at 5,642 metres, the highest mountains in Russia and Europe. From there we went to the skiing resort town of Dombai and took a cable car up the spectacular mountainside. I hired some skis and hit the kiddy slopes, literally. Naturally endowed with the co-ordination of a slug, I not only couldn't manage to stay upright on the slippery sticks, but appeared to have a magnetic attraction to trees. Four-year-olds zoomed confidently around my flailing limbs, giggling loudly.

Before returning to Olga's, I took a detour to Crimea to visit Dr Vitaly and Tatiana's sister, Natasha, in the Ministry of Defence Sanatorium in Gurzuf, on the Black Sea coast. It was luxurious indeed, and eye opening, a glimpse into the privileged world of the elite, like my mysterious night with Sveta in Moscow. On the way back to Moscow, I read my very first book in Russian on the train, a translation of George Orwell's *Animal Farm* — a fable-style parody of the progression of the Soviet dictatorship, from the exhilaration of the October Revolution to the despotism of Stalin. Several passengers asked to borrow it, and soon the wagon was buzzing. 'How did Orwell know what was going on here, while we had no idea?' 'What a stroke of genius to cast the leaders as pigs!' 'How did we put up with the lies for so long?' 'What kind of a country have we been living in?' I thought back to my conversations with Yulia and that first train trip to Khibeni — and felt very naïve indeed.

By now I knew I wanted to stay in Russia and began investigating work options. Just as I started to make useful contacts, I received a letter from my mum. She was going to visit Europe for the first time in her life, and had booked a flight to arrive in Frankfurt, Germany, on my birthday. I hadn't seen her in close to two years. By coincidence, Olga's brother, Igor, had received a scholarship to study conducting in Frankfurt, a stroke of luck in more ways than one. Not only did he have a chance to glean baton-waving wisdom from a renowned German conductor, he was paid a stipend in German marks. This left him relatively unaffected by Russia's hyperinflation and able to send money home to his wife and baby daughter in St Petersburg. Igor had been in Frankfurt for several months already and Olga was keen to see him.

We decided to go to Frankfurt together and took a train to Warsaw, where we stayed with Anna, the violist. By extraordinary coincidence we bumped into Tatiana and her son, Igor, at the market near Anna's flat. Tatiana had finally scraped together enough items to make her trip to Poland viable and was now trying to offload the combs and handkerchiefs from Irina's state shop in Vysokaya Gora to the openly antagonistic Poles. As a proud Russian, she was finding the experience deeply humiliating.

Now the Soviet empire was no more, the peoples it had oppressed for so long were unleashing their resentment on their former occupiers. Olga was apprehensive and we lied about her nationality as we hitchhiked west across Poland. It was something she'd already had plenty of practice at after her years of living in the Soviet satellite state of Czechoslovakia. Even though the Czechs were usually friendly, her father had always warned her to keep quiet, because 'you can never be sure how people will react'. I did all the talking, in abysmal pidgin Polish, telling our drivers that we were both Australians. Olga and I spoke English together. Once I accidentally used a Russian word instead of the Polish. The driver snapped, pulled over and threw us out.

We made it to Frankfurt airport just as Mum's plane landed. Olga found Igor's flat and we all stayed together with his wife, Lena, who had just arrived from St Petersburg with their baby daughter, Masha. Mum got straight into her inquisition. What exactly *was* I doing with my life? If I wanted to learn Russian then why didn't I come back to Melbourne and go to university? What was the point of all my wandering? My friends back home were finishing degrees, getting good jobs, mortgages, doing something with their lives. What was wrong with me? Why couldn't I just settle down somewhere and stick to something?

I was irritated. At twenty-three, I was absolutely confident that the life of a peripatetic bum was a fine and noble occupation. I was finding it endlessly fascinating, drifting into other people's lives, trying to understand what made them tick, learning languages, trying to piece history together. Opportunities kept appearing and I didn't want to miss the chance of some mind-bending encounter with a Tajik poet or a Tatar babushka, just for the sake of getting a sensible job and a mortgage.

Mum eventually returned home in despair, having completely failed to knock any sense into me, and I continued my wanderings. The soles fell off my boots and I wore plastic bags inside them to stop my feet getting wet. I let my clothes turn to rags and hitchhiked all over Europe, from Poland to Gibraltar, from Scotland to Vienna and Finland with a collection of mini-dictionaries in German, French and Spanish. Sometimes I rode in goods transport trucks, sometimes with a carload of noisy kids, once in a pig truck in the south of France. I got a terrifying 240 kilometre an hour lift in a Porsche on the German autobahn and the crazed driver took a photo of the speedometer while driving to prove it. I played Bach's Cello Suites transcribed for clarinet in the London Underground, slept in forests, worked as a roadie for rock bands, washed dishes, looked after kids and taught English. Then I ended up in the former USSR's great foe, the United States of America.

14

Grabification

One hangs the thief who stole three kopecks, and honours
the one who stole fifty kopecks.
Russian proverb

August 1995

The questions kept coming, bewilderment mixed with disapproval.

'Are you a communist? You'd better be careful over there. Don't you know they want to kill us all?'

It was three years since I had left Russia, and I'd ended up in a place that made even the Soviet Union seem normal. Palm Springs, California, was the Great American Dream in nightmarish tones. Part golf-course-covered haven for ageing celebrities living in high stucco-walled compounds filled with date palms and bougainvillea, part trailer park with mini-methamphetamine factories in every second mobile home, it was also home to health freaks who lived on wheat grass juice, tempeh and organic papaya slivers, an underclass of Hispanic illegals who cleaned the pools, tidied the gardens and picked the fruit, and armies of masseurs, cosmetic surgeons and entertainers who tended to geriatric movie stars. To the extent that anyone knew anything about Russia, they viewed it through a McCarthyist time warp. Nobody could understand why I had ever lived there. I was wondering how I could live any longer in Palm Springs.

I had found a job in the desert oasis playing with a jazz trio in a hotel casino owned by two dodgy American Indian brothers. 'Classical' music meant Frank Sinatra, Cole Porter and Andrew Lloyd Webber, but it paid better than busking and I didn't have to worry about being arrested. The town and I were a complete mismatch. I couldn't pronounce tomato and had my own fingernails. Compared to Russia, the southern Californians seemed utterly superficial — everyone was either mega-rich or aspiring to be, obsessed with image, glamour and the possession of status symbols: ritzy houses, luxury cars and yachts, designer clothing and wrinkle-free bodies. I longed to return to Russia, where life was simpler and less ostentatious. Or so I thought.

I was saving for my ticket back, playing endless stomach-churning show tunes in the Spa Hotel, when a group of Russians came into the restaurant. Excited, I mentally rehearsed my long-unused greetings for when our break came. While Bob the pianist tinkled away on his solos, I watched them, baffled, wondering how they could possibly afford a meal in a place like this. But they were nothing like the Russians I knew. They spoke loudly, very loudly. Both the men and women dripped with gold and sneered at the Mexican maître d' with sour-faced scowls. One man, with exceptionally fleshy jowls and no neck, carried a large black leather bag, which he placed by his chair leg. Perched on my high bar stool on a podium, I could see right into it. I gulped. It was stacked full of hundred dollar notes, tied in bundles. In the end, I was too shy to approach them. When they got up to leave we were still playing. The man with no neck walked past the end of the piano, nodded gruffly and stuck a tube of notes in our tip glass. At the end of the night we unrolled it. There were three $100 notes, one for each of us.

What had happened to Russia?

It was time to go back. Olga arranged another visa invitation, this time a 'business' visa through IKEA, which fortunately made the process a relatively painless one for her. Now, instead of listing my profession as a musician/music teacher, as I had for my first visa application, or English teacher, as for my second, I was officially a 'furniture consultant' — whatever that was. I flew to London to collect my new visa at the Russian Embassy.

In August 1995, I joined an Aeroflot queue at Heathrow Airport for my flight to Moscow. I could hardly believe I was returning to the same country. The frumpy 60s fashions of five years earlier had vanished, and while my fellow passengers still carried bulging shopping bags, this time they bore conspicuous insignias of Harrods, Armani and Versace. The Nouveaux Riche/New Russian/Novy Russkys had risen like scum on a pond. No longer did bossy airline staff rule the skies ... these brash, shrill and designer clad Novy Russkys had taken over, snapping their fingers and bellowing orders at the obsequious stewardesses who flitted around pandering to their demands. I felt sorry — well almost — for the flight attendants and tried to be extra courteous. My efforts were rewarded with a Soviet-style snarl, my polite request for water totally ignored. It was another lesson: in this new Russia, being nice gets you nowhere.

Five years ago, the novelty value of being a Westerner had afforded me a certain respect. Olga had even told me that Russians considered Westerners to be somehow superior, which was why everyone made such a fuss over me. But this was obviously a thing of the past. These Novy Russkys appeared to be on a mission to wow the world with their wealth, style and importance.

An old Soviet joke had once defined Russian business as 'stealing a box of vodka and selling it so as to have money to spend on drink'. In the new Russia, '*biznes*' meant stealing the factory. Once you got the factory, you automatically had wealth, power, respect and the right to advertise your superiority by being as obnoxious as possible. Affluence — real or illusory — was all important.

Boris Yeltsin had now been at Russia's helm for three and a half years, the self-styled great reformer and democrat guiding its transition to a market economy, one hand open for kickbacks and the other holding a shot glass. While his 'reforms' were obviously working for the Armani-clad Harrods' shoppers, Moscow's Sheremetyevo Airport remained as dreary and dingy as ever, the officials just as bad-tempered. The only noticeable difference was a small population of despondent African families and students sleeping on cardboard boxes in the dark corridors, unable to afford their deportation.

A mob of unshaven men in grungy leather jackets encircled me as I exited customs, shouting and tugging at my clothing.

'Taxi, taxi, only one hundred dollars.'

One hundred dollars! That used to be several months' wages. A taxi to Moscow couldn't possibly cost that. I pushed my way through the fug of vodka fumes and stale cigarette breath and found a money-changing booth, astounded to find that one US dollar was now worth almost 5,000 roubles. I walked to the minibus stop, passing the Novy Russkys' chauffeurs loading Louis Vuitton luggage into limousine boots. The closest metro station was a rambling forty-minute ride from the airport. I barely recognised the road I'd travelled down in the old Lada five years earlier. Gigantic billboards lined the route at 30 metre intervals, spruiking Mercs and Beemers, Japanese TVs and sound systems, insurance, Scotch whisky and skimpy lingerie. And the roads were so clogged the drivers had plenty of time to soak it all up. The woman next to me sighed as we inched our way forward. '*Probka*,' she muttered, indicating the chaos outside.

I thought *probka* meant 'cork', as in what's jammed into the top of a bottle.

'It does,' she replied. 'Just look at it.'

In the metro underpasses haggard old matrons stood behind trestle tables, peddling pornographic magazines and videos to passers-by. I glanced at some titles — *Sex with Dogs, Shit, Shit and More Shit* — and a whole row of girly mags with cover pictures so gratuitous they made Andrei's models look like a church choir. The young women around me tottered on lethally spiked heels, hem lengths had risen by a couple of feet, necklines had plunged and clothing in general had shrunk several sizes. It couldn't be true. In the tart stakes, the Russians had out-California-ed the Californians.

I was on my way to visit Nadia, and stopped at one of the kiosks outside her station at Chertanovo to buy her some food. There wasn't a queue in sight and prices were hundreds of times what I'd remembered. Everything in the kiosk was imported — yoghurts, preserved meats and sausages, bottled soft drinks, packets of biscuits and chocolates. Most appeared to have been mouldering there for weeks, gathering dust and passing use-by dates. The only locally produced and relatively dust-free items were a range of noxious-looking vodkas and beers. Babushki shuffled by with shopping bags, peering into the glass display counters. Occasionally one would interrupt a saleswoman busily filing her nails or plucking her eyebrows to ask for a price, before huffing up and skulking off at the answer. I settled for some half-mouldy fruit, rock-like bread and slightly furry cheese. It was hardly a fitting gift, but seemed the least likely of the available options to kill us.

Nadia was jittery. 'Come in quickly,' she whispered, pulling me into her flat and locking the metal door. 'It's not safe.' I gave her the bag of decaying foodstuffs. She was even more embarrassed than I was. 'You shouldn't have! It's so expensive now.'

Poor Nadia. Like millions of other pensioners in the former Soviet Union, she had dreamed of a peaceful retirement. Instead they were left bewildered and impoverished by the spiralling inflation that had gripped the country since the collapse. Prices had risen by 2,508 per cent in 1992, by 839 per cent in 1993 and by 215 per cent in 1994. This year they would increase by a further 131 per cent. Yet the official pension had barely risen a kopeck. Many of the elderly were literally starving, unable to afford more than black bread and tea, let alone medicine. Nadia was luckier than most as her nephew occasionally sent money from Canada. But the imported food in the shops was still too expensive for her. She could only 'look at and smell' these exotic new products. 'Meat, sausage, fish, they are not for us,' she sighed ruefully. And it wasn't just the pensioners who were struggling. All those on fixed wages — most of the working population — found themselves sinking further and further into financial hardship. Factory workers, coal miners, teachers, scientists and doctors — all were now trying to survive on wages below the poverty line, that were often never paid, or if they were, came months or even years late.

These new depths of destitution had come as an unpleasant shock to Nadia, who had eagerly awaited the improvements in living standards so anticipated after the collapse of the stagnant Soviet economy. In 1991, she had 1,000 roubles in the bank, which she received from selling a gold bracelet left for her by her sister, Tanya, in Cuba. It was then the equivalent of nearly a year's pension. Skyrocketing inflation rendered it worthless within weeks.

'But many I know lost much more,' she said, shaking her head. 'Some people were saving for their funerals so their families wouldn't have to search for money when the time came. But it was all wiped out.'

Nadia had few kind words for Yeltsin and his so-called 'young reformers', whose bold programs to transform the economy had wreaked such havoc on the ordinary people. As she, and they, saw it, Yegor Gaidar, the architect of 'shock therapy', had destroyed industry and agriculture while giving free rein to hustlers and crooks. And Anatoly Chubais, privatisation chief and former Chairman of the State Committee for Management of State Property, had simply given away the nation's vast assets.

The 'people's privatisation' program had begun back in 1992, with the aim of transferring as much of the state's property, industry and resources into private hands as quickly as possible. 'We need millions of owners, not a small group of millionaires,' Boris Yeltsin had proclaimed grandly.

Yeltsin and Chubais devised a scheme that promised to transfer the majority of state property to the population in a fair and equitable manner, via a voucher system. Somehow Chubais came up with an estimate of the value of all state property: the improbably precise figure of 150 billion roubles. This divided neatly into the estimated population of 150 million people, meaning each and every Russian citizen was entitled to 10,000 roubles worth of Russia's wealth. However, the real value of these vouchers, proclaimed Chubais, was more like 150,000 to 200,000 roubles.

'In time,' he declared, 'these vouchers will be worth the equivalent of two Volga sedans' — then the most expensive car in the country.

Initially the people supported Chubais' proposal, believing it would ensure the even distribution of Russia's resources. On 1 October 1992, 144 million citizens — Nadia among them — paid a token fee of 25 roubles and collected their vouchers from their local branch of the

State Savings Bank, Sberbank. The vouchers were to be used to purchase shares in officially designated medium-sized and large enterprises. But there was a serious glitch in the plan. Not a single state enterprise was willing to be privatised.

Keen to assist with the modernisation of Russia's economy, the US government funded the so-called 'Russia project' through Harvard University. Two Western investment banking consultants from Credit Suisse First Boston were engaged: Stephen Jennings, a 32-year-old New Zealander, and Boris Jordan, a 27-year-old Russian émigré. They chose the famous Bolshevik Biscuit Factory across the river from the Kremlin as their first target, and eventually persuaded management that privatisation would bring them new capital. Large crowds, including workers and management, turned up to use their vouchers to purchase shares in the factory, raising a total of USD$650,000. It was a steal. Jennings had recently negotiated the sale of a similar factory in Poland to Pepsi for USD$80 million. He and Jordan immediately realised that this fire sale of Russia's assets was 'the opportunity of a lifetime'.

By now, another flaw had appeared in the voucher-privatisation program — the vouchers were transferable. Few Russians really understood what stock ownership was all about — capitalism had after all had been the ideology of the enemy for the last three generations — so those who did recognise the worth of these pieces of paper had little trouble in relieving the poor and naïve of their newly obtained piece of the immense Russian pie. Even before the sale of the Bolshevik Biscuit Factory, millions of cash-strapped citizens had sold their vouchers to intermediaries at well below market price. Touts lurked in metro stations and underpasses, wearing placards advertising their readiness to pay cash for vouchers. Four thousand roubles (about USD$40) was the going rate, and for most people, the cash to buy a few bottles of vodka was infinitely better than something called equity.

For those who did understand the potential of the vouchers, amassing them became a national sport. Many factory directors and managers had been involved in black market operations during Soviet days and saw privatisation as a chance to not only pilfer a few extra sausages to sell on the side, but to grab the whole factory for themselves. The existing hierarchy ensured directors had little difficulty intimidating workers into handing over their shares, or selling them at rock-bottom prices. One common tactic involved simply threatening workers with dismissal if they didn't give their bosses their shares. As jobs often came with housing, healthcare and childcare, losing one's job meant losing everything. Another ploy was for managers to claim they had no money to pay salaries, thereby forcing workers to sell them their shares out of economic necessity. In many cases, the factory's assets had been whisked away to private foreign bank accounts. But brought up to be passive cogs in the Soviet machine, few workers understood their rights.

Nadia had queued for hours to buy her voucher. After extensive research she decided to invest it in Nedvizhimost Moskvy, a Moscow real estate company, which promised great returns for investors. She filled in their forms and queued again to purchase her share. But the guaranteed profit never materialised. She received one letter advising her that her dividend was ready for collection. After another day of queuing, she received the equivalent of around USD$4, less a 10 per cent fee. It was the first and last time she heard from the company. 'The company and the government lied to everyone,' she complained. 'There was no money coming from these vouchers. But at least I got something. Many people got nothing at all.'

Jordan and Jennings however would get rather a lot. They began acquiring vouchers on behalf of foreign and local investors, who were hoping to make a killing in Russia's new market economy. By 1994, Credit Suisse First Boston had reported a profit of $87 million from their Russian operations. A year later Jordan and Jennings left Credit Suisse and founded their own company, Renaissance Capital, with their headquarters in a former disco hall of a Moscow hotel.

The acquisition of vouchers was only one of a number of routes to phenomenal wealth in the Wild East. With local factories and industry almost at a standstill, shuttle traders continued to make fortunes importing consumer goods from China, Turkey and Poland. And the well-connected bosses and technocrats in the former Communist Party and KGB did very nicely for themselves too. Aided by the lack of laws and regulations, the bribe taking and back-door deals endemic amongst Soviet officials continued. Many of the powerful and privileged simply shifted the assets of their organisations off to their own Swiss bank accounts. Others established new banks and businesses in Russia, using government connections to win contracts. A new word appeared in the Russian lexicon: *'Prikhvatizatsiya'*, a blend of the Russian for 'grab' and English 'privatise'. In English it came out as 'grabification'.

The prevailing lawlessness was a godsend for the Mafia too. The predominantly ethnic Russian and Georgian *vory* quickly adapted to the new order, continuing to disseminate their 'live only by thievery' ideology. They had plenty of takers and the unemployed and disillusioned flocked to the Brotherhood in droves. New *vory* were crowned, many relabelling themselves as *biznesmen*, using legal businesses as fronts for drug smuggling, gambling, extortion and prostitution rings. Kidnapping and assassinations became everyday events as gangs fought for control of lucrative 'industries'. Petty crime was commonplace and Nadia told horrific tales of elderly neighbours being mugged in the streets right outside her flat. She wouldn't go out at night and she wouldn't open her door to anyone unless she knew who they were. Meanwhile, the ever blurry line between theft, state and business almost disappeared as connections between mafiosi, business and government grew ever stronger.

By June 1994, the voucher program had succeeded in delivering 70 per cent of state property into private hands. But the most desirable enterprises — energy, telecommunications and metallurgical industries — still belonged to the state. Yeltsin's administration was by now desperate for cash, with growing foreign debt and shrinking revenue as industries went belly up all over the country. Taxes were increased to an impossibly high rate, which only encouraged widespread evasion, while many defunct industries failed to pay taxes at all.

To raise capital, Yeltsin's government decided to auction off shares in these industries in a 'loans for shares' scheme. The idea was that in exchange for loans, the state would hand over packages of shares in Russia's biggest firms, worth many times more than the cash amounts received as collateral. If the government did not repay the loans by September 1996 then the lender acquired the stock. A small clique of extremely cashed-up successful entrepreneurs and bankers had made it their business to cosy up to Yeltsin and his circle. When the auctions began in the autumn of 1995, it was clear they were rigged to ensure these favoured and powerful few got the pick of the spoils. In less than a year, shares in much of Russia's industry were transferred to a few major banks and companies at ridiculously low prices. The financial barons who owned controlling stakes in the banks soon found themselves emperors of the finance, energy, media, industrial and telecommunications sectors.

A subclass of super New Russian was created, the unfathomably ultra-wealthy tycoons known as 'oligarchs', including Boris Berezovsky, a former mathematician who ended up with much of Siberia's oil and half a TV station; his one-time 'associate', Roman Abramovich, a black market trader in perfumes and deodorants who found himself with a controlling interest in a number of oil companies; Vladimir Potanin, a banker who got Norilsk Nickel, one of Russia's major producers of raw materials; and Mikhail Khordokovsky, a former computer importer then banker, who found himself with much of the rest of Russia's oil. And while the Russian government was close to bankruptcy, Yeltsin and Chubais were profiting handsomely from the chaos, showered with inducements from newly minted oligarchs grateful for their assistance in making them some of the world's richest men.

It was a time of plenty for foreign companies in Russia too. One of the English students I'd met on my first trip, Peter, was now working in Moscow as an auditor for a major Western accounting firm. His salary package included accommodation in the gothic-style 'Stalin' skyscraper at Taganskaya, just around a bend in the Moscow River from the Kremlin. From his twelfth-floor kitchen window, Peter had spectacular views over the river, the perfect vantage point to observe high-speed car chases along the embankment below. But compared to his year with a jolly Tatar family in Kazan, he was feeling lost and lonely in the big smoke. Originally built to house high-up party members and officials, Stalin's tower was almost oppressively grand, with two-storey high wooden entrance doors and soaring ceilings that made normal-sized humans feel like insignificant dwarves in their own homes.

Peter's job was to audit the accounts of one of Russia's mega oil and gas companies. The firm he worked for had recruited a number of Westerners experienced in oil industry audits, none of whom spoke Russian, and most of whom were there to collect the substantial 'hardship bonus' given to those prepared to endure life in Moscow. His firm was charging the Russian company a king's ransom to 'convert its financial statements to conform with international accounting standards'. Peter, as a humble accountant, below manager level, was finding the whole business rather questionable.

'When I've audited Western companies, I go through the figures and then ask the relevant people for supporting evidence to back up their claims. But here it's impossible. The company is so huge, that whenever I have a query, no one knows the answer, or even who to ask. If I did find something dubious then what do I do? The company would deny it and my managers would most likely tell me that we need to keep our client happy.'

Peter was feeling adrift and bothered. 'If no one can provide answers, then the firm is basically signing off on something that is very likely fictitious.' To Peter, the situation reeked of a 'you scratch my back and I'll scratch yours' arrangement. 'It's a totally different mentality. In the West, an auditor is there to provide assurance to shareholders. But here, the company needs a prominent Western accounting firm to say its figures are legitimate, and the accounting firm gets paid a fortune to take the risk of legitimising fudged numbers.'

Moscow was a swindler's paradise. Mafia groups grew and multiplied, expanding their ranks with unemployed police, former KGB, ex-sportsmen and ex-cons, preying on the starving and naïve. Sometimes they offered to 'help them out' by buying up their war medals, art works, family heirlooms and antique silver. Often their tactics were less subtle, using outright violence and intimidation. Scams and cons flourished. Other shysters would talk them into selling their newly privatised flats for a song, or a bottle of vodka, resulting in a new phenomenon, the *bomzh*.

BOMZh is an acronym for '*bez opredelyonnogo mesta zhitelstva*', which translates as 'without a specific place of residence' — in other words, a homeless person. There were *bomzhi* everywhere, teetering drunkenly through parks and metro stations, scrounging for food scraps and cigarette butts. I watched them scraping fragments of unburnt tobacco leaves from discarded cigarettes, re-rolling them in squares of filthy newspaper for a hit of nicotine. To drown their misery they bought bootleg vodka with their kopecks from begging. Often distilled in basements from typewriter or windscreen cleaning fluid, these cheap spirits were seriously nasty and regularly lethal. Stinking comatose bodies were becoming a frequent sight in the alleyways and tunnels of Russia's capital.

It was hard to tell who was more despised by ordinary Russians: Yeltsin, Chubais (now dubbed 'Father of the Oligarchs'), or the oligarchs themselves. As living standards of more than half the population plummeted below the poverty line — compared to a little over 1 per cent in the late Soviet-era — the thought of Boris Berezovsky flitting around in his private jet made their blood boil. By 1995, most Russians viewed the privatisation process as the theft of the nation's wealth by Yeltsin's mates. Nostalgia for the good old days washed over the hungry unpaid workers and elderly. They might have been slaves to a system, which denied them freedom and provided them little more than the bare necessities, but compared to this 'bandit capitalism' and so-called democracy, communism was starting to look not so bad after all.

15

Evil People

Fear the goat from the front, the horse from the rear,
and man from all sides.
Russian proverb

September 1995

'Ludi stali zlymi,' Tatiana lamented. 'People have become evil.' From Moscow I had travelled back out to Kazan to stay with Tatiana, shocked to find her noticeably aged, a shadow of her once vivacious self. As a true believer in the mightiness of Russian culture and inherent goodness of its people, she was finding her 'great country's' recent transformation deeply disturbing.

'The USSR wasn't so bad. Even though there was nothing in the shops, at least everyone could afford it,' she sighed. 'Now no one cares about other people any more. They only think about themselves and about getting rich, at the expense of their humanity.'

Tatiana's husband, Anatoly, had given up on his money-making activities, a pursuit requiring nerves of steel in the new *biznes* climate. Great fortunes came with great risk. Any moderately successful venture would attract the attention of Mafia thugs with thick necks and gold chains, often sporting prominent battle scars. For a cut of the profits, these burly blokes, known euphemistically as *krysha* (meaning 'roof'), would offer the entrepreneur their 'protection services'. Refusal was not an option, unless you were prepared to have your property destroyed, car blown up, family threatened, or perhaps be brutally maimed or even murdered. The more profitable the business, the more the Mafia wished to share in your success. Different *kryshi* controlled different 'industries': prostitution, the casinos, produce markets, alcohol distributors, drug dealers, clothes shops and the kiosks on the street. Even the begging babushki and street kids had to hand over a percentage of their proceeds.

The *kryshi* weren't a new phenomenon. Sergei, Tatiana's son, had had a brush with their ilk back in 1988, when his father was running his small trading enterprise. He'd been at home after school with his girlfriend when there was a knock at the door. Sergei opened it to find two huge guys. 'Can we talk to Anatoly Alexandrovich?' one growled. They were 'very polite', but the then fifteen-year-old Sergei understood from their size what they wanted. He told them his father wasn't home. 'Listen,' the guy said. 'We know you're there with a girl having fun, but tell your father we have to have a meeting.' Sergei told Anatoly, who went straight to the police. The police were 'very professional', and instructed him to go ahead with the meeting. Anatoly was bugged, the conversation recorded and the scary guys arrested.

But that was then. Just a few years on and it seemed the police were in on the deal. To supplement their miserable wages, they turned a blind eye to the thugs, who, after all, drove faster cars and sported far more powerful weapons. The pathetic sight of a couple of cops in a clapped-out Lada in lukewarm pursuit of an S-Class Mercedes was all too common. By the first corner the cops would be blinking like lost turtles, the fugitives long gone. Were these 'chases' just for show, I wondered, to give the people the impression that the law enforcement agencies were actively tackling crime, while in reality they were taking handsome bribes from the *kryshi*, drug dealers and pimps to allow them to continue business as usual.

Tatiana was only teaching a couple of mornings a week now and like all *budzhetniki* — people who received government salaries — she hadn't been paid in months. She told of children coming to school without warm clothes or even shoes. Many were hungry. Either their parents weren't receiving a salary, or if they were it was going on bootleg vodka, Baltika beer and Moldovan wine. Alcohol was one of the few affordable commodities which at least offered the bonus of temporary solace from their woes. Tatiana was despondent. She simply couldn't believe the state had abandoned its people.

'Before we knew the state would look after us. Now we suddenly have to look after ourselves, and most people don't know how to. We were never taught, and never ever thought we would need to. It's like a parent casting off its own children. People are still waiting for the government to do something to improve their lives for them. Most don't understand that it's up to themselves now.'

Everything about the new Russia appalled her. On television, the moralistic Soviet movies and upbeat news reports of bumper harvests had been replaced by the worst of the West. Tawdry soap operas like *Dynasty*, with plotlines revolving around lifestyles of extreme affluence and extreme malice, with promiscuous, green-eyed uber-bitches as heroines, had replaced *Skippy* and *Lassie* as the must-see foreign dramas. Salacious and often pornographic B-grade American flicks that were once banned were broadcast on prime time. Children's viewing hours were scheduled with sordid scenes of murder, lewd sexual acts, violence against women and drug use, as if the country had developed some morbid fascination with the dark side of human nature. 'How can people watch this depravity?' she despaired. 'What will happen to the minds of children who see this and think it is normal behaviour?'

The worst thing for Tatiana was the loss of her dignity. Only a few years ago she had taken pride in her beauty. Now it was a luxury she could no longer afford. Even a visit to a dentist to replace her two missing bottom teeth was inconceivable, let alone the purchase of hair dye, new clothes or make-up. Their flat too, once a source of gratification, was sinking into disrepair. The plumbing was leaking and they couldn't afford to fix it. Rather than be liable for damage to the shop ceiling below, she had turned off the water supply to the flat and stored cooking water in buckets in the kitchen. She was depressed — and defeatist. The injustices and corruption in the new Russia were apparent to all. But Tatiana and her equally bitter friends shrugged their shoulders. Their attitude was, 'Well, that's just how it is and there's nothing I can do about it.' I couldn't understand why people didn't protest, demonstrate, or rebel in some way against the corruption and chaos of the new regime. 'But it won't do anything except get people in trouble,' she said despondently. 'And people are so exhausted from just trying to survive that they have no energy left to complain.'

Walking to the shops, Tatiana and I passed a toothless old woman kneeling on the footpath, palm outstretched with some crumpled roubles in a scarf on the grimy cement. Her weathered face was beautifully photogenic, etched with lines of hardship, a once strong woman who had no doubt given her all for her country. I wanted to capture her image on film. Tatiana was horrified. 'Why would you want to take a photo of a poor old woman?' she hissed. 'This is our shame, our disgrace, and not something for people outside the country to see.'

Perhaps as a hangover of the days of hyperactive propaganda, everybody seemed to want to conceal or ignore the unsavoury reality. 'Keep the rubbish inside the house' was a phrase I heard often. It was a way of saying yes, we know bad stuff is happening, but it's one thing for us to discuss it in our kitchens, and quite another for foreigners to judge us. For the majority, keeping up the national image was more important than their own hardship.

Tatiana was dealing with her impoverished existence by withdrawal rather than protest. She and Anatoly had bought a humble wooden dacha in the village of Ilet in the neighbouring republic of Mari El. Ilet was just northwest of the Tatar border, off the railway line and surrounded on all sides by a birch-forested national park. In this tranquil setting Tatiana, the schoolteacher, endeavoured to grow enough vegetables to ensure self-sufficiency, while Anatoly, the engineer, worked at making the tumbledown shack liveable. Tatiana took me mushroom-picking in the forest behind their house. She knew the names of tens of different species which were edible and how to preserve them. Her spirits lifted as our baskets filled. While I cursed and swatted at the swarms of mosquitoes attacking me, I saw a glimpse of the effervescent woman she had been less than four years ago.

Besides mushrooms, the only subject that cheered Tatiana was her second son, Sergei. He had excelled in his law studies and even before his graduation he had begun work as a legal counsel to the Tatar government, or more specifically, the newly established and cumbersomely titled Tatarstan Regional Government International Cooperation Agency. His powerful boss had arranged his exemption from army service and 23-year-old Sergei was now busily drafting foreign trade regulations for Tatarstan, representing the agency before the World Bank and establishing and managing joint ventures in the USA, Germany, Hungary and India. But as one of only two ethnic Russians working in the Tatar dominated government, Sergei was finding the new order a challenge. After three-quarters of a century of ethnic Russian dominated Soviet control, the Tatars were determined to show that they were now the masters in their own territory.

It was exactly five years since Tatarstan had declared its sovereignty and the city was celebrating — or at least the Tatars were. They paraded down streets and through squares, many of their communist-era names replaced by those honouring Tatar heroes, poets, and historical figures. The signage on shops, public buildings and everything else was now bilingual, with Tatar given prominence. Tatar language was being taught in schools and spoken far more in the streets. On 30 August, a huge celebration took place in Kazan's main stadium to mark Tatarstan's 'Independence Day'. Thanks to Sergei's government connections his friends, including me, got some of the best seats in the house for the gala event. The best of Tatarstan was on show, from gymnasts and dancing girls in Tatar national costume to displays of giant vegetables, livestock and Kamaz trucks. All hailed the President, former Communist Party bureaucrat, Mintimer Shaimiev.

In fact, Tatarstan was not wholly independent, at least not in the way that the former republics of Central Asia, the Caucasus and the Baltics were now countries in their own right. Radical Tatar nationalists had pushed for Tatarstan — surrounded on all sides by Russia — to unite with the Orenburg and Samara districts to the south to create a large state stretching all the way to the border with Kazakhstan. But Shaimiev only needed to look to another former autonomous republic — Chechnya — to realise it was prudent to stay on Moscow's good side. Chechnya had been unwilling to compromise with Moscow on its demand for independence, and in December 1994 Yeltsin sent in Russian troops to show the recalcitrant Chechens who was boss. That bloody conflict was still raging and both Yeltsin and Shaimiev wanted to avoid a similar situation in Tatarstan. So in 1994, Shaimiev had signed a treaty with Russia, agreeing not to seek full territorial independence. Tatarstan would maintain responsibility for its own economic, cultural and political development while defence and foreign relations would be covered by Moscow. Shaimiev, who had made a big deal of pushing for cultural and linguistic revival to placate the nationalists, had saved his own skin. He now presided over an oil-rich territory of which he had full economic control. In true clan fashion, Shaimiev had stacked his government with relatives and mates. The language of government was changed from Russian to Tatar, and as few Russians had ever learned Tatar, it was an effective way of keeping ethnic Russians out of decision-making. The rise of the Tatars was well underway.

Tatiana and her university lecturer friend, Natasha Gelms (mother of Sergei's friend, the comely Katya), were unimpressed by the new Tatar domination. Both considered Tatar to be an inferior language to Russian and saw no point in learning it. 'You just can't compare Tatar literature with Pushkin,' declared Tatiana. 'And I don't need it in the shops. I was born here and I've spoken Russian all my life here and that's not going to change.'

I suspected that there was a hint of a sense of racial superiority in their attitudes, although it wasn't something they would ever admit to. For all their lives, ethnic Russians had been the ascendant race, and the USSR had been dominated by Russian language and culture. Now the roles had reversed and ethnic Russians were beginning to feel like second-class citizens in what they felt to be their land. 'The Tatars,' Natasha bemoaned, 'are taking over the key posts at the university, pushing Russians to the outer.' Sergei had already recognised the limited options in his new job and was in the process of applying for admission to an American University.

But matters were different for my friend Zulfia who I caught up with at her flat in Karl Marx Street. Connections — along with a keen intellect and buckets of charm — brought opportunities, and she had seized every available chance to find a niche for herself in the new market economy. She had heard about a student exchange scheme which offered the chance of a year in Turkey and two days later had left for the coastal town of Izmir. She studied Turkish at a faculty of Ankara University and worked as an interpreter for foreign businessmen at international fairs. On her return to Tatarstan she found a position in the Tatarstan Chamber of Commerce and Industry. Since Shaimiev's agreement with Moscow, Tatarstan had become one of the favoured destinations for foreign investment in the former USSR. Americans, Germans, Iranians and Turks in particular were pouring capital into the region, and Zulfia's Turkish, English, Russian and Tatar language skills ensured she was in demand. She would later become the head of the Investment Department, advising locals and foreigners on how to go about establishing joint-venture companies.

Zulfia had also set up an importing business, bringing in food and construction materials from Turkey to sell in Kazan. Things weren't going well, which was an 'only-in-Russia' blessing in disguise: no profit meant no Mafia attention. 'You have to be crazy to be successful in business in Russia,' she laughed. 'There are no laws and regulations to protect businesses. It is completely wild.' The nascent taxation system was also a nightmare. 'In the USSR,' she explained, 'there was no such thing as taxes as we have now. Now we have to pay almost 90 per cent of business profits in tax to the government. It's impossible to expand my business, let alone have anything for myself. If I had to pay off a *krysha* as well, I would be losing money.'

The only way *biznes* people could get ahead was to find ways to avoid paying tax. Most simply shipped their assets off to foreign bank accounts and employed dodgy accountants to fiddle the books. As a result, the banks of Switzerland, the Channel Islands and the Bahamas were bulging with billions of dollars of Russian money. Meanwhile the Russian government had nothing with which to pay wages and pensions, fund hospitals and schools and generally keep the country afloat.

Vildan the Tatar beekeeper was also faring well. Tatiana and I took a trip back to Saya — where I'd once braved a blizzard in a giant orange coat — to visit him, Nai'ilya and the boys: Rustam, Ruslan and Rushan, now ten, thirteen and fourteen. I barely recognised the place in its autumn colours. Tatiana had been right — they did remember my previous visit. The clip-on koalas I'd given them still had pride of place on the trinket shelves, along with the best tea set and framed portraits of great-grandparents. Nai'ilya welcomed us in with a gold-toothed grin and again the table filled with pickles, vodka and dishes of honey. Life was good for the Zainullins. Their honey was in demand and little by little Vildan had built up his business, constructing new hives and expanding production. No mafiosi could be bothered with him out in his little village, particularly if it involved taking their Mercs off road to get there. He proudly got out his new toy, a Video 8 Camcorder, and soon my every move was being captured on tape: from vodka toasts and honey tasting to a tour of his hives. But the best news of our visit was learning that his sister, Gulshat, had left the vile cheating Rustam in Uzbekistan, moved the kids back to Tatarstan and found a flat in a neighbouring village.

Within half an hour, we were on our way to see her, laden with baskets of food and jars of honey. Gulshat was momentarily stunned, then burst into tears, embraced me and wouldn't let me go. Life was tough, but she was ecstatic to be away from Rustam and the misery of Urgench. The children hadn't even asked about their father, and were happily making friends at school and learning Tatar. She had found a job as a seamstress. It didn't pay well, but thanks to brother Vildan's kindness they were surviving.

News of our visit spread quickly amongst Gulshat's new neighbours. A fellow villager came to offer his *banya* to us for the night — an invitation too good to refuse. It was a traditional style *banya*, a small wooden shed in the backyard near the chook-house, with a steam room, washing room and a dressing/resting/tea room. The 'boys' went first, which always seemed to be the way — I presumed it was to give the women time to prepare the food while the men were broiling themselves. A couple of hours later they returned, with shiny, red faces, flushed from intense heat, beating and vodka, ready to demolish the banquet we had so painstakingly laid out. Then it was our turn: Tatiana, Gulshat, Nai'ilya and me.

We disrobed in the dressing room and I self-consciously grabbed a towel to cover myself. The others were completely oblivious to our stark naked state, Tatiana continuing to lecture us all on the medicinal properties of pine needles, as if nothing had changed. Making a determined effort not to allow my gaze to sink below chin level, I donned a *shapka,* a conical mushroom-like felt hat, designed to protect one's hair from the fierce heat we were about to endure, and stepped into the steam room. Typically heated by a wood stove, the steam room in a Russian *banya* can reach temperatures of up to eighty degrees Celsius. Once we had adjusted to the heat, Nai'ilya ladled water onto hot rocks in a chamber on the metal stove top, and a cloud of steam filled the room. By now we were all sweating profusely, and it was time for the real fun to begin.

Tatiana ordered me to lie face down on one of the wooden benches. The others watched in amusement as she whacked me from top to bottom with a *venik,* a bunch of birch twigs tied together. Despite my protestations that my circulation couldn't be better, she continued her 'invigorating' beating with an almost sadistic intensity. Just as I was about to expire, she let me out for the 'cold treatment' part of the *banya* cycle. Preferable 'cold treatment' options include running outside and jumping in an icy river, or rolling in the snow. As neither were available I had to settle for pouring freezing water over myself in the washing room and attacking my pores with a vicious scrubbing cloth, before heading back in for another round.

Boil, beat, freeze, boil, beat, freeze was the torturous routine. The whole process was rather like banging one's head against a brick wall: the real pleasure comes when you stop. But I have never felt cleaner in my life than after a real Russian *banya.* When we finally left Saya — after lunch the next day — Vildan presented us with a honeycomb of dripping beeswax on a wooden frame. Tatiana was thrilled. And I was ecstatic too. The honey was great, but nothing beat finding out that Gulshat had managed to turn her former hellish life around.

Much to the chagrin of Tatiana, *biznes* and *marketing* (with a Russian accent) were the professions with prospects in the New Russia. Sergei's friend Marat had finished his law degree a few months earlier and found himself just such a line of work. In fact, he'd already made a small fortune. Marat had started out — just as oligarch Boris Berezovsky had done — by taking a train to Germany and buying an old Mercedes, which he then drove back to Kazan and sold for a handsome profit. On his next trip he bought a flashier Merc, and made an even bigger profit. And so it continued. When he wasn't dealing in second-hand German luxury vehicles, he'd begun to manage a small local rock band, arranging gigs in the new nightclubs which had sprung up around town. With his tight leather pants, crew cut and gold chain, he was every bit the suave and confident man–about–town. Marat knew everyone, everyone knew Marat, and no one would dare mess with him. The girls adored him too. Every time I saw him, he had some new and dazzling siren hanging off his arm, simpering, sighing and giggling inanely. It was so very Hollywood.

Andrei Bogdanov, the intense bespectacled photographer of ladies in lingerie whose work had been scorned by the authorities, was also finding himself in hot demand. Beauty, fashion and femininity were in vogue. These days, few young girls aspired to careers as doctors, teachers, musicians or engineers, opting instead for modelling, striptease, or prostitution. Andrei now had his own glamour photography studio, with queues of would-be supermodels rehearsing sultry pouts, hoping for a chance to hit the big time. He even had a manager, a chirpy Tatar with an impish grin called Azad, who seemed to be permanently glued to the phone, arranging for Andrei to shoot calendars for tyre factories and the like. The savvy Azad had ambitious plans for diversification. As soon as they'd raised the capital they would buy up one of the many ailing factories on Kazan's outskirts. 'We'll buy new machinery from Europe,' he declared, 'and make plastic crockery and cutlery. It's crazy that we spend so much on imported products when we are capable of making them here.'

But Andrei the *artiste* was focused on his photography. As well as his private studio, he also worked at a newly opened School and Agency for Models. Girls aged eleven to fifteen, who a decade ago would have been practising pirouettes in tutus and pointe shoes, were learning to strut the catwalk, starve themselves into emaciation and pose for Andrei's new Nikon. 'Our women here are every bit as beautiful as the French, maybe more so,' he opined. 'I'm sure we will soon be seeing Russian supermodels in Paris.' Meanwhile, he'd made enough to afford his very own VCR, handing over USD$300 for the joy of being able to watch pirated porn in his own home. 'Finally,' he told me, 'the government understands that there's no point in fighting it.'

Tatiana was dejected. 'No one knows what to believe in any more,' she complained. 'People have forgotten how to behave towards each other. We were told that our Soviet ways were wrong, and that the West was right after all. Then look at what we see of the West! This rubbish on the television. And so people think that is the right way to live and try to emulate that lifestyle.'

Or what they could see of it, through the prism of the low-rent southern Californian movie industry. The dynasty of the Tsars had fallen to the dynasty of the communists. Now they in turn had fallen to the Dynasty of Blake Carrington, the wealthy Denver oil baron star of the American prime-time soap. In a few short years Russia had become a dog-eat-dog world, where profit, money and business were no longer dirty words. They seemed to be the only ones that mattered.

16

Siberia, Misha and a Tale of Two Presidents

What's worse than living in Siberia?
Dying in it.

September–October 1995

As fellow descendants of exiles to an 'untamed frontier', Siberians seemed to feel a kinship with Australians. For centuries, the empire had banished its troublemakers eastwards into a territory so vast that Australia could nearly fit into it twice over. From the early eighteenth century, when the so-called Decembrists had challenged the rule of Tsar Nicholas I, to Stalin's deportations of millions into freezing purgatory during the 1930s and 40s, the word Siberia had become synonymous with harsh living conditions, excruciating temperatures, labour camps, ice and snow.

But now it was autumn. Yellowing birch forests alternated with tracts of swampland as the Trans-Siberian trundled 4,492 kilometres from Kazan to Irkutsk, where I was heading to visit Lake Baikal, the world's deepest, oldest and largest freshwater lake.

From my upper bunk in a *platscart* wagon I had a fine vantage point to observe the unfolding dramas of this random captive sample of humanity in the new Russia — and for months afterwards, my heart ached at the memory of the family tragedy I witnessed on that Moscow–Vladivostok express.

I'd joined the train in Ekaterinburg, after a brief stopover to visit friends of Zulfia's in the Ural's city where the last Tsar and his family had been murdered in 1918. A ragged young couple with two small daughters were already aboard and I noticed a stench of urine, bile and vodka pervading the area around their bunks. The parents were passing a dubious-looking bottle back and forth, taking turns at swilling its contents while the little girls looked on. Their almost toothless mother ignored them. The couple began to argue in the slurred and incomprehensible garble of the inebriated, then the man staggered to his feet and swiped at the woman. They fell to the floor and I saw blood seep from her head onto the wagon floor. An old lady nearby beckoned to the children, offering them tea and ginger biscuits.

This routine continued over the next five days as Siberia passed in a blur of forests, fields and villages, punctuated by broad rivers and identical mega-cities of concrete block suburbia — Omsk, Novosibirsk, Krasnoyarsk. The parents would rouse from their alcoholic stupors and glare sulkily at each other until the next opportunity came to purchase more booze from the vendors on the station platforms. They ate nothing but a few gherkins, and their girls, seven-year-old Lena and four-year-old Katya, may as well have not existed. The kindly babushka and I fed them, and she told fairytales to take their minds off their trashed parents. As we headed east the air grew chillier and the girls began to shiver in their thin skivvies and skirts. At Krasnoyarsk Station I bought them some warm clothes, tiny woollen stockings and warm jumpers.

As we approached Irkutsk, the babushka took me aside. 'Can't you take them?' she whispered. 'What will happen to them with parents like this? Adopt them, take them to Australia with you.' I wished I could. They were still babies: beautiful and innocent, with wispy blonde hair and trusting round, blue eyes. Their parents didn't deserve them. I racked my brains to think of some way to save them but couldn't come up with a remotely feasible plan. I disembarked in Irkutsk with a leaden heart. Lena and Katya pressed their small faces against the dirty window as the train pulled out of the station on its way to Vladivostok. I forced back tears.

At Irkutsk Station two young men in smart suits approached me, having decided for some reason that I seemed a good bet to give them directions to a hotel. Yuri and Oleg were nineteen-year-old Muscovites on their first-ever trip out of the capital. Yuri looked like he should have still been in school and Oleg was barely shaving, but they'd been sent to Siberia by a newly established Moscow bank with instructions to sell credit cards to the locals. The one oversight in this otherwise commendable plan was that neither of them seemed to understand how these mysterious plastic rectangles worked. The concept of being able to spend money you didn't have sounded too good to be true. Still, it was a job, and the travel was exciting, if only they could locate their hotel. So I found it for them. In gratitude they offered to smuggle me past the cantankerous key-minding *dezhurnaya* babushka and put a row of cushions on the floor for me to sleep on — a fortuitous offer considering I'd become so blasé about my impromptu wanderings that I hadn't even thought about where I was going to stay once I got here. Without official permission to be in Siberia, I couldn't take the risk of showing my documents to the hotel staff, making check-in impossible.

It was around 9 pm and we were munching into a packet of cardboard flavoured cheese puffs when the room phone started ringing. Yuri answered it and began to blush. 'No, thank you,' he said firmly, putting the receiver down. He looked genuinely shocked. 'It was reception, asking if we'd like some girls.'

A few minutes later it rang again. Oleg answered this time. 'No, really, NO!' he almost yelled.

But it was no use. The phone continued to ring, each time the offers becoming more detailed. 'Listen, we have all kinds of girls, blondes, Asians, tall ones, petite ones. You just tell us what you want and we'll find one for you.'

'But we don't want any,' shouted Oleg.

Finally the receptionist was fed up. 'What is wrong with you guys?' she demanded. 'You're away on a business trip. You are supposed to want girls.'

Yuri and Oleg clearly had a lot to learn about Russian *biznes* etiquette.

Reception then alerted the *dezhurnaya* on our floor to the peculiar behaviour of the two male guests who were refusing to enjoy the local talent. Suspicious and irritable, she barged into the room and sent me packing, out into the cold and dark September night with nothing but a tip that I may find somewhere warm to wait out the frosty night near the airport. Sitting at the bus stop I watched men buying beer, 'from the tap' at a kiosk. Some were handing over empty soft drink bottles to be refilled, but one only had a leaky plastic bag. He lurched away from the kiosk holding his mouth to the bottom of the filthy bag, sucking and gulping furiously.

The bus came, and sure enough there was a cavern of a dormitory by the airport, with a hundred or so canvas stretchers arranged in rows. It was now 2 am. A hunched old night-watch granny, fortunately unaware that she was supposed to check my passport, guided me through the snoring, snuffling, malodorous masses to an empty 'bed'. I curled up under a stinky blanket wondering what the hell I was doing. A few hours later I woke to a chorus of throat clearing and phlegm ejection. I'd come to Irkutsk to visit 'the pearl of Siberia', yet I was rapidly being surrounded by regurgitated oysters. It was time to get out of the doss-house and find the lake.

Baikal is a 50 kilometre hydrofoil trip southeast from Irkutsk, along the Angara River. I found the river station and bought myself a ticket to a village on the western shore of the lake, curiously named Bolshiye Koty (Big Cats). The hydrofoil was almost empty and the leathery captain beckoned me to sit with him.

'The lake has three hundred and thirty-six sons, but only one daughter,' he told me as we whoosed out of Irkutsk. 'That is, there are three hundred and thirty-six tributaries running into the lake, but this one, the Angara, is the only river coming out. From here it flows northwest and joins the Yenisei on its way to the North Sea.'

At the entrance to the lake he pointed to a huge stone jutting out of the water. 'The Shaman stone,' he said, adjusting his threadbare cotton coat. 'The Buryat people say that father Baikal threw that stone at his daughter Angara when she ran away to her lover, the Yenisei.'

Lake Baikal is said to contain up to one fifth of the earth's fresh water, enough to supply the entire world's population with fresh water for forty years. It is home to a range of creatures found nowhere else on the planet and possesses an almost mystical beauty, its crystal clear deep waters fringed in places by steep, densely forested banks, in others by barren rocky shores. So it was only natural that Soviet central planners should select an unspoiled site on its southern shore as the perfect location for the construction of a paper mill. Built in the 1960s to provide high-quality cellulose to the Soviet space program, the Baikalsk Pulp and Paper Mill had been pumping toxic effluent into Baikal's waters ever since, threatening the fragile ecosystem of the lake.

We left the river and entered the lake at the village of Listvyanka. It was a sparkling sunny day and the distant peaks across the lake were clearly visible. The captain waved to the southwest and pointed out Baikalsk. 'The factory still pours its waste into the lake, but no one there wants it to close or they'll lose their jobs.'

Considering the proximity of the factory, the water was miraculously pure. I was half-expecting a nightmarish scene like one I'd seen on my quick trip to Ekaterinburg: a small lake in the city centre so polluted that the surface was covered in a thick brown scum. Oxygen-starved fish made frenzied trails in the gunge as they gulped frantically for air. Many lay dead, and a few gypsy boys were busily scooping up the corpses to bake on their campfire. Baikal was pristine by comparison.

The captain steered the boat northwards to Big Cats, a cluster of wooden houses some 20 kilometres north of Listvyanka. We pulled in to the dilapidated wharf and a slightly built man with a grey beard and woollen beanie — scarily reminiscent of my father — approached the boat on a bicycle. The captain handed him some mail and introduced us. Vadim Maksimov was a marine biologist from the Ukraine who had spent the last twenty-five years in self-imposed exile in Bolshiye Koty, studying the lake's wildlife. He invited me to tea with his wife in their house perched on the hillside above the village. She disappeared into the garden and returned with bowls of fresh raspberries, and we sat on their verandah munching berries and admiring the now misty lake.

Baikal was Maksimov's obsession. To him it was a place of magic. Did I know it was filled with cadaver-eating amphipods, a kind of miniature shrimp that constantly purify the water? If one leaves a dead fish in the water, they will devour it in less than twenty-four hours and nothing will remain but the shadow of a skeleton. And the *nerpas* — the Baikal seal — are a complete mystery. No one knows how they came to be here, many hundreds of kilometres from the ocean.

His research showed that the lake had so far survived the pollution from Baikalsk, but he feared things were going to get much worse. He proffered more raspberries. 'Our biggest threat is the Chinese. Now that Russians have no money, they will sell our forests to the Chinese. They do not respect the environment and it will be destroyed forever.'

Vadim's laboratory was a wooden shed by the house, filled with jars of pickled worms, crustaceans, and fish with faces that belonged in horror movies, as well as dusty books and several microscopes. An old-fashioned typewriter on a desk was surrounded by reams of papers. There were some framed photographs on one wall: a young man in an old-fashioned diving suit, another of the same man standing in front of an odd-looking capsule. It was Vadim's son, also a scientist. 'He is studying the life at the bottom of the lake,' explained Vadim. 'In this capsule it is possible to descend over one mile and stay down long enough to collect samples like these.' Vadim blew some dust from his marinated worm collection. Below the display was a couch-bed, which he said I was welcome to use for the night. Relieved, I gratefully accepted. I'd become so accustomed to Russian hospitality that last night's misadventure had come as a rude shock.

I told Vadim about my father, and how when I was a child, each year he would take the family to live on a homemade boat on the Great Barrier Reef. He'd built his own underwater camera housings, tripods and microphones and was ardently devoted to filming the life on the reef. Watching him wrestle a heavy Arriflex camera and miles of 16 mm film had completely put me off ever wanting to make documentaries. But all of a sudden I wished I knew how to. Baikal was so extraordinary, and Vadim so passionate about it, that I wanted to learn how to tell his story on film.

Bolshiye Koty was like a flashback to the old days, isolated enough to have remained relatively immune to the influences sweeping the big cities. The village store was almost completely bare, but it didn't worry the few inhabitants of Big Cats, who were mostly self-sufficient. They fished for *omul,* a species of salmon abundant in the lake, and grew their own vegetables. A couple of cows wandered around the few dirt tracks between the houses and chickens hopped over piles of rusting machinery. Everyone knew everyone else, and their business.

Among the village's colourful characters was Elena Perelomova, a sixty-something former scientist. She lived in Irkutsk but her dacha, a two-room cottage with metal bunks, was here at Bolshiye Koty. Elena had the Asiatic features of the Buryats — the indigenous peoples of the region — and radiated a warm, gold-toothed smile. She'd never met an Australian, but had an intimate knowledge of Malaysia after having worked in a department dedicated to analysing satellite maps of the nations of the world. Elena had been assigned a section of Southeast Asia to monitor over a period of several decades. Now retired, she was spending more time out here, making raspberry jam and pickling tomatoes. It was hard to imagine this dear old lady had spent her working life spying on far-off lands. But not as strange as the stuffed head on her wall above her bed. It was some kind of cat, perhaps one of the village namesake Big Cats? It was certainly big — nowhere near the size of a Siberian tiger — but what made it truly frightening were its long protruding canine teeth. I should have known better than to comment on it. Seconds later Elena had removed the unfortunate beast's head from the wall and was pressing it into my hands. 'Please, take it with you back to Australia,' she implored. '*Na pamyat.*'

On my return trip to Moscow, one of my *sputniks* was an ethnic Russian descendant of an exile from European Russia. 'You know,' he said, cracking open a vodka bottle as the train pulled out of Irkutsk, 'we have a lot in common. Your country was built by convicts and criminals. So was Siberia. I propose a toast, to eternal friendship between Siberians and Australians.'

★ ★ ★

Many thousands of kilometres of train tracks later, Olga met me at the Moscovsky Station in St Petersburg, carrying a pair of windscreen wipers and a car radio. She was now the proud owner of a metallic blue Ford Sierra and was taking no chances of having bits of it pilfered by petty criminals. She had just returned from another trip to Australia with her parents where her father had been conducting the West Australian Symphony Orchestra. Sadly, her grandmother, Vera Nikolayevna, had passed away two years earlier, in 1993, and she was living on her own with Rizhok the cat in the family flat on Opochinina Street.

On my second night back in St Petersburg, Olga invited me to dinner with her new boyfriend, Misha (Mikhail), a Muscovite who also worked at IKEA. They chose a recently opened upmarket Indian restaurant called Tandoor, just across from the Admiralty Building near the Winter Palace. The last time I'd been in this area was three years ago, when Olga's father, Vladimir, had shown us the 10 metre square room he'd lived in as a young boy after the Great Patriotic War. Fifty years later we were eating real rogan josh served by real Indians with real turbans just one street away.

Misha was twenty-nine, with intelligent eyes and neat brown hair. He was shorter than Olga, but as she was a whisker shy of six foot, so were most people. Misha's mother, Galina, was a public servant and his father an engineer for a department responsible for the manufacture of oil and gas pipelines. Misha had grown up in Moscow, been the best Young Pioneer in school, and entered the Moscow Institute of Chemical Engineering in 1983. His major was a subject called 'chemical technology', which I gathered was a euphemism for the study of chemical and nuclear weapons. This institute, he explained, was one of a few places in Moscow which offered a 'military education'. Such an education came with the immeasurable benefit of exemption from the usual compulsory two years of military service. As the USSR was embroiled in a lethal campaign in Afghanistan at the time, this was indeed a matter of life and death.

'Nobody wanted to go to the army, and especially not to Afghanistan,' said Misha. 'We were told that we were fighting in Afghanistan for "peace in all the world and for friendship between peoples". But those who were returning from the front couldn't readjust to civilian life. Many had terrible physical injuries, others developed paranoia, imagining that the streets of Moscow were filled with enemies. Since childhood we'd been told we should "be happy that we were born here in the Soviet Union, and not in America". We had to be patriotic citizens, ready to defend our motherland. When I was very young I believed it. I remember an old communist came to our school and told us how to hide our Communist Party cards in secret pockets in our pants, just in case enemies came and tried to take them. I went straight home and asked my mother to sew such a pocket.'

Instead of being dispatched to the front in Kandahar, Misha was drilled by his officers in chemical and nuclear weapons studies four days a week, and learned soldiering skills on the fifth. After four years of this, and three months in a military base, he became a reserve lieutenant. But by now he knew better than to believe the anti-Western propaganda he'd been fed. His father had travelled abroad for work in the early 70s — accompanied naturally by the requisite KGB minders — and returned with stories that life beyond the USSR was nothing like they'd been told. In fact, his father had reported, it was rather good, something young Misha had pondered often while queuing for hours to purchase himself such simple childhood treasures as a Rubik's Cube. But he wasn't going to challenge the system, especially after one of his university philosophy professors was sacked for promoting the virtues of democracy. Instead Misha learned about chemical and nuclear warfare.

'You know, even though it was the time of the Cold War, we all knew there was no chance of nuclear war with the Americans. The Russians knew as well as the Americans that if there was to be a war, the whole planet would be affected and the nuclear fallout would last for thousands of years.'

When Chernobyl's nuclear reactor exploded in April 1986, it was Misha's officer lecturers who were dispatched to lead the clean-up operations. Luckily for Misha, he still had two years of study to go, otherwise he too would have been sent into the danger zone. When he'd finished in 1988 he was posted to a scientific research centre in Moscow to work on 'super-conductors'. He hated the place and his work and begged to be sacked. But rules were rules and Soviet law stated that all graduates would be sent to wherever the state wished for the first three years of their working lives. So he arrived at work at 11 am, left at 4 pm and studied English and Swedish to fill in time. Exactly three years later he left the job and found work as an interpreter.

In 1992 he went to live and study in Sweden. With no Russians around, his Swedish and English improved rapidly. After a year in Sweden his mother called from Moscow. Things were so bad in Russia, she told him, that he shouldn't bother coming home. But he didn't want to stay and began writing to different companies to ask if they could use his services in Moscow. In September 1993 he went for an interview at IKEA's Moscow office. He was offered a job, just as all hell broke out in the Russian capital.

For well over a year, Tsar Boris had been wrestling with his parliamentary deputies in the Duma (the lower house of parliament) for control over government, policy, banking and property. In March 1993, Yeltsin announced to the nation via a televised address that he was granting himself 'special powers' in order to push through his increasingly unpopular 'reforms'. The furious deputies attempted to remove him from office through impeachment, but didn't quite manage the two-thirds majority required. On 21 September, Yeltsin proclaimed that he was disbanding parliament and scrapping the constitution. He would rule by decree until a new parliament could be elected in December. Despite the obviously undemocratic nature of his actions, Yeltsin received strong support from the West, who believed he was trying to speed up the transition to a functioning market economy. Russia's Supreme Soviet, however, declared Yeltsin's act unconstitutional and swore in his vice-president, Alexander Rutskoy, as acting president. For several days, Russia had two presidents. Tens of thousands of civilians took to the streets in support of the deputies and in protest against corruption and the decline in living standards for which they held Yeltsin and his cronies responsible.

The mass uprising continued to grow into early October. The recalcitrant deputies refused to leave the White House, and Yeltsin responded by cutting off their phone lines, electricity and hot water. After much negotiation, Yeltsin won the support of the army generals and interior ministry troops, and ordered them to seal off the parliament with barricades and wire. But the excitement soon turned nasty. Misha was on his way for a haircut, driving up Leninsky Prospekt — the main arterial road running from the centre to the southwest, about three kilometres from parliament — when he saw the tanks come rumbling past. He sped home and turned on the TV, in time to see those very tanks in front of the White House. 'I thought it was a war. There was a huge queue of people coming out from the metro to defend the White House ... old and young, men and women, and they were all worked up. It was scary, but at the same time it was exciting, something new to see people protesting.'

President Number 2, Alexander Rutskoy, cheered on the crowds from the White House balcony, urging them to take control of the mayor's office and national television centre at Ostankino, some ten kilometres north of the city centre. Ruslan Khasbulatov, the speaker of the Supreme Soviet, called for the Kremlin to be stormed. By 3 October, several people were dead and many wounded. The country seemed on the brink of civil war. Yeltsin declared a state of emergency and sent interior ministry troops to defend Ostankino. Sixty-two people were killed that night. The television centre was severely damaged and television stations went off the air.

The next day Yeltsin ordered army tanks to shell the White House. By 5 October, the upper floors were burning. Troops began to occupy the building, floor by floor, forcing the deputies out. Rutskoy and Khasbulatov stayed on, before finally being taken away in buses. In the chaotic streets below, troops fired on unarmed protesters. By afternoon the uprising was completely suppressed, at the 'official' cost of 187 lives and 437 wounded. Unofficial estimates were closer to 2,000. This bloody 'Second October Revolution' showed that Russia was very much a presidential regime, and that he who controls the military controls the country.

Misha feared that IKEA and other Western companies might pack up and leave Russia altogether. But IKEA stayed, and on 18 October he began his new job as a delivery planner, liaising with suppliers from all over Russia to organise the transport of raw materials to the seaport in St Petersburg and beyond.

Following the storming of the White House, Yeltsin moved quickly to ban or sack everyone who had supported parliament: leftist and nationalist parties, regional councils that had opposed him, newspapers, even the chairman of the Constitutional Court. Rutskoy and Khasbulatov were charged with 'organising mass disorders' and imprisoned. He then announced that a new parliament would be elected in December, and a referendum held on a new constitution.

'Russia needs order,' Yeltsin had pompously declared to the people in a televised address to present his proposed new constitution. It would give him power almost on a par with the Tsars: he would be able to appoint the prime minister, government deputies, military leadership and members of a new security council, regardless of parliament's wishes. He could veto any bill and he couldn't be impeached. He could also dissolve parliament. That December, Yeltsin's new constitution was approved.

Olga had once had high hopes for Yeltsin. 'I thought he was very much one of the people. I heard a story that when he was the first secretary in Ekaterinburg he decided to improve public transport operations. So he took the person responsible for that in the city and forced him to come to his workplace by public transport. Then they realised how bad it was. So, we believed he could do a lot for the country.'

Now they were both unimpressed. 'Gorbachev was a weak man for the USSR,' said Misha. 'He didn't know what he was doing and was only afraid of losing power. But Yeltsin is a bastard. He is destroying the state. This is not democracy. There are no laws, only corruption. Okay, so there was bribery in the USSR, but it was nothing … kopecks … compared to what is happening now.'

Even Misha was starting to look back at the USSR with nostalgia. 'It was a good time, everyone was reasonably happy and everyone lived more or less the same. There were no poor people, and people just didn't think about money. It was safe on the streets and people didn't think about when they would eat. If you didn't work, the police would take you and first encourage you, then force you to work. If you were still lazy and drank too much, they would send you 100 kilometres south to Mozhaisk.'

Misha hadn't been lazy, and when IKEA was forced to close its Moscow office in July 1995, he was one of only three Russian staff members retained and relocated to St Petersburg, to work in the same office as Olga. They'd been together now for a few months and Olga was looking for a new home for her cat so she could move into his place.

As we demolished our surprisingly delicious Indian meal, they described a recent business trip to Sweden with some Russians from the provinces. 'They were amazed,' said Misha, 'to see "serve yourself" sugar, sauce and salt packets in Swedish restaurants.'

'How can this be?' they had asked him. 'This would be impossible in Russia. People would just take it all.'

Misha laughed. 'You know what? They were right.'

I looked around at the well-heeled and snappily dressed clientele of the Tandoor. Not a single one was pilfering condiments. But considering our bill for three was equivalent to a couple of months of the pension, I supposed anyone who could afford to walk through the door wouldn't need to.

Olga and Misha invited me to join them on a weekend trip to the village of Repino where they were pursuing a new hobby: horseriding. We drove northwest out of St Petersburg and along the Gulf of Finland, eventually pulling up at a grand former Dom Otdykha (House of Rest) picturesquely situated in a forest near the hamlet. 'Rest houses' had been a Soviet institution — a kind of compulsory team bonding camp. Every workers' collective — from propagandists to factory labourers — had their own designated place to 'relax' together with their colleagues, and this one at Repino had once been the holiday house for the cinematographers of Leningrad's official film studio, Lenfilm.

I imagined we would be taking a gentle trek through the woods, delighting in the passing scenery while sitting back on a placid steed. Instead, I discovered we had come to a riding school. A horse-faced woman swishing a whip showed us to our nags. For two hours we trotted round and round a small ring while she bellowed commands: 'Stand on your left leg, now right leg, face backwards, forwards, no hands, no feet!' If we were too slow to change positions, which I invariably was, she cracked her whip to make the horses go faster. It was excruciating. By the time we were allowed off, my vertebrae were so crushed I could barely walk and Olga was grimacing, clutching her bruised buttocks. Misha grinned at us as we hobbled back to the car and remarked cheerily, 'That was fun, wasn't it?'

Back in St Petersburg I caught up with Olga's friend Masha. She had remarried, this time to a half-Uzbek called Kim, and they were living in her grandparents' old flat, which she had inherited after the death of her grandfather. She had just given birth to a baby son, Yegor. I was amazed to hear that at the hospital she had been considered an 'old mother', and as such required special observation. She was twenty-six.

'In the Asian tradition girls should marry at fifteen or sixteen,' she explained. 'And in Russia, eighteen or nineteen is considered the optimal age for marriage and childbirth. So at twenty-six I am an old woman already.'

Financially, Masha and Kim were struggling. As a teacher she earned a pittance, and Kim only occasionally picked up casual work. Their flat was rundown, wallpaper peeling and pipes dripping, yet they couldn't afford to pay for repairs. And while Masha had realised some of her mountain climbing dreams, she was limping badly after a knee reconstruction following a skiing accident.

Natasha was also finding money matters a challenge, but seemed upbeat after finally completing her degree at Leningrad State University. She still practically lived on the university campus, teaching Russian to Chinese students and working on a thesis about social linguistics and Russian semantics. Natasha understood that she could have been far better off in a job with a company, Russian or foreign, but her passion for linguistics won out.

After four months in Russia I returned to Australia and enrolled in an English teaching degree. I spent a summer at Melbourne's Latrobe University doing an intensive TEFL (Teaching English as a Foreign Language) course, then headed back overseas. I visited an old friend in Japan and hitchhiked around that country, then went to Vietnam to meet up with some Belgian ethnographic film-makers I'd met in London, who I hoped would enlighten me on the mysteries of documentary making. I learned precisely nothing about film-making, but did discover the importance of having proper permits when shooting in lands ruled by totalitarian regimes. We were arrested in a highland village for illegally filming and put on a night train back to Hanoi — escorted by a guard — to be dealt with by the authorities. I was not happy. I hadn't known that they didn't have official permission to film in the area and was annoyed about having unwittingly been put in this position. Halfway back to Hanoi, we made a brief midnight stop at a small regional station. Noticing the guard and Belgians were all asleep I grabbed my bag and snuck off the train into a pitch black village. I eventually found my way to the Chinese border and walked into China with no idea what I was doing or where I was going — or what happened to the Belgians. Four months later I rode out of the western Chinese province of Xinjiang, and over the Khunjerab Pass into Pakistan, on a shoddily made mountain bike with only three working gears. It was now October 1996.

17

Rafael and the Mutant Elephant

Strange things happen. I was riding down the Karakoram Highway in Pakistan's Northern Areas on my defective Chinese bike, when I stopped at a village in the Hindu Kush Mountains, near the Batura Glacier. I noticed a backpacker with a small video camera and we got to chatting. Martin was Canadian, travelling around the world making short films for a TV show in Canada called *Race Around the World*, or whatever that is in French. He and seven others were traversing the planet, spending ten days in each of ten countries, producing a four-minute film in each one. It sounded extraordinary.

The next day I rang my mother in Melbourne. After we got past her initial fury at my failure to let her know where I'd been for the past six months, she told me about an ad she'd seen, seeking applicants for a new ABC TV series. It was to be called *Race Around the World*. I couldn't believe it. The ad asked for applicants to send a four-minute film to show what they could do. I bought a cheap Video 8 camera at a market in Lahore, smuggled in via Dubai to avoid import taxes, and tried to work out how to use it. In India I shot an embarrassingly amateur story about cows, found a place to edit it in Delhi, and with one finger painstakingly typed an application in a grungy 'communications office', the first time I'd been near a keyboard since

Basic Keyboarding classes in Year 9. On the eve of 1997, I sent my dismal cow film off to Sydney and headed out into the Rajasthan Desert to try to forget all about it.

A month later I was on my way back to Australia to do a crash-course in documentary making with fifteen other *Race Around the World* hopefuls at the Film and Television School in Sydney. And in April I set off on a 100-day spin around the planet, passing through Latin America, Mexico, Africa, the Middle East and Central Asia. Almost eighty flights later and nine stories out of ten into the trip, I was running to catch a plane from the Uzbek capital, Tashkent, to Bangkok, when my foot slipped into a pothole in the car park. My ankle snapped and instantly swelled up like an eggplant. I hopped into the airport terminal, dragging my possessions behind me, trying not to scream with pain. The airport nurse, a beefy peroxided Russian, tried to jab a needle into me. I yelped and pushed her off.

The flight was agony. I was wheeled off the plane and dispatched to a Bangkok hospital where an X-ray failed to reveal the fracture I would discover several months later. After a week on my back in a fluoro-lit, windowless white room in a backpacker's joint watching aerobics classes on Thai TV, I managed to stumble to the lift. The two young men already in it eyed my crutches curiously. One spoke with a distinctly Russian accent. By the time we reached the ground floor we were all shaking our heads in amazement.

Rafael was a Tatar and astounded to find that I'd not only heard of, but had been to, his republic of Mari El. Even more unbelievable was that the one place I had been — the village of Ilet, population 200, where Tatiana and Anatoly had their country house — was the very village where Rafael had grown up. He was twenty-five, with striking pale blue eyes, pale skin and black hair. His friend Akhmed was a 21-year-old Ingush from a village near the Chechen border, with wide brown eyes and a boyish grin. Both were studying at an Islamic university in Kuala Lumpur, along with ten other students from various Islamic areas of the former Soviet Union.

Nothing appeared particularly odd about a group of young men from Muslim republics being sponsored to study Islamic theology in

Malaysia. I assumed it was all part of the great opening to the outside world of the former Lenin-worshipping empire. To me, a worldly 28-year-old, Akha and Rafael seemed a couple of young innocents, lucky enough to find a way to travel beyond their native borders. Our light-hearted interaction mostly revolved around the inseparable pair teaching me Russian slang Olga had been too polite to mention, and our mutual alarm at what Thai girls could do on bar tops.

But their situation wasn't quite as straightforward as it first appeared. I gleaned from their conversation that they were on the run from a Malaysian businessman who'd done them over. They were both skint and facing expulsion from the university; however, going home without a degree wasn't an option. Rafael was the first person from his republic ever to study abroad and he was aiming high. In fact, he declared with a wry grin, he wasn't going back to Mari El to be anything less than the president of the republic.

Rafael was his mother's only child, the first of six of his father. He'd grown up alone with his mum and had started working at the age of ten, as a shepherd's assistant during the summer months, taking the village sheep, cows and goats out to pasture at 5 am and returning home at 9 pm. Often, he said, he had to defend the flocks from wolves, especially in autumn when the cubs were leaving their lairs. Sometimes he would have to sacrifice a sheep to a pack of wolves circling his herd. For his labours he initially earned himself a monthly wage of ninety roubles. By the age of sixteen, he was working alone, raking in 1,500 roubles per month, an astonishing sum for one so young. The average adult wage was around 140 roubles.

By the time he was called up to serve in the army in 1990 Rafael had saved 30,000 roubles, at a time when the USSR's flashest car, the Volga sedan, cost 15,000 roubles. Rafael wanted to buy a couple, but his mother was against it. As a good Communist Party member on a standard wage, she thought it would look bad if her young son was driving around in a flashy vehicle. When Rafael returned from military service in the Siberian city of Krasnoyarsk his entire childhood savings had been swallowed by hyperinflation. 'It was the blackest day of my life,' he recalled bitterly. 'I spent two years serving my country and came home to find I had nothing left from all those years of work.' His mother was sick with guilt. 'She felt so bad that she barely stopped crying for two years.'

During his time in the army Rafael had learned to cut hair. 'Everyone had to learn some profession. I had a choice of welding or hairdressing. I saw some guy cutting other people's hair and decided I didn't want him to touch mine. So I went to an officer and told him I would learn hairdressing. The hair clippers had been modified to be used for tattooing, by removing the top part and replacing it with a nail to make the cuts in the skin. So I had to learn to use scissors only.' He flicked his fringe, which slid straight back down over his face.

'After army I understood one thing ... that I have to leave my village because everyone there just drinks and does nothing.' So in 1992, Rafael moved to Kazan. On a visit to a mosque to make an offering, in the hope it would lead him to greater things, he met Valiulla Hazrat, the Deputy Chief Mufti of the Republic of Tatarstan. At that time Valiulla was busily translating religious texts he had collected from old Tatars into modern Tatar language, then printing and distributing them. He needed an assistant and offered Rafael a job. Soon after, a group of Arabs had come to Kazan to recruit students to study Islam abroad, and Valiulla Hazrat suggested that Rafael take their test.

Rafael's mother was Muslim and he knew the answers. But after doing the test he heard that no one was going to be sent anywhere. 'I followed those Arabs back to Moscow, sat there in their office and said I wouldn't leave until they sent me somewhere. All I knew was, I didn't want to go back to my village in Mari El. They made me pray with them and practise Islam.'

Rafael winked at a pretty Thai waitress and stroked his clean-shaven chin. 'I knew that it would be an Arab university, and I told those Arabs that I would study religion. I would have told them anything. Finally they agreed. But then I had a problem with the Russians. In the army I'd been sent to guard a secret installation. When I finished they made me sign a paper to say that I wouldn't leave Russia for five years. It was 1993 and I'd only left the army a year before. The KGB called me and asked what I was planning to do in Malaysia.'

(The Soviet security apparatus had been through a number of metamorphoses since the USSR collapsed and was now called the FSB, Federal Security Service. But Rafael still preferred its old, more sinister acronym.)

'I hadn't thought what to say so I told them I was going to be an artist — my name is Rafael, just like the famous painter — and that's what came into my head at the time. So the KGB guy asked me to draw an elephant with my left hand, and of course it was terrible. He told me it was ugly and they wouldn't let me leave the country. I went back to my village and was very angry. On the day that I was supposed to fly to Malaysia the KGB called me and said I had to come to Yoshkar-Ola (the capital of Mari El republic) immediately. They said that if I promised to give them information, then I would be allowed to go. So I agreed and went to Malaysia.'

Years would pass before I thought to grill Rafael further and ask the question: 'So who were the Arabs and why were they so generously paying for you to go to Malaysia?'

It was January 2007 and we were having breakfast in a fancy Japanese restaurant in Kazan. Rafael gave me one of his sardonic, almost conspiratorial smiles and smoothed his pinstriped suit. 'Put it this way. They weren't very known in the world back then, but they are now. A certain group wanting to spread an Islamic revolution in the world and it's best that my boss doesn't know about it or I'll lose my job.'

'Al Qaeda?' I suggested. 'Jemaah Islamiah?'

'Like I said, I think it's best not to say too much. But they weren't wild ones. They had normal eyes, not wild eyes. Even so, when I was in Malaysia I heard that they had been kicked out of Russia because they were Wahhabis [ultra-conservative Sunni Muslims].'

He sipped his coffee and went on.

'The KGB agents were everywhere. Every foreign embassy is full of them, even now, and they have to know what every Russian is doing. But Akha never realised. Russians would come up to him on the beach and ask him questions about the students, "What are they doing?" "Are they going crazy with this Islam?" The KGB guys are good psychologists and they tried to find out about our views.'

As far as I could tell, the KGB wouldn't have learned a lot from Akha and Rafael. The Arabs weren't giving them enough money to live on so they had found jobs in a hair salon. Rafael's blue eyes also scored him modelling work, and Akha's European looks got him a role as an extra in a movie with Catherine Zeta-Jones and another with Jackie Chan. The Dagestani students received good money to crawl around in the jungle dressed as UN soldiers for another movie. By the time I met them, in 1997, they hadn't attended classes in months and were saving to 'buy' a diploma to take home when their four years were up.

Then again, I might have been very naïve. Perhaps the KGB were right to suspect them of involvement in smuggling Russian nuclear, chemical and biological weapons into the hands of Al Qaeda? Perhaps there were two religious zealots lurking behind those smooth chins? But listening to them discuss the merits of the scantily clad Thai girls, somehow I didn't think so.

I shot my final story for *Race Around the World* in a Buddhist monastery in northern Laos, dragging myself around on crutches, counting down the days until it would all be over. By August I was back in Australia and immediately began plotting to find a way to get back to Russia. Eventually the Executive Producer of another ABC program, *Foreign Correspondent*, agreed to send me to Russia to shoot some 'postcard' stories. They would pay my airfares and lend me a camera, but for the rest I was on my own. Yet again Olga arranged an invitation for me. This time I was a 'consultant for a woodworking factory, coming to inspect a plant in the town of Syktyvkar some 1,000 kilometres northeast of Moscow'.

It was now November 1997. On my way I stopped to visit Akha and Rafael in Kuala Lumpur. They'd blown their savings in Thailand and were working as hairwashers in a beauty salon. Neither was in any hurry to go home. Rafael remained adamant that he would settle for no less a position than President of Mari El, so somehow he had to get a degree, whether or not he knew anything about what it was in. Akha's homeland of Ingushetia was teeming with refugees fleeing the brutal war in neighbouring Chechnya, and work prospects were grim.

He also knew his father was trying to find him a grim. 'I'm just not ready for all that,' he moaned to Rafael and me. He was even afraid to visit his family, worried that he would be roped in to a shotgun marriage and forced to stay. After sampling the high life of the glittering Southeast Asian capitals, life in his small native village of Sleptsovsk held little appeal.

On the plane back to Moscow, I encountered yet another face of the new Russia.

Stanislav Kucher was in his mid-twenties and presented a weekly current affairs discussion program on TV6 called *The Observer*. He couldn't believe I hadn't heard of him. 'Stas', as he instructed me to call him in a smooth American-accented drawl, had noticed my camera bag and asked if I'd been covering the same story they had: the Arms Expo in Malaysia where Rosoboronexport — Russia's defence export agency — had just concluded a number of sizeable deals to provide fighter aircraft, attack helicopters, missiles, tanks, and artillery to several nations in the area.

I shrank into my seat and confessed that I was merely going to Kazan to shoot a story about body art. Nevertheless, Stas invited me to 'have a drink' with his crew, who were lolling at the back of the plane in a haze of cigarette smoke, having in true Russian fashion seen a long trip as an occasion to get blotto and pass out. I counted four empty bottles of Black Label Johnnie Walker on the floor and two corpselike bodies slumped across some empty seats.

Stas introduced me to his colleagues, all seven of them. Apparently it took eight people to file a couple of reports: a producer, director, sound recordist, two cameramen (now snoring loudly), editor, and a wardrobe/make-up girl, plus Stanislav of course.

'So where's your crew then?' Stas asked me. 'I suppose you're picking one up in Moscow.'

'Umm, no … I shoot myself while I'm doing the interviews.'

Far from being impressed by my multitasking abilities, this revelation clearly diminished my status in Stas's eyes. In Russia, one did not command respect by doing many things at once, one did so by being important enough to delegate as much as possible to others — all of course except the really crucial part, which was having your mug on the box each week.

In Moscow, Nadia, who I was staying with, was astounded to hear that the 'famous' Stanislav Kucher had invited me for a drink on the plane. 'Oh, how wonderful! I watch him every week. He's so intelligent and handsome.' She almost turned to jelly when he called the next day. 'Perhaps he likes you?' she suggested breathlessly as she handed me the receiver. Whatever he thought, he did send his chauffeur to pick me up and deliver me to the tower at the Ostankino television centre complex in Moscow's north where he worked. At the revolving restaurant at the top of the tower he ordered the most expensive dishes and paid a violin and accordion duo to serenade us. Then he told me about his wife, Natalia, a beautiful ex-Olympic swimmer who'd studied in the States and was now writing a doctorate and lecturing at a Moscow institute. It was all very strange.

But it was to become stranger still. With his stated motivation of 'introducing me to people with connections', Stas continued to call and invite me to various parties and gatherings. I even had to buy a dress for a glitzy Christmas party at the Moscow Hotel, one of the city's grandest, where, he assured me, I would 'meet lots of arms dealers and politicians'. And so I did — so slippery and smooth they were almost dripping. Looking at them in their Armani suits with gold cufflinks I couldn't help but wonder what and who they'd ripped off, bumped off or paid off to have ended up here.

The 'thieves code' had undergone some revision in the past few years. Once, ownership of property by a thief had been punishable by death or mutilation. These days the crooks occupied prestige real estate, preferably with Kremlin views. A weekender on the Côte d'Azur and a private yacht were essential. Tattoos were out, so was prison time, while designer suits and chunky gold jewellery were in. And instead of shunning official authority, the massive profits of organised crime were purchasing political influence and a veneer of wholesomeness. A well-placed fat wad of cash or bank deposit could go a long way to keeping an illegal *biznes* ticking over. There was no way anyone on an official government salary could afford an Armani suit without a little help from his friends, and if that meant turning a blind eye to a prostitution ring, drug cartel, or extortion racket, then so be it.

Considering the extreme poverty of most of the country's population, the party's decadence was almost obscene. Waiters hovered amongst the throngs, pouring Bollinger into champagne flutes and proffering gold trays of hors d'oeuvres: huge dollops of red and black caviar on mini wafers, swirls of smoked fish and a multitude of other exotic delicacies. The women glittered with jewels and gold, extravagantly attired in Versace, Dolce & Gabbana and whichever other haute couture happened to be currently in vogue. Bling ruled.

I took a deep breath and smiled politely. A little routine began: Stas would introduce me as an Australian journalist (which was quite a stretch), boorish Mr Slime would make a quip about kangaroos and Australia having no winter, before laughing loudly into his champagne and wandering off to ogle the more seductively dressed Russian women. No one was about to drunkenly give me any juicy tidbits of information, and I couldn't think of anything diplomatic to say. Not that it really mattered. I was only here in Russia to do a story about body painting.

The bottomless Bollinger and sycophantic schmoozing eventually managed to bore even socialite Stas. He summoned his faithful friend and cameraman, Mitya, to take us on to a friend's flat to continue drinking. I was almost sick with terror as Mitya sped and skidded on the iced-over roads, completely oblivious to traffic lights and road rules. For the first time ever in Russia, I committed the grave offence of doing up my seatbelt. Normally this would be the direst of insults to a Russian driver, a sign that one did not trust their driving skills. Until now I had resisted the urge to put sense before pride, but not tonight. I still don't know how we didn't end up wrapped around a lamp post, nose down in the river or plastered onto the side of a building. Mitya was so drunk that I even managed to beat him at Scrabble … in Russian. The hostess was the only other remotely sober person around, and she was busily packing designer outfits into designer luggage while the drunks got louder and louder. She and her husband were off to Switzerland the next day.

'How nice! Is it for work, or holiday?' I asked.

Everyone laughed.

'They're going to visit their money of course. Why else do Russians go to Switzerland?' Stas said, looking at me as if I were a complete idiot.

Hanging out with Stanislav did little for my confidence, but it did offer an intriguing insight into the relationship between Russian politicians, business and the media.

'I'm going to show you our new apartment,' he announced on another occasion, between simultaneous conversations on two mobile phones in which he loudly dropped names of prominent Moscow politicians.

Stas's 'new' flat was in a grand Stalin-era building, with large rooms, high ceilings and tall windows fronting onto the prestigious Leninsky Prospekt. It wasn't so much a new flat, as an old one that had been completely gutted and presently in the process of what appeared to be a rather up-market refurbishment, with parquet floors, chandeliers and mountains of marble.

'So what do you think? It's going to be great when it's finished.'

I nodded, trying to compute the value of such a place in Moscow's dizzy real estate market. 'TV presenters must do very well here!'

'Well, you know, my salary is not so much really ... but you know how things work here. You help someone, they help you.'

It seemed quite simple. With his high-profile show on TV6, Stanislav was perfectly placed to sell the ideas, policies and virtues of the highest bidders. His mobiles rang constantly with calls from press secretaries and even politicians themselves to whom he chatted casually, on a first name basis, lining up 'exclusives' for next week's show. In the meantime his meagre salary was topped up by those grateful for his sympathetic spin, which fans like Nadia believed to be balanced and honest journalism. It was, he assured me, all normal practice. Otherwise how else could he afford his flat, renovations, or dinner in the tower at Ostankino?

I shouldn't have been surprised. It was solely thanks to a compliant media that Tsar Boris was still in power at all. Before the June 1996 presidential elections, the permanently inebriated and barely-conscious Yeltsin was one of the most loathed people in the country, with an approval rating in the single digits. Blamed for everything from the rise in violent crime, rampant corruption, the collapse of medical services, scarcity of food and fuel to plummeting life expectancy, there seemed to be no chance on earth that Boris Nikolayevich Yeltsin could possibly be re-elected as president of the Russian Federation. Except of course that it was in the best interests of his astronomically wealthy oligarch cronies to keep him there. So realising that Boris's future was looking about as dull as his alcohol-addled eyeballs, his mogul mate Boris Berezovsky decided to help out.

Berezovsky, 'the original oligarch', had begun his phenomenal business career selling computer software and Mercedes cars, before moving on to commandeer the assets of the state car manufacturer, Avtovaz; the state airline, Aeroflot; Sibneft oil; most of Russia's aluminium; and even the state's most influential TV station, ORT, as well as Stas's station, TV6. By cosying up to Yeltsin's chief of staff, Berezovsky had become close to the president's inner circle, the so-called 'Family'. With Yeltsin's re-election chances seeming as likely as him giving up the booze, Berezovsky swung into action, pulling out all stops to orchestrate the campaign. He formed a group of seven oligarchs who between them owned most of Russia's media outlets and ordered them to schedule 'all Yeltsin all the time'.

The bewildered Yeltsin was dragged back and forth across the country, making his best effort to stay awake for the cameras and mutter barely coherent phrases about the need to keep the communists from returning to power. His near catatonic image was beamed across the country and commentators began talking him up. Opponents were banned from speaking to the media, and any coverage of their policies was spun into scaremongering.

'Vote from your heart. Yeltsin will save us from the communists', was the message.

Incredibly, the manipulation worked its magic, and by the 16 June election, Yeltsin managed to garner enough votes to keep his job. It was a miraculous achievement by the propaganda machine, that a people whose lives had been so devastated by the policies of one man could be convinced to vote him in again.

Nadia was disgusted in her countrymen. 'How could they vote for him, after what he has done to this country?'

Life for her was a far cry from the wild excesses I'd been witnessing courtesy of Stanislav. Nadia still counted every rouble. Materially, little had changed for her, although her nephew had sent money for a new fridge, new wallpaper for the kitchen, and the ultimate luxury: a washing machine. For the first time in her life, Nadia didn't have to lean over a bucket in the bath to wash her clothes. But she was increasingly afraid of the world outside and too scared to leave her flat at night. She told tales of violent drug-crazed youths roaming the neighbourhood, robberies, muggings of the elderly, and even murders. Whenever I was out I called her constantly to reassure her that I was still alive.

But Nadia's life had improved in some small ways. She was at last able to learn about her religion, through a Jewish club that had opened in Moscow in 1995. A fledgling Jewish Theatre Company called Shalom had taken over a Soviet-era cinema building and Nadia was now a devoted audience member. She took me to see a play, and proudly showed me the new library and school that were part of the club. The rabbi was teaching her and others about the various Jewish festivals and rituals. Pesach and Hanukkah were her favourites, and although after a lifetime of Russian traditions she couldn't really get used to celebrating them, she was simply excited to learn what they were. 'Jewish life exists here now,' she said happily. New synagogues were opening up across the country, a Russian factory made matzoh, and Jews no longer had to hide their ethnicity.

She had also recently joined the Memorial society. Established a few weeks after Gorbachev had given a speech publicly denouncing Stalin in November 1987, Memorial had begun the momentous task of amassing data on the details of his victims. Branches were set up in the major cities and Gulag towns and the horrifying statistics of Stalinism were finally brought into the open. Many tens of millions had died:

executed, from starvation or torture in camps, or fighting the war. And then there were millions more survivors, like Nadia's father, Khaim, whose lives had been needlessly destroyed. It meant a lot to Nadia that her family's suffering had finally been recognised in this way.

Nadia's other wonderful news was that Canadian Tina was back in Russia and living in Moscow. It even looked like she was going to be around for a while. After completing a Masters degree in Russian and East European studies at Oxford, she had moved to Moscow and found a job editing a newsletter called *Capital Markets Russia*. She'd then met and married the Kiwi banker Stephen Jennings, who had once advised Chubais on the sale of the Bolshevik Biscuit Factory. His investment bank, Renaissance Capital, was doing spectacularly well, so much so that he had two full-time bodyguards shadowing him everywhere he went. High-profile contract killings were as common as caviar amongst Russia's business elite, and with reported profits of over AUD$100 million, Stephen couldn't afford to take chances.

Neither could Tina and their baby daughter, Sasha, a lovely doll of a child with eyes like big blue saucers. Since meeting Stephen, Tina hadn't even been on the Moscow underground. Her whole life had turned upside down. Sasha had a full-time nanny, they lived in a beautiful apartment, and Tina even had her own chauffeur. I gushed over their lavish flat and Tina looked almost embarrassed, explaining that this was a temporary one they were renting. They had bought four adjacent *kommunalki* — two up, two down — in a magnificent old building overlooking Patriarshiye Prudi (Patriarch's Ponds) in the exclusive Embassy district just north of the Kremlin. Tina described the renovations she was overseeing of their future penthouse palace, which included a sauna, gym, grand staircase with hand-wrought banister, Malaysian hardwood floors, a Moroccan themed master bedroom, and an ensuite and walk-in-robe for Sasha's bedroom. They were importing workers from Europe, and even the taps were made of gold. Stas's place seemed rather small and renovations quite humble by comparison. My jaw agape, I took the metro back to Nadia's. We folded out her wire stretcher for me to sleep on and marvelled at Tina's fortune.

18

Stripping for Fun and Profit

'There's nothing new in art except talent.'
Anton Chekhov

December 1997

Anton Chekhov was wrong. There *was* a new craze in art, and in the new Russia, naturally it involved nicely toned female bodies. Nikol had put a lot of work into hers and recently taken out second place in the Tatarstan women's bodybuilding championships. She struck a couple of bicep-bulging poses for my camera and jutted out her lower jaw in a toothy grin, lapping up the attention. It was a numbing minus thirty degrees outside, but she seemed happy enough to be standing around in nothing but a G-string while Alexander Busygin, a Kazan-based Russian painter and friend of photographer Andrei Bogdanov, got himself organised.

Busygin — who resembled a mischievous orthodox priest with his long hair and straggly beard — wasn't going to paint a portrait *of* her, he was preparing to paint *on* her. Obviously adept at overcoming the technical challenges posed by decorating an animate canvas, he began by covering Nikol in white from head to toe, before adding swirls and stripes in red, green and black over her entire body. If not for the white-blonde hair, she could have been an African tribeswoman.

'People do this everywhere in different ways,' said Busygin with a wink. 'I saw this kind of painting in Holland. And what about tattoos?

What are they if not a kind of body art? They're just permanent. Here they do it in prisons where there is nothing to draw on but skin. And women paint their faces every day. The whole cosmetics industry revolves around it.'

Andrei snapped prolifically with his Nikon while I filmed him, trying to come up with an angle for my 'postcard' story. Apart from the visual interest of Nikol's swirly bottom, there wasn't one. Busygin's wife, Olga, watched on, then disappeared and returned with a cutout newspaper article. 'As is already well-known,' she read, 'Kazan avant-garde artists are continuing in the traditions of the Peruvian Mayans, the historical roots of body art.'

Body art was the new craze in Kazan. 'Exhibitions' and competitions were being held in nightclubs across town and for Nikol — her stage name — they offered a welcome change from her usual job as a stripper. Dubbed the 'mother of Kazan strippers', she was a regular act at the Gentelmen Klub and a big hit with local *biznesmeny*. 'There's nothing wrong with showing off your body if it's beautiful,' she opined as Alexander put some finishing splotches on her buttocks. 'And if men want to pay me to dance striptease for them, then I have no problem with that.'

In her late twenties, Nikol had not only trained most of the other stripper-dancers in Kazan, she had fought with club owners to exempt 'her girls' from providing prostitution services as well as dancing. She was now saving up the roubles she collected in her G-string to study law at Kazan University.

Enthusiastic artists were having no trouble finding volunteers to expose flesh to their paintbrushes. But Tatiana was appalled by the phenomenon. 'Maybe somewhere in the world this could be considered art,' Tatiana sniffed. 'But not here on our soil. These New Russians might be very rich, but they are not cultured and have terrible taste. It's nothing but pornography.'

Whatever it was, Andrei the photographer saw commercial possibilities in the new fad. His next assignment was an advertisement for a local jazz club. He called one of his models, Adele, an attractive and busty student from the Theatrical Institute, to pose in nothing but sunnies and a tin of silver paint. I chatted to Adele as Andrei's make-up artist, Lena, covered her curves with a metallic sheen. She was from a small town in the Caucasus Mountains. 'Yes, my family is Muslim. I haven't told my mum and dad about this because I'm afraid they will think it's immoral.' Adele turned to admire her freshly silvered legs in the mirror. 'I consider myself a Muslim. I come from a family of believers, and I am a believer. I don't go to the mosque often enough, but in my heart and soul I'm a believer.'

'But in the Koran it is written that the woman should not even show the shape of her body?' I asked, bemused.

'Yes, I'm a sinner. In the Koran it is written that actors are sinners. Before they didn't even bury actors in the same cemeteries with ordinary people,' said Adele matter-of-factly, craning her neck to see her reflection. 'Maybe one day I will pay for this. But I think that Allah gave me this beauty and that I must do everything in my power to present myself as a woman to be admired, so that people will value and appreciate it.'

I passed on Tatiana's opinion.

'People do worse things,' she replied as Andrei handed her a tenor saxophone. 'They steal, sell drugs. People should develop themselves in other directions and not just think about filling their pockets with money. It is good that now there is a new generation of intelligentsia. In the old times there was no freedom of expression and now much has changed.'

Much certainly had changed. Back in the winter of 1991–1992, Tatiana had scolded me constantly for going out in minus twenty 'not dressed properly'. Because my enormous orange coat didn't come down to my knees, she informed me authoritatively, the icy wind would have a dangerous cooling effect on my 'woman's area'. Now, in 1997, young women were tottering through blizzards in miniskirts, stiletto ankle boots and fur jackets cropped at the midriff. It wasn't just Tatiana who was bothered by this trend toward near nudity. Ultra-conservative Wahhabi Muslims from Saudi Arabia who had come to Tatarstan to build mosques, hand out Korans and rekindle the faith amongst Tatars were appalled at the amount of female flesh on display and were entreating their women followers to cover themselves properly. The streets of Kazan were now an incongruous mix of goose-bumped bimbos and the occasional black-shrouded devotee of Prophet Mohammed (peace be upon him).

I discussed the arrival of the Wahhabis with Zulfia and her friend Alfia. Both considered themselves to be 'ethnic Muslims'. 'Historically, Tatars are Muslims, so that's what we are,' explained Zulfia. 'But we aren't strict. We don't think women should have to cover themselves up like this. It's not right.'

'Unless you are really ugly,' interjected Alfia. 'Then you should cover so other people don't have to look at you. While you are young and beautiful then you should show yourself off for everyone to admire.'

The Wahhabis had their work cut out for them here in Tatarstan. Armed with my tapes of naked women I headed back to Moscow.

Tatiana's son, Sergei, certainly appreciated the prolific eye candy. He had just returned to Moscow to take up a job with a top Western legal firm after a year and a half in the United States studying American Law. On finishing his degree in Kazan he'd written to a professor of Soviet/Russian Law at Emory University in Atlanta. The professor had invited Sergei to meet him in Moscow and been so impressed that he'd immediately offered him a place and free tuition. In addition, Sergei had been one of fourteen students to receive financial assistance through a fellowship program administered by the US government and partially funded by Hungarian-born financier and philanthropist George Soros.

'I guess I was an instrument of US foreign policy,' he said, with a new and distinctly American accent. 'The aim of the program was to expose Russians to US culture and education, and create a group of talented and energetic Russians who would be friendly to US interests. I guess you educate people in your country so you can create personnel to work in your businesses in Russia.'

Sergei soon found that little of his new knowledge could be applied back at home where bribery was an everyday part of life. 'The American legal system is well tested and well developed, but here the system and rules are too primitive.'

New laws were coming out fast but getting people to abide by them was another matter. Even Sergei the fledgling lawyer was contravening Russian law by his very presence in Moscow. It wasn't only foreigners who were required to register with the OVIR wherever they went. Since Soviet days a system of *propiski,* or residency permits, had been in place to ensure that every Russian citizen stayed where they were supposed to. As a Kazan native, Sergei was registered in that city, and was allowed three days in Moscow before he was, by law, obliged to inform the authorities. But OVIR's registration procedure for Russian citizens was every bit as exasperating as that for foreigners, and Sergei hadn't had time. There was also a chance he might be refused a much sought after Moscow *propiska,* and then he would really have problems. So he rented a flat on Tverskaya Street — the main boulevard running north from Red Square, now lined with luxury goods stores and ritzy restaurants — and hailed a gypsy cab (any old car with a driver eager to pick up money) to work each day in his smart tailored suit and hoped that no policeman would ever ask for his documents. He didn't seem worried. If they did, he would simply pay them off.

I was working on the same principle and hadn't yet registered my visa either, despite having been in the country for several weeks. Because my invitation had been made through IKEA in St Petersburg, a representative from the company had to take my documents to the registration office there. It was time to hotfoot it north and organise my paperwork before I got caught out.

Inflation had finally hit the railways, so I took a cheaper day seat rather than an overnight bunk for the eight-hour journey. A dishevelled young man sat to my right, twitching and scratching at a long row of scars on his arm. I offered him some chewing gum and he stared at me incredulously.

'Where did you get that from?' he asked.

'At the kiosk at the train station. You can get it anywhere.'

We got to talking. Yura had just been released from prison after serving a ten-year sentence for using heroin. Since 1987 he'd seen nothing of the world but the inside of his putrid cell. He chewed frantically on his gum, eyes darting anxiously. 'You can't imagine how people live there,' he muttered. 'Worse than animals. Six men to a cell meant for two, just over two square metres per person. You have to share a bed with some tuberculosis-ridden faggot coughing their lungs out all over you all night. There's no toilet and everyone just shits on the floor. Rats and cockroaches are running everywhere.'

Yura held out his arms for me to inspect and film his slash scars, the legacy of his multiple suicide attempts. I continued to film as he spoke. He'd completely missed the collapse of the Soviet Union and the world he had just re-entered bore only a passing resemblance to the one he'd known, in which chewing gum had been an almost impossible to obtain treasure. He was hoping to find his mother in 'Leningrad' and start afresh. But he seemed so disturbed it was hard to imagine him fitting into a normal society, if 1997 Russia could be described as such. I had no idea what I'd do with the footage, but it was infinitely more fascinating than the stories I'd been sent to film.

Olga and Misha were now married with a baby son, Artemy, who they affectionately called Tyoma. They were living in Misha's recently completed apartment on Leninsky Prospekt in a *spalny raion* on St Petersburg's southern outskirts. It was very IKEA, all blonde wood and white cotton, a world apart from the dark greens, greys and vinyl floors of her parent's Stalin-era flat on Vasilievsky Island. They had employed a nanny to look after eight-month-old Tyoma so Olga could return to work. She adored her chubby cherub and seemed ecstatically happy.

It was the day before New Year's Eve, too late for Olga to submit my passport and visa to be registered and returned to me before I needed to travel again. For my second 'postcard' I planned to shoot a short story about life on a long-distance train and had decided on a trip to Murmansk, at the northern tip of the Kola Peninsula. It would be a three-night return trip. Olga and I figured we would wait until after Orthodox Christmas on 7 January to worry about my registration.

Olga, Misha and I celebrated New Year's Eve on Leninsky Prospekt, popping the champagne cork as quietly as possible so as not to wake the sleeping Tyoma. St Petersburg was deathly still on New Year's morning as the city slept off its hangover. But I had work to do. I met up with Anton Labushkin, the former puppetry student who had been on the Khibeni trek back in 1990. He had agreed to accompany me on the world's northernmost railway, for a trip up the Kola Peninsula: past Lake Ladoga and Lake Onega, along the shores of the White Sea, over the Arctic Circle at the Gulf of Kandalaksha, and through the desolate tundra to Murmansk, the terminus station on the Arctic Ocean coast.

Our train, the *Arktika*, was already waiting when we arrived at the station and I was dismayed to find it almost completely empty. We were the only passengers in our entire wagon. How on earth, I wondered, was I going to shoot a story about vibrant Russian train life, when the entire population was too hungover to want to go anywhere? Desperate to find some characters we sidled up to our wagon attendants — *provodniki* — from the verb 'to accompany'. Normally there were two per wagon, sharing a sleeping compartment and job in alternating twelve-hour shifts. But today there were so few passengers that several had congregated in our wagon. They looked rather poorly, slumped around a laminate table, picking half-heartedly at shrivelled microwave dumplings. One guy with a wild shock of hair was making an evil-looking cocktail with raw egg and vodka shots.

We hovered at the doorway and a middle-aged woman with smiley bright blue eyes beckoned to us. We squeezed in and she introduced herself as Nadia Alexeyevna, also known as 'Mama Nadia'. She went round the group, introducing her 'family'. Those on duty were in uniform, those who weren't were in tracksuits (men) and floral aprons (women). The *provodniki* spend half their lives on the rails. The St Petersburg–Murmansk run was relatively easy: three days on to go there and back, then three days off to rest before doing it again ... and again ... and again. But those on the Trans-Siberian spent up to fourteen days straight on the move — cleaning stinking toilets, filling samovars, checking tickets and changing sheets — before they could get time off.

Mama Nadia had been a wagon attendant all her working life and couldn't imagine doing anything else. She gazed out the window as we clacked through a snowed under village.

'The window is our TV, with four channels. In winter our TV is black and white. In summer it's green. Autumn is incredibly beautiful — all the trees are different, all the trees are changing. I just love looking out the window. It's our television ... [we rumbled past a group of kids playing in the snow] ... with actors!'

The *provodniki* were lovely people, and the winter wonderland scenery photogenic, but I had no idea what the story was, beyond a snapshot of camaraderie in a community on wheels.

Winter days in St Petersburg were only a few hours long, but 1,438 train kilometres north in Murmansk they were non-existent, obliterated by the nearly two-month long polar night. From 2 December until the end of January, the sun never rises above the horizon. 'Daylight' is a faint bluish twilight making a brief appearance around midday. Inhabitants of the region in the sixteenth century declared: 'There are three *versts* [an old Russian unit of distance, approximately equivalent to one kilometre] from Kola to hell.' But that hadn't stopped Russians from choosing this location — the Arctic Ocean's only ice-free harbour — to build their largest city beyond the Arctic Circle.

These days Murmansk had a population of around 350,000, many employed by the Russian Navy at its Northern Fleet headquarters. Like St Petersburg, Murmansk had been honoured with Hero City status for its efforts in defending the country from the Germans during the Great Patriotic War. And like the southern city of Stalingrad, now Volgograd, most of it had been flattened by German bombers in the process.

It was mid-afternoon when we farewelled Mama Nadia and her brigade, and wandered off into the lamplit streets. In front of the main department store, mini-Michelin children played on a slide carved from ice. I tried to film some sculptors whittling away at giant blocks of solid ice, fashioning sculptures of castles and Disney characters. But it was so cold that my supersize camera batteries drained almost instantaneously. I tucked the excruciatingly icy spares into my undies to warm them, but my pain yielded little gain. Worse still, I was unable to operate the camera with gloves on, and without them I quickly lost all sensation in my fingers. Within a minute my fingertips had stuck fast to the frozen camera body.

By now it was dark again. I gave up filming and bought a local newspaper. On the front page was an article about the high incidence of poor eyesight in Murmansk's school children caused by nine months of living by fluoro alone. It was a cheery place. Anton checked in to a multistorey concrete box hotel, avoiding mention of the fact he was not alone. I waited outside, stamping my feet in the minus thirty-five degree frost. Once he had a *propusk* he came to get me. We confidently strode through the foyer and got into the lift. By the time we reached our floor, the key monitor *dezhurnaya* was waiting by the lift door.

'No visitors allowed,' she barked at Anton. She turned to glare at me. 'Where are your documents? Go back to reception immediately.'

We had no choice but to do as she ordered. The receptionist was a Soviet-era relic, with bouffed hennaed hair, a fearsome snarl and the charm of a bulldozer. She snatched my passport and began flicking through all sixty-four pages, filled with entry stamps and visas from Yemen, Ethiopia, China, Laos, Vietnam, Pakistan and Poland to Mexico, Peru, Botswana and India.

'Where is your Russian visa?' she demanded.

It was the question I'd been dreading. Russian visas are issued on a separate piece of paper and I'd kept it aside, hoping vainly that she might forget to ask. I fished out the crumpled green sheet and gave it to her. It took only a millisecond before she noted the absence of a registration stamp.

'What is your business here in Murmansk?' she snapped. 'This document states you are a timber industry consultant and that you are visiting Syktyvkar.'

'Oh, I'm just looking,' I stammered lamely.

She reached for the phone.

'Is there a problem?' I asked meekly, feigning innocence.

'I'm calling the customs and border police,' she retorted. 'Your visa is not registered by the appropriate authorities, and you have no permission to be in Murmansk.'

Demented butterflies flapped in my stomach as she dialled and waited for someone to pick up the phone. It rang and rang … and rang and rang. She glared at me venomously and replaced the receiver.

'I will keep your passport and visa here,' she snapped. 'When I contact the police I will send them for you. For now you can go to the room, but do not leave.'

We waited nervously, perched on the edge of rock-hard midget-sized beds. I didn't relish the idea of being arrested only three kilometres from hell. A gale outside hurled snowflakes against the window and the grimy toilet gurgled noisily. Anton looked worried.

'You know, Murmansk is a sensitive place. Our nuclear submarines are stationed at bases close by, and it's the headquarters of Atomflot, our fleet of nuclear-powered ice-breakers. People have always been suspicious of foreigners and now you are with a camera and without having your visa registered. I'm afraid we could have real problems.'

The hours passed. The snow continued to whirl and the toilet continued to burp. Anton went downstairs to see what was happening. The receptionist was still dialling the customs police, and still not getting any answer. She told Anton that she believed I should be deported.

'But why aren't the police answering?' I asked Anton when he returned.

'I think you should be very thankful it's 2 January. Of course they are all still hungover after the New Year. Let's hope they keep on drinking,' he said.

We didn't sleep that night. I stayed dressed and waited for the customs police to come and arrest me. By 9 am there was still no sign of them. It was nearly time for our train back to St Petersburg, but I couldn't go anywhere without my documents. We went downstairs and found the hennaed bulldozer had left and a young girl was now seated in reception. My passport and visa were on the desk in front of her. Anton nodded at me and began to chat to the girl. Once she was suitably distracted I leaned over, grabbed them and poked Anton in the backside. He said we'd be back soon and we walked out. As soon as we were out of sight of the hotel we bolted, skidding on the frozen footpaths as fast as we could, all the way to the station. We got to the train just in time.

Back in Moscow, with a freshly registered visa and lighter wallet, I went into the ABC's office to meet their Russia correspondent, Eric Campbell. He had just returned from a summer holiday in Sydney and invited me for a beer at an Irish-themed pub across the road from the office on Kutuzovsky Prospekt, just near Moscow's White House. It was my very first expat experience. I stared dumbly at the Western journalists and businessmen in suits with their mugs of Guinness and listened to Eric discuss Russian politics with an American friend of his, Eve, who worked for a US television network. When they asked about my stories I shrivelled into my seat. Body art and train trips were so embarrassingly trivial.

Eric had already been in Moscow for nearly two years and had a large circle of Western expatriate acquaintances. He introduced me to some of his friends — diplomats, journalists and businesspeople — and I discovered a whole new side of Moscow. At parties people spoke English and talked about places to buy Australian beef and beer. Most lived in secure compounds for foreigners, where guards would check your ID before you could enter. Eric's flat was at least six times the size of Nadia's. The expats frequented American-style diners I never knew existed, sipped lattes in five-star hotel cafes and shopped for groceries at an outrageously priced supermarket called Stockmans. Eric worked out in an extortionately expensive gym in the Radisson-Slavyanskaya Hotel not far from the ABC office.

But these places weren't only for foreigners. A burgeoning middle- and upper-class of Russians with cash to burn and a desire for only the best left many of the expats feeling positively underprivileged. Sergei's friend Marat had also now moved to Moscow and was doing very nicely managing several rock bands. He drove a new S-Class Merc, sported several latest model mobile phones and ate out in the classiest of establishments, always with new and ever more gorgeous girls. Age, wealth and responsibility had not changed Marat one bit. His girth might have broadened, but his grin was still cheeky, his eyes still mischievous, and I could still never quite tell when he was having me on. He was also a great repository of jokes, and his theme of the moment was the New Russian, stereotyped — not altogether unrealistically — as the uncultured oaf with more money than sense.

A New Russian goes to a car dealer and asks for a silver Mercedes 600. The salesman shows him the car, takes his money and asks curiously: 'Excuse me, sir, but didn't you buy the same car three days ago?'

'I sure did,' retorts the New Russian. 'But the ashtray in that one is full already.'

A New Russian is lying by his crashed car on the side of the road, weeping aloud. 'Oh, my BMW!' he wails. 'Oh, my BMW!'

A passer-by is shocked. 'How can you cry about your car when you've lost your entire hand?'

The New Russian re-evaluates the situation and resumes his cries. 'Oh, my Rolex!'

Two New Russians meet. One asks the other: 'Hey, Vasya, where did you get that tie?'

'At the Valentino store. It cost me $2,000.'

'You were conned! I know a place where you can get exactly the same tie for $5,000!'

An Austrian friend worked as a flight attendant for Lauda Air. She told tales of pompous and arrogant Novy Russkys, too poor to afford their own private jets, who chartered luxury planes to fly empty from Vienna to Moscow to collect them, their families and accompanying staff, and fly wherever they required, be it Majorca, the French Riviera or skiing in the Alps. 'They are the rudest people I've ever met,' complained Vicky. 'Especially the wives. They shout at the nannies and airline staff as though we are their slaves.'

Bizarrely, in a city bursting with glitzy designer clothing stores and prestige car dealers, many of the expatriate workers received a 'hardship allowance'. In Eric's case it seemed to go mostly towards funding the expanding waistlines of the *GAI-ishniki,* Moscow's traffic police. Foreigners were required to have special number plates on their vehicles to make them easily identifiable. Every time Eric so much as drove around the block in the ABC's car (not a Mercedes) he would be pulled aside by a baton-waving *GAI-ishnik.* I watched him hand over hundreds of US dollars for non-existent misdemeanours, just to save the trouble of going to the station. Interestingly, the *GAI-ishniki* never stopped Marat in his Merc — but on one occasion when I got a ride with Olga's husband, Misha, from St Petersburg to Moscow, his Jeep was flagged down no less than thirteen times by traffic cops lurking in the forests lining the route.

One of Eric's friends, Julie Lewis, was an Australian print journalist working for the English-language *Moscow Times* and freelancing for *The Australian.* I told her about my recent trip to Kazan and my observations of the revival of Tatar culture there over the past few years. She wanted to find out more and I offered to arrange a trip.

'Bring her, of course,' gushed Zulfia when I called to ask if she'd have room for two.

Zulfia was now living with her new boyfriend, a Tatar businessman who had come to her at the Chamber of Commerce and Industry last autumn seeking advice on starting a joint venture business with an American. She had bewitched him in an instant with her magnetic charm and enormous brown eyes. And her man, Ildar, once star graduate of the Chemical and Mechanical Engineering faculty of her alma mater, had won her over with his intellect. 'His name is even listed on the university honour roll,' said Zulfia with pride. Ildar was not a tall man, with a build and complexion that suggested he enjoyed a good meal and a whisky or two. Given that much Russian wheeling and dealing was conducted over lengthy meals washed down with vital relationship-forming spirits, it appeared business was going well.

Or rather it had been. Ildar had hooked up with a sixty-something American who had seen the potential to make a motzah by selling US-made furniture right here in Tatarstan. With local factories barely able to put together a footstool, there were plenty of cashed-up customers happy to splash out on imports. Phase two of their plan was to reinvigorate a Russian factory with American technology. It all sounded perfectly plausible and even downright sensible. A functioning and properly run Russian factory would provide jobs and manufacture goods that were in demand. It was exactly what the country needed after years of relying on expensive imports that the majority of the underpaid and often unemployed population couldn't afford. But like most business propositions in Russia more complex than outright theft, Ildar and his partner were struggling to get their project off the ground.

While fledgling businesses were drowning in red tape and bureaucracy, mosques new (and old) were sprouting up around the republic by the hundred. Julie and I visited the newly refurbished Nurulla mosque on Kirov Street, one of the few whose original 1840s building had been preserved. In 1929 the Central Executive Committee of the Tatar Republic had ordered it to be closed. Its minaret was demolished and the building was used for apartments and offices until 1992, when it was handed back to the faithful. It had since undergone extensive renovation and the minaret had been rebuilt. A young mullah took us to a room where a group of old women sat cross-legged, poring over Korans in Arabic. A wizened babushka with twinkling eyes was happy to talk.

'During Soviet times we would go out and hide in the forests to pray,' she croaked. 'I am nearly eighty years old, and only now I am able to learn Arabic. I feel like I am born again, to be able to come freely to the mosque and to study Islam openly.'

In the main hall, men in embroidered skullcaps were praying: standing and kneeling, leaning forward to touch their foreheads on the ground, kneeling and standing again. The majority were in their late teens and early twenties.

'Many young people are coming to us now,' the mullah whispered when the prayers were over. 'This society we live in is very amoral. Many young people are getting involved in bad things, in drugs, drinking, sex. There is much poverty, unemployment and violence.

People now are too concerned with attaining wealth and possessions. These young men are searching for something different and are finding the answer here in Islam.'

Ildar and Zulfia invited Julie and me to the village of Izma, northeast of Kazan, where Ildar had relatives. With no family or friends in the country until now, it was Zulfia's first ever visit to a Tatar village, and the city girl was shocked by the primitive conditions. 'I mean, it's very interesting, but I can't imagine how they live there like that! But I suppose it's what they're used to, and maybe our city lives seem strange to them too.'

Ildar's mother, Alfira — a robust and powerful woman both in figure and personality — ushered us all inside the wooden cottage.

'Please meet my favourite mother-in-law of my future husband,' Zulfia announced to Julie and me in English. Alfira, who had no idea what Zulfia was saying, smiled a thin-lipped gold-toothed smile and seized me in a vice-like hug.

I now understood that a *banya* was an essential part of a visit to country Tatarstan — but it was a ritual Julie was yet to experience. Zulfia, Alfira, Julie and I crunched through the deep snow to the shed behind the house. Not one to waste time on ceremony, the burly Alfira gestured to Julie to get her gear off. Soon Alfira was mercilessly flogging the sweating, prostrate Julie with a bunch of dried birch leaves. I glanced over at Zulfia who gave me a conspiratorial wink: 'I think it's going to be a tough relationship with my mother-in-law,' she whispered. 'She is very strong and wants everything to be her way. But I just say "yes, of course" and then do what I want anyway. Still I know she likes me. She's always saying to Ildar's sister Gulnara, "Listen to Zulfia".'

Zulfia considered herself lucky not to have been born a century earlier. Her great-grandmother and great-grandfather's marriage back in 1910 had been arranged by their relatives. Aged sixteen and seventeen respectively, the first time they had seen each other was at their own wedding. According to tradition, the new bride moved into the house of the husband's family and become the house-drudge, looking after the entire family. 'But it wasn't just Tatars and other ethnic Muslim nationalities who had this tradition,' Zulfia explained. 'Even though the Russians were Christians, they did exactly the same.'

Julie needed to be back at her desk at the *Moscow Times* office by Monday morning. Zulfia dropped us at the station on Sunday night. The station's LED thermometer read minus thirty-five degrees as we shuffled into the ticket hall. Alas, there were no tickets for the next train to Moscow. 'Just get on it anyway,' advised Zulfia. 'If you give the *provodnitsa* some money, she'll find you a place somewhere. Don't worry.' I told her we'd be fine and she left.

The train soon emerged from the darkness, lights and horn blaring as it pulled alongside the icy platform. Passengers disembarked, others boarded, clinging to each other and their bags to avoid slipping on the ice. Julie and I picked a wagon without too much activity, and as the horn sounded announcing the train's imminent departure, we clambered aboard. The wagon attendant glared at us and I realised too late there was at least one woman in Russia who wouldn't take bribes.

'Tickets,' she demanded as the train began to gather speed.

'Umm, we don't have any,' I stammered. 'We have to be in Moscow in the morning ... can't we ... ummmm ... buy a ticket from you?'

'Not under any circumstances,' she yelled and yanked the '*Stop Kran*', a long metal lever which signalled to the driver to make an emergency halt. The train slowed down just as our wagon was passing the end of the platform. 'Get out!' she yelled, pushing us down the steps. I jumped, landing on my still fragile ankle on the slippery ice.

It wasn't until 4 am that another train came through on its way to Moscow and we hauled our frozen bodies aboard. Julie was late for work and my ankle was purple again. I checked my emails and found one from the Executive Producer at *Foreign Correspondent* wanting to know where I was and when I was planning to bring their camera back.

I took my tapes and sheepishly returned to Australia to edit my postcards.

★ ★ ★

I was frustrated. I wanted to do stories on important issues, but no one took me seriously. My next gig was a trip to South America for an ill-fated budget travel show. While Brazilian witchcraft, Bolivian silver miners and the magical and medicinal properties of llama foetuses were all fascinating, I craved the chance to be able to investigate something more meaningful. In July 1998 I decided to return to Pakistan with my own camera. I spent several weeks in and out of Afghan refugee camps around Peshawar with members of a group called RAWA (Revolutionary Association of the Women of Afghanistan), filming with victims of Taliban violence, sickened to the core by what I saw and heard. Then I headed north to the town of Chitral, which I had visited a little over a year earlier to film for *Race Around the World*. This time I wanted to collect material for a story about the Kalash people, a unique ethnic group living in the Chitral district. From Pakistan I had a flight booked from Islamabad back to Moscow.

19

Fortune and the Beggar

'Any idiot can face a crisis. It's the day-to-day living that wears you out.'
Anton Chekhov

August 1998

Krylov was nineteenth-century Russia's Hans Christian Andersen, a celebrated poet whose wise and witty fables have entertained generations of Russian children. 'Fortune and the Beggar' tells of a miserable pauper who trudges from house to house. He wonders why the wealthy, despite all their riches, are rarely happy with their lot and constantly trying to amass more and more wealth, often gambling in foolish ventures. One day, Dame Fortune appears before him and offers to help.

'Hold out your sack and I will fill it with gold coins — on one condition. Whatever remains in your bag will be pure gold, but whatever falls on the ground will turn to dust. Your bag is worn, so be careful not to overload it.'

Overjoyed, the beggar opens his sack and watches as Dame Fortune fills it with gold. It soon grows heavy, bulges and is dangerously close to splitting.

'Is it full enough?' asks Dame Fortune.

'No, not yet,' answers the beggar. 'Just a little more.'

At that moment, the sack bursts open. The treasure falls to the ground, turns to dust, and Dame Fortune vanishes, leaving the beggar as poor as ever.

★ ★ ★

Few in Yeltsin's Russia were paying heed to Krylov's cautionary tale. Those who could continued to fill their sacks with gold, promptly squirrelling it away offshore. For those enjoying the good times, they just kept on rolling — and Renaissance Capital, led by Tina's husband, Stephen Jennings, was no exception. After reporting record profits of nearly USD$100 million in 1997, in June of 1998 the company threw an extravagant party at Kuskovo, the opulent eighteenth-century summer palace of Count Sheremetyev on the outskirts of Moscow. Sparing no expense to entertain their investor guests, Renaissance hired models in period dress and even flew in a US water-skiing team to do a stunt show on the lake.

Within two months, the Kuskovo party would be remembered as the zenith of the excess of Russia's wild cowboy capitalism. In August 1998, the Russian government defaulted on its debt repayments, the share market crashed and the rouble lost 70 per cent of its value. I watched the Russian financial collapse on *BBC World* from Chitral, where I was hiding under a burqa from furious locals out for Western blood in retaliation for recent US airstrikes on neighbouring Afghanistan. The world seemed to be going mad.

A friend from Peshawar escorted me back south, me masquerading as his covered and mute wife on a hair-raising fourteen-hour minibus ride. Hurtling down the mountains on narrow winding roads high above a river, the end seemed nigh. Would I be strung up by raging extremists, or would our van fly off the rocky path and tumble a hundred metres into the river below? Fortunately, neither scenario eventuated, and a couple of weeks later I flew to Moscow. It was now mid-September.

Since leaving Moscow in February of that year, I'd kept in contact with Eric, the ABC's Russia correspondent. When I told him I was coming back to Russia, he offered to pick me up at the airport. I walked out of the terminal, still in full Pakistani dress — a baggy *shalwar kamiz* suit with a shawl over my head and pulled across my face — which for some reason I wasn't ready to remove after two months of covering. I saw him pacing neurotically up and down outside the airport, his ear glued to his mobile. He was exhausted after frantically filing round the clock for weeks and didn't even recognise me.

My wad of 50,000 rouble notes left over from my last trip had not only shrivelled into worthlessness in the past six weeks, they were also obsolete. In an attempt to ease the psychological sting of hyperinflation, the rouble had been 'redenominated' earlier that year, meaning the last three 0's were removed. But my pain was a mere pinprick compared to the millions of Russians who lost their entire life savings — in many cases all over again — when banks began collapsing right, left and centre. In a few short weeks, Russia's emerging middle class had been all but wiped out.

The word *krizis* was on everyone's lips. To me it had come as little surprise, the only wonder being that it hadn't happened sooner. Several years had now passed since Tsar Boris had handed over most of the country's wealth to his dodgy mates, who had popped it into their offshore bank accounts and purchased luxury yachts and French castles rather than paying taxes. The flagrant corruption and rampant tax evasion had been catching up with the government, which had no money to pay either its foreign debt, or its *budzhetniki*. As the pensioners, teachers, factory workers and doctors got poorer, the International Monetary Fund kept trying to bail Russia out, pouring tens of billions of dollars into government coffers. The hungry pensioners saw none of it. Many billions evaporated, whisked away by crooked officials to fund their lavish lifestyles. But the debt didn't.

Industry was at a standstill, and most *biznes* seemed to involve laundering dirty money through importing products few could afford. In May of 1998, miners, pensioners, teachers and nurses across the country began to protest, calling for Yeltsin's resignation. But Tsar Boris continued to bumble along drunkenly, seemingly oblivious to the unrest around him. On 14 August he went on holidays. So did Olga, Misha and Tyoma.

'We were in Greece and didn't even know what was going on in Russia,' Olga recalled when I caught up with her. 'We heard there was some crisis, but didn't know any details until we got back. I went to the supermarket to get food and found it was closed. When it opened again two days later, prices had gone up four times. It was really frightening. I wanted to buy some sunflower oil but it had gone up from 20 roubles to 80 roubles. I felt like bursting into tears and left without buying anything.'

While Olga, Misha and Yeltsin had been off relaxing, the government had run out of money. It defaulted on its foreign debt and the Reserve Bank could no longer afford to prop up the rouble at 6.3 to the US dollar. On 17 August, the rouble had begun to plummet. Anyone with savings or who received their income in roubles — which was almost everyone — was in trouble. As they watched the value of their roubles shrink once again, prices shot up.

'Everyone was buying up all the *kasha* [porridge oats],' said Olga. 'Our population is trained for such periods of hunger. So when the dollar went up, everyone panicked and invested their money in *kasha*.'

Fear set in across the nation. People rushed to change their roubles into dollars, and soon the dollars ran out. Banks began folding en masse, leaving bewildered customers furious and bankrupt, with no one to sue and nowhere to turn to retrieve what was left of their money. And in true Russian style, 'new' banks — mostly reincarnations of the old ones, owned by the same old bankers — popped up like mushrooms, carefree and immune to the wrath of their former clientele.

Olga and Misha were in the lucky minority. They were still working for IKEA and received their salaries in dollars, so after Olga got over her initial shock at this new bout of hyperinflation, she realised they were largely unaffected by the sinking rouble. They had no savings, so lost nothing. And it even seemed possible that they might at last be able to break into the skyrocketing Russian real estate market.

In January of 1999, the family had relocated to Moscow and were now renting a cramped two-room flat near Belyayevo Metro in the city's southwest. Misha had inherited a one-room bedsit near the Tryokhgorka Textile Manufacturers from his grandmother, who had once been an employee of the factory. It was a cupboard of a place with barely enough room to swing a hamster, let alone squeeze in a family, so they decided to put it on the market and take up IKEA's offer of an interest-free loan to buy themselves a basic two-bedroom flat near the 1905 Metro station.

'We never could have managed to buy our place if it hadn't been for the crisis. But no one could afford to buy real estate, so there was no competition,' explained Olga.

Misha's parents hadn't fared so well. Their minuscule pensions had all but disappeared and without help from Misha they wouldn't have been able to put food on the table, let alone buy medicine. Nadia too only got by thanks to help from her nephew. Millions of other pensioners found themselves in dire financial straits yet again.

Renaissance Capital wasn't spared either. The seemingly invincible company, and recent mega-party host, was suddenly worth a fraction of its pre-*krizis* value. But Stephen Jennings was undeterred. He bought out his partner, Boris Jordan, and took control.

I began shooting a story about the newly established Moscow Rescue Service, Sluzhba Spaseniya, hoping to get some dramatic footage to show the producers at *Foreign Correspondent*. Sluzhba Spaseniya was an amazingly hi-tech outfit for Russia, with well-equipped and trained teams responding immediately to calls for assistance — quite a novelty in this normally chaotic city. I spent several 24-hour shifts with the crews as they raced from grisly car accidents to rescuing distraught babushki who'd locked themselves out of their security-doored flats with a pot of porridge burning on the stove.

The crews were a good-natured bunch from various walks of life, attracted to the service by both the excitement factor it offered, and the promise of wages they had no hope of even receiving in their trained professions. Andrei was a doctor who had added abseiling, fire fighting and breaking and entering to his skill base and got a job with the Sluzhba. Georgiy was a teacher who'd handed back his chalk and now got a buzz racing the rescue vehicle at lethal speeds through Moscow's streets. Alexei Saraikin, at twenty-three, was one of the younger members of the service.

'It's been exceptionally busy since the *krizis*,' Alexei told me over a cup of instant noodles he had insisted on buying for me. I knew his already meagre salary was shrinking by the day, and was touched by his generosity. 'There are more robberies, more domestic violence, and more people injured,' he went on. 'People are depressed and despondent. And I think people are drinking more to forget about their problems and there are more car accidents.'

Alexei was a fresh-faced veteran of the war in Chechnya. He had desperately wanted to join the KGB's elite commando unit, Alfa, one of a number of Spetsnaz (elite special forces) groups. Formerly known as 'Antiterrorist Group A', Alfa had been set up in July 1974 by Brezhnev's successor, Yuri Andropov, after eleven Israeli athletes were killed at the 1972 Olympic Games in Munich, to enable the KGB to respond to similar incidents in the USSR. But Alexei had failed to get a place after answering back to a senior officer, thus blackening his name for life. After his tour of duty in Chechnya, Alexei had become addicted to the adrenaline rush of work involving mutilated bodies. Sluzhba Spaseniya was the only outlet he could find to satisfy his cravings.

I saw a lot of bodies in my time on patrol, mostly being prised from wrecked vehicles by Russia's only set of 'jaws of life'. Blood and gore had always disturbed me — I'd had to give up early teen ambitions of a veterinarian career after fainting into a partially speyed cat on an operating table at my first work experience job — but I found that somehow I managed to get used to it. Russians in general seemed relatively immune to the sight of entrails and splattered body parts. I supposed it was because their history was full of it: bloody wars, bloody revolutions, bloodthirsty autocratic rulers with their bloodthirsty security services and armies.

Whatever the reason, the higher powers at Moscow's Sluzhba Spaseniya felt their work would make compelling television viewing. They had employed a cameraman to document their more dramatic rescues and were in the process of developing a prime-time TV series to rival the hit reality show, the graphically gruesome *Dorozhny Patrul* (*Highway Patrol*). This twice-daily horror-fest featured police trawls around Moscow, close-ups of blood-soaked corpses, drug raids and bolting prostitutes. The punters loved it.

There may have been a fascination with the maimed and dead, but most Russians seemed to have little compassion for the down and outs. I was walking through the underpass between Leningradsky and Kazansky Stations with Kumi, a visiting Australian friend, when an old woman crashed down the steps and landed in a lifeless heap at the bottom, blood trickling from under her matted hair. Passers-by turned away and ignored her. I had no phone and asked a couple if they could call an ambulance.

'Who cares?' one answered. 'Look at her, just some old drunk. Look at the state she's in. She's an animal, not a human anymore.'

I remembered there was a first-aid room in Leningradsky Station and ran there to get help. A matron with bright red lips and a pressed white coat was filing her nails. She slowly lifted her head and glared at me.

'Please come quickly,' I urged, puffing from my run. 'A woman has fallen and hurt herself.'

'Where?' she snorted, returning her attention to her nails.

'Down the steps into the underpass. Please hurry, she's bleeding badly from the head.'

'We only work in the station,' she snapped. 'That's not my area. Go and find someone else.'

Disgusted, I ran back to Kumi and the still motionless woman. Hundreds of people must have passed them while I'd been gone, yet all had turned away. Blood from her smashed head was dripping into a grate. She stank of decay: urine, unwashed clothes, stale alcohol. But still she was a human being. Eventually the station police came and I begged them to call for help.

'Our ambulance service is overworked as it is,' he sneered. 'Why should they bother with "that"?'

We couldn't believe we were witnessing such heartlessness. But one of the cops did call, I suspect more to get rid of us and clear the way as peak hour was approaching. At last an ambulance came.

★ ★ ★

Kumi was flying to St Petersburg the next day and Alexei offered to borrow a friend's car to drive her to the airport. On the ring road we passed a terrible three-car accident. Alexei screeched to a halt and jumped out. A man's leg had been all but ripped off at the knee and was pulled between two cars, with a sinew stretching over a metre. The man's young son was trapped in the back seat of the smashed car. Within minutes Alexei had everything under control, emergency services on the way and the man free. He lay silently staring at his stump in a state of shock.

Once the ambulance arrived and he'd helped remove the boy, Alexei returned to the car. Unable to look, Kumi had curled up on the back seat. Alexei was grinning. 'Sorry about the delay,' he said cheerily. 'But I couldn't leave them there.' He slammed his foot down and headed for the airport. Kumi and I looked at each other. After our utter disbelief at the callousness we'd experienced the day before, Alexei had restored our faith in humanity. But this being Russia, it wouldn't be long before I would lose it again.

Rafael had returned from his four years in Malaysia just in time for the *krizis*. He'd decided the time had come to realise his political ambitions and was renting a room near Perovo Metro on Moscow's eastern outskirts, traipsing from one party headquarters to the next with his laminated Muslim theology degree, newly purchased in Malaysia, trying to persuade someone, anyone, to give him a job.

'They've never seen a degree from another country before,' he moaned. 'They were smelling it, biting it, trying to see if it was real. Then they told me that they had begun by sweeping streets and that I should get out.'

So he did. He tried his luck with Yabloko, the Russian United Democratic Party, and with the loony ultra-nationalist Vladimir Zhirinovsky's Liberal Democratic Party. He offered his services to parties so minor that no one had ever heard of them, let alone voted for them. But no one needed or wanted him. Unable to get so much as a toe on the rung of the political ladder, Rafael found work in Moscow's construction industry. But the few roubles he was earning didn't even cover his rent. He was despondent, in his particular wry way.

By November he had no option but to return to Mari El and live with his mother. He couldn't bear it and called his old friend Valiulla Hazrat, the Deputy Chief Mufti in Kazan who had been responsible for his Arab-sponsored 'study' in Malaysia. Rafael showed Valiulla the certificate he'd bought with his hairwashing money and begged the mufti for work. At first Rafael helped the Deputy Mufti with paperwork, for the pitiful salary of 500 roubles a month. He only got paid twice. If it hadn't been for his aunty, Rafael would never have got by.

Aunty had just moved to a two-room flat, but still had a room in a *kommunalka* in Kazan, a communal apartment where fourteen people shared one toilet and a kitchen. She offered it to Rafael. There was no sink to wash in, the place was crawling with cockroaches, a teenage junkie lived in the stairwell and most of the lights didn't work. But at least Rafael had a room to himself: 6 metres long and 2.5 metres wide. A family of four lived in the room next to his, the parents and two grown-up sons sharing a space the same size. One son slept on a fold-out armchair, the other on the floor. The one who slept on the chair had a medical condition and could have avoided army service, but he chose to go anyway so he could escape the cramped conditions at home.

Valiulla had by now published all the books he thought necessary for a Muslim revival and was ready to move on to other ventures: halal restaurants, halal shops, and a hair salon to cater for newly strict Muslims. The Tatar government was giving the Muftiat back its buildings that had been confiscated during the Bolshevik revolution, and Valiulla allowed Rafael to set up a hair salon in a decrepit old place near Kazan's Kamal Theatre.

'There really aren't many rules for cutting hair, except that a man must cut a man's hair, and a woman must cut a woman's,' explained Rafael. 'Still, it's a great location, near the railway and bus stations, and I get a lot of work.'

Despite the ancient roof sagging threateningly over his clients, Rafael began to turn a profit. He even managed to open a bookshop at one end of his salon. By February 1999, he was earning 20,000 roubles a month from both businesses (around USD$800) and had to employ an assistant to help him keep up. One of his regulars always came at closing time and would ask if he'd like a ride home. On one of these occasions the client told Rafael 'he knew everything'. Rafael asked him if he was KGB (as Rafael still called the FSB). He was. The spook asked about the other students back in Malaysia, but Rafael knew nothing, other than that they were religious but not violent. 'It's so stupid that the KGB is still controlling everything and everybody,' he muttered.

Everything and everybody except the Mafia.

Just as Rafael's business began to take off, he had some visitors. Five of them — big ones, with battle scars and bulging pecs, who informed Rafael they would like to share in his profits. Half of his proceeds would do nicely for a start. Rafael refused and went home as usual after work. He knew that the guys were from the *krysha* who controlled the businesses on his street. That night they destroyed everything. They burned all his books and the hair salon was razed. The lost books alone were worth about two months' wages. Rafael was unemployed again, but remarkably philosophical.

'It's just life here. Everyone goes through it.'

My two-month visa was due to expire and to renew it, I had to leave the country. The closest and easiest option was to take an overnight train to Tallinn, the Estonian capital, where I could get a new visa issued in two days.

It turned out I wasn't the only one wanting to leave Russia. Eric had read about a town called Ivangorod — on the Russian–Estonian border, some 100 kilometres to the southwest of St Petersburg — which was begging to do so too. In the days of the USSR, Ivangorod in Russia and Narva in Estonia had been more or less one town, sliced in two by the Narva River. Many families had members living on both sides. The collapse of the Soviet Union had left them citizens of different countries with very different fates. On the Russian side, the standard of living had declined steeply. Many of Ivangorod's factories had closed, unemployment was rampant, workers unpaid and social services deteriorating. But in Narva, things were looking up. Most

Estonians had been reluctant captives of the Soviet Union and since gaining independence, their economy had boomed. The Russians in Ivangorod figured they could enjoy the same benefits as Narva if the map were redrawn around them. A group of concerned citizens had signed a petition calling on neighbouring Estonia to take it over. It was a vain hope. Russia had no intention of giving up its territory and Estonia had no desire to take over a decrepit Russian town. But it seemed a powerful example of how bad things had become in the Russian provinces.

Eric thought Ivangorod's woes would make a good story for *Lateline*. His bureau cameraman had just left Moscow, so we decided to go together, with me shooting and translating for him. First we would go to Tallinn to do some interviews and get my new visa — a journalist one this time — through the ABC. On our way back to Moscow we would pass through Ivangorod and film there.

It wasn't going to be easy. In theory our journalist visas permitted us to go anywhere on the territory of the Russian Federation, but the border service made its own rules. Filming a border was an offence and if caught we would most likely have to hand over the tapes, or be expelled. We decided to pose as tourists and join the throngs of Estonians who queued daily at the border to take advantage of Ivangorod's cheaper prices. I packed my digicam and tripod in a backpack.

The border crossing was a bridge over the Narva River, flanked on both sides by medieval forts. It took six hours to get through the passport queue and five minutes to walk into Russia. Yuri Gordeyev, the leader of Ivangorod's secessionist push, was waiting for us at the end of the bridge, stomping his boots in the snow. Short and stocky, with thick grey hair, a bushy moustache and a black leather jacket, he reminded me of an ill-tempered bull.

'I've been here for six hours,' he said gruffly. 'First thing, we need to go and register you with the local police.'

This seemed total madness, but Yuri was not to be argued with. Ten minutes later, as a ruddy-cheeked cop pored over our documents, I wished we had put up more of a protest. Yuri the loud-mouthed was obviously known to the police as a local nutter and it seemed he'd brought us here to prove to the cops just how important he was — so important that journalists had come all the way from Australia to talk to him.

So much for our tourist cover.

The head officer took Eric's business card, examined it closely and compared it with his visa. He shook his head gravely.

'There is a problem. Look. The name on the visa is different to the card.'

Sure enough, the Cyrillic transliteration of Campbell was different: the card included the silent 'P', the visa didn't. Two hours and many phone calls later we were released, with a stern warning not to film anything. It was now dark and Yuri drove us to Ivangorod's only hotel.

The receptionist was glued to the TV set and looked taken aback when I asked for a room. I got the feeling we were the first customers she'd seen in weeks.

'Don't you know anybody in town you can stay with?' she grumbled.

'No we don't. We'd like a room here.'

She looked at us warily. 'You won't like it,' she warned. 'There's no heating and no hot water.'

We had no choice. She led us up four dingy flights of stairs, down a dingy, unheated corridor to an even dingier room with two narrow single beds. It was about two degrees below zero inside. The sheets were putrid and bathroom equally so. The rusting pipes yielded no hot water and the faeces encrusted toilet barely flushed.

'We'll take it,' I said.

We hadn't eaten all day and the irritable receptionist waved us towards the 'restaurant'. A young couple sat at a white plastic table on white plastic chairs, sharing a bottle of beer and a packet of chips. The girl had straw-yellow hair with black roots, blue eye shadow and bright red lipstick. Fashions might have been changing in Moscow, but not in the provinces. Cheesy pop blared from tinny speakers. A glass case displayed blocks of chocolate, bottles of Baltika beer and cheap vodka.

A sullen waitress appeared and handed us a menu. It offered the usual fare: *borsch* (beetroot soup), *shchi* (cabbage soup) and various types of rissoles with mashed potatoes or macaroni. We ordered, the waitress scribbled on a pad and left. Half an hour later she returned — empty-handed. '*Nyeto* ...' she said. They didn't have a single thing we'd ordered.

We tried again. Again, she returned with nothing. 'Okay, bring us whatever you have!' I begged, ravenous and exasperated. Finally, she returned, with one bowl of cold greasy noodles.

Back in the freezing room, we donned every item of clothing we had. The beds were shorter than me, with solid wooden ends. At 5'4" I only had to bend a little, but Eric had to curl up in foetal position. By the wee small hours I managed to drift off.

At 3 am, someone began bashing on the door, and a man's voice demanded we open it immediately. I opened it a crack and four paramilitaries burst in. The receptionist, suspicious of the foreigners she was harbouring, had contacted the police, who had called the border guards. It took an hour to convince the thickset thugs in camouflage gear to put their machine guns down. Eventually they left, with another warning not to film the border.

Early the next morning, Yuri arrived at the hotel to take us on a whinge-tour of his broken down town. Jammed in the back seat of his scrap-heap fodder Lada — which had neither functioning suspension, nor a front passenger seat — we passed rows of abandoned, derelict and bankrupt factories while Yuri spewed forth a litany of complaints.

'This factory used to employ twelve hundred people,' he shouted as we bumped along. 'Now it officially employs three hundred and twenty but only about forty people work there.'

Yuri was delighted to have an audience and we sensed again that most considered his crusade ridiculous. It was one thing to grumble and complain in private to friends and neighbours, but anyone who did so publicly was certain to be regarded as a bit of a hare brain. Even so, Yuri had persuaded 740 of the town's 13,000 residents to back his plea to join Estonia.

'I collected these signatures as a protest to show Moscow how badly we live,' he said showing us a several page long yellowing petition.

At the local market, Belarussians sold cheap towels and tablecloths — produced in Belarus's still heavily subsidised state-run factories —

to the day-tripping Estonian bargain hunters. Once the comparatively high standard of living of the Belarussians had made them the envy of the rest of the Soviet Union. Now they were amongst the poorest in the Commonwealth of Independent States with average wages down with those of Tajikistan, a blighted republic neighbouring Afghanistan. Flogging linen to Estonians in Russia was the only way many Belarussians could survive.

But the Russians in Ivangorod couldn't compete. I filmed a Russian babushka, Nina Vyeser, who hadn't received her pension for three months. She was unsuccessfully trying to sell Russian newspapers to the Estonians, in a futile attempt to make enough to buy some shoes.

'We don't get pensions, there's no work, my daughter hasn't worked for five years, what kind of life is this?' she moaned. She pointed to her feet, clad in sandals and socks. It was below zero. 'Winter is coming and I don't even have anything to wear.'

Narva's residents had been trying to help their neighbours across the river, but their patience was running out. The Narva City Council had attempted to set up an aid program to send food parcels and medicine to Ivangorod, but it needed special permission from the border service to transport medicine across the bridge. After months of bureaucratic delays and last-minute refusals, Narva was considering suspending the program. There was also a chance that Ivangorod could lose its electricity supply, which was produced on the Narva side of the river. The Russians were years behind in their payments and the Estonians were threatening to turn it off.

Ivangorod may have been a basket case, but the border service clung to the idea it was guarding a vital strategic stronghold. It was a criminal offence to film the bridge across the Narva River, which made no sense as we had filmed it openly from the Estonian side. We had to sneak into the medieval fort and lean over the parapet to get a shot from the Russian side.

The head surgeon at Ivangorod hospital, Natasha Khilkevi, showed us around the institution she was trying to run without funding or equipment, the strain of her task apparent on her young face. I filmed as we squelched along the cracked linoleum floors in our regulation (filthy) white coats and slippers, peering into wards painted in lime green where glassy-eyed patients stared sombrely at the ceilings. It was lunchtime, and a nurse was doling out some kind of gruel from metal buckets.

'Normally relatives would bring food for the patients, but many of them can't afford it so we try to give them something,' Dr Natasha explained, pointing at the pigswill sloshing into enamel dishes.

Since the financial crisis had begun three months earlier, none of the doctors had received their salaries of USD$35 a month. The hospital was almost out of medicine. In the operating theatre she pointed to a glass of syringes. 'We have to use needles many times over. Of course, you're not supposed to, as there's a risk of AIDS, but we have no choice.'

The operating table was covered in torn, stained vinyl and the light bulbs had blown. Next stop was the delivery room. The centrepiece was a table with iron leg shackles. A set of medieval looking metal instruments hung from hooks on the walls. In the corner was a metal bucket with *Abortsii* (abortions) painted in dripping red on the side.

I winced, grateful that I would never need to rely on a place like this. Or so I thought.

An American physician asked his Russian colleague: 'Is it true that there are cases in your country where a patient was treated for one disease, only to have the autopsy reveal another cause of death?'

'Absolutely not. All our patients die from the diseases we treat them for.'

Out in Kazan, the *krizis* had destroyed Ildar and his American partner's furniture business. As the rouble deflated, they'd been forced to put up their prices. With many potential customers losing all their savings, demand for such extravagances as imported furniture dried up overnight. Fortunately for Ildar, he hadn't borrowed much, but thousands of other small-time entrepreneurs watched their dollar bank loans expand to mind-boggling proportions. With no sales, they had no hope of paying the banks back. A tide of bankruptcies spread across the country.

Undeterred, Zulfia and Ildar decided to put their last kopecks towards a wedding bash. They tied the knot on 11 December 1998, the same day her parents had married back in 1965. I was invited and took the train out from Moscow for the festivities — a great night of wild music, dancing, vodka and a feast, which continued late into the night and all the next day. I was due to catch the 8 pm train back to Moscow. Zulfia was just about to take me to the station when in a fit of crazed merriment, her brother, Zofar, grabbed me round the waist and spun me upside down. I yelped. By the time he got me right side up again I had a stabbing pain on my right side under my ribcage and my head was spinning. I sank to the floor in a dizzy blur.

My imminent train journey was a fourteen-hour trip, alone on a bitingly cold and blizzardly night. Wedding guests crowded around to offer opinions.

'She shouldn't catch the train tonight. It might be appendicitis, and if it is then you only have twenty minutes to get them out before they burst and kill you.'

'Oh great,' I thought, writhing in agony.

I was carried to a couch and lay there for a while, hoping the pain would subside. It didn't. Zofar and Zulfia bundled me into a car and headed for the hospital. They dragged me through the snow and shouted out at the emergency desk. A man in a soiled white coat with a mouthful of gold and decaying teeth appeared and tried to focus on us with bleary eyes. He reeked of vodka. Zulfia asked where the doctor on duty was. 'Yeah, that's me,' he slurred. Zulfia explained what had happened. When he heard I was from Australia he perked up and turned to peer at me.

Zulfia helped me into the examination room. Two other doctors were slumped over a table, sleeping off the effects of the empty bottle in front of them. A poster of the Grim Reaper holding a syringe hung on the wall behind them, the sinister letters СПИД, Russian for AIDS, across it. The first doctor shook the others awake. They decided they would need to rule out appendicitis first and spoke quietly to Zulfia. She came over to me.

'They are just going to give you an injection in your backside and in twenty minutes they'll know if it's appendicitis or not.'

She went back to the doctors and whispered something. They sprang to life, apparently eager to see some Australian buttocks up close. In horror I noticed some syringes in a slime-filled beaker on a scungy bench. The doctor pulled one out, wiped it on his sleeve and stuck it in a vial, all with the Grim Reaper looming behind him.

'No!!!!' I yelled, as they pulled down my pants and jammed it into my bum.

'Don't worry, it'll all be fine,' Zulfia said reassuringly.

The doctors started to snigger.

'Don't you have needles in Australia? We've seen plenty of backsides before. Yours is no different.'

The doctors left with Zulfia and a gnome of a babushka in a dirty frayed coat came into the examination room. She carried a dirty plastic drinking straw, a dirty test tube and a rusty scalpel.

'I'm going to take some blood to do some tests,' she said.

Before I could protest, she took my left middle finger and hacked at my fingertip with the rusty scalpel until blood flowed. She stuck the straw on the wound and sucked. When the straw was full, she spat it into the test tube, handed me a cotton wad to put on my bleeding finger and walked off.

The Grim Reaper was staring straight at me. I'd lost the energy to argue, and figured if I was going to get AIDS, then I probably already had. The gold-toothed doctor returned and led me to a different room. Another babushka appeared. She took a couple of sheets of yellowing A4 paper from a stack by the bed, and lay one where I was to put my head, and the other under my bottom. They were printed on one side, some kind of official documents dated around nine years earlier still bearing the insignia of the USSR. She apologised for only covering part of the bed, but 'the hospital couldn't afford more paper so they had to try to make it last'.

Dr Gold Tooth came in and began to prod deep into my abdomen.

'Where does it hurt?' he asked.

Everywhere hurt. He looked at his watch.

'Well, it's not appendicitis, otherwise we'd know by now. You need to go upstairs to the gynaecology department.'

Zulfia came in to see me.

'I have to go for a bit,' she said. 'But don't worry, you're in good hands. They'll call me if anything happens.'

The only thing Kazan's hospital had on Ivangorod's was that it was bigger. It had the same grungy lime-green corridors leading to the gynaecology rooms and the same torn and stained vinyl-covered beds with metal foot shackles. There was even an identical enamel bucket with the word *Abortsii* painted in the same dripping red.

I knew abortion was an everyday procedure in Russia. Ildar's dentist sister had had ten of them and calmly told me it was 'just their way of contraception'. She was surprised I'd never had one. So were the two 'gynaecologist' babushki who eyed me up and down when Dr Gold Tooth ushered me in.

'Here comes another stupid one,' I could hear them thinking. Dr Gold Tooth explained I had abdominal pain, but it wasn't appendicitis. Blood tests were normal. 'Apart from the babushka spit,' I thought to myself. The women adjusted their headscarves, ordered me onto the bed, locked my ankles into the shackles and began poking around with a large metal probe. I felt blood gushing and begged them to stop. They laughed.

'What's wrong? Haven't you ever been with a man before?'

They found nothing. Bruised and humiliated I was led to a ward. It was still snowing outside and a streetlight cast an eerie green glow over the room. A tap dripped into a filthy sink. Three middle-aged women occupying the other beds woke as I came in.

'Don't worry dear,' said one. 'The doctors here are the best you'll find anywhere. Look at the job they've done on me.'

She pulled open her floral nightdress to reveal a freshly sewed incision from her belly button straight up to just below her third chin. The stitches were huge criss-crosses in thick black thread. I was miserable, scared and wanted desperately to escape to somewhere with sterile instruments and sober doctors. Then I felt guilty. This was all the locals had and who was I to deserve better?

Just as I lay down, Dr Gold Tooth, now almost sober, came to tell me there was a phone call for me, in his office. I staggered down the corridor, clutching my stomach. It was Eric. Zulfia had called him in Moscow to tell him what happened and passed on the hospital number. He sounded as if he were worried sick. I assured him I'd be fine — although I wasn't sure I believed it myself. I hung up, flopped in a chair in Dr Gold Tooth's office and struck up a conversation to distract myself. He'd been an army doctor and spent eight harrowing years in Afghanistan treating wounded soldiers. 'I can never forget the things I saw there,' he said bitterly. 'No one can imagine what hell it was.' I was the first Australian he'd ever encountered and he apologised for the lack of facilities.

'I haven't received my salary for nearly a year now,' he sighed. 'And we have to buy our own equipment and uniforms too.' He plucked at his worn out coat. 'But it's better than in Afghanistan.'

I returned to my creaky hospital bed and spent the rest of the night tossing and turning. Gradually the pain faded. Zulfia and Zofar came to get me in the morning, bringing the vodka and chocolates the doctors had apparently requested while I'd been out of earshot. Gold Tooth and the other doctors, all now sober, were ecstatic at their night's earnings. He patted me on the shoulder as I hobbled to Zofar's car.

'It really was good to meet you. You must come and visit us again!'

The Russian playwright, Anton Chekhov, had once written: 'Doctors are the same as lawyers; the only difference is that lawyers merely rob you, whereas doctors rob you and kill you too.'

As Zulfia drove me to the train station to get a new ticket, I thanked my lucky stars he'd been wrong on both counts.

20

The Ballet Mafia

When money speaks, the truth remains silent.
Russian proverb

February 1999

On the stage of the Bolshoi Theatre in central Moscow, a resonant bass voice rang out from a bulging female fat-suit, naked but for a cook's apron around its waist. The gigantic cook waved a gigantic ladle in defence of three papier-mâché oranges on wheels with whom a hypochondriacal prince, cursed by an evil witch, had fallen madly in love. More inflatable figures, life-size puppets, acrobats and bodybuilders appeared. Premiered in December 1921 in Chicago, Sergei Prokofiev's rumbunctious opera, *The Love for Three Oranges*, was an extraordinary spectacle: an absurd plot, set in an absurd kingdom, with absurd characters behaving completely absurdly. Which is probably why it was still a box-office hit in the eighth year of the reign of Tsar Boris the Sozzled.

After months of grovelling letters to the director of Russia's most famous opera and ballet theatre, I'd finally been given permission to film both a performance and backstage. In my pitch to the Bolshoi's press secretary, I'd raved about how I'd come to Russia long ago because I'd been so inspired by its brilliant artists. My story, for *Foreign Correspondent,* was going to be 'a glowing report on the incredible talent of Russian singers, dancers and musicians'. My fawning bore fruit. As well as allowing me to shoot *The Love for Three Oranges* they'd organised for me to film with their rising young ballet star, Svetlana Lunkina.

The stunning Sveta had been singled out as a great talent the moment she arrived from the Moscow Choreographic Academy. Within three months at the Bolshoi the Audrey Hepburn lookalike was performing the title role in *Giselle*, the youngest ballerina ever to do so in the company's history. I met Sveta at a rehearsal where she was being coached by one of the Bolshoi's living legends, former prima ballerina Yekaterina Maksimova. Now sixty, Maksimova still moved like a woman twenty years her junior and had only given up the stage eight years earlier. Sveta was practising a *pas de deux* with her partner, who had the unenviable task of holding her exceptionally tall (for a ballerina) yet delicately boned body over his head and running around in circles. Maksimova stopped them every couple of seconds, bellowing: 'It's really very ugly when you do it like that!' Sveta was undaunted. Studying with Maksimova had been her 'most treasured wish', even over dancing at the Bolshoi.

Now, at the tender age of nineteen, Sveta's dreams had been realised. She was performing lead roles to critical acclaim at a theatre which had once been an icon of the Soviet empire. But unlike the stars of the past, Sveta was church-mouse poor. Back in Stalin's day, limber and lovely prima ballerinas like Galina Ulanova and Maya Plisetskaya had been the darlings of Stalin and the communist elite, needing only to pick up a phone to get whatever their hearts desired. But now, in March 1999, the base wage for performers at the Bolshoi was a lowly 700 roubles a month, around USD$35. With Moscow rapidly shooting up the 'world's most expensive cities' list, that amount barely covered a basic restaurant meal. I took Sveta and her sixteen-year-old sister, Yulia, also studying to be a dancer, out for coffee and cake. They blushed with embarrassment when I picked up the 200 rouble bill.

'It really is difficult here in Moscow now,' said Sveta, her eyes wide with concern. 'We don't make enough not to worry. I do it because I love it, but if there's something I'd like to do, like go to the ballet or go somewhere to dance then I need money. Then I start to think ... well dancing is wonderful, but in reality, you somehow need to make money.'

With Sveta performing to capacity crowds night after night, it seemed ludicrous that she should be so poorly paid. But with the country's economy in tatters, funding for the arts was no longer a priority. It didn't help that, unlike previous generations of Russian leaders, Tsar Boris apparently preferred to get plastered than turn up to ogle the finest specimens of perfectly proportioned and elastic limbed dancers his country had to offer. As Americans were busy condemning their recently impeached president Bill Clinton for his affair with White House intern Monica Lewinsky, Russians were shaking their heads in bemusement. 'What's the big deal?' was the general consensus. 'They should be thankful to have a president who can get it up.'

Performers everywhere were counting kopecks. Once I'd flagged down an old Lada outside the Moscow Conservatorium and noticed a French horn case on the back seat.

'It's impossible to survive in Moscow on our wages,' the horn player/driver complained. 'So when I'm not rehearsing I work as a gypsy cab driver. Fortunately I bought this car years ago when we used to tour abroad with the orchestra. I wish I'd emigrated like everyone else. You go to any orchestra in the world and you'll find it's full of Russians. No one cares about music here any more.'

While musicians, singers and dancers eked out poverty-line existences, a Ballet Mafia was making a killing from the performers' talent and toil. Scalpers skulked outside the theatres and concert halls, touting tickets at inflated prices to balletomanes and opera lovers unable to buy seats at the box offices. And they couldn't get seats at the box offices because the scalpers had snaffled the lot before they went on sale to the public.

I sidled up to a cagey dude with a close-clipped head pacing around one of the columns of the Bolshoi's portico, proffering crumpled tickets to foreigners from the inside pocket of his leather jacket. His name was Igor and he had once been a dancer. Now his acquaintances in the theatre helped him to acquire a wad of tickets for each performance. There were, he told me about fifty scalpers working around the Bolshoi — twenty in front of the theatre, and another thirty doing shifts in front of the official box office by the entrance to the nearby Teatralnaya Metro station.

'It's not an easy business,' he grumbled. 'We have to pay off the police and the *krysha*, $100 a month to the cops and $400 to the Mafia, so that's $500 a month just to be able to stand here.'

He offered me a front row seat for *Swan Lake*, at the bargain price of USD$250. I examined the ticket, noting the box office price in small print: 100 roubles, the equivalent of USD$5. Even with his police and Mafia payouts, Igor only needed to sell a few tickets a month to be ahead of Sveta financially. It was no wonder he'd given up the long hours and blistered toes of the stage.

But while Sveta accepted this blatant fraud with a graceful resignation, I was annoyed and frustrated on her behalf. I tried to discuss the scalpers with the Bolshoi's Director of four years, the charismatic Vladimir Vasiliev. Together with Sveta's teacher, Elena Maksimova, Vasiliev's wife, the pair had once been the Bolshoi's most famous *pas de deux*. Now Vasiliev had the job of keeping the company afloat. Sitting behind a large oak desk in a smart suit with a neatly buttoned waistcoat, Vasiliev had the aura of a man enjoying his power. He stroked his straw-blond goatee and peered haughtily down his nose at me.

'The black market in tickets is an evil which must be fought against,' he replied with well-practised slickness. 'The scalpers must be eliminated, put in prison, but the laws say otherwise.'

Vasiliev folded his arms and made it clear he did not wish to discuss the matter further. I couldn't help feeling he must somehow be profiting handsomely from the current arrangements. His main concern was the state of the theatre building itself; the magnificent nineteenth-century Russian neoclassical masterpiece — with its huge 2,000-plus seat, five-tiered auditorium sumptuously decorated with glittering chandeliers, gold stucco and plush red velvet furnishings — was in a bad way. The dilapidated electrical wiring was a fire hazard, and the stage and equipment were in urgent need of repair. Almost nothing had changed, Vasiliev told me, since the theatre had been rebuilt in 1856 after fires had destroyed the previous two theatres built on the same site. Not even the Bolshoi's managers had caught up with the times.

'It is the age of computers and internet,' he complained, 'yet here we are still using the abacus.'

At the time I met her, Sveta was performing the lead in a ballet based on *Anjuta*, a story by Anton Chekhov written in 1886. It's the saga of a poor girl forced to marry a rich official to help her family out of their money troubles. She does so reluctantly, leaving her poor student beau distraught. But Anjuta soon begins to revel in her new position in society. Her husband even encourages her flirtations with men of influence in order to advance his ambitions. In the final scene, the now contented Anjuta is moved by seeing her forgotten destitute father, brothers and sweetheart in the town square.

Anjuta was a tale with contemporary resonance in a Russia which seemed to be morphing back into a society eerily similar to the one Chekhov had known. It was now more than six months since the financial crisis had practically annihilated Russia's middle class. But the elite, whose fortunes were safely offshore when the rouble went into freefall, appeared to have remained relatively unaffected. This was fortuitous indeed for those poor folk who could no longer conceive of life without their maids, nannies, beauticians and chauffeur-driven limousines. It was also lucky for the organisers of Russian Fashion Week. Without the patronage of the mega-wealthy they would no longer have an event. Curious to see what effect the crisis had had on Moscow's late twentieth century bourgeoisie, I went to one of Fashion Week's catwalk shows in the Great Hall of Europe's biggest hotel, the Rossiya, with Julie, the Australian journalist I'd taken to Kazan.

We picked our way through the mass of limos jostling for parking space outside the monstrous concrete building behind St Basil's. Inside, the hall was packed with the snappily dressed and perfumed wives of the super-rich, here to check out the latest designs of two local favourites, acclaimed dressers of pop-stars and presidential wives — Valentin Yudashkin and Igor Chapurin. We watched on as a stream of emaciated six-foot tall prepubescent models minced and hip-swivelled in ridiculously skimpy cuts of furs and silks. Yudashkin and Chapurin were brought on stage to rapturous applause. Then it was time for a champagne break.

Julie wanted to talk to some of the audience members. Trying not to sneeze from the overpowering aromas of hairspray and Chanel No. 5, I approached a group of movie star look-alikes and eavesdropped.

'Some of Yudashkin's clothes are okay, but I only shop on the Champs-Elysees,' sniffed one dolly, flicking her locks, shampoo commercial-style.

Julie nodded to me. I took a deep breath and introduced myself, feigning confidence as they spun on their stilettos to peer down at the dowdy foreigner in cargo pants.

'How has the crisis affected you?' I asked a walking advertisement for Prada. Her name was Nastya.

'Not at all.' She laughed.

'How can that be?' I asked.

Nastya looked at me as if I were totally daft.

'Of course my husband was not so stupid as to keep *our* money *here*. We have enough put away for generations.'

The others all nodded.

'We were smart enough to marry smart men.'

So was Tina. Little by little, Stephen Jennings was pulling Renaissance Capital out of the red. By the second half of 1999, he even managed to turn a profit. The rest of Russia wasn't doing too badly either, primarily thanks to rising world oil prices. The crisis also gave a boost to local industry as the rouble's devaluation made imported goods prohibitively expensive. But the gap between the haves and have-nots only seemed to widen.

The disparities were obvious everywhere. In Soviet times, the GUM department store on Red Square had been the place to pick up tractor parts or perhaps a bar of coarse soap if you were lucky. Now lavishly refurbished, GUM boasted swanky outlets for every luxury brand imaginable. You could buy French cosmetics, German technology, Italian leathergoods, and stop for a meal of exorbitantly priced sushi after working up an appetite trying on thousand-dollar shoes. Security guards patrolled the entrances, hustling anyone who didn't pass their '*feis-kontrol*' tests back out into the icy winds.

'Face-control' was something I had never encountered outside Russia, effectively a kind of wealth/class/race discrimination. It gave thuggish doormen the right to refuse entry to anyone they considered wasn't well-dressed or good-looking enough. Failing to pass 'face-control' meant you were too ugly and/or poor to be considered socially acceptable in whatever circle you were attempting to enter. This had never been an issue for me before, as I'd never had any great urge to frequent the haunts of the mega-wealthy, except on the invitation of Marat or Stanislav who had muttered quiet words to convince bouncers to let me through. But Eric and I had now become an item and he enjoyed checking out the local nightlife and eating out at places more chic than the local *pirozhki* kiosk. He dragged me around to snooty shops — where standoffish sales staff peered at me as though I were dog poo on their designer footwear — and made me update my shabby old wardrobe of holey jeans, jumpers worn through at the elbows and hiking boots. Soon I was the reluctant owner of a couple of short dresses, boots with heels and even some stockings — ready to hit the town's hotspots, dance on bar tops and ogle the posh people.

Right on the doorstep of these security-patrolled shrines to wealth — the swish stores, upmarket restaurants, opulent hotels and nightclubs — was Russia's wretched underworld. Ragged and filthy street kids, some as young as five, scampered through metro tunnels and back alleys like frightened wild creatures. Many clutched plastic bags with yellow glue in the bottom, inhaling and exhaling from their poisoned balloons. Dazed babushki and one-legged Afghan war veterans slumped against the cold tiled walls of the metro passageways, holding out cups in scabby hands to collect kopecks from passers-by. There seemed no hope for them. No one cared.

The wealth–poverty gap was every bit as pronounced in St Petersburg as in Moscow. A new friend, an Indian woman named Gayatri, invited me to stay with her and her husband, Nitin, who had an executive position with the multinational blade and razor giant, Gillette. Along with a substantial salary came a whole-floor apartment on the bank of the Neva River, just a couple of buildings up from the Winter Palace. For a monthly rent of USD$20,000, Nitin and Gayatri's residence could almost have been mistaken for a suite in the Hermitage. From the panoramic river views, glossy parquet floors, thick velvet drapes, antique furniture and lavish furnishings, right down to the silver teaspoons, the place oozed affluence. Even my guest room was nearly 100 square metres. Yet a few short blocks away, homeless kids caught ducks on the canals to eat, bunking down in attics, basements and stairwells. It was thirty-five degrees below zero.

I caught up with old friends, eager to find out how they were faring. Masha and her Uzbek husband, Kim, had moved again — via a complicated exchange arrangement, which had taken a year to organise, involving eleven property swaps on one day — into a run-down old flat in the Petrograd district with Kim's elderly mother. This new flat was bigger, but a hundred years older and in an even worse state than the last one. Money was tighter than ever, but somehow they were getting by. Four-year-old Yegor was a handsome boy and Masha was still managing her yearly climbing expeditions.

Olga's brother, Igor, now conducting the orchestra of St Petersburg's Musical Comedy Theatre, was little better off. 'Classical music is not valued like it used to be,' he told me dejectedly. 'The young generation, the "Pepsi generation", just wants to listen to pop songs, and to the Novy Russkys, Mozart and Beethoven are just some dudes who wrote the tunes for their mobile phones. The main problem is that the audiences who used to come to concerts in Soviet times were the educated, the intelligentsia. But they are the ones who became the poorest after the collapse of the USSR. They were too proud to make money by trading and as inflation rose and their incomes fell, they had no money to go to concerts or the theatre.'

And Olga's friend Natasha had temporarily abandoned her academic pursuits in St Petersburg to teach Russian at a university in Brittany, France. She was able to send money back to Russia to help out her mother, Irina, who was still lecturing at the military academy. But Irina was disillusioned and bitter.

'Yeltsin has built criminal capitalism here. Only the strong and dishonest can thrive in such a society as this. People get so upset when they see some neighbour who got terrible marks at school and can hardly string two words together but is now rolling in money. At the same time, the pensioners live terribly. People who have worked hard their whole lives can barely survive, so naturally it arouses hatred when they see rich people. This makes tensions in the society.'

But she could understand why people didn't protest.

'When perestroika began people were so sick of communism, the empty shops and queues. They wanted to believe that things would be better. Now they are full of disappointment and too exhausted to protest. For seventy years people were too frightened to protest. The fear is in their genes — the older generation will never do it. Yeltsin was only re-elected because all the ads scared people into voting for him, threatening that the communists would return if they didn't support Yeltsin. Now people are disappointed and a whole generation is disinterested in politics. Young people today aren't interested in political or spiritual matters. All they care about is money.'

I followed Svetlana Lunkina's career, glad to see that her measly salary was no obstacle to her following her ballet dream. She became one of the Bolshoi's great stars, touring the world with her beloved company to critical acclaim. Sveta also found love, in the form of a Muscovite banker with a golf club business who promoted ballet stars on the side. While she mightn't have had high-up politburo members catering to her every whim, it was good to see that the post-Soviet elites could still appreciate her beauty and talent.

21

Romance in the 'Stans

'My wife and I were happy for twenty years.'
'Then what happened?'
'We met each other.'

Back in 1997, as part of my *Race Around the World* trip, I'd revisited Central Asia for the first time since leaving the rioting Tashkent in 1992. The fun started in Islamabad International Airport: two months, seven countries, three continents and forty flights into my tour of the Third World. First a Pakistan International Airline (PIA) official informed me that my ticket to the Kazakh capital, Almaty, was unconfirmed. Then a customs officer pronounced my Kazakh visa invalid. I talked my way through with the aid of some of Australia's new plastic currency that neither believed was real.

I cut an outlandish figure. All my luggage had gone missing a month earlier on my race odyssey and I'd landed in the Kalahari Desert without even a change of undies. Since then I'd been in an Ethiopian highland village, a remote town in northern Yemen and the Hindu Kush town of Chitral, none renowned for their shopping opportunities. I was carrying my possessions in a cardboard box, and wearing a dusty Pakistani *shalwar kamiz*, an Ethiopian turban around my shoulders, mud-caked boots, and a torn sarong from Botswana over my unwashed hair.

After five hours on a crowded minibus from Peshawar, Hindi film music blaring, I'd arrived in the outskirts of Islamabad at 1 am to find that for some incomprehensible reason, no hotel in the area would accept foreigners. I'd spent the remainder of the night flopped in various scungy hotel foyers until I'd been evicted, and now felt as good as I looked.

So I was surprised when a clean-cut young Pakistani wearing a smart Western suit in the airport check-in queue offered to buy me a coffee — and even more so when he spoke Russian. Arshad was twenty-seven and 'descended from Iranian royalty'. He lived in Peshawar in the North-West Frontier Province but had studied aeronautical engineering in Moscow for six years. There he had fallen in love with a nineteen-year-old Russian divorcee, and against his father's advice had married her. Arshad had brought his Russian princess back to Pakistan, they'd had a son, then she decided she'd had enough. She'd returned to Moscow, and taken their son with her. Now Arshad was on his way to get him back.

Arshad showed me photos of his son's first birthday party his wife had sent him from Russia. His now ex-wife was twenty-one but looked about thirty, with peroxide-whitened hair, blue eye shadow, dark painted lips and thick foundation.

'My father warned me about divorced women, and about Russians,' he said ruefully. 'He said they wouldn't take marriage seriously, and they won't have any problems about ending one a second time. I didn't believe him … but he was right.'

Arshad wasn't the only South-Asian male I would meet that day with marriage issues. As I strapped myself into my wobbly PIA seat, my neighbour began to prod my arm. He was a handsome man in his late thirties, dressed in Western clothing and very agitated.

'Please, Madame, I am a businessman from Iran and I want to ask you for help.'

He showed me a card. His name was Amir and he had offices in Tehran and Malaysia.

'I am a good man. I have a job, my own company. I used to be a sports champion in Iran. I am a good Muslim, but I am missing one thing in my life. I have never met a woman I wanted to make my wife until now.'

I'd spent enough time in Pakistan and India to be used to guys falling madly in love at first sight of my passport. But this time I was filthy and attired like a bag lady, carrying my few remaining possessions in a cardboard box. Surely this could not be a declaration …

'And now she is here, on this plane, the most beautiful girl I have ever seen. I will die if I cannot make her my wife,' he went on.

I shifted uncomfortably in my seat.

'But I can't talk to her. You see, she is travelling up there in front with her mother and sister. I have been watching her in waiting room and I have never seen such beauty. But it is not our custom to talk directly to a girl. You must go to her mother, give her my card and say that you have known me for years, that I am a trustworthy and respectable man, that I will make a fine husband for her daughter.'

I gulped.

'How can I do that? I don't know you, I don't know her. I would be too embarrassed.'

He was crestfallen.

'But you must, I beg you, please, in the name of Allah.'

The captain's voice boomed out from the loudspeaker.

'*Insha'allah,* we shall be landing in Almaty in three hours.'

God willing, we shall be landing in three hours.

The other passengers settled back in their seats for takeoff. *God willing.* Each time I heard this it made me fidgety. What happens if God isn't willing? I supposed that at least I wouldn't have to ask a woman I didn't know if a man I'd only just met could marry her daughter.

Amir didn't let up. I swallowed my embarrassment and resolved to help him out. How could I selfishly deny him the glorious future he had already planned out? I lurched up the threadbare floral carpet to the row he had indicated. A very, very large and fierce-looking woman sat in the aisle seat. Next to her sat her two equally buxom and fearsome-looking daughters. The younger of the two, Amir's new true love, had a bad case of acne. The mother turned sharply to look at me, her bearded jowls wobbling.

'Ummm,' I stammered pathetically holding out the card. 'My very good friend, who is on the plane with me, has asked me to introduce his good self to you and your daughters.'

She looked like she might erupt.

'You go back and tell him right now that we are Pashtuns. If I even catch him looking at my daughters I will tell my husband to kill him.'

After a couple of extended visits to Pakistan's North-West Frontier Province, I knew all about the Pashtuns — a tribal people, renowned for their strict code of honour which includes swift revenge for perceived injustices — indeed, it was the Pashtuns who had kicked the British army out of Afghanistan. I gulped again.

'But ...'

'Now go away and don't bother us again.'

The daughters smirked at my headdress, clearly enjoying watching their mother in action. I slunk back to Amir to break the news.

'It's not looking good,' I began.

'What did she think? Did she take my card?' he asked eagerly.

'I really think you should give up on this ...'

'Did you tell her that I am a wrestling champion of Iran?'

Against my better judgement I went back to my new Pashtun friend. She took one look at me and drew a deep breath. Her formidable chest heaved ... and I scuttled back to my seat.

'I'm so sorry, but there is no hope.'

Amir sank into a morose stupor and barely spoke for the rest of the flight. He bade me a melancholic farewell in Almaty airport, with furtive longing gazes towards the girl he would never have as his wife.

The Pakistani customs official was right — I did not have a valid Kazakh visa, and Kazakh customs officials were determined to milk me for everything they could. I hadn't actually intended to shoot anything here. My original idea was to transit through Kazakhstan on my way to neighbouring Kyrgyzstan. But after the *Race Around the World* producers back in Sydney told me to cancel my shoot in Cambodia, which was suffering a sudden bout of unrest, I had to find a new story in a new country and thought I might as well stop off here. PIA kept the plane waiting on the tarmac while I solved the matter with a 'visa extension' fee.

A Pakistani businessman was also having difficulties with his wife and son's visas. The immigration officials spoke no English so I translated for him. When their problems were sorted out, they offered me a ride into town. Shahid Khan was from Karachi and working in Almaty for the Dutch airline company, KLM. This was the first visit for his wife, Pervin, and his eight-year-old son. By the time we got to the city they had asked me to stay with them. Exhausted after my previous sleepless night and with no idea where I was going, I gratefully accepted.

Shahid lived in a U-shaped concrete apartment building, with a dusty central courtyard for the kids to play in. Minutes after we'd arrived, his exuberant Chechen neighbour, Razit, turned up on the doorstep with her three children and a plate of cakes. Despite the language barrier, Razit had befriended Shahid, feeling sorry for him on his own in a strange country. She hugged Pervin and chattered away. Pervin smiled and nodded politely, obviously not understanding a single word. I was quickly roped in as translator. Razit insisted that I come to stay with her. She had a bigger flat than the Khans and her husband never came home.

Razit's flat was newly renovated, with swirly pastel wallpaper and pink glass chandeliers. Her husband had been a lawyer before opening a successful computer business and now drove a BMW, sent the kids to private schools and had bought a state-of-the-art stereo and a cellular phone. But behind her bubbly exterior, Razit was miserable. For the third time that day I became an agony aunt to a total stranger. We sat in her kitchen and she poured cups of tea from her samovar, telling me how her husband hadn't been home for two weeks. She knew he was having an affair, and so did everyone else. She was humiliated and there was nothing she could do about it.

From her third-floor kitchen window Razit pointed to various flats. There was the Kazashka (a Kazakh woman) over there on the fourth floor, with her constant stream of lovers, a different one every night. There was a man called Rustam who she thought had said he was Libyan, but his Russian was bad so she couldn't be sure. He often waved to her from his window. One day he had given her his phone number. He was old, but not too ugly, and Razit wondered if he was after her. Lily upstairs was also a Chechen, and she was having an affair with a Kazakh removal man. Shahid was the only decent man around. He'd lived here alone for two years and had never once had women guests. Pervin was lucky to have such a good husband.

Razit's parents had been deported to Kazakhstan at the end of World War II after Stalin had declared the entire Chechen population to be Nazi collaborators. Every last Chechen had been forcibly removed from their homeland at the northern foothills of the Caucasus Mountains and packed into freezing cattle trucks for the long journey into exile. Without food or heating, tens of thousands had perished on the way. Her recently deceased parents had been among the survivors and Razit had been born here in Kazakhstan. She had no relatives left back in Chechnya and little choice but to remain as part of the large Chechen diaspora in Almaty. The Chechens were treated as second-class citizens, but they were proud of their ethnicity and kept up their traditions. Suddenly Razit brightened.

'There's going to be a wedding this weekend. Come with me and you can meet my people and see how we dance … how we are far, far away from our homeland, but still we keep our traditions alive. You can film it.'

Razit's eldest daughter, Laila, was thirteen going on twenty. She saw her mother's torment and understood she was suffering. Laila did almost everything around the house and looked after her younger sister, Elvira, and little brother, Rashid. The two younger children bounced around excitedly, peeking into the small flip-out screen on my camera as I watched through my tapes from my last story and tried to write a script. Rashid was particularly intrigued by the images of the Afghan refugee family I had filmed in northern Pakistan. He thought their hats were funny. Laila was pensive. She missed her father and feared he had forgotten them.

The day of the wedding arrived. Razit's spirits lifted and she spent the afternoon curling her hair and doing her make-up. I asked her if it was a 'love marriage' or an arranged marriage.

'It's a Chechen wedding. The young man's friends and relatives went around to the girl's house this morning to steal her.'

'What do you mean, "steal"? Does she know the man she is marrying? Is she happy about it? Why do they have to steal her?'

It sounded barbaric.

'This is just our tradition. Sometimes girls are stolen against their will, but usually it is agreed beforehand that the friends of the groom will come to take her at a certain time,' Razit explained. 'She can refuse if she wants to, but it is considered bad luck to refuse. Maybe no one will ever ask her again if she refuses once. After she is stolen, she is taken to the house of a relative of the groom to settle certain formalities in private between the families and a mullah. The groom himself is not there. Tonight there will be music and dancing.'

That evening a friend of Razit's picked us up and drove us to the wedding party. Little Rashid held my hand as we entered a courtyard lit with fairy lights. A line of young men sat on chairs along one wall, a row of beautiful young girls, elegantly attired in velvet and taffeta, sat opposite them. Most appeared to be in their late teens. A musical trio — accordion, hand drum and some kind of primitive oboe — pumped out pulsating and energetic dance music while an older man strode between the rows of youngsters brandishing a cane which he used to tap pairs, first a boy, then a girl. The anointed couple would diligently rise and dance together as the others watched on, clapping in time to the music. We watched a young girl in slinky scarlet velvet, eyes cast down, slowly swivelling her hips, her feet gliding, arms out level with her shoulders, twirling her wrists high in the air. Her partner stamped his feet in rapid-fire stomps, thrusting his arms around wildly as if attacking an invisible swarm of flies.

'A Chechen woman must be like a swan; graceful, smooth, elegant, sensuous,' Razit whispered. 'And the man must be bold and strong, like an eagle. But the most important thing is that the girl and boy should never, ever touch each other. In our culture, to touch is a great sin.'

Most young Chechens would meet their prospective partners at wedding parties like this one, making eyes at each other across the dance floor while pretending to be absorbed in the couple dancing between them. I could only hope that this marriage would work out better than Razit's. When I left Almaty ten days later, her husband still hadn't come home.

Bishkek, the capital of the small mountainous country of Kyrgyzstan, was a four-hour taxi ride west from Almaty. I shared a vintage Lada peppered with bullet holes with a churlish Kazakh in military fatigues and a Kyrgyz television producer. His name was Bolot, Russian for bog or swamp, and I couldn't help wondering if that had ever been an issue for him.

Our driver cheerfully regaled us with tales of the car-jackings and murders that he'd witnessed on this, the Almaty–Bishkek road, over the past few weeks. The 'army' guy raved about the fortune he was making 'exporting' used German cars. And both the driver and Bolot listened, mesmerised, as he described how the German Social Security system gives money to the unemployed.

'How can a government give people money for doing nothing?' the driver asked, dumbfounded. 'At least the car-jackers are working for their money.'

There was no border checkpoint between the two countries, and therefore no one to stamp my passport to show I'd left Kazakhstan or entered Kyrgyzstan. I wondered out loud if this might be a problem. They all laughed.

'No one cares. And if anyone asks, you pay them something and they will forget you were ever here,' advised Bolot.

The taxi driver left us outside the TV station where Bolot worked. He invited me in and a couple of heavily made-up newsreaders in tailored bright orange suits poured sickly cherry liqueur into goblets for us to drink with them. The Kyrgyz had finer and more Oriental features than the swarthy Kazakhs and the women looked like delicate porcelain dolls. Bolot showed me the studio where he produced a 'music morning' every Sunday with Western video clips. His face fell when he realised I knew nothing about pop music. He'd been hoping to get me in as a guest. I couldn't imagine anything more nerve-racking than being put on the spot about my favourite band on live-to-air TV, in Russian.

But then I heard about Bolot's uncle. He was allegedly a world-famous dentist, whose party trick was to remove up to fourteen teeth at one time, without an anaesthetic. I thought he might make a great story subject, until Bolot explained that he performed this great feat by using hypnosis on his patients. Gold or stainless steel teeth might be fashionable in this part of the world, but I preferred to keep my own.

Bishkek was a nondescript Soviet town with the same old drab apartment buildings found everywhere in the former USSR. From Bishkek I travelled east, along the southern shores of the sparkling turquoise Lake Issyk Kul, literally 'warm lake'. Ringed by snow-capped mountains, Issyk Kul is the world's second largest mountain lake. I stopped in the village of Barskoon on the lake's southern shore, to track down some friends of friends, the Tynayevs.

Ishen Tynayev struck a Genghis Khan-style figure, exceptionally tall for a Kyrgyz shepherd, with long black hair and high cheekbones. While independence had bought extreme poverty to most Kyrgyz, Ishen had been one of the few who'd managed to improve his lot. He had learned reasonable English and found a job at the Kumtor Gold Mine — a joint venture project co-owned by the Kyrgyz government and a Canadian company, Centerra Gold — just upriver from Barskoon. Ishen had also set up a small tour company with his wife, Gulmira, taking the occasional intrepid group of foreigners on horseback into the magical Tien Shan (Heavenly Mountains) range around the lake.

Gulmira too spoke English and had caused quite a stir in Barskoon by not only shunning the traditional headscarf and cutting her hair short, but by becoming the first woman in the village to wear jeans. She took me to meet her neighbours, the Babakanovs, an elderly couple and their extended family, who put me up for the night on the floor of their wooden cottage with the grandkids. Their hospitality was so overwhelming I had to beg them not to slaughter their best horse to mark my visit.

On the next day, Gulmira, her brother, Rashid, and I rode up into the foothills of the Heavenly Mountains to visit relatives who spent their summers as their ancestors had done, living in a round felt yurt while watching over their sheep grazing on lush mountain grasses. Alamkul the shepherd was thrilled to have news of the world beyond the hillside and rushed to pour us some *kumiz,* fermented horse milk. He was intrigued to meet his very first Australian, but appalled to hear I was twenty-eight and unmarried. Alamkul quickly offered to send a number of sheep, horses and goats to my family in exchange for me marrying his son, in what Gulmira assured me was a pretty good deal for such an old bride.

Almost two years later, in March 1999, I returned to Kyrgyzstan with Eric and an ABC crew. It was nine years since my first trip to then Soviet Central Asia, and history was fast being rewritten. Back in 1990, official propaganda described 'the great happiness of the Central Asian peoples on their liberation from their Tsarist oppressors by the Bolsheviks'. These days it was the Soviets who had become the big bad bogeymen of Kyrgyz history. The Tsarist colonisers were still regarded as cruel exploiters of the people and natural resources of the region, but unlike the Soviets, they had at least allowed the practice of Islam.

We arrived in the Kyrgyz capital, Bishkek, in time for Muslim New Year, Nouruz, which had replaced the Great October Revolution celebration as the party of the year. Instead of a show of Soviet tanks and artillery, red flags and war veterans dripping with medals, the assembled masses were treated to a vibrant display of dancers in national dress, horsemen with pointy white felt hats and even a yurt assembly demonstration. President Askar Akayev watched on proudly.

But this show of nostalgia for the traditions of the pre-Soviet Kyrgyz was like a colourful party mask, a distraction from the grim reality of the new era of independence. As everywhere else in the former USSR, living standards of the majority had fallen, social services were crumbling and government corruption was endemic. In Central Asia, where wealth, power, politics and family dynasties have always been intertwined, many complained (quietly) that President Akayev was styling himself as a feudal Khan, channelling the country's assets to his family and friends. Almost a year earlier, his son Aidar had married Aliya Nazarbayeva, the daughter of the Kazakh president, a partnership eerily reminiscent of past deals to cement alliances between Khanates.

Gulmira was in Bishkek for the Nouruz holiday, but she was circumspect about the new-look post-commie Kyrgyzstan. The previous May there had been an awful accident involving a truck carrying nearly two tonnes of sodium cyanide, which had crashed through a bridge over the Barskoon River on its way to the World Bank funded Kumtor mine site. It wasn't until several hours after the incident that residents of Barskoon had been told about the poisoning of their water source. Several people had died, hundreds fell ill and thousands had to be evacuated. Despite widespread contamination of land, water, livestock and produce around Barskoon, most villagers had received little, if any, compensation. As part of a Soviet-style spin operation, doctors at Barskoon's hospital had apparently been ordered by officials to attribute only four of the deaths to the cyanide spill. Furious villagers protested as the Kyrgyz government and Centerra Gold quickly resumed work at the mine, making fortunes for themselves, while the locals queued up at the hospital presenting skin rashes, sores and other ailments.

We spent the night in a magnificently appointed suite in a Bishkek hotel, which included a splendid dining room furnished with a ten-seater table and cabinet filled with china crockery and silver cutlery. The carpet, velvet curtains and flock wallpaper were all a matching dark crimson. Amidst such extravagance it was almost a shock to find the bathroom was just as antiquated and putrid as every other Soviet-era hotel. Breakfast was an all-white 'heart attack special', consisting of a cup of sour cream, a dish of ricotta-type cheese with cream on top, white bread with slabs of white butter, tea with an inch of undissolved sugar at the bottom of the glass, and a poached egg covered in salt with an anaemically pale yolk.

Eric and the ABC crew had hoped to go out to Barskoon and up into the mountains with Gulmira and Ishen. But it was still too cold. Gulmira suggested we return in a few weeks when the snow had melted and spring foliage had bloomed. There were no flights out of Bishkek that day, so we decided to take a taxi to Almaty and fly back to

Moscow on the first flight the following morning. We'd spent approximately three hours on Kazakh territory — from 1 am to 4 am — before arriving at Kazakh airport customs. But because there'd been no border checks when we'd driven in, we had no stamp to say when we'd arrived. We filled in the customs declaration, stating we had USD$3,000 cash.

'Where is your customs declaration form for entry to Kazakhstan?' demanded a surly customs officer as he scanned the completed form.

We didn't have one. There'd been no one at the border to check our passports at 1 am, let alone give us a customs form.

'Well how do we know you haven't earned this money in Kazakhstan and are trying to leave without paying tax?' he snarled.

I showed him the stamp to say we'd only entered Kyrgyzstan two days earlier.

'That is no proof of anything. You must pay us half the money in taxes or you cannot leave the country.'

I was furious at such bare-faced extortion. We had no choice but to pay up or miss the flight. And we couldn't even complain to the official in charge. He *was* the official in charge.

By the time we made it back to Barskoon it was late May. Gulmira and Ishen had been waiting for us for weeks. So had Ishen's grandfather, Suyumbek. Every winter he trained a young eagle to hunt for small mammals, which it could spot running across the snow from a great distance, and bring its prey to him. After the winter hunting season was over, he released the eagle back into the mountain skies.

This year I had asked him to let us film as he set his eagle free. But when we finally got to Barskoon, a month later than promised, the poor bird's flight muscles had wasted from lack of use. We followed as Suyumbek carried the giant creature on horseback up into the mountains. On a grassy hillside high above Issyk Kul, the eagle sat on Suyumbek's leather arm shield, digging in its talons as the old man swooshed him round like a firestick, trying to remind him of the feel of air beneath his wings. But the eagle was either unwilling or unable to leave the man in the white felt hat who had enslaved him for the past winter. Clinging to its master, the creature seemed to fear independence and what that would bring.

'I have kept him too long,' said Suyumbek. 'He has forgotten how to fly by himself and now he can't live without my help.'

The image seemed an apt metaphor for the psychological upheaval experienced by the ordinary people of the former USSR. I remembered something Tatiana had told me: 'For all our lives we were told the state would look after us. So many people took a long time to believe that this help was gone and that we really had to look after ourselves. They just kept waiting for someone to give them things.'

Finally Suyumbek's eagle flapped off, clumsy and reluctant, hardly the scene of joyful liberation I'd anticipated. He stayed close by as we rode on up through the forested mountainside.

After some hours we came to Alamkul's yurt, the same one I'd visited two years earlier. The family remembered me and their daughter Almira hurried to pour cups of *kumiz* for us all from a bag made out of a sheep's stomach hanging by the yurt door. Eric politely tried not to gag as he picked out the hairs and dubious looking crusty floaters from the potent fermented mare's milk.

Life had changed little on the Tien Shan foothills. But eighteen-year-old Almira seemed forlorn. When she went out to milk the horses Alamkul told me how last year she had been 'bridenapped', a good old Kyrgyz tradition, rather like the Chechens, in which a young man and his mates 'abduct' a young girl he likes and marries her immediately. Almira hadn't minded the bridenapping — he was a nice enough guy — but after she had two miscarriages, his family had sent her back here. Her prospects for a future other than life with her parents in their yurt were gloomy.

Over a plate of boiled lung from a freshly slaughtered sheep, Alamkul told us that despite the supposed new 'freedoms', life under the Soviets had been better.

'Back then we were more equal. Now those who have property and money live well and have everything. But those who don't live worse.'

After the shoot, Eric and I spent a couple of days at Barskoon's sanatorium. In Soviet days, holidaying workers and their families had 'relaxed' here, enjoying Issyk Kul's sandy beach, with its spectacular mountain backdrop. Accommodation was still in small wooden dormitory huts, and the old daily schedule was still up on the wall outside the communal dining hall. All guests had had to follow the strict regime of exercise and activities, beginning with reveille at 6 am. It reminded me of a girl scout camp, only this had been for adults. Thankfully those days were long gone and we were able to sit on the beach without officious sanatorium staff ordering us to play volleyball. Instead we watched local men wearing nothing but budgie smugglers and traditional felt hats ride their horses up and down the beach.

Eric went back to Moscow and I had to return to Australia. He was after all the ABC's Russia correspondent, so I'd had to find somewhere else to work and planned to shoot a film about Muslim women in Indonesia. Again I took a taxi from Bishkek to Almaty. Not wanting a repeat of our official extortion at Almaty airport two months earlier, this time I made sure I filled in a customs form at the Kazakh border. As we approached Almaty the driver asked me where exactly I wanted to go.

'To the airport,' I replied.

He laughed.

'There is no airport any more. It burned down yesterday.'

I could barely hide my joy. Was it karma at work, divine retribution to put those grasping custom's thugs out of business? My plane left a few hours late, but at least my wallet was intact.

22

Rancid Fish and Dirty Games

The fish always rots from the head downwards.
Russian proverb

While I was off in Australia and Indonesia, the twists and turns in the soap opera that was Russian politics became ever more erratic. Since March 1998, Tsar Boris had been playing musical chairs with his prime ministers, hiring and firing them every few months. From 1992, the former Gazprom chief, Viktor Chernomyrdin, had held the post, overseeing the nation's economic ruin while mysteriously building up an astronomic personal fortune from his paltry prime ministerial salary. But on 23 March 1998, Yeltsin demanded Chernomyrdin's head, and installed the bookish 35-year-old Sergei Kiriyenko in his place.

In mid-August, the rouble began its nosedive. Days later, Yeltsin sacked Kiriyenko, declaring that only Chernomyrdin could bring the country back from the brink of financial *krizis*. Considering he'd sacked Chernomyrdin just five months earlier after blaming him for the country's woes, it appeared to the bemused public and his livid Duma deputies that Yeltsin had at last completely lost his marbles.

One of the few powers Yeltsin's constitution had left the Duma was the right to approve a new prime minister. And the Duma was in no mood to accept the return of Chernomyrdin who they despised as much as Yeltsin. After a couple of weeks of posturing, Yeltsin was forced to put up a compromise candidate, the dour Foreign Minister and former director of the Foreign Intelligence Service, Yevgeny Primakov, who took up the position on 11 September 1998. Conservative and patriotic, Primakov was popular with the commies and nationalists. Remarkably for a Russian political figure, he even had a reputation for personal honesty. It wasn't long before Yeltsin began to feel insecure about Primakov.

Boris's paranoia wasn't helped when the Duma communists began moves to impeach him for, among other things, destroying the Soviet Union and invading Chechnya. There was never any hope of the impeachment getting through the tortuous legal processes that Yeltsin's appointees controlled, but it added to his already deplorable image problems. And if this wasn't enough, yet another unexplained bout of ill-health landed Yeltsin in hospital again.

Yeltsin struck back from his hospital bed, firing, among others: his head of Presidential Administration and the deputy in charge of the Special Services. But Primakov was undaunted. He authorised the Prosecutor-General, Yuri Skuratov, to begin an investigation into Yeltsin's oligarch mates, including Boris Berezovsky, Anatoly Chubais — the former Chairman of the State Committee for Management of State Property — and Pavel Borodin, a member of the Presidential Administration accused of corruption related to an extravagant refurbishment of the Kremlin.

Skuratov dutifully produced a damning report on Russian money in Swiss bank accounts. Tsar Boris was worried. His deputies were still trying to impeach him, and if the increasingly popular Primakov should get into power, who knew what might happen? It was vital to find a loyal presidential successor who would guarantee Yeltsin and his inner circle, the 'Family', immunity from prosecution once he left office. It was also crucial to halt Skuratov's corruption investigations, which had now come way too close to the 'Family' for comfort.

Skuratov had to go. It was time to spice up the show. In February 1999, in a time-honoured Russian tradition, *kompromat* (compromising material) was produced and sent to Skuratov. After watching a videotape of a man with an uncanny resemblance to himself frolicking with two prostitutes, Skuratov resigned. But in a surprise twist, the Federal Council (upper house of parliament) rejected his resignation.

Too many people were enjoying watching the oligarchs squirm in the wake of his reports to let him go. Eventually Yeltsin had no choice but to fire his pal Berezovsky, once Russia's richest man and former presidential tennis partner, from his position as Executive Secretary of the Commonwealth of Independent States.

Just as Skuratov issued a warrant for Berezovsky's arrest, the tape of him with the prostitutes was leaked to state television. The Minister of the Interior, Sergei Stepashin, and the Director of the Federal Security Service (FSB), Vladimir Putin, held a joint televised press conference to discuss the matter. Putin calmly outlined how expert FSB analysis — including measurements of the offending member — had proved the authenticity of the tapes, and that the man on the tape was indeed Skuratov. But again the Federal Council refused to let Skuratov resign.

Yeltsin was incensed. The presidential press service claimed that 'such an important post [as Prosecutor-General] cannot be held by a person letting himself be used in a dirty game', a bold statement considering Yeltsin's own record. Primakov's popularity soared still further and on 12 May 1999, Yeltsin sacked him. The chubby-cheeked interior minister, Sergei Stepashin, was reluctantly sworn in as Prime Minister a week later, despite telling Yeltsin he didn't want the job.

Meanwhile, on Russia's southern border, trouble was brewing — again. Yeltsin's 'small victorious' war in Chechnya, which he'd begun back in December 1994, had raged on for nearly two years with horrific loss of life on both sides. In late August 1996 a deal known as the Khasavyurt Agreement was brokered between a gruff Russian general, Alexander Lebed, and the Chechen leader, Aslan Maskhadov. However, not everyone was happy with the ambiguous terms of the proposal, which delayed a decision on the status of the republic for a five-year period. Many Russians felt they had made a humiliating retreat after 'losing' Chechnya, while many Chechens were equally discontent at not having achieved complete independence. But at least the bloodshed had stopped. Democratic elections had been held in January 1997, and Aslan Maskhadov sworn in as President of the Republic of Chechnya.

The fragile peace didn't last long. On 4 August 1999, Islamic radicals clashed with interior ministry troops in Chechnya's neighbouring republic of Daghestan, killing four. Prime Minister Stepashin flew to the Daghestani capital, Makhachkala, to sort things out. The next day, the infamous Chechen commander, Shamil Basayev, and his deputy, a Saudi mujahid called Khattab, led over a thousand heavily armed fighters from Chechnya eastwards into Daghestan. Basayev announced his plan to unite Chechnya and Daghestan into an Islamic Caliphate and heavy fighting immediately broke out.

On 8 August, Stepashin returned to Moscow where Yeltsin promptly fired him, naming Vladimir Putin, the 46-year-old director of the FSB, as his new Prime Minister. This Putin, however, wasn't just any old new Prime Minister. This time, Tsar Boris announced to the stunned masses that the little-known former KGB spook with the piercing, blue-eyed stare was his chosen successor as President. Now widely viewed as a national embarrassment, an endorsement from doddering Boris, whose approval rating was around 2 per cent, should have been the kiss of death for Putin's political ambitions.

To most Russians, Vladimir Putin had seemingly sprung from nowhere. Few paid much attention to him; it wasn't as if he was ever really going to be President. Olga's husband, Misha, thought he seemed okay. 'At least he's educated.'

He was. The new Prime Minister had graduated from Leningrad State University (LSU) in International Law. Then, this long-time fan of intelligence officer characters in Soviet movies joined the KGB and the Communist Party. After a decade of training and working for the KGB in Leningrad and Moscow, Putin was promoted and sent to Dresden in East Germany. When the Berlin Wall came down he returned to Leningrad. He took up a position in the International Affairs department at LSU and began to cultivate important connections, in particular with his former lecturer and now mayor of Leningrad, Anatoly Sobchak. During the coup attempt on Gorbachev in August 1991, Putin resigned from the security services and began to work for Sobchak as his Deputy for External Economic Affairs.

In charge of foreign investments, Putin surrounded himself with former KGB mates and expertly schmoozed everyone who mattered.

When Sobchak, accused of financial impropriety, failed in his re-election bid in 1996, Putin thoughtfully arranged for the ex-mayor's escape abroad. Chubais and others in Moscow were impressed. Such loyalty to a former boss was an admirable quality indeed, just what the Kremlin needed, given many of its senior figures seemed likely to face the same fate as Sobchak. Putin was invited to work in the Presidential Property Management Department under Pavel Borodin, a powerful 'Family' member who would soon be wanted by the Swiss on corruption charges.

Rung by rung Putin ascended the political ladder. In 1997 he was made Deputy Chief of Presidential Staff, and in June 1998, he became Deputy Chief of Presidential Administration for Relations with the Regions. Six weeks later he was made head of the FSB, Yeltsin's incarnation of the KGB.

'I have come home,' Putin declared as he took up his new post.

Two weeks later the financial crisis hit Russia. But Putin not only survived Boris's purges, he networked his way still further into favour. By March 1999, in addition to his role as Chief Spook, he became Head of the Security Council. Now he was Prime Minister.

Confronted with the crisis in Chechnya and Daghestan, steely-eyed Prime Minister Putin launched major combat operations, vowing to crush the rebels in a fortnight. But the fighting dragged on and intensified. Federal forces attacked villages in Daghestan, a car bomb destroyed a military housing building killing sixty-four people, and the Russian Air Force began bombing 'rebel bases' inside Chechnya.

It was what happened next that both sent conspiracy theorists into a frenzy, and secured Putin's rise. In the middle of the night of 9 September, ninety-four people were killed when a massive explosion destroyed a building on Guryanova Street, on the southeastern outskirts of Moscow. Another bomb on the 13th killed 119 people on a nearby highway, Kashirskoye Shosse. Three days later, seventeen people were killed in an explosion in the southern town of Volgodonsk. Putin immediately blamed the Chechens, declaring famously that he would pursue them anywhere, even 'waste them in the shithouse'. His approval ratings soared as many Russians, fed up with the incoherent and unpredictable Yeltsin, saw Putin as just what Russia needed, a strong, resolute and decisive leader.

Olga was at the family dacha in Tryokhgorka, north of Moscow, with Misha and two-year-old Tyoma when they heard news of the bombings. She didn't believe for a second that the Chechens were responsible.

'Of course it was the government,' she said matter-of-factly. 'It's their way to frighten people and lead them to think and do what they want.'

And what the government needed was for Putin to win the upcoming presidential elections, so Yeltsin, the 'Family', and his crooked mates could all be granted immunity from imminent prosecution and avoid a potential grisly Ceausescu-style end.

On 22 September, an old woman saw FSB officers planting explosives in an apartment building in Ryazan, southeast of Moscow, fuelling speculation amongst many of Yeltsin's opponents that the FSB had indeed been responsible for the Moscow and Volgodonsk apartment bombings. A day later, Putin's replacement as FSB head, his old mate Nikolai Patrushev, announced it had been a training exercise and Putin's rise continued unabated.

The very next day he ordered the bombing of the Chechen capital Grozny. At the beginning of October, Russian forces poured into Chechnya, prompting a flood of refugees to flee west into neighbouring Ingushetia with spine-chilling reports of murder and torture by Russian soldiers. Yeltsin and the 'Family' stood behind Putin all the way. But they were worried.

Despite his increasing popularity, Putin's victory in the forthcoming presidential elections was anything but certain. Primakov, the former Prime Minister, had joined forces with Tatarstan President, Mintimer Shaimiev, and Moscow mayor, Yuri Luzhkov, in a party called Fatherland — All Russia (Otechestvo — Vsya Russiya, or OVR). By the December 1999 Duma elections, Primakov was number one on the list and Yeltsin's succession plan was looking dubious. Yet again, oligarch Berezovsky came to the rescue. Together with various (and highly corrupt) regional leaders, ministers and even a world champion wrestler, he formed a new movement to support Putin, which would later become the Unity party. Berezovsky's media empire went into overdrive to propagandise Unity and discredit Primakov and Luzhkov, and yet again, it worked. Primakov and Luzhkov's OVR party was crushed, and Primakov was out of the presidential race.

As the end of the millennium approached, the threat of catastrophe from the Y2K bug sent Russians into a spin. Russia was predicted to descend into chaos on the stroke of midnight as the nation's archaic computers crashed and malfunctioned. Potential doomsday scenarios circulated: central heating systems would fail, water would freeze in pipelines causing plumbing pipes to burst and crack. Telecommunications would cease to operate and the country would be plunged into darkness. People were preparing for the worst, stocking up on food and bottled water in anticipation.

It wasn't only the Russians who were panicking in the face of impending calamity. The Australian Embassy evacuated its entire personnel to Manchester, and the ABC insisted its employees move to the Metropol, a five-star hotel opposite the Bolshoi Theatre, and a block from Red Square. Once the only hotel in Russia to have hot water, refrigerators and lifts, the Metropol now boasted its own generator. Should the rest of the country come grinding to a standstill, we could at least have hot showers while everyone else died of hypothermia and starvation outside.

I had returned to Russia in November 1999 and was now living with Eric in the ABC flat. It was midday on New Year's Eve and I was packing some things together to take to the Metropol that night, with the Russian Channel One television news on in the background. Suddenly Tsar Boris appeared on screen, seated at a desk as if ready to give an official address. This was something new. Traditionally Kremlin leaders gave a minute-long televised speech to the nation at two minutes to midnight. For the last minute of the year the country froze before an image of the Kremlin tower clock ticking over before popping the corks of their *Sovietskoye Shampanskoye*.

But it was still daytime. I watched in disbelief as Boris Nikolayevich Yeltsin, the president who not so long ago had fought several attempts by his deputies to impeach him, voluntarily announced his resignation. Prime Minister Vladimir Putin would be acting President for the next three months until elections could be held. I called Eric, who was just preparing to leave the office for the Metropol, to see if he'd heard the news.

He couldn't believe it. Yeltsin couldn't have chosen a more inconvenient time to quit. Over his four years as a correspondent, Eric had compiled thirteen obituaries for old Boris, ready to run the minute the news came through that his latest heart attack, flu or stomach ulcer had finally bumped him off. I'd watched Eric several times, panicking to get yet another one ready every time old Boris was taken off to hospital. But now he'd gone and resigned, on the very day that Eric couldn't run the story. The ABC had just begun a 24-hour broadcast special for the New Millennium and he couldn't break into the broadcast with a news report. Eric would now have to prepare a new story to send through the next morning.

All our Millennium Eve plans went out the window. I phoned Olga, who had invited us for dinner at their flat, and asked if she and Misha would mind if Eric filmed their reaction to Yeltsin's resignation. Even as I asked the question I knew what her answer would be.

'I'm sorry,' Olga apologised. 'We just can never be sure in this country what might happen. Who knows what the future holds and if we may get in trouble for an opinion we express now.'

They didn't want to say it to the camera, but Olga and Misha had mixed feelings about Yeltsin's departure. On one hand they were glad to see the back of the embarrassing drunkard who had comprehensively screwed up the country. On the other they were apprehensive. Might it be a case of the devil you know? Putin would certainly be a very different leader. But who knew what the former spook had in mind for the country?

It was still only early afternoon, but barricades were already being erected around the city centre to prevent vehicle access during the evening celebrations. Eric and David, the ABC's new cameraman, packed a camera kit and editing machine, and we left for the Metropol. Moscow Mayor, Yuri Luzhkov, had gone all out with the street decorations: banners, tinsel and giant baubles were strung up across the city, towering *yolki* (New Year's trees) and enormous Grandfather Frost (the Russian Santa) figures loomed over every square. Crowds of revellers were already streaming into Red Square, rugged up against the cold and clinking bottles as they strolled. In Manezh Square, rows of extra *toi-tois* (portaloos) were being set up. With a leak in a *toi toi* costing more than a beer, I wondered how many cash-strapped Muscovites would opt to spend their hard earned roubles on the former.

The Metropol was one of Moscow's finest hotels, recently restored to its pre-revolutionary glory in immaculate and intricate detail. Our room even had its own luxurious ensuite, with surfaces so sparkling it was hard to believe we were still in Russia. Even the sheets were crisp and white, with no evidence of previous occupants. But there was no time to savour any of it. There was work to do.

We headed out into the half-sozzled crowds, now cheerfully throwing champagne bottles and lighted rockets at each other. It wasn't a good time or place to be trying to find sober English speakers willing to comment on Yeltsin's resignation.

'We're in Russia so I'll only speak Russian,' one guy shouted as I dodged a lighted flare, about to explode at my feet.

'Who cares?' yelled another, waving a freshly opened champagne bottle and spilling most of it down my front.

At one minute to midnight, everyone turned to the Spasskaya Tower clock and began the countdown. I waited for the city to black out on the stroke of twelve. Five, four, three, two, one … Thousands more champagne corks shot into the air, bells chimed and fireworks cracked over the Moscow River. And the lights stayed on. The months of panic over Y2K had been for nothing.

Acting President Putin was nowhere to be seen. He'd had a busy day. After signing a decree granting Boris Yeltsin full immunity from prosecution, he'd flown to Mozdok, on the Russian border with Chechnya. While his people were busily downing sweet bubbly he was flying over Chechnya in a military helicopter with his wife and FSB crony, Nikolai Patrushev.

The Putin era had begun.

PART THREE

Putin

(For God, Tsar and the Fatherland)

23

Pride and Prejudice

'The nationalist not only does not disapprove of atrocities committed by his own side, but he has a remarkable capacity for not even hearing about them.'
George Orwell, from 'Notes on Nationalism', 1945

Ingushetia, January 2000

It was my first trip to a war zone, and while we hadn't even left the Nazran Airport car park, a fight was about to break out. I had flown down with Eric and his cameraman, David Martin, who were covering the refugee crisis for ABC News, but I was going to work independently with Bentley Dean, a filmmaker friend from Australia.

I'd come to the wintry and muddy republic of Ingushetia in the north Caucasus to shoot a story about refugees fleeing Russian bombs in neighbouring Chechnya. When I'd told Akhmed — Rafael's buddy whom I'd met in Thailand — I was going to his homeland, he sent a message to his family. 'Don't worry,' he'd assured me. 'My family will guard you with their lives. It is a matter of honour for us Ingush to protect our friends.' Akhmed was still in Malaysia, but his brothers, Magomad and Badruddin, his father, and two of his four sisters had come to the airport to collect us.

But Ruslan Aushev, the Ingush president, had other ideas. Following a spate of kidnappings of foreigners — including one which had ended with the grisly beheading of three Britons and a New Zealander working for a British telecommunications company in December 1998 — Aushev's government had decreed that all foreigners must be accompanied by official government guards and drivers, at the extortionate rate of USD$150 a day, each. And the only place we would be guaranteed safety was at the Assa Hotel in Nazran, the Ingush capital.

An official in a slick suit flanked by guards told Magomad and Badruddin to go home. They began to fume and Badruddin looked ready to punch the bureaucrat right in his smirking face. Magomad, the eldest, a swarthy twenty-something with a distinct whiff of vodka on his breath, pulled me aside and hissed: 'You can't trust these people. They are Mafia and just want your money. I mean it. How do you know they are not just going to kidnap you? I have promised Akhmed you will be safe and I can *not* let you go with these people. You know you can trust me.'

He had a point. I trusted Akhmed's brothers, mainly because I trusted Akhmed. But Eric wasn't convinced Ben and I should go off on our own. The smug official swaggered over to me and growled: 'How do you know you can trust these men? How do you know they won't kidnap you?'

In the end I was outnumbered. To pacify the now ropeable Magomad, I told him we'd do as the authorities demanded today but would be in contact soon. The official allocated us a burly young 'security guard' in camouflage gear called Adam, and a battered Lada with a truculent driver named Ruslan. Eric, David, Ben and I jammed in, camera gear and bags wedged around us. Adam squeezed in after us, lay his AK-47 on my camera bag and we sputtered off to the Assa.

A posse of bulldog-faced OMON (Otryad Militsii Osobogo Naznacheniya, Special Purpose Police Squad) heavies waving Kalashnikov assault rifles stood at the entrance, malicious enough to deter the most ambitious of would-be kidnappers. But the hotel was full. The BBC and Reuters had permanent bookings for many of the rooms. French, Scandinavian, German and American journalists had taken all the others. Adam, who seemed trustworthy, and Ruslan, who didn't, began to argue in Chechen. Finally Ruslan turned to me.

'Okay,' he said gruffly. 'We will take you to a house for tonight. It will cost one hundred US dollars each, plus one hundred for Adam. Meals will be extra.'

I translated for the others. They were not happy, nor remotely confident it would be safe. The creepy Ruslan seemed just the kidnapping type. But we had little choice. We were already captives. I turned up the charm, hoping he would think us too nice to murder.

Ruslan took us to an Ingush family home; a weatherboard cottage behind a high sheet-metal fence with an elaborately welded gate painted in a pale blue-green. Chickens scattered as our overloaded vehicle groaned into the slushy yard. I was relieved to see a woman in a headscarf carrying water in a bucket up onto the verandah. Surely they wouldn't behead us in front of their women? A couple of the chooks weren't so fortunate, appearing some time later in a stew. Adam tucked into a hearty serving and fell fast asleep, draped over a chair in his camouflage gear with his Kalashnikov on his lap.

'Well this is good,' muttered Eric.

Judging by his snores, Adam had a good night's kip. But Eric and David remained on edge, wrestling with satphones, microphones and laptops for most of the night to file radio reports. We survived intact and returned to the Assa in the morning, managing to wangle a couple of beds and a patch of floor space in one of the BBC's rooms.

Our woes were nothing compared to those of the estimated 170,000 Chechens who'd fled to Ingushetia over the last three months to escape the Russian bombardment. Hundreds more were arriving every day. The lucky ones had crowded into derelict railway carriages and cattle sheds. The rest were freezing, filthy and hungry in tent camps with pit toilets and little fresh water. A tanker came daily to dish out soup. It was heart-wrenchingly awful.

I trudged numbly through the mud at Karabulak camp, 20 kilometres northeast of Nazran, on the Sunzha River. A group of ragged children followed in my wake, staring up at me hopefully with dirty and desperate faces. I had nothing to give them, no food, no toys, no clothes, no hope. I tried to convince myself that I was here to record this horror so people 'back home' would know what was going on. 'Maybe someone will see it and be able to help,' I kidded myself, trying to find some moral justification for my lack of practical assistance. A woman spotted me, called out and waved me over.

'Help us please,' she cried, pressing a charred remnant of a photo into my hand. 'My tent has burned down. We have lost everything. Even our passports, documents, photos … they're all gone.'

In a frayed cardigan, floral skirt, rubber boots and headscarf, Manash looked around sixty. She clutched my arm and led me to the pile of ash that had been her family's makeshift home. A tear rolled down her cheek. She wiped it with her scarf, sniffed, then ushered me into the neighbouring tent where she was now staying. A young woman stirred a pot on a primitive wood stove, a toddler with terrified eyes huddled on her lap. The stove was a fire hazard, but the eight adults and several children who shared this damp, cramped space would have been chilled to the bone without it. Manash showed me the tattered dressing gown she'd been wearing as she fled from her burning tent. Along with the fragment of the photo of her son, it was all she had left in the world.

'My house in Chechnya was burned down, and now my tent here has burned too,' she wailed, her gold teeth glinting. 'But I feel nothing compared to the pain I feel at the slaughter of our young men. The Russians say all our men — from ten to sixty — by day they are civilians, and by night they are terrorists. Our poor boys, and those poor, young Russian boys, who are being killed for nothing. It's so sad. We are like trapped animals. They've put us in a cage and locked the door. They murder us, make us paupers, strip us in public, kill our men.'

Manash paused. I could almost see her thoughts racing, memories surfacing. She sighed and stared into the camera lens.

'Zhirinovsky [the ultranationalist leader of Russia's Liberal Democratic Party] and the Russians say that it's not our land. Why isn't it Chechen land? Who are we? Did we grow out of the earth? Did we fall from the sky? We had grandfathers and great-grandfathers. We had a language, history, culture. What are we then? Wolves? Animals? Why are we being punished like this?

'We don't make tanks. We don't make planes. What do we have? Our land. We have never invaded Russia. We have never bombed a

Russian city. But I will never forget the night the Russian forces came to my village. The next morning there were forty-two corpses. The Russians bombed everything. What are our men supposed to do? They are defending the honour of our women, our children, our elderly. Of course our young men are becoming, as the Russians say, bandits, terrorists. The Russian Army is making them into bandits.'

A boy in grubby trousers and a brown beanie came into the tent: Manash's nephew, Mausa. He was thirteen, but had a kind of choirboy innocence that made him seem far younger. Manash instructed him to take me to the camp's makeshift school. Mausa took my hand and escorted me along a slushy path between rows of mud-spattered tents. The school tent doubled as a psychiatric clinic for the hundreds of traumatised children in the camp, many of whom had witnessed parents and relatives tortured, raped and even murdered in front of them. The children were drawing and making plasticine models, the hell of their recent experience apparent in their wide eyes. Mausa showed me some of his creations; a fighter plane which dropped plasticine bombs and a man with an RPG, a rocket-propelled grenade launcher. Now he was working on a Chechen tower, 'like the ones in the mountains my ancestors used to live in'. Other children had drawn battle scenes; Chechen fighters taking Russian prisoners-of-war and Russian helicopters flying over a shepherd with his flock.

Kheda, the 23-year-old woman who ran the school, told me how even the very young children could identify all the various planes and weapons. 'They know about tanks, military helicopters, mines, grenades, and which guns are for shooting what.'

A small girl came over to us whimpering, and buried her face in Kheda's skirt. She looked about four. Kheda stroked her hair.

'Every time a plane flies overhead she runs to me. I understand her because I have seen the same things. But I saw it as an adult and it is much harder for a child. I don't know how they are going to get through this and have a normal life.'

Adam, our guard, had been trailing after us. Mausa and his friends surrounded him, pleading to have a turn at firing his AK-47. I asked Mausa if he knew how to use it. He laughed. 'Of course we all know how to use a gun,' he said. 'It's our tradition. My father taught me to shoot when I was eight.'

The Chechens have always been the most rebellious of the Russian Empire's minority groups. Their ancestral heartland spreads north from the Caucasus mountain range, a rugged territory of steep ravines and deep gorges, into the lowlands around the Terek and Sunzha Rivers. Like the Pashtun tribes of Pakistan's wild North-West Frontier Province, the Chechens are renowned for their volatile natures and hot tempers.

Chechen society is organised into tightly knit clans known as *teips*, based on family relations and ownership of land. *Teips* elect leaders from amongst their elders who are responsible for decision-making, and clan members are obliged to look after and out for each other. Society is governed by a rigid code — a complex system of traditional laws called *adats* — in which honour and hospitality are all-important and killing to avenge an insult is not only acceptable but necessary. Blood feuds can last for generations. When Akhmed's brothers promised to protect me with their lives, I believed them.

The Russian autocratic model of an all-powerful leader who treated his or her subjects as slaves was anathema to the Chechens. For centuries they fiercely resisted foreign rule and attempts at assimilation. Many of their *adats* were at complete odds with the Russian and later Soviet criminal codes. But any Chechen who put Soviet law before tradition was despised by his Chechen brothers and considered to be weak and contemptible. This conflict between loyalty to legal codes was often used to explain why many Chechens became involved in crime: what was a crime to a Russian was perfectly legitimate to a Chechen.

At the end of the Great Patriotic War, Joseph Stalin accused the Chechen and Ingush people of collusion with the fascists. Considering that Chechens had been fighting alongside the Russians against the Nazis, and the German army hadn't even reached Chechnya, this was a spurious claim, but no one dared argue with the Man of Steel. On 'Red Army Day' in February 1944, soldiers had rounded up the entire Chechen and Ingush population, loaded them into open cattle wagons and deported them east to Siberia and Central Asia. Between one-third to one-half of the Chechen population died before they were finally allowed to return to their ancestral lands in 1957. Those who survived never forgot.

During the 1980s Chechen gangs took over many of Moscow's hotels, restaurants and car dealers, becoming a strong presence in the organised crime wave that overtook Russia in the early 1990s. Then, in October 1991, as the USSR was collapsing, the defiant former Soviet Air Force general Dzhokar Dudayev declared his native Chechnya independent. He later expelled the Russian Army, which scuttled out leaving the place full of weapons, planes, tanks, artillery and ammunition. Chechnya soon became a magnet for bandits, gangsters and racketeers. The ensuing chaos and lawlessness weakened Dudayev's authority and a struggle began amongst the *teips*.

In December 1994, Yeltsin cracked down on the mutinous state, sending in Russian federal forces to carry out a brutal campaign of bombing and destruction. Malnourished and undertrained Russian troops, many of them teenage conscripts, hammered into the fledgling republic. They quickly became cannon-fodder for the weapons-savvy Chechens and were slaughtered in their thousands. Despite the carnage, Russia's generals continued to pour troops into the region. But the feisty Chechens, transformed by the two-year war from a motley band of rebels into an effective and formidable guerilla army, ultimately managed to force Russia into negotiation. The human cost of the victory was horrific: human rights groups estimated somewhere around 200,000 Chechen civilians lost their lives in those two years. And the survivors had a new reason to despise the Russians.

Now, in February 2000, the gloves were off again. With federal forces under the command of Vladimir Putin, this time the Russians were adamant they would show the unruly Chechens who was boss.

At the Ingush–Chechen border post, groups of refugees waited nervously, hoping to spot family members in the overloaded vehicles entering Ingushetia. Others were trying to cross back into their war-torn homeland to find relations and bring them to safety. Russian soldiers jabbed them back from the road with their rifle butts.

'Not even Hitler did this,' wailed an old man in a tall grey fur hat at anyone who would listen. 'The Russians came with their planes, murdering people. When I was fighting in Germany it wasn't this bad. We never shot at civilians. Not even Stalin did this.'

A Russian soldier barked at him to shut up. Bentley and I went over to the old man. He was trembling — with fury, fear and frustration.

'I fought for the Soviet Union for three years,' he said bitterly. 'And now no one remembers. No one respects me. They have destroyed my house, killed my son.'

Another elderly man joined us, nodding as he listened. Aslan was eighty years old. He lived in Nazran but had family in Chechnya and was trying to get back to rescue his grandchildren. He began to sob.

'I need to get there and save the children before they kill them. When my mother died, I didn't cry. When my father died, I didn't cry. But now I am crying.'

His chances of getting through the border seemed slim. The Russian border guards had been instructed to treat all Chechen males as suspect, even this fragile octogenarian. But Aslan had a plan to pass the ten Russian checkpoints between this border and Grozny. He surreptitiously opened his jacket front to reveal a bottle of vodka tucked in an inside pocket.

'With this I can do it,' he said, sniffing.

He began to weep again.

'They shouldn't be murdering innocent children. But they are bombing the innocents. Kill the guilty, but spare the women and children. Buses are hit by rockets as they are driving along the road, killing everyone. You need to go there yourself, then you will see and feel what is happening.'

I wished I could. But Russian authorities were refusing to allow foreigners, especially journalists, to enter Chechnya. We were told it was for our own good, that they couldn't guarantee our safety. But most of us suspected the real reason was that the Russian government didn't want the outside world to know that their federal forces were shelling homes and massacring civilians.

During the 1994–1996 war there had been relatively free media access. Russian and foreign journalists were able to file uncensored reports telling both sides of the conflict, even if they contradicted official Russian government propaganda. The Russian public knew that while generals boasted of the strength and valour of their army, in reality, many of its soldiers were hungry, poorly trained and ill-equipped. The public heard of atrocities committed on both sides and knew that the main victims of the bombardments were defenceless children, women, and elderly.

But with Putin now at the helm, the media was forced back into its Soviet-era role, as government propagandists. A few approved journalists were permitted to cover the 'anti-terrorist operation', under the strict control of the Defence and Interior Ministries. Information about the conflict was both restricted and censored, and guidelines were given to reporters on every detail, right down to the terminology used. Chechens were no longer 'field commanders', 'rebels' or 'fighters' as they were in the first war, now they were 'bandits', 'terrorists' and the historical enemies of the Russians. A *zachistka,* literally 'cleansing', was now described as a 'mopping-up operation'. Across Russia, Acting President Putin's ratings were rising by the day as state media dutifully reported on the success of the campaign and the heroism of the Russian Army. There seemed little chance of telling the other side of the story, first hand, without being able to get into Chechnya.

The creepy Ruslan offered to sneak us in, 'for a price', but my gut told me that the price to get out again might be more than we could afford. Ben and I had to find a way to get around without Ruslan. I'd met a team from Human Rights Watch who were collecting eyewitness testimonies from refugees staying in the cattle sheds on Nazran's outskirts. They introduced me to an incongruous pair, a Chechen, Magomad Magomadov, and a Russian, Viktor Popkov. Magomadov was a lawyer and human rights activist, with a warm smile, neatly trimmed ginger beard and round white skullcap. Viktor Popkov was a religious scholar, dressed in the flowing dark robes of an Orthodox priest, with a chest-length white beard to match.

Magomad and Viktor were about to visit Verkhniy Alkun, a village on the Ingush–Chechen border, to investigate claims of atrocities against civilians. They agreed to take Ben and me along. Magomad lent me some of his sister's clothes and I pulled my hair into a bun and tied a scarf at the nape of my neck in the local style. We gave Adam and Ruslan the slip, met Magomad and were soon driving up into the hills, past fallow fields, bare-branched winter forests, clusters of wooden cottages and the occasional weatherboard mini-mosque. Apart from the Russian soldiers at regular checkpoints, the area seemed deserted. Each time soldiers flagged us down, Magomad told them I was his sister. I nodded, keeping my eyes downcast as they inspected the car, hoping they couldn't hear my heart pounding.

Verkhni Alkun was at the northern foothills of the eastern Caucasus Mountains. Magomad pulled up near a shepherd's hut at the edge of the forest and a ragged man, bent double, scuttled to greet us. The crack of gunshots came from the direction of the forest.

'Don't let the bandits see you,' he hissed in Russian. 'Quick, come.'

'He means the Federal Forces,' whispered Magomad, hurrying us inside. 'The woods are full of snipers.'

The scruffy and unshaven shepherd, Salambek, was a relative of Magomad's. For the last fifteen years he'd lived in the hills on the Chechen side, but had recently fled to this abandoned hut with his family after Russian soldiers destroyed their house and slaughtered their cattle. Several other men, two women and assorted children were crowded into the hut's single room. Salambek pulled out a packet of photos and handed them to Magomad, his hands shaking.

'Look here. See what the soldiers have done to these people. They've not only killed them but cut off their ears, pulled out their teeth, smashed in their faces and gouged out their eyes.'

Magomad, Viktor and I examined the grotesque images, nauseating in their barbarity. Viktor took notes as Salambek told how parachutists had landed at the village of Al-Khoroi in early December and killed everyone they could find. Most of the victims were shepherds, a few were refugees from Grozny. Next to the bodies were beer and vodka bottles, cigarette butts and even syringes, leftovers from where the killers had partied after their massacre.

'None of these men were rebels,' said Salambek. 'Now there is no one left there at all except for the Russian Army.'

Salambek's wife, a handsome woman with a careworn face, joined in. 'Of course there's no one left. They've been bombing for three months. They've killed everyone.'

Salambek and his brother had buried most of the bodies. Flicking through the photos, he found one of a tractor with a rocket through its roof, and another showing a crater in the ground. Magomad studied the pictures closely and turned to me. These images, he said, were documentary evidence of the types of weapons being used by the Russians, in this case, 'extremely powerful bombs, which explode deep in the ground after being dropped from a plane'.

'You see,' said Magomad, 'if a man has no cattle, no tractor, no house, then he has no means of survival. When they are completely starving, the Russians will bring them humanitarian aid, and that person will say out of hunger, "Yes, give me a grain of wheat and I will agree to be part of Russia".'

Salambek punched the air with his fist. 'If one of my sons agrees to stand under the Russian flag while I'm alive, then I will kill him myself,' he shouted. 'Let those Russian bastards who are destroying us know that. Even if they kill all of us, we will not be ruled by the Russians.'

He sank into a chair and put his face in his hands.

Magomad took me aside. 'You can see why he is so angry. He put all his energy and hopes into this land. He built a house for his children so they would have something to inherit. Yet in one hour it was all destroyed. From that moment, all Russia became his enemy. We don't know the people living in Archangelsk, Rostov, Sverdlovsk. It's not them sending us rockets. First Yeltsin and now Putin are sending us rockets.'

Salambek sat up. 'They say Chechens bombed an apartment building in Moscow. But the Russians are bombing and killing a whole nation and not one Russian stands up and protests. One building was bombed and they say all Chechens are bad, that we are bandits. But when they have been destroying us for years, no one says this is bad.'

It was dark when we left Verkhniy Alkhun to return to Nazran. I felt sickened by what we'd seen and heard, repulsed by this incomprehensible brutality. Even Magomad and Viktor, both accustomed to the horrors of war, were quiet. Our silence was broken by Viktor, addressing Magomad. 'I am ashamed to be Russian,' he said in a whisper. 'I wish that I was Chechen and you were Russian. That would be easier for me, because then you would be killing me and not the other way around.'

Viktor was intimately familiar with this region and its people. During the first war he'd collected money to buy sacks of flour and bravely hauled it into Chechnya himself to distribute to starving civilians. He'd also taken a video camera to record what he saw. It had very nearly cost him his life. 'The rebels thought he was working for the FSB,' explained Magomad, 'and the soldiers thought he was working for the Chechens.'

But Viktor had survived and presented his footage, findings and suggestions to the Russian authorities, who were unimpressed by his recommendation that they acquaint themselves with the Geneva Convention. He firmly believed that Russia's actions in Chechnya were far more serious than isolated, or even widespread, cases of human rights abuses. 'Their politics are directed towards the destruction of the Chechens and the loss of their dignity,' he declared. 'It is nothing less than political racism and political genocide.'

Magomad agreed. 'Putin is like Nero. He burned down Rome, blamed the Christians, then had an excuse to begin a war against them to strengthen his power. It's the old principle used by all cruel leaders. To increase your power, create an evil at home, then present yourself as the protector of the people from this evil, just as Hitler did. Putin is acting like this. He blew up apartment buildings in Moscow to create a reason to blame the Chechens. But when he tried to do the same in Ryazan, an old woman saw what was going on and called the police. He covered it up by saying it was sacks of sugar. What kind of person would kill 185 people just so they could become president? He is a terrifying man.'

Magomad readily admitted that not all his fellow Chechens were blameless, but it was the stereotyping of his entire people that pained him most. 'Yes, there were the hostages, the executed Brits, the crime. But that was just a few people, not the whole nation, and not the government. Putin shouldn't say "all Chechens", they just need to say the names of the people who have done this without mentioning their nationality. This is not a war against terrorism, it's a war against an ethnic minority. It's a political game and we are the pawns. They just keep moving us around on the board.'

Back in Nazran, Magomad managed to convince the sinister Ruslan to find someone else to work for. Eric and David had returned to Moscow and Ben and I felt a lot safer with Magomad as our guide. During the first Chechen war, Magomad had worked in the Public Prosecutor's office of Chechnya's interim government. After Aslan Maskhadov was elected President in January 1997, Magomad had been the republic's Deputy Prosecutor for criminal investigations. He'd also headed an anti-kidnapping task force, negotiating the freedom of hundreds of kidnap victims. Now he was working as a legal expert for the International Helsinki Federation for Human Rights and the Chechen Committee for National Salvation, trying to help victims of abuses bring their cases to the European Court of Human Rights in Strasbourg. The Russian authorities did not like him one little bit.

But I did. For someone who had witnessed so much tragedy, Magomad was magnetically cheerful and had an extraordinary capacity for enjoying life. One of his nieces, a refugee from Grozny, was getting married and he invited Ben and me along. I filmed the eighteen-year-old bride putting the final touches to her hair and make-up, while younger children danced around her to the accompaniment of an old uncle's accordion.

Suddenly a car full of teenage boys screeched to a halt outside the house, the groom's mates coming to collect her. Relatives and friends piled into their cars and began to hoon after the bridal vehicle. Magomad zoomed along too, dodging potholes and lunatic drivers. The most sought after position, he explained between hair-raising swerves, was the one right behind the bride. All the drivers were vying for that place and usually there were lots of accidents. It was total mayhem but Magomad was cackling like a kid on a roller coaster. Then the gunshots began. I stuck my head out the window to see passengers in the cars around us firing their Kalashnikovs into the air.

'This is how Chechens carry on, even when they're on Russian territory ... quietly and with dignity!' laughed Magomad. 'For Russians it's a crime to fire guns, but for Chechens, it's our tradition. We shoot when we're happy — just for the noise, for the effect! Some cultures have fireworks, but when we're in a good mood, we shoot! We even fire guns when we're dancing, it's no big deal.'

It wasn't a custom compatible with high-rise housing developments and casualty rates from errant bullets had soared as the Soviets constructed twelve-storey buildings in Chechen cities and towns. Authorities had attempted to ban these exuberant outbursts, but with little success. Luckily out here there were only fields. The shooting continued when we arrived at the groom's house. The bride tiptoed through the slush in her fluffy white gown and was led into a room with a long table laid out with a humble banquet. She stood meekly in the corner, eyes down and face covered by a light veil, forbidden to eat or speak while the wedding guests devoured the spread. The groom was nowhere to be seen. After the meal the party moved on to a nearby house for dancing.

The dance routine was just as I'd seen in Kazakhstan with Razit, although slightly less formal. This time everyone danced to the infectiously energetic accordion: small children, older people, Magomad ... and me. An elegant middle-aged woman in a tight-fitting emerald velvet dress, with hair slicked in a tight bun and come-hither eyes, was particularly taken with Ben and pulled him up to do his best eagle impression. For a few hours it seemed everyone had forgotten there was a war going on.

'You see how wild and passionate these Chechens are,' said Magomad. 'They are explosive, open, easily provoked, kind-hearted and generous. From love to anger for these people is just one step.'

I believed him. As the music and dancing reached fever pitch, our host pulled a pistol from his jacket and began shooting into the floor. I leapt up in fright. Everyone else fell about in hysterical laughter.

★　★　★

Just as the Soviets had failed to stamp out the Chechens' love of guns, they had been unable to annihilate Islam, which had taken hold towards the end of the eighteenth century after being brought to the region from Daghestan around 1650. Initially the mountain people had supported the Bolsheviks, but they soon revolted, and the area became a hotbed of Islamic anticommunist activity. In 1937 the Soviets purged the Chechens' religious leaders. Magomad described how mosques had been destroyed and imams hunted down, imprisoned or shot. 'But it was one thing to destroy a mosque, and quite another to wipe out a religion. It simply went underground, into the hearts and souls of the people.'

Magomad's father had been one of many secret mullahs who had hidden his religious beliefs from the authorities. Yet while he had considered the Soviet state satanic and the Communist Party to be messengers from the devil, he never tried to argue with his young son, Magomad, who learned about the glorious history of the Soviet Union at school.

'In fifth grade I told my father that the twenty-sixth congress of the Communist Party was going on, and soon we would have communism,' Magomad recalled. 'I told him that Lenin had promised that soon there would be money and everyone would live well. Naturally, I believed what I learned at school. My father just laughed.'

Magomad dutifully became a Young Pioneer and joined the Komsomol, but by the time he'd finished school in 1982, it was obvious to him that *Das Kapital* didn't explain everything. The opening of the Iron Curtain had been a time of revelation. Until then, for Magomad there had been 'no West, no East, only the Soviet Union'. Everyone else had been simply 'our enemies'. Now people were free to worship and new mosques were sprouting up everywhere. He took me to visit Nazran's main mosque where I noticed the majority of worshippers were males in their late teens and early twenties.

'People are returning to religion more and more since the war started,' he whispered as we watched solemn young men praying fervently. 'When people see death every day, they understand that life is short. The more you witness death, the more you begin to wonder what comes after. Usually youths study, enjoy themselves and don't think about death, and it is the old who turn to religion. But look around and you see here it is wall-to-wall young people.'

It was the young who were taking up arms against the Russians too. Magomad arranged for me to talk to a handsome twenty-year-old *boyevik* (resistance fighter) who instructed me to call him Mustafa. As a child, Mustafa's father had told him stories of his ancestors: his grandfather, great-grandfather, all the way back to his great-great-great-great-great-great-grandfather. He knew where they had come from, where they were buried and what they had done. To Mustafa, as to all Chechens, the memory of their ancestors, their history, their deeds and their land was part of his identity. 'They would rather die than stand by and watch their homes being razed, their people massacred and their territory destroyed.'

Mustafa permitted us to film, but only in silhouette and with his voice disguised. 'Our motherland is in peril,' he hissed with palpable fervour. 'They are bombing and murdering us and we can't let this go unpunished. Every self-respecting male should take up arms and fight for his people and motherland against the enemy. It doesn't mean we are thirsty for blood. We are simply defending our people. When we were children we read Russian textbooks, which told us that to fight for your motherland is sacred. But now when we do this they say we are terrorists. But we are fighting for our freedom. Russia thinks we are a wild people who cannot think for ourselves and that we need them to protect us. But look at the methods they are using to "defend us". The truth is that they are afraid to lose the Caucasus. If Chechnya becomes independent, then other regions may try to secede and Russia does not want to lose its territory. They also want to have control of the gas pipeline, which passes through Chechnya, without having to share any of the billions of dollars of profits they will make from this. So we must stand up to them.' ·

Ben and I returned to Moscow to get a Russian perspective on the Chechen situation. I tracked down Alexei Saraikin, the friendly young veteran of the first Chechen war I'd met when filming with the Moscow Rescue Service. We arranged to visit him at the one-room basement flat in south-central Moscow he was sharing with another Chechen veteran, also called Alexei. Buff and hulking Alexei 2 obviously spent a lot of time pumping the iron stacked in the corner of their small space, and since returning from the war had found work as a security guard.

The Alexeis had been called up for military service in 1994. Both were eighteen and neither had ever held a weapon, yet they were immediately posted to Chechnya. 'No one took the first war seriously,' Saraikin said ruefully. 'We thought it would be easy — just boom, and it would be over. But although we knew how to fight in the forests, in the fields, in the desert — we had no experience of urban warfare. It has its own particular tactics and we didn't fight properly that time. This time they are doing it right.'

I tried to imagine this gentle young man on the tattered couch in front of me dressed in military fatigues, brandishing a gun in the streets of Grozny. I couldn't. Instead, I remembered him helping people in distress, his kindness to strangers, his compassion for others. Now I was triggering painful memories in him and I saw how, like Mustafa, the scars of his experience ran deep. The Alexeis loathed the Chechens every bit as passionately as the Chechens loathed the Russians.

Saraikin told of seeing Chechens grabbing machine guns from dead soldiers, slaughtering Russians en masse and decapitating them with daggers on the streets. He grimaced. 'They aren't human, they're beasts!'

Alexei 2 described how while 'cleansing' a village, local women began screaming at him to go home. 'This provocation puts pressure on your psyche and many soldiers can't cope. But the civilians are to blame. They're a cunning people and impossible to trust, even the children and elderly. They say they are men of their word because they are mountain people, but they will never face you, they will just stab you from behind. There's a wolf on their flag, but they aren't wolves, they are jackals.'

The Alexeis were offended by what they saw as 'one-sided' Western media coverage of the conflict which they believed portrayed the Russians as bloodthirsty thugs, and the Chechens as 'innocent, oppressed and long-suffering victims who just want their republic'.

'It's an historical fact that they've always been slitting each other's throats,' Saraikin muttered. 'It's been going on a long time. The only time there's ever been order there was when Stalin was in power and sent them all to Central Asia. Russia needs a dictator.'

The Alexeis were great Putin fans and couldn't wait to vote him in as president at the upcoming election. They saw him as a strongman, the 'iron fist' Russia so sorely needed to unify the country after the disastrous anarchy of the Yeltsin years. At last, they thought, Russians were regaining their patriotism and had a leader they could respect. Putin's decisive actions in Chechnya had played a big part in boosting national pride. They wouldn't have a bar of the theory that he had ordered the bombing of the apartment buildings in Moscow. 'It's a completely ridiculous suggestion,' said Saraikin. 'He's just a normal guy. He wouldn't do something like that.'

While Putin could do no wrong in their eyes, Saraikin feared Russians in general were indifferent to the fate of 'their boys', losing their lives by the thousands in the far south. He took me to the Tomb of the Unknown Soldier — the eternal flame which burns beside the Kremlin Wall in the Alexandrovsky Gardens — a memorial to Soviet soldiers killed in the Great Patriotic War, including his grandfather. Women in furs posed for photos while their children giggled at the stony-faced pair of soldiers on either side of the monument. Alexei stared at the flame.

Did I know, he asked, that there was no memorial to the soldiers killed in Afghanistan, or those killed in Chechnya? Thirty-seven soldiers from his unit had not returned from Chechnya, their ultimate sacrifice unrecognised but for a small plaque at a military base. The apathy of the Russian populace terrified him. 'If our society continues to be like this,' he mused, 'then who knows what will happen here.'

The September 1999 apartment bombings unleashed a new wave of anti-'black' sentiment across Russia. Arriving back from Malaysia, Akhmed found himself right in the thick of it. Though he was hardly 'black' by any objective standards, his olive skin and brown eyes marked him as a southerner, a *chernozhopiye*, or 'black arse'. I had no idea how serious this was until I invited him for lunch at Eric's (our) apartment. Four hours after he'd said he would arrive, there was still no sign of him. At last a call came through from the security guards at the compound gate and a sneering voice asked if I really did know this Akhmed. A few minutes later he stood on the doorstep, his face bruised and clothing dishevelled.

'Akha! What the hell happened to you?'

He laughed.

'It's my black arse. Every time I walk out the door some cop comes up and asks to see my documents. I'm supposed to go and register with the police, but I know they'll just beat me and want a big bribe. So I haven't registered and they arrested me for not having my registration stamp. I only had to spend a couple of hours at the station, then they took all the money I had and let me go. Anyway, I'm going to Ingushetia tomorrow.'

Akhmed was remarkably unfazed at his treatment by the Moscow police, more concerned about what lay in store at home. It seemed his father had found him a bride. Akhmed was not impressed. He had no intention of going back to live in his native village and certainly wasn't ready to get hitched. 'So, I guess it's going to be a short visit,' he chuckled. 'My dad doesn't know I'm coming so I'll have to get away before he has time to organise the wedding.'

He wasn't sure what he was going to do. He had many friends among Moscow's large Chechen diaspora, but many of them were finding the heightened xenophobia of the ethnic Russian population unbearable. He thought he might have to find a way to go back to Malaysia.

'You know the most ridiculous thing?' he said. 'In Moscow I'm black, but in Asia I'm white!'

Akhmed invited me to meet his friend Timur in a seedy billiards hall near Novoslobodskaya Metro on the north of the Garden Ring Line which circled Moscow's centre. Now in his early twenties, the morose Timur had fled Chechnya during the first war. Akhmed told him about his detention and Timur shrugged. For him, xenophobic persecution was a daily reality. He thought Akha had got off lightly. The last time he'd been arrested, he'd been beaten, handcuffed and hung from hooks in a prison cell until he lost consciousness. He wasn't sure if he'd been released because they realised they made a mistake, or because his lawyer had paid a bribe. Either way, he was despondent.

'It's pointless to argue with the police. They represent the authorities, and if the police are against you and the people in power are against you, it means you can never be right. If the authorities want to destroy an entire nation they will do it. It's easily done.'

The 'nation' Timur spoke of was his own people, the Chechens. He might have been a Russian citizen with a Russian passport, born on the territory of the Russian Federation, but to ethnic Russians he would always be a Chechen — and never 'one of them'. In English we use the word 'Russian' to refer both to ethnic Russians and to citizens of the Russian Federation. In Russian there are two separate words: *Russky* is an ethnic (Slavic) Russian, while *Rossiyanin* refers to a citizen of Russia. Timur and Akhmed were *Rossiyaniny,* but not *Russky,* and it was this distinction which sealed their fate as second-class citizens.

Hiding one's ethnicity was next to impossible. It was written on the fifth line of the title page of every Russian passport — a document it was against the law to leave home without. Almost everything required showing one's passport: applying for a job, a place at a university, renting an apartment, setting up a bank account. The word 'Chechen' in Timur's ID meant he'd been refused admission to university and couldn't get a job. He knew many Chechens who were changing their names to avoid harassment. It was the fault of the media and the politicians, he said, who were demonising his people. But he had no energy to fight the discrimination that was ruining his life.

'I don't want to fight for Chechen rights. I just want to have a normal life like everyone else. I don't want to live for a fight. I want to live for my future family. But if I am completely honest, I no longer want to marry and have a son who will suffer here in Russia. He would just become another tortured soul.'

An intelligence test was given to the OMON, which involved different shaped and sized holes and pegs. In conclusion, the OMON can be divided into two groups: the extremely stupid and the extremely strong.

Travelling on the Moscow metro, I saw OMON special police everywhere, pacing in camouflage flak jackets, thumping rubber batons in their palms, ready to pounce on anyone with remotely dark skin. Ben and I decided to secretly film them 'at work'. We selected Kievsky Station as a hotspot of OMON anti-black arse action, rolled my little camera in a coat, and loitered. Operating under the motto: 'We know no mercy and ask for none', the OMON were doing their maxim proud, lurking at the top of the escalators, swooping on every olive-complexioned person they saw, grabbing them roughly and demanding documents. It was clearly an extortion racket and we got some good shots of frightened Trans-Caucasians and Central Asians handing over wads of cash.

But we lingered too long. Just as I noticed we'd been spotted, a mean-mouthed cop strode up, demanded our documents and ordered us to come to their office. Realising we were in trouble, I gabbled away, explaining that we were filming to show what a fine job the OMON were doing carrying out these important security checks in such dangerous times. Meanwhile, Ben furtively changed the camera tapes, replacing our footage with a blank. The OMON knew better than to rough up foreigners, but I could imagine the terror of being at their mercy. Following an interrogation and lecture — we should have known that we were not allowed to film in train stations without permission (which is never granted), nor were we allowed to film police without permission — I offered them the (blank) tape from the camera, hoping they wouldn't check it. They didn't, and we bolted.

Chechens fleeing the Russian attacks found themselves hopelessly trapped. Magomad divided his time between the village of Sleptsovsk on the Chechen–Ingush border, and a rented flat in a northern suburb of Moscow, now home to many of his relatives. Fifteen people — five adults and ten children — were living in a two-room apartment, among them the only son of his sister, whose father had been killed in the first war; a young woman with three small children whose husband had disappeared; and his sister-in-law with her two little daughters, who had been on their own since his brother had been arrested by the

Russian Army in 1995 and hadn't been heard from since. Sister-in-law was in the kitchen crying into the phone to her younger brother in the Siberian town of Krasnoyarsk. Their older brother had disappeared two months earlier after being arrested for not having his documents in order and both were sick with worry.

All were practically under house arrest. None but Magomad were registered with the authorities, and without proper documents they were too afraid to leave the safety of the flat. He had made acquaintance with the local police and convinced them to allow two of the women to shop at the nearby kiosks and some of the children to play in the yard below. But none would risk travelling by public transport, the children couldn't attend school and one of the women had not left the flat for more than three months. According to Magomad, information about every Chechen in Moscow was on an FSB computer. His flat too was closely monitored by the security bureau, and the details of my visit would most definitely be recorded.

'Here they really love and respect us!' he joked. 'You come here and no one pays any attention to you. We arrive and immediately they demand our passports, registration cards and want to know our business. You know, when a head of state arrives in England, he is met by the Queen and by the parliament. When we arrive in Moscow we are met first by the military police, then the police, then the FSB. "Why have you come?" they ask. "Who are you? What do you want to do here? Maybe you want to blow something up? Maybe Putin? Maybe an apartment block?" ... But look around you, look at these "terrorists"!'

The children sat quietly, following my every move with attentive, curious eyes. Magomad beckoned his twelve-year-old nephew, Yusup, to sit next to him on the sofa. He had told me that his nephew had witnessed Russian soldiers kill his father, and that he had taken care of him since that terrible day. He put his hand on the boy's shoulder. 'In Chechnya,' he said proudly, 'Yusup was already a champion of karate.'

Yusup forced a smile. 'I told my uncle that I wanted to go back and live in Chechnya,' he whispered. 'I don't like it here with the Russians and I miss my home.'

Tears welled in his eyes. Magomad patted him and motioned that he should go to his cousins.

'This stress is difficult for an adult to cope with, let alone a child. Every day he sees what is going on at home on the television. Imagine how hard this is for him to understand. But the main thing is that we are alive. We have a lot in common with the Russians. We grew up with their culture and we respect it. If we could respect each other's differences then we may be able to coexist. But they oppress us because of these differences. They don't understand us and they don't want to understand us.

'If we cannot keep the land where our ancestors are buried, we will become gypsies, and then the Chechen people will vanish.'

I turned on the news that night to see another report of Russian triumph: one more Chechen village razed, more 'bandits' eradicated.

It was hard to feel optimistic.

24

The Unfairer Sex

Putin's resounding election victory in March 2000 surprised no one. A few opposition politicians and human rights activists bleated about the death of democracy and return to dictatorship, but they were drowned out by the media's adulation for Putin — a man's man with a steady hand and a black belt in karate, a president who could restore Russia's dignity after eight years of Yeltsin's anarchic and corrupt 'democracy'. The new consensus was that Russia could do without *demokratiya*. The country needed order, and Putin was happy to oblige.

Olga was among the sceptics. 'I never believe what I'm hearing in the mass media any more,' she said. 'But the people in the regions only ever hear the opinion of state TV, and many of them believe what they hear. They voted for Putin because they didn't know about anyone else. They had no choice. But to me it was so unnatural, so obvious, so strange, that when Yeltsin resigned he said, "Okay, I'm going, and here's the person who will replace me." And yet, we are supposed to be a democracy.'

Such criticism was now considered almost heretical. Once outspoken journalists, politicians and even oligarchs now kept their opinions to themselves. The colourful dissenters of the Yeltsin era melted into insignificance, many eventually lining up behind Putin. The rest were dismissed as nutcases.

★   ★   ★

Eric and I left Russia just before the election. His Russia posting was over and we decided to go travelling for a few weeks before heading back Down Under. Craving sunshine, sea and cheery faces, we flew first to Cuba where we met up with Nadia's younger sister, Tanya, who still lived in Havana, despite having divorced her Cuban conductor husband years earlier. Tanya fantasised about returning to Russia but short of sharing Nadia's couch in her 12 square metre bed-sit, she would never be able to afford a place to live. Cuba's fragile centrally controlled economy had collapsed completely along with the USSR, which had propped it up by buying Cuban sugar at ridiculously inflated prices. But at least Cuba had sun and salsa.

From Havana — lycra and bikini capital of the world — we back-tracked to a snow-bound Moscow, changed planes and flew to Syria, without even leaving the airport. I switched overnight to long sleeves, long skirts and headscarves, ready to soak up the mosques, ancient monuments and exotic Middle East. In Damascus we discovered eerie echoes of Moscow. Stalls in the main souk offered priceless Russian icons, ecclesiastical statues in gold and silver, antique incense burners and candelabras, that could only have been smuggled out of Russia. And 'gentlemen's clubs' advertised one of Russia's other major exports to the Middle East — long-limbed glamour girls who danced on sheikhs' laps and around poles on bar-tops, wearing even less than the Cubans.

We had to return to Moscow for our flight back to Australia. The plane out of Syria felt like a Moscow nightclub, carrying a large contingent of chic young platinum blondes in figure-hugging ensembles conspicuously sporting Prada bags. Blue fur jackets were in vogue this season too. At Damascus International Airport I'd watched a couple of these foxy dames receiving wads of cash from local men. And in Moscow's Sheremetyevo Airport I ducked into the toilet near the immigration checkpoints to see those same women wrapping their cash in cling wrap and disappearing into the cubicles. It can't have been a comfortable way to avoid declaring cash to Customs.

The Syrian-based starlets seemed a lot happier than the prostitutes lining Leningradskoye Shosse, the main highway north to the airport and St Petersburg. For years now this area had been a favoured zone for women touting for business from passing drivers. It was a depressing scene: spaced-out young girls shivering in mini-skirts, stomping their stilettos in the snow to keep warm, pimps in black Mercs parked menacingly under nearby trees, and obnoxious looking clientele cruising slowly by.

I'd often wondered how many of those girls were there by choice. In a widely publicised survey of Moscow high school girls in the early 1990s, 60 per cent had said they would exchange sex for hard currency. I couldn't believe this was true. SBS's *Dateline* program had broadcast my story about Chechnya and agreed to commission another. I decided to look at how women's lives had changed since the collapse of the USSR. Ten years had passed since Yulia, Tatiana and Sveta had attempted to make a real Russian woman out of me: a woman who cared about her appearance, who knew how to cook delicious meals, who was prepared to give up her own selfish pursuits in order to serve a man and make him happy. I was used to the fact that Russians viewed women differently, but still, I couldn't help cringing when I saw newspaper ads for secretaries which specified: 'Long legs and no inhibitions essential'. Before Eric and I had even found a place to live in Australia, I was on my way back to Russia.

A Novy Russky brings a beautiful girl into a jewellery shop and asks for the best necklace in stock. He rejects all the cheaper items, finally settling on a USD$1 million ruby necklace. 'Wrap it for her,' he orders, 'and bill my bank next week.'

The shop manager is confused. 'I'm sorry, but we can only deliver the necklace when the bill is honoured,' he says apologetically.

'Are you sure it can't be done sooner?' the Novy Russky shrugs.

'Sorry, sir,' says the manager. 'Okay, we'll get the girl's address and deliver the necklace the moment you've got clearance.'

The next week the shop manager calls the Novy Russky. 'I'm sorry, sir, but your bank rejected payment.'

'That's okay,' says the Novy Russky. 'I still had a fantastic weekend.'

Marina Pisklakova was a vivacious blonde thirty-something with an American husband, and one of the first women in Russia to carry out research on Russian women and their position in society. Her findings had troubled her so greatly that she established a crisis centre in Moscow called ANNA (Association No to Violence) for women fleeing domestic violence. I sat with her now in her office.

Until Marina began her work in 1989, there had been no such thing as women's studies in the USSR. Soviet propaganda declared that men and women were equal and that was the first and last word on the subject. Even before the revolution, Lenin had often written and spoken of the need for women to be 'emancipated'. On gaining power he declared that in his communist utopia, women would be liberated from the selfish drudgery of child rearing, housework and cooking by communal kitchens, laundries and childcare, enabling them to put their energies into the more noble service of the motherland. But the first part of his plan never fully materialised, so while women were forced to work outside the home, tradition dictated that they were also responsible for all the household chores. Many women did become respected scientists, academics, engineers, musicians and even cosmonauts, but many more were saddled with the double burden of factory or field work and home duties. The Soviet rhetoric of equality had always been an illusion. Now perestroika had brought a return to the ways of the pre-Soviet past.

In her impeccable American-accented English, Marina explained how Russia's patriarchal society also had 'some elements of the Muslim culture, from the time of the Tatar invasion'. In the sixteenth century there had been a set of rules called *domostroi* (household), which gave instructions to a man on how to discipline his wife and servants using physical punishment. *Domostroi* included the following tips: 'Don't beat her face or you won't be able to show her in public'; 'Don't beat her stomach if she is pregnant or you could harm the baby'; and 'Don't use your fist, use a whip. It is more painful and she will learn better'. Women were locked up in their houses and forbidden to leave without permission from their husbands or brothers. All property belonged to the men.

'You never found books on *domostroi* during the Soviet era, but since perestroika they have been republished several times,' said Marina. 'It was a way of coming back to our roots, to our traditions. And in those instructions it says: "And after you beat her, show her how much you love her." And that is why we have a saying: "If he beats you it means he loves you." It's one of the main myths in Russia and a major contributor to the problem of domestic violence.'

Marina went on to quote horrendous statistics. Domestic violence was common in 13 per cent of families. Every year in Russia, 600,000 crimes were committed against women, and more than 14,000 women were killed by their husbands. There were no Soviet-era figures: officially, domestic abuse didn't exist. But Marina was certain that murder rates of women had increased with perestroika as life had become more stressful and access to weapons easier.

Her Moscow crisis centre was a suite of plain and simply furnished rooms where counsellors offered legal advice, sympathy and shelter to victims of aggression. Several graphic anti-violence posters hung on the white walls, alongside certificates of gratitude and achievement. As Marina and I talked, a pretty and petite blonde with dark circles under her tear-stained eyes came into her office.

Snezhanna had been divorced for two years, but still shared a room with her ex-husband in his parents' flat. She had nowhere else to go. Her ex-husband abused and beat her regularly and she was distraught. Two days earlier he had kicked and beaten her, grabbed her throat and tried to strangle her. Their eight-year-old daughter had heard her mother's terrified screams and ran to find her father standing over her battered and bloodied body. The police had confronted her ex-husband, but he denied everything, telling them he'd been asleep and had no idea who'd beaten her. Her daughter's testimony was judged irrelevant as she was a minor. A friend told her about the crisis centre and finally she had mustered the courage to come.

'My ex doesn't even think he's done anything wrong,' she sobbed. 'When I try to defend myself, he laughs in my face. I'm afraid to be in that apartment.'

Marina summoned one of her counsellors, Violetta, and they began to fill in complaint forms about lack of police action and make arrangements for a temporary placement for Snezhanna and her daughter. Violetta passed tissues to the weeping Snezhanna, repeating, over and over: 'Don't blame yourself. It's not your fault.'

Snezhanna's response, Marina explained, was typical. 'In our society, women are responsible for the emotional atmosphere in a family. And if a woman is abused then it is considered to be her fault. She has failed as a woman. She has failed as a wife. The typical question she would be asked is: "What did you do wrong? Why can't you create an atmosphere where your husband will be satisfied?"'

As well as violence in the home, sex crimes were rampant, on the rise, and also blamed on women. Marina believed that girls' upbringings had a lot to do with it. 'It is not normal for women to show they don't like something. Girls are brainwashed from a young age that they must be tolerant, nice and ready to please. And then when they are raped, men accuse them of provocation. The standard defence in any rape or violence case is that "the woman provoked the man" and therefore deserved what she got.' With the assumption always that it was somehow the woman's fault, it was little wonder that few victims spoke up.

Marina's views made her an object of passionate hatred by many Russian men. When she'd bravely agreed to appear on TV talk shows to discuss the issue of domestic violence, male interviewers accused her of radical feminism. Livid male callers to the programs hurled abuse at her, live on air: 'What right do you have to meddle in the affairs of a family?' they screamed. 'These matters are strictly between a husband and wife. You should keep the rubbish inside the house.' The host sat by and nodded in agreement.

Remarkably, Marina kept her cool. She was used to such invective, and she was used to the fact that many men believed it was their right to manipulate women's lives. 'After the loss of twenty million citizens in the Second World War,' she explained, 'Soviet women had been coerced into reproductive services, commanded to churn out offspring, with medals awarded to those "Heroine Mothers" who produced ten or more children. Abortions were illegal, yet women were only allowed six months of maternity leave before they were required to return to the workforce.' More recently, Gorbachev had come up with a plan to counter rising unemployment in the general population. One of its key features was a propaganda program to promote the idea that women belong at home. Some officials even declared that no women should have jobs until all the men were employed. Marina considered this simply another form of manipulation.

'They declared women had been used too much by the state, so now they had the right to go home, stay home, take care of the children and fulfil their natural predestination. But it's not giving women a choice whether to work or stay home, it's telling them again what to do.'

Tens of thousands of women found themselves without work, leaving many in wretched financial circumstances. At the same time, a movie called *Interdevochka* (*Intergirl*) hit the cinemas, becoming Russia's biggest domestic box-office hit of 1989. Depicting the glamorous life of Tatiana, a nurse by day and foreign-currency call girl earning big bucks from visiting rich Westerners by night, *Intergirl* caused a sensation. Although the heroine ultimately came to a sticky end, many women, seduced by the images of her indulged and sophisticated lifestyle, began to see prostitution as a legitimate means to improve their circumstances.

Officially the Soviet Union had been a puritanical and morally conservative nation. Prostitution, like homosexuality and drug addiction, officially 'did not exist'. But it had long been commonplace for women to exchange sexual favours in return for gifts, goods from hard currency stores, or even a grocery-shopping trip. Stalin, Brezhnev and other leaders kept mistresses, providing them with apartments and privileges. And now, with thousands of women needing work, *Intergirl* Tatiana became a role model. The world's oldest profession was suddenly an alluring and empowering lifestyle choice.

Mass media also played a part in sexualising Russian culture. Once strictly censored, newspapers and magazines freed by glasnost began to pack their pages with nudity, erotic images and articles about sex. Advertisers draped scantily clad females over every possible product and a tidal wave of pornography flooded the country. Nightclubs and casinos sprung up in every city, featuring strippers, pole dancers and call girls. Even family restaurants had strip shows.

It was a backlash, Marina explained, against the prohibition of seventy years of Soviet rule. 'First things swing to the opposite extreme before they return to something normal. During the Soviet era, the image was of a woman as a workhorse: having babies, running a family, working full-time and participating in public life. But after perestroika, Russian media companies began to show foreign movies from the 1950s, 1960s and 1970s. These movies portrayed the woman as either the perfect housewife or the pouting starlet, and it was still totally normal to slap a woman across the face if she did not obey. The new image that was created for Russian women was a kind of cross between a nice wife, prostitute and businesswoman. And for an average person to see the difference between the real world and the world on television is very difficult.'

Most of my friends were from the intelligentsia class, sufficiently educated and well travelled to see through and ignore the emerging stereotype. But by the early 1990s, the image of the sexy, promiscuous vixen had become the ideal for many young Russian women. The advertisements I'd seen for female office assistants stipulating that applicants must be attractive and *bez kompleksov,* literally 'without hang-ups', was a polite way of saying, 'only women prepared to shag the boss need apply'. In another survey of that era, Russian women ranked prostitution eighth in a list of the top twenty jobs. But only a few of Russia's new prostitutes enjoyed the glittering lifestyle of the *interdevochka.* Many worked the streets, plying their trade in toilets, stairwells and the back seats of cars. Often they were raped, became hooked on drugs, and caught and spread diseases while earning a pittance. None of this stopped young women from aspiring to the profession.

I spent a night with my hidden camera on Novy Arbat Street, a boulevard running east from the Kremlin, renowned for its casinos, nightlife and hookers strutting their stuff. They were everywhere, in spiked heels and leopard print, hot-pink furs or skin-hugging slinky black, leaning nonchalantly against lampposts, flagging down cars and jumping in when a deal was done. It was all completely open. City police strode past the pimps illegally parked on the curbs in their Mercs with tinted windows and gave them friendly nods. I shot a series of wobbly zooms of car-window negotiations from my armpit, and wondered how I could meet some of the girls. But each time I approached them, their pimps and chauffeurs gave me the evil eye. The business might have been going on under the cops' noses, but prying journalists were another matter. I had no idea what they might do to me, but with enormous sums of money at stake, I didn't want to find out. I moved on quickly.

As exclusive clubs and bars opened across the country in the early 90s, there were myriad other opportunities for Russia's beautiful young things to profit from their looks and charm. The Novy Russkys, eager to flaunt their newfound wealth, saw being surrounded by gorgeous, fawning females as much a status symbol as having the latest model Porsche. But these new post-Soviet elites weren't content to merely emulate wealthy Western lifestyles through the acquisition of luxury goods and bacchanalian displays of sexual liberation. They took hedonism to new extremes. By the late 90s, the flamboyant leader of the Liberal Democratic Party, Vladimir Zhirinovsky, was starring in soft-porn flicks and had penned his own book, *The A to Z of Sex*. I'd been with Eric to its launch — in a raunchy Moscow strip joint called Dolls — astounded by the spectacle of bikini-clad mannequins wrestling a giant python on stage, and rendered speechless by Zhirinovsky's suggestion that men too poor to buy flowers for their beloved should present them with jars of their own sperm to use as face cream. A Moscow restaurant served sushi laid out on a naked girl's body. And nightclubs like the infamous Hungry Duck were hotspots of debauchery where the sight of inebriated young girls copulating with strangers under tables was as common as the drug deals in the toilets. The sleaze factor of the new Russia was off the scale. The daggy New Year's disco I'd been to in the Lenin Library in Kazan seemed a lifetime ago.

I headed back to the Tatar capital to visit Nikol, the striptease dancer I'd met while filming my 'body art' story. She was now sharing a bed-sit with one of her protégés, 'Brenda' (her stage name), who'd come to Kazan three years earlier from a village in the neighbouring republic of Bashkiria, to study at the Chemical Technology Institute. Her family were unable to support her, so she had taken a job as a waitress at a local nightclub, Arena, where Nikol performed regularly. For weeks, Brenda watched Nikol's act in admiration then begged her to teach the tricks of the stripping trade. Soon she was gyrating in a G-string on stage too. Nikol still aspired to study law and the girls were now plotting a way to get to Greece, hoping they could find better paid work in clubs there.

'The stereotype of a Russian woman is that she wants to find some rich husband who will support her,' said Nikol over a dish of boiled potatoes in their cupboard of a kitchen. 'But in reality, often it doesn't work out. Usually they end up with some drunkard who cheats on her. So we want to be independent, and that's why we want to go to Greece to make money.'

It wasn't going to be easy. Even getting a work visa invitation for another country was a bureaucratic nightmare. The girls desperately needed to find 'contacts' who could help smooth the way. I accompanied them to one of the clubs they worked at in Kazan, an intimate and depressingly shabby place with twenty or so ogling, overweight and balding clientele. After much negotiation I was allowed to film, but only after swearing I wouldn't point my camera at the patrons. Leggy Brenda performed an erotic little number, displaying extraordinary flexibility as she disrobed to the swooning strings and Shirley Manson's sultry vocals of the theme song to the previous year's James Bond movie, *The World is Not Enough*. She flung her clothes into the audience, honed in on a fat guy in a tight suit and slithered all over him until he stuffed a wad of notes into her G-string.

'Lots of rich and influential businessmen come to this place,' she wheezed, puffing from her exertions in the dressing room backstage. 'Many have connections, and we are working on getting them to help us. It's the only way to do anything in this country. Everybody who is wealthy here started with nothing and gradually moved up … but you can never be sure with the help of who or what. It's just the way it is.'

Another popular route out of Russia for women was via international marriage agencies, which had been growing and multiplying across the country since the mail/internet order bride business began in the early 1990s. When I'd lived in Palm Springs in 1993–95 I helped a male friend to write letters to girls in Russia and the Ukraine, and to translate their replies. They reminded me of childhood correspondence with pen friends: 'my hobbies are x', 'my favourite colour is y', 'do you like horses?' But the women were also keen to sell their wifely potential: 'I like very much cooking'; 'I want a husband to look after, a family and a happy home'. Some were as young as eighteen, the oldest was thirty. Many had been married before and had children.

My Palm Springs friend did eventually go to Russia. He stayed with Olga in St Petersburg and interviewed his correspondents one by one, increasingly disillusioned by each meeting. A barbie-doll/hooker wasn't what he'd had in mind, but that was what he found. Then one day on Nevsky Prospekt, he bumped into a captivating Belarussian factory worker called Sveta who lived in a dormitory and spoke no English. They married a year later and are still happily together.

In Kazan, Zulfia's secretary, Rosa, dreamed of finding such contentment as Sveta. A sweet-faced Tatar in her late twenties with a twelve-year-old daughter, Elvira, she lived in a small flat on the outskirts of Kazan with her parents. Mild-mannered Rosa didn't want to talk about why her marriage failed, but knew for certain she didn't want another Russian or Tatar husband. Men here had too many problems — they were unemployed, poorly paid, depressed and angry — and she didn't 'want to live with such a man'.

Rosa was so disillusioned with men and life in Russia that she had signed up with an international introduction agency in Kazan. I went along with her for her first meeting with the agency's manager, Elena Fyodorova, an American TV evangelist lookalike in a tailored suit, slathered with make-up and sporting a bottle-blonde bob. Elena spoke in low and soothing tones, oozing care and concern as she ushered shy Rosa into her office. Her desk was piled with stacks of photos of girls, and catalogues of available men.

'So you want to find an independent and stable man who can protect you from the difficulties in life?' she asked, cocking her head to one side.

Rosa's face flushed with such excitement I thought she might burst. 'I'm just like any woman. I want to make a happy family. But men here are so busy with their problems.'

Elena turned her attention to me. 'Now I think I represent the majority of Russian women when I say that they would like to completely devote themselves to their husbands, children and families. From what I know, Western women aren't like this. They want to be independent, to "realise themselves", and this frightens men, I think. Do you agree?'

I gulped. 'I suppose you'd have to ask a man that question.'

Elena was kind of scary.

'Now,' she continued with a dramatic flourish, returning her gaze to Rosa. 'Here we have many serious problems. It's no secret that our men don't get paid much. And many of our men, in the opinion of our women, are rather lazy and like to drink too much. We women are all the same. We don't want to think about politics. Of course some women have businesses, but most dream about being women — that is, having a husband, children, family.'

Rosa nodded meekly. Elena wasn't the sort of person you'd argue with. She handed Rosa some forms to fill out and explained that she would have to pay 1,000 roubles, the equivalent of a week's wage, to join the 'club', and then she would be allowed to look at the catalogues. If she wished to write to any of the men pictured, she had to pay an additional 400 roubles (AUD$25) per address. There was no guarantee she'd get a reply. It was also necessary for Rosa to get a suitably sensational portrait taken. Elena handed her a stack of photos from her desk and suggested she peruse them for fashion, hair and make-up ideas.

I looked over Rosa's shoulder as she flicked through the pictures. Women of various ages struck sultry poses, the younger ones dressed to reveal their wares, proudly jutting out their best attributes. Every hair was sprayed into place, their foundation thick, cheeks rouged, mascara immaculate and pouting lips painted to perfection. Rosa sighed. She wasn't tall, or particularly slim, or in the least bit glamorous. She was pretty, with short brown hair and smiley eyes. And she longed to find a caring man who would love her and appreciate her delicious Tatar pies. But she would have to compete for their attentions with a horde of barbie dolls. She paid her money, set a date for her photoshoot and began to look through the catalogue of wife-hunters.

It was hard to know where to start. Rosa had never travelled further than Moscow. Apart from Tatar and Russian, she knew no other languages. But she'd seen 'life' in the West in Hollywood movies. Even state TV had been showing *Santa Barbara* for years. They were enticing images — and the only way West for Rosa was via an international marriage agency like Elena's.

I listened as Elena continued her sales pitch, filling Rosa's impressionable head with tales of happily-ever-after romance. One former client was now in Denmark, another with a 'lovely German' called Thomas. An Australian 'looking for a Russian bride' was due to arrive in Moscow shortly to meet 'Gizelle', one of the women on her books. They'd been corresponding for two months and he was sure to take her back with him.

'You tell me what you want, and we will work out a program to find a man for you,' Elena said in her cool reassuring voice. 'You must learn about the psychology of Westerners so you will feel comfortable. We even have the services of an image-maker, who will make you the way Western men prefer.'

Rosa nodded, overwhelmed. Ira, another prospective bride, arrived and together they flipped through the agency's catalogues, picking out men who took their fancy, giggling like schoolgirls. Ira liked the tall ones, Rosa the kindly ones. I didn't want to spoil their enthusiasm by mentioning the horror stories of Marina at the crisis centre. One had been of an acquaintance who'd married an American through an agency like this one. This woman had moved to the States with her young daughter, to find it was her daughter the man was interested in. Other catalogue brides found themselves forced into sexual slavery and prostitution. Despite the risks, thousands of women were signing up.

Once a month Elena took a busload of women from Kazan to a club in Moscow to participate in a kind of bride expo. Rosa had been to one before, with a different agency. She estimated there'd been about seven hungry women per foreign male. Without English or spectacular looks, poor Rosa's dance card had remained empty. But she hadn't lost heart.

After leaving the office, Rosa invited me to her home to meet her family and her daughter, Elvira. Together we planted potatoes in their nearby vegie patch, and picked tomatoes and cucumbers for lunch. Rosa and Elvira wore traditional coloured scarves as we worked in the hot sun. It could have been a scene from a Soviet movie set on a collective farm. They were a close-knit family and her parents had never even travelled as far as Moscow.

Over lunch, I began to ask what they thought of their daughter's desire to find a foreign husband and emigrate. Rosa pinched me under the table and changed the subject. She hadn't told them, she whispered later. They would be afraid, and miss her terribly. She would wait until Elena had found someone for her and everything was arranged.

I'd seen Elena as a shyster, making a fine business for herself, selling dreams and fairytales to desperate women. But Rosa had fallen for her promises, hook, line and sinker.

As we parted, she pressed an envelope into my hands.

'Can you take my photo to Australia with you?' she whispered. 'Perhaps someone there will want me?'

25

East Beats West

'I cannot forecast to you the action of Russia. It is a riddle wrapped in a mystery inside an enigma: but perhaps there is a key. That key is Russian national interest.'
Winston Churchill, from a BBC radio broadcast made in London
on 1 October 1939

June 2000

My trip to Kazan to see Nikol the stripper and Rosa the internet bride was my first since my ill-fated visit for Zulfia's wedding. She and Ildar were still happily married, and being summer, were 'relaxing' out in the country at her family's dacha. For almost a decade, Zulfia had implored me to 'come to Kazan in summer when it's really beautiful'. Now I'd finally made it, I just didn't get it. Winter was stark, dramatic, pristine, with glistening snowflakes and vivid azure skies … except, of course when it was grey and slushy or gripped by a biting blizzard. Tatarstan in July was as exotic to this Australian as a hazy suburban Melbourne backyard overgrown with weeds and swarming with mozzies; the murky Volga River as inviting as a swamp. But for her it was a welcome respite from the bone-chilling cold months. And at least there was no risk of freezing to death if your car broke down on a country road.

Zulfia's beloved mother, Nai'ilya, had recently passed away after a long illness that not even Kazan's best doctors could cure. Her father,

Kayum, was quietly digging out his pain in a plot of potatoes and cucumbers. Their city flat was overflowing with freshly harvested vegetables from their country garden waiting to be pickled or stored in bags on the balcony for winter. Her brother, Zofar, was newly married and she was thrilled with her sister-in-law, a feisty and down-to-earth girl who worshipped Zofar. We three girls squatted in the dacha's vegetable garden, picking fat strawberries and inhaling the aroma of ripening tomatoes. Now this was more like it.

Zulfia sniffed the air contentedly. She had recently returned from six months in North Carolina courtesy of a US Department of Commerce study grant.

'I didn't learn much, but I learned I don't like America.'

'Why not?' I swiped at a persistent fly.

'They don't have a strong history and past like we do. They don't respect their history like us Europeans.'

In Australia I had always felt deprived of a cultural identity. Even as a fifth generation Anglo–Scottish Aussie I considered my family to be squatters on Aboriginal territory. I was born in Australia, but what was my culture? I had no traditions, beliefs or land that had been passed down from my ancestors. There was nothing I could identify with as 'belonging' to my family's past, apart from a 'Traill Pavilion' in the town of Montrose, Scotland, which my Great Uncle Ralph had reported was little more than a toilet block. But Zulfia knew exactly where she belonged — here in Tatarstan on the banks of the Volga. Her family tree had been cut off by the Soviets and she couldn't trace her ancestors further than her grandparents, but she had a strong sense of herself as a Tatar and all that went with it — from its language, poetry, heroes and history, right down to traditional recipes for apple pies and *chak-chak* (a doughy Tatar sweet).

Since coming home from the States, she'd moved on from the Tatarstan Chamber of Commerce and Industry and set up her own independent consultancy, hoping to use her knowledge of doing business with foreigners to make some money. Travelling abroad was fun, but home, family and the motherland were best. I related my tale of creepy Elena and her internet bride agency with its 'image-making 'service' to transform her clients into whatever she thought it was that Western men prefer. Zulfia shook her head.

'I know Rosa is looking for a foreigner to marry, but I couldn't do that. Once I thought I could, but now I know it's impossible. With someone from your own culture you understand each other. You experienced the same things, you were both Pioneers, you watched the same movies, listened to the same music. But I hope she finds happiness.'

Rafael from Mari El/Malaysia was also looking for a partner, but not by choice. His mother had gone apoplectic on noticing he had put some blonde streaks in his hair and decided he was gay. She left her village in Mari El and moved in with his aunt in Kazan, vowing not to leave until he found a wife. 'What am I going to do?' Rafael wailed. 'I'm twenty-nine. I don't want to get married. But I can't have my mother here, telling me what o do!' He'd ordered her to find women for him to meet and so far had gone on blind dates with twelve of them; the daughter of her hairdresser, daughters of friends, daughters of auntie's friends ...

'So you know what I do? After a date I say to her, "Yes, she was very nice, but you know what? When I went to drop her home, I walked her up to her flat and it was so messy I couldn't believe it. I really can't marry someone who isn't tidy." My mum of course instantly agrees. It's the woman's job to keep a house nice, and if a young woman is untidy then she's a bad bet as a daughter-in-law.'

I rolled my eyes.

'Yeah, yeah. I know. You Western women expect men to do work around the house. These Hollywood movies have ruined everything. Even our women are getting crazy ideas. They're starting to think men should be present at childbirth, that they should clean. It all used to work fine, women did all the work in the home, but now ... Luckily, my mum still believes in the old ways, so when I make up bad habits, she is satisfied that the girls are unsuitable.'

While Rafael was managing to avoid marriage, he wasn't appeasing his mum either. It had been seven months and he was desperate. On the upside he had found a new job. After having his political and presidential ambitions cruelly dashed by his multiple job rejections in Moscow, he had finally made his move into Tatarstan's circle of the fabulously moneyed and politically powerful. Rafael may not have learned much about theology in Malaysia, but his English was good, a fact he'd casually mentioned to his doctor. The doctor, who knew 'everyone in the republic', just happened to have a 'friend' in need of an English speaker to organise an 'international event'.

The friend turned out to be in the very top echelons of the Tatar elite. His hobby was racing — not those prissy Formula 1 vehicles that whizzed aimlessly around in loops, but rally cars and eight tonne, 800 horsepower Kamaz trucks that he mowed over rocky tracks at 200 kilometres an hour. 'It reminds him of the potholes in Kazan,' added Rafael in an attempt to justify his new patron's eccentric pastime. 'It's a sport for rich people. They have heaps of money and motor racing is a good way to waste it.' This wealthy Tatar needed someone to organise his participation in European and Middle Eastern championships.

So while Rafael hadn't fulfilled his dream of becoming President of the Republic of Mari El, he was now the proud Executive Director of the Federation of Motorsports of Tatarstan, with the laughable monthly salary of 900 roubles, or USD$30. 'Of course I can't live on that,' he said wryly. 'So I arranged for the hot water heater to explode and asked my boss for money for repairs. I got it fixed very cheaply and kept the difference.'

I couldn't blame him. His new boss flew in a private jet and bought $300,000 cars that he'd prang in one race. The mechanics got paid so little that they could only feed their families by stealing tyres from the workshop and selling them. But Rafael did get some perks: a natty pinstriped suit, the latest model mobile phone and a newly wallpapered office with his very own secretary.

Since Rafael and Zulfia were both accommodation challenged, they had arranged for me to stay with a friend and colleague of Rafael's, Galina, a single mother with two children. Galina lived in a shoebox two-room flat, halfway up one of a proliferation of ubiquitous 1970s towers in an outer Kazan suburb, and worked long hours as an accountant at the Federation of Motorsports with Rafael. Her thirteen-year-old daughter, Sasha, did most of the housework, cooking, shopping and looked after her little brother, Ivan. She wouldn't let me lift a finger to help. Sasha was mature beyond her years, practical, sensible and responsible. Still, I couldn't help raising an eyebrow when she told me she was learning to load and fire an AK-47 at school as part of a new Putin initiative to equip Russia's youth to defend the motherland, should it be necessary.

It was only a few months into Putin's reign, but national self-esteem had already lifted. Gorbachev had been weak and insipid, Yeltsin a doddering embarrassment, but Putin, with his glistening pecs and don't-mess-with-me glare, was the country's pride. After years of Yeltsin, the population was exhausted, disillusioned and apathetic. All most wanted now was calm and stability — no more devaluations, hyperinflation or financial crises, no more coups, terrorism or wars, and perhaps even less crime, corruption and cronyism.

To a people weary of chaos, the bland bureaucrat Putin promised security and order, and few seemed to mind when he brought his trusted mates, an equally dull bunch of forty-something yes-men, down from St Petersburg to take up prominent posts in the Kremlin. Many of these new players had links to the army or security services and were known as *siloviki* — from the Russian *sil* meaning 'power'. These 'power people' were of Putin's mould: Soviet-minded suits who believed in control. There was barely a ripple of opposition as Putin began to boost the powers of the security services and military. Russia might have been democratic in theory, but the reality was as bureaucratic as ever. The result was a strange hybrid: a people who wanted freedom as long as someone else decided what to do with it.

Officials no longer spoke of reform, modernisation, progress and democracy. The new buzzwords were stability, order, greatness, sovereignty, power and patriotism. Ordinary people had given up thinking Western ways would make them rich, while those who had become rich, the Novy Russkys, wanted to show they were better than the West. Russia's barons might send their kids to school in London and Geneva, buy villas in the south of France and fly in private jets, but they were scathing of their adoptive lands.

Increasingly, Russians considered Russian and Western culture to be incompatible. In 2000, a survey revealed that almost 70 per cent of respondents thought Soviet rule had made Russians different to other people. They believed that Russia was predestined to follow its own 'special path', and this path required a strong leader, powerful government, and superpower status. There was palpable nostalgia for the days when the world had feared the Soviet empire. It seemed most people valued their country's power and prestige above their own rights and freedoms.

Putin's KGB past marked him as a prime candidate to restore Russia's rightful place on the world stage. A man might leave the KGB, but the KGB would never leave the man. And the KGB's raison d'etre was to seek and destroy those who sought to destroy the motherland. Putin was a patriot. He may not have been able to remedy his nation's domestic chaos, but at least he could restore some dignity to his citizens by rebuilding Russia's international image.

Since the demise of the USSR, Russian frustration with American global supremacy had been increasing. No longer was the US seen as the Promised Land where jeans, bubble gum and Pepsi flowed freely. I often heard disgruntled citizens claim that the West had deliberately set out to bankrupt Russia by saddling it with massive debts through International Monetary Fund (IMF) and World Bank loans. The US was believed to have sponsored Yeltsin's corrupt privatisation. Western NGOs like Greenpeace were said to be sabotaging industry and revealing state secrets. And NATO was not only seducing former Soviet bloc states, it was committing genocide on Russia's Slavic brothers in Serbia.

Now settled in Moscow, Olga was sceptical about the creeping anti-Western sentiment. 'It's the usual story in this country,' she said frankly. 'Pick someone outside your circle and blame them for the problems. It's always easier to find external enemies than to admit your own faults.'

NATO's decision to bomb Serbia in March 1999 had been a turning point. As the war over Kosovo dragged on, Russian officials encouraged people to hurl eggs, tomatoes and abuse at the US

Embassy on Moscow's Garden Ring Road, accusing the Americans of genocide against their Slavic brothers. City authorities organised buses to take Moscow University students to the site and Serbian diplomats even provided them with ripe and rotting ammunition. Demonstrators waved banners: 'Yankee Hands Off Yugoslavia'. Russian state media gleefully covered every detail.

I ran into Stanislav Kucher, the smooth host of the national current affairs show, *The Observer,* I had met on the plane from Malaysia. He was enjoying a bout of moral superiority.

'When NATO dropped the first bomb on Yugoslavia, that's when the United States brought the Cold War back,' he said pompously. 'Now it's clear NATO is not just an aggressive organisation. It is a criminal organisation!'

I visited Stas's long-suffering wife, Natalya — whom I had befriended after the Moscow Hotel arms dealers' Christmas party — at the elite Anglo-American high school where she taught. Her wealthy students shared similar anti-US sentiments, despite speaking and dressing like characters from *Beverly Hills 90210.*

'America is trying to start World War Three,' one boy told her, when she asked their thoughts about the Kosovo war.

'America wants war with Russia,' said another.

One of her students was a perky, eleven-year-old girl called Anastasia, whom the other students treated like a celebrity.

'I think that NATO are murderers,' she said. 'And this is not just because the Serbs are our friends, but because they are people. You people don't understand who you are killing.'

She was Mikhail Gorbachev's grand-daughter.

Putin was steadily overturning what was left of the pro-West stance of Gorbachev and Yeltsin. The Kremlin's rhetoric wasn't overtly anti-Western at first, but it emphasised US plans to build a missile defence shield and the expansion of NATO into the former Soviet bloc. Putin made a point of visiting what the US saw as 'rogue states' of North Korea, Iran, Syria and Libya, cementing alliances and discussing, among other things, sales of Russian arms to these countries.

'Well, you never know,' Sasha in Kazan had replied when I'd asked who she thought she might have to shoot with her AK-47. 'But I think it's important we are prepared, just in case we *are* invaded.'

I stifled a smile, remembering Yuri in Ivangorod. He would have gladly given all his gold teeth to be invaded by Estonia. But Sasha, bursting with youthful patriotism, was taking her military classes seriously. I couldn't help fearing this new brand of defensive nationalism might erupt into something ugly. Weapons training for teenagers and anti-Western propaganda seemed a dangerous mix.

Some felt Putin wasn't going far enough. He might have been more openly anti-Western than Yeltsin and Gorbachev, but hard-line communists were already feeling he had betrayed their trust. In Moscow, I tracked down a group calling themselves the Avant Garde Red Youth, a feisty bunch of disgruntled neo-Stalinist youths. They were so unimpressed with their new leader that a group of fifty or so kids met regularly in a south Moscow basement to discuss plans for another communist revolution. Masha, a diminutive fifteen-year-old blonde in a red and black Stalin T-shirt, explained the reasons for their disappointment.

'People voted for him because they believed he wasn't like Yeltsin or Gorbachev. They thought he was a patriot who would follow a communistic path of development. The oligarchs thought he would follow a democratic, capitalist path. In the end he leaned that way because he is making money for himself.'

Pretty Masha and her Red Youth comrades now believed that not only was revolution the answer, but that Joseph Stalin had been the greatest leader of the twentieth century.

'When Stalin was in control,' declared Masha, 'the USSR was a strong country which inspired fear and respect. He was a great man, a real leader, our ideal. We need a strong hand like him to rule our country.'

'But what about the twenty million of his own people killed under his rule?' I asked.

'Well he only killed people who were causing problems,' she replied with frightening conviction. 'They needed to be dealt with firmly.

Now the media tries to fool people, to portray Stalin as some kind of tyrant. If he was so bad then why would people have got together to shout "For Stalin and the Motherland"? He did so much for our people. There were no illegitimate children, no crime, no drug addicts, not so many drunkards. Wages were decent, there were jobs, the pension was adequate and education and medicine were free. Now you can only get a higher education if you have a lot of money for bribes, and even if you have an education you can't get work without connections. So we young people can't even think about having families because we don't know how we're going to live ourselves, let alone feed our children.'

Masha introduced me to her boyfriend, a scruffy kid with a Che Guevara pin on his lapel who went by the name of Chekist, the term once given to members of the Cheka, Stalin's secret police.

'We need to get the people to rise up,' Chekist declared with the passion of a hormonal seventeen-year-old. 'They need to understand that they are not living, but existing ... existing in such conditions where they have no rights. People should have the right to a decent job. You find street sweepers and shop girls have engineering qualifications ... but the people just sit and sleep. They say, "Oh, a revolution — there'll be Gulags and repression." The TV shows such rubbish they are afraid that if there will be communism they'll all be put up against the wall and shot. But if you go into the provinces you'll find people there wishing there was still the Gulag to send all those who are driving around in their fancy Jeeps to, while their own children are dying of hunger.'

'The US doesn't want us to be a strong power,' added Masha. 'They are trying to bring us down however they can. But this American/Western path isn't acceptable to us. Those at the top were only pro-Western because they got money from the West. Where did those oligarchs and officials get their money from?'

The meeting concluded with a graphic song about 'going to the Kremlin to hang our Red Flag', which included the following stanza:

Moscow will be set on fire …

We'll look on laughing at how our enemy is convulsing in red hot basements

We'll build our Gulag on their bones and sweat.

It's time to burn the bridges and the treasury.

My bed is groaning because I'm dying in the society of the bourgeoisie …

A lot of shouting about Stalin and the motherland followed. When I told Nadia what I'd heard, she was horrified.

Meanwhile, my own country was hosting the Olympics and I watched the closing ceremony on Russian state TV. The commentators seemed baffled by the laid-back presentation, devoid of mandatory displays of mass precision. And when Kylie Minogue appeared on a giant thong, they were totally stumped. 'What the …?' they asked each other. Then one finally got it. 'It's a *tapochek!* Australia's most famous songstress is riding into the stadium on a house slipper!'

It was now ten years since my first visit to the Russian capital, and the city was almost unrecognisable, thanks to billions of laundered dollars flowing in from a variety of dodgy sources. Much was rumoured to be IMF loan money on its return from a Swiss holiday. Mayor Yuri Luzhkov had been spending up on massive construction and renovation projects involving quarries full of polished marble. Casinos flashed neon 24/7. Queue-free shops and roadside kiosks groaned with hundreds of brands of beer and vodka, chocolates, chips and cigarettes. Sparkling designer clothing and luxury goods stores lined the boulevards: Prada, Fendi, Hermes, Louis Vuitton. The roads were gridlocked with chauffeur-driven Mercs, Beemers and limousines. At the same time, those whom the IMF loans were intended to assist — the *budzhetniki* (pensioners, teachers, nurses, miners, state employees) and those who had fallen through the cracks (street kids and the homeless) — eked out ever more tenuous existences alongside the glitter.

I caught up with Marat, Sergei's old law school friend from Kazan, who had been busily building up his management portfolio of popular rock bands since I'd last seen him. I asked what he thought about international institutions giving loans to Russia. He laughed.

'The Russian mentality is such that when you're given money, some of it simply must stay in your pocket. Perhaps in three or ten generations, Russia will change and people will start thinking differently. It's a matter of psychology. You foreigners, you think in a different way. When you build, you want the place to look good and be convenient for people. But the first thing our people think of is what they can steal.'

Marat never beat around the bush. He had just bought himself a new toy, his third Merc, this one a silver 600 model, which he deftly manoeuvred through the inner-city congestion, simultaneously talking on two mobile phones and playing me a CD of one of his bands' latest releases.

'So what do you think?' he asked when he'd finished his calls. 'Will they like it in Australia?'

Unlike Sergei and Olga, Marat had never learned English. His wealth and success had not come from long hours of toil for a Western company, but rather in the traditional manner; networking, bartering favours and schmoozing. Over the years he had built up an extensive network of connections across the country. Once he'd dropped a visiting Australian friend of mine at the airport. After Marat had a quick chat with a mate high up in Aeroflot, she was upgraded to business class for her flight to New York. And when another friend — a Russian who had immigrated to Australia at the age of eleven then decided to return at thirty — asked me for help finding work, I put her in touch with Marat. Within weeks she had a job at a TV station, hosting Russia's first-ever incarnation of the romance/quiz show, Love at First Sight.

Marat took me to a nightclub off the prestigious Tverskaya Street, just near Pushkin Square, where one of his groups was performing. 'It's okay, she's Australian,' I heard him whisper to the face-control bouncer, who nodded dumbly as if my nationality excused the fact that my boots didn't have stiletto heels and my outfit didn't come from a boutique in London's Knightsbridge. No longer were Westerners treated with the respect and mild envy of just a few years ago. Now I felt like some backward primitive and provincial peasant, gawping at the sophisticated socialites. Marat ushered me past the well-heeled and intoxicated clubbers into the sound engineer's room where we could at least hear each other speak. He beamed.

'You could say that today, people who have money are feeling pretty good. I can say for myself that I'm doing quite okay. There's a saying: "How are you?" "I drive a Mercedes." "I see."'

He ducked out for a chat with his lead singer, Maxim Leonidov, who was taking a break between sets. I gazed into the dimly lit spaceship-like interiors of the club, its walls and ceilings lined with what looked like hammered sheets of aluminium. Young women clutching cocktails tottered up metallic steps in pin-thin heels, groomed, manicured, sprayed and worked out to perfection. From what I could tell from peering through shop windows on Tverskaya, one of their sexy little dresses would have cost more than a teacher's yearly salary, and that didn't include jewels, shoes and a bag. Even a drink in this place cost an average week's salary for a *budzhetnik*; a bottle of champagne, two months. Yet it was packed, with Hollywood celebrity clones clinging to men who made cane toads look handsome. It seemed so unjust and topsy turvy to me. But to Marat it was simply an immutable fact of life.

'There never was a time in Russia when everybody was equal. That's just an invention people believed, especially abroad. And of course, our government kept repeating that the people of Russia were all brothers and sisters, that everybody was equal, that we all shared the food from one common pot. Communism! Hurray!'

In retrospect, I couldn't believe I'd ever been dumb enough to fall for the caring-sharing propaganda. It was no wonder Yulia had looked at me like I was a raving idiot when I told her how great her country was on my first visit. I cringed at the memory. Wide-eyed, I had blinded myself to the bleeding obvious: the communist state was a criminal state, whose officials twisted their ideology to disguise all kinds of despicable activities. And those who had run it hadn't changed their spots with so-called democracy, only their suits.

26

A Nuclear Wasteland

'Man has been endowed with reason, with the power to create, so that
he can add to what he's been given. But up to now, he hasn't been
a creator, only a destroyer. Forests keep disappearing, rivers dry up,
wild life's become extinct, the climate's ruined, and the land grows
poorer and uglier.'
Anton Chekhov, *Uncle Vanya*

October 2000

A monstrous, wrinkled, yellow face squinted at me from a jar of formaldehyde. I peered around it, realising in shock that this pickled human foetus had two heads. The specimen bottle next to it contained another 'baby', this one with the back of its skull missing. The label read '*anencephalia*', the medical term for 'no brain'. Dr Gennadi Brukhin, the prim Head of Histology and Embryology at the Chelyabinsk State Medical Academy, tapped on the glass.

'This is a relatively widespread mutation. They have a head, but no brain — the skull is open,' he explained matter-of-factly.

Dr Brukhin moved on to the next jar. I concentrated on framing my shots, the only way I could keep from feeling queasy. 'This one is an extremely unusual foetus which we received two years ago,' he continued. 'It's like some kind of monster. See its enormous head? The eyes are hidden and there is practically no stomach. We did a post-mortem, and there are very few organs and only one kidney.' He crossed the room and pointed to another specimen. 'This one they call a "mermaid" — the bottom end is joined up and the head is very large.'

I'd been brought to this fluoro-lit chamber of horrors by Milya Kabirova, a sweet-faced woman from a nearby village. She examined the grotesque bottled fish-like creature and turned to Dr Brukhin. 'I have a friend who gave birth to a baby like that, but it was taken away immediately,' she said quietly. 'It wasn't that one was it?'

Dr Brukhin couldn't say. Milya sighed and looked at me.

'Every time I come here I am glad that we were unable to have children. I can't imagine how terrible it would be to give birth to such a monster.'

For many women in the Chelyabinsk region, southeast of the Ural Mountains, the nightmare of discovering their babies were fatally deformed was too often a tragic reality. Dr Brukhin had been collecting these mutant aborted and miscarried human foetuses for the past two decades, and suspected the mutations were linked to exposure to radiation. Milya and her environmental activist husband, Gosman, had been carrying out their own investigations, and had no doubt that enormous doses of radiation were responsible for the high incidence of mutants in their native territory. But authorities were tight-lipped.

I'd met the couple a few weeks earlier through a mutual friend in Moscow. Their terrible tale made my blood run cold and they'd invited me to Chelyabinsk to film their story. I booked a ticket east, on a rickety Chelavia Tupolev, which appeared not to have been serviced, let alone cleaned, for several years, and took off towards what Gosman described as the 'most radioactively polluted place on the planet'.

From 1945 to 1948, Stalin's police chief, Lavrentiy Beria, oversaw the construction of a nuclear plant at the southern end of the Ural Mountains, a thousand kilometres east of Moscow. Built in total secrecy by 70,000 prisoners, Mayak (Lighthouse) was at the heart of the Soviet Union's nuclear weapons program, with five reactors initially used to produce and refine plutonium for use in nuclear weapons. Workers lived in a nearby 'closed city', known as Ozersk, or Chelyabinsk-65 — a Soviet-era code name referring to its distance from (65 kilometres) Chelyabinsk. The Soviet Union's first nuclear bomb was produced here, and later the facility reprocessed spent fuel from reactors and decommissioned weapons. Forty per cent of the country's nuclear arms stockpile was assembled at Mayak.

Operations at the complex were carried out with total disregard for the environment, and from 1948 to 1951, almost three million curies of toxic radioactive waste were pumped into nearby lakes and the Techa River, the only water supply for the residents of the thirty-eight villages built on its banks. Gosman and Milya were born in one of these villages, Muslyumovo, 47 kilometres downstream from Mayak. They and their parents had no idea that the river they drank from and played in was a radioactive waste dump.

But things were to get much worse. In September 1957, when Gosman was a baby, his parents heard rumours of an accident upstream. Locals had noticed a kilometre-high plume rising from what appeared to be an explosion at the mysterious facility nearby. Soon after this, more than two hundred people in the region died and thousands more became seriously ill. Without explanation, most of the villages along the Techa River were evacuated and more than 10,000 inhabitants relocated. But the 4,500 residents of Muslyumovo were left where they were.

Milya's father was employed as a policeman, charged with keeping villagers away from the river. No one told them why the water was out of bounds, and in the hot months children found ways to sneak past the policemen and swim. People drank the river water, used it to water their gardens and wash their clothes. They caught fish in it and their livestock drank from it. In 1962, five years after the accident, Milya's policeman father died from severe leukaemia. He was forty-four. Milya was two, the youngest of seven children. Her widowed mother was offered work by the state collecting water samples from the river. The children helped her and they often kept jars of water in the house.

A decade after the explosion, there was a third disaster. Since 1951, the main dumping basin for toxic waste from Mayak was a bog called Lake Karachay. In 1967, a severe drought caused Lake Karachay to dry out. Gale force winds spread five million curies of radioactive dust across 25,000 square kilometres.

Most of the world knew little or nothing about the 1957 accident until 1991, when thirty-four years too late, the Kremlin finally admitted to the disaster. The cooling system for a storage tank containing tens of thousands of tonnes of nuclear waste had malfunctioned, causing a massive explosion, which released over twenty million curies. Radiation covered over 1,000 square kilometres and around 80 million cubic metres of radioactive liquid had poured into the Techa River. Over a quarter of a million people had been affected. It was the Soviet Union's worst nuclear disaster until Chernobyl, which was rated at Level 6 on the International Nuclear Events Scale of 0–7.

Suspecting something was seriously wrong with their village, Gosman and Milya had left Muslyumovo in their early twenties. Milya's mother had already died, along with two of her siblings. Three others were seriously ill. Gosman found work as a plumber in the industrial city of Chelyabinsk where they now lived in a small flat with their fourteen-year-old adopted son. He met me at Chelyabinsk's airport and we rattled off in his beaten up old Zhiguli. Milya had prepared a couch for me and we sat down to a supper of black bread, sickly sweet tea and pickled cabbage. Both talked non-stop, reeling off grim statistics: cancer rates, radiation levels, genetic mutations, laughable financial compensation and barbarously dismissive authorities. Gosman was brusque and determined, Milya charming and persuasive.

With scant funding from various foreign organisations, the Kabirovs were trying to win compensation for surviving victims of the 1957 catastrophe and to convince the government to relocate those still residing in the radioactive zone. But they were fighting a losing battle. The government still refused to acknowledge that some of the most highly contaminated zones had been affected at all.

The next morning, Geiger counter in hand, Gosman took me to Argayash, a region downwind from Mayak that according to the authorities was perfectly habitable. It looked tranquil enough, with swathes of freshly harvested wheat fields, picturesque autumn forests and gaggles of geese wandering around rough-hewn wooden cottages. Villagers waited at a bus stop. An elderly couple clopped by in their horse-drawn cart. We pulled over at the edge of a village and Gosman gestured with a stocky worker's hand to three tall chimneys sticking up from the forest like matchsticks ... Mayak.

'This,' he said gravely, 'was the most secret facility in the Chelyabinsk region, maybe even in all of Russia.' All around us, he said, was a huge concentration of plutonium, 'one of the most terrible carcinogens'. Just a few metres away an old woman was digging up beets in her garden. An elderly man was chopping firewood. Gosman asked him where it had come from and he waved to the forest between his house and the chimneys.

Gosman turned back to me, his pockmarked face resigned. 'There's so much radioactive pollution here it's even dangerous to be here, let alone burn wood from the forests, grow wheat and potatoes, pick berries and mushrooms, fish and raise livestock. The land is completely poisoned, yet people live here and sell their produce by the roadside without any checks. They have no choice. People have nowhere to work and need to live somehow. They think it's better to die from radiation tomorrow than of starvation today.'

I was uncomfortable. Just a few kilometres back we'd bought some potato *pirozhki* at a village store. I felt guilty for even thinking about myself when tens of thousands of people had no option but to poison themselves daily. Gosman read my mind, and gruffly reassured me that he'd checked them with his Geiger counter. I made a silent resolution to avoid eating.

Gosman drove closer to the ominous smoking chimneys, into the village of Novogorni, the site of the power station which provides electrical energy to Mayak. Just weeks earlier, there had been a major accident in the Ural power network. The Novogorni station had been affected and Mayak had been without power for a full twenty-two minutes. Fortunately, the emergency generator had been turned on just in time to avert a major catastrophe, but Gosman was scathing about the professionalism of the engineers.

'They don't know what they're doing. To do this job you have to be a highly trained expert. But it seems that in this country, just anyone can do it. They said it couldn't happen but it did, and there was very nearly a massive disaster.'

A Soviet anecdote came to mind:

An officer falls asleep on duty, right in front of the red button*. The colonel comes in and the officer reports: 'Nothing's happened during the duty, comrade Colonel.'

'What do you mean nothing's happened? Nothing's happened? Then where the hell is Belgium?'

(*The 'red button' was the main control of the USSR's nuclear armoury. Pressing it would herald the start of World War III, almost certain to result in MAD — Mutually Assured Destruction.)

MAD had once seemed almost an amusing term — a relic of the Cold War — but out here, suddenly it didn't seem quite so funny any more.

Over dinner that evening back in Chelyabinsk, Milya played me a tape she had secretly recorded on a dictaphone smuggled into a village clinic. A nurse listed the shocking disease and mortality rates in the Argayash region: 72 per cent of the population have diseases of the central nervous system, 50 per cent have diseases of the digestive system, 38 per cent have blood diseases, and every fifth person is an invalid. Incredibly, this information was still considered a state secret, even now, nine years after the collapse of the Soviet Union.

'Of course it's a secret,' said Milya, with obvious frustration. 'It's very convenient for the government not to acknowledge that these illnesses are due to radiation. If they did, they would have to pay compensation. Our goal is to convince the government that the region is polluted and to have it included in the regions that receive welfare.'

The next day Gosman and I drove to Muslyumovo, his and Milya's native village. A memorial forest of young birches on its outskirts was marked by a simple wooden archway, carved with the words: 'We warn. We remember. We grieve.' Next to the forest was one of Muslyumovo's six cemeteries. They were all full. Gosman pointed out the graves of his grandparents, Milya's parents and two brothers, and many other relatives. All had died from various forms of cancer. Beyond a sign with the universal symbol for radiation was the Techa, an innocuous-looking, peacefully flowing stream. Birds twittered and yellowing birch leaves fluttered gently to the ground.

Gosman stared at the river he had played in as a child, then happily ignorant of the colourless, odourless and tasteless radiation which contaminated its waters. If he had known what the consequences would be, he told me ruefully, he never would have come here.

'The secrecy has only caused harm. They haven't killed a single enemy with their atomic bomb, but a huge number of our local population here in Muslyumovo have died and are continuing to die. And even though we all know of the dangers here, authorities still have not relocated residents.'

It was a chilly autumn day and Muslyumovo showed little sign of life. A shroud of doom hung over derelict and abandoned buildings. A few cows wandered around, idly munching at tufts of grass. Once a policeman had patrolled a barbed wire fence which cordoned off the river, but now both were gone. Gosman held his Geiger counter to the grass a few metres from the riverbank in the centre of the village. The reading was 652 microroentgens, sixty-five times higher than normal acceptable level. We trudged through the mud down to the riverbank and he measured again. Here the reading shot up still further, to 952 microroentgens. A cow stood ankle deep in the sludge, slurping the toxic water. It would return to its owner later to be milked, said Gosman, milk which village children would drink, poisoning their bodies with strontium, cesium and plutonium.

'The animal should be shot and left right here. But when it is killed it will be eaten. There have been calves born with two heads and one without an anus. Another had five legs. People are afraid but what can they do? No one has any money, the collective farms are gone and the pensions are kopecks. Here they receive "ecology money", compensation for living in an irradiated zone. It's only around 40–200 roubles a month (AUD$2–10), but if they leave, they lose this money. They live here voluntarily, but are economically bound to stay. If they leave they have to find money to buy a new house, and they won't receive any money or medicine. Our laws are so ridiculous that people are forced through economics to live in an environmentally polluted area.'

We dropped in to visit one of Gosman's old school friends, Rafid Magludtovich. Gaunt and sallow, he looked at least twenty years older than his forty-three years. Rafid invited us in and proffered tea and berry pie, made with 'our irradiated berries, what else?' I tried to think of an excuse not to partake that didn't sound precious, but I couldn't. Rafid and Gosman began to discuss the fates of various relatives and classmates while I nibbled at a slice of radioactive cake and sipped from a mug of radioactive tea.

Eric, an old school friend, had died from stomach cancer. Another friend, Marat, had died a slow, tortured death from skin cancer, as had both his parents. Their neighbour, Galya, was dying of stomach cancer. Rafid had already undergone four operations: three on his stomach and one on his spine. Now doctors were telling him he needed another on his spine. But no doctor would admit that his problems were caused by radiation. His monthly welfare payment while in hospital was 33 roubles, less than AUD$2. He couldn't afford essential medicines, let alone support his family.

Rafid's wife, Gulfira, was only forty-four but also looked much older: emaciated and fragile with dull, exhausted eyes and pallid papery skin. Like all the other villagers, she had lost all her teeth by the age of thirty. Their eldest son had been born with one enormous kidney, and the other shrivelled like a walnut. Rafid and Gulfira were certain it was a birth defect caused by radiation, but doctors claimed otherwise. Their daughter had problems with her heart and kidneys and the youngest had a compromised immune system. Even a scratch would lead to hospitalisation.

Gulfira had just lost seven relatives in a four-month period, including her father from lung cancer and her mother from stomach cancer. Her maternal uncle had died of heart problems because they couldn't afford a 40,000 rouble operation. Her younger brother had died from a heart attack at the age of thirty-four after his heart had swollen to 1.2 kilograms, four times the normal size. Her cousin had died at the age of twenty-two from kidney malfunction. While her grandparents were still alive well into their eighties, most of their children were already dead.

'My grandmother can't even cry any more. At the last funeral she could only shake. I'm so tired of burying people. We just finish forty days of mourning and there's another one. We are waiting for our turn to come to die. But we don't want to.'

Gulfira shook her head.

'Everyone who lived near the river, it's the same story. There isn't enough paper to write it all down. In every family there is grief. There isn't a family where people aren't dying of cancer. All I want is that my children live, that's all. I think about all these statistics ... that each generation a life is twenty years shorter.'

'So we've already outlived our time,' Gosman laughed.

'We try to joke and laugh,' sighed Gulfira. 'But mostly we cry. All we want is for the children to get an education so they can get out of here. If they had told us when we were children, we would have left. But they didn't tell us. Even the policemen who chased us away from the river didn't know. They just got an early pension and died too.'

'Back then, atomic energy was something amazing,' said Gosman. 'It was an achievement for Lenin, for the USSR, and we were patriots. But the reality is, it's hell. Now those people who rant on about the motherland are my personal enemies.'

For Gosman and the villagers of Muslyumovo, the ultimate insult was the realisation that they had been used as human guinea pigs, forced to languish and suffer in a radioactive zone so scientists could study the effects of radiation on a captive population. In 1961, four years after the accident, an Institute of Biophysics was set up in Moscow, with a branch in Chelyabinsk (now called the Ural Institute of Radiation Medicine). Masquerading as doctors, scientists and researchers visited Muslyumovo regularly to take blood from the inhabitants for analysis. They even went to schools and took blood from young children without asking their parents, using huge needles meant for animals. The villagers were told that these 'doctors' were 'doing research to find out where their diseases came from', but the test results and medical records were kept secret.

'They never gave any kinds of results. They just said, "Yes, there are abnormalities, but it's nothing to worry about,"' Gulfira recalled. 'But how can there be nothing to worry about when everyone is dying from cancer?'

Many critically ill villagers, thinking they were being taken to hospital, were transported to the Institute of Biophysics in Moscow. Gosman's aunt had died there and family members had whisked her body away for burial before she was dissected. His uncle, who had been a policeman guarding the river, died there too, from leukemia. When his father was being examined in the Institute they could hear dogs barking in the next room. A neighbour who was dying from throat cancer had also been sent there for tests. She never returned. Even now, whenever a baby was born in the village, their details were immediately registered with the Institute of Radiation Medicine, who added them to family trees showing diseases and mutations within each family.

'We were an experiment,' Gosman muttered bitterly. 'A whole institute works on us. The government knew in the 1960s that it was dangerous for people to live here. But they didn't want to resettle people. If they were to move us, they would have to look all over the country to find us rabbits and investigate what is happening to us. But this way they have a whole village where they can come and do analysis. To keep sheep and rabbits was more expensive than to keep us all in Muslyumovo. We don't take a kopeck from the government. We feed ourselves! How many theses and dissertations were written about us? How many "Heroes of the USSR" received their awards for destroying their own people? And the Director of the Institute of Radiation Medicine sold the results of the research to the Americans* and received a grant of USD$120,000, and an award for "Fellowship amongst Peoples". Ha! They get rich from our suffering. And we can't even afford medicine.'

(* The data collected by the Institute from the irradiated populations of the Chelyabinsk region was given to the US Defense Nuclear Agency's Armed Forces Radiobiology Research Institute in Bethesda, Maryland in 1992. Statistical results showed hugely increased rates of cancers, genetic abnormalities and death, undeniable proof of the catastrophic effects of the Mayak disasters on the health of the surrounding populations. The report was unclassified, with unlimited distribution, yet even now, in 2000, the Russian government and local doctors were continuing to lie to the locals affected.)

Gosman and I left Rafid and Gulfira sitting sombrely at their kitchen table. He wanted to visit his mother who lived nearby. We passed crumbling concrete low-rise flats, sidestepping puddles on the unsealed road. Chickens scattered in a flurry of feathers. Gosman's mother shuffled to the door and let us in, embracing her son weakly. Now seventy-two, she had lived in Muslyumovo all her life. She had raised eleven children and brought out her 'Heroine Mother' medal and certificate from an old chest to show me. His father, long deceased, had been the youngest of fourteen. But like many of their generation, Gosman and Milya were sterile. At first they'd been upset. Now they were both relieved.

'Many people here now envy us. "Thank God you don't have children," they say to me, "otherwise you would be suffering like we are." That's why we adopted our son from the orphanage, so we could save him from a life of poverty.'

We drove on to Milya's childhood home, long deserted and slowly collapsing from neglect. Anything of value had been looted. Gosman showed me the potato patch, which they still used even though the soil was heavily contaminated. My instinct would have been to get as far away as possible from this toxic place. Gosman knew it was irrational, but for him this weed-infested patch of hell was his home.

'It's my motherland. I still want to come back, to remember my childhood. Once people lived here, children played, it was a happy home, full of joy. Milya's family worked hard to build this place, and now no one will ever live here again. It's so sad. But it's even sadder for the little kids who still have to grow up in the village.'

In 1996, Gosman's anger at Mayak led him to found an environmental protest group, which he called Techa after the river through Muslyumovo. When Techa unsuccessfully tried to sue Mayak for compensation for the victims, Gosman was asked dismissively by the lawyer for the weapons plant: 'Well, what does it matter if two or three people died if we saved the world from nuclear war?'

Gosman was furious. '"But those two or three people ... that is me, my family, my aunt, my brother, my father," I shouted at him. They

February 2000 – A war wedding: the young Chechen war refugee bride has just arrived at the groom's house in an Ingush village, as the groom's relatives and friends play music, dance and fire Kalashnikovs into the air in celebration. (Photo: Bentley Dean)

July 2000 – Any train trip involves a farewell committee. (Front row, left to right) Rafael, Sasha, Galina with son Ivan, as well as (back row, left to right) Rafael's secretary, Reseda, Zofar and his new wife, and Zulfia come to see me off at Kazan.

With 'Nikol' (stripper and would-be lawyer) in the one-room flat she shared with fellow stripper 'Brenda' in Kazan. (Photo: 'Brenda')

Trying to squeeze a rugged-up fourteen-month-old Nik into the tiny lift at the ABC's apartment on Kutuzovsky Prospekt, Moscow.

A memorial board near Moscow's White House commemorates victims of the October 1993 stand–off between Yeltsin and the Russian parliament. Yeltsin ordered troops to fire on civilians protesting in support of his opponents, resulting in 187 deaths. Communist sources claim the number killed was closer to 2000.

Sergei in August 1991. On the day of the coup against Gorbachev, Sergei was on a family holiday on a cruise ship on the Volga River. He'd just finished his first year of Law at Kazan State University. (Photo taken by ship's photographer)

Interior Ministry police harassing a Tajik illegal ('black arse') at the entrance to the Alexandrovsky Sad Metro station in central Moscow.

Many of the 177 stations in the Moscow Metro network are decorated with social–realist art; this mural is on the platform at Borovitskaya.

January 2007 – Olga's local shop in Moscow, near 1905 Metro station. Entire walls stocked with alcohol are typical of shops across the former USSR.

January 2007 – Olga, Tyoma and Misha at their newly completely grand *dacha* at Tryokhgorka on Moscow's northwestern outskirts.

January 2007 – Nadia posing next to a calendar showing the sanatorium just outside of Moscow where she had gone with a friend to 'rest' at New Year.

January 2007 – The latest trend in wedding transportation in the new Russia. A local poses while the wedding party has its photo shoot at the Mikhailov Palace in St Petersburg.

January 2007 – Stuffed local wildlife is a feature of the Yolki Palki chain of all-you-can-eat Russian cuisine restaurants which sprung up all over post-Soviet Russia.

January 2007 – A pensioner poses with a wax figure of Empress Catherine the Great outside the main department store on St Petersburg's Nevsky Prospekt. Russia's royals are now back in vogue after 75 years of damnation by the communists.

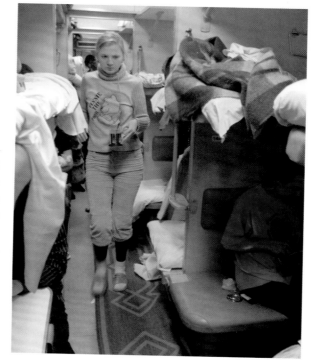

A *platscart* wagon – the cheapest travel option favoured by students – on the 'Tatarstan' night train between Moscow and Kazan.

January 2007 – Rafael in the kitchen of his aunt's *kommunalka* where he lived for several years. He shared this space with thirteen others to cook, wash and do laundry.

January 2007 – Kazan. Rafael in his office where he is the Executive Director of the Federation of Motor Sports of Tatarstan.

January 2007 – Revisiting the Tatar village of Saya. Left to right: me, Tatiana, Vildan the beekeeper, his daughter-in-law, Elvira, and wife, Nai'ilya. Note the obligatory bottle of vodka in the foreground.

proclaim that they have saved the whole world from nuclear war. But we had our own ethnic group here — the Meshary — and now we are almost extinct.'

For his protestations, Gosman was put under constant state surveillance. Secret police tapped his phone and his activities were monitored.

As if past woes weren't enough, the Russian parliament was now, in October 2000, considering a new bill to allow the import of up to 20,000 tonnes of nuclear waste into Russia. Most was destined for Mayak. It seemed an absurd proposition given the extent of the existing problems, but with a deal reported to be worth up to USD$21 billion I could imagine officials rubbing their hands in eager anticipation, already perusing French real estate and ordering catalogues of the latest private jets.

The Kabirovs were violently opposed to the bill and this past summer Gosman and six others had held a demonstration on the Techa River. Seventy police had attended and videoed everything. Another recent protest, against Finnish waste being brought to Mayak, resulted in the Finns reconsidering, and Gosman had found himself in yet more trouble. He showed me a document from the FSB, which accused him of doing great harm to the region and country. His crime was having damaged the economy by 'stating the truth about the environment'.

One of Gosman's colleagues, the head of the Movement for Nuclear Safety, Natalia Mironova, had collected a staggering 2.5 million signatures from Russian citizens against their country becoming the world's nuclear waste dump and calling for a nationwide referendum. But the government claimed that some of the signatures were invalid, and refused to hold the referendum. Gosman was livid.

'There will be such a concentration of radioactive materials here in one place. If there would be an accident like there has just been with the power network with all this extra radioactivity stored here, it would be enough to cause a global catastrophe. They say, "We'll bring in the waste from other countries, get money, and then we'll help people." But we don't believe them. They will receive the money and again it will disappear into the pockets of the officials, again they will add to the foreign debt, and again there could very easily be a huge accident and the entire population here could perish once and for all. Our officials, our ministers, our President will sell anything for dollars. They've already sold us.'

Had anything changed since Soviet times? Back then, the communist elite ruled from the moral high ground of an absolute and unquestionable ideology. These days, authorities claimed to have a mandate from 'the people' via the democratic process. But everyone understood that those in positions of power had clawed their way up by anything but democratic means, and that gaining a political post was nothing to do with serving the people, and everything to do with serving oneself. Greens like Milya and Gosman, who genuinely acted in the public interest, were a nuisance to the authorities, who preferred to keep their corrupt behaviour away from public scrutiny.

In July 1999, Putin, then FSB chief, advised his secret police to crack down on international environmental groups, declaring that, 'unfortunately, foreign intelligence services, under the guise of diplomatic missions, actively use environmental groups as covers for espionage'. All across the country, environmental activists and journalists who exposed the dangers of Russia's nuclear industry were being hounded, portrayed as unpatriotic traitors determined to sully Russia's image. *Svoboda slova* (free speech) had been reduced to a meaningless patter, overtaken by the more traditional mantra of 'Keep the rubbish inside the house'. The government was happy to tolerate 'free speech' that praised it and its policies, but anything critical was deemed destructive to the nation's self-esteem.

Mayak was only one of a number of nuclear perils in the vast Russian Federation. From the Arctic North-West to the Pacific Far East, Russia's neglected fleet of nuclear-powered submarines was now haunting the citizens it was supposed to protect. When the USSR collapsed, initially many environmentalists had been optimistic that the end of communism would lead to greater openness in dealing with the issue of nuclear safety. By now all hope had evaporated, and some prominent whistleblowers had even been accused of treason.

It seemed nothing short of insanity that potential environmental catastrophes should be considered state secrets. In Vladivostok, journalist Grigory Pasko had been held in detention for over a year, accused by the FSB of revealing 'secret military information' after working with Japanese documentary makers on a film about the dumping of radioactive nuclear waste into the Sea of Japan by Russia's Pacific Fleet. And in St Petersburg, retired naval captain Alexander Nikitin was in the midst of a long-running trial for 'treason through espionage'. Formerly a nuclear safety inspector working with Russia's Northern Fleet of nuclear-powered submarines, Nikitin had assisted a Norwegian environmental monitoring organisation called Bellona with a report on the navy's dumping of nuclear waste into the Arctic Sea north of Murmansk. Amnesty International declared Nikitin a prisoner-of-conscience, the first since the demise of the Soviet Union.

I travelled back to Murmansk, at the tip of the Kola Peninsula in the Northern Polar Circle, to meet with activists from Bellona, this time making sure my documents were in order. Since the mid-1980s, Norwegian scientists had been trying to ascertain just what was going on in their secretive neighbour's backyard. Their conclusions were disturbing: the nuclear waste deposits and dilapidated nuclear submarines of Russia's Northern Fleet posed a grave threat to the region.

With the collapse of the USSR, the situation worsened. As economic and political crises ravaged the country, there was little money or political will to deal with the problems. Bellona began to map the nuclear sites on the Kola Peninsula and in the early 90s they had been given permission to open a small office in Murmansk. Their work had attracted international attention, along with resources to fund the decommissioning of the subs, to build storage facilities for reactor compartments, and to rehabilitate the environment.

Sergei Fillipov was a twenty-something local in a jaunty beret who had run Bellona's office since 1994. He took me to a bleak windswept hilltop overlooking Murmansk's harbour. It was still early autumn yet temperatures hovered around a bitter ten below zero. A biting wind sliced into my exposed nose and my uncovered fingers turned numb.

Kola Bay was like a gigantic scrap car yard, an apocalyptic nightmare of half-submerged rusting hulks. And this was just a fraction of the problem. Russia had the largest nuclear fleet in the world, with more than 150 nuclear powered submarines, ice-breakers and navy ships in and around Murmansk alone. Here in front of us, said Sergei, and at the nearby Northern Fleet headquarters at Severomorsk, many of the subs and ships were already in a bad way, and deteriorating rapidly.

'Their reactors are still on board, in danger of melting down and leaking. But they are still in the water and we can't get them out of the subs. Radioactive waste has been dumped into the sea near here. There is the highest concentration of nuclear reactors held in such conditions anywhere in the world and there could easily be a disaster. We even joke that if something should happen here, then it won't be our problem.' He stopped and laughed. 'We'll simply disappear, and it will be an international problem.'

Sergei took me on a 'nuclear hell' tour of his hometown, a blur of rust and ice, crumbling concrete, and more rust and ice. Churning winds whipped snow into mini-tornadoes. Murmansk was miserable enough at the best of times, without the looming threat of a Chernobyl or Mayak type disaster. As we passed the high iron gates in front of the FSB office, Sergei casually mentioned that most of Bellona's computers were still in there. They'd been confiscated back in 1996, two years after Nikitin had begun his investigations into the dumping of nuclear waste by the Northern Fleet. Sergei, along with all the other Bellona staff, had been taken in for interrogation. He glanced in his rear-vision mirror.

'They really believe that we environmentalists are using our work as a cover for espionage,' he said with a wry grin. 'They'll be keeping an eye on us now, don't worry.'

I was enjoying the rush of defying the authorities to get a story, albeit from my now relatively immune position of accredited foreign correspondent. The worst that could happen to me was that I would be deported and my tapes confiscated. But for Alexander Nikitin in St Petersburg the situation was deadly serious. Despite his research having been carried out with the knowledge of the Northern Fleet commanders, he had been arrested by the FSB regardless, and spent ten months in pre-trial detention in a maximum-security prison. And while his report merely compiled information already publicly available, the government portrayed him as a traitor to the motherland, and a seller of state secrets. Legal proceedings against him dragged on for years and only now, in October 2000, had been resolved with a full acquittal.

Sergei called Nikitin who was back at work in Bellona's St Petersburg office and he agreed to meet me. I booked a flight from Murmansk to St Petersburg and Sergei dropped me at the 'International Airport', a shabby shed way out in the tundra past a giant bronze hammer and sickle. The building was filled with chain-smoking men in bad suits and skivvies, already into the vodka and cards at 8 am. I could barely contain my joy when the flight was delayed an hour ... then another hour ... then another. Soon the haze of stale smoke was so thick I could bear it no more. I paced around outside, stamping my feet to stop them freezing, lugging my camera gear with me for safety.

We boarded at midnight, well over fourteen hours after the flight was scheduled to depart. My stomach was growling, head throbbing, feet almost frostbitten and I could think of nothing but flopping into my seat, getting some food and going to sleep. Alas, it was not to be. My seat was broken and after a precarious takeoff clutching the arm rests, I had to stand for the entire flight. Dinner was a boiled lolly. By the time I arrived at the hotel I'd booked near St Petersburg's Moscovsky Station it was 3 am and staff had given my room to someone else. I trudged around the snowy streets trying to find somewhere to stay. By 5 am I was halfway back out to the airport at the Pulkovo Hotel. For a mere USD$200 I got to spend three hours in a drab room with a broken window. It was so cold I could only huddle and shiver until the buffet opened. Never had beetroot and garlic salad for breakfast tasted so good.

I could hardly complain about a delayed flight to a man who'd spent ten months in a Russian maximum-security prison. Exhausted as I was, I was slightly awestruck to be meeting the former naval engineer with the gravelly voice and bushy moustache I'd seen so often on television news reports. Despite his recent acquittal, Nikitin felt the matter was far from over. He had few kind words for Putin and his crackdown on NGOs. After all, it had been on Putin's watch as the head of the St Petersburg FSB that Nikitin had been prosecuted.

'Of course it's uncomfortable for the authorities to have people around who understand the issues, and whose positions don't coincide with their own,' Nikitin growled. 'The government has its own interests, which usually don't coincide with the interests of NGOs. We want to ensure that before projects are approved, the effects on the health of the people and environment are properly studied. For the government, the most important thing is money. So they are trying to get rid of these activists using those methods which they tried to use to get rid of me.'

It was a David and Goliath battle in which David was locked up before he could find his slingshot. I returned to a Sydney still jubilant about the success of the Olympics, despondent about the state of the world. A few weeks later I saw an article about Muslyumovo in the *Sydney Morning Herald* written by an acquaintance in Moscow whom I'd told of my trip. I then learned that the BBC had decided not to report the story as it was deemed too dangerous to visit the region without full protective gear. The boots and jeans I'd been wearing while trudging after Gosman along the banks of the Techa were sitting in my cupboard. In a panic I dug them out and threw them away.

By December the Russian government approved the bill to import waste to Mayak. Nikitin and the Kabirovs battled on. Milya and Gosman kept in contact and my heart sank when I heard a few months later that Gosman had been diagnosed with a life-threatening blood disorder.

Back in sunny Australia for my first Sydney New Year's Eve since a trip in my teens, I found it hard to adjust to the carefree ways of my native land. I finished editing my film about Muslyumovo and immediately started plotting ways to leave again. Finally I persuaded *Dateline* to let me go to Afghanistan, where the Taliban had taken over all but the northwest corner of the war-torn country. At the same time I convinced Eric that he would love working in China as the ABC's Beijing correspondent. In March 2001, we packed up our flat and while Eric moved to China, I headed off to the last bastions of Northern Alliance-controlled Afghanistan.

Two months later, after spending my thirty-first birthday running for cover on the frontline between the Taliban and Northern Alliance troops in the Shamali Plains, I joined Eric in Beijing. We moved into one of the ABC correspondents' flats in a guarded compound reserved for foreigners just across the road from the 'Friendship Store', the Chinese version of the Soviets' 'Beriozka' shops. To the north, surrounding nearby Ritan Park, were streets lined with embassies — the Ethiopians, Poles, Americans and Bulgarians. Beyond the park, shops and markets supplied goods to Russian traders, plump Siberian women who bought up truckloads of plastic toys, fur coats, imitation designer handbags, shoes and coats to send back to Novosibirsk and Krasnoyarsk. Russian 'students' in short skirts waited outside cheap hotels and nightclubs at all hours, hoping to 'meet people to practice their English with'. Rickshaw drivers bellowed *poekhali!* (let's go!) at me in pidgin Russian.

The Soviet Union's swift descent into chaos had proved a great boon to the Chinese Communist Party (CCP). At the slightest hint of criticism of their authoritarian regime, the CCP pointed to the former superpower as an example of how democracy could ruin a perfectly good country. The English language *China Daily* was filled with a plethora of sordid tales of homelessness, unemployment, street kids, drug addiction, alcoholism and prostitution in the former USSR, all great propaganda for the CCP, who declared it was the result of weak leaders allowing the people too much freedom.

By May 2001, as far as I could tell, the only thing remotely 'communist' about the world's most populous nation was its one-party government. The once vaunted 'dictatorship of the proletariat' was now a dictatorship of old fuddy duddies with their trousers belted above their belly buttons who kept the immense People's Liberation Army (PLA) on hand to 'maintain social order'. Any Chinese citizen who thought that democracy mightn't be such a bad thing only had to remember the PLA's brutal crushing of pro-democracy student demonstrators in Tiananmen Square in June 1989 to ensure they kept their frustrations in check.

Meanwhile across the country — just as in the former USSR — enthusiastic new entrepreneurs, who not so long ago would have been publicly shamed and sentenced to decades of hard labour and thought reform, were embracing business, taking over state enterprises and amassing fortunes. Just two weeks before the International Olympic Committee (IOC) was due to announce the host country for the 2008 Olympic Games, President and leader of the CCP, Jiang Zemin, made the stunningly hypocritical announcement that capitalists could join the Communist Party.

I was in Beijing on the night of the IOC's decision to award China the Games, at a party held by the Australian Embassy on the roof of a grand hotel near Tiananmen Square. As word came that China had won its bid, the capital screamed in ecstasy. Millions of joyous citizens raced into the square, waving red flags and shouting until the wee small hours. At 5 am the police moved in and shooed away the revellers. By 6 am, teams of workers were spraying the character for 'condemned' on buildings through the city. Soon after, the cranes were at work, demolishing whole districts of ancient courtyard houses in central Beijing while residents stood angrily by, powerless to save their homes. Promised compensation disappeared into the pockets of corrupt officials and the newly homeless couldn't even complain. They had no choice but to sacrifice their family homes for the national image, just as the Meshary of Muslyumovo had no choice but to sacrifice their health and future for their nation's security.

Had anything changed since the feudal empires of China's and Russia's pasts? Marxist and Maoist communist revolutions had overthrown one set of all-powerful rulers only to replace them with another. The Marxist and Maoist rhetoric of equality had proved to be just that: rhetoric. Were these imperial attitudes impossible to eradicate? Was genuine democracy and respect for human rights anathema to Chinese and Russian culture?

* * *

In China I was *persona non grata*. The Chinese Ministry of Foreign Affairs didn't recognise de facto relationships so I couldn't get an official visa to accompany Eric. My only option was to get a one-month tourist visa and leave the country every four weeks to get a new one. The Chinese government was notoriously controlling of foreign media and the ABC was afraid that I might compromise Eric's position by potentially reporting on sensitive issues for *Dateline* from China. I had no choice but to commute elsewhere to work. Even so, Foreign Affairs ministry officials quizzed Eric about the 'SBS correspondent in Beijing' just to remind him that they knew exactly who I was.

Just after the Olympic announcement, my visa expired. Eric was already miserable in his new posting. I'd persuaded him that living in Beijing would be fun — but try as I might to be positive, I had to concede that our new life under constant surveillance was not quite as I'd anticipated. And if I was irritated at having to self-censor emails and phone calls, it was even more frustrating for foreign correspondents trying to cover China. Big Brother watched closely, meticulously monitoring everything they did and said with a forest of spying antennae. I left Eric trying to locate his Chinese producer, who'd disappeared under mysterious circumstances after meeting with a dissident, and flew back to Moscow.

And so began a routine of spending short enough periods in Beijing to convince the Chinese that I wasn't living there, and a heck of a lot of time flying back and forth over Siberia on eight-hour Aeroflot flights full of Chinese businessmen with phlegm issues.

It was a dream come true.

27

Russian Roulette

More people are drowned in a glass than in the ocean.
Russian proverb

June 2001

The Chinese Communist Party was right about one thing — post-Soviet Russia was a hotbed of social decay. Its people weren't an endangered species just yet, but since the collapse of the USSR, the mortality rate had shot past the birth rate, average lifespans had plummeted and the population had already fallen by over five million. Demographic experts were predicting the decline to continue by a further one million a year.

The statistics should have been sobering, but sobriety was not the Russian way. Dismal health care, depression- and poverty-induced suicides, epidemics of HIV and STDs, homicides and car crashes had a lot to do with it, but the prime cause of premature death in Russia was alcohol. According to official statistics, three million of Russia's 145 million citizens were alcoholics. But with an estimated adult per capita consumption of between 14 and 18 litres of pure alcohol annually, experts believed the real figure was closer to ten times that — a whopping thirty million whose lives were ruled by the bottle. Alcohol-related deaths were estimated to be somewhere between 500,000 and 750,000 annually, 40,000 of those from alcohol poisoning. The country was literally drinking itself to death.

Consumption of alcohol has been a Russian national pastime for centuries. The supreme social lubricant, vodka toasts cement friendships, business deals and marriages. Toasts signify hospitality, mark births and deaths, successes and failures ... they praise the beauty of nature, a woman, the wisdom of a leader. If you didn't drink to it, it probably didn't happen. Russia without vodka was as inconceivable as China without chopsticks. Legend has it that Grand Prince Vladimir of Kievan Rus (the predecessor to the Russian state) chose Christianity as the official state religion back in 988, because it allowed believers to drink every day, not just on holidays.

I arrived back in Moscow from Beijing in time for the summer solstice on 23 June. Traditionally, the shortest, lightest night of the year was celebrated with an ancient pagan harvest festival called Ivan Kupala, involving music, dancing and most importantly, the communal consumption of moonshine spirit called *samogon,* literally 'self-brew'. I met up with some arty friends at an Ivan Kupala party in a large yard behind a Bohemian club/weird modern art gallery called Dom, off Pyatnitskaya Street. This district — just south of Red Square — was favoured by students and alternative types, but I hadn't expected to find party-goers leaping through a huge bonfire after sculling home-brewed spirits from a bucket. I couldn't help gasping as half-pickled revellers narrowly avoided tripping head first into the blaze. There wasn't an Armani suit to be seen. It was just like the old days, only much, much wilder.

A film-maker friend of a friend, Andrei Silvestrov, had invited me to join in the fun. He introduced himself as a 'part-time philosopher', and with his thick beard and twinkling eyes looked every bit the part. Ivan Kupala, Andrei explained, was a pre-Christian festival, a time for fertile women to attract mates and get themselves up the duff. 'So it's absolutely natural that everyone gets warmed up with some *samogon,'* he declared, taking a large swig from the metal pail being passed around the eager crowd.

'In the West,' he shouted over the roar of the fire, 'people are preoccupied with sex. In Russia, we are preoccupied with alcohol. They're basically the same thing. The sex begins when the alcohol ends. Anything that's the other way around is a Western perversion. There is an opinion, which many of my friends support, that sex is not "manly". In fact, it's a rather silly thing to do. Of course you have to, what can you do? But fancy wasting your life on that stuff! There are far more masculine activities, like drinking vodka with your friends!'

Some young guys began to play drums. Girls made garlands of flowers and put them in each other's hair. They danced, swinging each other around by the arms, whooping loudly. It could have been a scene from a nineteenth century painting ... except for the onlookers sending texts from their mobile phones. Andrei watched the girls and turned to me with a mischievous look.

'The women are trying so hard to make themselves beautiful ... all to attract the men. But the men are preoccupied with more important matters. That's why the women look after their figures, spend all their money on clothes and make-up, because otherwise they have no chance.'

I considered Andrei's theory. Did Russian men really, genuinely see women as frivolous, twitty things, only to be dealt with as a matter of necessity once the serious business of drinking was done? As I wondered whether there might not be a grain of truth in his commentary, a large wooden coffin was lowered onto the bonfire.

'Ivan Kupala signifies the victory of life over death,' Andrei continued. 'Only drinkers can possibly understand the meaning of life. To quote Descartes, "I think therefore I am." So death is the moment when you cease to think and to exist. And the frequent consumption of alcohol leading to loss of consciousness is the natural attempt of a human being to experience victory over death.'

As the night wore on, the imbibers of the wicked home brew began to drop like flies. I could only hope they were experiencing victory over death, although many were doing fine impressions of the real thing. Ever since my own victory-over-death vodka binge with Tatiana (which had ended with me falling off the train) I'd been wary of the 'little water'. And my memory of the skull-splitting morning-after agony was so awful that I had little trouble in stopping after just one sip of the paint-stripping *samogon*. But being an almost non-drinker in

Russia was even less comprehensible than vegetarianism. While worrying about animals was ever so slightly understandable, there was no earthly reason why I should not drink. In fact, my wowserliness marked me out as being a slightly suspect human being.

Andrei, his friend Pasha and I wandered off to a crowded nearby *pelmennaya*, a Soviet-style shot bar/ravioli café with no chairs. The small, round laminate tables were at chest height — little more than a platform from which to shovel in a few steaming *pelmeni* and slam down your empty glass. It was all very utilitarian: eat, drink and run. 'It's a kind of social paradise,' enthused Andrei, still remarkably articulate and coherent after already downing what must have been nearly half a litre of almost 50 per cent proof plonk. 'Everyone comes here — businessmen with their Mercedes 600s, artists, even homeless people.'

Pasha clapped Andrei on the back and grinned. 'Drinking with someone is the highest possible expression of your trust. It can't get any higher. A toast to our friendship!' They clinked shot glasses, tapped my glass of water and gulped down another 100 grams each. I smiled dopily and took a sip of H_2O, in a feeble attempt at solidarity.

The flipside was that not drinking with someone was tantamount to saying you didn't trust them. My refusal to slurp myself blotto was regularly interpreted as such, often correctly. So to avoid letting the person I didn't trust get offended by thinking that I didn't trust them, I'd developed a complicated and well-rehearsed medical explanation as to why this pathetic Australian couldn't sink shots with the best of them. Luckily Andrei didn't take it personally when I politely declined to sup myself into a coma. After all, I was only a woman, and a foreigner at that. Obviously I had inferior alcohol-intolerant genes.

Ivan Kupala might have been a fun night out, but there was a sinister, and tragic, side to Russia's drinking fetish. For far too many Russians, the line between a bonding toast and a destructive dependency had blurred away. In the eleven years since I'd been coming here, the average life span of a Russian male had dropped nine years, from sixty-four to fifty-five. It was a shocking statistic, primarily attributed to the country's love of the bottle.

Alcoholism in Russia was hardly a new phenomenon. In Soviet days it was blamed for high rates of divorce, suicide, accidents and worker absenteeism. But according to Dr Oleg Zuikov, a Moscow-based narcologist studying chemical dependency in Russian society, it was tolerated by the totalitarian authorities for a very good reason: a permanently inebriated workforce was much easier to control.

In May 1985, two months after taking office, Mikhail Gorbachev began an anti-alcohol campaign, in a vain attempt to wean his countrymen off their addiction to the bottle. Alcohol prices were raised, sales restricted, distilleries and wineries closed down. Drinking in public and on long-distance trains was banned and those who were caught were prosecuted. But Gorby's 'dry law' was a dismal failure. While there was some improvement in public health, the campaign was political suicide for Gorby.

'Vodka was a way to manipulate people,' Dr Zuikov explained. 'It was a political instrument. To deny the citizens of a totalitarian state their vodka was to destroy the totalitarian state. People had to get drunk, otherwise it was impossible to have power over them. How could you take away the vodka? There was nothing left. No moral values. To take away their treasured vodka and not give anything in return, naturally Gorbachev provoked the destructive process. People began to think about something other than vodka. At this point even the ordinary people realised the absurdity of the state system.'

Gorbachev soon became known by the derogatory moniker *Mineralny Sekretar* (Mineral-water-drinking Secretary), instead of the *Generalny Sekretar* (General Secretary). More seriously, the state lost billions of roubles in revenue. Black market producers leapt in to fill the void, often manufacturing bootleg booze in unsanitary conditions from dangerous substances. Poisonings increased as hard drinkers turned to whatever they could get their hands on. Vodka even became a currency in its own right, used in the barter of goods and services: one hour of plumbing equalled two bottles of vodka. In 1987, the dry law was abandoned. By the end of 1991, the USSR, and Gorbachev, were no more.

Soon after, the new government lifted its monopoly on alcohol production. Hundreds of new producers got to work. Some were legitimate, most weren't. Criminal networks set up bodgy bootleg operations in basements and garages, brewing up often lethal concoctions from industrial chemicals, anti-freeze and window cleaning fluids. Shops and streetside kiosks across the country soon overflowed with cheap fake plonk, convincingly packaged with carefully forged labels. The temptation offered by cut-price grog was more than *Russky* livers could bear.

On my first trip in 1990, public drunkenness was rare. Alcohol was available, but drinkers had to queue so long they'd be sober by the time they got their next fix. But now, in 2001, beer was cheaper and easier to find than a bottle of water. Vodka and other spirits were available anywhere, anytime, for a sum even a beggar could afford. Sometimes the whole country appeared to be plastered. On a summer evening stroll through the capital I watched youths congregating in squares and pedestrian underpasses listening to rocking buskers and sinking beers. The middle-aged drank vodka in parks and grounds around their buildings. Bulbous-red-nosed *biznesmeny* and politicians toasted themselves in airport cafés and fancy bars, while twenty-something young 'professionals' had a 'few for the road' at street kiosks all over the city. I even saw primary school aged kids obviously inebriated and proud of themselves.

To me, the omnipresence of swaggering drunks seemed a depressing waste of human potential. Yet to most locals, it was background noise: something to ignore, tolerate or laugh at. Most worryingly, to many it was a matter of national pride that Russians could drink everyone else under the table.

Not even the police seemed to take the problem seriously. I talked my way into a patrol wagon at the Taganskaya police station in the southeast of Moscow's centre, and was rewarded with a wild night cruising the boozing hotspots, sirens blaring, watching the cops move the drinkers on and collect the worst cases in the back of their paddy wagon. But while they carried out the motions, the police had plenty of sympathy for the intoxicated.

'It's the Russian soul,' one told me, jumping back into the wagon after scraping a comatose couple off the grass. 'It's that simple. In

World War II you got 100 grams before an attack. That's how we won the war. Thanks to spirits. The whole Army was drinking. It's just a fact of life.'

The most conspicuous lost causes were the homeless, the *bomzhi,* flopped in metro tunnels, dingy doorways and across park benches. As a rule, the sober and sheltered snubbed the *bomzhi,* averting their gazes as they passed. Most considered Russia's estimated four million *bomzhi* to be little more than animals, wretched creatures who had lost all self-respect and dignity. Apart from the old woman who'd fallen down the stairs outside the Leningradsky Station underpass that I'd tried to help with Kumi, I was as guilty as the rest in ignoring the blundering and wasted who inhabited the dark corners of the capital. But now I wanted to find out how they had sunk so low. So on a cool June midnight I ventured out with a Belarussian friend, another Pasha.

Moscow at night didn't feel safe any more. Eric and I had come out of a restaurant in central Moscow with friends one night a year earlier to find a freshly stabbed, squirming body in a bloody puddle on the footpath. Brave as I thought I was, pulling out an expensive camera in a dim back alley was asking for trouble. Pasha and I flagged down a car and headed for Kursky Station, just east of the city centre. The major train hubs were favoured stomping grounds for the dispossessed. With trains arriving and departing throughout the night there was a constant stream of people, 24-hour kiosks, large waiting halls for transit passengers and lots of nooks and crannies to sleep in.

We wandered around the skips and rubbish dumps at the back of the once pleasant park adjoining the main station building. A gang of kids who couldn't have been more than about seven years old slunk in the shadows, watching us warily, sucking at plastic bags with globs of yellow glue in the bottom. A pair of cops strode by and shouted at them. 'Get out of here you snotty stinkers!' They scattered, melting into the darkness.

Four *bomzhi,* three men and a woman, were dragging sheets of cardboard into an alcove by a door. Pasha approached and asked one of the men if they would talk to us. His face was swollen and bruised. The others looked little better. He told Pasha they hadn't had a drink that night, and if we could get them something, then yes, they'd talk to us. We left them arranging their makeshift beds and ducked into the station for some vodka and food. It felt wrong to be buying alcohol for alcoholics for the sake of an interview, and I wrestled with my conscience as we tried to select a non-bootleg brand that at least wouldn't kill them.

Sasha, Sergei, Galya and Volodya's battered faces lit up appreciatively when we returned, and Sergei noted that we'd got decent vodka. Normally, he said, they couldn't care less whether it was potentially lethal cleaning spirits, as long as it numbed the brain. They eagerly cracked open the bottle and wolfed into the bread, cheese and sausage, oblivious to my filming. It was heartbreaking to see human beings reduced to such a state.

'The young kids beat us up,' said Volodya, pointing to his smashed face. 'There were seven of them. They were stoned, out of it on that stuff that they sniff. We four were sleeping at night and they attacked us with sticks. They just do it for fun, like entertainment. It's terrifying. They are everywhere and we have nowhere to hide from them. And there's nowhere to go to get fixed up.'

He rolled up a putrid and torn trouser leg to reveal a thigh-length bruise from a kick so hard it had split open the skin. The wound was festering and he dripped a few drops of our vodka onto it, wincing in agony. My conscience improved marginally as I convinced myself that Pasha and I were providing necessary pain relief.

Volodya had been living on the streets for three years already, after 'losing' his flat to conmen. He'd survived three winters but doubted he'd make a fourth. 'Summer is okay, but in winter you may as well put up a cross for us. Hopefully we'll just die over there by the fence and to hell with it all.'

Alcohol had taken on a new significance for Volodya since the collapse of the USSR. 'Before, two comrades would meet and chat, for pleasure. They would share a toast, drink to something, for a beautiful girl, for nature. Then they would get up and go to work, and so there'd be no smell they would clean their teeth. They felt a sense of responsibility. But now, who are we working for? For Putin? For Yeltsin? A man doesn't want to work. His life has become pointless. Now people drink without joy. Just so your thoughts don't work. Everything is expensive: bread is expensive, meat is expensive. You don't know whether to buy bread, meat or have a 100 gram shot. So you have 100 grams and at least your head is clear.'

Fifty-year-old Sasha had been released after twenty-six years in prison for 'robbing from the state' to find his mother had passed away two days earlier and her flat was now occupied by thugs. Devastated and with nowhere to live, he'd hit the bottle, hard. That was around six months ago, he thought ... or was it two? After a couple of shots his face relaxed.

'Vodka is the only thing that calms my soul. I was given my freedom, then they took away my flat. Where should I go for help? To the President? Ha! Why is this happening? No one will give us a job. We can't ride in transport because we stink. The police beat us, the kids attack us, people kick us out from everywhere. They don't even consider us as humans.'

He took another swig.

'My soul is burning. I can't bear it. Everything is disgusting. This life forces us to drink. When you drink it extinguishes the pain ... the pain ... it numbs the pain. You feel good. Then again you need to drink and you have to search for it. You have to beg someone to pour you some. Sometimes they punch you in the face, sometimes they pour you some. This is how we live.'

He lay down on his cardboard and sighed loudly. I wanted to understand, I wanted to help, but realistically there was nothing I could do for any of them — nothing more than record this miserable moment of their abject existence. And was there any point in that?

Forty-year-old Sergei was an ex-builder, who'd also been tricked into signing away his flat to *biznesmeny*. They'd come to his door, got him drunk and asked him to sign ownership documents. When he sobered up and realised what he'd done it was too late. The new owners of his flat pushed him out at gun point and he'd been on the street ever since, drowning his sorrows with Volodya and Sasha. He pulled a notebook out of his pocket and announced he would like to read us a poem. Clearing his throat he began:

'Why mama did you give birth to such a terrible son?
I've upset everyone, my mother and sister.
Now I sit and remember how much trouble it was to bring up such a terrible son.
You gave to us all your life.
You brought us up without a father, willingly giving us your love and beauty.
Now I have lived to my grey years and I can't forgive myself.
I hate myself.'

Sergei closed the notebook and fumbled with a cigarette lighter. I couldn't think of a thing to say. The woman, Galya, reached over and laid a scabby hand on his shoulder. 'We won't let you down, I promise,' she whispered hoarsely.

At forty-nine, Galya was a physical wreck with legs and feet so swollen she couldn't fit shoes onto them. Her bare feet were cracked and filthy, soles split, face puffy and bloated. She'd sold her flat to pay debts. The proceeds long drunk, Galya had been homeless for months. Her grown-up children had no idea where she was, and she didn't think they'd even care. She prepared a cigarette, carefully prising unburnt leaves from a collection of butts into a small square of newspaper, which she rolled and lit.

'Maybe I brought them up not to care about me,' she mused after a long drag. 'Or maybe life has just become like this. Everyone lives for themselves.'

She paused. 'If only we had a flat. But they took it away.'

'You'll get your flat at the cemetery,' Volodya chimed in.

'What cemetery?' scoffed Galya. 'They'll just burn us somewhere.'

'Who's going to waste a fire?' Volodya said bitterly. 'In Mitishek cemetery there's a brother's grave for us *bomzhi*. They just tip the bodies in on top of each other.'

There was silence. Sasha held the bottle up to the distant streetlight and shook it. There was just enough for one last round.

'Thank you,' he said solemnly to Pasha and me as we readied to leave. 'Now our souls are calm and we can lie down. If the kids don't come and beat us tonight, then we will sleep like angels.'

It was the most hellish and precarious of existences. Their only aid came from the Salvation Army, who dished up bowls of soup from the back of a van in front of the train station. Sometimes other church groups handed out old clothes. Another charity ran a bus service to take bodies out to Mitishek cemetery for burial.

Equally disturbing was the number of youths with drinking problems. Some were homeless, some were children of alcoholics, but many were from stable middle-class backgrounds, openly encouraged to drink by advertisements blatantly glamorising beer in particular as a vital part of social interaction. Dr Zuikov, the narcologist, blamed this for a frightening increase in teenage alcoholism.

'It's horrifying. Beer is depicted as something trendy, even as "good for you"! A significant percentage of our young people don't consider beer to be alcohol. They even think it is part of a healthy way of life! This is a paradox. Beer is the gateway to alcoholism. It shouldn't be part of youth culture, but it's happening. Teenagers and even children are becoming alcoholics.'

I didn't have to look far to find underage drinkers. Teens and tweens with bottles were everywhere: frolicking in the fountains near the Manezh underground shopping complex next to the Kremlin, loitering in parks, courtyards and subterranean pedestrian crossings. On a sweltering summer afternoon I strolled through Victory Park, just north of Moscow's centre. A group of kids splashed in a pond beneath the soaring column commemorating Russia's World War II heroes, soaking themselves and each other to the skin. Most were holding bottles of beer, gulping it down like water. A couple of babushki loitered nearby, waiting to pounce on the discarded bottles, worth a few kopecks from recyclers.

I introduced myself to some of the kids: Maksim, a well-dressed and handsome fifteen-year-old boy, and two younger girls, Yulia and

Ksenya, both wet through and giggling hysterically. All three were very merry and clutched bottles of Doctor Diesel beer. Maksim waggled his bottle and made a disapproving face. 'It's not my favourite brand. The best are Klinskoye and Old Miller, but they don't have any at the kiosk. Still, it's drinkable and I wanted a drink.'

Russian law prohibits under-eighteens from purchasing and consuming alcohol, but to Maksim it was a joke. He handed his now empty bottle to a grateful babushka, gestured for me to follow him to one of the kiosks in front of the park's war museum and calmly bought three bottles of Lowenbrau.

'See, it's that easy,' he said as we walked away. 'Even eight-year-olds can buy beer. No one asks anything, and if they do, you just say it's for your dad.'

I returned to the kiosk and asked the woman if she knew she'd just broken the law. She slammed the window in my face. I told Dr Zuikov about my experience.

'Of course she sold it to him,' he said. 'If we had a law-abiding state, then she would obey the law. It's not a question of her being afraid of punishment, it is a question of her moral attitude to the situation. But now when everyone is doing it, she is simply following the normal standard of morality, and this is the level of morality of our state.'

This lack of morality, according to Dr Zuikov, was at the root of contemporary Russia's ills.

'In our totalitarian state we were told we were living not for ourselves, but for the sake of society ... whatever that was. Something abstract, the Politburo ... some sort of silliness. But then they said, "No, that was all wrong and now you need to live only for yourselves, to earn money." So men became like wolves and for the last decade we have been living like this. This is why people will sell alcohol to children, and why the government allows advertising of alcohol everywhere. People care more about making money than they do about the nation's health.'

And, Dr Zuikov believed, it was the legacy of three-quarters of a century of totalitarianism that had crippled the population's ability to resolve its problems.

'When people grow up in a paternalistic state, they become very passive. So until recently there was a general attitude that the state should solve our problems. But what is that state? Is it Putin? There are 145 million of us. Can he solve all our problems? The government officials say yes, we can solve your problems, just give us money. So the bureaucracy grows and the problems remain.'

Money certainly wasn't going to Russia's public health system. High-end private clinics with the latest gadgets and medicines charged huge sums to treat the wealthy, but ordinary citizens couldn't afford thousands of US dollars for medical attention. Rundown hospitals were ill-equipped to deal with the epidemic of alcoholics, and if my Kazan experience was anything to go by, they even seemed to be staffed by them. Only a handful of state-run narcological hospitals offered detox and rehabilitation programs. After much pleading I was given permission to visit one on the outskirts of Moscow, on the condition that I would not film the patients or the wards.

It was a typical Soviet-era institution, gloomy and neglected, with flaking green walls and corroded downpipes — just the kind of place that would drive one to drink. A bad-tempered babushka in a tattered white coat led me to a flight of worn stone stairs and puffed loudly as she hauled her mass upwards. I sneaked a glimpse into some of the wards as I followed her down a dim corridor. Sets of dull eyes stared blankly out at me from sunken beds. Some patients were hooked up to intravenous drips. At the end of the corridor, the babushka ushered me into a room. 'Dr Vladimir Batishev, Psychiatrist', read the plaque on the door.

Dr Batishev stood up wearily from his desk. 'Ah yes, welcome to the nuthouse,' he said with a dry smile, wiping his hand across his forehead. 'Not just this place,' he added, nodding to indicate the building around us. 'I mean Russia.' He waved me to a chair and I set up my camera. Dr Batishev and his office was all I had been given permission to film.

'I have no idea why they won't let you film here, apart from the fact that there's nothing to show,' he said apologetically. 'I can't understand why this subject should be so secretive. It's the KGB, the FSB, up there, playing games, saying everything needs to be closed. "Don't show anything to anyone," they tell me. But why, I don't understand. You only have to look on the internet to find out anything, but here it's all forbidden. I have no rational explanation for this. For an ordinary, healthy psychologist it's completely illogical.'

Dr Batishev made no secret of his concern for his country's future. The official government figure, he said, of three million alcoholics only counted those who sought treatment at the state's narcological centres. By his reckoning, only one in ten either acknowledged their problems or got treatment specifically for their alcoholism. Often alcoholics would seek treatment for alcohol-related illnesses — mainly neurological diseases or problems with the liver, kidney and heart — yet doctors were unable to give a diagnosis of alcoholism, in case the patient complained. The actual number of drinkers with a problem, estimated Dr Batishev, was more like thirty million.

'The outlook is very bleak. Basically two generations — those born in the 70s and 80s — we could say that they are dying out. Mostly it's the men, because not all women drink, but because of these social circumstances which encourage drinking to excess, we could say that we have lost them. It's our second national disaster. The first was World War II, where every family suffered. Now it is alcoholism and narcotics, from which practically every family is suffering. There is evidence. There are statistics from the ambulance service, which is constantly dealing with junkies and alcoholics. There are even thirty cases reported each year of children under seven who are dependent on alcohol. But no one acknowledges the problem. These narcological centres are a shambles. The officials don't know what to do, and they squash the people who do, like this.'

He ground his thumb into the desk and twisted it.

'The country is indifferent to what's going to happen. No one cares. To resolve the problem you have to use your head ... and people aren't accustomed to using their heads in Russia.'

It was time for Dr Batishev to have a session with one of his patients, here in his office. He left and returned a few minutes later with a solidly built, unshaven man with a pasty, fleshy face. 'This is Dimitry. You can ask if he minds if you film,' he said.

Dimitry had no objections. He was thirty-two and had worked in construction, on many of the skyscraping residential towers going up in Moscow's suburbs. His had been a two-bottle-a-day habit, two 750 millilitre bottles of vodka that is, while operating a crane to lift steel beams into place twenty floors up. All his drinking partners were already dead, and Dimitry's liver was shot. But the drinking wasn't his fault.

'I have always been for sobriety,' he told Dr Batishev. 'But you know, it's like some kind of black force. Some sort of demons jumped on me.'

'And they grabbed you by the hand and led you to the bottle, eh? What a nightmare!' said Dr Batishev, nodding. 'And what awful things did they do?'

'That's always what happens. In my time of weakness they come and jump on me and pour vodka down my throat. And then they leave and I am alone,' said Dimitry dully.

'With vodka?' Batishev asked. 'So basically you are pro-sobriety, and if there were no demons, then everything would be all right?'

The discussion continued in this vein. Dr Batishev listened patiently, trying to lead Dimitry towards the idea that he would have to take some personal responsibility for ridding himself of the demons. Little seemed to sink in and eventually Dr Batishev took Dimitry back to his room.

'In alcoholism, everyone is guilty but the person himself,' he said when he returned. 'It's either demons or supernatural forces. But you can see the person does not take any responsibility for his own actions. In our political system it's the same thing. No one wants to take responsibility for anything. The whole country is like this.'

The next patient, Mitya, was a 25-year-old with broken teeth and a thick scar across one cheek. He told Dr Batishev he had just spent a month living in the forest near his family's dacha after they kicked him out because of his drinking. While in the forest, he and a companion had drunk more than two litres of vodka a day, each, on an empty stomach.

'Vodka is high in calories, so I told myself it was enough to stay alive,' he told Dr Batishev. The good doctor was unfazed, and yet again it seemed as though he was talking to a wall.

'These mental disturbances are one of the worst things that comes with alcoholism,' he told me after Mitya's session. 'The main aim of these people is to make things worse for themselves. According to our studies, one alcoholic drags down two relatives, who also end up with the same mental disturbances. So ninety million people are set on making things worse for themselves. Right now in our country, we don't need an FSB guy in charge, we need a good shrink, preferably with experience in chemical dependency, to bring this nuthouse back to normal!'

The plane back to Beijing was jam-packed with a Russian football team and their offsiders. Each and every one had picked up a litre of duty free spirits, and the toasting began even before we left the ground. I was wedged between a couple of nearly seven foot players, clacking their plastic cups right over me. I shrank into my seat, wishing I could share my recent experiences with these cheerful young lads. But I knew it wouldn't make one jot of difference. By somewhere halfway across Siberia, the bottles were empty and the snoring began. All around me, livers were being pickled and psychoses were developing.

It was the 'Russian soul'.

28

Shooting Up … The New Russian Roulette

'A single death is a tragedy. A million deaths is a statistic.'
Joseph Stalin

'You fell in love with a country that no longer exists, at a time a new one was being born,' Zulfia philosophised. 'And like a mother, you never stop loving your child. You might get furious with it, it might drive you crazy, but you forgive it and keep loving it.'

I considered her opinion over a cup of tea. Zulfia was usually right. She was one of those 'born wise' types, who dealt with tragedy, injustice and chaos in a rational, matter-of-fact kind of way. I would get bogged down in sorrow, sympathy, and frustration, but she knew exactly what was within her power to change. Maybe that was what kept her happy, while I would snap with irritation at the idiocy around me. 'It's no wonder your country is such a bloody disaster,' I muttered to saleswomen who ignored my attempts to buy something. Then there were the OVIR clerks who made people queue three hours and come back three times to register a visa, bank tellers who wouldn't give me money and con-artist black marketeers who wouldn't accept less than ten times what an item was worth. Once, fuming after spending five hours trying to pay my journalist friend Julie's phone bill, I walked home screaming, 'Fxxx you all and your stupid country!' — in English, just in case. But Zulfia was right. The place drove me insane, yet I didn't stop loving it — which, I suppose, says something about me.

There were so many far more pleasant places to be, with decent weather, appetising food, polite people, clean air, spectacular nature and fascinating histories. But then I'd listen to some Rachmaninov or Shostakovich and remember why I'd come here in the first place. It was the Russian soul, that soul which thrived on excess — an excess of talent, of melodrama, of revolutionary fervour, of blind patriotism ... of alcohol. Nothing about the country or its history was mediocre or ordinary. It was dramatic, violent, a place of awful ugliness and divine beauty, of extraordinary genius and blockhead stupidity. It was a place you felt alive, even if under constant emotional assault. While other places were 'nice', Russia was extreme — and schizophrenic.

For many of my friends, the parting of the Iron Curtain had brought opportunities to earn good money with Western companies, drive imported cars, travel freely, read previously banned literature, and buy pineapples at their local supermarket — not unlike what my life could have been, had I chosen to stay home. But I hadn't, and was finding it fascinatingly confronting to delve into the darker side of Russia's past and present. So while Olga and Misha went on holidays to Turkey and France, I headed for the Caucasus and Minsk. And while they enjoyed nights out at an exorbitantly expensive Ukrainian restaurant with a courtyard full of live farmyard animals — chickens, sheep, rabbits, a cow and even a babushka in national dress — I sought out drunkards, street kids, persecuted Chechens.

It was Nadia who had planted the seed for my next story. 'You should do something about drug addicts,' she'd suggested when I'd dropped in to see her on my last trip. A pensioner friend's son was a junkie. He'd stolen everything she had, given up his studies, couldn't hold down a job and couldn't be left alone. Nadia's friend had spent a fortune on treatment programs but nothing had worked. It sounded just like addiction anywhere — except that being Russia, everything about the problem was so much more intense.

I talked to Pasha, the Belarussian friend who had helped with my alcoholism film. In the 80s he'd picked poppies from the fields near his village in Belarus, and together with friends had prepared *chernuskha*, 'black opium', which they'd injected using old syringes. Nearly all of those friends were now dead or in prison. Pasha had moved on but had been left a life-long reminder of his youthful folly — hepatitis C. By 2001, hepatitis was as common as a cold to intravenous drug users, a trivial inconvenience they were all infected with. The real concern was HIV/AIDS, which was spreading faster in the former Soviet Union than anywhere else in the world. Most of its victims were young intravenous drug users, but instead of trying to help them, the authorities were locking them up.

Pasha agreed to find some users who would consent to be filmed and in July 2001 I returned to Moscow, again from Beijing, to make my next disheartening foray into Russia's seedy underbelly.

Slava was an ex-junkie who after years on heroin, and several in prison, was now working with a Dutch-funded NGO called Harm Reduction. A fidgety fellow with intense eyes and close-cropped hair, he and other ex-users patrolled the subterranean passages in Moscow's centre where junkies went to score, handing out condoms and pamphlets about HIV, STDs and hepatitis. One of the hottest patches to pick up a range of illicit substances was the square of tunnels linking the corners of Lubyanka Square, right in front of the FSB headquarters.

Pasha and I fitted Slava with a radio microphone and trailed behind him with my mini-camera wrapped in a coat. There were cops everywhere. Moscow's tunnels had always been considered strategic 'objects', and therefore illegal to film or photograph. But, Slava warned, the city's *militsiya* would be pussycats compared to the drug mafiosi. Under no circumstances should we get caught filming them. We paced around, following Slava and his colleagues, Yulia and Vlad, while feigning interest in the wares of the various stalls in the tunnel: religious icons, woman's lingerie, pirate videos of Hollywood action flicks.

We soon identified a dealer lurking in a dark nook near a stairway. Transactions were brief, a furtive exchange of roubles for small packages, mostly obscured by a leather jacket and crowds of pedestrians passing between us and him. We edged closer and I pretended to inspect a triple E cup lacy red bra, while peering into the camera's fold-out screen to check I had him in frame. I glanced up and he caught my eye. He stared hard, then looked down at my coat. If one was hunting for something suspicious, a small lens might have been visible. His eyes narrowed and I saw him puff up like an angry cat. My heart began to pound and Pasha grabbed my arm. 'Move, fast, NOW!' he hissed. We did, and were quickly swallowed by the crowd.

Above ground we found Slava, Yulia and Vlad earbashing some teens. The young trio was flying high and their attention wandered as Slava tried to enlighten them about Russia's harsh drug laws and their potential punishment. The laws were draconian indeed: mere possession of a poorly washed spoon or cap where heroin was prepared could put you in prison. And sharing a hit, or even a joint, was 'dealing', with a sentence of seven to fifteen years, plus confiscation of all one's possessions.

Across the road loomed the nerve centre of the secret police. The kids nodded sombrely, took a handful of condoms and swaggered off. Slava, Yulia and Vlad were done and ready to leave. Yulia and Vlad disappeared into a tunnel leading to Detski Mir, the huge children's toy emporium, which fronted the northwest of Lubyanka Square. Slava, Pasha and I went the opposite direction, surfacing in a small leafy park. Slava strode briskly, nodding greetings to an assortment of dodgy types seated on benches throughout the park. 'Dealers,' he muttered through clenched teeth. 'You can get anything you want here.'

If Russia's traditional poison was alcohol, post-Soviet freedom brought a whole new range of toxins. Bubble gum, yoghurt and Pepsi quickly lost their thrill factor and the young flocked to try anything and everything new. Getting high, or attaining *kaif* — a state of sensory nirvana and blissful oblivion — took on a whole new meaning. Mafia groups set up a lively trade in drugs: from marijuana and LSD, to heroin and cocaine. Narcotics became all the rage: from Russia's glam new nightclubs to seedy back alley and kitchen table shoot-ups. And it wasn't just bootleg alcohol that was potentially lethal. The white powder proffered by dealers was often mixed with chalk, sugar and sometimes more dangerous substances. Inexperienced users had no idea of dosages. In 2001 alone, 104,810 Russians died from drug overdoses and related problems.

'There never used to be heroin in Soviet days,' said Slava as we walked. 'People made *chernushka* from poppies, but that was all. When perestroika and democracy came, drugs like cocaine, heroin and ecstasy appeared. And recently people started using ephedrine to prepare methamphetamine, *vint* [Russian for 'screw', as in the kind used by carpenters; in Australia we call it 'ice']. It's everywhere. But the authorities don't even admit there's a problem. Instead of doing something useful, like allowing us to set up a needle exchange, they arrest the users. Because of this, many diseases are spreading.'

Slava flagged down a car and took us to visit a friend, Roman, who lived just off the ring road in Moscow's inner east. He came down to let us in, glanced around nervously and hurried us into the foyer, which stank of stale urine, and into the lift, which reeked of vomit. Roman lived with his mother, but assured Slava she was out of town. Even so, he twitched at every noise and spun his head to the door. Their poky two-room flat overlooked the railway line, a modest abode with floral wallpaper in muted pinks, tacky crystal ornaments and the usual fold-out couch/bed. A bunch of dusty cloth flowers stood in a vase on the kitchen table, where Roman was in the middle of something resembling a chemistry experiment. Several small bottles and dishes were open and an acrid smell filled the room.

'Listen, Slav,' Roman said anxiously. 'Come here and smell this.'

They leaned over a small aluminium saucepan on the stovetop and sniffed.

'It's supposed to be Soutan, but I don't think it is,' muttered Roman, referring to a cold and flu medicine containing ephedrine.

'You're right. It's not. It's calendula. My mother uses it.'

'Shit!' said Roman. He checked his watch. 'Okay, it's only half past nine. We can go to Pharmacy Number One and get some from the guards. They sell the right stuff. They wouldn't dare lie or they'd get sacked.'

Roman's desperation was palpable. He called a friend with a car. We all piled in and drove back to Lubyanka. Pharmacy Number One, once

Moscow's main apothecary, was on a pretty side street with cobblestones and wrought-iron lamps, leading to Red Square. Sure enough, the security guards were carrying out a vigorous trade in pills and potions. Just down the road, Slava pointed out a babushka in an overcoat, another reliable source of Soutan. Roman's eyes lit up. A few minutes later, with two bottles of Soutan — one from the guards, one from the granny — we were on our way.

Roman was a good-looking guy in his early twenties who had once trained as a dancer and choreographer. Now he had two prison terms to his record and no job, well, not really. He directed the driver around some winding back streets and ordered him to stop in front of an entrance to a low-rise brick building. We sat in the dark and waited ... and waited. Eventually Roman returned, jubilant, jumped into the car and made a quick phone call.

'To Proletarskaya,' he commanded the driver (a metro station southeast of the centre, just beyond the Garden Ring Road). Roman turned to us.

'The guy I've just been to see, who I took some things to, he's the general director of a company which sells accessories for mobile communications.'

'And he uses drugs,' added the driver.

'Yeah,' said Roman. 'He uses drugs, he has lots of money and he trusts me. Almost every day he gives me a thousand, two thousand, three thousand ... and this is how I can afford to keep using.'

It was midnight when we arrived at the flat in south-central Moscow where Roman's friends, Natasha and Kolya, were staying. I'm not sure what I was expecting, but this wasn't it. They seemed too ... ordinary. Natasha was twenty, a natural down-to-earth beauty in baggy overalls, a rare make-up free Russian woman. Her smile was infectious and I warmed to her immediately.

Roman emptied his pockets and Natasha bounced up and down excitedly at the sight of the Soutan. While she began to bustle around looking for saucepans and other paraphernalia, Kolya filled a syringe from a saucer. He switched off the lights and sat on the edge of the folded out couch. Natasha lit a cigarette and sat with him as he

407

injected himself. Kolya slumped backwards moaning, holding the syringe in his motionless hand. I felt queasy. I'd never witnessed anyone shooting up before and my alarm must have showed on my face.

'Don't worry,' Natasha said reassuringly. 'He's experiencing euphoria. Now he's just used unclean, second-hand drugs, but it will pass soon. What we're preparing now will be better.'

After a while Kolya stood up and shook himself. He took the syringe to the kitchen, washed it under the tap and put it on the table. Meanwhile Roman had stripped to the waist, revealing a spectacular display of tattoos, covering almost every inch of his torso, back and front, and his arms down to his wrists. He showed me his arms, pointing out how the tattoos followed his central veins.

'That's to hide the needle tracks. When the cops stop you, and they stop you all the time, they check your veins. If they see evidence of needle use they can take you straight away. They can plant drugs on you. They use them as an excuse to extort money from us. The drugs police don't get paid much, so that's how they make their money, through robbing users. They can do anything they want because they know you can't go anywhere to complain. And why do they send users to prison? They only harm themselves with drugs. They aren't dealing. But our prisons are full of them. And many of them have had drugs planted on them. They could get off if they didn't admit to it, but many are beaten and forced to confess that the drugs are theirs.'

A complex chemical procedure was under way, involving petrol, cough medicine and some kind of acid. For hours they mixed, dissolved, boiled and distilled and at last Roman triumphantly poured a small quantity of white and yellow powder onto a wad of newspaper. 'The white is ephedrine, the yellow is acid. The acid soaks into the paper and leaves pure ephedrine.' He folded the paper, put it inside a book and sat on it. It was now about 4 am and the sky was beginning to lighten. I was fantasising about my bed, they were buzzing.

Roman had begun smoking marijuana with friends at sixteen then moved to other drugs. One day a friend offered to prepare ice for him. Roman handed over the money, the friend brought the ingredients to his mother's flat and taught him how to make it. At the time he was in his first year at the Russian State Academy of Physical Culture. But his promising career ended abruptly with an accident on a dance tour, which irreparably damaged the tendons in his knees.

Kolya trained as a swimmer at the same Academy and told a similar story. He was full of freaky facts. 'When people use ice, sometimes they don't sleep for four to five days and don't want to eat either. Some people's brains stop working properly and occasionally people kill themselves. But for others, like us, it's okay. You shoot up and come down in twenty-four hours — just like cognac. I had a friend who did this for twenty-six days in a row and didn't sleep or eat. He was okay.'

It didn't sound very 'okay' to me. Or perhaps I was just ultra-conservative and ultra-unadventurous. Natasha's story disturbed me most. She'd been a classical violinist until a police beating left her so badly injured she could no longer play. After two operations on her spine and knee, in a state of depression she began to experiment with cocaine and LSD. Since then she'd tried everything, 'every drug I've ever heard of'. She believed that many users were 'like us', talented people who had been denied an outlet for their genius in this world, 'so drugs help us to find a place'.

Roman opened the book. After another hour of mixing and dissolving, the ice was ready. Natasha filled Kolya's already used syringe from the saucer, laughed and waved it at me. 'My happiness!' She kissed the loaded needle. 'Mine and his,' she grinned, turning to kiss Kolya on the cheek. She turned off the lights and sat on the couch. Kolya injected her and she lay back and exhaled loudly. Kolya refilled the syringe and shot up himself. Then it was Roman's turn. But he couldn't get the needle to penetrate his skin. He jabbed and stabbed but his skin was too scarred.

'My veins are finished. I've used them all up.'

Kolya sat up, pupils like black holes. He leaned over Roman and jammed the syringe hard into his arm. Roman sank back, a look of calm spreading over his face for the first time since we'd met, eight hours ago.

'Ah ... *kaif*,' he sighed.

As far as they knew, Roman, Natasha and Kolya didn't have HIV. They knew it existed, and they knew it was transmitted by sharing needles. But it didn't stop them. They reasoned that if they only shared syringes with close friends then they wouldn't contract the disease. And it was exactly this mentality that was assisting the Grim Reaper in his murderous rampage on Russia's drug users.

The United Nations estimated that as many as two and a half million Russians were intravenous drug users. In the past year alone, the number of HIV-infected people had exploded from 80,000 to 195,000, the highest growth rate of the epidemic in the world. Yet as few of those in the high-risk category bothered to get tested, experts believed the real number to be closer to a million. It was another demographic catastrophe in the making, but it barely registered with the government. The entire federal budget for dealing with AIDS was a paltry USD$6 million, enough to treat around 500–600 infected people.

How could a country be so blasé about a pandemic? And how could users be so apathetic about the risks to their lives? Slava helped me track down a young HIV-positive couple in the outer Moscow sleeping district of Solntsevo. Once a sleepy dacha village named after the Russian for 'sun', these days Solntsevo was best known for the powerful Mafia gang, the Solntsevskaya Bratva (Solntsevo Brotherhood). Formed in the mid-1980s by waiter turned petty criminal, and later Gulag prisoner, Sergei Mikhailov, the *bratva* had taken over southwest Moscow's underworld and was now spreading its tentacles worldwide. Calling himself a *biznesmen*, rather than a *vor-v-zakone*, godfather Mikhailov had built up an empire of crime, running extortion rackets and prostitution rings, laundering money, dealing in arms, stolen art, cars and nuclear materials — and drug trafficking, of course. He was arrested in Switzerland in 1996 but by the time his trial began in November 1998, all key witnesses had been murdered. The trial was aborted.

The sun shone brightly over Solntsevo the day I made the trek out by local train to meet 23-year-old Lena and her husband, Sergei. But not even the vivid summer greens, blues and yellows could disguise the dead-end-of-the-world gloom of a place with no hope. Like any other sleeping district in any other Soviet city, Solntsevo was a grey stone jungle — row after row of blocks of flats in various stages of dilapidation, surrounded by overgrown grass and piles of rubbish. Children played on buckled slides, watched over by attentive babushki. Drunks sprawled across broken benches. Plastic bags danced over the weeds in the light breeze. It wasn't hard to see the appeal of joining the *bratva* or getting high.

I wandered around in search of Lena's flat, no easy task thanks to a ridiculously complicated address system. A cluster of buildings was called a 'house', with an individual building in that group given a 'korpus' number. Then there was an entrance number and often an entrance code to gain access, a floor number and finally a flat number. So an address, written in reverse to ours, typically followed this format: Street 'X', Dom 1, Korpus 2, Podyezd 3, Kod 4567Y, Etazh 8, Kv 16.

Eventually I located the two-room flat Sergei and Lena shared with her mum and their three-year-old son, Nikita. Lena welcomed me in. Moving with the gait of the chronically fatigued, she offered me a seat on a saggy couch, tea and ginger biscuits. Her pretty features were hardened by blotchy, sallow skin and bleached hair hacked short. She sat next to me, nursing her cup of tea. At almost a decade younger than me, she was already a mother, and suffering a terminal disease.

'It's terribly serious,' she sighed, shaking her head. 'There's an epidemic of HIV out here. Kids have nothing to do. There are no clubs where they can get together, and they are bored. So they look at the kids who use drugs and think, "well, I will be cool if I use them", and that's how it starts. Now practically all those who used drugs are infected with HIV. And not just HIV, but HIV and hepatitis C. Many even have hepatitis A and B on top of this. But no one thought about this and now it's too late.'

Lena was fifteen when she started using. Not because she had any kind of problem, but because everyone she knew used drugs. She too wanted to try and was soon addicted. Then she met Sergei, married, and within a month was pregnant. A month after Nikita was born she started using again. They lived with friends in a rented flat and there were drugs everywhere. She and Sergei began to feel unwell and went to a clinic for blood tests. Lena smiled dourly, revealing yellowing teeth.

'When we went to get the results, they said, "Yes kids, you have HIV." We laughed … yes, we laughed. Maybe it was because we didn't want to show our fear in front of each other. But after that we were hysterical for a month and drank heavily. Then we went back to drugs again, but told all our friends openly that we had HIV and they shouldn't use our needles. Then the family problems began. My mother took Nikita away, and I left Sergei and went to live with them. But I kept using because one of my friends sold drugs and everything was nearby. I was in such a bad way that I started to steal things from my mother. Finally she demanded I get treatment and I understood that beyond prison or death there could be nothing else.'

Lena agreed to a home detox program, which left her unconscious and hallucinating for two weeks. Since then she had been clean and clear-headed enough to realise she had sentenced herself to a premature death.

'I knew nothing about the risks when I started using. I knew there were different types of hepatitis, but when you are in a bad way and need a dose, you just don't care about these things. You don't use drugs because you get pleasure, you do it because you have to in order to function. No one in this state cares about getting infected.'

The door opened and Sergei entered with little Nikita, a blond cherub on a plastic trike. Lena waddled on her knees to embrace her son who beamed and threw his arms around her neck. She held him tightly and he began to giggle.

'Thank God Nikita isn't infected too. I don't think I could have forgiven myself.'

Lena had worked with Slava at Harm Reduction for a while, but found it too distressing to be confronted daily with young teenagers 'destroying their brains and bodies'. She now helped HIV-infected women through a Canadian-funded AIDS organisation. But she admitted she and Sergei were in the minority.

'We are trying to do something for our future, for the future of our child. But the majority we know aren't doing anything. If they hear there's heroin around, they run for it. It's quite terrifying to think of what lies ahead.'

Nikita tugged at his mother's arm and begged her to come outside with them. We walked down to a nearby stagnant pond, choked with rushes and humming with the buzz of flies. A half-disintegrated car roof stuck out of the water on a rakish angle. Lena and I watched as Sergei tried patiently to teach Nikita to skim stones. It should have been a happy scene, two young parents with the child they adored, tossing pebbles on a sunny day. But behind Lena's wistful smile I could see she was fighting a welling sadness at their inevitably tragic future. She read my mind.

'If everybody tried to do something it might be possible to change the situation. But as no one wants to do anything, and everyone is waiting for somebody else to do something for them, then it's unlikely things will change.'

29

A Baby, a Bomb and Big Brother in Berlin

The world was about to be shaken. In September 2001, I returned to Uzbekistan for a glittering tenth-anniversary-of-independence extravaganza with Eric, who was using it as an excuse to get a journalist visa. Behind the fireworks, flags and giddy displays of Uzbek patriotism, President Karimov was running one of the nastiest dictatorships in the former Soviet Union. Eric's intention was to dutifully film the celebrations — a gala of military parades, tractor displays and five thousand nubile dancing girls — then sneak off and meet with dissidents and human rights activists. Many had been horribly tortured for heinous crimes like visiting mosques, publishing religious pamphlets or criticising Karimov. As Karimov's henchmen tapped their phones and monitored their movements, no local fixers were willing to risk contacting them. I played 'Anna', the interpreter, sneaking off to public phone booths to make cryptic phone calls and organise clandestine interviews. My decade-old love affair with exotic Uzbekistan ended abruptly as I spun lies to sleazy officials and heard sickening stories of police barbarity.

After Ingushetia and Afghanistan, it felt strangely routine to be asking victims of intimidation to describe the details of their torment, to produce the goriest photos they might have as evidence, to point out the dents in the wall where police had rammed their heads, and to ask them to do it again for a close-up cut-away of the blood stain. I practised detachment, questioning dispassionately while feigning deep shock and concern. My focus was to ensure there was a suitably tight and dramatic sound bite to sum up the 'talent's' terror. It wasn't that I didn't care. I just couldn't afford to let myself be swept up in their tales on location, lest I seize up with pity, anger and a burning desire to throttle President Karimov. I learned to bottle my emotions, at least until replay time. All our interviewees told the same story: Karimov branded anyone who opposed him as an 'Islamic terrorist'. After a couple of weeks visiting torture targets, we concluded this was simply a ruse to allow Karimov to crack down on political opponents.

After a quick side-trip to the toxic dust-covered northwestern town of Nukus, where I shot a story for *Dateline* about a crumbling museum crammed with priceless Soviet avant-garde artworks, we returned to Tashkent. The hotel receptionist was ashen-faced. 'What's happened?' I asked, glancing up at a TV monitor behind her, which showed a tall building burning. 'Haven't you heard?' she asked wide-eyed. 'There's been a plane crash in America.'

It was September 11.

The next day we flew to Moscow. Putin had been the first foreign leader to call President George Bush to express his commiserations and understanding. 'Russia knows directly what terrorism means,' Putin told his countrymen later in a televised address. 'And because of this, we, more than anyone, understand the feelings of the American people. In the name of Russia, I want to say to the American people — we are with you.' Shocked Muscovites flocked to place wreaths, candles and messages of condolence outside the US Embassy, the very same building which demonstrators had pelted with eggs and tomatoes in protest at the US 'aggression' towards Yugoslavia just over two years earlier.

That chill in US–Russian relations had already begun to thaw. It was just over three months since George Bush Junior had gazed into Putin's stony eyes and declared he was 'able to get a sense of his soul'. When Bush began rallying allies for his assault on Afghanistan, Putin put up his hand to help. Russia's spy chief offered his services, declaring the attacks 'proved the global nature of the threat of international terrorism and the need for joint action to prevent it'. Russia and NATO announced they were 'united in their resolve not to let those responsible for such an inhuman act go unpunished'. Even the FSB declared they were investigating the attacks and would hand over 'any significant information to our colleagues in Washington'.

Human rights activists cringed as Putin declared on national television that Bin Laden's people were connected with the events now taking place in Chechnya. 'We know his people are present there and our American partners cannot but be concerned about this circumstance.'

My Chechen friends were miserable. Magomad — my guide to Ingushetia — had been travelling regularly to the European Court of Human Rights in the French city of Strasbourg to present evidence of war crimes committed by Russian troops against Chechen civilians. He saw Putin's linking of the Chechen rebels with Bin Laden and Bush's 'global war on international terrorism' as a cunning ploy to force the West to support Russia's 'anti-terrorist campaign' in the Caucasus. Sadly for the Chechens, the shocked world nodded understandingly and the already muted international criticism of the Chechen war faded further.

Magomad also had some terrible news. In April 2001, his Russian friend Viktor Popkov, the eccentric bearded religious scholar and human rights activist who travelled with us around Ingushetia, had been shot while trying to deliver food aid in Chechnya. He had died two weeks later from his injuries.

Not all of Russia's elite were sympathetic to America's suffering. Some proclaimed that America deserved what they got, that the attacks were the 'price they had to pay for playing the role of the world's single superpower'. As the ashes settled over the World Trade Center, Russian newspaper editorials pondered almost gleefully: 'Why is anti-Americanism so strong all over the world? Why do so many people hate them?', followed by a 'we told you so'. 'Russia has been warning the world for years about the threat of terrorism. We told them, and they didn't listen.' Some papers even mocked President Bush's behaviour, declaring that 'it didn't fit the image of a fearless Texas cowboy'. 'He was running — from Florida to Louisiana to Nebraska. America remembers JFK, who never left the White House during the Cuban Missile Crisis; and even King George VI, who remained with his subjects in London when German bombs were raining on the city during World War II.' There were calls too for the US to revise its military doctrine and scrap its recently revived 'Star Wars' missile defence shield plans.

The new alliance was always going to be a rocky one. Russia had long been an ally of the Arab nations and purveyor of modern weapons to Syria and Iran, countries considered 'rogue states' and supporters of terrorism by Washington. Contracts worth up to USD$10 billion were in the pipeline. A number of influential Kremlin officials were rumoured to make handsome personal profits from these deals and were vehemently opposed to closer ties with the Americans. Many of Putin's senior generals were unimpressed too. Permitting American planes to use bases in Central Asia — considered Russia's sphere of influence — was allowing the old enemy too close for comfort. Putin ignored them. For the first time in history, the US military flew, invited, into the former USSR.

I spoke with Russian soldiers who had fought in the bloody decade-long conflict with their southern neighbour. They thought the Americans were barking mad. 'The Afghans are experts at partisan warfare. If the Americans stay there then the Afghans will show them!' Lieutenant Colonel Yuri Shamanov warned presciently. 'They will be beaten up everywhere they go ... from behind. There will be no frontline. There will be no battles. But the Afghans will bite from behind. The Americans will never win.'

Retired military journalist Iona Andronov was even more forthright when I asked his opinion on the impending invasion. 'We retreated from Afghanistan with shame. What happened to the great British Empire? Three times they went to Kabul, three times they were forced to retreat, losing almost their entire army. So if the Americans wish to do that, they are stupid.'

The US did start bombing Afghanistan, and by October, President Bush heroically announced that the Taliban were history. I wanted to be there to see what happened. Just before Christmas 2001, I arrived at Bagram Air Base, just north of the freezing Afghan capital, with USD$10,000 in my underwear to deliver to the ABC's makeshift bureau in Kabul. Initially it seemed the Afghan veterans in Russia were wrong. The US military — droping bombs from miles up — were annihilating the 'enemy' without suffering a single casualty on their side. Spin doctors wrote off civilian deaths as tragic accidents, unavoidable in the battle against the medieval, barbarian Taliban. But as I watched old warlords being handed new ministerial posts, Afghanistan's future seemed dark.

I spent two months with women, mullahs, refugees, soldiers and government ministers. I also met the remarkable American journalist Elizabeth Neuffer, who had written award-winning books and covered wars in Africa and the Balkans. Now, in her mid-forties, she was injecting herself daily with hormones, hoping they would help her fall pregnant. As I talked to Afghan women, craving lives free from war, hunger and violence, I began to question myself. Like the Chechens, the victims of Mayak, the persecuted Muslims of Uzbekistan, all they wanted was a peaceful, secure existence with enough to eat, a roof over their heads, and possibly even education and health care. Many thought I was crazy. Why was I spending my child-bearing years deliberately seeking out horror? Suddenly my biological clock began to tick, and I realised I didn't want to find myself in Elizabeth's situation.

Four months later — in mid-April 2002 — Eric and I were sitting in a doctor's surgery at the outrageously expensive American Medical Center in Beijing, awaiting test results. An obese Texan regarded me solemnly.

'You're definitely not pregnant,' he declared. 'We think there may be some hormone imbalance, which will require further investigation. One of our specialists will contact you to arrange an appointment.' I nodded. 'But don't worry,' he said, showing us to the door. 'My wife and I tried for eight years, and she became pregnant with twins at forty.'

Two weeks passed before I found the courage to slink into a Chinese pharmacy with a hopelessly inadequate phrase book. I performed some elaborate charades to a bemused audience of white-coated salespeople. Eventually one began to giggle and handed me a pregnancy test kit. I paid and scuttled out. Halfway home I peeked at the box, and realised I had no idea how to use it, or interpret the result. I had no choice but to return for another round of humiliation.

The Texan was wrong. Eric was overwhelmed at the prospect of fatherhood — and my anticipated elation quickly turned to fear. Beijing was one of the world's most polluted cities. If even a quick stroll across the road to the Friendship Store filled my nostrils and eyes with black grime, how much lead would I ingest in a twenty-minute pedal to Tiananmen Square? Then the grisly nightmares began. Dr Brukhin's collection of mutant foetuses came to life, clawing and gnashing toothless gums in their glass formaldehyde-filled prisons. Would that radioactive pie I'd eaten mean my own foetus might end up with no brain? The first ultrasound was hardly comforting. I appeared to be gestating a shrimp. The doctor assured me it was totally normal.

I now felt for the victims of Muslyumovo and Chernobyl on a whole new level: a sick-in-the-guts terror of knowing that due to circumstances beyond their/my control there was every chance that their/my child would have some awful genetic mutation. Relatively I'd only had a minute fraction of the exposure to radiation that they had. But all they, and now I, wanted was to have the best chance possible to give birth to a healthy child, and bring it up in peace. I'd willingly chosen to go to these places: so many others weren't so lucky.

Comatose with the fatigue of early pregnancy, I returned to Moscow to finally finish my story on junkies and Russia's HIV epidemic. A mile above Siberia in an Aeroflot toilet, the nausea set in. It was downhill from there. I staggered around Moscow with my camera gear, trying not to regurgitate my *pelmeni*. I interviewed a Russian Orthodox priest about his 'detox through spirituality' program and hung out in rehab centres. It was all depressing.

I still had a tourist visa for China, which had to be renewed monthly. It hadn't been a problem until now as I was travelling constantly. But as I stood for five long hours in a queue of pushing and shoving traders at the Chinese Consulate in Moscow, I began to wonder how long I could keep this up. Two months later, in July 2002, Eric and I got married back in Sydney. Now instead of the Consulate queues I had to line up for medical tests in Beijing to prove I wasn't bringing HIV, TB or any one of a host of other diseases into the country. At last I got a visa that would last until after the birth. Or so we hoped.

While I was obsessing about the health and normality of the shrimp, Madame Ren from the Chinese Ministry of Foreign Affairs was obsessing about Eric. He was constantly in trouble for 'provoking Foreign Ministry minders', asking 'impertinent questions' and putting 'malicious stories' to air, which were allegedly damaging Australian–Chinese relations. In September, he was threatened with expulsion. He had three months to learn to play by the rules, otherwise we would have to leave China — and D-day was the shrimp's due date, 24 December.

Much as I approved of Eric's refusal to kowtow to the Foreign Ministry's demands that he report 'the truth', I didn't relish the thought of a twenty-hour flight with a bulging, squirming belly. We decided that there was only one option. Eric would have to swallow his pride and be nice to Madame Ren.

At the same time, an ultrasound revealed I had placenta praevia, a potentially serious complication where the placenta covers the cervix. As the foetus grows, it can rupture the placenta, causing haemorrhaging. I was told I shouldn't go further than twenty minutes away from a good hospital, so that last minute dash to Afghanistan I'd been contemplating was out of the question. Thankfully, the ultrasound image also showed a baby with all its bits and pieces in the right places. It even had a brain.

On 15 December 2002, winter hit Beijing, white powdery snow transforming the choked grey city into a crispy clean wonderland. I hadn't seen my feet in weeks and had given up riding my bike after being knocked off by a pushy rickshaw driver a month earlier. But suddenly I was full of energy. I dragged Eric off on a 10 kilometre walk and just as we got home, the contractions began. Ten hours later in a

Beijing hospital, a Chinese nurse handed me a wailing, splotchy creature with a cone head and mashed up face. I stared at my newborn son in horror.

'Oh dear,' was my first thought. 'I hope something changes, otherwise he's going to get a really hard time at school.'

We called him Nicholas.

I was besotted with our spotty little child. All my plans to 'just put him in a pouch and get back on the road' evaporated the instant I first held him. I was perfectly happy — until Eric came home one night with some 'great news'. He was flying to London the next day to do a chemical weapons training course. If, or when, the US invaded Iraq, as looked bound to happen, he'd be ready to cover the conflict. Wasn't that exciting? My heart sank. I couldn't believe he really wanted to go to Iraq.

For me, everything had changed. I understood the thrill of being where the big story was. Only a year ago I'd been in Kabul as Hamid Karzai was inaugurated president. Now my world had shrunk to focus on my tiny boy and I didn't want Eric to go to war, not just yet anyway. Still, I wasn't going to stop him and have him resent me for it.

In March 2003 we flew back to Australia. Nik was not quite three months old. Eric went straight to Canberra to get an Iranian visa, and I flew to Melbourne to stay with my family. Four days after Eric left Australia, the US began bombing Baghdad. Eric was now in Kurdistan in Northern Iraq, with a Paris-based freelance Australian cameraman, Paul Moran. On 24 March he called me at my parents' house. All was fine, he said. He and Paul, who had a six-week-old baby daughter, Tara, were being extra careful. That night I watched his report on the news. Baby Nik seemed to pay extra attention when he heard Eric.

At 1 am the phone rang. I staggered up to get it but the answering machine clicked in before I got there. My mum and dad were standing in their bedroom doorway. I grabbed the receiver just as Eric's distraught voice boomed through the house. 'I'm okay,' he cried, 'but Paul's dead, Paul's dead.' My heart stopped. A million thoughts flooded my head. His poor child ... baby Tara ... she will never know her father … his wife … and where was Eric? Would he get out safely or was he in the middle of a battle somewhere and this would be the last time I ever heard from him? Was Nik about to lose his father too?

Eric was in shock. He tried to explain what had happened but didn't make much sense. They'd been filming at a checkpoint near a base of the Kurdish Sunni Islamist group, Ansar al-Islam, he said, when a suicide bomber pulled up next to Paul. Five people had died instantly in the explosion. Eric had miraculously escaped almost uninjured. Then he had to go. There was no number I could call him on as his satphone had been melted in the blast. The line went dead.

I was numb. My parents sat in stunned silence. Nik slept through it all. I pulled myself together and began to make phone calls to Eric's sisters and father to let them know what had happened before they heard it on the radio. All the while my heart was breaking for a woman in Paris called Ivana and her tiny baby, whose lives had suddenly changed forever.

It took a week for Eric to get back to Australia with Paul's body. Ivana left Tara in France with her parents and flew to Iran to meet Eric and Paul as they left Iraq. The entourage arrived at Melbourne's Tullamarine Airport in the middle of the night, Eric shattered, with a bloody bandage around his head, Ivana shell-shocked yet calm. Her inner strength and resilience were phenomenal. At Paul's funeral in Adelaide a week later she gave an eloquent tribute to her beloved husband before hundreds of mourners. And at the wake afterwards, it was she who was comforting Paul's grieving relatives and friends. 'I lived in Belgrade during the war in Yugoslavia,' she told me. 'And I know for sure that women are the real men.'

We didn't return to Beijing for more than six months. Eric was suffering post-traumatic stress and Nik ended up needing two operations to remove a rare form of tumour I had discovered growing through a toenail. As we waited in the oncology ward at the Royal Melbourne Children's Hospital for him to recover from his anaesthetic, I couldn't help wondering if my trip to Muslyumovo had anything to do with it.

Incredibly, none of this killed our wanderlust. Eric was determined to get back to work. And as I watched little Nik crawling around, I began to think about how I could take him with me on shoots. My mum looked after all of us, overhearing our conversations about getting back overseas. She said nothing but I got the feeling she thought we were completely bonkers. In September we returned to China, to Nik's outgrown baby clothes and cot and change table, unused for six months. We packed up our flat there and in December I dragged Eric and Nik off to Berlin to do my first post-birth story. Nik had just turned one.

It was supposed to be a quirky piece about an eccentric new Russian reality TV series. The days of 'Big Brother' conjuring up an Orwellian image of Stalin-era surveillance had long passed in Russia. Here, as everywhere else, *Big Brother* was a TV experiment, wildly popular with audiences and contestants alike. This particular show was the typical BB set-up — twelve young people chosen from thousands all over Russia, eager for the overnight fame and prize money that came with allowing oneself to be publicly humiliated. All they knew was that they would spend one hundred days in a purpose-built house with a group of strangers, with cameras documenting their every move. Each week they would vote out one person, and the survivor would receive USD$1,000 a month for the rest of their lives.

'A Russian prize,' the heavily pregnant 25-year-old series producer, Masha Shaikevich, half-joked between puffs on her fifteenth cigarette that morning. 'They won't have to work for the rest of their lives.'

But being Russia, there was an extreme twist. In an effort to boost ratings of what was by now a tired old format, an executive at the TV channel, TNT, had come up with a novel idea. Instead of the audience watching contestants sitting around eating all day, wouldn't it add some excitement if they had no food? The network's bosses leapt at the concept and now that black joke had become reality.

Soon after, the twelve were blindfolded and put on a charter plane, to an unknown city in an unknown country. After a lavish banquet on their first night in what to most was palatial accommodation, the TV crew removed every skerrick of food from the house. For six days they had nothing to eat but vitamin drinks, and nothing to do but to speculate on where they might be.

Just as contestants began to hallucinate about *pelmeni* and fried eggs, they were instructed via a booming voice to select two of their group to be taken out to find food. Nastya and Karina, with cameras and microphones hidden in their hats and backpacks, were taken into the mystery city and deposited next to the monument to the unknown soldier at Berlin's Brandenburg Gate, once the dividing line between East and West. A bevy of digicam operators shadowed the pair as they begged for food. They had no passports, no money, and neither spoke a word of German. Eventually a Russian man in a supermarket bought them some bread.

From that day, participants were deposited in the city on a regular basis, forced to use whatever talents they had to find money for the essentials: alcohol, cigarettes and sometimes even food. Producers had carefully cast a stripper/law student, a singer and an artist. There was also a medical student, a Spetsnaz officer and an ex-con. Lyuba, the stripper, had lined up regular work at a Russian-owned nightclub. Others were going batty.

Called *Golod*, meaning 'Hunger', the show was causing an uproar in Germany. Lurid newspaper stories accused the show's producers of imprisoning and starving the contestants. Politicians called for it to be banned. *Golod* was over a month into production when I took Nik into the converted Siemens factory on Berlin's western outskirts. One hundred plus chain-smoking Russians filled the aircraft-hangar-sized shed, peering at TV monitors linked to the hundreds of cameras inside the 'house' in the centre of the building. I fought off a migraine as Nik toddled around playing with cigarette butts. The show's producers were excited.

'What a great idea for a Christmas special! Let's put the baby into the house and see what the kids do when they wake up and find him there!'

I was dubious. 'He's going to be terrified and start crying.'

'That's okay, you can go in there with him.'

This wasn't the idea. I was coming to do a story about them. Now they wanted to make Nik and me their story. But I had a problem.

Along with my smoke-induced migraine I had tummy trouble after some dodgy Chinese takeaway the night we arrived. So dodgy that I was ducking to the toilet every few minutes.

'Are there cameras in the toilets too?' I asked Masha.

'Of course,' she said matter-of-factly. 'There isn't a single camera-free place in the house. We have to be able to watch them everywhere, to make sure they aren't doing anything illegal.'

That clinched it. No way was I going to have my bowel problems viewed by the legions of camera operators, editors and line producers churning out a daily hour-long episode.

The contestants were less concerned about having their intimate moments captured on digicam. Even so, some were finding the strain unbearable. Masha and her team turned their attention to reviewing the previous night's footage. Ksenya, an intoxicated redhead, was waving her fists at the cameras, screaming.

'I'll do whatever I want! I hate you all, did you get that? You're all moral mutants because you're doing all this to us,' she screeched and burst into hysterical laughter. 'I'm a bad girl! I'll destroy the furniture, I'll do whatever I want and try to stop me!'

Masha pressed pause.

'Put that in,' she nodded to an editor, and hit the play button.

The scary voice spoke, which I now knew was Masha in the control room going through some computer distortion. 'Ksyusha [diminutive of Ksenya] ... put the microphone in front.'

A drunken breakdown made for riveting viewing. It would be a pity to ruin it with substandard audio. Ksenya did as she was bade and continued, her voice now cracking between tears and laughter. 'I don't want to be a superstar! I hate you all, because you get into the soul and torture us.'

It wasn't just the contestants who were feeling tortured. Back in Kazan, Karina's boyfriend, Sasha, was going insane with jealousy as he watched his beautiful TV reporter girlfriend flirting with the boys. First he went to TNT in Moscow and demanded her removal from the house. They refused. Karina had signed a contract and there was no backing out. Sasha, a wealthy businessman used to getting his own way, could bear it no longer. He hired a private detective and arrived in Berlin with an entourage of heavies and threatened to kidnap her. Not the type to be intimidated, Masha had a brainwave.

'Okay, you can kidnap her,' Masha told Sasha. 'But we're going to film it.'

So the unsuspecting Karina was sent onto the streets with Lyuba the stripper. Soon after, a black Mercedes with tinted windows pulled alongside them. A twin pair of thugs leapt out, grabbed Karina, threw her into the car and sped away. Lyuba was beside herself with panic. The crew played along with the story and by the time they got back to the Siemens factory, Lyuba was a weeping, quivering basketcase.

Meanwhile, kidnapped Karina was driven into the Berlin night by men she assumed were Mafia and taken to a fancy restaurant. Sasha was waiting in a private room with flowers, gifts, a diamond ring at the bottom of a glass of champagne and a proposal of marriage. She agreed immediately, quit the show, and returned to the *Big Brother* house that night with a blow-up doll as a present for the guys in the house. The wedding was a week later.

If starvation, breakdowns and a kidnapping weren't enough to keep audiences hooked, then a subtle bit of nudity helped to maintain interest. The free-for-all porno fest of the Yeltsin era was now a thing of the past and Putin's censors were cracking down on naked flesh. But when a Russian nightclub in Berlin offered to pay three of *Golod*'s contestants thirty euros each to get their gear off for an 'artistic evening' of body painting, the producers made sure they were bussed there on time. For Lyuba it was all in a night's work, but Natasha, the young mother from the provincial Ural town of Tyumen, had to swig half a bottle of vodka before she found the courage to doff her kit.

'But it wasn't striptease,' Masha explained. 'And the main thing was that it was dark so we could show it on air.'

My stomach woes continued and Nik and I never did become *Golod*'s Christmas special. We had flights booked to leave Berlin for Barcelona on the afternoon of Christmas Eve, where we planned to spend the silly season with friends. But while I'd made spectacular progress with weight loss, shedding four kilos in four days, I was way behind schedule with filming. I spent our entire last night bent double in the bathroom, by now so weak I could hardly stand. In desperation I asked Eric to use his university German to find a doctor, hoping to be prescribed some magic pill to keep me going until the flight. Eric disappeared, promising to call for an emergency visit, leaving me in a floppy heap on the bed wrapped in a dressing gown.

Minutes later the door burst open and several Schwarzenegger lookalikes in fluoro emergency outfits rushed in, one with an oxygen tank, another with a fire hose.

'*Was? Was?*' (What? What?)' they shouted, ready for heroic action.

Eric puffed in behind them.

'Ummmm, *Sie hat ein schlect* ... ummm ... *magen* ... (She has a bad stomach),' Eric mumbled.

There was a stunned silence.

I pulled my gown tightly around me and eventually one spoke.

'Well, drink lots of water then,' he said.

They turned and left.

By January 2004, we were back in our old flat on Kutuzovsky Prospekt, just near Moscow's White House. Eric was to ease himself back into work by filling in between correspondents for four months and I was planning more *Dateline* stories. I was excited. In a strange way it felt like we had came home. Olga dropped in with Tyoma, now six, and a bag of his baby toys and winter clothing for Nik. Tina's chauffeur picked us up in a snazzy new Merc with individual DVD players built into the backs of the seats and took us to a playgroup with her youngest daughter, Katya. Her eldest, Sasha, now seven, was learning piano and Tina had arranged for her to audition for a place at the prestigious Gneisen Academy, a hothouse conservatorium for the musically gifted. Ultra-talented children from all over the entire country vied for places and the competition was intense. Tall and lanky like her father, Sasha was a beautiful child, comfortably bilingual, but not particularly keen on piano practice. Along with piano, she was learning figure skating and having private ballet tutorials with one of the Bolshoi's leading teachers. Tina couldn't imagine bringing her kids up anywhere else. I agreed wholeheartedly.

But without my own private army of staff, my enthusiasm for life with Nik in Russia quickly turned to sheer exhaustion. Insulating a squirming toddler from a minus twenty degree winter was no easy task. To add to the challenge, the apartments in our compound were heated to a sweltering thirty degrees. 'It is a special courtesy to the foreigners,' explained Ira Stelliferovskaya, the ABC's office manager. While Olga complained of draughts in her flat and constantly worried about Tyoma catching cold, Nik lived in nothing but a nappy. Venturing outside meant preparing for a fifty degree drop in temperature. I dressed myself first: leggings under my jeans, a thermal top, jumper, padded vest, thick woollen scarf, beanie, two pairs of socks and thick boots, all topped with a down-filled coat which reached to my knees. Bulging like a Michelin man and soaking with sweat, I started on Nik, who thought it hilarious to run around the flat while I wrestled him into stockings, several layers of clothing, a scarf, hat, Tyoma's padded snowsuit and a sleeping bag.

Once he was wrapped like a stuffed sausage I wrangled him into his pram and battled with the flat's two front doors. Then came a war with the doors of the minuscule lift from our ninth-floor flat which opened just wide enough to fit the pram, as long as I jammed them open with my feet. Usually they snapped shut as the pram was halfway in. 'Why,' I wondered in frustration every time I tried to leave the flat with Nik, 'couldn't Soviet architects have designed bigger lifts?' I now understood why Tina and Stephen had installed a super-sized elevator to get to their penthouse apartment. By the time I got past the heavy double wooden entrance doors with their vicious springs, I was ready to pass out.

Our second-hand Peg-Perego hadn't been designed with deep snow in mind and pushing it to the shop was an ordeal. The wheels got bogged in the snow, which varied from a fresh, fluffy, white quicksand texture, to slushy grey muck, which sprayed up over my jeans. Riding over a newly deposited yet carefully covered dog poo was a particular joy. The local 'supermarket' was heated like a sauna, so I would bolt up and down the aisles of chocolates, frozen *pelmeni*, and sickly, fizzy drinks hoping to locate some edible fruit and vegetables before Nik woke up in a sweat. If produce had once rotted because it took so long to get to the market, now it went rotten because no one could afford it. And forget BYO shopping bags. Every item was cling-wrapped to death on polystyrene trays. There was more wrapping than food. Shopping was still horrendous. Worst of all was that I could only fit enough food on the handles of Nik's pram to last a day or two, so this debacle became a daily routine.

Until now I'd quietly considered Tina's chauffeur and round-the-clock nannies to be an extravagant indulgence. But as I stood on Kutuzovsky Prospekt in the sludge with Nik in his pram contemplating just how I was going to get anywhere or do anything, I developed a whole new appreciation for hired help. I couldn't drive, and I didn't have a Russian licence, a car, the will or intestinal fortitude to tackle the gridlock and road rage in front of me even if I did. I considered flagging down a car, but getting a baby and a pram into some exhaust-belching Zhiguli with a greasy spare tyre taking up the entire boot was a daunting prospect. And what if we got picked up by some suspect guy who might drive off with the pram, or worse, with Nik. Taking a pram on the sardine-can metro wasn't an option. And Tina had three kids! What did Russian mums do?

The answer was simple. Babushki. There was a plus to having live-in parents after all, or at least devoted babushki living nearby. I needed to find one. Nadia adored Nik, and I knew she would love to look after him, but it was too much to ask. She lived too far away, was terrified of travelling by metro or taking a car, and was too fragile these days to take on my boisterous thirteen-month-old. I'd already had the blood-curdling experience of coming out of the bathroom to find him standing on the windowsill, opening the window to a snow storm, nine floors up. In desperation I followed up handwritten advertisements for nannies pasted on noticeboards and began my interviews. There was brusque, ultra-strict Lyuba, an ex-engineer, and Tanya, an ex-university lecturer with a blonde coif sprayed stiff under her mink fur hat. Both were trying to subsist on pensions, and exuded visible bitterness at having been reduced to looking after rich folk's spawn. Then there was Khazbika, an ebullient Chechen recommended by Magomad, whose hourly rate was, for some reason, three times more than the others. All were bossy, overbearing and seemed unlikely to listen to my requirements that Nik eat something other than lollies and do something other than being parked in front of the television.

Eventually Olga came to the rescue, offering me the services of Tyoma's babysitter, Galya. In her late thirties, Galya was a gentle soul, married but sadly childless. She loved children and worked twenty-four hour shifts for a paediatric ambulance service. Her salary didn't even cover basic expenses so she nannied for Olga on the days when Misha's mum couldn't make it. Galya picked up Tyoma from school, played with him, and cleaned and shopped for Olga, who was stuck in snail-paced traffic each night, returning home from work at IKEA's new mega-store in Khimki out by the airport in Moscow's far northwest.

Galya kindly offered to squeeze a few hours of Nik-sitting into her hectic timetable. It was a revelation. I could dash to the shop while she built block towers with Nik, and she even agreed that fruit and vegetables were good for children. At last I could consider working, as long as I could arrange interviews for times she wasn't at Olga's or her ambulance job.

3 0

Black Widows and Skinheads

February–March 2004

The first big news story after our return to Moscow was a rush-hour suicide bombing in a metro tunnel, a colossal explosion which wrecked part of a train between Avtozavodskaya and Paveletskaya stations in the city's southwest. Forty-two were killed, 250 injured, and Chechen rebels immediately copped the blame. The fugitive deposed Chechen president Aslan Maskhadov denied involvement, but that didn't stop Putin declaring him the mastermind.

'We do not need any indirect confirmation. We know for certain that Maskhadov and his bandits are linked to this terrorism,' pronounced Putin at a press conference. 'Russia doesn't conduct negotiations with terrorists … it destroys them.'

Eric was still having nightmares and flashbacks to the suicide bombing that had killed Paul in Iraq almost a year ago. I worried about how covering this incident would affect him, but he was determined to prove he could cope. Despite the bombing occurring only a few kilometres from our flat, I felt no fear. Neither motherhood, nor what had happened to Eric, had yet put me off wanting to do stories on the tragic and macabre. It was time for another story about Chechnya.

Magomad was in Moscow and I invited him over to hear his take on the current state of affairs in his homeland. It was five weeks out from the Russian presidential elections on 14 March and Putin, the unrivalled favourite for a second term, had been declaring for some time that the situation in the war-torn republic had stabilised.

Russian journalists still carefully adhered to Putin's script: the war was over bar the occasional 'mopping-up operation', it was safe for refugees to return and Chechen civilians were gratefully accepting Russian money to rebuild their homes. In March 2003, a referendum had been held in Chechnya, in which the population had voted to remain part of the Russian Federation. Then in October 2003, the powerful Kremlin-backed clan leader, Akhmad Kadyrov, had been elected president. Everything was, apparently, back to normal. So why were foreign journalists still kept on short leashes, herded around on official tours, if they were allowed in at all?

Magomad arrived with a box of chocolates and I beamed as I introduced him to Nik. I might have made a film about the Chechen conflict, but giving birth to a son was an infinitely more respect-worthy accomplishment. In Chechen culture, motherhood was the true destiny of a woman, and the production of a son the ultimate achievement. Magomad too had become a parent since I'd last seen him. When we'd met back in 2000, Magomad — still single at thirty-five — told me about Alissa, the girl he planned to marry. He just had to wait until she turned seventeen, which she did later that year. Their first daughter, Malika, arrived at the end of 2001, and their second, Amnat, less than eighteen months later. Alissa and the girls were back in the Ingush border village of Sleptsovsk with his family while Magomad was on one of his regular visits to Moscow.

Since 2002 he had been participating in discussions with, among others, the Russian Duma and the Russian National Committee for the Cessation of War and Establishment of Peace in Chechnya. When I told him about the news reports from Chechnya I'd been watching, he shook his head.

'No one believes the referendum or election were free and fair,' he said, stroking his ginger beard. 'The Russians have handed over control to Kadyrov, who does what they want. But his troops, the Kadyrovtsi, are even more evil than the Russians. There are still disappearances and murders, only now the Russians can say that it's the Chechens fighting amongst themselves. I personally know of many families who have lost their sons and fathers to Kadyrov's soldiers. And I know women, bereaved wives and mothers — "black widows" — who are prepared to sacrifice themselves.'

In October 2002, a group of forty to fifty Chechens, including a number of young war widows, had taken part in a mid-performance siege of the Dubrovka Theatre in Moscow. They held almost nine hundred people hostage until Russian special forces stormed in two and a half days later, gassing everyone and executing the Chechens. Up to two hundred people died in the bungled rescue, including many children. In July 2003, two more young Chechen women who had lost close relatives had blown themselves up at a rock festival in Moscow's Tushino Stadium, killing fifteen.

I looked over at Nik, who was furiously pressing buttons on the phone. He smiled at me and I tried to imagine what it would be like to lose him to a gang of armed, masked thugs. I could almost understand what might drive a mother or wife, despairing and demented in her loss, to strap herself with explosives and kill people in revenge. Almost.

It was too dangerous for me to contemplate going to Chechnya, and I was still breastfeeding Nik. So together Magomad and I hatched a plan. He was afraid of being on camera again as Russian, and now Chechen, authorities were unimpressed by his reports to the European Court of Human Rights, and he feared for the safety of his young family. But a female relative of his would be prepared to smuggle my tiny camera into Chechnya. I would explain to her how to use the camera and what to ask. She would go to acquaintances who had lost husbands and sons, find out their stories and record them for me. For her own safety, she would remain anonymous.

The next day Magomad brought a middle-aged woman in a headscarf, who I will call Mariam, to our flat. My mother had just arrived from Melbourne and she watched on as Mariam and I compiled a gruesome list of instructions.

- *Go to your friend whose sister was killed in the Dubrovka Theatre siege.*
- *Film damage to Grozny.*
- *Interview families whose men have been killed or abducted by Russian troops and Kadyrov's soldiers.*

Nik drove a plastic tractor around our feet as I explained how to change tapes, fit a microphone, charge batteries, use a mini-tripod and frame shots. Mariam seemed overwhelmed and a little frightened, but assured me she could do as I needed. I gave her money for air and bus fares and she promised to return as soon as she could.

Now I had a real babushka to sit with Nik, I set about finding a Russian ex-soldier who would agree to talk about the war from his side. After days scouring personnel lists, copying names and numbers of veterans living in the Moscow region, I found a recently returned mercenary who agreed to be interviewed *if* I paid him USD$200, filmed him in silhouette and swore not to disclose his real name. I left Nik with my worried mum and headed to a friend's flat on the Moscow River embankment for our night-time rendezvous, expecting to find some brute of a man who got his kicks from massacring women and children. Instead I found a sensitive and thoughtful youth who'd found himself a player in a vicious game because there was no other work around.

Now twenty-three, 'Yura' had been conscripted at eighteen and served his two years compulsory service in Kaluga. Returning from the army he couldn't afford the bribes to get a higher education and found work as a barman. Most of his friends became drug addicts and/or alcoholics, many with HIV and Yura realised he didn't want to end up that way. The only job he could find other than bartending was as a mercenary, a *kontraktnik,* fighting for Russia in Chechnya. But ten months' 'service' in the mountainous area around the village of Shatoi had left him disillusioned and disturbed by what he'd been forced to do. Unlike the two Alexeis — the veterans of the first Chechen war who I'd met in Moscow back in February 2000 — Yura had come to see the war from both sides. He understood it was only logical that the terrified village boy who had stared at him in his black mask, armed with grenades, a knife and a gun would grow up to despise Russians. And he couldn't blame the Muslim Chechens for their fury at the drunken Russian soldiers who tanked themselves with vodka and fired indiscriminately into villages.

'They are normal people and we need to understand them. It's a war on their homes, their children, their families. They are afraid too. Yes, they do bad things and I'm not saying that it's good that they blow things up. But you can understand that if since childhood people have been barging into their houses and interfering in their lives that they are not going to like Russians after that. It's Russia that is creating the terrorists.'

But Yura didn't blame the Russian soldiers either. He described being dropped into the mountains by helicopter in winter with nothing but a summer uniform, gun and bullets. With no money or food he and the other soldiers had no choice but to loot, kill livestock and steal from civilians.

'How are they supposed to live? Of course they will loot and steal. But who is guilty here? Who sent those soldiers there without proper uniforms, without food? You have to eat. You have to wear something. But no one gave them anything. So they go to some house, get in a fight and kill some people, then those that are left want revenge — blood for blood. So what do they do? Put explosives on themselves and go to some rock concert, a theatre, a train and blow themselves up ... just as they are doing in Iraq. The war there will go on a long time too. It's just the same as in Chechnya.'

I hadn't expected this at all. The Alexeis had been so black and white in their allegiances to Russia, so certain in the rightness of their cause, the perfect propaganda poster boys for Putin's anti-terrorist campaign. For them, service in the Russian Army was the supreme sacrifice for the motherland. For Yura it was a farce.

'Everyone drinks vodka all the time. It's the only way their nerves can handle it. One night a guy in the next room to ours drank so much he pulled the pin from a grenade. Two were killed, four were hospitalised and everyone else just kept watching television. It was completely normal that soldiers got drunk and killed each other. Many soldiers even sell their weapons and ammunition to the Chechens so they can buy dope.'

He produced a dub of a mate's 'home video' and asked if I'd like to see it. The grainy VHS footage revealed a shabby dormitory seething with scrawny, half-naked, shaven-headed youths — up to thirty in one room, said Yura — slamming shots of bootleg vodka. The cameraman leered in for close-ups. 'Say hi to your mum,' came an invisible voice. Scarred faces loomed into frame, grinning drunken, broken-toothed grins. Barely out of their teens, many looked half-deranged. The more testosterone-fuelled did chin-ups for the camera, which zoomed in on their bulging biceps. Others wrestled each other, boxed, did karate kicks, anything to burn up tension. And this, explained Yura, was the good side of life in the Russian Army. No one bothered to film the hazings, the torture and humiliation meted out by senior officers on their young charges.

But the ultimate affront for Yura was the discovery that he wasn't being paid the amount promised in his contract. He had signed up to receive 30,000 roubles a month, roughly USD$1,000, yet was paid only 11,000 roubles. This war, he believed, was a money laundering arrangement for 'someone high up'.

'I was there for ten months, and each month I didn't receive 20,000 roubles I was supposed to. That's 200,000 roubles! There are very, very many *kontraktniki* there and where is that money going? And they are not only laundering money through soldiers, but through selling weapons too.'

I asked what he thought of Putin's claim that the war was over. He was scathing.

'Ha! Russian soldiers are still being killed in Chechnya every day, yet the television shows nothing. The subject is closed and what they do show is all lies. We watched the news when we were in the mountains and it was just ludicrous to us. It was so staged. People are killed there all the time. I was very offended when after the Kursk went down [a nuclear cruise missile submarine which sank in the Barents Sea in August 2000, killing all 118 on board], for a year everyone was saying, "Oh those poor marines, they drowned." But why is everyone silent about the thousands of soldiers who have been and are still being killed in Chechnya?'

Yura didn't know what he was going to do now. He had recently married and dreamed of a family and 'normal' job. But employment prospects were remote and he was contemplating going back to Chechnya for another tour. As I trudged home after our meeting, headlong into a blizzard, I felt profoundly sorry for Yura. He seemed a genuinely nice guy and deserved a decent future. But there wasn't one for him here.

Mum was relieved when I returned. She was finding everything about Moscow confronting: the minus twenty degree temperatures, the overheated apartment, walking on the icy footpaths and the incomprehensible language. We couldn't walk down the street without worrying about icicles dropping from buildings and impaling us or Nik's pram. We took to shopping in an open-air market so I wouldn't have to worry about Nik sweltering in his Arctic suit. Even this made Mum fearful, after she was bailed up by aggressive, uniformed guards for trying to take a picture of a man pushing a trolley-load of frozen sturgeon. And while the market vegies looked good, I had to warn her they could be smothered in chemicals and we shouldn't buy them. The UHT milk gave Nik eczema and there was no way of knowing whether other produce was safe. It was difficult for Mum to get to the tourist attractions she wanted to see, and if she did she worried about how she'd get back. The metro might explode and a taxi driver could whisk her off anywhere and she wouldn't have a clue what was happening. She didn't feel safe and my going out late at night to meet mercenaries was not making her feel any better. She could only wonder why on earth I was voluntarily spending my sixth winter in this awful place.

A few weeks into her stay, my old school friend Mardi came to visit too, making our home one very crowded flat. Company gave Mum courage and they flew off to explore St Petersburg for a week.

Galya looked after Nik while I filmed an anti-war demonstration in the square in front of the Lubyanka (the FSB's headquarters), sifted

437

through hours of gruesome amateur footage of the aftermath of massacres of Chechen villagers and interviewed an evasive Russian government official who assured me that Chechnya was now a land of peace.

Three weeks after I'd given her my camera, Mariam returned from the Chechen capital, Grozny. She shuffled wearily into our flat, dropped a plastic bag of tapes on the table and handed me back the camera. The experience had been far more dangerous and distressing than she could have imagined. Even as a Chechen, possession of a video camera had made her an object of suspicion and she'd quickly learned to hide it in a scarf. Anyone who saw it bombarded her with questions: 'Why are you filming? Are you a spy? Why do you want to know what we think? How can we trust you?' A girl had recently been abducted from her home at 3 am after an interview she gave to French television was broadcast, and many of those Mariam had hoped to interview were terrified that Kadyrov's men or the Russian special forces would do the same to them or their children. It had taken all her diplomatic skills to convince them that nothing bad would come of it.

As we watched the tapes, I felt a great weight of responsibility. Some of these people had risked their lives to talk and I must ensure their identities were protected. The interviews were in Chechen, and Mariam translated each story roughly into Russian as we went.

There was 'Koka', a 47-year-old Grozny native who'd fled to an Ingush refugee camp with his family when Russian bombs began raining on his hometown in late 1999. He'd recently been ordered to return to Chechnya but didn't believe it was safe. Just three weeks earlier, his cousin had been killed by Russian troops on her way to a wedding. Koka loathed the Russian military with a near psychotic passion and believed that after all that had happened, independence was the only option.

'Musa' and his six family members were also refusing to leave the Ingush camp that had been their home for the past four years, despite threats of violence from local authorities.

'There are still murders every day,' Musa cried. 'Kadyrov's special forces are working with the Russians. I have a seventeen-year-old son and I have to stay here. I only receive a small pension of 1,300 roubles a month [around USD$40]. If they took him and killed him I would need to buy back his body. How could I afford to? I only have enough for cigarettes.'

The camps were even more dismal than they had been four years ago. Mariam's images showed frayed and worn tents, haggard women scrubbing clothes in buckets of dirty, icy water, and kids playing in snowdrifts. Yet few of the camp's inhabitants were prepared to risk returning home. Once we began to roll the tape Mariam had shot in Grozny I could see why. She'd climbed to the twelfth floor of a bombed out apartment building and, concealing the camera, had done some wobbly pans up and down the neighbouring streets. Her camerawork reflected her terror, frantic crash zooms in and out of gutted buildings as she tried to capture every inch of the destruction before a sniper fired at her. The devastation was total. I glanced up from the small screen at Mariam and saw she was shaking.

'When I agreed to do this, I never thought that as a Chechen I would need anyone to look out for me. But when I started, I realised what a mistake I'd made. It could have cost me my life.'

In Grozny she'd recorded a weeping sixty-year-old widow whose two sons had been abducted in the night, leaving her with eight grandchildren under eight to care for. Her sons had never been heard from again. Mariam had also found a friend of one of the women hostage-takers who had been killed in the Dubrovka Theatre siege in Moscow. Afraid to give her name, the 22-year-old had been arrested by Russian troops for having 'terrorist connections'. They'd let her off with a warning and she was now in hiding. Mariam's dimly lit shot showed only a pair of brown eyes staring out of a black-bandaged head.

'They told me that this scarf I wear means I am a Wahhabist and a threat,' the girl said, her voice muffled by her hijab. 'But I think it is genocide against our people. They don't want us to survive. Now that many young Chechen women have blown themselves up they are afraid of us too. They see every Chechen as a threat, whether they are male or female.'

Mariam asked her if she would consider becoming a *shahidka*, a martyr.

'I have had the opportunity,' the girl replied serenely. 'But it seems Allah didn't want it so I'm still alive. Maybe Allah spared me for a different mission.'

'What if it would mean the deaths of innocent civilians?' carried on Mariam.

'Civilians are dying anyway. If an innocent person dies then I think that with the help of Allah, they would go to heaven too. I would sacrifice myself so that people would think, "We can't go on like this. This has to stop. Look, even girls are sacrificing themselves for their people." It's already been seven years of the destruction of our people. If it keeps going on then all girls, out of desperation and misery, will do anything.'

It was a pointless waste of human life. Yet the longer it continued, the more convinced each side became that their desired outcome could be the only possible solution. The Chechens continued to accuse the Russians of genocide, and the Russians declared the Chechens were terrorists. With every death the passion, rhetoric and blaming grew stronger.

High on the Russians' list of evildoers was one Akhmed Zakayev. Now living in exile in London, Zakayev had an impressive and unorthodox resume: renowned Shakespearean actor; Chechen Minister of Culture; rebel commander; security adviser; peace negotiator; Deputy Prime Minister; and special envoy to President Aslan Maskhadov. Recently he had added: friend of Vanessa Redgrave, who was sponsoring his stay in Britain; and one of Russia's most wanted men.

I bundled up Nik and my camera gear and headed to London to meet the man the Russians alleged was behind the Dubrovka Theatre siege. If travelling alone with a full camera kit plus tripod had been a challenge before, adding an adventurous fourteen-month-old with pram, toys and winter clothing was ridiculous. Even before we boarded I'd managed to lose him down a luggage chute at Sheremetyevo Airport while checking in our mountain of paraphernalia. Nik toddled up and down the aisle for the entire four-hour flight and by the time we arrived in London at 4 am Moscow time, I was a bleary-eyed wreck.

Zakayev was perfectly charming, a Chechen Richard Burton. He calmly declared that Vladmir Vladmirovich Putin was a war criminal who must take responsibility for the genocide of the Chechens. All terrorist acts in Moscow — the apartment bombings, the theatre siege, the metro — along with those in other cities, were the work of the Russian special forces. Yes, some Chechens had been involved, but their acts were a response to having lost relatives to Russian barbarity. Aslan Maskhadov was still the rightful elected leader of the Chechen authorities and he was still his special envoy. Akhmad Kadyrov was no more than Putin's homicidal hatchetman and no good would ever come of his rule. And no, he, Zakayev, wasn't a terrorist.

Two months later, on 9 May, President Kadyrov was killed in an explosion during a Victory Day parade in Grozny's main stadium. Immediately the Kremlin appointed his unlovely son, the shifty-eyed 27-year-old Ramzan, to the post of Deputy Prime Minister. In three years he would be President. Magomad would spend the next winter locked up in a Grozny prison while a petrified Alissa bore their third child. Peace in Chechnya seemed an impossible fantasy.

In the meantime, back in Moscow after my meeting with Zakayev, I found myself in a skinhead's bedroom. He was showing me his favourite trophy, a gold tooth he'd knocked out of one of the people he'd beaten.

'See, it's a tooth, a human tooth, made of gold,' he laughed excitedly. 'He was unconscious and I wanted to take something to remind me of him.'

Usually he just souvenired their hats. The buff, tattooed nineteen-year-old pulled a shoebox from his bedroom cupboard and waved his headwear collection at me one by one, identifying them as he went.

'This is from a Rasta. This is what the trans-Caucasians wear. This is what rappers wear, those ones like monkeys. This is a Muslim's cap, they wear these hats around and pray, Allah Akhbar and all that shit.'

Maxim, who preferred to go by his street name, 'Tesach' (Hatchet), lived with his mum at the rich end of town. His bedroom was plastered with posters of bodybuilders — and his hero, Adolf Hitler. Their flat, in northwest Moscow's Krilatskoye district, was just a few buildings away from Boris Yeltsin's apartment. His mother pottered in the kitchen, baking biscuits, while Tesach bragged to me of his conquests. She seemed scared of him.

'People say that skinheads are fascists or Nazis but in actual fact we are racists. Racism is a love of one's race, nothing more, nothing less. I don't see anything bad in that. Our goal is for the supremacy of the white race on the whole planet. Not like now where we are ashamed to say that we are white, that we are Aryans. We need to stand up proudly and say "We are Aryans" and kill all negroes and Chinese, Jews and trans-Caucasians. Just kill them all so there are none left. We will kill a lot of people because only seven per cent of people on the planet are white.'

It was the September 1999 Moscow apartment bombings that ignited the architecture student's murderous rage against non-Slavs. His girlfriend had been asleep in her bedroom on Kashirskoye Shosse when a massive bomb blast flattened the building. As he picked through the rubble of her home, dust still rising from the ruins, he realised it was his 'destiny' to fight the scourge of non-Slavic immigrants to the Russian Federation.

'When I knew that Chechens had done it I hated them so much I wanted to kill them all. One of my classmates said, "Let's go to the market and have a pogrom, kill some trans-Caucasian." They all said yeah, yeah, but no one went. They were all afraid. So I went alone onto the street with a knife, wild with fury. I was young back then, and saw a group of people who said, "Come along with us and kill some trans-Caucasians." They were skinheads. After I had killed one then I understood that was what I needed to do.'

I gulped as Tesach went on, telling me how he now believes it is his patriotic duty as a Slav to 'cleanse' Moscow of non-Russians — Azerbaijani traders, African students, Central Asian passersby. The police never stop him.

'They see us going down the street and say, "Good on you skinheads. I'd do the same thing but I can't, I'm in uniform."' Tesach chuckled. 'They understand we are cleansing the city of this black-arsed scum.'

I'd met this bitter young man at a skinhead rally outside Moscow's White House. Galya was working so I'd had to take Nik with me, pushing his pram through the snow in minus twenty degree temperatures, camera gear on my back. An assortment of neo-Nazis, ultra-nationalists and Slavic supremacists watched on in bewilderment as I unpacked my camera, rocking Nik's pram back and forth with my foot to keep him asleep.

To gain Tesach's confidence, I found myself telling the story of Eric being caught up in a suicide bombing in Iraq. My bald Aryan toddler with round grey-blue eyes was the ideal prop, even in a beanie with his eyes shut. 'He nearly lost his father thanks to Islamic extremists,' I said, pointing at my chubby sleeping son and feeling decidedly unclean. 'So I understand how you feel.'

Since then, Tesach had come to trust me enough to invite me to film with his friends. He took me to a suburban basement gym where he pumped iron with mates 'so they'd be prepared for battle'. When the security guard tried to stop me bringing in my camera, Tesach had reassured him. 'It's OK, she's one of us.' He puffed up his chest as I shot him striding purposefully through suburban metro stations, daggers in his eyes at anyone darker than Putin.

'Basically all normal people support us. If you're beating a trans-Caucasian in the metro they start to say, "What are you doing?" Then they see it's a Caucasian and say, "Oh one of them, then it's OK."'

Shockingly there was some truth to Tesach's staggering assertion. Xenophobia against non-ethnic Russians was becoming almost mainstream in Russia as hundreds of thousands of migrants from the independent states on the edge of the old empire flocked to Russian cities in search of work. Once they had all been Soviet citizens. But after the USSR's collapse, society began to split along ethnic lines. As jobs became scarcer and crime rates rocketed many *Russkys* (ethnic Russians) began to openly resent their former comrades. The most despised were the darker-skinned peoples from Central Asia — the Tajiks and Uzbeks who provided cheap labour on construction sites — and those from the Caucasus region — Georgians, Armenians, Azeris — who ran most of the market produce stalls, selling fresh fruit and vegetables from the warmer southern republics. The Tajiks sold drugs, and the stereotypical Chechen was a mafiosi who controlled hotels and restaurants. To Tesach, they were all 'black-arses'.

To prove his point, Tesach played me a videotape of his group's leader, a mean-mouthed thug who went by the name of 'Buz', being interviewed on the popular weekly prime-time Sunday night current affairs show *Namedni* (*The Other Day*).

From a comfortable studio chair, Buz gave his take on the recent murder of an Azeri vegetable vendor, brutally bashed to death at his stall by a gang of teenage skinheads.

'We really approve of this murder. In fact, it is humanitarian to kill hundreds of enemies as soon as possible so they understand where their place is,' he stated with chilling assurance. 'Russians are dying out. We are in a state of war. Murders, slavery, it is all from the blacks. We will raise a generation of heroes who have their songs, their martyrs. For us this is a real war for the whites and nothing will stop it, not even bullets.'

The interviewer nodded. The tape momentarily went black, then another story began. A blonde presenter in a tailored suit began to read from her notes, enunciating her words crisply.

'Our poll showed that seventy per cent of Russians support the deportation of Caucasian people from large Russian towns.'

Tesach flicked the tape off and gave me a chilling stare.

'You see how many people agree with us?'

Tesach and his hard-core neo-Nazis had recently split off from another of Moscow's many ultra-nationalist groups, the People's National Party. The PNP were openly racist, led by the suave and egomaniacal forty-something Alexander Sukharevsky. Describing his philosophy as 'Russist', Sukharevsky claimed to have 15,000 followers across Russia. They invited me to attend a meeting at their headquarters near Belorussky Station in central Moscow. I watched on as Sukharevsky, a forceful orator, preached to his entranced young audience of the need to create an ethnically pure Russian state.

'Russian people always stand for justice,' he bellowed to the enraptured teens. 'It's in our mentality, it's in our blood. But our Asians don't have such an understanding of justice. They have different genes … God created them differently. For them the most important thing is to rule their neighbour, to beat him up, to become his master.'

The PNP was planning an initiation ceremony in a forest on the outskirts of Moscow and I asked if I could go along. Noticing Sukharevsky's dubious look, I again told the story of Eric in Iraq. That settled it.

A few days later I left Nik with Galya and caught a train out of Moscow with forty or so tattooed teenagers with shining pates. Some carried black flags with swastikas, others bore the double-headed eagle insignias of Imperial Russia. Others had banners with the Russian Orthodox cross.

'This shows that God supports us,' explained its bearer, a bleached-blonde girl with a black armband.

From the station we trudged for kilometres through a birch forest deep in snow. The kids marched and chanted alternately: 'Slava Rossiya' ('Glory to Russia') and 'Nasha Rodina — SSR!' ('Our Motherland — USSR!'). They seemed to be working themselves into some kind of frenzy and my gut churned in trepidation. Might they possibly be leading me out into the wintry wilderness to perform some freaky sacrifice of the invading Antipodean?

We finally reached a clearing and the contingent assembled in rows before Sukharevsky. He stood solemnly, flanked by flag-bearers, inhaled deeply and began his spiel.

'Jews and Muslims and our enemies say that this is a swastika,' he roared over the wind. 'No, I say. This is more than a swastika. It is two swastikas — a left and a right swastika. It is the cross of final and irreversible triumph.'

The mesmerised teens nodded, many apparently overcome with the intensity of the moment. Sukharevsky went on, appointing one of his protégés, a macho eighteen-year-old called Ines, as the PNP's head of the Moscow region.

'Dignity, honour and purity of blood, and propagandising the word of Russism, of a pure white race in Europe and the whole world. That is your challenge!' he shouted at Ines.

'I believe until death,' Ines yelled in response.

The initiation was followed by a pagan Slavic ritual involving ancestor worship, sword fights in costumes of ancient Rus, declarations of future victory and the blessing of swastikas. The kids downed berry wine to cement their oaths. A comely brunette called Lena explained that they could never, ever drink the grape-based variety. 'Grapes are grown in the south, and we will only consume the foods of our ancestors.'

Lena was a seventeen-year-old law student who had taken her oath of lifelong allegiance to the PNP three years ago. She saw the elimination of non-Slavs from her motherland as her patriotic duty.

'I don't think there's any other way. We need protest so that the government will introduce certain measures. If it doesn't, then we will prepare a mass Russian protest and agitate all towards a national revolution. I want my white children to have a bright future, that they live in a normal Russian community. I want them to be free people who respect their history and their people. I don't want them to become slaves to these black-arsed idiots. I want that if I let them go to a concert that they return alive and well, and that nothing happens, not in the metro or at the concert.'

Lena would have been wearing fluffy white bows in kindergarten when I first heard the Soviet rhetoric of fraternal harmony between all ethnic groups. I remembered Olga's brother, Igor, telling me how it 'really was true, that in the USSR, everyone was friends'. How could things have changed so much? What had happened to this country?

A few days earlier I'd met an effervescent Armenian woman, Natalya Amirova, whose husband, Artur, had been bashed to a pulp by skinheads as he came out of a metro station. He died two days later in hospital. Ten months on, Natalya, a bottle-blonde Russian speaker who had fled violence in her homeland a decade ago, was afraid for her and her children's lives. Their haven had become a hell-hole and they had nowhere to escape. We sat on her couch in the shabby bedsit she shared with her son and daughter on Moscow's periphery and she showed me her passport. I noticed that the 'fifth line', indicating *natsionalnost* (ethnicity) was no longer there. But its removal from official Russian identification documents had not helped Artur.

'Look, see, we are Muscovites, Russian citizens. But the skinheads see that your skin is darker, that you are from the Caucasus, that you are black ... and they beat you anyway.'

Natalya's son, Jan, had survived his own attack and now rarely left the flat. The only work he could find was packing bread into bags at a nearby factory. Her twenty-year-old daughter, Sabrina, was too spooked to go further than the grounds around their building. Without official residency documents, and with their Caucasian looks, accents and names, the Amirovs had no chance of finding decent work. Natalya supported them all by working as a hairdresser for other refugees.

'I earn money myself. I don't even want the kids to go outside, to go where they could earn more money, because they would need to go into the city and to go out like that means that every day I'll be sitting here, praying, and waiting to see whether they will come back alive or not.'

I'd recently seen a spine-chilling TV news report about a nine-year-old Tajik girl who had been bashed to death by skinheads in St Petersburg. Tesach thought it was a good thing.

'She only would have grown up to sell drugs like her father or do some other shit. Why feel sorry for a rat? Some said why kill a little rat when she hadn't done anything? But she would have grown up to do something, so why not kill her while she's small?'

Even Lena, the future lawyer and mother, agreed.

'I was very glad that they killed her, although some ordinary people said that it was bestial, that it wasn't fair for five people to kill her, that it was inhuman to do that to a nine-year-old girl who couldn't fight back. But as a result of them killing her, her mother said that she wouldn't come back to Russia, so that is already a plus. We have done something with our actions.'

I listened in horror as they spoke so clinically of the murder of a child, swallowing my disgust and nodding so they'd continue talking. Tesach's group weren't stupid. They knew the money-making potential of selling footage of their rallies to foreign journalists and made sure each and every action was documented in a saleable format. I agreed to pay USD$100 a minute for images of a gang march past the Kremlin. Stomping black boots, ranting and chanting, swastikas flapping. They'd even hired a decent cameraman for the shoot.

I was in a panic, finishing interviews, packing up the flat to leave Moscow and return to Australia. Mum had gone home, Galya was sick and Eric was in Georgia. Unable to pick up the tape, I asked Maksim to bring it to our flat, completely forgetting I had asked Magomad to help me translate the Chechen interviews that afternoon. Magomad and I were painstakingly rewinding and re-listening to a sobbing widow's terrible tale, him translating into Russian, me into English, when the phone rang. The skinheads were downstairs.

A terrible vision flashed before me: my friend Magomad's bloodied corpse lying on our floor, little Nik watching his final death throes. I begged Magomad's forgiveness and led him, the former Deputy Prosecutor for the Chechen Ministry of the Interior, to the now empty wardrobe in Nik's room.

We flew out of Moscow the next day. For the first time, I wasn't sorry to leave.

31

Putin and Politkovskaya

Stalin and Truman are arguing whether there is more freedom in the USSR or in the USA. Truman says: 'In the USA, anybody can shout, "Down with Truman!" in front of the White House.' Stalin replies: 'Anybody can shout, "Down with Truman!" in Red Square too.'

October 2004

Journalist Anna Politkovskaya didn't go out of her way to make friends. The likelihood of such a forceful personality surviving to a pensionable age, let alone dying a natural death, was as unlikely as a peace agreement in Chechnya. And if it wasn't the FSB, Chechen or Russian bandits, or any one of the myriad others she had managed to infuriate who were going to kill her, then for one brief moment it might almost have been me. I'd been warned of her 'capricious' and difficult nature, but given that she'd agreed to an interview, I didn't imagine she'd direct her fury at me.

'We work under conditions where there is no kind of freedom of speech and that's it,' she snapped when I asked her to describe the hazards for journalists in Putin's Russia. 'There's no point in telling you the details. The West isn't interested in these things. They just need good conditions for trade and that's it. But that we are working like somewhere in an African state, where there's a dictator, that doesn't concern you. I explain the details constantly, but then Western leaders come here and hug and kiss Putin anyway.'

With that she turned her back and continued flicking through her emails. I pressed pause on my camera and contemplated my options. I'd come all the way to Moscow from Sydney, thirty-five miserable hours squirming in economy class via Frankfurt, to do a story on the muzzling of Russian media. Anna Politkovskaya, the fearless heroine journalist of one of the few remaining independent newspapers in Russia, *Novaya Gazeta,* was to be the central figure.

I'd long admired her gutsy reporting, particularly from war-torn Chechnya. Politkovskaya was one of the few Russian journalists who defied government media restrictions on reporting from the republic. Despite being detained, harassed and once subjected to a mock execution, she continued to carry out her investigations. She had even talked her way into the besieged Dubrovka Theatre during the October 2002 hostage crisis and relayed the separatists' demands to the media outside.

Now I was finally sitting next to her, camera poised to shoot, and she wouldn't even look up from her computer screen. I wanted to pack up and get the hell out of there, but I couldn't. Somehow I had to convince her to talk. I cleared my throat and tried again.

'Have the dangers increased since Putin came to power?'

She rolled her eyes. I knew it was a dumb question, but I needed her to answer it, preferably in a complete sentence, without scowling and while looking at the camera. Even twitching seven-year-old glue-sniffing street kids had been easier to interview.

'Of course it's dangerous,' she replied haughtily. 'When Putin came to power the authorities didn't permit anyone to enter Chechnya and cover the war who didn't work with the military. But it doesn't mean anything, because it's part of our profession and I don't think it's a tragedy. Either you work as a journalist in Russia and understand that it's a risky profession ... when a miner goes into a mine he also knows that he might be killed, so it's the same for us.'

A whole sentence — hooray! Buoyed by this success, I went on. What I needed her to describe was how she'd just been poisoned on a flight from Moscow to the North Ossetian town of Beslan. A month earlier, on 1 September, the first day of the new school year, a group of armed men and women seized Beslan School Number One, taking children, teachers and parents hostage. Politkovskaya immediately called Aslan Maskhadov (still considered Chechnya's president by his supporters) and asked him to negotiate with the hostage takers. She then boarded a flight to cover the unfolding drama for *Novaya Gazeta*. But she never made it to Beslan. While hundreds of journalists reached the town unhindered, Politkovskaya fell unconscious on the plane after drinking a cup of tea. When more than three hundred hostages, most of them children, died two days later in a bungled attack on the school, Politkovskaya lay in a hospital ward. Medical tests suggested she was poisoned.

In short, she had every reason to be cranky.

The former USSR was rapidly gaining a reputation as one of the world's most dangerous places for journalists, with 148 dying of unnatural causes since 1992. It wasn't clear who the culprits were because most of the murders were never officially investigated. Oleg Panfilov, at Moscow's Centre for Journalism in Extreme Situations, had done his own research, concluding that while some were the work of *biznesmeny* eliminating pesky reporters who'd exposed their devious doings, many more could be linked to the authorities.

Murder was at the extreme end of silencing critics. A far easier method was squeezing their employers. One of Putin's first acts on assuming the presidency was to set his tax police onto Vladimir Gusinsky, an oligarch who owned the closest thing Russia had to an independent national television network, NTV. His business affairs were no dirtier than any other oligarch, but it sent a message that meddling with politics would not be tolerated. Within months Gusinsky was in exile and NTV had been taken over by a Kremlin-owned company. NTV's news managers were sacked and once-critical programs were tamed or axed.

A recent casualty was a panel show I used to watch called *Svoboda Slova* (Freedom of Speech). The host was a personable, sharp-witted journalist called Savik Shuster who led lively and often unruly debates on controversial subjects to an audience of millions. But in July 2004, the high-rating show was canned without explanation. I wondered if officials were even embarrassed by the symbolism of closing a show called *Freedom of Speech*.

Savik Shuster was happy to talk about what happened. Then again, he didn't have much else to do with his time. He was still employed by NTV, but doing 'special projects'.

'There wasn't an official reason for axing the program,' he told me in his office at Ostankino. 'One reason they gave was that I was being promoted to deputy general director responsible for documentary films. So basically it's the usual story in Russia where you demote by promoting. But I think that a program like that cannot exist now, because it's absolutely uncontrollable from the point of view of the Kremlin, it's impossible to control, it's live, and whatever happens, happens.'

To the Kremlin, control was everything. Journalists were in a state of paralysis. Simply observing and reporting on events had become a risky business. For Shuster, the coverage of the Beslan tragedy — the biggest news story of the year — was yet another example of the state attempting to manipulate reporting to suit their purposes.

'Here at NTV, nobody took any decisions because they were afraid: "What should we show? What shouldn't we show?" Everybody was waiting for a decision to come from the Kremlin, and therefore it was a mess. People, viewers, the country, they did not understand the proportions of a possible tragedy because immediately there was an order to say there were 354 hostages.'

In fact there were over a thousand. The residents of Beslan knew the figure given in state broadcasts was a blatant lie, and even the journalists knew it was a gross underestimate. But government orders and fear of punishment won out over truth. Some families of the trapped hostages were so furious at the Russian journalists for giving false information they beat them in the street.

'We have no journalism any more,' lamented Shuster. 'The press is absolutely disoriented. It doesn't know how to function because nobody knows where censorship begins and where it ends.'

When federal security forces began to storm the school's gymnasium in the early afternoon of 3 September, the other two national TV stations began playing movies. Only NTV continued to broadcast live. Russian troops were shown firing from tanks into the building where the hostages were trapped, causing a wall to collapse which potentially resulted in mass fatalities. That footage was never seen again. Every subsequent report carefully doctored the story to avoid the fact that the military was likely responsible for the deaths of one hundred people.

Three weeks after the Beslan tragedy, President Putin addressed journalists at a press conference.

'In your hand is a powerful informational tool which is able to both divide and unite the world community. I am certain that in these conditions of a global terrorist threat, when people are killed, the mass media cannot be simply observers.'

To Shuster, Putin's pronouncement reeked of the old days, when media was nothing more than a propaganda tool for the Kremlin. 'Journalists', or rather 'propagandists', were given the task of portraying their leaders as infallible and heroic fathers of the nation, defending the motherland from implacable and cunning enemies — be they counter-revolutionaries, Nazi Germany, the capitalist West with its nukes, or any number of other evils threatening Soviet utopia.

In the Yeltsin years, television had experimented with investigative journalism and critical scrutiny of politicians. But now the daily news was becoming uncannily reminiscent of Soviet days. First came a chronicle of the leader's day: Putin visiting a collective farm, Putin shaking hands with foreign dignitaries, Putin signing important documents, Putin doing a spot of karate … The message: 'Our strong, fit leader has everything under control and he even has time to care about the little people.' Then would come the stories of the wicked enemies hell-bent on the destruction of the motherland — international terrorists, Chechens, NATO, the US …

At least viewers knew their strong, fit leader had it all under control.

'We are now at a critical point,' Anna Politkovskaya had told me when she finally realised I wasn't going away. 'Will democracy be not even remembered in a year? Will mass media just carry out a purely decorative role as they did in the Soviet Union … to tell of the success of the authorities and of nothing else? If democratic freedoms will be preserved, then it's possible that the press may develop, but at the moment I don't believe it's likely.'

Few Russians seemed to want to hear Politkovskaya's message. Many saw her criticism of their country's leaders and their actions as traitorous and destructive. 'Keep the rubbish inside the house', was a mantra I heard regularly. They were almost as hyper-sensitive to foreigners. I had often felt people's hackles rise defensively at the slightest negative comment about their country — its history, traditions, rulers and their policies — as if it were a personal slight against them as an individual. It seemed bizarre to me. It wasn't that I didn't like my country, but if someone said something against Australia, it never affected me personally. Back home, whingeing about politicians — past and present — was a national sport. But in Russia it was not only unpatriotic — it was downright dangerous.

Politkovskaya nevertheless felt a calling. Despite the entreaties of her anxious children for her to leave the profession, she felt she would be a traitor to do so.

'I personally believed things would get better, that the war would end and then I could have the right to live peacefully,' she told me. 'But every year gets more complicated than the last. So I explain to my children that I can't stop, because that would mean betraying people. Less and less newspapers write about what I and my colleagues are writing about. To leave journalism would be a great present for the Kremlin. So I have written my will and prepared my children for the fact that at any moment they may be left alone, without me. They have all instructions from me in this case.'

It was dedication way beyond anything I could imagine.

I returned to Sydney and squeezed Nik. I could understand Anna's fierce determination to make a difference, to write about what was really happening: the injustice, the corruption, the nepotism. But if she, with her international profile and shelves full of awards, wasn't managing to make a jot of difference, what could I hope to do? Her children were already young adults. Nik wasn't even two. And though

I desperately wanted to tell the Chechen story, back in Australia no one really cared. There was infinite appetite for reports on American misdeeds in Iraq, but Russian atrocities in Chechnya didn't hold the same appeal to producers.

My mum had been looking after Nik while I was away and flew back to Melbourne the day I arrived in Sydney. We had no childcare and Eric was back at work, planning a trip to South America for the ABC's *Foreign Correspondent* program. I took Nik into SBS and plonked him in front of the bank of monitors in the newsroom where he could watch BBC World, CNN, or any number of international TV news broadcasts, while I tried to write a script and edit my story. Jet-lagged and fatigued, I didn't feel well. At home I worked until late into the night after I'd put Nik to bed, then was kept awake by strange throbbing and aches in my body. Something wasn't right.

It would be months before I finally got an accurate diagnosis of the cause of my painful joints. By then I couldn't lift Nik, could barely hold a knife or even a pen, and walking was agony. My left knee was so swollen I could hardly bend my leg and in the mornings I was so stiff that just getting out of bed was a monumental struggle. The GP prescribed insoles for my shoes. Nothing improved. In desperation, I googled 'swollen joints'. The words 'Rheumatoid Arthritis' popped onto the screen and I read the list of symptoms. I had every single one, bar a positive blood test result for 'rheumatoid factor'.

Two days before my thirty-fifth birthday in April 2005, I sat nervously in the GP's office. Eric had left for five weeks in Africa the day before. The doctor scanned his printout from the pathology laboratory.

'Ah, yes,' he said. 'You've tested positive for the rheumatoid factor. I'm afraid there is no cure. You'll have to see a specialist.'

Images from my past flashed before me. RA was in my family. Both my paternal grandparents had it. A great aunt on my mother's side was so severely afflicted she'd been confined to a wheelchair from the age of twenty-one. I remembered visiting Great Auntie Bon in her nursing home, a hunched and shrivelled old lady with hands twisted like claws. She hadn't walked in decades. I thought of Granny and Grandpa Traill

455

— their bulbous knuckles and gnarled fingers, their walking sticks and in-home care. But they hadn't got it until they were in their sixties. I was only thirty-four. My boy was only two.

I was unable to speak. The doctor arranged an urgent appointment with a rheumatologist and I hobbled home. I'd taken a job at the ABC, organising logistics for a documentary series about the re-creation of a one-hundred-year-old car rally from Peking to Paris. In just six weeks I was supposed to fly to Beijing to spend two months crossing Eurasia. I called in and explained what had happened. As word got around, the house filled with flowers. That night I sat alone with Nik feeling like I was in a funeral parlour. He could see I was sad and patted my knee. 'Mummy ... you'll be okay.'

The rheumatologist filled me with steroids and within days I was pain-free enough to take the trip — sixty days of bumping and rattling through northern China, the Gobi Desert, across Siberia to Moscow and on to Paris.

But the steroids were a temporary fix. When I returned, I started a new regime of scarily named 'Disease-Modifying Anti-Rheumatic Drugs', which would prevent the crippling bone deformation characteristic of RA. Without them, the rheumatologist said, I would be crippled in five years. The drugs made me throw up and my hair fall out. They weakened my immune system and I kept getting sick. My knee continued to swell and the doctor had to drain out the fluid with a fat needle. There were X-rays, bone scans and constant blood tests.

Eric was back in Russia and I struggled to look after Nik. Mum came up to stay and help out — but I was worn out and depressed. I lay on the couch watching Nik play, thinking of all the things I'd wanted to do with him. My future seemed to have vanished. Was my son only ever going to know his mother as a cripple?

Eventually the drugs began to work their magic. The dull aching never completely faded but I realised I had no choice but to learn to live with it. I kept telling myself I would get back to film-making one day, but deep down I knew that if I ever did, it would be a long time away. For now, I was Nik's mum. Finally I managed to accept that that was enough.

In early October 2006, exactly two years after I'd met Politkovskaya in Moscow, she was assassinated. I was in Bali with Eric and Nik at a writer's festival when I heard she'd been found shot dead in the lift of her apartment building, a pistol and four shell casings beside her body. The identity of her assailants was a mystery. I felt numb. As a person there was no doubt she'd been difficult. But as a journalist she'd been extraordinary.

More than one thousand people attended her funeral, mourning not just her death, but the end of free speech.

32

Moscow Revisited

January 2007

It was a national holiday but it felt like a war zone. I woke to the sound of rockets whistling through the air, some exploding with ear-splitting cracks outside my window near the Kremlin, others thudding and booming on the outskirts of town. Whoops rose from the street, followed by the sound of glass shattering.

The alcohol-fuelled pyromania had begun at around 5 pm on New Year's Eve, as crowds of sozzled Muscovites stumbled toward Red Square, letting off fireworks as they shouted, sang and smashed vodka bottles on the pot-holed alleyways. In my jet-lagged delirium I dreamed the Nazis were invading again, and half-expected a shell to blow a hole in the side of the building.

The mayhem was still going on five days later as I waited for Olga on the kerb of Bolshoi Znamenski Lane in central Moscow, admiring the golden domes of the Christ the Saviour Cathedral. The original had been the world's biggest Orthodox Church until Stalin ordered its demolition in December 1931. Rebuilding had taken a decade and cost USD$250 million, much of it rumoured to be laundered money from Mafia tycoons. Encased in bronze, gold and white marble it was almost an exact replica of the 1860s Tsarist cathedral, save for the three-storey underground car park the BMW-driving Church boss, Patriarch Alexei II of Moscow and All Russia, had demanded.

Olga pulled up in her slush-splattered Peugeot, jumped out and we embraced. Tyoma, now nine, sat in the back seat with a neighbour's son, Artur. Both boys were madly pressing buttons on their beeping mobiles. Tyoma grunted a 'Hi!' in my direction. A year and a half had gone by since Olga and I had seen each other, when I'd passed through Moscow on the Peking to Paris expedition in June 2005, but with cheap phone calls and email, that time had flown. Today she seemed unusually weary as we drove north through Moscow on amazingly traffic-free eight-lane roads.

On a typical weekday it would take an hour and a half to drive the 26 kilometres from her home to her work at Khimki, out near Sheremetyevo Airport. This had been her routine for seven years, ever since the world's largest IKEA store opened in 2000, incongruously located behind a row of iron crosses marking the limit of the Nazi advance in December 1941. With a daily dose of three hours of road-raging Muscovites, it was no wonder she looked drained.

It was 5 January 2007, and the country was still hungover after the whopping 'New' New Year celebrations. And with 'Old' New Year coming up on 13 January, there would soon be yet another excuse to crack open a bottle of vodka or three. As of the previous year, President Putin had decided that with such an excess of revelry and alcohol-related absenteeism, he might as well declare extra-long national New Year holidays. I'd picked the wrong time to visit old friends. Those who could had fled the madness of one of the world's most expensive and congested cities — Olga and Misha to their dacha, Sergei to the Seychelles. Even Nadia was enjoying a 'rest' in a sanatorium near Moscow. But those who couldn't get out were still drunkenly setting off fireworks, oblivious to the fact clocks had struck midnight five days earlier.

Olga didn't think much of the new super-long holiday. Everything was shut, there was nothing to do and all but the very rich had run out of money. Even the ice-skating rink on Red Square was prohibitively costly for most. The country seemed to be going crazy with boredom.

We were heading to her family's dacha at Tryokhgorka, just north of Moscow. I hadn't been there for years, but dimly remembered a humble weatherboard cottage, painted dark green, surrounded by Misha's mother's flower and vegetable garden. The sunflowers had almost glowed in the summer sun as insects buzzed impatiently around their petals. The toilet was a pit in a shed outside and accommodation snug. Misha had been toiling away out there every weekend for the last five years and I was keen to see the results.

I'd also been looking forward to a crisp white Russian winter — sort of. But something very strange was going on. I'd come prepared for the usual nostril-hair snapping temperatures of minus twenty degrees and below, but in the few days I'd been here so far it had barely dipped below zero. What little powdery snow that had fallen on New Year's Eve had quickly melted into black puddles. Now I was sweating, both disappointed and relieved. It was my first winter here since being diagnosed with rheumatoid arthritis, and I was unsure how my aching joints would react to extreme cold. And if this one degree heat wave continued, I wouldn't get a chance to find out.

Olga couldn't understand it either. The previous winter temperatures had hovered around minus thirty-five for seven weeks in a row. Every time she wanted to go anywhere she had to dig her car out from a snowy tomb, and then it wouldn't start. This winter was the warmest in a hundred years. It had even been raining all December. Was it global warming? What was a Russia winter without snow?

A fit of hysterical giggles came from the back seat. We turned to find the boys peering at Tyoma's new mobile phone/camera/MP3 player, his much nagged-for New Year's present. Olga had tried to convince him he didn't need it, but he was the only kid in his class without one. Now it was playing a chirpy song with George Bush's head on a dancing demon stick figure.

'Bush is such an idiot,' sniggered Artur.

Times *had* changed. In 1990, young people idolised the US. These days a ten-year-old's ridicule knew no bounds. Back then, there was a decade-long waiting list to get landlines installed. Now, I'd just read in the *Moscow Times*, mobile penetration into the country had reached 100 per cent. Even the reindeer herders in the Arctic north were carrying phones on their dog sleds.

The forest of billboards along the freeway's edge was denser than ever: bikini-clad models with mobile phones or cigarettes, busty blondes in lacy undergarments sprawling over glossy sports vehicles. Behind them were mega-stores selling building materials, garden tools, even a motorbike showroom. Just before a complex of almost completed apartment towers, a sign indicated the turn-off to Tryokhgorka. I blinked. The countryside had vanished. Tryokhgorka was now practically a suburb of Moscow. Five new skyscrapers stood in a staggered row, each twenty-five storeys high, looming up from what was once a field of sunflowers and potatoes. They were, explained Olga, yet another project of Moscow mayor Yuri Luzhkov's wife.

The fearsome Elena Baturina owned a construction company, which curiously seemed to win almost all the city government's building contracts. She was now the richest woman in Russia, with an estimated fortune of more than three billion US dollars. And with Moscow's soaring real estate prices — already among the highest in the world — she was growing ever wealthier.

We turned off onto an unsealed road into the once sleepy village, now overshadowed by the towering flats.

'Nobody is happy about it, but nobody is doing anything,' Olga mused. 'It's the Russian way. We sit in our kitchens and complain, but do nothing.'

At the edge of the village, she pulled up at a high metal fence and opened a gate, revealing a three-storey brick house. No trace remained of the original cottage, inherited by Misha's mother from elderly childless relatives who had worked in the Tryokhgorka textile factory in the 1930s. Misha came to greet us; his hair neatly combed as always, jeans pulled high. The boys disappeared and Misha showed me through their new home, built from plans bought online from a St Petersburg architect. The ground floor had a large room devoted to an expansive heating system for the whole house, plus a bathroom and several storerooms. The next level had a kitchen and dining area overlooking the neighbouring woods in one direction, and a spacious living area with balcony and study with views towards Ms Baturina's new high-rises in the other. The top floor had three generous bedrooms and another bathroom. I looked out over the 'village', now a sea of similarly imposing houses, many with three-metre-high fences, barbed wire, CCTV surveillance, armed guards and savage Rottweilers. The old Tryokhgorka had all but disappeared.

Despite their pride in their new house, Olga and Misha were gloomy. Over bowls of *pelmeni,* Misha described how the once peaceful forest next to the house was now devoid of wildlife, bar packs of roaming feral dogs. One had attacked and bitten Tyoma. There was rubbish everywhere: broken bottles, abandoned cars and stinking bags of household garbage. Illegal hunting and fishing were wiping out Russia's wildlife. Pollution was worsening by the day. He told of Chinese traders bribing Siberian police to turn a blind eye to their illegal wood felling. Whole forests in Siberia and the Far East were fast disappearing on trains to China. I'd seen them as I'd crossed Mongolia a year and a half earlier — twenty or thirty wagons long, stacked high with logs. Trucks laden with twisted metal were following the same route: stolen pipelines, copper wires, anything of value. In Siberia I'd even seen an entire road being pilfered. We'd tried to drive along a remote back road, only to find a crane lifting giant slabs of steel-reinforced concrete into the back of a truck.

'Our government is only concerned with the oil and gas industry,' said Olga. 'They don't put any money into developing the country. But most people aren't educated enough to understand what is going on. They expect the government will do the right thing. But the government doesn't care. They aren't looking long term. They just think, "Well, I'll be dead anyway so I may as well do what I like now."' She shrugged her shoulders. 'A couple of weeks ago, I heard an opinion on Ekho Moskvy — the alternative radio station — that the government thinks that a population of twenty-five million in Russia [of a current population of 142 million] is enough to run the oil and gas pipes, and everyone else can just die.'

I could hardly believe I was hearing this from Olga. Even she had lost faith. People had changed, said Misha. The country had changed. Everyone was afraid, no one trusted anyone and no one had time to be friendly or helpful. Olga had driven her car into a ditch by the road a couple of times, trying to let pedestrians by, and become bogged. Once people would have stopped to help. Now it was every man for himself.

'And this business with the Georgians is just ridiculous.'

'What business with the Georgians?'

The day before I'd been mystified to find Moscow's normally bustling markets almost empty. Bare tables bore signs indicating the spaces were for rent. I assumed the big supermarket chains were putting the little guys out of business, or perhaps everyone was on holidays. Instead, Putin had decided to retaliate after Georgia's president Mikhail Saakashvili arrested Russian officers in Tbilisi, and threatened to kick out Russia's military base and join NATO.

'After the row, police cracked down on Georgians,' said Misha. 'They closed casinos, declaring that gaming tables that had been there for ten years were illegal, and then they threw all the Georgian traders out of Moscow. There's even a boycott on Georgian wine and mineral water. My mum went to buy some shoes from a Georgian with a stall on the outskirts of Moscow and he was packing up to leave. Even the tandoori bakery near our flat is empty. Putin says that it's about protecting the interests of "native Russians". But I think it's just stupid propaganda.'

I could just imagine Tesach the skinhead and Lena the Russist rubbing their hands with glee. But I couldn't see them hawking tomatoes.

Tyoma and Artur were still playing with their mobiles. I asked Tyoma — the grandson of a renowned orchestral conductor — what his favourite music was.

'Black Eyed Peas. They play one of the tunes on my phone.'

He and Artur scuttled off to twiddle with their toys. Misha was vexed.

'We're sending Tyoma to a private school because there are so many problems in the public system — kids of alcoholics and junkies, fighting in the classes. Kids go to class drunk, they sell drugs in the schools. The teachers hardly get paid so they don't turn up and have to take bribes from the kids. But his school is full of rich kids and sometimes he feels left out. There are only seven kids in his class, and one, Anton, is the son of a Novy Russky who sells up-market vehicles — Land Rovers,

Jaguars, Volvos and Mercedes. They have a fifteen-room flat and Anton even has his own cook, nanny and everything money can buy. When Tyoma went to his house, he was dropped back at school in a convertible. The teachers are having lots of problems with Anton's rudeness, but there's nothing they can say as his father is so rich.'

Money talked louder than ever. While Baturina had been able to erect her monumental eyesore without a hitch, it had taken Misha's mum three years of queuing at various departments to 'register' their new dacha. And 'having someone' who could help out with visas, passports and registrations, for a fee of course, was vital to ensure that your requests were actually dealt with. Finding a trustworthy doctor was also crucial. Everyone knew that they received payment from pharmaceutical companies to prescribe expensive medicines, so knowing an honest medic was essential to 'make sure you weren't filled up with too many chemicals'.

After dinner we watched the NTV news. The lead story was about a fisherman who might have disappeared under the ice on Lake Baikal, or possibly not. Then followed a rambling piece on writer Anton Chekhov's crumbling house in Yalta, with interminable close-ups of peeling wallpaper and cracked walls, hardly a novel sight for the average Russian. The international news informed viewers that snow had fallen in the French Alps, and a new tourist attraction in South Africa offered the opportunity to feed white sharks from an underwater cage. That report concluded with a shot of a one-legged man hopping down a beach. The final story was announced, from Israel. At last, I thought, something serious. But alas ... NTV's story from that troubled land showed an English former air stewardess called Lucy, who had set up a farm for homeless and abused donkeys.

We hoped the content was merely a sign of a low-ratings period. Next came an American infomercial, dubbed in Russian. 'Our "natural bra" will solve all your problems,' crooned a sexy female voice. 'You'll look like a princess in any outfit. It's a saviour. If nature has given you problem breasts, we can solve your problems with these silicon cups. You will feel your femininity, you will look so sexy.'

Misha turned off the TV.

'Yeltsin did do some good things,' said Olga. 'He brought freedom of speech to the media and journalists were able to be critical. Remember *Kukli*?' she asked, referring to a weekly satirical puppet show which lampooned politicians with rubbery caricatures. 'Every Friday we were glued to the TV to watch it. It felt okay to criticise him. But now the media is on a short leash, everything is controlled. We only ever hear that everything is okay. Only Ekho Moskvy and the foreign stations show what is really going on, and only a few people can access those.'

Just as troubling was the flood of serials and documentaries praising the marvellous deeds of Lenin and Stalin. Over the past two decades, the telling of Soviet history had made a full circle, from hero worship to condemnation, and back again. The first time around, Olga had believed. Now she knew better.

'They brought nothing but pain and destruction to our country, yet now they are being made into heroes again. Young people, who never heard about the purges, who never saw the queues, they think Lenin and Stalin are true heroes.'

Even Tyoma's state-approved Russian history books were giving the under-tens a strong message about the greatness of their nation's bloodthirsty former autocrats. Olga showed me his textbook, open at a page on Ivan Grozny (Ivan the Terrible), 'Russia's first dictator,' she said. 'It seems this country can't function without one. Perhaps it is because the country is so large that we need strong leaders like Peter the Great, Ivan the Terrible and Stalin. But they all killed for power, and they're still killing for power.'

The following night was Orthodox Christmas Eve, 6 January. I took a train back to Moscow to attend a service led by Patriarch Alexei II, at the Christ the Saviour Cathedral. I was staying at Sergei's empty flat, just a block away, and left half an hour before it was due to start to find the streets cordoned off and busloads of OMON riot police on the prowl.

The queue for the service was just like the old days. Once I'd lined up for bread and the site of this church had been a swimming pool. Now bread went stale in the shops and the people queued for religious salvation. But first they had to pass through a metal detector. The waiting throngs snapped photos of each other on their mobiles, posing in their designer apparel. My coat was seven years old, I had no mobile and was relieved to note some equally unfashionable babushki. But the real surprise on this holiest of eves was the profusion of gangsters with long leather coats, crew-cuts, hi-tech phones and chunky gold jewellery.

After passing the security checks I was swept along through the grand wooden doors and into another queue where people were busily filling out forms. I picked one up. It was titled 'Plenary Indulgences'. Below was a list of options with prices. You could pay the priest to pray for your health, for one month, or three months, or if you signed up for a year you'd get a discount. If you wanted him to pray for others as well, that was extra. Everyone was stuffing envelopes with roubles and dropping them into tall wooden boxes. A thick-necked thug posted his bulging envelope, let out a loud sigh and stepped away lightly, in apparent relief.

The cathedral was chock-full, and despite the cavernous marble interiors felt frighteningly claustrophobic. I wedged myself next to a bearded babushka and let the glorious chanting wash over me. Too short to see any of the incense-swinging action, I could only look up at the breathtaking artisanry: shining new frescoes, an enormous white central altar inlaid with green and pink marble, and a gleaming golden tabernacle.

It was just over seventy-five years since Stalin had ordered the original Cathedral to be dynamited as his ultimate attack on the Orthodox Church. He'd planned to build a monumental 'Palace of the Soviets' on the site, but the foundations kept sinking into the nearby Moscow River. Eventually his successor, Nikita Khrushchev, had the hole turned into the world's biggest public swimming pool. Now the Cathedral was back, tonight teeming with snappily dressed politicians — including Mayor Luzhkov — flanked by bodyguards muttering into their sleeves. Had all these former Communist Party members, once avowedly atheist, really become true believers? Or was this just some elaborate attempt to convince the public that they were good and god-fearing folk, when everyone knew they were corrupt and duplicitous? How could anyone tell?

All I knew was that the more I knew about Russia, the less it made sense.

The transformation of the communist, atheist USSR to capitalist, Orthodix Russia was remarkable. In the sixteen and a half years since my first visit, Moscow had morphed from a dowdy, rundown backwater to a showy, brazen metropolis with more billionaires than anywhere on the planet, and an official ranking of world's most expensive city, 'beating' London, New York and Tokyo.

Even flats in the dilapidated suburban high-rises, with their cracking concrete slab walls and drooping steel-framed balconies, sold for well over USD$4,000 per square metre. The closer one went to the Kremlin, the higher the price. A 'new' apartment in the centre could cost a minimum of USD$8,000 per square metre, and that only got you a floor and walls. Kitchens, bathrooms, even wiring and plumbing were all extra. Yet even at these outrageous prices, property developers were having no trouble finding takers, with new projects sold out even before foundations could be laid.

Construction magnates and their Central Asian labourers had been working overtime since I'd passed through in June 2005. Cranes hovered over building sites planting space-age glass and steel mega-structures. The ornate façades of the gas-works buildings on the embankment opposite the Kremlin were freshly restored. Three-storey high tarpaulins painted with stone window frames and entranceways hung over nearby building works.

Many Soviet-era eyesores had disappeared or were in the process of doing so. The unsightly 3,200-room Rossiya Hotel, which had once stood next to St Basil's Cathedral, had been reduced to a pile of rubble, revealing five miniature onion-domed churches behind the demolition site. And to the north of Red Square, the former Intourist Hotel — another concrete travesty I'd seen detonated a few years earlier — was replaced by a marble and granite faux-nineteenth-century hotel. Once a prime pick-up zone for hookers, there was no longer a prostitute in sight.

The girls might have gone, but the underpass from Red Square still reeked of urine and vomit. Young homeless men, their faces puffy and purplish-red, eyes bruised and swollen, lay amongst broken bottles on cardboard boxes inside the metro entrance. Holiday revellers held their noses, stepped around the bodies, and headed to a Christmas fair in front of the State Historical Museum to guzzle *medovukha* (mead, a traditional winter honey-based drink) and stuff themselves with *pirozhki* and caviar. There was a yurt, shooting gallery, Russian crafts and animal-shaped helium balloons, and very nearly a pleasant carnival atmosphere.

Strolling northeast towards the Lubyanka, I looked into boutique windows: Tiffany, Zegna, Roberto Cavalli, Armani, Dolce & Gabbana — all empty bar bored security guards and salesgirls admiring their own reflections. I crossed Lubyanka Square to the Detski Mir (Children's World) Emporium, where Misha had once queued for hours in the snow to buy a Rubik's Cube. On my first visit, the shelves had been almost bare. Now you could find every type of toy imaginable — life-sized stuffed animals, an antique merry-go-round, child-sized Porsches. Locals were buying up big and I took photos to show Nik. I wandered on through Kutnetsky Most, scanning menus on café windows, contemplating stopping for a coffee. A caffeine hit was a minimum AUD$6, a sliver of cake AUD$10, and there wasn't a spare seat anywhere. In 1990, I hardly had any money but felt like a millionaire. Now Moscow was a city of millionaires and I was a poor Westerner.

Sergei was doing rather better than me. He wasn't a millionaire, but part of the middle class earning enough to live comfortably in Moscow. He was also in the minority doing so honestly. On Orthodox Christmas Day he returned from his Seychelles holiday with his girlfriend of three years, Nastya, and her mother, brother and brother's partner. Nastya's brother ran a pension fund and according to Sergei was 'very rich'. He lived in an expansive flat on elite Arbat Street, had just bought two new cars and was considering getting himself a private jet. Nastya lived with her mother and worked for her brother. 'And she's not spoilt,' said Sergei. 'She doesn't ask me for things all the time.'

They showed me pictures from their trip to paradise, Nastya in a bikini, svelte and bronzed in sultry poses against various exotic backdrops. The beaches were deserted, fringed by tropical vegetation and a turquoise ocean. Why, oh why, did I keep coming back to Russia when there were places like that in the world? After dinner at Sergei's local, a German-style pub called To Beer Or Not To Beer, Sergei produced a DVD of Sasha Baron Cohen's movie, *Borat*. The spoof had outraged the Kazakhs, and been banned by the Russians, but Sergei had gone straight out and bought a pirate copy from a metro kiosk. He laughed himself silly — there was little more amusing than watching Americans make fools of themselves.

Sergei was working for one of Moscow's main legal firms, White and Case. Now a senior associate, he represented clients such as Gazprom, ExxonMobil and Texaco in mergers and acquisitions, restructuring and joint ventures. At Emory University he'd learnt to dot the i's and cross the t's on contracts that ran to hundreds of pages. His thoroughness didn't always impress Russian businessmen, who still preferred a few paragraphs and a bottle of superior vodka or two to clinch their multi-billion-dollar deals. They were learning, but as with all aspects of Russia's judicial system, there was a long way to go.

'It will take generations to create an atmosphere where people will abide by the laws. In the USSR, enforcement was built on fear. But now there is less fear, and a lack of law-abiding culture. The traffic police for example, they all take bribes all the time. Everyone takes and gives bribes. Every single thing you need to do in Russia involves paying someone off. It's just how it is.'

'Take Lika, for example,' Sergei said, referring to his ex-girlfriend, a winsome dancer with a penchant for designer fashion. 'Her father worked for the presidential administration so it only took a couple of phone calls to connections to get her a place studying law in a prestigious university. However, her case was an exception because she was very smart and did deserve a place.'

Sergei was confident that the situation was changing. 'Consider taxes. As systems of state control and management are being put in place, the state is becoming stronger, and now has more power to enforce its laws.'

He regularly worked fourteen-hour days and spent weekends in the office, yet seemed to be thriving on his diet of stress and cocktail liqueurs. He'd amassed a formidable collection of Armani suits and silk ties and bought himself a black BMW, but Moscow's traffic was so deplorable it was faster to walk. After a decade in the capital, he was finally looking at purchasing an apartment and had found one of interest near Barrikadnaya Metro, just off the Garden Ring Road. At USD$700,000 for 75 square metres, he thought it could be a good buy.

Sergei wasn't missing Kazan at all. After once being one of only two *Russkys* working in the Tatar government, he was glad now to be surrounded by Russians. With his qualifications and impeccable English he could have emigrated to the US but decided against it. 'Why would I move somewhere, when I know that I could never accept the mentality and values of that country?' Russia was home, and nowhere felt more like home than the Russian capital.

His youthful admiration for the West had vanished. 'I used to look at the West and US in particular as the highest standard for human morals and real democratic values. Unfortunately, now the West has completely disavowed itself. I may have reservations about the current environment in Russia, but it seems that Russia now looks noble compared to the West.'

The war in Iraq was a case in point. While Russia supported the 'global war on terror', it had vehemently opposed the March 2003 invasion of Iraq. 'Russia said that Iraq had no weapons of mass destruction. It was obvious to many people here that it was simply because of oil. It was ironic because when I was telling that to my smart and very well-educated American friends, they were telling me that they had to do it for democracy! Why is it that only now people in the West have started to admit that it was because of oil?'

Under Putin's leadership, Sergei felt Russia was finally showing its muscle. Putin was no longer allowing Russia to be ordered around. He was standing up to Western aggression, saying what he thought about NATO expansion into former Soviet states and what everyone believed to be Western-sponsored 'colour' revolutions against pro-Russian governments: 'Orange' in Ukraine, 'Rose' in Georgia and 'Tulip' in Kyrgyzstan. The missile defence base in Poland was clearly an act of aggression, and the UK was harbouring Russian and Chechen terrorists.

With cable TV, Sergei had access to hundreds of foreign news channels. He regularly watched BBC and CNN and felt Western media was becoming increasingly anti-Russian. CNN was 'one-sided' and Americans now so 'brainwashed they didn't even realise it'. Even the BBC was biased. With some pride he showed me 'Russia's CNN' — a new state and oligarch-funded TV channel — which ran Russian news and current affairs in English. The plan was to broadcast worldwide to counter anti-Russian propaganda. We watched a story about a priest, murdered in the Sverdlovsk region on Christmas Eve while trying to save icons being stolen from his church. I can't say it left me with a warm and fuzzy glow.

But Sergei was an optimist. 'I look at Russia from an historical perspective. Of course there were black pages in our history but I am proud of what Russia and Russians have done and achieved during the last several centuries. The economic crises of the early 90s were very short in terms of history, and I never understood why Westerners looked down on Russia. I think it indicates ignorance of history, and arrogance, which is not a good thing. I may not like many things that are happening in Russia now, but they do not affect my patriotic feelings as they are deeply rooted in respect for the Russian culture, intellect and scientific achievements.

'Economic growth has been impressive during the last few years and the country has developed dramatically. People's income and wealth have grown substantially. You can see the birth and development of a middle class. And despite cutting back on democracy, there is more or less political and economic stability in the country. Even the birth rate is starting to rise. If Russia is managed well during the next decade, with its vast natural resource base, it may become among the biggest economies in the world.'

★　★　★

Nadia too was now back from her New Year's 'rest' and I took the metro to visit her. It was a half-hour ride from the centre and all around me, female commuters were reading. The elderly lady opposite — wearing a leopard-skin patterned tracksuit, matching coat and a fluffy pink beret — was engrossed in a book entitled *Everything about Vegetables*. To my left, a voluptuous matron with a frizzy henna-red mop was glued to *100 Greatest Mistresses*. To my right, a pallid and studious librarian type was up to Lesson Four in an Arabic textbook. And the woman leaning over me clutched the daily paper. Bearing the headline 'Powder of Death', the article praised Moscow's special services for foiling another terrorist attack on the Moscow metro. All the men were asleep, and drooling.

A platinum blonde in five-inch stilettos with a sequined cat-print handbag leaned against the door, tapping on her mobile. She scowled when I tried to squeeze past to exit the wagon. Snow had finally fallen, blanketing Chertanovo's ugliness and squeaking underfoot. A billboard promoting the film *Babel* was the only colour against the concrete grey of construction sites. Cate Blanchett stared stonily into the oncoming traffic. Once we'd been in the same class at Methodist Ladies' College in Melbourne. Now her face was on a billboard in a bleak Moscow suburb, and I was there looking at it.

I crunched up the main road, bemused to see a hundreds-long queue of pensioners holding plastic bottles, snaking around the new wooden church on the corner of Nadia's street. I eavesdropped on those joining the end of the line and learned the wait for Holy Water was around three hours. Next to the church elderly believers were funnelling water into their receptacles from white plastic drums. Police guarding the proceedings clutched their own containers, already filled. I looked through the iron fence at the frenzy of the faithful, jostling and splashing for their share of the magic liquid, then proceeded on up the street. Just past the church was an emergency services truck, parked in the middle of the road with a large hose under it, leading to the church grounds. The other end was attached to a fire hydrant. These poor old folk were freezing their feet off for a bottle of bog-standard non-potable city tap water.

Nadia wasn't so superstitious. Now seventy-five, she was still sprightly, but noticeably more fragile than when I'd last seen her. She chattered excitedly about her week's stay at a sanatorium in the woods outside Moscow, a Christmas gift from her nephew. She'd gone with a friend and the friend's adult son and they'd just brought her copies of photos they'd taken. Every detail was covered, from the bland twin room she'd shared with her friend, the plastic vines decorating the eating hall, to the moustachioed 48-year-old son who'd never managed to find a wife, standing solemnly in the snowy forest. It had all been lovely.

She'd made 'my favourite' dish for lunch — boiled buckwheat, fried in butter, with pickled cabbage on the side. It was traditional peasant fare, an early 90s staple when little else was available. Back then I'd been young and hungry. Now suburban supermarkets offered wide selections of reasonably priced items, yet Nadia still stuck with what she knew. Was it because her life had been so filled with upheaval and tragedy that she now clung so dearly to routine and order?

Her one big adventure had been a trip to Israel. Just as the war began in Iraq, hard-up tour operators began offering USD$500 all-inclusive packages to the Holy Land. Her nephew bought her a ticket and persuaded her that it was the perfect time to go. He was right. Her group had been the only tourists, they'd stayed in the best hotels and were treated like heroes. And there wasn't a single terrorist act the whole time she was there.

Otherwise, life was plodding on. Her Jewish club was in limbo after the theatre they used as a meeting place found a new director who'd put it up for rent. She and the club's forty-five other elderly singles were missing the club and optimistic they would find a new venue soon. Her monthly pension was now the equivalent of USD$160. Without her nephew's help she would be starving.

'Even under Stalin, prices for food, gas and electricity got cheaper each year,' she said. 'But now it's impossible to manage.' She loved Mayor Luzhkov for providing free transport to all pensioners and giving them 100 roubles (a little under USD$4) a year towards their phone costs — even if it did cost 200 roubles a month — and worried about how they would be treated once his term ended.

She was also concerned about Tina, who had mysteriously declared she couldn't return to Moscow after a holiday at the family's house in Slovenia last summer. Just before they'd left, Tina had collected Nadia in a limousine and taken her out to see her and Stephen's new country 'cottage'.

'It was like a palace, on enormous grounds with guards, barbed wire and cameras everywhere,' she said, gasping at the memory. 'I heard it cost ten million dollars. Everything was so luxurious, there was white marble everywhere, even the door handles were made from gold.'

Tina's disappearance was most peculiar. I'd caught up with her in 2005, and over lunch she'd told me she'd finally almost completed her Doctor of Philosophy at Oxford University and was working with Sotheby's, setting up an art auction house in Moscow. I emailed her to see what had happened, and never heard back.

Olga and Misha's holiday break had finally finished and they were back in their city flat. I had taken over Tyoma's bottom bunk. I returned from my visit to Nadia and told them about the queue for Holy Water I'd seen at the church. Olga picked up a soft-drink bottle filled with water from their kitchen bench, and waved it at me.

'We've got some too. Misha's dad has retired now so he queued up and got this for us. He brings me some every week.'

I tried to be open-minded. They'd recently seen a documentary, which 'proved' prayer can alter the molecular order of water. The film told the story of a priest, imprisoned during Soviet times, who was given dirty water to drink. He'd blessed it, it became pure, and that was how he'd survived. Olga and Misha didn't know how it was so, but it really was true. Misha told me how some years ago the Patriarch had blessed all the water from Moscow's taps on the same day. His aunt had taken water on that day and bottled it. On the next day she'd also taken water from the same tap. The blessed water stayed pure, the other turned green. This water Misha's father had brought them, even though it came straight from the city's water supply, was blessed and therefore holy.

The Baptism of Christ was coming up on 19 January, which was why everyone was stocking up on the magic H_2O. Olga was also fasting because the next Sunday was Eucharist. In Orthodoxy, fasting didn't mean starving oneself, it meant abstaining from meat, alcohol and cooking with oil, the rationale being to make food as tasteless and unpleasureable as possible. Olga seemed to fast an awful lot, which always worried me as she was naturally so thin. How often did she have to avoid these foods? She got out her religious instruction manual and we began to count.

Firstly there was Advent, the forty days leading up to Christmas, from the 28th of November to the 6th of January. Next came Lent, from the 6th of March until Easter. The exact date depended on the moon. Then there was the 'Peter and Paul' fasting, which started around the 19th of June (depending on the date of Easter) until the saint day on the 11th of July. There was also the Uspenski fast, for the two weeks leading up to Madonna's death on the 28th of August. Plus, of course, every Wednesday and Friday for the whole year.

That was a lot of days that the 80 per cent of Russians who claimed to be Orthodox were not supposed to be eating meat or fish, let alone drinking alcohol!

I'd booked a ticket on the midnight train to St Petersburg and ordered a taxi to the station. My driver, Bakhadir, was a forty-year-old Uzbek who'd been living in the sleeping district of Vykhino for the last five years, because Uzbekistan was 'corrupt and very poor'. He was sure President Karimov was deliberately keeping people in poverty so they didn't make trouble. Most only survived by growing their own food. The 'old days' had been 'much better'.

'In the USSR there was stability. You knew there would be free kindergarten, free schooling, free flat, and free health care. The state provided work with a salary of 120 roubles a month, plenty to feed a family on. When you retired you'd get a pension of 120 roubles a month, enough for food and clothing. You could even build your own place, but if it was too fancy then the authorities would question you about where the money came from. People were much more equal than now.'

Like hundreds of thousands of other Uzbeks, Tajiks and Kyrgyz living in Russian cities, Bakhadir had been unable to find work at home. He had two children to support, a son in grade 8 and a daughter in grade 6, plus two elderly parents. After working as teachers in secondary schools all their lives, their pension was the equivalent of USD$12 a month.

Bakhadir estimated that at least 80 per cent of *priyezhii* (immigrant) workers in Moscow were there illegally. Most provided labour on building sites for monthly wages of around USD$200, trapped in a vicious cycle of exploitation. Bosses used their illegal status to keep wages low and conditions miserable. Up to five hundred workers would be virtual prisoners on any given site, afraid of leaving lest they be caught by the police and fined or deported. They even slept there, bunking down in the partially constructed building as soon as there was a floor. The police knew exactly what was going on, but received hefty bribes from the developers to keep away. Almost all the workers' pay went on basic survival rations, the rest went back to their families.

Official registration was a nightmarish procedure. Bakhadir told me he'd seen thousands of people in one queue, sleeping upright in the cold so as not to lose their places. Often desperate would-be workers followed up suspect ads in the metro and free newspapers offering 'assistance with registration and work permits'. Everyone knew these permits were a scam, but most immigrants felt they had little choice other than to go *levoi* (left), slang for 'dodgy' or 'not via the proper channels'. Still, it was risky. Cops easily identified fake documents, demanding bribes of 1,500–2,000 roubles if the papers weren't in order. And when someone couldn't pay up, they were put behind bars for up to two months while the cops checked out their details.

If that wasn't enough, ethnic Russians treated them like animals, complaining that these 'black-arsed Central Asians' were taking their jobs.

'But they would never do such back-breaking work for so little money,' Bakhadir fumed. 'We are here building their city for nothing and people are making huge profits from our labour.'

Lenin should have been turning in his mausoleum.

33

Extreme Makeover

I shared a *coupe* to St Petersburg with a fifty-something couple returning home after New Year with friends in Moscow. Marina was a mathematician with the physique of a ballerina who managed to make even a puce velvet dressing gown look elegant. She fussed over her grumpy physicist husband, Yevgeni, proffering him items from our 'supper' trays — plastic boxes with bright red salami, noxious-looking pate, plastic-wrapped peanuts, crackers and chocolate. He examined each tidbit as if it were poison, rejecting everything but a teabag and lump of sugar. This collection of chemical concoctions was meant to be a sign of progress. All I could see was waste.

It was pitch black when the train pulled into St Petersburg at 8 am, and a dull grey twilight when I checked into a hostel at the Winter Palace end of Nevsky Prospekt two hours later. Natasha had invited me to stay, but I didn't want to put her out. She was now married to a computer programmer who worked for an American company and they had a two-year-old son, Feodor. They dreamed of buying their own place, but prices were rising faster than they could save, so they were still living with Natasha's mum in the old family flat.

The hostel was a cheaply renovated former *kommunalka* with an irritable receptionist who made no secret of the fact she thought the job beneath her. Begrudgingly she offered me breakfast — another inedible affair comprising a packet of Nescafe 3-in-1, a slice of stale white bread and plastic-wrapped cheese. She scowled at my untouched plate with a thought bubble: 'You spoilt Westerner ... how can my life have come to this?'

I had some Amex traveller's cheques to cash in, and dropped in to a small bank in central St Petersburg. The ditzy teller had never heard of Amex, or traveller's cheques, and it took some persuading to convince her to show them to her superiors, who fortunately confirmed they were worth something. An hour later I hadn't moved. She'd taken my passport, immigration card, visa and even written down the address of the hostel. Customers in the ever-lengthening queue behind me were bristling.

'What's going on? This is Soviet service!' complained a pasty-faced woman.

'It's our fault, we only have ourselves to blame,' said the woman behind her. 'I voted for Yeltsin. We all did.'

She stepped in front of me and shouted into the microphone on the customer's side of the bullet-proof glass wall between us and the bank staff. Another teller appeared with a 'complaints book'. Perhaps things *had* changed. Were Russians beginning to stand up for themselves? The complainant looked at me and in perfect English revealed she was a professor in comparative literature and had worked in British and American universities, including a long stint at Oxford.

'You would never tolerate this in Australia, would you? When will people learn that their job is to serve clients, and not the other way around?'

Olga had made a similar observation: 'It's as though salespeople take a sadistic delight in telling you they don't have something in stock, or no, they can't help you.'

Salespeople weren't the only breed who still loved to make life as difficult as possible. Masha had been battling with bureaucrats for over a year now to be allowed to sell the apartment she shared with her son, Yegor, now eleven, her estranged husband, Kim, and his elderly mother. She'd spent weeks in offices, and her entire teacher's salary on fees and bribes, but hadn't yet managed to get all the required stamps on the stack of necessary documents to be able to proceed.

We were sitting at the kitchen table in the flat Masha was so desperate to leave. It was even grungier than I remembered. An air of decay and squalor pervaded the entire building: mouldy wallpaper sagged from the walls, the floorboards were rotting, plumbing leaking, windows broken and paint flaking. Masha's relationship with Kim and his mother had soured to the point that they could barely stand the sight of each other, passing silently in the corridor between their rooms to use the putrid toilet or make a cup of tea in the grimy kitchen.

They couldn't sell the place because it hadn't yet been privatised. This was a ridiculously involved process at the best of times, but in Masha's case had been made even more complex by the fact that the previous residents had made an unregistered alteration to the premises, unlawfully moving the toilet from the bathroom to what had been a cupboard. In an attempt to legalise her relocated toilet, Masha had forked out several months' wages to an engineer to draw up a plan, to plumbers, electricians and innumerable bureaucrats at the Bureau of Privatisation and the mysterious but apparently vital Inter-Estate Commission. She was waiting for one last signature.

'I have no idea what these people do apart from taking bribes. There are so many departments, and I've spent weeks queuing to get these stamps and signatures. Without them I can't get a passport for the flat.'

It seemed absurd. And why did a property need a passport?

'Without the passport I can't privatise it, and without privatising it we can't sell it. It would be easier to just break everything and put the toilet back where it was!'

I thought back to when I'd tried to tell Yulia how great her country was. These days I kept my mouth shut, thankful that in Australia I'd never had to bribe officials for anything.

Money was a problem, and her personal life far from ideal, but Masha had somehow retained her dogged zest for life. Despite a second knee operation in 2004, a full replacement this time, she still lived for mountaineering. Her knee wasn't perfect, but she'd recently completed training as an instructor, and led an expedition to the Caucasus Mountains for a twenty-day trek each year.

She had no regrets about the end of the USSR. She'd never believed in communism and was glad that people were now free to work as they chose. She told me about a book she'd been reading, a theory of the history of the Russian state, by Lev Gumilov, son of the famous poetess Anna Akhmatova. Gumilov proposed that different ethnic groups have varying levels of passion/activeness, and that in order to make significant societal change, these levels have to be very high. Most Russians, it seemed, had run out of passion.

'After the shock of the 1990s, Russians are even quieter and more subdued than before,' she said. 'They have no more energy to go onto the streets and protest. They all understand that the people who were in power before divided the power and wealth between them, and the ordinary folk are too afraid to protest.'

I asked what she'd thought of Galina Starovoitova, a courageous and outspoken politician and ethnographer, fatally shot at the age of fifty-two outside her St Petersburg flat on the Griboyedov Canal Embankment in November 1998. Starovoitova's cold-blooded murder had stunned me, but to Masha it hadn't been unexpected.

'She was a trusted politician, a clever woman who people liked and respected. She proposed sensible laws that were in the common people's interests. But it's always the case in our history, that people who stand up for change are eventually ostracised, isolated, then if they don't change their ways, eliminated. People knew she was strong and that those in politics are always taking risks with their lives. There's a lot of adrenaline in Russian politics and few people are able to handle the strain. In our version of democracy it's always understood that if you do something to upset those with power and money, they can easily pay money to have you killed. In the case of Starovoitova, she was killed for doing something, not for saying anything. Look at Zhirinovsky. He is always saying things, but never actually does anything. He's the "Wedding General". In Tsarist times it was vital to have generals and important people at a wedding to make it official, so they were invited along just for show. That's all an opposition politician can ever be here. Just for show.'

It was little wonder that most Russians now appeared to equate democracy with anarchy, a lawless free-for-all in which the rich and powerful triumphed. The democratic experiment on Russian soil had failed and the 'vertical hierarchy' of the country's autocratic past had returned. Most Russians now believed their nation needed to be ruled by an iron fist, and Putin was it, the highest link in the chain of vertical power he often spoke of. He was making Russia great, standing up to evil NATO, the US and the West, showing them Russia was once again a country that inspired fear and respect. The pre-revolutionary motto 'For God, Tsar and the Fatherland' could almost be revived for Putin's reign — Russians must obey God in Heaven, the Kremlin on earth and love their country above all else.

Perhaps, as Olga had said, there was no other way. Lenin had seen that 'For God, Tsar and the Fatherland' was a recipe for keeping the masses under control and his revolution had been intended to shatter that hierarchy. But his 'dictatorship of the proletariat' had soon became a reinvention of the same theme, demanding individuals subvert their desires for the good of the whole: the leader, the ideology and the nation.

I picked my way down the half-collapsed stairs in Masha's building, thinking about something I'd read recently. It was a claim by a Russian biologist-geneticist who had calculated that the genetic loss inflicted upon the Soviet Union from the 1917 revolution through to Stalin's death in 1953 would take a further five generations to restore. So many of the nation's best brains had been lost to Gulags, executions and war that he predicted 'there would not be an influx of physical and mental energy into the nation until the year 2025'.

There had certainly been an impressive influx of energy put into the renovation of Putin's hometown, dubbed Russia's capital of crime in the late 1990s. The year 2003 saw the 300th anniversary of the great city's founding and money had flooded in, enabling hundreds of crumbling historic buildings to be restored to their original splendour. Nevsky Prospekt was lined with upmarket stores supplying the essentials to discerning residents of the Venice of the North: high-fashion boutiques like Fendi, Canali and Versace, alongside shops trading in hunting paraphernalia — guns, knives, ammunition, camouflage outfits, stuffed reindeer, foxes and even an eagle. One place in Passazh Arcade offered foot-high Putin replicas, lead soldiers in pre-revolutionary uniforms, and stuffed fully-grown bears.

Cultures clashed everywhere. A fancy sushi restaurant just up from the Admiralty building on Nevsky bore a plaque stating that Vladimir Ilyich Lenin had once given a speech here. And just behind the colonnaded Kazan Cathedral, one of Russian Orthodoxy's most sacred and revered places of worship, was the hip new Ice Bar. For a mere 300 roubles (AUD$20) entry, those passing face-control were given an extra thick coat and pair of *valenki* (felt peasant winter boots Sergei had once laughed at me for wearing) and the privilege of sitting on a stool carved from ice at a bar carved from ice in a room carved from ice. A rugged-up barman poured ice-cold vodka shots from a liquor cabinet carved from ice. I could see the novelty value of such a place in sub-tropical Sydney where few would ever experience ten below zero. But here anyone could sit outside and drink vodka in minus ten degrees — for free!

I stopped in at the plush Hotel Astoria across from St Isaac's Cathedral where I'd once met the now deceased mayor and mentor of Putin, Anatoly Sobchak. Next to the lift, a plaque listed famous guests: Rasputin, Naomi Campbell, Tony Blair, Luciano Pavarotti, George Bush, Yesenin (an early twentieth century Soviet poet who'd killed himself in the hotel), the world-renowned cellist and conductor Mstislav Rostropovich and his soprano wife, Galina Vishnevskaya, Russian pop idol Alla Pugacheva, Elton John (his name was next to Rasputin's), Prince Charles, American dancer Isadora Duncan, and Elizabeth Taylor. St Petersburg was *the* place to visit.

The Stroganov Palace on Nevsky Prospekt — formerly the residence of one of St Petersburg's wealthiest aristocratic families — was now a chocolate museum, with an African doorman. Every day, an athletic Senegalese physics student donned nineteenth-century white livery to stand at the entrance. Inside, one could buy almost anything — moulded or carved from any shade of chocolate: chocolate busts of Lenin, chocolate chess sets, chocolate weapons and chocolate Ferraris.

There was a distinct revival of interest and pride in pre-revolutionary history. From newly refurbished palaces of the aristocracy to a wax Catherine the Great seated on a bench in front of the Gostiny Dvor department store, St Petersburg had re-embraced its Tsarist past. Bridal couples posed for wedding photos in front of the bronze statue of Peter the Great on a rearing horse on the banks of the Neva River. Another favourite backdrop for newlyweds to take their snaps was The Church of the Saviour on Spilt Blood, St Petersburg's nineteenth-century version of St Basil's in Moscow, built on the site of Tsar Alexander II's shooting in March 1881. (He died a few hours later in the Winter Palace.) I saw another wedding party pull up outside the Mikhailovsky Castle in a stretch-limo Hummer decked with flowers.

Retro Soviet was also in vogue. I watched a young couple toast each other from plastic cups in front of the Aurora — the battleship from where the shot was fired to signal workers, peasants and soldiers to storm the Winter Palace in October 1917 — while a friend took their portrait. A Soviet-themed restaurant in the Petrograd district featured Lenin busts and propaganda posters.

Historical revisionists had been busy. At Dom Knigi, the book mega-store opposite the Kazan Cathedral where I'd once bought social-realist posters and language tutors with texts glorifying communism, one could now buy everything from translations of Robert Massie's *Nicholas and Alexandra* and glossy coffee table books depicting the sumptuous lives of Russia's aristocrats to Soviet histories praising the great wisdom of Lenin and Stalin.

I arranged to meet Natasha in the bookshop's new café for coffee. Once I'd been able to shout her and Olga train tickets to the Ukraine for a couple of dollars. Now a couple of anaemic cappuccinos and a stale slice of cake cost the equivalent of her daily salary as a university lecturer. But somehow her family was managing — and she was on her way to pick up her mum from the airport after a week-long holiday in Egypt. Now that getting a passport for foreign travel was less painful — bribes and connections were still necessary, but at least people could leave — package tours to Crimea and Central Asia were a thing of the past. The hot destinations for Russia's lower middle classes were Turkey, Greece, Spain and Egypt, with all-inclusive trips available for a few hundred dollars.

Natasha was upbeat. Her husband was a good, kind man who didn't drink and earned a reasonable salary, which allowed her to pursue her work at the university. Her son, Feodor, was a delight, even if he was two. She wasn't sure what she was going to do with him as soon she would be required to spend more hours at work. A place in a private kindergarten cost a minimum of 12,000 roubles a month, yet she only earned 10,000. And even if they could afford it, she didn't want Feodor to go to childcare with Novy Russky children where she feared he would learn the ways of the spoiled. A child psychologist friend was inundated with cases of disturbed young rich kids. One mother had complained that her five-year-old son had two rooms full of unopened gifts yet showed no interest in any of them. The mother had been astounded when the psychologist suggested the parents should take some time to play with their child.

'The husbands are always away ... working, whatever that is ... and the wives are frantically trying to keep themselves beautiful. They spend all their time at the gym, the hairdressers, the nail salon, the beauty therapist and shopping for clothes because they are petrified that if they lose their looks their husbands will leave them for their mistresses. And all the Novy Russkys have mistresses. It's an essential part of the "gentlemen's set". They need a fancy city apartment, a place on the French Riviera, a multistorey dacha, a selection of cars — perhaps a Mercedes limousine or a Cadillac, a Land Rover for hunting, a Lamborghini or Maserati for the girlfriend — and a mistress or two, otherwise a man cannot consider himself a true gentleman. So the official wife always feels her position is under threat and tortures herself to keep gorgeous ... and they never pay any attention to their children. It's no wonder the kids are so messed up.'

She gazed out the window, over to Kazan Cathedral.

'Ah, and the other mark of a gentleman is that he should go to church.'

Natasha didn't share Olga's faith in Orthodoxy and sniffed at claims that eight out of ten Russians were now true believers. To her, Orthodoxy seemed primarily about superstition and rituals that helped bad people feel better about themselves, or good people feel they were suffering for a reason.

'I'm sure there are some genuine priests, but they are the exception. For the most part, it's just an official institution to make money. The church doesn't help people, it just plays on their superstitions. Go into any church and you'll see bandits in there, people who kill others. And Putin is always shown in a church, crossing himself. I don't believe they are true believers.'

I'd had similar thoughts watching a service in Kazan Cathedral the previous day. The priests were young, plump and dripping with gold, and hungry babushki were spending their precious pensions on candles and offerings.

'Russians are so superstitious that when a Novy Russky gets himself a new office, a new car, a new flat, the first thing he does is invite a priest to come and bless it. The priests make a lot of money from this. Friends of mine built a new dacha. The toilet broke and the stove didn't work, but instead of getting a plumber, they called a priest.'

Back in 1588, the English Ambassador to Russia, Giles Fletcher, had lambasted the Russian Orthodox Church, criticising the cosy relationship between church and state and observing that 'the people give what little money remains after the state's taxation to the monasteries out of fear and superstition'. 'The common people,' he wrote, 'were robbed constantly, both of their hearts and money by tyrannical and greedy rulers.'

Lenin believed that capitalists embraced religion because it taught them 'to practise charity while on earth, thus offering them a very cheap way of justifying their existence as exploiters, while selling them moderate-priced tickets to well-being in heaven'. In 1990 this had seemed a blasphemous criticism of a long-suffering institution. But I sensed Natasha thought it close to the mark. She gestured to the bustling street outside.

'It looks like Europe, but really it's a banana republic!'

Natasha left to collect her mother and we arranged to meet again. I stepped out into the 3 pm twilight and walked up the Griboyedov Canal to what had been Galina Starovoitova's apartment. I vividly remembered the night she was assassinated, my shock at the cold-blooded gunning down of a principled and intelligent woman. She was the kind of person Russia needed to steer it down a path of justice and equality, a democrat in the proper sense of the word. A former ethnographer, she was known for her work to protect ethnic minorities. But like Anna Politkovskaya, her criticism had threatened too many. Eventually I located the place she'd died, indicated by the smallest of signs stating that she had lived in this building. There was no mention that she'd been murdered.

Russia was covered in memorial plaques and gravestones marking lives cut short. The most spectacular I'd seen were in a graveyard in the forest outside Ekaterinburg: monuments to gangster victims of a Mafia shoot-out. Relatives had honoured their violent ends with larger-than-life statues carved in polished granite. One bandit had the keys to his Mercedes dangling from his hand. Across the road was a memorial to those killed in Stalin's purges, thousands upon thousands of names whose lives had ended in 1937–38. To stand out in death in post-Soviet Russia, one had to be rich, powerful or both. Galina Starovoitova had merely been dangerously decent.

Olga's parents, Vladimir and Nelli, were in town, and invited me to a concert Vladimir was conducting at the Kapella. The recently refurbished hall of Vladimir's childhood music school was sold out for the performance, which featured an extraordinary twenty-year-old pianist, Miroslav Kultyshev, playing Prokofiev's Piano Concerto No.2. I sat with Olga's brother, Igor, and he was pleased to note a large turn-out of young people in the audience. A decade ago Igor had worried about the future of classical music in his homeland, fearing the kids of the 90s had been led astray by Pepsi and pop. Now he seemed more positive.

But for most musicians, a career in today's Russia still meant an almost certain life of poverty. In Soviet times, a profession in classical music had been a plum job with privileges, decent pay and respect. These days an average orchestral musician's monthly wage was 3,000 roubles, about AUD$120. Those in the St Petersburg Philharmonic and the Mariinsky Theatre earned more, but the performers at Igor's

Musical Comedy Theatre would starve if they had to rely on their base salary. Most took teaching work to feed themselves. Incredibly, the high standards had been maintained, despite many of Russia's best fleeing the country in search of better-paying work.

Vladimir, too, was more optimistic about Russia's musical prospects than I'd seen him in years. He and Nelli were continuing to travel the world, while he worked with orchestras from Siberia to Perth, where he was the principal guest conductor of the West Australian Symphony. We met up the day after the concert in Konditerei, an old-style café on the Hermitage end of Nevsky Prospekt. Vladimir selected a plate of *studen* for himself, a wobbly jelly made from boiled animal innards, and tucked into it enthusiastically.

'Did you see the crowd last night? At last things are improving for the intelligentsia and the audiences are coming back. Now our problem is that because tickets are very cheap, the orchestras are struggling to get enough money.'

Fortunately, finding food in St Petersburg's centre was no longer the challenge it had once been. Cafés, restaurants and bars offered every kind of cuisine imaginable — if only one could afford it. The fanciest eateries I could manage were Yolki Palki's, a chain of kitsch theme restaurants decked out like log cabins, decorated with moose heads and stuffed roosters, with grouchy youths in traditional embroidered frilly white-and-red outfits as wait staff. The Sizzlers of post-Soviet Russia, Yolki Palki's trademark is an all-you-can-eat wooden cart, strung with artificial ivy and piled with pickled cucumbers, pickled garlic and pickled herrings, plus a hundred and one combinations of dishes involving beetroot, cabbage and potatoes. Another new fast-food outlet offered Russian fare: borsch, *pelmeni* and grated beetroot salad. It was just like a Soviet canteen, but staffed by greasy-haired students and decorated with funky orange laminate and Macca's-style backlit photos of the dishes on offer. The food was identical, but the blaring doof-doof house music almost burst my eardrums. I felt a strange nostalgia for the days when white-coated roly-poly babushki scowled and mumbled as they weighed out serves of grated pickled cabbage and totted up bills on an abacus.

I took another trip down memory lane on a bus out to Tsarskoye Selo (Tsar's village), where Catherine the Great had one of her summer palaces. Restoration work had been going on at the palace since the Nazis bombed it to a shell during World War II and had almost been finished in time for St Petersburg's 300th anniversary. For the first time I saw the reconstructed 'Amber Room', a garish space with walls and ceilings decorated in carved translucent orange. Portraits of the Imperial family hung throughout the palace and the tourist shop sold busts of the now canonised last Tsar. Books on the Romanovs in all major languages filled the shelves.

The cloakroom attendant asked where I was from. 'Oh, Australia!' she cried, barely able to contain her excitement. 'Tell me, how is Kylie? Is she better? Has she married Olivier yet? And what was the real story about Michael … what's-his-name? … Hutchence, that's right! How did he die? Is it true it was from a drug overdose? And how is Nicole getting on in her new marriage? Does she ever get to see those children she adopted?'

Kangaroos, nor Australia having no winter, didn't rate a mention. She was devastated when I couldn't answer a single question.

'Women just love celebrity gossip,' Natasha told me when we next met up. 'I once took a bus to Finland, all women on a shopping trip. For the whole journey they discussed nothing but Princess Di and whether she should leave Charles or not.'

We were sitting in a Middle Eastern themed café with her friend, Inge, a university lecturer who studied religious sects in Russia. With their short hair, conservative dress and make-up free skin, Natasha and Inge stood out in style-central St Petersburg where the female uniform was fur coat and hat, stiletto heeled boots and trowelled-on face paint. We ordered cappuccinos and baklava, and the conversation turned to the lamentable state of a sexually liberated Russia where alcohol was cheaper than water.

Inge told us a story about a male friend of hers who had been driving through a village near Yaroslavl, east of Moscow, a few years back. Two women had approached him and offered to pay him for sex. They wanted to have children, they told him, but all the men in their village were alcoholics. Natasha and I were speechless. We both knew the provinces were in a bad way, but this was almost unbelievable. On my trip across Siberia in June 2005, I'd been dismayed to witness a dying countryside — thousands of kilometres of uncultivated fields, dilapidated machinery, abandoned shells of houses and factories, and villages lifeless bar a few elderly women and drunkards. The young men who should have been driving tractors, working in the factories and rebuilding houses sat pathetically by roadsides, inebriated and obnoxious. They were hardly sperm donor material, let alone potential fathers. Would-be mothers loitered around truckstop cafés in tight skirts hoping to earn a few roubles from drunken passers-through.

It was the same story in the sleeping districts of suburban St Petersburg and the village where Natasha's husband's grandmother lived: unemployment, poverty, depression, alcoholism, substance abuse, plummeting lifespans, declining birthrate, HIV, prostitution. In 1990, Leningrad (as it was then) had more than five million inhabitants. Sixteen years later, the population had shrunk by a million, 20 per cent — and there hadn't even been a war.

Like Natasha, Inge had been fortunate enough to find a husband who kept away from the bottle. She too had a toddler son. At thirty-seven, they were considered practically geriatric mothers. Inge's husband was an academic specialising in alternative theories of evolution, and was living in Germany. It was only thanks to her husband's wages that she was able to keep her position at the university. For twenty-two hours of lectures a week she received a base rate of 7,000 roubles a month, plus an extra 3,000 because she had a Masters degree. This gave her a total of about AUD$400 a month. Basic living expenses for her and her son were at least three times that. She would like to have another child but couldn't afford to.

'What can people do? If someone comes up with a scheme to get money, to take bribes, or not to pay taxes, then it is not considered a crime. Everyone does it. There is no other way to get by.'

Property ownership was an impossible fantasy, unless you were lucky enough to inherit something. A carcass of a new three-room flat on the edge of town was a minimum of USD$260,000. With no floors, walls, windows, plumbing or wiring, it would take at least another $100,000 to make it habitable. Only those with oil money could afford to buy property and these outer suburban developments were often snapped up as a money laundering opportunity.

'No one who works honestly could ever afford their own place,' concluded Inge ruefully. 'It's just how it is here.'

Regardless of financial problems, keeping up one's image was more important than ever. Inge had gone to buy a plane ticket to visit her husband, only to be refused entry to the KLM office because her coat wasn't smart enough. Female university colleagues had derided her flat-heeled footwear as 'uncultured'. I stuck my hiking boot out from under the table and they shook their heads. As always, I failed the shoe test. Having the right clothing, footwear and car, explained Inge and Natasha, was worth great sacrifice. People living in *kommunalki* would mire themselves in debt to buy a classy vehicle. A woman would spend every last kopeck on an expensive fur coat while letting her teeth rot away. Lipstick was more important than food.

The government had its priorities 'all wrong' too. Officials sent their children to the UK and US to study, and scant resources went to local educational institutions. Inge's poorer students worked long hours to support themselves. One was a belly dancer, another worked in a hospice. But the rich kids just bribed their way through to a degree. One girl had missed an exam because she had a solarium appointment. Hospitals were just as bad. The rich went to private clinics or flew abroad for treatment, while the hoi polloi had no choice but to rely on rundown and under-staffed hospitals.

It was little surprise people had turned to religion. If the state was no longer going to provide the basics, then perhaps God might. Despite a 1997 law banning any religion that had not existed in Russia for fifteen years and did not have a certain number of followers, many 'foreign' sects continued to operate in Russia. Inge had made a comprehensive study of her compatriots' quests to find meaning and salvation post-communism. Many had fallen for the Scientologists, who charged followers 320,000 roubles for a course to change their lives. There were Moonies, Quakers, Mormons, Christian Scientists,

Hare Krishnas, Hindus, Kabalah (a favourite of businessmen), Neo-Yazichniki (pre-Christian Russians), Seventh Day Adventists and Baptists — the list went on and on.

But most were Orthodox, and that was how the state seemed to like it. Officially the church and state were separate, but according to Inge, the Orthodox Church was 'very friendly' with the government, particularly the Ministry of Defence and the Ministry of the Interior. Now every prison and every hospital had a priest. The *politruks* (army propagandists like those I'd met in the academy in Lvov) of Soviet days had disappeared in 1991 and now it was Orthodox priests who were specially trained to work with the military. She told me of a soldier who had been kidnapped, tortured and killed in Chechnya, allegedly for his refusal to accept Islam. He'd later been canonised as a martyr and even had an icon dedicated to him.

Every conceivable kind of quack, from faith healers to fortune tellers and occultists, filled newspaper advertisement pages with tempting offers for the down-and-out and gullible. You could sign up for a course in esoteric psychoanalysis, which claimed to teach you how to get what you wanted just by imagining it — be it a mink coat, Porsche or oligarch husband. You could 'Buy a Diploma', 'Return your Husband to the Family', or 'Cure Venereal Diseases through Hypnosis'. My personal favourite was 'Call this Number to Correct Your Destiny'.

'Same day abortions' was another common theme in the classifieds. Abortion remained the usual method of birth control, with an average of eight to ten per woman. The contraceptive pill was rumoured to make you fat, so it was far better to get pregnant and have an abortion. Natasha had met a woman at a party, who'd boasted of having eighteen terminations before deciding to keep a son. 'It was as if she was talking about trips to Italy!'

And only yesterday she'd been at the hair salon, with the hairdressers chatting over her head about their recent abortions. One had paid 800 roubles, the other only 500. 'Damn,' the first had said. 'I could have bought new shoes with that 300!'

Some women even deliberately got themselves up to duff to improve their skin, then had an abortion at twelve weeks. And both had heard stories of East German women swimmers who got knocked up before major races so the flood of hormones would improve their speed. Remembering the lethargy of the first trimester of my pregnancy I thought this seemed rather far-fetched, but Inge and Natasha were adamant it was true.

Not all women managed their abortions in time. Natasha had given birth to Feodor in a public hospital. After the birth, she was taken to a large ward with a public phone next to her bed. The woman in the neighbouring bed came to use the phone. 'She put money in and dialled,' recalled Natasha. 'Then I heard her say, "Hi! Yuri ... I've just given birth to your daughter!" There was silence and she hung up. Then she dialled again. This time she said, "Hi! Pavel ... I've just given birth to your daughter!" Silence again. Only on her third call did she find a guy who agreed that he might be a father.'

On my last night in St Petersburg, I went to the circus. The show was based around the story of Peter Pan, with all the circus arts cleverly woven into the plot. I watched in awe, wishing Nik was with me. Children and adults gasped as trapeze artists dressed as pirates whizzed above us, flinging each other around with no safety nets and often no ropes. A trio of elephants performed improbable balancing tricks on giant steel balls; acrobats, jugglers and clowns were all worked into the story as the children and Lost Boys. The kids loved it, until the magician came out, dressed as Captain Hook. He popped Tinkerbell into a box and sawed her in half with a chainsaw. It was all too much. St Petersburg might have been Russia's crime capital but the children still had illusions.

34

Epiphany

As I had done so many times before, I bought a *platscart* ticket for the 'Tatarstan', the 8.20 pm to Kazan from Moscow's Kazansky Station. Sheets now cost so much that few passengers could afford them. The 'no sheet, no mattress, no blanket' rule still held, so half the wagon made do with bare, vinyl-covered bunks. I stared out into the blackness as the train pulled out of the station, hit by a wave of nostalgia for my old life of wandering. I wondered if I'd ever be able to drag Nik from his Lego and take him with me to Tatarstan.

I began to check out my *sputniks*. I had an upper bunk and for now was sitting at the foot of the bed underneath, occupied by a tearful, heavily pregnant Kyrgyz girl. Opposite was an Armenian woman, sharing her bunk with her moppet of a daughter who looked about four, Nik's age. Two men took up the aisle beds.

We got talking. Zhenya was twenty-two and eight months pregnant, on her way to her parents' home in the Siberian city of Omsk to give birth. Her family had moved there eight years ago from Jalalabad in Kirghizia (she used the old Soviet name for her republic, now the independent State of Kyrgyzstan). She'd married a Kyrgyz man in Omsk but he'd had to travel 2,700 kilometres east to Moscow to find work, stacking shelves in the Hypermarket, an enormous supermarket on the edge of the city. His employers provided him with a cheap bunk in a squalid room with nine others. He wouldn't be able to come to Omsk for the birth and Zhenya doubted he would see her or the baby for at least a year.

Zhenya's hopes for a better future lay on eventually having a second baby. In an attempt to counter Russia's plunging birth rate, Putin was now offering a 250,000 rouble (about USD$9,200) baby bonus to couples who procreated a second time. To Zhenya it was an incredible sum, well worth having a baby for. The Armenian agreed, but saw herself as too old. I took her for about forty-five. She was thirty-two. Zhenya pulled her coat over herself and dozed off. She had a bumpy four days ahead before she'd be back on terra firma and I hoped she'd make it in time.

I turned to eavesdrop on the two men. The younger was skinny, with clippered hair, smashed teeth and a scarred face and was returning home to Bashkiria (a republic neighbouring Tatarstan) after two years 'on contract' with the army in Moscow. He'd just quit his job as a soldier because he could no longer afford to keep it up.

'Just imagine,' he told his *sputnik*, 'we were paid 4,000 roubles [about USD$150] a month and had to buy our own food. They gave us a place to sleep, in a dormitory for four, but it was nothing. And now they tell us they can't provide free transport any more. So all my money goes on food and there's nothing left to visit my parents.'

'Ha!' scoffed the *sputnik*, revealing toothless gums. 'Our country has nothing to be proud of. Everything is a disaster — agriculture, industry, even the army.'

The newly retired soldier was thoughtful.

'I heard that American soldiers are paid eighty times what we get. Do you think they would take a Russian?'

Zulfia picked me up at the train station, bubbly as ever. No matter how long elapsed between visits, it always felt like we'd seen each other only yesterday. She hadn't changed a bit, but Kazan was almost unrecognisable. The city streets were gridlocked and swarming with police because, Zulfia explained, President Putin was in town. It was Tatar President Mintimer Shaimiev's seventieth birthday and Putin had come to present him with an Order 'For Merits to the Fatherland'. Roadblocks had paralysed the city to allow the 59-strong presidential entourage — including cooks, guards and a wardrobe adviser — to pass unhindered.

Kazan had been one big demolition zone cum construction site when I'd stopped by in mid-2005 on the way to Paris. At the ripe old age of 999, the city had been preparing for its millennium anniversary by flattening much of its past. It was a tragedy — whole districts of hundred-year-old wooden houses in Kazan's centre had been razed, to be replaced by soulless modern flats and office buildings. Everywhere, old Kazan was either crumbling away or being given a helping hand by heavy machinery. Glass, granite and steel shopping complexes, car showrooms and space-age metro stations were sprouting like mushrooms from the rubble.

Now 1001, Kazan boasted a new bridge across the Kazanka River and a new racetrack — for horses in the summer and cars in winter. Opposite the kremlin was a reflective-glass pyramid housing posh boutiques and swanky restaurants. But the city's most striking addition was the sparkling Turkish-style Kul Sharif mosque inside the kremlin, its four towering minarets now dominating the skyline of the ancient citadel. The original mosque, part of the 'castle of the Kazan Khans', had been destroyed on the orders of Ivan the Terrible back in 1552, and this ostentatious reconstruction made a bold statement: 'The Tatars are back'.

To me, it was brash and out of place, better suited to a Star Wars set or a contemporary desert city like Dubai. The interior was even more disappointing. Entry to the huge space was only permitted with a tour guide, so we peered in from the doorway. It was completely empty. The Kul Sharif might be Tatarstan's biggest mosque, but it was only for show. Nobody went there to worship, except on official occasions.

Zulfia had a busy day planned. Friends had invited her, Ildar and me to their dacha for a banquet in celebration of Shaimiev's birthday, and of course we couldn't go empty-handed. We stopped outside a supermarket near her flat — which I remembered from the days of queues, black bread and beetroot — and paid a crotchety man with a notepad to keep an eye on the car. In the foyer, we passed through a metal detector, had our handbags sealed into plastic bags and were given a once over by a pair of security guards before we could even enter the store.

Eyes popping, I followed Zulfia, marvelling at displays that made the average Australian Woolies look positively Soviet. There was a tank of live sturgeon, a deli display with tens of varieties of smoked horse meat and another devoted to offal, tongues and feet, neatly cling-wrapped on polystyrene trays. I counted over fifty brands of honey, hundreds of kinds of canned fish and preserved meats and an entire wall of the traditional Tatar sweet, *chak-chak*. The whisky aisle stocked a mind-boggling array of bottles, including several with price tags upwards of USD$1,000. Zulfia selected a fine Scotch malt for Ildar and I quickly reassessed my plan to pay for our purchases. I took my camera out and snapped a few pictures. Seconds later a guard had me by the arm.

'*Nyelzya*,' he barked. ('It is forbidden.')

'But why?'

'It's the rules. Put your camera away.'

I felt a familiar irritation rising within. What kind of a country was this, where cops turned a blind eye to skinheads bashing people to death and journalists were murdered for critical reporting, yet supermarket guards harassed people for taking a photo of a fish tank?

'It's okay,' said Zulfia after I'd put my camera away. 'After the apartment and metro bombings in Moscow, security is much tighter. But no one minds. They understand it has to be this way.'

We pushed our trolley load of artery-clogging food to the checkout. Zulfia was unfazed by the exorbitant total. Ildar now had a 'really good salary' as the deputy director of one of Kazan's major aircraft factories and money wasn't a problem. They went on five-star European holidays and were looking to buy a house in the country. Zulfia considered her work — as a lecturer in International Economics at the Kazan State University — 'just like a hobby'. It suited her perfectly, only four days a week, the longest from 9 am to 3 pm. She'd finished a PhD a few months ago and also did some consultant work, writing and public speaking on the side, mainly to fill in time while Ildar was away.

When Ildar had taken on this job five years earlier, the factory hadn't made a plane in years. Now, Zulfia said, he'd recently clinched contracts to sell eighty-six aircraft to Iran and Syria. The one flaw in an otherwise excellent plan was that the factory was only capable of producing two planes annually.

News of his sales came as a relief to me. In June 2005 Ildar had given me a folder of promotional material for his company and an invitation to an expo in Moscow, which I'd promised to pass on to my brother Richard who works for Qantas. I had done so, but Richard was less than optimistic that Qantas would be keen on Russian-made aircraft, even if they were cheap. I'd felt bad. Zulfia, Zofar and Ildar had done so much to help the Peking to Paris expedition: Zofar had arranged workshop facilities at Kazan's Gazprom headquarters (Tatneft — where he now held a high post) and Ildar had roused aircraft engineers into action on a Sunday to produce a spring for a 1907 model Itala. I owed them one, and had hoped Richard might convince his employers to sign up for a plane or two. Now I was off the hook.

We drove out of Kazan and through Derbuiskhi, one of hundreds of factory towns hurriedly moved westwards from European Russia when the Germans invaded in 1941. The factory here produced binoculars and night vision instruments. It was already dark when we arrived at the dacha. Zulfia's friend Nelli bustled us in from the cold and we unpacked our offerings while she pulled a stuffed home-grown squash out of the oven. It was so big she'd had to cut it in half to fit it in. A vivacious brunette with laughing eyes, Nelli was dressed remarkably casually in a baggy man's shirt over leggings. Her husband, another Ildar, was a well-known Tatar artist and had even painted the official portrait of President Shaimiev's wife. My eyes went straight to the one painting in their house I could see, a large canvas above the master bed with a reclining curvaceous nude. Ildar chuckled. 'No, not that one … that's *my* wife.' The rest of his works were being hung at a soon-to-open exhibition in Kazan.

Ildar, forty-one, was a quiet, reflective type, with funky square-rimmed glasses and a permanent sleepy smirk. After studying for seven years in Leningrad, he'd returned to Kazan to find his work in demand

and had since managed to make a respectable living. He took me on a tour of the three-level log house he and Nelli had built. The basement boasted a table tennis room, cold storage for vegetables and *banya*. On the next level was the kitchen and lounge. A wild baby boar skin, which he'd shot himself, took pride of place on the wood panelled walls above the sofa. An Orthodox icon hung opposite. Liya, their dreamy fifteen-year-old daughter, was curled up on the couch, her head buried in a book, and their adopted stray Russian spaniel, Coxy, gambolled up and down the stairs.

More guests arrived: Mansour, a jocular former client of Zulfia's who owned a chain of hardware and furniture stores, and his shy second wife, Alkechek. Now forty-six, Mansour had once trained as a radio engineer. In 1985 he'd been posted to the Soviet Army barracks near Weimar, Germany, where he'd been ordered to set up television signals so troops could watch *Vremya* (the evening news). He'd barely left the barracks, been prohibited from communicating with locals, and seen nothing of Germany. On returning to the queue-ridden USSR, he'd seen the potential to profit from the demand for consumer goods and began to import wallpaper, bathroom fittings and general hardware from Europe. His timing was perfect and he made a fortune. Now he owned six mega-stores and was not in the least concerned that IKEA had just opened its first outlet in Kazan right next to one of his.

'They won't do well here,' he opined. 'Their products are too expensive for ordinary people, and those who have money prefer Italian and Chinese style furniture. IKEA is too minimalist for most people here. We have a 50 square metre lounge room with nothing but a TV, couch and plants. My parents can't understand it. "Where is your display cabinet full of plates and crystal?"'

Like most who'd set up businesses in the early 1990s, Mansour had his share of Mafia/protection racket dramas, but he'd somehow retained his boyish energy. He was the most un-*biznesmen*-like *biznesmen* I'd ever met.

Zulfia's Ildar finally turned up after a stressful day of multi-million dollar negotiations and we sat down to Nelli and Zulfia's banquet.

Nelli began to fill our shot glasses for a toast and I put my hand over the top of my glass. She raised an eyebrow.

'I can't drink,' I explained, 'on doctor's orders.'

There was a collective gasp.

'What?'

'Ever?'

'Never?'

'No!'

A moment of sympathetic silence followed. But it *was* President Shaimiev's birthday and he did need to be commemorated. Zulfia's Ildar made the first toast: 'To our wonderful President Shaimiev, with our deepest gratitude for the wonderful opportunities we have had thanks to his wise leadership.'

The whisky and vodka levels dropped quickly. Mansour declared we would one day all go sailing on a yacht in the Whitsundays. Zulfia's Ildar had just been reading about Lenin's brain, which had apparently been dissected after his death.

'He had used five per cent of its capacity. Normal people use only 2.5 per cent. Did you know that every second there are 1,600 impulses going to the brain, yet with all that we are only capable of making one decision?'

'Ah,' said Ildar the artist, stroking his designer stubble. 'That would be … "To drink, or not to drink!"'

He sculled another whisky and disappeared downstairs to check the *banya* was ready. It was, and the men descended to broil and beat each other.

The women's conversation drifted to the subject of ancestry. They were impressed I could trace my relatives back to seventeenth-century Scotland. Zulfia knew no further back than her grandparents. Landowners at the time of the revolution, they had fled from Tatarstan to the Azerbaijani capital, Baku, where her grandmother became an ardent communist. Her father was two at the time. Zulfia wanted him to help her find his birthplace, but he refused. She knew her ancestral lands were somewhere around here, but exactly where seemed likely to remain a mystery.

It was a long night of munching, beating, sweating and barbecuing kebabs in the snow. By 3 am we were surrounded by empty bottles and Mansour was playing songs on his guitar. I was contemplating a nice long sleep-in when Ildar the artist came up with an idea. First thing in the morning, we would all go to a nearby lake to celebrate the Orthodox Epiphany with a quick dip. Nominally they were all Muslims, but I supposed if they were Russified enough to indulge in the 'little water', then marking the baptism of Christ — which worshippers believe is when the Holy Spirit descended on Jesus in the form of a dove — was no more incongruous.

I was half-asleep as Zulfia skidded her car off the main road and down an icy hill the next morning. We were going to a 'magic lake', she said, so magic that no matter what the air temperature was in winter, the water was always four degrees, 'warm enough to swim!'

It didn't sound like bathing weather to me, but hundreds of locals had flocked to the curiously ice-free, blackish-blue lagoon with just that in mind. We traipsed through the snow and I watched the faithful taking their extremity-shrivelling plunges from wooden platforms built along the bank — some stark naked, some in bathing costumes. Babushki, *biznesmeny* and buff bodybuilding types crossed themselves and descended into their 'River Jordan'. From our party, only Mansour and Ildar the artist were brave enough. The rest of us watched on, cruelly laughing as they howled in anguish.

Andrei Bogdanov, the glamour photographer, came to meet us at the lake. One autumn long ago, he and I had taken a boat down the Volga from Kazan to the island of Sviyazhsk. It was here, in 1551, that Ivan the Terrible had ordered the construction of a fortress from whence to carry out his assault on the Tatar capital. Sixteen churches, a monastery and convent were also built on the island in that century, several with timber from forests thousands of kilometres away, floated over on rafts.

Until 2006, Sviyazhsk had only been accessible by boat during summer, or by a hair-raising and prayerful drive across the ice in winter. But a new road now connected the four hundred remaining inhabitants of the windswept isle to the Volga shore, meaning it was now possible to visit without risking a frigid and waterlogged end. Andrei and I left the others at the lake and drove to Sviyazhsk. A stinging gale whipped around us, buffeting Andrei's car as we crossed the causeway. A rusted-out hulk of a ship jutted up from the frozen river. Far beyond, out on the river, three young men fed a fishing net out through an opening in the ice. They would check their catch in the morning.

We followed a rocky track around the barren shoreline and came to a freshly built wooden pier, leading out to a walkway framing a square cut in the river ice. A ladder hung down into the black water, an Orthodox cross nailed above it. Andrei walked out to the hole, splashed his face and crossed himself.

Once 4,000 people had eked out an austere existence on this bleak island. Now most had left for the comforts of the city — gas, running water, sealed roads and electric street lamps. Of the original churches, only six remained, and they were in a poor state. The others had been bombed, vandalised or demolished, their icons and artifacts looted during the 1930s and 40s. But things were changing. The first sign of life we saw was a bulldozer shifting a pile of snow-covered bricks over to a whitewashed stone chapel where workers were repairing a collapsed wall.

Andrei drove on to another church in the centre of the island. A weatherworn babushka trudged through the grounds, pails of water dangling from each end of a curved stick balanced across her shoulders. There were, she told us, some original 1561 frescoes remaining in this church, but the building was locked during winter to prevent damage from the extreme cold. She directed us to the old monastery, further up the road.

Andrei knew the place well. He pointed out the ruins of the old monastic cell buildings, looming eerily in the bluish-grey twilight. In Soviet times they had been used as a 'psychiatric hospital' for the mentally ill and politically suspect. As a child, Andrei had seen the bars on the windows. Some 'famous thriller' had been shot in these grounds 'with mad people wandering in the background'. The hospital had been closed in the early 1990s and the buildings abandoned until 2004 when the land was returned to the church. A grand procession and ceremony had been held to reconsecrate the grounds. But now the place was almost deserted.

A young novice strode briskly towards us, dark robes flowing behind him. For a religious hermit he was remarkably chatty.

Did we know that scientists had been to analyse the water from this well? Yes, they have, and incredibly it has no smell, no colour and no taste, therefore it is real Holy Water. And did we know that it's possible to find 500-year-old coins and bones around the shore of the island?

He invited us to the evening service he was about to attend in the main church, with Sviyazhsk's three monks and four other novices. We seized the opportunity to thaw our frozen toes and followed the pealing bells to the only church renovated enough to have heating. The monks seemed irritable as they swung their incense before the icons. I hoped it wasn't because of us and held my breath in the quiet bits just in case. All of a sudden, a tacky song came blaring from my pocket. I'd completely forgotten that Zulfia had given me a mobile phone, so she could 'keep track' of me in Kazan. I raced out, tripped down the stairs — and missed the call. Andrei came to find me and we decided to make a run for it before the mad monks got madder.

We drove back to Kazan in pitch darkness. Andrei had few compliments for the clergy, believing most of them were just 'in it for the money'. He'd once done a photo shoot for the head priest at one of Kazan's main churches who 'was interested in nothing but wealth. He even drove a Mercedes!'

'Do you think he bought it with money from babushki?'

'Not necessarily. The church has private sponsors, and often it's rich criminals who donate to the church, hoping to save their souls. The state also gives them money to use for restoration and often priests take some for themselves. It's the same with museums. The directors take money and use it to buy themselves flats and cars. They work for the church because it is considered a respectable and dignified job with status.'

Andrei took me back to his house/studio, a free-standing wooden building which he hoped wouldn't go the way of the city's other old houses, 'all being demolished for profit with no respect for our history'. As always, his pad was a hangout for gorgeous chicks, and, as ever, he seemed immune to their charms. His best friend was a slobbery brown boxer. He handed me a stack of calendars and catalogues, his past year's work. Most involved girls, or vehicles with girls draped over them. My favourite was a black-and-white calendar for an oil company that featured the same model painted glistening oily black all over, against a black backdrop. A shaft of light picked up one plane of curves in each pose. There was a subtlety about it that said 'art' rather than 'objectification of women'. Andrei agreed, but he was paid — a lot now — to do as clients wished. Judging by these examples, clients wanted tarts. Occasionally he got to do something different — a catalogue for a millionaire horse breeder in Samara and a portrait of a Merc-driving priest — but his staple was girls, girls, girls, and at least it paid for his annual windsurfing holidays in Egypt.

'My' phone rang again. It was Rafael, who'd tracked me down via Zulfia.

He picked me up the next morning in a new silver SUV. He'd told me in an email that he'd had some heart trouble, but although he looked tired, he joked and smoked as always. We stopped in at one of Kazan's three Japanese restaurants for coffee and breakfast.

Rafael had eventually found a wife. On the fifteenth blind date arranged by his mother he'd met Lilya, a strong-willed girl with long lashes who took an immediate dislike to him. Rafael rose to the challenge and decided she would be the one. They were married two months later. Their son, Adam, was two weeks older than my Nik. Now they all lived in one room in Lilya's parents' flat. Until a month ago, Lilya's sister and two children had been living there too. Rafael was hoping it wouldn't be for much longer. He'd bought some land 9 kilometres from Kazan five years ago and was building a house there.

He still worked at the Federation of Motorsports of Tatarstan and now earned a respectable thousand euros a month. He travelled regularly to Europe to organise his boss's participation in various events there. The boss flew in at the last minute on his private plane.

'Where does he get the money?' I asked.

Rafael gave me a 'duh' look.

'He just has to make a call, give his bank account number and the money appears. You know how it is here!'

Rorting the system was an industry in itself. Rafael told me about guys who lined the route between Kazan and Moscow with computers and printers ready to churn out fake receipts for hotels, petrol, car washing. 'So people hand in these receipts then stay somewhere cheap, do everything on the cheap, and that way they can save money.'

The Federation's mechanics were continuing to pilfer tyres to sell to supplement their minuscule salaries. Despite Rafael's entreaties, his boss refused to increase their wages, and so the tyres kept disappearing. Now Rafael was letting them repair other people's cars in the Federation's workshop so they could pick up some extra cash. Scamming and scheming were the natural order of things.

Mafia groups remained a powerful presence in the city. Every time Rafael parked his car anywhere at all, he had no choice but to contribute to their coffers. If you didn't pay up, they trashed your car, and after his hair salon experience he knew they meant business. Protection and extortion rackets, prostitution rings and drug runners were part of society's fabric. Even those mafiosi who wanted to get out and earn 'honest' livings were finding it near impossible. Rafael knew one guy 'with a huge scar across his face' who had been trying for years to escape the tentacles of the gangs. 'But he doesn't know anything else. He's got no education.'

Scarface had set up a legitimate flower business, but couldn't compete with the big supermarkets. Rafael even had an ex-Mafia driver living in his half-built country house. The guy was a distant relative of his wife's and had been on the run for seven years. Rafael hadn't wanted to shelter him, 'a Tatar who hates every other race on the planet', but Lilya's uncle had assured him that he wasn't a bad guy, 'he'd only been a driver'. Rafael checked police records, found it was true, and for the last ten months, Gangster X had been working for him as a guard.

'There's no way I'd harbour anyone wanted for murder. But this guy was very young, and if he can keep out of trouble for the next two years then he'll be able to come back out in the open. So he stays in the house all day and only ventures out in pitch darkness, wrapped in a scarf and hat.'

Rafael hadn't heard from Akhmed in ages. 'He comes back from Malaysia every year and says he's going to get married. His father chooses him a wife, then he runs away. It's the same each time. No one knows where he is now!'

He invited me to his new office, in the Traffic Police building. Security was tight, with ID checks and a metal detector before we even got to the lift. Rafael's floor was all FSB. The day before the millennium celebrations in August 2006, the FSB and Ministry of Internal Affairs buildings burned down in mysterious circumstances. 'Now they are renting rooms all over town, and unfortunately right opposite my door. I can't get away from them!'

That night I met Lilya and Adam. She was lovely, naturally pretty and down-to-earth, not at all what I'd expected after Rafael's uncomplimentary description of the woman he'd married. Seeing four-year-old Adam giggling away with a plastic toy pistol made me miss Nik intensely. I called him the next morning (courtesy of Rafael's boss) and told him I'd bring him back to Russia one day. Tyoma and Adam would teach him how to make snowmen. There was a pause. 'Well, make sure you pack an old carrot,' he said. 'We'll need that for the nose.'

Rafael wanted to show me his work-in-progress. We drove out of Kazan, passing pretentious McMansions with snow-covered cupolas. Hundred-year-old *izbas* with painted window frames lined the main road, but Rafael doubted they would be there for long. His half-constructed house overlooked the river in a 500-year-old Christian Tatar village. Directly opposite was an Orthodox Church, the Church of St Paul, the saint of water. To Rafael, the Muslim, this was a bonus. 'It means the river water will stay pure!' Unfortunately, the holy water was also a prime attraction for many of Kazan's gangster barons, who had built country retreats right next door.

One day, Rafael's 'money-sink' would be an eye-catching, if eclectic, abode. His Tajik carpenters had constructed striking 'Samarkand-style' windows with elaborate geometric patterns framing the glass panels. But this aesthetic triumph was somewhat tainted by their insistence on painting the living room salmon pink and the kitchen lime. For a novice in construction it seemed to both Rafael and me that perhaps things weren't being done in the right order. While the walls downstairs were painted already, the top floor was nothing but a few joists, rough wooden beams slicing the space horizontally. But the gangster didn't mind.

Rafael helped me track down Tatiana at her dacha in Mari El. She sounded almost hysterical, and promised to come to Kazan at once. 'And we must visit Nai'ilya and Vildan in Saya,' she cried. 'If only I could find a car.'

Rafael offered me the services of one of his mechanics, Rinat, a cheerful Tatar in a peaked cap, and the next day we drove over to meet her at the old flat on Sibirsky Trakt. Tatiana was a jittery, frantic with anxiety about my seeing the state of the place. She and Anatoly now lived permanently at Ilet, and their Kazan flat had sunk into dereliction. A flood in the flat above had ruined the bathroom and kitchen ceilings, but neither they nor the neighbours could afford repairs. The wallpaper she'd so proudly redecorated with before Ian the Welshman's stay in 1990 hung off the walls. Sacks of rotting pumpkins lay on the peeling linoleum floors of the dining room where I used to sleep. In Sergei's former bedroom, piles of string bags bursting with sprouting onions sat next to a heap of law texts which had fallen through a shelf broken by their weight. Her prized collection of Russian literature was thick with dust and she wouldn't even let me look into the other room.

She disappeared for a moment and returned with a photo album. I reminded her Rinat was waiting below, but she pressed me into a dusty dining chair and opened the embossed grey book. The here and now disgusted her, but in these moments frozen long ago, she was beautiful and she was happy. In her wedding photo she could have been a Bond girl, with cheekbones, eyes and figure to send Roger Moore into a frenzy. And in another, taken just over twenty years later, she posed with her son, Igor, outside a Moscow military base. He was nineteen, tall and handsome in his uniform. She wore a floral print summer dress, strappy sandals and a coy smile. 'You know,' she said, 'I am forty years old in this picture. But when I visited Igor, his officers would announce that "his sister was here to see him". Can you imagine that?'

It was hard not to feel her pain. She had been a striking woman, but this past decade and a half of hardship had shattered her physically and emotionally. Her huge hands were rough and calloused, her face red and puffy, from crying or alcohol I couldn't say. When she spoke, she stretched her bottom lip up to hide her missing teeth. Nothing gave her joy anymore, not even her grand-daughter, Katya, whom she had so adored as a pink-cheeked five-year-old. Igor's wife, Natasha, had left him two years earlier and taken Katya to live with her parents. Tatiana had hardly seen her since, and because she had no money to buy her presents, the now seventeen-year-old Katya had little interest in her.

Tatiana was so miserable and agitated that it was becoming hard to be with her for long. She clung to me as if I could somehow bring back the past. Perhaps I reminded her of a time when she had the means and energy to entertain friends and family with grand banquets, to have foreigners stay, to take pride in her appearance, to afford blue eyeshadow and lippy.

I wanted to be more supportive, but honestly didn't know what I could do. She bristled with anger at the loss of her dignity and she wanted compensation from the people who had taken it from her. She wanted justice where there would never be any and her rage was eating into her soul. Every happy memory had turned sour.

'Remember Irina at Vysokaya Gora? And beautiful Zhenya, her daughter?'

I did, a gorgeous girl with waist-length honey hair.

'Well, she is an invalid now. She was in a terrible car accident and her spine was damaged. She's only twenty-five but her life is destroyed. Vitaly, Irina's boyfriend, left and Irina cares for Zhenya alone. Then Irina lost her job at the state shop and now she has to work in the bazaar, standing outside all day. It's tolerable in summer, but in winter it's terrible. Poor Irina's heart can't take all this stress and I am afraid she will have a heart attack.'

It was awful. Tatiana and Irina had believed in communism, believed they would be looked after. And the truth — that they were on their own in this dog-eat-dog world — was an unbearably bitter pill to swallow.

At last I got her to the car and introduced her to the amiable Rinat. I asked him to stop 'for a minute' at a supermarket so I could buy something to take to Vildan's family. Tatiana had always been indecisive, but at almost sixty she was impossible. She snubbed everything I chose: 'too expensive', 'not a tasty brand', 'they wouldn't like it', or 'what is it?' She spent fifteen minutes discussing salami brands with deli staff, another quarter of an hour selecting and rejecting different kinds of juice. At the checkout she wailed about the cost (I was buying) and made sure everyone knew of her misery. An hour later we were back in the car. Rinat gave me a wink of solidarity.

The entire journey was one long tale of woe. She and Anatoly had put all their energy into building their dacha in Ilet. They'd moved there full time ten years ago 'when people began stealing things' whenever they left. Five years ago that house burnt down and they lost everything. Sergei bought them a new house, but she hated the location — between the road and the railway line. To make matters worse, someone had to stay there all the time because people came and stole things, anything — a bag of sugar, a packet of grain, a glass. It made her furious because she'd worked so hard for everything.

I would hardly recognise Ilet now, she said. While Novy Russkys were defiling the place with ostentatious multistoreyed houses, many inhabitants made a living selling berries, mushrooms and *veniki* (bunches of leaves for *banyas*) by the roadside. She and Anatoly received a combined pension of 3,700 roubles a month, around USD$120, which she collected on flying fortnightly visits to Kazan. It was only thanks to Sergei that they weren't completely destitute.

Anatoly had hit the bottle hard and never quite got himself together after losing all his money in the 1992 devaluation. Now, she said, he spent his days watching TV. She couldn't bear to watch it — 'all shooting and sex'. 'They put a tiny blurry square over the nipples, but otherwise you can see and hear everything. It's disgusting. I don't want to hear other people having sex. Every channel you turn on, all during the day, that's all you see — guns and sex!' Anatoly's parents had just died, but they had nothing to leave them.

We passed a new red brick building, which Rinat told us was a kindergarten. Jolted back to her rosy past life as a teacher, Tatiana sniffed. 'In Soviet days, children were polite and disciplined. These days kids in first grade take pornography to school and all they talk about is buying and selling.'

Rinat interrupted to ask Tatiana for directions. Soon we were completely lost. Even when we were obviously going in entirely the wrong direction, Rinat politely deferred to Tatiana's erratic instructions. Eventually a collective farm worker pointed us to Saya and an hour later we located Vildan's house — to find no one home. It was dark and at least minus twenty. In a flurry, Tatiana bashed on the neighbour's door. A beaming babushka with only two teeth beckoned us in, sat us at her table and filled it with slabs of white bread, bowls of cream, berry jam and gingerbread. Vildan and Nai'ilya, she thought, were off preparing for the wedding of their second son, Rushan, which was to be held in Kazan the next day. Just as we got settled, Vildan burst in to drag us to his place.

The Zainullins were prospering. Vildan had worked hard to expand his bee-keeping business and now produced five tonnes of honey a year, which he sold to a bottling company in Moscow. He was currently experimenting with making beeswax candles, *medovukha* (mead) and harvesting pollen as a sideline.

Since my last visit, which we calculated to have been nearly eleven years ago, they'd extended and revamped their humble cottage. It was now double the size, with an internal *banya* and attached indoor poultry coop, which provided covered access to the pit toilet without having to walk through the snow. To a family accustomed to a freezing trek to relieve themselves, this was progress indeed. Nai'ilya had gone all out with the interior decoration, plastering the walls with glittery pink floral wallpaper and positioning pink plastic flowers in pink plastic baskets on every available surface. She'd selected swan motif tiles for the bathroom and fruit for the kitchen, all set off by turquoise floral curtains and a flowery pink porcelain chandelier (not wired in), hanging next to a fluorescent light.

Vildan slapped a bottle of vodka on the table with a mischievous wink. Hard work was keeping him fit and he hadn't aged at all.

Business was so successful he even had a mobile phone, with an 'Ode to Joy' ring tone to a disco beat. Nai'ilya was limping, but otherwise her usual dynamic self. Their three sons were now twenty-four, twenty-three, and twenty-one, and not only was second son getting married tomorrow, first son already was and grandchild number one was on the way. It didn't seem so long ago that they were all shy little boys, peeking nervously at the strange foreigner with the gifts of clip-on koalas. And yes, they still had them in their display cabinet, next to the best tea set.

Nai'ilya disappeared into a side room and led out a pale girl in a penguin-patterned dressing gown, their pregnant daughter-in-law, Elvira. She'd barely kept food down in weeks and had just come out from Kazan, hoping the country air would help. Elvira was a village girl (but not from Saya) who'd moved to Kazan to study literature. She'd met Ruslan, five years her junior, while he was training at the police academy. When she wasn't suffering morning sickness, Elvira worked as a television reporter for a show called *Road to Riches*, a brainchild of Tatar President Shaimiev himself. The idea was to promote friendship between the various ethnic groups in Tatarstan, and Elvira specialised in stories about cross-cultural weddings and feast days of Tatarstan's Afghans, Chechens, Assyrians and Georgians. It was a pleasant change from the xenophobia of Moscow.

I asked Vildan about his sister, Gulshat. He'd bought her a flat in a neighbouring village and she worked as a cook in a Kazan factory canteen. Her son, Radik, was studying at Kazan State University and her daughter, Gulnaz, was a talented pianist, in Year 11 at a special music school. Gulshat had never married again. Rustam, her horrid ex-husband, had been contracted to drive a fully laden Kamaz truck from Kazan to Uzbekistan eight years ago. Neither Rustam, nor the truck, had ever been seen again.

I'd developed a nasty cough in Kazan and Vildan was concerned. He was a helpful type, and told me he had a sure-fire cure, which I hoped had something to do with honey. But no, the Tatar remedy for a chronic cough was to submerse my head in a bucket of hot water, then move it to a bucket of cold, then back to the hot and so on. I made a conscious effort to restrain my outbursts of spluttering and promised I'd try it after dinner, hoping he'd forget. He did.

I helped Nai'ilya set the table with freshly gutted herring, sausage, *pelmeni,* home-grown potatoes and dried apricots. Vildan brought in scoops of different varieties of honey and we sat down to dinner and more news. Ruslan (number one son, Elvira's husband) was working as a policeman. Rushan (number two) had finished university last year and was teaching the Tatar language in Kazan. Their youngest, Rustam, was studying to be an economist. Getting three village boys to university had been quite an achievement. I showed them photos of Nik and we all congratulated ourselves. All except Tatiana, who was trapped in her web of gloom and determined to tell everyone about it.

We were all sympathetic, but after a while Nai'ilya had had enough. She switched on the television, to a gruesomely graphic documentary about 'hypnotist-shamans' who rip cancerous tumours from living bodies with their bare hands. Vildan leapt up, fished around in a drawer and produced a dusty Video 8 tape. It was the home movie he'd shot eleven years ago with me and the boys, aged ten, thirteen and fourteen.

I'd always been acutely self-conscious about being filmed. I could never watch my own stories and the sound of my voice makes me cringe. But this was intriguing. I'd obviously forgotten the camera was rolling, most likely thinking that given I was out in a Tatar backwater with a population of 270, neither I, nor anyone I knew, would ever see it. The family roared with laughter watching our old selves, Elvira chuckling at the sight of her husband as a fourteen-year-old. She rang him at the police station in Kazan to tell him the Australian was back. I watched myself at twenty-six, chatting in Russian to Tatar kids in the middle of nowhere. I'd spent so long in this country; trying to make sense of its, engrossed in its music, loving and hating it.

After dinner, Nai'ilya led me to a bed. I slept fitfully, waking in the dead of night with a bursting bladder. In pitch darkness I groped my way through the house, donned the oversized felt boots by the door, and stepped gingerly into the black hole that was the chicken's quarters. Somewhere beyond the irritated poultry was my destination, a deep wide hole piled high with frozen excrement. Suddenly I panicked. What if I couldn't find it? What if a loose-fitting *valenok* should fall in? What if *I* fell in? Seized by fear and burning need, I squatted in the straw. There was a brief moment of relief ... then a chicken attacked my bum.

Back in bed, wounded buttock stinging, I wondered if Russia would ever be normal. It would certainly never be dull. Every day here was a roller-coaster ride — from despair to exhilaration and back again. I tried to find a glimmer of hope in Tatiana's misery. But she, like so many others, was trapped by circumstances which offered little promise of a happy ending. So much about this land was harsh and unjust. I thought of Gosman, Milya and the villagers of Muslyumovo, cruelly sacrificed by callous authorities ... of the tens of thousands of young conscripts sent to their deaths in far-off wars ... the Chechen civilians caught in the crossfire of brutal battles ... the tragic story of Nadia's father and brother, and the millions like them ... the impoverished, unemployed, depressed and hopeless who turned to the bottle or needle for solace.

'Romantics carry revolutions,' Natasha's mum in St Petersburg had told me once, 'but the fruits of revolutions are taken by dishonest people.'

Why did it always have to be this way? Our *sputnik* on the train to the tundra back in August 1990 had been right when he complained that with such vast resources, Russia's people should have been well off. Why couldn't Roman Abramovich put some of his colossal wealth towards fixing his country instead of buying USD$300 million yachts and an English football team? Why couldn't authorities compensate innocent victims of nuclear disasters? How could they turn a blind eye to the tragedy of Chechnya ... the murder of journalists ... the corruption and violence? Why couldn't the law protect all citizens and not merely the rich and powerful? How could people be so accepting of their lamentable situations?

But then here were Vildan and Nai'ilya, contentedly plodding away, enjoying their small triumphs, their family and friends, a vodka toast, a plate of pickled herring, a spoonful of honey. Rafael had finally found himself a niche in the new order, so had Andrei, Zulfia, Olga, Marat and Sergei.

My years in Russia had shown me the best and the worst of humanity. Since that fateful Aeroflot flight seventeen years earlier, perched precariously on a broken seat, I had lost my certainty about almost everything — except that injuries to my backside were apparently inevitable. All those youthful illusions about the worthiness of communist ideals had well and truly evaporated. The more I had experienced and learned of Russia and its people, the more it seemed that it was the past that was the key to its present.

Whatever I had witnessed, Russia was now part of me. Back in Australia, I missed my friends, *pelmeni*, snow and extraordinary concerts. I wanted Nik to learn Russian, to build snowmen with Rafael's son, Adam, to see the acrobats at the circus and to experience the warmth and friendship I had felt from so many. I wanted to take him on the Trans-Siberian, to the Registan in Samarkand, to the Hermitage in St Petersburg. Above all, I wished that one of those esoteric psychoanalysts advertising their services in the classified pages of St Petersburg's local papers could come up with a magic cure to 'correct Russia's destiny'.

But maybe it wouldn't be necessary. 'No matter how bad things are,' Natasha's mum had said, 'Russia is the kind of country that will always survive. Russians are survivors.'

EPILOGUE

July 2009

Two and a half years after my last visit, my friends are all surviving, despite the global financial crisis wreaking havoc on Russia's economy.

In May 2009, Olga moved to Sweden where she is working as a 'sourcing developer' for IKEA in the town of Almhult. Tyoma will join her soon and Misha is looking for a job. Her father, Vladimir, is the principal guest conductor of the Voronezh and Saratov orchestras and continues to tour the world, mainly to Australia, the USA and Europe. Igor has left St Petersburg's Musical Comedy Theatre in search of new challenges and has recently been conducting his father's orchestras.

Masha never did manage to sell her flat and is still living with her son, her ex-husband and his mother in St Petersburg. She is teaching English, and continues to go mountain climbing each year, this summer to Kyrgyzstan. Natasha is working at St Petersburg University, teaching Russian as a foreign language and researching four days a week. Five-year-old Fedor stays home with a nanny. Natasha, Fedor and her husband haven't yet managed to buy their own place, so still live with her mother, and are spending the summer holidays at the family dacha.

Rafael and Lilya finally finished their country house, evicted the gangster and moved out of her parent's flat in May 2008. Adam is now six, and baby daughter Saphia just turned one. Rafael is still working for the Federation of Motorsports and is currently in Norway lining up a competition for his boss. Akhmed is living it up in Malaysia. His father passed away last year and now, according to Rafael, 'there is no force on the planet' that can make him marry. Zulfia and Ildar have moved to the country near Kazan. She continues to work at Kazan University and he is selling aircraft.

Magomad has returned to Ingushetia with his wife, Alissa, and their four children. His elderly father refused to leave his motherland, so Magomad, as the youngest son, must stay at home to care for him. He continues his work as a lawyer with an organisation called Chechen Mothers, offering legal advice to families of 'disappeared' persons. Chechnya, he says, is now safer than it was, and once a week he travels to Grozny. The rest of his family has emigrated to Europe — some to France, the rest to Holland and Belgium. His sister, Madina, has become a well-known Chechen rights activist and spends much of her time in Moscow and Europe.

His nephew, Yusup, who I met as a fragile twelve-year-old back in 2000, was due to be married to a French girl in August 2008. I was invited to the wedding, but couldn't make it. The day before the appointed date for the ceremony, all the relatives were already there when news came that Yusup's maternal uncle had been killed in Chechnya. The wedding was postponed. As of July 2009, he is preparing to enter university and is expecting his first son.

Yulia has been living in Magdeburg, Germany, for the last ten years. She never did manage to find a job as a pharmacist and after a year on welfare, was allocated work shifting rocks in a Jewish cemetery. She now works as a cleaner in a roadhouse and looks after her eighty-year-old mother. But according to her friend Elena in Melbourne, Yulia has no regrets about having left Russia. Dima excelled at his studies in physics at Gottingen University and completed a PhD in robotics in Israel. He is now back in Germany where he is coming to the end of a three-year tenure at Gottingen. Much to Yulia's displeasure, he isn't 'finding the work exciting', and dreams of returning to Moscow to become a soccer commentator.

Renaissance Capital has become Russia's biggest investment bank and Stephen Jennings has now expanded operations into Africa, his 'second once-in-a-lifetime opportunity'. He is Russia's wealthiest foreigner and was reportedly the world's richest Kiwi. Tina is back at Oxford, turning her thesis on 'The Rise of State Corporatism in Russia' into a book.

Sergei bought the flat on Barrikadnaya. He is currently working as Special Counsel at Baker Botts LLP, a US law firm, advising clients on mergers, acquisitions and oil and gas transactions. He's still with Nastya, and 'life is good, but currently a bit challenging. The crisis is no doubt affecting Russia.'

His parents, Tatiana and Anatoly, 'are getting old and are not in good health'. They've left their house in Ilet and returned to their old flat on Sibirsky Trakt in Kazan. Sergei supports them. In Moscow, Marat is managing an ever-growing portfolio of rock bands and pop singers, but complains that the crisis has slowed demand for his performers. He hasn't married, and has swapped his Mercs for a Lexus and Toyota.

US President Obama has just been to visit Putin's successor, Dimitri Medvedev. Sergei is optimistic that the US and Russia are at last genuinely serious about improving relations. 'Obama is much better than Bush!' he wrote. But Sergei seems less positive about Russia's future than he was two years ago, when oil prices were soaring and the country was booming.

'In a few words,' Sergei wrote, 'Russia is complicated. I am not sure what is going on and where Russia is going.'

Meanwhile, I haven't been going anywhere. But I'm starting to teach Russian to Nik (now six) and am hoping to take him for a visit next winter.

GLOSSARY

In transliteration, I have attempted to use the English orthography which represents the Russian sounds most closely, except in the case of words already existing in English, such as 'soviet'.

apparatchik — 'agent of the apparatus', colloquial term for a full-time, professional functionary of the Communist Party or government.

BOMZh — *bez opredelyonnogo mesta zhitelstva*, without a determined place of residence, abbreviated to its initials, *bomzh*, to refer to homeless people.

budzhetniki — people receiving salaries or pensions from the state.

coupé — second-class wagon on train. Individual compartments with four bunks.

dezhurny/dezhurnaya — 'on duty'.

Duma — lower house of parliament.

dynya — a honeydew melon, grown in Central Asia.

gostepriimstvo — hospitality.

homo sovieticus — pseudo-Latin for 'Soviet human', a term coined by Soviet writer Alexander Zinovyiev as a critical reference to people with a mindset characterised by: passivity, lack of initiative, indifference, avoidance of individual responsibility.

kommunalka — communal apartment with rooms off a long corridor.

krysha — literally 'roof', refers to mafia groups running protection rackets.

nomenklatura — elite subset who held key administrative positions in Soviet era.

Novy Russky — 'New Russian', Nouveau Riche.

platscart — third-class train carriage with open–plan bunk arrangement.

plov — pilaf — Uzbek dish cooked in wok usually containing meat, rice and pumpkin.

politruk — a person whose task was to encourage 'correct thought' amongst the members of the armed forces.

provodnitsa/provodnik — train wagon attendant.

Rossiyanin — a citizen of the Russian federation.

Russky — an ethnic Russian.

soviet — council.

spalny raion — 'sleeping' district, suburban area with flats but few amenities.

spekulyant — trader in goods and currency.

Spetsnaz — *Voyska spetsialnogo naznacheniya* — elite special forces troops.

svoboda slova — freedom of speech.

talony — ration cards.

tapochki — slippers.

tubiteika — skull cap.

valyuta — hard currency.

venik — a bunch of twigs, for sweeping, or of leaves, used for beating flesh in banya.

vor — thief.

Acronyms

CHEKA — Chrezvychainaya Komissiya, ChK (Extraordinary Commission). The first of the Soviet state security organisations, created by Lenin in December, 1917.

FSB — Federalnaya Sluzhba Bezopasnosti (Federal Security Service).

GULAG — abbreviation of Glavnoye Upravleniye Ispravitelno–trudovykh Lagerei i Kolonii (Chief Administration of Corrective Labour Camps and Colonies). System of forced labour camps.

KGB — Komitet Gosudarstvennoy Bezopasnosti (Committee for State Security).

KIM — Kommunisticheskaya Internatsionalnaya Molodyozh (the International Communist Youth).

NKVD — Narodny Komissariat Vnutrennikh Del (People's Commissariat for Internal Affairs).

OMON — Otryad Militsii Osobogo Naznacheniya (Special Purpose Police Unit).

OVIR — Otdel Viz i Registratsii — Department of Visas and Registration (a department of the Ministry of the Interior).

ACKNOWLEDGEMENTS

I have so many people to thank ... for their inspiration, generosity, help, friendship and encouragement — Pamela Bloom, my clarinet teacher; Blair Munro, sadly no longer with us, for teaching me Cyrillic on AYO tours; Olga Verbitskaya for inviting me to her homeland and going along with all my hare-brained ideas, and her family — father, Vladimir, mother, Nelli, brother, Igor, and husband, Mikhail Kulikov — and friends, Natasha Maroussenko and Masha Kondratova in St Petersburg; Elena and Alissa in Melbourne for 'introducing' me to Yulia in Moscow; Nadia Shenker, Sergei Stepanov, Marat Khairutdinov and Ira Stelliferovskaya at the ABC's Moscow office; Sasha Petrov at Human Right's Watch; Oleg Panfilov at the Centre for Journalism in Extreme Situations; Nadia Rodova and Tina in Moscow; Zulfia and Zofar Kadayev, Ildar, Rafael, Galina, Tatiana Stepanova, Vildan and Nai'ilya Zainullin in Kazan and Saya; Magomad Magomadov, the late Viktor Popkov and Madina Magomadova; and Akhmed Barakhoyev in Malaysia.

In Australia, Paige Livingston, Mike Rubbo, Di Haddon and Richard Fidler gave me my start at film-making on *Race Around the World*; Amos Roberts, Martin Butler, Pottsy and Wayne helped put my stories together at *Dateline*; Anna Chen Chow got me to and from places many people have never heard of, even when the airport had burnt down.

Without Pasha Radetzki I never would have been brave enough to do many of the things I did. I must also thank Eve Conant, Monica Attard, Bentley Dean, Dr Roy Allison, Peter Chew and Peter and Svetlana Lumb.

Thanks to Amruta Slee at HarperCollins for seeing a book in my sketchy notes, and to Lydia Papandrea and Patrick Mangan for casting their critical eyes over my manuscript. Kind friends too — Catherine and Margaret Ingram, Gabrielle Deakin, Nick Byrne, Sarah Lightfoot, Mardi Trompf, Peter Bucknell, Ian Gason, Claudia Rowe and Jenni de Jager, and in particular Eric Campbell, Carol Traill (Mum) and Mick Matheson have read drafts and offered suggestions. Francis Merson and Katya Kalashnikova have generously corrected my Russian transliterations.

And to Josephine Parrett and Jason Burgess, Jan Van Dyk, Don Close, Anthony Fletcher, Perry Garofani, Kaye Morehen, Clare Harley, Ainslie and Alastair Macgibbon and especially Carol and Alastair Traill — thank you so very much for keeping Nik out of trouble while I was swimming in paper.

Lastly, I must thank Nicholas Campbell for his (almost) unwavering patience while boring old mummy has been stuck at the computer instead of playing with Star Wars Lego. (And no, you can't read it until you're older!)